COMBAT SPORTS

COMBAT SPORTS

An Encyclopedia of Wrestling, Fighting, and Mixed Martial Arts

David L. Hudson, Jr.

GREENWOOD PRESS

Westport, Connecticut ◆ London

Library of Congress Cataloging-in-Publication Data

Hudson, David L., 1969–
    Combat sports : an encyclopedia of wrestling, fighting, and mixed martial arts / David L. Hudson, Jr.
      p. cm.
    Includes bibliographical references and index.
    ISBN 978–0–313–34383–4 (alk. paper)
  1. Hand-to-hand fighting.   2. Mixed martial arts.   I. Title.
    GV1111.H84   2009
    796.8—dc22   2008052479

British Library Cataloguing in Publication Data is available.

Library of Congress Catalog Card Number: 2008052479
ISBN: 978–0–313–34383–4

First published in 2009

Greenwood Press, 88 Post Road West, Westport, CT 06881
An imprint of Greenwood Publishing Group, Inc.
www.greenwood.com

Printed in the United States of America

The paper used in this book complies with the
Permanent Paper Standard issued by the
National Information Standards Organization (Z39.48–1984).

10 9 8 7 6 5 4 3 2 1

To Mike Rodgers, Hunter Pierce, Charles Welfel, and Flattop—great combatants and even better friends.

CONTENTS

LIST OF ENTRIES

GUIDE TO RELATED TOPICS

Fletcher, Frank
Gibbons, Mike
Hamsho, Mustafa
Hart, Eugene "Cyclone"
Tiberi, Dave

Mixed Martial Arts Organizations
Affliction
Elite XC
International Fight League (IFL)
PRIDE
Ultimate Fighting Championships (UFC)

Olympic Gold Medalists (Boxing)
Benvenuti, Nino
Casamayor, Joel
Gonzalez, Paul
Kacar, Slobodan
Leonard, Sugar Ray
Papp, Laszlo
Randolph, Leo
Reid, David
Savon, Felix
Spinks, Leon
Spinks, Michael
Stevenson, Teofilo
Taylor, Meldrick
Whitaker, Pernell

PRIDE Champions
Emelianenko, Fedor
Gomi, Takanori
Henderson, Dan "Hollywood"
Nogueira, Antonio Rodrigo
Silva, Wanderlei

PRIDE Fighters
Aoki, Shinya
Barnett, Josh
Filipovic, Mirko "Cro Cop"
Fujita, Kazuyuki
Overeem, Alistair
Silva, Wanderlei
Vovchanchyn, Igor
Waterman, Ron

Promoters
DiBella, Lou
King, Don

McIntosh, Hugh
Parnassus, George
Rickard, George Lewis "Tex"
Warren, Frank

Puerto Rican Boxers
Benitez, Wilfred
Rosario, Edwin

Referees
Hazzard, Larry
Lane, Mills
McCarthy, John
Mercante, Arthur, Sr.
Pearl, Davey
Steele, Richard

Sambo
Arlovski, Andrei
Emelianenko, Fedor

Sanctioning Bodies (Boxing)
International Boxing
    Federation (IBF)
International Boxing
    Organization (IBO)
World Boxing Association (WBA)
World Boxing Council (WBC)
World Boxing Organization (WBO)

San Shou
Le, Cung

Savate
Gordeau, Gerard

Strawweight Champions (boxing)
Alvarez, Rosendo
Lopez, Ricardo
Vorapin, Ratanapol Sor

Streetfighters (Brawlers)
Abbott, David "Tank"
Slice, Kimbo

Submissions/Techniques
Anaconda Choke
Gogoplata
Ground and Pound
Guard
Kimura, Masahiko
Triangle choke

Super Middleweight Champions (Boxing)
Barkley, Iran
Calzaghe, Joe
Collins, Steve
Eubank, Chris
Ottke, Sven

Trainers
Arcel, Ray
Benton, George
Blackburn, Jack
Dundee, Angelo
Futch, Eddie
Mayweather, Floyd, Sr.
Mayweather, Roger
McGirt, James "Buddy"
Miletich, Pat
Roach, Freddie
Steward, Emanuel

UFC Champions
Couture, Randy
Franklin, Rich
Frye, Don
Gracie, Royce
Hughes, Matt
Jackson, Quinton "Rampage"
Liddell, Chuck
Ortiz, Tito
Pulver, Jens
Serra, Matt
Severn, Dan
Shamrock, Frank
Shamrock, Ken
Sherk, Sean
Silva, Anderson
St.-Pierre, Georges

UFC Heavyweight Champions
Arlovski, Andrei
Barnett, Josh
Coleman, Mark
Couture, Randy
Mir, Frank
Nogueira, Antonio Rodrigo
Smith, Maurice
Sylvia, Tim

UFC Fighters (other)
Abbott, David "Tank"
Alexander, Houston
Bisping, Michael
Evans, Rashad
Florian, Kenny
Hamill, Matt
Herring, Heath
Huerta, Roger
Lesnar, Brock
Machida, Lyoto
Taktarov, Oleg
Trigg, Frank

Ultimate Fighter
Bisping, Michael
Evans, Rashad Griffin, Forrest
Jardine, Keith
Leben, Chris
Lytle, Chris
Serra, Matt

Uncrowned Champions
Burley, Charley
Goldberg, Benny
Langford, Sam
McAuliffe, Jack
McFarland, Packey
Scott, James
Stribling, William Lawrence "Young"
Williams, Holman

Undefeated Fighters
Barry, Jimmy
Hinton, Jemal
Kim, Ji-Won
Marciano, Rocky
Marsh, Terry
Mesi, Joe
Sithbanprachan, Pitchit
Womack, Rickey

Welterweight Champions (Boxing)
Armstrong, Henry
Benitez, Wilfred
Breland, Mark
Brown, Simon
Corbett III, Young
Cuevas, Pipino

INTRODUCTION

For centuries humans have engaged in various forms of combat sports for any number of reasons: military training, entertainment, physical exercise, or necessity. Human nature enjoys the visceral thrill of seeing two combatants engage in face-to-face conflict and near life-or-death struggle. Whether for the love of violence or just a thrill-seeking nature, many live vicariously through boxers, kickboxers, wrestlers, and mixed martial artists. Nothing in the world of sport compares to a vicious knockout, a powerful body slam, or a technically superior submission of an opponent.

Combat sports have a long and storied tradition that traces back to ancient times, including the great civilization of Greece and the mighty Roman Empire. These civilizations bestowed special honor on the top combat specialists of their time, whether they be the pankrationists of Greece in the early Olympiad or the gladiators of ancient Rome. Such honor is not the exclusive domain of Western civilization; the origins of much martial arts tradition—whether it be karate, kung fu, or judo—reside from the rich, and at times mystical, tradition in the Eastern world.

Arguably, the two most popular combat sports today are boxing and mixed martial arts (MMA). Boxing arose from ancient Greece in the seventh century b.c. The great writer/poet Homer wrote about a progenitor of boxing during those times. Modern boxing arose in England in the seventeenth century and gradually developed into a worldwide phenomenon. The nineteenth century witnessed the Marquis of Queensberry Rules, which provided for a ring, rest between different rounds, and various other rules. Toward the end of the nineteenth century, bare-knuckle boxing gave way to gloves as the sport sought to become more humane. Boxing was often a respected sport; President Theodore Roosevelt viewed it as healthy exercise for young men.

Boxing entered its heyday in the 1920s when popular heavyweight champion Jack Dempsey became a hero of Ruthian proportions, rivaling the Babe as the greatest sports hero of the day during the so-called Roaring Twenties. Radio and later television brought an even greater audience and following to the sport that sportswriter A. J. Liebling once called "the Sweet Science."

However, boxing suffered from what W.E.B. Du Bois called the "problem of the color line." Many great African American boxers never received a title shot and were relegated to lower-paying matches with each other. White society would not accept a black champion—certainly not in the heavyweight division. When the controversial and flamboyant John Arthur "Jack" Johnson broke the color barrier by capturing the world heavyweight title in 1908 (in Australia of all places), white society responded with a virulent degree of racism. Johnson's victory over the former undefeated James J. Jeffries on July 4, 1910, touched off race riots nationwide and led to the banning of fight films.

Yet, slowly progress was made, as the second African American to hold the most coveted title in sports was Joe Louis—a man canonized by many as an American hero particularly after felling his German rival Max Schmeling in the first round in their rematch. Sportswriter Jimmy Cannon famously referred to Louis as a "credit to his race—the human race." But, boxing has always been about more than the United States and more than merely black and white. The Latino community supports boxing more passionately than another group. The Philippines and Indonesia follow boxing with a fervor unknown to most North America.

Another form of combat sports has taken the world by storm, particularly in the last 15 years. In 1993, a relatively frail-looking Brazilian named Royce Gracie won something called the Ultimate Fighting Championships—a "no holds barred" tournament featuring combatants of various fighting disciplines—Muay Thai, savate, kung fu, karate, wrestling, boxing, judo, jiu-jitsu, and others—competing in no-time limit matches to the finish. Gracie—a member of the most famous fighting family in Brazil—showed the world that ground fighting or grappling could overwhelm those who merely engaged in stand-up punching and kicking.

Mixed martial arts, like boxing, also had historical roots tracing to ancient Greece. Pankration was an Olympic sport in 648 B.C., and these early combatants engaged in fighting standing up and on the ground. Today, numerous organizations—including the enormously successful and popular UFC—provide millions of fans with bouts that feature cages, gloves, and rounds. Mixed martial arts has become arguably the fastest growing sport in the world. Its adherents stretch all over the globe from Russia to Japan to Brazil to Europe to the United States.

This book focuses on boxing and mixed martial arts—the two most popular and widely practiced combat sports. But, it also provides information about a variety of other combat sports, including kickboxing, savate, sambo, sumo wrestling, and Greco-Roman wrestling. It does not cover the popular subject of professional wrestling because that product offers fans entertainment packaged in preordained outcomes rather than traditional sport.

This encyclopedia, which organizes entries in alphabetical order, provides information about top boxers, leading mixed martial artists, promoters, writers, fighting organizations, great fights, and submission holds. The hundreds of entries listed in the following pages provide a snapshot of the entry and a "Further Reading" section that should help the fan, the researcher, the historian, and any others hoping to learn more about combat sports.

Combat sports hold a special place in my heart, as I have served as a licensed boxing judge for more than a decade, even judging a couple world title fights. I regularly write about boxing and mixed martial arts for Fightnews.com and have authored a previous book on boxing. I truly hope you will gain a greater appreciation of combat sports or more knowledge about one of your favorite combatants. Thank you for reading this book and/or using it as a research tool.

Note: Ultimate Fighting Championship®, UFC®, The Ultimate Fighter®, the Octagon®, and Zuffa® are all registered trademarks and the protected intellectual property of Zuffa, LLC.

ABBOTT, DAVID "TANK" (1965–). Tank Abbott is a mixed martial artist known for his heavy hands and outrageous actions. Abbott achieved fame as a brawler or pitfighter not versed in many grappling and submission skills. But, he did not need many of those skills early in his career, as his powerful right hand bombs inflicted major damage. He also had a wrestling background that he used to his advantage early in his career.

He burst onto the mixed martial arts (MMA) scene at **Ultimate Fighting Championships (UFC)** 6, knocking out 350-lb. John Matua in 18 seconds. As Matua's body writhed in pain, Abbott mimicked Matua's near-lifeless motion. In his next bout, he kayoed Paul Varelans, grinning as he mashed his opponent against the Octagon fence. After the bout, Abbott told commentator Jeff Blatnick that he better turn the tape off of the fight, as he was "starting to get sexually aroused." He lost in the finals of UFC 6 after 17 minutes to Russian **sambo** expert **Oleg Taktarov.** Abbott's brawling, take-no-prisoners style endeared him to UFC fans, but his lack of conditioning led him to lose many fights that he possibly could have won.

He nearly won the Ultimate Ultimate 96, kayoing two opponents before falling in the finals to **Don "the Predator" Frye.** Physically strong, Abbott allegedly bench pressed more than 600 lbs. He has lost more fights than he has won at the top levels of MMA, dropping fights to **Maurice Smith,** Kimo, **Dan Severn, Frank Mir,** and **Paul Buentello** among others. He did have an impressive showing in May 2005, when he knocked out Wesley Correira in the first round. In February 2008, a 42-year-old Abbott faced street fighting phenom **Kimbo Slice** in a main event for **Elite XC** and lost in 43 seconds.

Professional MMA Record:	10-14
Championship(s):	None

Further Reading

Dayton, Morinyanga. "Abbott knocks out 'Cabbage' in 1st round." *The Honolulu Advertiser,* 5/8/2005, p. 1C.

"Portrait of a Serial Brawler: Tank Abbott." *FightSport,* April 2008, pp. 64–67.

Wall, Jeremy. *UFC's Ultimate Warriors Top 10.* Ontario: ECW Press, 2005, pp. 27–42.

ABRAHAM, ARTHUR (1980–). "King" Arthur Abraham is, at the time of this writing, an undefeated middleweight champion known for his iron chin, indomitable will, and courage in the ring. Born in 1980, in Yerevan, Armenia, Abraham currently resides in Berlin, Germany.

He turned pro in 2003 and two years later moved into position for a world title shot by defeating the highly regarded Howard Eastman from Great Britain. He later defeated the highly regarded Kingsley Ikeke in the fifth round to win the vacant **International Boxing Federation (IBF)** middleweight championship. He has made eight successful defenses, including two wins over tough contender Edison Miranda. In his first bout with Miranda, Abraham overcame a broken jaw to win a unanimous decision. Speculation abounds that Abraham will test his skills against **Kelly Pavlik** or **Joe Calzaghe** in the near future.

Professional Record:	28-0
Championship(s):	IBF middleweight, 2005–

Further Reading
Lewis, Ron. "Abraham proves his mettle with savage display of power." *The Times*, 5/28/2007, p. 28.
Official Web site: http://www.arthur-abraham.de/
Sheehan, Pat. "Arthur's the King of Pain." *The Sun*, 5/25/2007.

ABU DHABI COMBAT CLUB. A famous combat club created by mixed martial arts aficionado Sheik Tahnoon Bin Zayed Al Nahyan of the United Arab Emirates. The Shiek became an avid fan of mixed martial arts after watching the first UFC event in 1993. He created the combat club and invited top practitioners from many combat styles to train at his facility. In 1998, the Club hosted the world-renown Abu Dhabi World Submission Fighting Championships, which seeks to determine the best grapplers in the world. These championships do not allow for striking, but focus on grappling and submission holds.

Numerous top mixed martial artists have competed in the championships, including **Mark Kerr, Matt Hughes, Tito Ortiz, Antonio Rodrigo Nogueira, Jeff Monson** and others.

Further Reading
Abu Dhabi Combat Club Official Web site: http://www.adcombat.com/

ACCAVALLO, HORACIO (1934–). Horacio Accavallo was one of the greatest flyweight champions in history and one of the greatest fighters ever from Argentina. This southpaw great lost only 2 times in more than 80 professional bouts. Born in 1934 in Parque Patricios, Argentina, Accavallo turned pro in 1956 and did not lose until his 23rd bout when he traveled to Rome to face Italian flyweight champion Salvatore Burruni and lost a decision.

In March 1966, Accavallo traveled to Tokyo to face **World Boxing Association (WBA)** flyweight champion Katsuyoshi Takayama, whom he defeated by split decision over 15 rounds. He successfully defended his title three times—against the great **Efren Torres** and tough Japanese fighter Hiroyuki Ebihara twice—before retiring as champion. His only other loss was a nontitle bout against Kiyoshi Tanabe when he suffered a bad cut on his eyebrow, causing the referee to halt the bout.

Professional Record:	75-2-6
Championship(s):	WBA flyweight, 1966–1968

Further Reading
United Press International. "Accavallo Keeps Title on Decision." *Los Angeles Times*, 7/16/1966, p. A7.
United Press International. "Accavallo Keeps Flyweight Title." *The New York Times*, 12/11/1966, p. 255.

Former super bantamweight champ Clarence "Bones" Adams unloads a hook to the body of opponent David Martinez in their May 2007 bout. Adams won a unanimous decision. Courtesy of Chris Cozzone.

ADAMS, CLARENCE (1974–). Clarence Richard "Bones" Adams was a former world super bantamweight champion known for his quick hands and excellent boxing skills. Born in 1974 in Henderson, Kentucky, Adams turned pro at age 15 in 1990 against the infamous journeyman Simmie Black—a fighter with more than 150 professional bouts.

Adams rose through the ranks, compiling a record of 26-0-1 to earn a title shot against **International Boxing Federation (IBF)** bantamweight champion **Orlando Canizales.** Adams boxed well, winning several rounds before suffering a dislocated jaw and losing in the 11th round.

In his next two fights, he also lost to Frankie Toledo and Jeff Trimble because he dislocated his shoulder in both fights. Most fighters would have retired, but "Bones" kept fighting, and several years later in March 2000, he gave a boxing lesson to Nestor Garza to win the **World Boxing Association (WBA)** super bantamweight title. He successfully defended his title three times before vacating it to face **Paulie Ayala.** "Bones" lost a 12-round split decision and then lost by unanimous decision in the rematch. He last fought in 2008 in a bout that ended in a no-contest.

Professional Record:	43-6-4
Championship(s):	WBA super bantamweight, 2000–2001

Further Reading
Hudson, David L., Jr. "Clarence 'Bones' Adams: No Ordinary Fighter!" *Fightnews*, 2/19/2002.
Lebreton, Gil. "Lean years left 'Bones' hungry for success." *Fort Worth Star-Telegram*, 8/4/2001, p. SP 1.
Watkins, Calvin. "Fighting has been Bones Adams' life; Ayala's opponent started boxing before the age of 5." *The Dallas Morning News*, 2/24/2002, p. 1B.

AFFLICTION. Affliction, or Affliction Clothing, is a California-based company best known before 2008 for its popular t-shirts, which became popular in mixed martial arts (MMA) circles. Several mixed martial fighters and boxers sport Affliction shirts and now have their own Affliction shirts bearing their names.

Tom Atencio of Affliction announcing a partnership with Oscar De La Hoya's Golden Boy Promotions in September 2008. Courtesy of Chris Cozzone.

In 2008, Affliction Clothing became more intimately involved in mixed martial arts as it promoted a major mixed martial event entitled Affliction: Banned. The show featured MMA's reigning pound-for-pound great and heavyweight kingpin **Fedor "The Last Emperor" Emelianenko,** former two-time **Ultimate Fighting Championships (UFC)** heavyweight champion **Tim Sylvia, Andrei Arlovski, Josh Barnett, Matt Lindland,** and other MMA notables.

The July 19, 2008, event featured the rock band Megadeath, famed boxing announcer Michael Buffer, and many of MMA's top heavyweights. Affliction hopes to continue promoting high-profile MMA cards and presumably compete with industry leader UFC for supremacy in MMA. The company's next major show took place on January 24, 2009, headlined by a clash between Emelianenko and Arlovski.

Further Reading
Herman, Gary. "Q & A with Affliction Vice President Atencio," cbssports.com, 12/17/2008, at http://www.cbssports.com/mma/story/11178228
Official Site: http://www.afflictionclothing.com/banned_july19/
Taflinger, Neal. "Affliction: The Biggest Card of All Time." *FIGHT!* (July 2008), p. 28.

ALCINE, JOACHIM (1976–). Joachim Alcine is a former junior middleweight champion born in Haiti who resides in Canada. Born 1976 in Guitana, Haiti, he moved to Montreal, Canada, as a youngster. He didn't start taking boxing seriously until age 17, but he proved to be a quick study.

He turned pro in 1999 and first began to attract attention in the boxing world in 2004 with victories over Fernando Hernandez and Stephane Quellet. He followed that up in 2005 with wins over Carlos Bojorquez and former junior middleweight champion Carl Daniels. In June 2007, he finally received a world title shot against undefeated champion Travis Simms. Alcine dropped Simms in the sixth round en route to a unanimous decision victory. With his win, he became the first Haitian-born fighter to win a world boxing title. He made one successful defense before losing his title to Daniel Santos in July 2008.

He regularly spars and works out with mixed martial arts superstar **Georges St.-Pierre.**

Professional Record:	30-1
Championship(s):	WBA junior middleweight, 2007–2008

Further Reading
Todd, Jack. "He's fighting for poor kids: When Joachim Alcine was growing up in Haiti, his family was so
   poor that he didn't sleep in a bed." *The Gazette* (Montreal), 2/12/2005, p. C1.
Todd, Jack. "Boxer inspired to make history." *The Gazette* (Montreal), 7/7/2007, p. D1.

ALEXANDER, HOUSTON (1972–). Houston "the Nebraskan Assassin" Alexander is a
light heavyweight mixed martial arts (MMA) artist who fights in the **Ultimate Fighting Championships (UFC).** Born in East St. Louis, Missouri, Alexander's mother moved the family to
Omaha, Nebraska, when Houston was eight years old. He earned letters in football and wrestling in high school. He possesses a lethal stand-up game, featuring devastating power in both
fists.

He began his professional career in 2001 in an Extreme Challenge event losing via submission to Jason Medina. He rebounded with several victories, earning a UFC contract in 2007. In
his first fight in the UFC, he devastated favorite **Keith "the Dean of Mean" Jardine** with a first-
round stoppage. In November 2007, he lost to **Thiago Silva.** In his next bout in 2008, Alexander
suffered a devastating kayo loss to fellow striker James Irwin who stopped him in eight seconds.
At the time of this writing, he lost his third straight bout to Eric Schafer. He hopes to revitalize
his career in 2009 and beyond. Though he has lost three straight bouts, Alexander remains a fan
favorite given his explosive, aggressive style.

Professional MMA record:	8-4
Championship(s):	None

Further Reading
Franck, Loren. "The Dirty Dozen: Lifestylin' With the UFC's Houston Alexander." *Elite Fighter* (March
   2008), pp. 32–34.
Frazer, Bear. "Houston Alexander: The Assassin Stays Sharp." *Fight!* (December 2007), pp. 58–60.
Morgan, Adam. "Houston Alexander Interview: 'My Ground Game Is Just As Good As Anyone in the
   UFC.'" Five Ounces of Pain, 9/28/2007, at http://fiveouncesofpain.com/2007/09/28/houston-
   alexander-interview-my-ground-game-is-just-as-good-as-anyone-in-the-ufc/
Official Web site: http://www.houstontheassassin.com/

ALEXIO, DENNIS (1959–). Dennis "the Terminator" Alexio was one of the greatest kickboxers of all-time, compiling an unbelievable record of 70-2 with 65 stoppages. Alexio also
boxed professionally, compiling a record of 5-1. His only two losses in his illustrious kickboxing
career were to Don "the Dragon" Wilson and Stan "the Man" Longinidis. He lost to Longinidis
in 1992 only 13 seconds into the bout when he blocked a leg strike with his shin, breaking the
bone in the process. The fight had to be stopped. Alexio was recognized as the heavyweight
kickboxing champion by at least four different sanctioning organizations during the height of
his career, including the World Kickboxing Association and the Karate International Council
of Kickboxing (KICK). In addition to his devastating striking ability, Alexio had a great chin.
Alexio discovered his love for martial arts early in life as a youngster in Vacaville, California,
where he lived his early years before moving to Hawaii. Alexio often entered the ring in a grass

skirt as a tribute to his Hawaian culture. Once in a 1994 match in California, officials told him he had to remove the skirt or face disqualification. Alexio stripped down to his gym shorts and kayoed his opponent.

Alexio's popularity extended beyond the realm of sports when he entered the cinematic world, starring in the karate movie *Kickboxer* with Jean Claude Van Damme.

Professional Kickboxing Record: 70-2
Championship(s):   International Karate Federation Champion, 1998–2003

Further Reading
Dayton, Morinaga. "Amp Hoping to Stun Alexio." *The Honolulu Advertiser*, 5/7/1999, p. 1D.
Graswich, R. E. "Kick Boxing Faces Test in Return Here," *The Sacramento Bee*, 4/30/1998, p. E1.

ALI, LAILA (1977–). Laila Ali is arguably the most recognizable female boxer in the history of the sport. The daughter of **Muhammad Ali,** Laila turned pro in 1999 and compiled an undefeated record of 24-0 with 21 stoppages. She last fought in February 2007.

Born in 1977 in Miami Beach, Florida, to Muhammad Ali and his third wife, Veronica Porsche, Laila graduated college from Santa Monica College and later owned a business. She later turned her attention to boxing to much fanfare.

In 2002, she defeated Jacqui Frazier-Lyde—the daughter of her father's most famous rival **Joe Frazier.** She also defeated the tough Valerie Manhood twice and overwhelmed the smaller **Christy Martin** in 2003. She failed to fight some of the other top female fighters of her time, such as Ann Wolfe, Leticia Robinson, and **Lucia Rijker.**

Professional Record: 24-0
Championship(s):   WBC Female World Super Middleweight Champion, 2006–2008; WIBA World Super Middleweight Champion, 2002–2008

Further Reading
Ali, Laila with David Ritz. *Reach!: Finding Strength, Spirit and Personal Power.* New York: Hyperion, 2002.
Official Site: http://www.lailaali.com/

ALI, MUHAMMAD (1942–). Muhammad Ali is not only the most famous boxer of all-time but may be the most recognizable face in the world. A former three-time world heavyweight champion, Ali has transcended the sporting world and become a cultural, global icon.

Born in 1942 in Louisville, Kentucky, as Cassius Marcellus Clay, legend has it that he turned to boxing after a local bully stole his bicycle. Clay developed into a fine amateur, culminating in his winning a gold medal in the light heavyweight division at the 1960 Rome Olympics.

He turned pro later that year with a decision win over tough Tommy Hunsaker. He overwhelmed most of his early opponents with his catlike quickness and overwhelming hand speed. Clay attracted a following in part to his fistic prowess but in part to his braggadocio—part of which he borrowed from the wrestler Gorgeous George. In several fights, Clay would call the round in which he would finish his opponent. For instance, he predicted that former light heavyweight champion **Archie Moore** "would fall in four." Sure enough, Clay stopped Moore in the fourth round.

After a pair of tough wins in 1963 over contenders Doug Jones and **Henry Cooper,** Clay received a title shot against the formidable champion **Sonny Liston**—a feared champion who had destroyed **Floyd Patterson** with two successive first-round stoppages. Clay entered the ring as a heavy underdog in their 1964 encounter, but his speed overwhelmed the champion. Liston quit on his stool at the end of the seventh round. Clay justifiably and proudly proclaimed: "I shook up the world."

Later that year, Clay announced his conversion to the Nation of Islam and adopted the name Muhammad Ali. From 1964–1967, Ali was at his peak as a fighter. He successfully defended his title nine times, defeating the likes of Floyd Patterson, **George Chuvalo,** Henry Cooper, **Cleveland Williams,** and **Ernie Terrell** with relative ease. However, he refused induction into the armed services for Vietnam, famously proclaiming: "I don't have no personal quarrels with those Viet Congs." He also decried the war, saying: "The white man sent the black man to kill the yellow man."

He was stripped of his title in 1967 and later convicted for willfully refusing induction into the U.S. Armed Forces. Ali spent the next few years in exile, relegating to giving speeches on college campuses. In 1970, he received a license to fight in Georgia against contender **Jerry Quarry.** After another win over the tough **Oscar Bonavena,** Ali faced off against undefeated champion **"Smokin' Joe Frazier** in a bout billed as "the Fight of the Century."

The bout was close, but Frazier dropped Ali with a thunderous left hook in the 15th round and won a unanimous decision. After Ali dropped another decision to **Ken Norton,** some speculated he would never regain the heavyweight championship.

In 1973 and 1974, he won rematches with Norton and Frazier, putting himself in line to challenge heavyweight champion **George Foreman,** who had steamrolled his way through the division. Once again a heavy underdog, Ali faced Foreman in the legendary **"Rumble in the Jungle"** in Kinshasa, Zaire. Ali employed his famous "rope-a-dope" strategy, laying on the ropes and allowing Foreman to exhaust himself. Ali finished Foreman in the eighth round to regain his championship.

He successfully defended his championship 10 times, often narrowly escaping defeat. In 1975, he defeated Frazier in their famous rubber match called the **"Thrilla in Manila."** He also defeated Norton in their third bout by close decision in 1976. In 1978, Ali lost his title to underdog **Leon Spinks** by split decision. Seven months later, he defeated Spinks by unanimous decision to become the first man to win the heavyweight title three times. He retired after the Spinks bout but came out of retirement to face **Larry Holmes.** He was beaten badly over 11 rounds. He finally retired in 1981 after losing to **Trevor Berbick.**

Once hated for belonging to the Nation of Islam and his antiwar stance, Ali later became a cultural hero. The punishment he absorbed in his illustrious career no doubt contributed to his Pugilistic Parkinson's Syndrome. His hands shake, and he speaks quite slowly, if at all. However, he surprised the world by lighting the torch at the 1996 Atlanta Olympic Games.

To many boxing fans, Ali will forever remain "the Greatest."

Professional Record:	56-5-1
Championship(s):	WBC Heavyweight, 1964–1967, 1974–1978, 1978–1979; WBA Heavyweight, 1964, 1967, 1974–1978

Further Reading

Ali, Muhammad, with Richard Duncan. *The Greatest: My Own Story.* New York: Random House, 1975.
Bingham, Howard L., and Max Wallace. *Muhammad Ali's Greatest Fight.* London: Robson, 2004.
Brunt, Stephen. *Facing Ali: Fifteen Fighters, Fifteen Stories.* Guilford, CT.: Lyons Press, 2004.
Cottrell, John. *Man of Destiny: The Story of Muhammad Ali/Cassius Clay.* London: Muller, 1967.

Early, Gerald, ed. *The Muhammad Ali Reader*. New York: Harper Perennial, 1999.
Hauser, Thomas. *Muhammad Ali: His Life and Times*. New York: Simon & Schuster, 1992.
Hauser, Thomas. *The Lost Legacy of Muhammad Ali*. Toronto: Sport Media Publishing, 2005.
Marqusee, Mike. *Redemption Song: Muhammad Ali and the Spirit of the 60s* (2nd ed.). London: Verso, 1995.
Remnick, David. *King of the World: Muhammad Ali and the Rise of an American Hero*. New York: Vintage Books, 1999.
Zirin, Dave. *Muhammad Ali Handbook*. London: MQ Publications, 2007.

ALVAREZ, ROSENDO (1970–). Rosendo Alvarez was one of the toughest fighters in boxing's smallest divisions. Born in Nicaragua in 1970, Alvarez turned pro in 1992 and won his first 19 bouts before facing unbeaten **World Boxing Association (WBA)** minimumweight (or strawweight) champion Chana Porpaoin. Alvarez won a 12-round split decision in Thailand to capture the title in 1995.

He made four successful defenses of his title before a unification about with **World Boxing Council (WBC)** champion **Ricardo Lopez.** After the bout ended in a technical draw, the two fought a rematch in November 1998. Alvarez lost a split decision.

Alvarez later moved up to the junior flyweight division and won a world title by defeating Bebis Mendoza by split decision in 2001. He made several successful defenses of his title before eventually moving up to the flyweight division. He retired after losing to **Jorge Arce** in 2006.

Professional Record:	37-3-2
Championship(s):	WBA Minimumweight, 1995–1998; WBA Junior Flyweight, 2001–2004

Further Reading
Feour, Royce. "Light makes right: Lopez takes crown." *Las Vegas Review-Journal*, 11/14/1998, p. 1C.
Smith, Timothy. "Two Unbeaten Little Guys Square Off in Big Bout." *The New York Times*, 11/12/1998, p. D2.

ANACONDA CHOKE. The anaconda choke is a powerful submission move in mixed martial arts in which one combatant places his opponent in a headlock while locking one of his opponent's arms. The combatant then rolls over to the side of his opponent, squeezing the opponent's head into his body. This places intense pressure on the opponent's head causing a submission. Brazilian jiu-jitsu specialist and former **PRIDE** and **Ultimate Fighting Championships (UFC)** heavyweight champion **Antonio Rodrigo Nogueira** has used this submission move in professional competition to great advantage. In a 2008 UFC bout, Japanese mixed martial artist Yoshiyuki Yoshida submitted Jon "the War Machine" Kopenhaver via the anaconda choke.

Further Reading
Rousseau, Robert. "Top 20 Submission Moves in MMA." *ExtremeProSports.Com* at http://extremeprosports.com/MMA/submissions.html

ANGOTT, SAMMY (1915–1980). Sammy Angott was a former world lightweight champion who fought the best fighters of his era, including all-time greats **Henry Armstrong, Willie Pep,** and **Sugar Ray Robinson.** Born in 1915 in Washington, Penn., as Salvatore Engotti, Angott turned pro in 1935 and fought in 1950.

He is best known for handing the masterful Pep his first defeat in March 1943 via 10-round decision. In 1939, he defeated contenders Aldo Spoldi, Petey Sarron, Davey Day, and **Baby**

Arizmendi. That landed him a title shot in 1940 against Day for the NBA lightweight championship. He won a 15-round decision. Later that year he defeated **Bob Montgomery.**

He also captured the world lightweight title in 1941 with a victory over **Lew Jenkins.** During part of his career, he coached boxing at Washington and Jefferson University. His son Sam Angott, Jr. played professional baseball.

Angott lost three times to the great Sugar Ray Robinson—hardly a mark of dishonor. Angott earned his posthumous induction into the International Boxing Hall of Fame.

Record:	98-27-8
Championships:	NBA Lightweight, 1940–1941, 1943–1944; Lightweight, 1941–1942.

Further Reading

Nichols, Joseph S. "Pep Outpointed by Angott; Suffers First Defeat in 63 Professional Fights." *The New York Times*, 3/20/1943, p. 19.

Roberts, James B., and Alexander G. Skutt. *Boxing Register: International Boxing Hall of Fame Official Record Book* (4th ed.). Ithaca, NY: McBooks Press, Inc., 2006, pp. 272–275.

ANTUOFERMO, VITO (1953–). Vito Antuofermo was a tough brawler who clawed his way to the world middleweight championship, winning fights through sheer determination and an iron jaw. Born in Italy in 1953, Antuofermo moved with his family to the United States when he was 10 years old.

He turned pro in 1971, compiling a record of 17-0-1 in his first 18 bouts. In 1973, he suffered his first setback to master boxer Harold Weston, Jr. He rebounded with 18 straight wins before back-to-back losses in 1976—one to future junior middleweight champion Maurice Hope.

In 1979, he captured the world title with a surprising 15-round split-decision victory over **Hugo Corro** in Monte Carlo, Monaco. In his first defense, he entered as a heavy underdog to **Marvelous Marvin Hagler.** Antuofermo battled his way to a draw, retaining his title. He lost the belt in his next fight, dropping a split decision to Britain's Alan Minter. He then dropped the rematch to Minter. In 1981, Antuofermo failed to regain his title, losing to the then-champion Hagler in the fifth round due to cuts. He retired for good in 1985, after losing to undefeated Canadian prospect Matthew Hilton.

Record:	50-7-2
Championship(s):	Middleweight, 1979–1980

Further Reading

Katz, Michael. "Antuofermo Counts Out a Rocky Boxing Career." *The New York Times*, 12/8/1981, p. D27.

Matthews, Wallace. "A Comeback for the Cash." *Newsday*, 8/31/1993, p. 120.

Poliquin, Bud. "Vito's Face: The Look Launched 1,000 Gasps." *The Post-Standard*, 6/10/1991, p. E1.

AOKI, SHINYA (1983–). Shinya Aoki is a Japanese-based mixed martial artist known for his extreme flexibility, superior submission skills, success in the ring, and yellow spandex pants. Born in 1983, this former police officer began his professional mixed martial arts (MMA) career in 2004 at DEEP and then moved to Shooto competitions. He won the Shooto middleweight championship in February 2006 with a win over Akira Kikuchi. He has also had great success in **PRIDE,** defeating the likes of Jason Black, Clay French, and Joachim Hansen. He is known as the "Tobikan Judan" or "the tenth degree black belt in jumping locks."

Aoki achieved great recognition for his victory over Hansen at PRIDE Shockwave 2006, when he submitted his opponent **Joachim Hansen** with a **gogoplata**—a rarely used submission technique in actual fighting competition. Aoki then further cemented his reputation as one of the most creative mixed martial artists with a gogoplata submission win over Katsuhiko Nagata in 2008. Both those gogoplata submissions were called by *FIGHT!* Magazine as among the "10 sickest submissions of all time."

Professional MMA Record: 19-3
Championship(s):   Shooto Middleweight Champion, 2007

Further Reading
"Shinya Aoki: "I am not interested in ADCC at all." *FightSport* (August 2007), p. 30.
Yu, Al. "Baka Survivor: An Introduction to Lightweight Phenom—Shinya Aoki." *FIGHT!* (August 2008), p. 34.
Zeidler, Ben. "10 Sickest Submissions of All Time," *FIGHT!*, October 2008, pp. 94–96.

ARAGON, ART (1927–2008). Art Aragon was the original "Golden Boy"—many years before **Oscar De La Hoya** popularized the nickname. Aragon was a popular lightweight contender who never won a world title but won 90 bouts and defeated several champions during his long career.

Born in 1927 in Belen, New Mexico, Aragon moved to Los Angeles and was forever linked to the "City of Angels." To this day, many consider him to be the most popular fighter ever in the city. Blessed with a powerful left hook and good looks, Aragon made for crowd-pleasing fights and for good newspaper copy, as he was linked to several famous Hollywood starlets during the course of his career.

He made his professional debut in 1944 against Frenchy Rene. He fought better competition as his career progressed. One of his highlight performances was a dramatic 12th-round stoppage of Enrique Bolanos in 1950. In August 1951, he won a 10-round split decision over world lightweight champion **Jimmy Carter** in a nontitle bout.

However, in the only title shot of his career, Aragon lost a rematch to Carter in November 1951. Dropped twice, he went the distance but lost a unanimous decision. In 1955, he twice defeated future world welterweight champion Don Jordan over 10 rounds. He finally retired in 1960.

His career was not without controversy. He was charged and convicted of bribing an opponent $500 to throw a fight, though the conviction was overturned on appeal.

Professional Record: 90-20-6
Championship(s):   None

Further Reading
Pugmire, Lance. "Art Aragon, 80, colorful L.A. boxer." *Los Angeles Times*, 3/26/2008, at http://www.latimes.com/news/obituaries/la-me-aragon26mar26,0,646322.story
Whorton, Cal. "Past Incidents in Boxing Life of Golden Boy Aragon Recalled." *Los Angeles Times*, 2/21/1954, p. B11.

ARCARI, BRUNO (1942–). Bruno Arcari was one of boxing's greatest junior welterweight champions of all time though his name is underrecognized in the sporting world. He lost only twice in more than 70 professional bouts and never lost his world title in the ring. Born in 1942 in Latina, Italy, he turned pro in 1964 inauspiciously. He lost his debut bout against Franco Colella. He then won 10 straight bouts before losing to Massimo Consolati for the Italian junior welterweight title.

Arcari never lost again in a pro career that lasted until 1978. He won the **World Boxing Council (WBC)** welterweight title in 1970 with a unanimous decision win over Pedro Adiques of the Philippines. He successfully defended his title nine times, including an impressive kayo win over Joao Henrique of Brazil in 1972. He vacated his title in 1974 after defeating Antonio Ortiz and moved up to the welterweight division.

He never lost at welterweight, though he drew with a tough Rocky Mattioli in 1976. He retired two years later after defeating Jesse Lara. He should be inducted into the International Boxing Hall of Fame.

Professional Record:	70-2-1
Championship(s):	WBC junior welterweight, 1970–1974

Further Reading
Associated Press. "Junior Welterweight Title Won By Arcari on Decision." *The New York Times*, 2/1/1970, p. S6.
Associated Press. "Arcari Keeps Title By Knocking Out Henrique in 12th." *The New York Times*, 6/11/1972, p. S13.

ARCE, JORGE (1979–). Jorge Arce is one of the best little men in boxing and a former two-time junior flyweight champion. Born in 1979 in Los Mochis, Mexico, Arce turned pro in 1996. In 1998, he defeated Juan Domingo Cordoba over 12 rounds to win the World Boxing Organization (WBO) junior flyweight championship. He made one successful defense before facing former champion **Michael Carbajal.** Arce was far ahead on the scorecards but was kayoed in the 11th round. He then proceeded to win 23 straight bouts—many by knockout. He did not lose a bout after his loss to Carbajal in 1999 until 2007.

He rebounded to win the **World Boxing Council (WBC)** junior flyweight title with a sixth-round kayo of Yo-Sam Choi. He then made seven successful defenses before moving up in weight to the flyweight division. He defeated **Rosendo Alvarez** in 2006 in a WBC flyweight interim

WBC flyweight champion Jorge Arce celebrates a successful defense of his title against Hussein Hussein in March 2005. Courtesy of Chris Cozzone.

title bout. In 2007, he lost a 12-round decision to Cristian Mijares for the WBC super flyweight title. He remains a bona-fide threat in the lower weight classes.

Professional Record: 51-5-1
Championship(s):   WBO flyweight, 1998–1999; WBC junior flyweight, 2002–2005

Further Reading
Alderson, Brent Matteo. "Jorge Arce Tunes Up Another." *The Ring Extra* (August 2006), pp. 56–61.
Arias, Carlos. "Arce wins the chase." *Orange County Register,* 1/28/2007.

ARCEL, RAY (1899–1994). Ray Arcel was one of the greatest trainers in boxing history known for his longevity in the sport, keen eye, and emphasis on proper conditioning. Born in 1899 in Terre Haute, Indiana, his family moved to New York, which became his lifelong home. He began training boxers at Stillman's Gym in the 1920s.

He trained 19 world champions, including such greats as **Ezzard Charles, Benny Leonard, Tony Zale,** and **Roberto Duran.** His first champion was bantamweight Abe Goldstein in 1924. Arcel was also known as "the Meat Grinder" for training so many heavyweight opponents of the great **Joe Louis.** The last world champion he worked with was **Larry Holmes,** whom he helped train in preparation for a title defense against **Gerry Cooney.**

Further Reading
Berger, Phil. "Ray Arcel, Trainer Who Handled Many Boxing Stars, Is Dead at 94." *The New York Times,* 3/8/1994, p. B8.
Edes, Gordon. "Arcel Has the History of Boxing in His Head." *Los Angeles Times,* 3/1/1983, p. D1.
Jarrett, John. *The Champ in the Corner: The Ray Arcel Story.* London: Tempus Publishing, Ltd., 2007.
McCormick, Bill. "Noted Fight Trainer Tells How to Avoid 'Balloon Tires.'" *The Washington Post,* 3/16/1937, p. 18.

ARGUELLO, ALEXIS (1952–). The Nicaraguan-born Arguello dominated the lower weight classes in the 1970s and early 1980s, capturing world titles in three weight divisions—featherweight, super featherweight, and lightweight. Known as "the Explosive Thin Man," Arguello possessed was a classic boxer and puncher who consistently ranked among the pound-for-pound top fighters of his generation. He turned pro at age 16 in 1968, losing his pro debut in a first round technical knockout. Though he lost two of his first four fights, Arguello improved rapidly. He lost his first title bout to the clever Ernesto Marcel by a 15-round decision in 1974. Later that year, Arguello captured his first title by kayoing **Ruben Olivares** in the 13th round to win the **World Boxing Association (WBA)** featherweight title.

He added the **World Boxing Council (WBC)** super featherweight championship with a tough 13th-round victory over the skilled **Alfredo Escalera.** He successfully defended his title eight times with victories over future champions Rafael "Bazooka" Limon and **Bobby Chacon.** In 1981, he overwhelmed England's Jim Watt to capture a 15-round decision by a wide margin. In his first defense, he defeated the popular **Ray "Boom Boom" Mancini.** In 1982, he challenged undefeated junior welterweight champion **Aaron Pryor** for the WBA junior welterweight crown. In one of the great action fights of all time, Pryor rallied to win in the 14th round. Arguello valiantly tried to avenge the defeat in 1983 but lost again. He retired but returned to the ring in 1985 with a win over a nondescript opponent. His great career earned him enshrinement in the International Boxing Hall of Fame in 1992. He returned to the ring yet again for one fight each in 1994 and 1995.

Record:	80-8
Championship(s):	WBA featherweight, 1974–1977; WBC super featherweight, 1978–1980; WBC lightweight, 1981–1983

Further Reading

Anderson, Dave. "The Hawk and the Dove." *The New York Times*, 11/12/1982, p. D19.

Hoffer, Richard. "Arguello Wins It Just for Arguello." *Los Angeles Times*, 2/10/1986, p. SP 3.

Murray, Jim. "A Mere Triple Crown Isn't Enough for Arguello." *Los Angeles Times*, 10/21/1982, p. F1.

Poliquin, Bud. "Arguello: Class Act Among Champions." *The Post-Standard*, 6/12/1988, p. D1.

Vecsey, George. "Arguello Wanders into Ring History." *The New York Times*, 11/16/1981, p. C1.

ARIZMENDI, BABY (1914–1963). Albert "Baby" Arizmendi was a popular featherweight champion from Mexico known for his smiling face and killer instinct in the ring. Born in 1914 in Tamaulipas, Mexico, Arizmendi turned pro in 1927 at the age of 13. He won the Mexican bantamweight title in 1931 with a win over Kid Pancho.

In October 1932, he won a decision over Newsboy Brown for the world featherweight title—at least as recognized by the California Athletic Commission. However, in February 1933, he lost to **Freddie Miller,** who was recognized as champion by the New York Boxing Association (NBA). In November 1934 and January 1935, he defeated the great **Henry Armstrong** by decision in consecutive bouts.

He later lost to Armstrong for the world welterweight title in 1939. He retired in 1942 after suffering four straight losses.

Professional Record:	71-26-13
Championship(s):	Featherweight, 1932–1933

Further Reading

Lowry, Paul. "Baby Arizmendi, Mexican Hero." *Los Angeles Times*, 11/22/1932, p. A9.

Owe, Kay. "Baby Arizmendi Takes Another Hurdle When He Battles Claude Varner at Olympics." *Los Angeles Times*, 2/28/1932, p. F5.

Roberts, James B., and Alexander G. Skutt. *The Boxing Register: International Boxing Hall of Fame Official Record Book* (4th ed.). Ithaca, NY: McBooks Press, Inc., 2006, pp. 85–86.

ARLOVSKI, ANDREI (1979–). Known as "the Pitbull," Andrei Arlovksi is a former **Ultimate Fighting Championships (UFC)** world heavyweight champion known for his stand-up striking skills and overall athleticism. His quickness and power have led to some quick knockouts, including an amazing 15-second knockout of **Paul Buentello** in 2005.

Arlovski grew up in Minsk, Belarus, where he became interested in weight lifting and later **Sambo,** a Russian combat sport. In 1999, he became Sambo world champion. He began competing in mixed martial events in Europe, catching the attention of UFC talent scouts. He made his UFC debut in November 2000 with a first-round submission win over Aaron Brink. He then suffered consecutive losses to **Pedro Rizzo** and **Ricco Rodriguez** in 2001 and 2002.

He rebounded with three straight knockout wins between 2002 and 2004 over Ian Freeman, Vladimir Matyushenko, and Wesley Correira to earn a shot at the heavyweight title. He captured the world title earlier in 2005 with an Achilles submission lock over **Tim Sylvia.** He lost his title to Sylvia in the rematch next year. He also lost the rubber match to Sylvia. However, Arlovski has won four straight matches in his quest to regain the title, most recently a win at UFC 82 over Jake O'Brien. In July 2008, Arlovski—no longer with the UFC—fought on a fight card promoted by

Affliction. Arlovski defeated Ben Rothwell to cement his status as one of the world's top heavy-weights in mixed martial arts. He later defeated Roy Nelson to move closer to a bout with **Fedor Emelianenko** in January 2009, where Emelianenko stopped Arlovski in the first round.

Arlovski also plans to launch a professional boxing career in 2009, as he has been working with famed boxing trainer **Freddie Roach**.

Professional MMA Career:	14-6
Championship(s):	UFC Heavyweight Champion, 2005–2006

Further Reading
Goodlad, Terry. "Beware of the Pitbull." *Flex*, 10/1/2005, pp. 147–154.
Modrowski, Roman. "Arlovski no longer missing in action." *Chicago Sun-Times*, 2/28/2008, p. 70.
Official Site: http://www.arlovski.tv/
Villarreal, Adam. "You Can't Cage This Pitbull." *Tapout*, No. 24 (2008), pp. 41–45.

ARMSTRONG, DAVEY (1960–). David Lee Armstrong was one of the best amateur boxers and the only U.S. boxer to compete in two successive Olympic Games. In 1972, Armstrong lost to Enrique Rodriguez. Undeterred, Armstrong continued dominating in the amateurs, including a gold medal at the 1975 Pan-American games. He made the U.S. Olympic squad in 1976 and lost a controversial decision to eventual gold medalist Angel Herrera in the quarterfinals. Armstrong continued in the amateur ranks, chasing the Olympic dream, but he was foiled by the U.S. boycott of the Moscow Olympics. Armstrong turned professional in 1980 and compiled a record of 24-3. He never received a shot at a world title. He retired in 1983.

Professional Record:	24-3
Championship(s):	None

Further Reading
Gutskey, Earl. "For These Six, Quest for Gold Didn't Pan Out." *Los Angeles Times*, 9/15/1983, p. SD_B1.

ARMSTRONG, HENRY (1912–1988). "Hammering" Henry Armstrong was one of the greatest fighters in boxing history. He simultaneously held world championships in the feather-weight, lightweight, and welterweight divisions—perhaps the greatest accomplishment in boxing history. Born in 1912 in Columbus, Mississippi, as Henry Jackson, Armstrong turned pro in 1931 and lost his professional debut. In fact, Armstrong lost three of his first four bouts. He quickly improved and dominated his opponents with an all-out aggressive assault on his opponents.

He won the featherweight title in 1937 by stopping Petey Sarron in the 6th round. In 1938, he first won the welterweight championship by decisioning **Barney Ross** over 15 rounds. In his very next fight, he added the lightweight title with a 15-round decision win over Lou Ambers. In 1940, he attempted to add the world middleweight title but managed a draw against the power-punching Ceferino Garcia. From 1938 to 1940, he successfully defended his welterweight title 19 times before finally losing a 15-round decision to **Fritzie Zivic** in 1940. He retired in 1945 after a decision loss to Chester Slider. In retirement, he traded punching for preaching and became a Baptist minister.

Record:	151-21-9
Championships:	featherweight, 1937–1939; lightweight, 1938–1939; welterweight, 1938–1940

Further Reading

Armstrong, Henry. *Gloves, Glory and God*. Westwood, NJ: Fleming H. Revell Company, 1956.

Dettloff, William. "The Ten Greatest Title Reigns of All Time." *The Ring* (April 2005), pp. 65–76, p. 70.

Evans, Gavin. "The 20 Greatest Welterweights of All-Time." *The Ring* (February 2008), pp. 63–84, 65.

Hawn, Jack. "The Only Preacher Who Ever Held 3 World Titles." *Los Angeles Times*, 8/28/1977, p. E1.

Vidmar, Richard. "Down in Front: Little Dynamite." *The Washington Post*, 8/3/1938, p. X19.

ARUM, BOB (1931–). Bob Arum is one of the greatest promoters in boxing history and the founder and chairman of Top Rank Boxing, the Las Vegas, Nevada-based promotional company. He has promoted more than 9,000 fights in 22 countries across the globe.

Born in 1931 in New York City, Arum obtained his undergraduate degree from New York University and his law degree from Harvard. He then worked as a district attorney in New York City and then as a lawyer for the U.S. Department of Justice during the John F. Kennedy and Lyndon B. Johnson administrations.

Arum's first boxing promotion was the 1966 bout between champion **Muhammad Ali** and challenger George Chuvalo. It was the first fight that Arum had ever seen live. Arum learned a little about boxing when he headed the tax division of the U.S. attorney's office in New York, a position from which he had to hold up the purse of the first **Floyd Patterson-Sonny Liston** heavyweight title fight.

Arum later represented Lester Malitz, a television executive who produced boxing. In that capacity, Arum hired NFL running back Jim Brown to be a boxing announcer for Malitz. Brown, who became friends with Arum, told the Harvard-trained lawyer that he should become a boxing promoter. Brown later introduced Arum to Muhammad Ali.

That meeting led to a fruitful relationship for Arum and Ali, as Arum promoted more than 20 Ali fights. He also promoted other great fighters, including **George Foreman, Oscar De La Hoya, Sugar Ray Leonard, Julio Cesar Chavez, Floyd Mayweather Jr.** and **Marvin Hagler.**

Promoter Bob Arum raises the hands of two warriors, Manny Pacquaio (left) and Erik Morales (right) after their March 2005 bout. Courtesy of Chris Cozzone.

Arum and Top Rank remain a leading force in professional boxing today.

Further Reading
Berkow, Ira. "Arum is Proven Ringmaster," *The New York Times*, 4/7/1987, p. D33.
Iole, Kevin. "Remembering the first fight after 40 years," *Las Vegas Review-Journal*, 4/25/2006, p. 1C.
The History of Top Rank and Bob Arum: http://www.toprank.com/about

ATLAS, TEDDY (1956–). Teddy Atlas is a world-class boxing trainer, commentator, and respected voice in the sport of boxing. Born in 1956 in Staten Island, Atlas trained as an amateur under the guidance of the legendary trainer **Cus D'Amato.** He learned many tricks of the trade from D'Amato but had to leave the camp after a dispute over D'Amato's star fighter, **Mike Tyson.**

He later trained numerous world champions, including heavyweight champion **Michael Moorer.** The intense Atlas achieved fame for his inspirational speeches to Moorer when he defeated **Evander Holyfield** for the heavyweight championship in 1994. Atlas also trained **Barry McGuigan,** Michael Grant, and Donny LaLonde.

Further Reading
Atlas, Teddy, and Peter Alson. *Atlas: From the Streets to the Ring: A Son's Struggle to Become a Man.* New York: Ecco, 2006.
Singer, Eric. "A Perfect One-Two—Atlas: Too Demanding, Moorer: Too Unyielding." *The Ring* (March 1997), pp. 19–21, 69–71.

ATTELL, ABE (1884–1970). Abraham Washington Attell was one of the finest featherweights in the history of boxing. In 1910, *The Washington Post* called him "unbeatable." He held some version or claim to the featherweight title for more than a decade in the early part of the twentieth century. Born in 1884 in San Francisco, California, Attell turned professional in 1900.

He learned quickly with a trilogy of bouts against the great **George Dixon.** In 1903, he defeated Johnny Reagan to win the featherweight championship. He held a claim of the title until 1912 when he lost to Johnny Kilbane. In 1908—while featherweight champion—he challenged lightweight titlist **Battling Nelson.** Attell earned only a draw but insisted that he actually won the fight. His last professional fight was in 1917. He was indicted but never convicted in the 1919 Black Sox scandal where players on the Chicago White Sox conspired to throw the World Series. *The Ring* magazine senior writer William Dettloff rates Attell's featherweight reign as the third greatest in boxing history. He died in 1970 at the age of 85.

Record:	91-9
Championship(s):	Featherweight, 1903–1912

Further Reading
Bodner, Allen. *When Boxing Was a Jewish Sport.* Westport, Conn.: Praeger, 1997.
Dettloff, William. "The 10 Greatest Title Reigns of All Time." *The Ring* (April 2005), pp. 65–76, 68.
"Only One Abe Attell." *The Washington Post*, 12/11/1910, p. S2.
Roberts, James B., and Alexander G. Skutt. *The Boxing Register: International Boxing Hall of Fame Register* (4th ed.). Ithaca, NY: McBooks Press, Inc., 2006, pp. 60–61.

AYALA, MIKE (1958–). Mike Ayala was a talented top contender in the featherweight division who never won a professional world title. Born in 1958 in San Antonio, Texas, Ayala had a decorated amateur career, winning national Golden Gloves and AAU titles. Instead of trying out for the 1976 Montreal Olympic Games, Ayala turned pro a year earlier in 1975.

In 1979, he challenged **Danny "Little Red" Lopez** for the **World Boxing Council (WBC)** featherweight title, putting forth a valiant effort. In many rounds, Ayala's superior boxing skills prevailed, but the power-punching Lopez kept coming. Lopez eventually stopped Ayala in the 15th and final round in a bout *The Ring* magazine later called its "fight of the year." In 1985, Ayala received another world title shot against Juan Meza for the WBC super bantamweight title. He lost in the sixth round. Ayala's last bout was in 1991. He is the older brother of the talented but very troubled **Tony Ayala, Jr.**

Professional Record:	45-6
Championship(s):	None

Further Reading

Hobson, Logan. "Boxer Mike Ayala Has Last Chance." *United Press International*, 5/21/1983.

Whisler, John. "Product of a Glove Affair: Mike Ayala never became a world champ, but he feels like one after getting his life in shape." *San Antonio Express News*, 6/16/2001, p. 1D.

AYALA, PAULIE (1970–). Paulie Ayala is a former world bantamweight champion known for his good boxing skills, persistence, and courage. Born in 1970 in Fort Worth, Texas, Ayala turned pro in 1992 and won his first 25 bouts, earning a shot at **World Boxing Council (WBC)** bantamweight champion Joichiro Tatsuyoshi in Tokyo, Japan. The referee penalized Ayala a point for a headbutt that caused a severe cut on the champion. The champion could not continue, so the fight went to the scorecards, where the champion prevailed.

The next year, Ayala received a second world title shot against undefeated **World Boxing Association (WBA)** bantamweight champion **Johnny Tapia.** Ayala won a close unanimous

Paulie Ayala (right) does battle with the great Marco Antonio Barrera in June 2004. Ayala, who moved up in weight to the featherweight division, was stopped in the 10th round. It was his last pro fight. Courtesy of Chris Cozzone.

decision to capture the belt. He made four successful defenses, including a controversial decision win over Tapia in their rematch. He later moved up to the super bantamweight division, and in 2001 and 2002, he won two decisions over **Clarence "Bones" Adams** for the **International Boxing Organization (IBO)** super bantamweight title. In 2002, Ayala moved up in weight again and challenged **Erik Morales** for the WBC featherweight title. He took tremendous punishment from Morales but went the distance. Ayala retired in 2004 after losing to **Marco Antonio Barrera.**

Professional Record:	35-3
Championship(s):	WBA bantamweight, 1999–2001

Further Reading
Iole, Kevin. "Ayala-Tapia II: Controversy Everywhere . . . Except Between the Ropes." *The Ring* (March 2001), pp. 38–41, 96.
Iole, Kevin. "Ayala Battles Bones: A Remarkable Win For An 'Unremarkable Guy.'" *KO* (August 2002), pp. 36–40.
Lebreton, Gil. "Career Move: Paulie Ayala, 34, knows tonight's fight can make or break him." *Fort Worth Star Telegram*, 6/19/2004, p. 1D.
Official Web site: http://paulieayala.com

AYALA, TONY, JR. (1963–). If talent determined championships, many boxing experts believe Tony Ayala, Jr. would have been a dominant champion. The man known as "El Torrito" or "Baby Bull" had all the skills and power to reach the top of the boxing world. Unfortunately, Ayala could not control his personal demons and spent the bulk of his prime years behind bars.

Born in 1963 in Fort Worth, Texas, he turned pro in 1980 and was regarded as one of the sport's top prospects. Initially, he did not disappoint, as he reeled off 16 straight wins before signing to face champion **Donald Curry.** However, the 19-year-old Ayala was arrested and convicted of sexually assaulting a neighbor woman. He was sentenced to 35 years in prison.

Ayala was paroled in 1999—16 years later. He returned to the ring and had some success against journeyman opponents. In 2000, he lost to former world champion Yory Boy Campos in an exciting slugfest. In 2003, he lost to Anthony Bonsante in the 11th round. In 2004, Ayala received a 10-year prison sentence for repeated parole violations. Even after his initial release in 1999, Ayala could not control his personal demons.

Professional Record:	31-2
Championship(s):	None

Further Reading
Katz, Michael. "Tony Ayala's First Interview Behind Bars." *The Ring* (June 1983), pp. 70–71.
Maher, John. "Fighting for a second chance; Boxer will try to fend off his past." *Austin American-Statesman*, 4/23/1999, p. C1.
Smith, Greg. "Tony Ayala Jr.: The Best Prospect of All-Time." *The Sweet Science*, 6/10/2005, at http://www.thesweetscience.com/boxing-article/2228/tony-ayala-best-prospect-all-time/

BAER, MAX (1909–1959). Max Baer was a former world heavyweight champion known for his devastating right hand, showmanship, and less than exemplary training habits. Born in 1909 in Omaha, Nebraska, Baer turned professional in 1929 and won most of his early fights by knockout. In 1930, he knocked out opponent Frankie Campbell who later died. Apparently, Baer hit Campbell in the back of the head during the bout. Manslaughter charges were brought against Baer and later dropped by the district attorney's office. Baer later paid for the college education of Campbell's children (Ehrmann, 71).

In 1933, Baer upset **Max Schmeling,** stopping him in the 10th round. The next year, he won the world heavyweight title by battering the Italian giant **Primo Carnera** around the ring for 11 rounds. He lost the title via 15-round decision in a major upset to **James J. Braddock.** He never received another title shot and suffered kayo losses to **Joe Louis,** Tommy Farr, and Lou Nova. In retirement, he acted and refereed boxing matches.

| **Record:** | 72-12 |
| **Championship(s):** | Heavyweight, 1934–1935 |

Further Reading
Burns, Edward. "Max Baer, the fighting clown." *Chicago Daily Tribune*, 6/23/1934, p. 15.
Ehrmann, Pete. "The Truth About Max Baer." *The Ring* (February 2006), pp. 68–73.
Fleischer, Nat. *Max Baer: The Glamour Boy of the Ring.* New York: C J O'Brien, 1942.
Roberts, James B., and Alexander G. Skutt. *The Boxing Register: International Boxing Hall of Fame Register* (4th ed.). Ithaca, NY: McBooks Press, Inc., 2006, pp. 62–63.

BALLAS, GUSTAVO (1958–). Gustavo Ballas was a former junior bantamweight champion who went undefeated in his first 54 professional bouts. He won more than 100 professional bouts in his career that spanned from 1976 to 1990. Born in 1958 in Villa Maria, Argentina, Ballas turned pro and went on an amazing winning streak.

In September 1981, he dominated Sok-Chul Bae over eight rounds to win the **World Boxing Association (WBA)** title. Unfortunately, for Ballas he lost the title in his first defense via a

15-round split decision to Panamanian fighter Rafael Pedroza in a bout held in Panama City. Ballas failed in two subsequent world title bouts, losing to **Jiro Watanabe** in 1982 and Jesus "Sugar Baby" Rajos in 1987.

Professional Record:	105-9-6
Championship(s):	WBA junior bantamweight, 1981

Further Reading
Odd, Gilbert. *Encyclopedia of Boxing.* New York: Crescent Books, 1983, p. 14.
United Press International. "Ballas Takes Title." *The New York Times,* 9/14/1981, p. C7.

BARKLEY, IRAN (1960–). Iran "the Blade" Barkley was a warrior who captured world titles in three different weight divisions—middleweight, super middleweight, and light heavyweight. He is best known for two victories over **Thomas "the Hitman" Hearns** and close decision loss to the legendary **Roberto Duran.** Born in 1960 in the Bronx, Barkley turned pro in 1982.

In 1987, he received his first world title shot, but lost a decision to **Sumbu Kalambay** for the **World Boxing Association (WBA)** middleweight title. The next year he entered the ring as a heavy underdog against Hearns. He kayoed the champion with a devastating right hand. He lost the title in his next defense against Duran in one of the all-time great fights. Duran floored Barkley in the 11th round and captured a split decision.

In 1992, Barkley overwhelmed Darrin Van Horn for the **International Boxing Federation (IBF)** super middleweight crown. Later that year, he upset Hearns again to add the WBA light heavyweight title to his collection. He lost the super middleweight title in 1993 to James "Lights Out" Toney. In 1994, he lost to Henry Maske for the IBF light heavyweight title. After 1994, his career went into decline.

He retired in 1999 after a series of losses at heavyweight.

Professional Record:	43-19-1
Championship(s):	WBC middleweight, 1988–1989; IBF super middleweight, 1992–1993; WBA light heavyweight, 1992

Further Reading
Berger, Phil. "Barkley Stuns Hearns in 3d." *The New York Times,* 6/7/1988, p. D27.
Matthews, Wallace. "He Has the Eye of the Tiger: KOs Van Horn in 2nd." *Newsday,* 1/11/1992, p. 84.
Mullan, Harry. "Barkley the Blade has the cutting edge to blunt the thrust of Benn." *The Sunday Times,* 8/12/1990.

BARNETT, JOSH (1977–). Josh Barnett is a top-flight mixed martial arts heavyweight best known for his performances in **PRIDE.** Born in 1977 in Seattle, Wash., Barnett turned pro in 1997. He won his first seven bouts, including an upset of **Dan Severn** at Superbrawl 16 in February 2000. He suffered his first professional loss in February 2001 to **Pedro Rizzo** at **Ultimate Fighting Championships (UFC)** 30: Battle on the Boardwalk. He rebounded with three straight wins in the UFC, including an upset defeat of UFC champion **Randy Couture** in March 2002 at UFC 36: Worlds Collide. Barnett became the youngest man to capture the UFC heavyweight championship at 24.

Unfortunately, he was stripped of the title for testing positive for steroids. He left UFC and fought in Pancrease and K-1. Barnett became famous in Japan with his performances in PRIDE. He defeated Alexsander Emelianenko (brother of Fedor), **Mark Hunt,** and **Antonio Rodrigo**

Nogueira. The one fighter he had trouble solving was **Mirko Filopovic** (better known as Mirko "Cro Cop") who has defeated Barnett three times. Barnett fought seven times in 2006, but then remained inactive until July 2008 when he resurfaced at an **Affliction** fight card. Barnett looked impressive in kayoing former rival Pedro Rizzo with a powerful left hook. He remains one of the top heavyweights in the world, according to most experts.

Professional MMA record:	24-5
Championship(s):	UFC Heavyweight, 2002

Further Reading

Caplan, Sam. "5 Oz. Exclusive Interview: Josh Barnett talks Affliction; fighting Fedor; Gina Carano vs. Shayna Baszler; and more," *Five Ounces of Pain*, 5/27/2008, at http://fiveouncesofpain.com/2008/05/27/5-oz-exclusive-interview-josh-barnett-talks-affliction-fedor-gina-carano-vs-shayna-baszler-and-more/

Kalstein, Dave. "The Baby-Faced Assassin," *FIGHT!*, October 2008, p. 46–56.

Official Web site: http://www.joshbarnett.tv.com

Yu, Al. "Josh Barnett Playing the Field." *MMAWeekly.com*, 7/16/2007, at http://www.mmaweekly.com/absolutenm/templates/dailynews.asp?articleid=4335&zoneid=13

BARRERA, MARCO ANTONIO (1974–). Marco Antonio Barrera was one of the best boxer-punchers of the 1990s and early 2000s who continues to fight at the time of this writing. Born in 1974 in Mexico City, Barrera turned pro at age 15 in 1989 and won his first 43 professional fights.

In 1995, he won the World Boxing Organization (WBO) super bantamweight title with a 12-round decision over Daniel Jimenez. He made seven successful defenses, including a back-and-forth thriller over Kennedy McKinney. He lost in his eighth defense to Junior "Poison" Jones and then also lost the rematch. In 1998, he regained the WBO belt with a stoppage of Richie Wenton in 1998 and then made two more defenses before meeting **World Boxing Council (WBC)** champion **Erik Morales.** In a classic, Barrera lost a 12-round split decision. In 2001, he easily outpointed previously unbeaten **"Prince" Naseem Hamed** with a masterful boxing display. Then, in 2002, he gained a measure of revenge by outpointed his rival Morales in another close fight to capture the WBC featherweight title. He also defeated Morales in the rubber match to win the WBC super featherweight crown—a title he held until a 2007 loss to **Juan Manuel Marquez.** Barrera has twice lost to the Philippine sensation **Manny Pacquiao.**

Record:	65-6
Championship(s):	WBO super bantamweight, 1995–1996, 1998–2000, 2000; WBC featherweight, 2002; WBC super featherweight, 2004–2007

Further Reading

Donovan, Jake. "Marco Antonio Barrera: What's Done . . . What's Left To Do." *The Sweet Science*, 4/9/2005, at http://www.thesweetscience.com/boxing-article/1907/marco-antonio-barrera-done-left/

Goldman, Ivan. "Pretty Good for a 'Washed-Up' Fighter: Barrera Beats Morales in a Classic." *The Ring* (April 2005), pp. 26–31.

Stradley, Don. "Who's Really Number One? Has Barrera Passed Chavez As Mexico's All-Time Best?" *The Ring* (October 2006), pp. 50–55.

Thompson, Trae. "Unfriendly Rivalry Adds Chapter." *Fort Worth Star Telegram*, 11/25/2004, p. 3D.

BARRY, JIMMY (1870–1943). Nicknamed "the Little Tiger," Jimmy Barry stood only 5-2' inches tall and weighed barely a 100 pounds, but he looms large in boxing history. Born in 1870 in Chicago, Illinois, Barry turned pro in 1891 and fought until 1898. He never lost a professional bout, compiling nearly 60 wins and approximately 9 draws.

In his most famous fight, Barry kayoed British fighter Walter Croot in the 20th round at the National Sporting Club in London. Croot later died from injuries suffered during the bout. English authorities initially charged Barry and his second Tommy White with manslaughter, though the charges were later dropped after a coroner's report indicated that Croot died from a skull fracture sustained when he hit the canvas. The tragedy affected Barry as a fighter.

Professional Record:	59-0-9
Championship(s):	World Bantamweight title, 1897–1899

Further Reading

Associated Press. "For Manslaughter: Barry and His Second Are Both Jailed." *Los Angeles Times,* 12/8/1897, p. 2.

"Jimmy Barry Wins." *Chicago Daily Tribune,* 12/7/1897, p. 6.

Roberts, James B., and Alexander G. Skutt. *The Boxing Register: International Boxing Hall of Fame Official Record Book* (4th ed.). Ithaca, NY: McBooks Press, Inc., 2006, pp. 64–65.

BASILIO, CARMEN (1927–). It is fitting that former welterweight and middleweight champion Carmen Basilio was born in Canastota, New York,—the site of the International Boxing Hall of Fame, for Basilio, a former onion farmer, was one of the true ring greats.

Born in 1927, Basilio turned pro in 1948. He won his first world title in 1955 when he stopped Tony DeMarco in the 12th round. Basilio showed his toughness, body punching and all-around boxing skills in winning the title. "He's real tough, a hard hitter, and a strong body puncher," DeMarco said. "He threw some good punches and I went to pieces."

He lost a disputed decision to Johnny Saxton, but won the rematch to regain his title in 1956. Then, in his greatest ring triumph, Basilio moved up in weight and defeated the legendary **Sugar Ray Robinson** to win the middleweight crown in a thrilling 15-round split decision. The *Chicago Daily Tribune* reported that the bout "matched any fight in any era and in any weight division." He lost to Robinson in the rematch and failed to recaptured the middleweight title from **Gene Fullmer** and Paul Pender.

Professional Record:	56-16-7
Championship(s):	Welterweight, 1955–1956, 1956–1957; Middleweight, 1957–1958

Further Reading

"Basilio's Career Started in Army." *The New York Times,* 2/23/1957, p. 21.

Cowans, Russ J. "Saxton Beats Basilio to Regain Title." *The Chicago Defender,* 3/24/1956, p. 17.

Evans, Gavin. "The 20 Greatest Welterweights of All Time." *The Ring* (February 2008), pp. 63–84, 69.

Roberts, James B., and Alexander G. Skutt. *The Boxing Register: International Boxing Hall of Fame Register* (4th ed.). Ithaca, NY: McBooks Press, Inc., 2006, pp. 290–293.

Sheehan, Joseph M. "Loser Threatens to Punch Referee." *The New York Times,* 6/3/1960, p. 32.

Smith, Wilfrid. "Carmen Wins Middleweight Title on Split Decision After 15 Furious Rounds." *Chicago Daily Tribune,* 9/24/1957, p. B1.

United Press International. "Basilio Victory But In Vain." *Chicago Daily Tribune,* 6/11/1955, p. B1.

Youmans, Gary B. *The Onion Picker: Carmen Basilio and Boxing in the 1950s.* Syracuse, NY: Campbell Road Press North, 2007.

BASSEY, HOGAN (1932–1998). Hogan "Kid" Bassey was a former world featherweight champion and the first man from Nigeria to ever win such a world title in any weight classification. Born in 1932 in Calabar, Nigeria, as Okon Bassey Asuguo, he turned pro in 1949 and three years later moved to England.

In 1955, he won the British Commonwealth featherweight championship by kayoing Billy Kelly in Belfast. Two years later in 1957 he defeated Miguel Berrios of Puerto Rico to earn a world title shot against Cherif Hamia in Paris. He later that year captured the world featherweight championship. He successfully defended his title against Ricardo Moreno and then stopped the great **Willie Pep** in a nontitle bout in 1958. The next year, he lost his title to **Davey Moore,** "the Springfield Rifle" in 1959. After losing a rematch to Moore, he retired.

Professional Record: 59-13-2
Championship(s):   Featherweight, 1957–1959

Further Reading
Associated Press, "Kid Bassey Stops Hamia For Title." *The New York Times*, 6/25/1957, p. 34.
Brady, Dave. "Bassey Upsets Barrios And Earns Title Bout." *The Washington Post*, 4/27/1957, p. A14.
Daley, Arthur. "The Kid From Nigeria." *The New York Times*, 10/28/1958, p. 43.
Kahn, Alex. "Davey Moore Captures Title from Kid Bassey." *The Chicago Defender*, 3/28/1959, p. 24.

BATTLES ROYAL. Battle royal is a combat sports term that involves an event where multiple fighters are placed in an arena in an every-man-for-himself brawl. The term surfaced in Roman times when gladiators fought each other until one was left alive. Unfortunately, the practice surfaced in the United States, primarily amongst slaveowners who would force their slaves into such brutal brawls often blindfolded. Such boxing greats as **Tom Molineaux, Beau Jack, Jack Johnson,** and **Joe Gans** fought in such events—largely to the amusement of all-white audiences.

Further Reading
Ashe, Arthur, Jr. *A Hard Road to Glory: A History of the African-American Athlete: Boxing.* New York: Amistad Press, 1993.
Johnson, Jack. *In the Ring and Out.* Whitefish, MT: Kessinger Publishing, 2008.

BECERRA, JOSE (1936–). Jose Becerra was a former world bantamweight champion from Mexico who packed a big punch for a little man. Born in 1936 in Guadalajara, he turned pro as a teenager in 1953 and built a big following in his native country. He usually fought in Mexico but would occasionally fight in Los Angeles at the Olympic Auditorium and the Sports Arena as well.

In 1959, he dominated Frenchman Alphonse Halimi, stopping his foe in the eighth round to win the world bantamweight title. In his next fight, he defeated Walt Ingram in a nontitle bout. Ingram died from injuries suffered during the bout. Becerra then defeated Halimi in a rematch. Behind on points, Becerra unleashed a powerful double left hook that felled the Frenchman. He then outpointed Kenji Yonekura in another title defense. He retired while still bantamweight king in 1960 after losing a nontitle bout to Eloy Sanchez at a higher weight.

Professional Record: 71-5-2
Championship(s):   Bantamweight, 1959–1960

Further Reading
De La Vega, John. "Becerra Knocks Out Halimi in Ninth." *Los Angeles Times*, 2/5/1960, p. C1.
United Press International. "Brain Injury Fatal to Ingram, 25, in Loss to Bantamweight Ruler." *The New York Times*, 10/27/1959, p. 44.
Wolf, Al. "Hardest Punch Ever: Becerra Says Double Left Hook Used to Knock Out Frenchman." *Los Angeles Times*, 2/5/1960, p. C1.

BELFORT, VITOR (1978–). Vitor "the Phenom" Belfort is a Brazilian jiu-jitsu expert who once held the **Ultimate Fighting Championships (UFC)** light heavyweight title and a championship in the Cage Rage organization. Born in 1978 in Rio de Janeiro, Belfort trained under the legendary Gracie family, specifically Carlson Gracie. He turned professional in mixed martial arts (MMA) in 1996 at the age of 19. He defeated Jon Hess in Superbrawl 2 in 12 seconds. In his next fight, he fought in the UFC in 1997, stopping Tra Telligman in the first round. In October 1997, he suffered his first loss in MMA to **Randy Couture** at UFC 15: Collision Course.

In 1999, he traveled to Japan to face the legendary Kazuri Sakuraba in **PRIDE** 5, losing a decision. He returned to the UFC in 2002, losing to **Chuck "the Iceman" Liddell** by decision. In 2004, he defeated Couture at UFC 46 in 49 seconds to win the UFC light heavyweight championship. In the rubber match, he lost to Couture at UFC 49 in the third round. He then fought in PRIDE for several bouts in 2005 and 2006. In September 2007, he won the Cage Rage light heavyweight title with a win over James Zikic. In 2008, he defeated Terry Martin a bout promoted by Affliction.

Professional MMA Record:	18-8
Championship(s):	UFC Light Heavyweight Title, 2004; Cage Rage Light Heavyweight, 2007

Further Reading
Iole, Kevin. "Fight no match for Belfort's physical pain." *Las Vegas Review-Journal*, 1/25/2004, p. 4C.
Official Web site of Vitor Belfort: http://www2.uol.com.br/vitorbelfort/2007/

BENITEZ, WILFRED (1958–). Wilfred Benitez remains the youngest pugilist to win a world boxing champion when he outpointed **Antonio "Kid Pambele" Cervantes** to win the **World Boxing Association (WBA)** junior welterweight championship at age 17. Benitez, who had turned pro at 15, won championships in three different weight divisions—junior welterweight, welterweight and junior middleweight—by the age of 22. He holds win over world champions Cervantes, Bruce Curry (Bruce was Donald's brother), **Carlos Palomino,** Maurice Hope, and the legendary **Roberto Duran.**

Benitez lost to fellow greats **Sugar Ray Leonard** and **Thomas "the Hitman" Hearns.** His career went into rapid decline after losing to the tough **Mustafo Hamsho** in 1983. He made an ill-advised comeback in 1990, winning 2 out of 4 fights against limited competition. He suffers from encephalopathy.

Benitez was best known for his unnaturally gifted defensive skills. Called "Radar," Benitez could casually stand right in front of an opponent and make him miss punch after punch. Even Duran—never one to speak well of opponents—called him a fine boxer after dropping a decision to Benitez in January 1982. Benitez's greatest shortcoming was a lack of discipline, as he often trained only a few days before even major bouts.

Professional Record:	53-8-1
Championship(s):	WBA junior welterweight, 1976–1977; WBC welterweight, 1979; WBC junior middleweight, 1981–1982

Further Reading
Amdur, Neil. "Benitez Shows New Maturity in Win." *The New York Times*, 2/1/1982, p. C1.
Baker, Richard. "Clinging to Yesterday: The Sad Saga of Wilfred Benitez." *The Ring* (April 1991), pp. 32–33.
Brady, Dave. "Benitez Champion on Split Decision." *The Washington Post*, 1/15/1979, p. D1.

Hudson, David L., Jr. "The Under appreciated Champion." *Cyber Boxing Zone Journal*, July 2000, at http://www.cyberboxingzone.com/boxing/box7-00.htm#benitez

Kindred, Dave. "Benitez Is All Attention." *The Washington Post*, 11/28/1979, p. D1.

BENN, NIGEL (1964–). Nigel "the Dark Destroyer" Benn was a warrior who brawled his way to world championships in the middleweight and super middleweight divisions. Known as "the Dark Destroyer", Benn possessed great power and an indomitable will. Born in 1964 in Ilford, England, he turned pro in 1987 and won his first 22 bouts before losing to Michael Watson.

He captured the World Boxing Organization (WBO) middleweight in 1990 with a kayo win over Doug DeWitt. He then blasted **Iran Barkley** in one round before losing his title to **Chris Eubank.** Benn then moved up to the super middleweight division, winning the **World Boxing Council (WBC)** belt in 1992 by stopping Mauro Galvano in the fourth round. He defended his title nine times before dropping a split decision to Thulani Malinga in 1996. In perhaps him most notable bout, he squared off against power puncher **Gerald McClellan,** who battered Benn nearly to defeat in the first round. However, the courageous Benn rallied and stopped McClellan in the 10th round. McClellan suffered debilitating injuries and brain damage as a result of the bout. Benn retired after two losses to **Steve Collins** for the WBO super middleweight title.

Professional Record:	42-5-1
Championship(s):	WBO middleweight, 1990; WBC super middleweight, 1994–1996

Further Reading

Allen, Neil. "Benn Is Leaving Nothing to Fate." *Evening Standard*, 2/25/1994, p. 70.

Benn, Nigel. *Dark Destroyer*. London: Blake Publishing, 2001.

Berger, Phil. "Benn Stops DeWitt." *The New York Times*, 4/30/1990, p. C9.

Rendell, Jonathan. "Benn in the U.S.A.: The Dark Destroyer and the Black Pack." *The Independent*, 4/29/1990, p. 20.

BENTON, GEORGE (1933–). George Benton was a former middleweight contender known for his counterpunching, fine defense and inability to land a title shot. Benton was one of the more avoided fighters in the 1950s and 1960s because his boxing skills could make more powerful punchers look bad. Benton is best known as a world-class trainer who has worked with world champions such as **Pernell Whitaker, Evander Holyfield,** Mike McCallum, **Meldrick Taylor,** and **Leon Spinks.**

Born in 1933 in Philadelphia, Benton turned pro at age 16 in 1949. He defeated some future world champions in his career. For example, in 1960 he outpointed future junior middleweight champion **Freddie Little** over 10 rounds. In perhaps his finest performance, he outpointed future middleweight champion **Joey Giardello** over 10 rounds in 1962. He never received a world title shot and finally retired in 1970.

After his career ended, Benton began training fighters. He studied under the legendary **Eddie Futch,** serving as a cornerman for **Joe Frazier** in the legendary **"Thrilla in Manila"** battle against **Muhammad Ali.** Benton later became the head trainer for Main Events, working with fight manager Lou Duva.

Professional Record:	61-13-1
Championship(s):	None

Further Reading

Cyber Boxing Zone profile: http://cyberboxingzone.com/boxing/benton.htm

Eskenazi, Gerald. "Thomas Outpointed by Benton After Winning 19 Bouts in a Row." *The New York Times*, 7/21/1963, p. 120.

Gustkey, Earl. "After Benton's Finishing School, Biggs and Holyfield Are Ready for Pros." *Los Angeles Times*, 11/15/1984, p. F7.

BENVENUTI, NINO (1938-). Nino Benvenuti was a former Olympic gold medalist and world champion in the junior middleweight and middleweight divisions. Born in 1938 in Trieste, Italy, Benvenuti won 120 amateur bouts without a loss in his native country. He culminated his Olympic career with a gold medal at welterweight in the 1960 Olympic Games.

He turned pro later that year and amazingly won his first 65 bouts. In June 1965, he faced countryman Sandro Mazzinghi for the vacant world junior middleweight championship. Benvenuti won in the 6th round. He also defeated Mazzinghi over 15 rounds in a rematch. He lost the title to South Korean Ki-Soo Kim in Seoul.

In 1967, Benvenuti traveled to the United States to face **Emile Griffith** for the world middleweight title. He outboxed Griffith over 15 rounds to win the title. He lost a rematch a little more than a month later via another 15-round decision. In March 1968, he won the rubber match over Griffith in New York, dropping his rival in the 9th round for a close win. Benvenuti retained his title until losing to the great **Carlos Monzon** in November 1970. He retired in 1971 after another loss to Monzon.

Professional Record:	82-7-1
Championship(s):	Junior Middleweight, 1965–1966; Middleweight, 1967, 1967–1970

Further Reading

Associated Press. "Benvenuti Wins Decision, Rematch No. 3 in the Offing." *Los Angeles Times*, 3/5/1968, p. B1.

Brady, Dave. "Benvenuti Takes Title on Decision." *The Washington Post*, 3/5/1968, p. D1.

Cazaneuve, Brian. "Catching Up With . . . Nino Benvenuti." *Sports Illustrated*, 8/4/2003, p. 12.

Katz, Michael. "Benvenuti Ready for Monzon Fight." *The New York Times*, 5/8/1971, p. 21.

BERBICK, TREVOR (1954–2006). Trevor Berbick was a former world heavyweight champion known for being **Muhammad Ali's** last professional opponent and for losing to **Larry Holmes** and **Mike Tyson** for the world heavyweight championship. Born in 1954 in Port Anthony, Jamaica, Berbick represented Jamaica in the 1976 Montreal Olympics after relatively little amateur experience. He lost in the first round to eventual silver medalist Mircea Simon of Romania.

He turned pro later that year and stayed in Canada for his professional career. He won his first 11 bouts before losing to fellow prospect Bernardo Mercardo in the first round. In 1980, he kayoed former world heavyweight champion John Tate, which helped earn him a title shot against heavyweight kingpin Larry Holmes in 1981. Despite being a heavy underdog, Berbick took the champion the full 15 rounds. In December 1981, he defeated Muhammad Ali over 10 rounds in Nassau, Bahamas, in Ali's last professional bout. However, in 1982 and 1983, he lost back-to-back decisions to Renaldo Snipes and S.T. Gordon.

In 1986, Berbick revived his career with an upset win over undefeated **World Boxing Council (WBC)** champion **Pinklon Thomas.** In his first defense, he faced young contender Mike Tyson who stopped him in the second round. He battled legal controversies, including a 15-month prison stint for attempted rape and deportation from the United States in 1997 for parole violations. However, he continued fighting until 2000, retiring after winning a 12-round decision over Shane Sutcliffe. Tragically, Berbick was murdered in 2006 by his nephew and another young man.

Professional Record: 49-11-1
Championship(s): WBC Heavyweight, 1986

Further Reading
Strachan, Al. "Surprising Berbick lasts 15 rounds; Holmes promises Canadian fighter will get a rematch." *The Globe* and *Mail*, 4/13/1981.
Welsh, Jack. "Berbick's the Boss . . . WBC Version." *The Ring* (June 1986), pp. 28–32.

BERG, JACKIE (1909–1991). Born Judah Bergman, Jackie "Kid" Berg was reared in the Whitechapel section of London where he earned the nickname "the Whitechapel Whirlwind" for his nonstop action in the ring. In 1930, he defeated the great **Kid Chocolate** in a highly anticipated bout in America. The next year he defeated Mushy Callahan for the world junior welterweight championship.

He is perhaps best known for his trilogy with fellow Hall of Famer **Tony Canzoneri.** Berg defeated Canzoneri in their first meeting in 1930, but Berg lost the next two bouts—losing his junior welterweight title and failing to win Canzoneri's lightweight belt.

He retired in 1945 after 21 years of professional boxing.

Professional Record: 157-26-9
Championship(s): Junior Welterweight, 1931

Further Reading
Cyberboxing Zone profile: http://www.mmafighting.com/interviews/2007/11/01/paul-buentello-interview-a-headhunter-sure
Harding, Jack, and Jackie "Kid" Berg. *The Whitechapel Windmill.* London: Robson Books, 1987.

BERGER, PHIL (1943–2001). Phil Berger was a boxing writer for *The New York Times* and the author of many boxing books, including *Blood Season: Mike Tyson and the World of Boxing.* Born in Brooklyn in 1943, Berger graduated college from John Hopkins in 1964 and earned a masters degree in creative writer from Hollins College in 1965. He wrote several screenplays and later served as an editor for SPORT magazine. He covered boxing for *The New York Times* as a freelancer and then as a reporter from 1986–1992. He also authored other books on boxing, including *Punch Lines: Berger on Boxing* (1993), and collaborated with former heavyweight champions **Joe Frazier** and **Larry Holmes** on their autobiographies.

Further Reading
Berger, Phil. "Phil Berger, 58, Sportswriter and Author." *The New York Times,* 3/14/2001, at http://query.nytimes.com/gst/fullpage.html?res=9901E3DF1F3AF937A25750C0A9679C8B63
Berger, Phil. *Punchlines: Berger on Boxing.* New York: Four Walls Eight Windows, 1993.

BERGER, SAMUEL (1884–1925). Samuel Berger was an American heavyweight boxer whose claim to fame was capturing a gold medal at the very first Olympics for which boxing was an event—the 1904 St. Louis Olympics. Berger turned professional after the Olympics but only fought for two years. He showed great promise in 1905, stopping Jim Casey and Bill Richards in the first round. However, in 1906 he lost to Al Kaufmann. He later assisted his friend and professional heavyweight champion **James J. Jeffries** in his negotiations. He also would box exhibitions with Jeffries.

Professional Record:	2-1 (sources divided on Berger's actual record)
Championship(s):	None

Further Reading

Profile at Cyber Boxing Zone: http://cyberboxingzone.com/boxing/berger-sam.htm

Profile at International Jewish Sports Hall of Fame: http://www.jewishsports.net/biopages/Samuel-Berger.htm

BISPING, MICHAEL (1979–). Michael "the Count" Bisping is an English-based top-ranked light heavyweight in the **Ultimate Fighting Championships (UFC)** and a winner on *The Ultimate Fighter* series. Bisping possesses excellent striking skills, quick hands, a good chin, and a quick mind. His ground game is underrated.

Born in Cyprus in 1979, Bisping began training in combat sports at 8 years of age. He competed in a no-holds-barred event at age 15.

He turned pro in mixed martial arts in 2004 and in his third pro bout captured the Cage Rage light heavyweight championship. He received his big break a couple years later when he competed on Season 3 of *The Ultimate Fighter*. He won the competition in the light heavyweight division with a win over Josh Haynes.

He won his first four fights in the Octagon before dropping a split decision to **Rashad Evans**. After that loss, Bisping dropped down to the middleweight division where he has won several fights in a row. He hopes to challenge UFC middleweight kingpin **Anderson "Spider" Silva** in the near future.

Professional Record:	17-1
Championship(s):	Cage Rage Light Heavyweight, 2004–2005

Further Reading

Evans, Ant. "Count's move gives middleweights more blood." *UFC.com*, 12/14/2007, at http://www.ufc.com/index.cfm?fa=news.detail&gid=9204

Hudson, David L., Jr. "Bisping vows to end 'Dooms' Day." *Fightnews.com*, 6/1/2007, at http://www.fightnewsextra.com/cc/ufc85/11-bisping.htm

Taflinger, Neal. "Bisping Re-Mixed," *FIGHT!*, October 2008, at p. 72–74.

BIVINS, JIMMY (1929–). Jimmy Bivins was a former top contender in the light heavyweight and heavyweight divisions who fought in the 1940s and 1950s. Though he defeated numerous former world champions, Bivins never received a world title shot.

Born in 1929 in Dry Branch, Georgia, Bivins turned pro in 1940, fighting out of his hometown of Cleveland, Ohio. He won his first 19 professional bouts before dropping a decision to Anton Christoforidis, a fighter Bivins defeated several times. In 1945, Bivins stopped the great **Archie Moore** in the sixth round in perhaps the greatest triumph of his ring career.

He fought the best of the best, including bouts with **Jersey Joe Walcott, Ezzard Charles,** and **Joe Louis.** He was inducted into the International Boxing Hall of Fame in 1999.

Professional Record:	86-25-1
Championship(s):	None

Further Reading

Christopher, Sam. "Bivins credits wife, farm for longevity." *Ocean County Observer*, 3/20/2007.

Ferguson, Bob. "Back in the day; Boxing legend Bivins still fighting the good fight." *Call and Post*, 8/27/2003, p. 6B.

Maxse, Joe. "Boxer Bivins Is Swinging at 85." *Cleveland Plain Dealer*, 12/7/2004, p. D2.

BLACKBURN, JACK (1883–1942). Jack Blackburn was a former great lightweight boxer who is better known for his expert training of the great heavyweight champion **Joe Louis.** Born in 1883 in Versailles, Kentucky, Blackburn turned professional in 1901 and often fought much larger men. He fought frequently through 1908, but was arrested in 1909 for murder of three people, including his wife.

Convicted of manslaughter, he served nearly five years in prison. Upon his release, Blackburn returned to the boxing ring in 1914 where he fought for nearly a decade more. During his boxing career, he faced the likes of **Joe Gans, Sam Langford,** "Philadelphia" Jack O'Brien, **Mike Donovan,** and Ed "Gunboat" Smith.

Blackburn achieved lasting fame as a trainer, working with fighters such as Sammy Mandell, Charles "Bud" Taylor, and Louis, who affectionately referred to Blackburn as "Chappie." He was elected to the International Boxing Hall of Fame as a trainer in 1992.

Professional Record:	102-26-18
Championship(s):	None

Further Reading
Potts, Barry. "Real Black Menace to Be in Louis's Corner." *Los Angeles Times*, 2/10/1935, p. 26.
Profile by Cyber Boxing Zone: http://cyberboxingzone.com/boxing/blackburn.htm

BLUE HORIZON. The Blue Horizon is a club in Philadelphia that showcases boxing events with fan-friendly viewing. Built in 1865 as a private residence, the building later became a fraternal lodge (Collins, 26). In 1960, boxing promoter Jimmy Toppi purchased the building and named it after himself. He changed the name in 1961 after the 1940s song "Beyond the Blue Horizon." Famed promoter J. Russell Peltz promoted shows at the Blue Horizon for many years beginning in 1969. An amazing number of former world champions have fought at this famous venue, including: **Matthew Saad Muhammad, Bernard Hopkins, Fernando Vargas,** and **Tim Witherspoon.**

Further Reading
Chevalier, Jack. "Blue Horizon has housed Moose, a church, boxing." *Philadelphia Tribune*, 2/11/2003, p. 7L.
Collins, Nigel. "The Blue Horizon." *The Ring* (March 2001), pp. 26–27.
Official Web site: http://www.legendarybluehorizon.com/html/boxing.html

BODZIANOWSKI, CRAIG (1961–). Craig "the Gator" Bodzianowski achieved fame in boxing for fighting for the world cruiserweight championship on a prosthetic leg. Born in 1961, Bodzianowski turned pro in 1981 and won his first 13 fights. Then, in 1984, he suffered terrible injuries in a motorcycle accident, which caused him to lose part of his right leg.

Amazingly, Bodzianowski returned to the ring in December 1985 with a prosthetic limb. He won four more fights before losing a majority decision to Alonzo Ratliff. In 1990, "the Gator" challenged **World Boxing Association (WBA)** cruiserweight champion **Robert Daniels** for the title. He lost a unanimous decision over 12 rounds. After losing to Daniels, he won seven straight bouts before retiring in 1993. He lost only four times in his professional career—all by decision.

Professional Record:	31-4-1
Championship(s):	None

Further Reading
Fitzgerald, Mike. *Tale of the Gator: The Craig Bodzianowski Story.* Milwaukee, WI: Lemieux International, 2000.

Smith, Sam. "Bodzianowski Up to the Challenge: Amputee Kayoes Hard Puncher Enis." *Chicago Daily Tribune*, 4/7/1986, p. 5C.

Thomas, Pete. "One Legged Fighter Takes Strong Stand." *Los Angeles Times*, 4/21/1986, p. SP 3.

BONAVENA, OSCAR (1942–1976). Oscar Bonavena was a rugged heavyweight contender from Argentina in the 1960s and 1970s known for his rugged style, iron chin and irrepressible personality. Born in 1942 in Buenos Aires, Argentina, Bonavena made his pro debut in 1964 at Madison Square Garden in New York.

He rose through the ranks, defeating the likes of Tom McNeeley, Dick Wipperman, and Rudolpho Diaz. In 1966, he lost a 10-round split decision to **Joe Frazier.** In 1967, he lost a decision to **Jimmy Ellis** in a heavyweight title elimination bout. The next year he fought Frazier in a rematch for the world heavyweight title, losing a decision.

In 1970, Bonavena battled the great **Muhammad Ali** in and out of the ring. Outside the ring Bonavena taunted Ali, enraging the comebacking ex-champion. Ali defeated Bonavena in the 15th round, the only time Bonavena was ever stopped in his professional career. He fought in the 1970s, winning seven straight times before being shot by a bodyguard outside a Nevada brothel.

Professional Record:	58-9-1
Championship(s):	None

Further Reading

Anderson, Dave. "Frazier Outpoints Bonavena and Retains Title." *The New York Times*, 12/11/1969, p. 58.

Anderson, Dave. "Ali Stops Bonavena on 3 Knockdowns in 15th Round." *The New York Times*, 12/8/1970, p. 64.

Clarke, Norm. "Sex, boxing, murder at the Love Ranch." *Las Vegas Review Journal*, 11/30/2007, p. 3A.

BONJASKY, REMY (1976–). Remy Bonjasky is one of the greatest K-1 fighters and kickboxers to ever grace the ring. Born in 1976 in the Surinam, his family moved to the Netherlands when he was five years old. As a youngster his favorite sport was soccer, but a leg injury forced him to sit out a season. Then, he watched the movie *Bloodsport* starring Jean Claude Van Damme and became hooked on martial arts and kickboxing.

Known as "the Flying Dutchman," Bonjasky has mastered the Muay Thai discipline. He made his K-1 debut in 1999 and has captured numerous championships. He won the K-1 World Championship in 2003 and 2004. In 2007, he reached the finals of the K-1 World Grand Prix Championship but lost a narrow decision to Peter Aerts. He holds wins over **Ernesto Hoost, Ray Mercer,** Francois Botha, Ray Sefo, **Bob Sapp,** and many others.

Professional Kickboxing Record:	65-14
Championship(s):	K-1 World Grand Prix Champion, 2003–2004

Further Reading

Official Web site: http://www.remhttp://en.wikipedia.org/wiki/Paul_Buentello—Referencesybonjasky.com/

Profile at "Fans of K-1": http://www.fansofk1.com/fighter?fID=3

BOWE, RIDDICK (1967–). Riddick "Big Daddy" Bowe was a former world heavyweight champion known for his fine offensive firepower and proclivity to engage in excellent action fights. Though he sported an enviable 42-1 record, it is testament to Bowe's immense talents that many considered him an underachiever.

Born in Fort Washington, Maryland, in 1967, Bowe won a silver medal at the 1988 Seoul Olympics, losing to **Lennox Lewis** in the gold-medal match. He turned pro in 1989 and showed great promise. In 1992, he defeated **Evander Holyfield** in a 12-round unanimous decision to win the heavyweight title. He made two successful defenses before losing the title in a controversial 12-round majority decision to Holyfield. In 1995, he won the World Boxing Organization (WBO) heavyweight title with a won over Herbie Hide. Later that year, he won the rubber match against Holyfield. In 1996 he engaged in two brutal wars with Andrew Golota. Inexplicably, Golota—ahead on the scorecards—hit Bowe low several times and was disqualified in both bouts. The first Bowe-Golota match ended in a riot breaking out in the ring and in the stands in Madison Square Garden. Bowe retired after the second Golota bout. He later served time for allegedly kidnapping his former wife and kids.

Bowe made a comeback in 2004, winning two fights against nondescript opposition. He remains one of the great enigmas in boxing history, as he compiled a great record but could have accomplished much more.

Record:	43-1
Championship(s):	WBC, IBF Heavyweight, 1992–1993; WBO Heavyweight, 1995

Further Reading

Berger, Phil. "It's Unanimous: Bowe Knows Boxing." *The New York Times,* 11/15/1992, p. S1.

Farhood, Steve. "Riddick Bowe's Promise: This Time I'm Whipping Golota's Ass!" *The Ring* (January 1997), pp. 40–42, 57.

Farhood, Steve. "Riddick Bowe's Career in Perspective: The Underachieving Overachiever." *The Ring* (October 1997), pp. 24–27, 58–59.

Gildea, William. " 'Big Daddy' Bowe Keeps Title Quest in the Family." *The Washington Post,* 10/23/1991, p. G1.

BOZA-EDWARDS, CORNELIUS (1956–). Cornelius Boza-Edwards is a former junior lightweight champion known for several incredible wars he fought with such fighters as Rafael "Bazooka" Limon and **Bobby Chacon.** Born in 1956 in Uganda, Boza-Edwards emigrated to London, England, in 1974 at the age of 17. He turned professional at age 20 in 1976 and won his 27 of his first 28 bouts before facing the legendary **Alexis Arguello** in 1980. The much-more experienced Arguello stopped Boza-Edwards in the eighth round.

Undeterred, Boza-Edwards rebounded and challenged Rafael "Bazooka" Limon for the **World Boxing Council (WBC)** junior lightweight champion in 1981. Boza-Edwards dropped Limon in the 5th round en route to winning a 15-round war. In his first defense, Boza-Edwards defended his title against the popular Bobby Chacon who nearly kayoed the champion in the early rounds. Boza-Edwards showed his amazing ability to withstand punishment and began to inflict damage on Chacon in later rounds when the fight was stopped.

The two wars with Limon and Chacon took their toll on the champion who lost the belt in his next defense against Rolando Navarette in the 5th round. In 1983 he fought a fight-of-the-year rematch e with Chacon for a championship but lost a tough 12-round decision. Boza-Edwards dropped Chacon in the first round, but Chacon rallied down the stretch to capture the decision. Boza-Edwards retired in 1987 after losing to Jose Luis Ramirez in an attempt to capture the WBC lightweight title. In retirement Boza-Edwards has become a top trainer, working with such fighters as Peter Okhello, Brian Magee, and Orlin Norris.

Professional Record:	45-7-1
Championship(s):	WBC junior lightweight, 1981

Further Reading

Feour, Royce. "Boza-Edwards' 83 classic with Chacon still amazes." *Las Vegas Review-Journal*, 11/29/2003, p. 13C.
McGowen, Deane. "Arguello Stops Boza-Edwards." *The New York Times*, 8/10/1980, p. S6.
Rodda, John. "Boza takes world title." *Manchester Guardian Weekly*, 3/15/1981, p. 24.
Smith, Red. "Truculent Weekend." *The New York Times*, 6/1/1981, p. C3.

BRADDOCK, JAMES J. (1905–1974). James J. Braddock was a former world heavyweight champion best known for his upset of **Max Baer** to capture the title. An unlikely champion, Braddock's name and his rags-to-riches story has become a part of cultural lore due to the recent hit movie *The Cinderella Man*.

Born in 1905 in New York City, Braddock turned pro in 1926 and progressed through the ranks a light heavyweight. In July 1929, Braddock faced **Tommy Loughran** for the world championship, losing a 15-round decision. Braddock lost a series of bouts over the next several years, usually by decision to larger men in the heavyweight division. By 1934, the former light heavyweight contender had been forced to stand in a bread line to feed his family. However, he received the opportunity of a lifetime as an opponent for promising young heavyweight Corn Griffin. Braddock stopped the youngster in the third round. He then defeated contenders **John Henry Lewis** and Art Lasky to earn an improbable title shot against Baer.

Braddock outboxed Baer over 15 rounds to win a unanimous decision. In his first title defense, he lost to **Joe Louis,** though he managed to drop Louis in the first round. Braddock's management shrewdly bargained that in exchange for defending the title against the formidable challenger, Braddock would future 10 percent of Louis' future ring earnings as champion. After his title loss, Braddock only fought once more, defeating Tommy Farr by decision.

Record:	46-23-4 (11 no decisions)
Championship(s):	Heavyweight, 1935–1937

Further Reading

DeLisa, Michael C. *Cinderella Man*. London: Milo Books, 2005.
Evans, Gavin. "Great Career Comebacks: How 10 Fighters Reinvented Themselves and Changed Boxing History." *The Ring* (October 2005), pp. 55–65, 62.
Hague, Jim. *Braddock: The Rise of the Cinderella Man*. New York: Chamberlain Brothers, 2005.
Schaap, Jeremy. *Cinderella Man: James J. Braddock, Max Baer and the Greatest Upset in Boxing History*. New York: Houghton Mifflin, 2005.

BRAMBLE, LIVINGSTONE (1960–). Livingstone, or Ras-I, Bramble was a former world lightweight champion known for his toughness, eccentricities and good boxing skills. Born in 1960 in St. Croix, Virgin Islands, Bramble turned pro in 1980. He marched to the beat of his own drum. For example, he had a dog named "Snake" and a pet snake named "Dog." But, Bramble was also an excellent fighter.

In only his seventh pro fight, he showed future promise by stopping the previously unbeaten prospect Kenny "Bang Bang" Bogner in the seventh round. He dropped a decision to Anthony Fletcher but continued to rise the lightweight ranks with wins over Jerome Artis, Gaetan Hart, and Rafael Williams.

In June 1984, he entered the ring as a heavy underdog to popular **World Boxing Association (WBA)** champion **Ray "Boom Boom" Mancini.** However, Bramble cut Mancini, battered and bloodied him and eventually stopped him in the 14th round. He defeated Mancini by a close decision in a rematch and then dispatched Tyrone "the Butterfly" Crawley in another successful defense. He lost his title to the talented **Edwin Rosario** in 1986.

He never received another world title shot and entered the realm of journeyman status, losing many a decision to rising prospects over the years. His last pro bout was in 2003. He now works as a personal and boxing trainer in New York.

Professional Record:	40-26-3
Championship(s):	WBA lightweight, 1984–1986

Further Reading
Katz, Michael. "Mancini Challenger is a Puzzle." *The New York Times*, 5/30/1984, p. B11.
Katz, Michael. "Bramble Takes Mancini's Title." *The New York Times*, 6/2/1984, p. 43.
O'Brian, Joseph D. "Another Flake Arrives." *The Ring* (May 1985), pp. 20–23.
Welsh, Jack. "Bye-Bye Boom Boom." *The Ring* (May 1985), pp. 32–39.

BRELAND, MARK (1963–). Mark Breland was one of the greatest amateur boxers to ever lace on a pair of gloves. He compiled a record of 110-1, culminating with an Olympic gold medal in the 1984 Los Angeles Olympics in the welterweight division. Born in Brooklyn, New York, Breland began amateur boxing at age 14 and quickly developed into a future champion. His only amateur loss was a disputed 3-2 decision loss to Darryl Anthony.

He turned pro in 1984 after the Olympics and won his first 18 bouts before capturing the **World Boxing Association (WBA)** welterweight title in 1987 with a seventh-round stoppage of South African boxer Harold Volbrecht. He lost the title in his first defense to **Marlon "the Magic Man" Starling.**

Breland regained the title by demolishing South Korean Seung Soon Lee in the first round to win the WBA title. He made three successful defenses before losing to the rugged Aaron Davis. He retired in 1991 after suffering a sixth-round loss to Jorge Vaca. Breland made a comeback in 1996–1997, winning five straight fights against limited opposition. Breland has stayed in the boxing game, serving as a trainer for several world-class boxers. He also acquitted himself as a fine actor in the 1983 movie *The Lords of Discipline.*

Professional Record:	35-3-1
Championship:	WBA Welterweight, 1987, 1989–1990

Further Reading
Berger, Phil. "Breland Finds Pro Style with Knockout Punch." *The New York Times*, 2/6/1987, p. A28.
Feinstein, John. "Breland Beats Count and Opponent." *The Washington Post*, 7/30/1984, p. D1.
Gutskey, Earl. "Breland is Cast as Gold Medalist." *Los Angeles Times*, 5/8/1983, p. B3.
Gutskey, Earl. "104 and 1: Near Perfect, Stringbean Mark Breland Packs Heavyweight Right-Hand Punch." *Los Angeles Times*, 7/26/1984, p. 11.
Remnick, David. "Breland Plans to Turn Medals to Gold." *The Washington Post*, 11/14/1983, p. C12.

BRENNER, TEDDY (1918–2000). Teddy Brenner was one of the sport's greatest matchmakers. For years he matched boxers at Madison Square Garden, which for a time was the mecca of boxing. Born in 1918 in New York, Brenner began arranging fights in New Jersey for his friend Irving Cohen. In 1947, Brenner began his association with Madison Square Garden.

He later worked at the Garden as assistant matchmaker to Al Weill under the direction of the International Boxing Club. Brenner later resigned, alleging that Weill and the IBC had told him to match boxers for a fixed fight.

In 1952, he began serving as matchmaker for the Eastern Parkway Arena in Brooklyn. In 1959, he moved back to Madison Square Garden after the IBC dissolved. He later became president of Madison Square Garden after the death of Harry Markson. He later worked for **Bob Arum's** Top Rank, Inc. as an advisor.

Further Reading
Brenner, Teddy, and Barney Nagler. *Only the Ring was Square*. Englewood Cliffs, NJ: Prentice-Hall, 1981.
Eskenazai, Gerald. "Teddy Brenner Dies at 82, Matched Boxers at Garden." *The New York Times*, 1/9/2000, at http://query.nytimes.com/gst/fullpage.html?res=9407EFD7103BF93AA35752C0A96 69C8B63
Matthews, Wallace. "Matchmaker, Matchmaker . . . Brenner Turned the Garden into Mecca of Boxing." *The New York Post*, 1/11/2000, p. 098.

BREWSTER, LAMON (1973–). Lamon "Relentless" Brewster is a former world heavyweight champion best known for his powerful left hook and his shocking upset of **Wladimir Klitschko** in 2004. Born in 1973 in Indianapolis, Brewster showed great potential as an amateur, winning a silver medal at the 1995 Pan-American Games. However, he failed to make the 1996 U.S. Olympic team, losing to DaVarryl Williamson and Nate Jones at the Olympic Trials.

He turned pro in 1996 with a first-round destruction of Moses Harris. He won his first 11 bouts by knockout and won his first 23 bouts overall before a decision loss to Clifford "the Black Rhino" Etienne in 2000 in an HBO-televised bout. Later that year he suffered another decision loss to Charles Shufford.

He rebounded and began to resurrect his career, including a win over former amateur nemesis Nate Jones. In April 2004, he faced the heavily-favored Klitschko for the World Boxing Organization (WBO) heavyweight title. Even more daunting was the fact that Brewster had just months ago lost his former trainer Bill Slayton (who also worked with former champion Ken Norton), who had passed away from an illness. Klitschko dominated the early rounds, but Brewster withstood the onslaught and kayoed the champion in the fifth round. He made three successful defenses against Kali Meehan, Andrew Golota, and Luan Krasniqi. The defense against Golota was most impressive, as Brewster dispatched him in the first round.

Brewster lost his title to Sergei Lyakhovich in 2006 and then lost in a rematch to Klitschko in 2007. He hopes to regain his past glory in 2009 and beyond.

Professional Record: 34-4
Championship(s):   WBO Heavyweight, 2004–2006

Further Reading
Donovan, Jake. "Lamon Aimin for Respectability." *The Sweet Science*, 5/19/2005, at http://www.thesweet science.com/boxing-article/2097/lamon-aimin-respectability/
Slezak, Carol. "Brewster: Nice guy in a punky business." *Chicago Sun-Times*, 5/17/2005, p. 111.
Woolever, Phil. "A Step Up in Class: Brewster Shocks Klitschko." *Boxing Digest* (July 2004), pp. 28–29.

BRIGGS, SHANNON (1971–). Shannon "the Cannon" Briggs is a former world heavyweight champion known for his devastating power and inability to live up to his potential. Born in 1971 in Brooklyn, New York, Briggs turned pro in 1992 and kayoed his opponent in the first round—a feat he would accomplish 26 more times in his career.

Briggs won his first 25 pro fights until a shocking 3rd-round kayo loss to fellow unbeaten prospect Darroll Wilson. In 1997, he won a dubious 12-round majority decision over **George Foreman.** Many ringside experts felt that Foreman deserved the nod. Nevertheless, Briggs' decision win earned him a shot at heavyweight champion **Lennox Lewis,** who stopped Briggs in the 5th round.

In 2000, Briggs dropped an 8-round decision to journeyman Sedreck Fields in a bout in which Briggs simply was not active enough. After losing a 10-round decision to Jameel McCline in 2002, many thought that Briggs' days as a top heavyweight were over. However, he kept winning and earned a shot at World Boxing Organization (WBO) champion Sergei Lyakhovich in November 2006. Down on all three scorecards, Briggs scored a dramatic last-round kayo to win the title. Unfortunately for him, he lost the title in his first defense against **Sultan Ibragimov.**

Briggs provides boxing commentary for ESPN2's Friday Night Fights when primary analyst **Teddy Atlas** (a former Briggs trainer) is unavailable.

Professional Record: 48-5-1
Championship(s):   WBO Heavyweight, 2006–2007

Further Reading
Berkow, Ira. "Briggs Stays Focused on Learning Process." *The New York Times,* 3/14/1996, p. B20.
Kimball, George. "Title win was a Briggs heist." *The Boston Herald,* 11/12/2006, p. b29.
Rosario, Andrew. "Shannon Briggs . . . For Real." *The New York Beacon,* 1/7/1998, p. 24.

BRISCOE, BENNY (1943–). "Bad" Benny Briscoe was a fearsome puncher in the middleweight division and one of the best fighters to never win a world championship. He had the misfortune of laboring in the division during the reign of the great Argentine champion **Carlos Monzon** and the Colombian great **Rodrigo Valdez.**

Born in 1943 in Augusta, Georgia, Briscoe served as a caddy at the Augusta National Golf Tournament, once caddying for President Dwight D. Eisenhower. Later he moved to Philadelphia to live with an aunt and focused on boxing. He turned pro in 1962 and pounded his way to becoming a top contender.

In 1972, he challenged the great Monzon for the world middleweight title, losing a unanimous 15-round decision. He staggered the Argentine champion in the 9th and 14th rounds but could not finish the champion. In 1974 and 1977, he lost to Valdez in two more shots at the middleweight crown. In the first bout he was stopped on cuts—the only loss of his career in which he failed to go the distance—and the other he lost a decision.

He fought many great champions and contenders in his career, including **Luis Rodriguez, Emile Griffith, Marvelous Marvin Hagler, Vito Antuofermo, Eugene "Cyclone" Hart, Eddie Mustafa Muhammad,** and Vinnie Curto.

Professional Record: 66-24-5
Championship(s):   None

Further Reading
Anderson, Dave. "Briscoe, Caddie Turned Boxer, Recalls Eisenhower's $100 Tip." *The New York Times,* 12/12/1967, p. 62.
Associated Press. "Monzon Keeps Middleweight Title by Outpointing Briscoe." *The New York Times,* 11/12/1972, p. S26.
Fernandez, Bernard. "Bashful Briscoe due Hall induction." *Philadelphia Daily News,* 2/13/2007, p. 58.

BRITTON, JACK (1885–1962). Jack Britton was a former world welterweight champion who held the title on three different occasions. He is best known for his incredible rivalry with fellow welterweight champion **Ted "Kid" Lewis.** Britton and Lewis fought each other an astonishing 20 times with 12 listed as no-decisions.

Born in 1885 in Clinton, New York, as William J. Breslin, Britton learned to fight on the street. He turned professional in 1905 at age 19 and lost his first two professional bouts. He won 104 bouts in a career that lasted until age 45 in 1930.

Britton won the welterweight title from Mike Glover in 1915 but lost it later that year to Lewis. He regained the title from Lewis in 1916 but then lost it to Lewis later in the year. Britton won the title for a third time by stopping Lewis in the ninth round. He held the title until losing a decision to **Mickey "the Toy Bulldog" Walker** in 1922.

Professional Record:	104-27-21 with 190 no decisions.
Championships(s):	Welterweight, 1915, 1916, 1919–1922

Further Reading
"Britton Outpoints Lewis." *The New York Times,* 10/18/1916, p. 12.
Evans, Gavin. "The 20 Greatest Welterweights of All Time." *The Ring* (February 2008), pp. 63–84, 76.
"Jack Britton Makes Monkey of White." *Los Angeles Times,* 7/5/1913, p. III3.

BROUGHTON, JACK (1704–1789). Known as "the Father of Boxing," Jack Broughton held the largely unofficial title of English champion for more than a decade in the eighteenth century. Broughton is better remembered for devising a set of boxing rules that served as a key progenitor for modern boxing.

Born in 1704 in Cirencester, England, Broughton earned the English championship by defeating George Taylor in 1738. He held the title until losing to Jack Slack in 1750. In 1741 Broughton defeated George Stevenson. Tragically, Stevenson died after the bout. Two years later, Broughton introduced a set of rules for boxing called "Broughton's Rules." These rules prohibited hitting an opponent on the canvas or ground. They also provided that a felled man had 30 seconds to rise to his feet.

Broughton was beloved in his native country so much that Westminster Abbey became his resting place upon his death in 1789 at the age of 85.

Professional Record:	Unknown
Championship(s):	English Champion, 1738–1750

Further Reading
Roberts, James B. and Alexander G. Skutt. *The Boxing Register: International Boxing Hall of Fame Register* (4th ed.). Ithaca, NY: McBooks Press, Inc., 2006, p. 18.

BROWN, JOE (1926–1997). Joe "Old Bones" Brown was a former world lightweight champion who fought professionally for nearly 27 years. Born in 1926 in New Orleans, Brown had one professional bout in 1943 but then served in World War II.

He resumed his career in 1945 and fought numerous top fighters, including **Sandy Saddler,** Freddie Dawson, and Johnny Bratton. He improved and received a title shot in 1956 against Wallace "Bud" Smith. Brown overcame a broken right hand in the 2nd round to win a 15-round decision. He then handled Smith more easily in the rematch, stopping him in the 11th round. He held the title for several years until finally losing it to **Carlos Ortiz** by decision in 1962. He fought until age 44 in 1970. *The Ring* magazine listed him as the sixth greatest lightweight of all time in September 2001.

Professional Record: 104-44-13

Championship(s):   Lightweight, 1956–1962

Further Reading

Cowans, Russ J. "Brown Stops Lopes in 11th." *The Chicago Daily Defender*, 12/5/1957, p. 24.

Dettloff, William. "The 20 Greatest Lightweights of All Time." *The Ring* (September 2001), pp. 49–69, 55.

Hand, Jack. "Brown Bags TKO Over Smith in 11th." *Los Angeles Times*, 2/14/1957, p. C1.

"Joe Brown Beats Bud Smith for Title." *The Chicago Defender*, 9/1/1956, p. 18.

Roberts, James B., and Alexander G. Skutt. *The Boxing Register: International Boxing Hall of Fame Register* (4th ed.). Ithaca, NY: McBooks Press, Inc., 2006, pp. 312–317.

BROWN, PANAMA AL (1902–1951). Born Alfonso Teofilo Brown in Colon, Panama, Panama Al Brown may have been the greatest bantamweight champion in boxing history. Possessing an enormous reach for a bantamweight Brown displayed fine boxing skills. Born in 1902 in the Canal Zone, a young Brown wanted to box after watching U.S. military men spar with each other.

Legend has it that he smuggled his way to New York City on a fruit boat. He turned professional at age 20 and won his first 17 bouts. In 1929, he faced Vidal Gregorio for the vacant bantamweight title. Brown won a 15-round decision handily. He owned a kayo win over **Battling Nelson.** He defended his title around the world for the next six years before finally losing to Baltazar Sangchili in Spain by decision. In 1941, he pled guilty to possession of heroin. He finally retired in 1942.

Record: 123-18-10 (4 no decisions)

Championship(s):   Bantamweight, 1929–1935

Further Reading

Carr, Harry. "'I've Been Hungry Too Often; I Can't Get Fat,'" *Los Angeles Times*, 1/4/1932, p. 11.

Dawson, James P. "Brown Wins Bout on Foul in Fourth." *The New York Times*, 2/9/1930, p. S6.

Neil, Edward J. "Brown Nears Bantam Title." *The Washington Post*, 7/14/1929, p. M20.

Roberts, James B., and Alexander G. Skutt. *The Boxing Register: International Boxing Hall of Fame Official Record Book* (4th ed.). Ithaca, NY: McBooks Press, Inc., 2006, pp. 78–79.

Williams, Edgar. "Al Brown Scores Kayo in 8th Round." *The Chicago Defender*, 4/23/1938, p. 8.

BROWN, SIMON (1963–). Simon Brown was a former world welterweight champion known for his good all-around skills, powerful left hook and great chin. Born in 1963 in Clarendon, Jamaica, Brown turned pro in 1982 and won his first 21 bouts before losing a split decision to fellow future champion **Marlon Starling** in 1985. Three years later Brown squared off against Tyrone Trice for the vacant **International Boxing Federation (IBF)** welterweight title. Brown rose from a 2nd-round knockdown to eventually prevail in the 14th round in a fight-of-the-year candidate.

He successfully defended his title seven times and then added the **World Boxing Council (WBC)** belt with a 10th-round stoppage of Maurice Blocker. Brown lost his title to **James "Buddy" McGirt** in 1991. In 1993, Brown shocked the boxing world with a fourth-round kayo of **"Terrible" Terry Norris** to win the WBC junior middleweight crown. After one successful defense, he lost his title by decision in a rematch with Norris. Brown lost in three more attempts at world titles: to Vincent Pettway in 1995 for the IBF junior middleweight crown, to Lonnie Bradley in 1996 for the World Boxing Organization (WBO) middleweight title and to **Bernard Hopkins** in 1998 for the IBF middleweight crown. He finally retired in 2000 after losing his sixth straight bout.

Professional Record:	47-12
Championship(s):	IBF welterweight, 1988–1991; WBC welterweight, 1991; WBC junior middleweight, 1993–1994

Further Reading

Goldstein, Alan. "Bell in way of Brown's shot at 3rd title; At 34, Mount Airy fighter seeks to turn back clock." *The Baltimore Sun*, 9/11/1997, p. 6C.
Jenkins, Sally. "Brown Turns His 'Nice Face' Toward Curry's Title." *The Washington Post*, 6/29/1986, p. B3.

BRUNO, FRANK (1961–). Frank Bruno was a powerful former world heavyweight champion known for his courage, power, and weak chin. Born in London in 1961, Bruno turned pro and won his first 21 fights—most of them by kayo within a couple rounds. In 1984, he fought **James "Bonecrusher" Smith** and outboxed the American for 9 rounds. However, in the 10th round, Smith kayoed Bruno.

The big Brit kept winning and earned a title shot in 1986 against champion **"Terrible" Tim Witherspoon.** Bruno lost in the 11th round. He failed in his next two attempts to win the world title, losing to **Mike Tyson** in 1989 and **Lennox Lewis** in 1993. Finally, in September 1995, Bruno won the world championship with a 12-round unanimous decision over **Oliver McCall** in Wembley Stadium in London. Bruno lost his title in his first defense against Tyson in the third round.

Professional Record:	40-5
Championship(s):	WBC Heavyweight, 1986

Further Reading

Clarke, Nigel. "My Crowning Glory; Frank Bruno's Verdict On His World Title Date with Destiny." *Daily Mirror*, 9/2/1995, pp. 34–35.
Frost, Bill. "Bruno savours his defeat of critics." *The Times*, 9/4/1995.
Shapiro, Jonathan. "Frank Bruno: The Man Who Would Be King." *The Ring* (July 1986), pp. 16–19.

BUCHANAN, KEN (1945–). Ken Buchanan was a former world lightweight champion from Scotland—some say the greatest fighter the country has ever produced. A stylish boxer, Buchanan held the title until running into a Panamanian nightmare named **Roberto "Hands of Stone" Duran** in 1972.

Born in 1945 in Edinburgh, Buchanan turned pro in 1965 and won his first 33 bouts. In his 34th pro he lost a questionable hometown decision to Spanish fighter Miguel Velasquez in Spain. He rebounded with several consecutive wins to land a title shot against **World Boxing Association (WBA)** champion **Ismael Laguna.** Buchanan won a 15-round split decision in Puerto Rico. He made two successful defenses before losing in the 13th round to Duran.

In 1975, he received another world title shot—losing a decision to Japanese boxer Guts Ishimatsu over 15 rounds in Tokyo, Japan. He retired in 1982.

Professional Record:	61-8
Championship(s):	WBA lightweight, 1970–1972; WBC lightweight, 1971

Further Reading

Associated Press. "Buchanan Rallies to Outpoint Laguna for Lightweight Title in Puerto Rico." *The New York Times*, 9/27/1970, p. S4.
Buchanan, Ken. *Buchanan: High Life and Hard Times*. London: Mainstream Publishing, 1986.
Buchanan, Ken. *The Tartan Legend*. London: Headline Book Publishing, 2000.
Dettloff, William. "The 20 Greatest Lightweights of All Time." *The Ring* (September 2001), p. 49–69, 65.

BUENTELLO, PAUL (1974–). Paul "the Headhunter" Buentello is an American mixed martial artist who specializes in hand and leg strikes. Born in 1974 in Amarillo, Texas, Buentello turned professional in mixed martial arts in 1997. After years of fighting in less well-known organizations, Buentello first fought in the **Ultimate Fighting Championships (UFC)** in 2005 at UFC 51: Super Saturday with a first-round knockout of Justin Eilers. After another win in the Octagon in UFC 53: Heavy Hitters, Buentello challenged **Andrei Arlovski** for the UFC heavyweight championship at UFC 55—the Fury. Unfortunately, for "the Headhunter," Arlovski landed a heavy right hand which kayoed Buentello, who fell on top of Arlovski.

In 2006, Buentello started competing in the Strikeforce organization, blasting out former UFC legend **David "Tank" Abbott** in only 43 seconds. In November 2007, he faced **Alistair Overeem** for the vacant Strikeforce heavyweight title but lost in the second round.

Professional MMA Record: 27-10
Championship(s):   None

Further Reading
Official Web site: http://www.paulbuentello.com/
Rousseau, Robert. "Paul Buentello Interview: A Headhunter for Sure." *MMAFighting.com*, 11/7/2007, at http://www.mmafighting.com/interviews/2007/11/01/paul-buentello-interview-a-headhunter-sure

BURLEY, CHARLEY (1917–1992). Charley Burley was an African-American fighter who was a top contender in the welterweight and middleweight divisions but never received a title shot. Born in 1917 in Bessemer, Pa., Burley turned pro in 1936 and won two of three fights with the tough **Fritzie Zivic.** He often had to fight much larger men—such as **Ezzard Charles, Archie Moore,** or Jimmy Bivins—because fighters in his division refused to face him. Some speculated that even the great **Sugar Ray Robinson** avoided Burley who was dubbed by some as "the uncrowned champion." Fighter and later Hall-of-Fame trainer **Eddie Futch** called Burley the finest boxer he had ever seen. *The Ring* magazine recently listed him as the fourth greatest welterweight of all time.

Professional Record: 83-12-2
Championship(s):   None

Further Reading
Evans, Gavin. "The 20 Greatest Welterweights of All Time." *The Ring* (February 2008), pp. 63–84, 67.
Otty, Harry. *Charley Burley and the Black Murderers Row.* Liskeard, Cornwall, UK: Exposure Publishing, 2006.
Rosenfeld, Allen S. *Charley Burley: The Life and Hard Times of an Uncrowned Champion.* Bloomington, IN: AuthorHouse Publishing, 2007.
Roberts, James B., and Alexander G. Skutt. *The Boxing Register: International Boxing Hall of Fame Register* (4th ed.). Ithaca, NY: McBooks Press, Inc. 2006, pp. 322–325.

BURNS, TOMMY (1881–1955). Tommy Burns was the shortest man to ever win the world heavyweight championship, standing only 5'7". Born in Canada in 1881 as Noah Brusso, he later fought under the name Ed Burns and then Tommy Burns.

He turned pro in 1900 as a lightweight. He steadily moved up in weight, winning the Michigan middleweight title in 1902. He then moved up to light heavyweight, losing a decision in 1904 to "Philadelphia" Jack O'Brien.

Burns received the opportunity of a lifetime when heavyweight champion **Marvin Hart** agreed to give him a title shot. Burns, who possessed quick hands and a powerful left hook, decisioned Hart over 20 rounds. The *Chicago Daily Tribune* reported that Burns won all 20 rounds, often outlanding Hart by a 10 to 1 ratio.

He then defeated his rival "Philadelphia" Jack O'Brien to gain broad recognition as world champion. Burns made 11 successful title defenses against foes such as O'Brien (twice), Fireman Jim Flynn, James Moir, Bill Squires (three times), and Bill Lang. He then agreed to face **Jack Johnson** for the title in Sydney, Australia. Burns fought courageously, but the bigger Johnson defeated him easily over 14 rounds.

Burns took a year off after the Johnson fight, returning to the ring in 1910 to defeat Bill Lang for the vacant British Empire heavyweight title.

Professional Record: 48-6-8 (2 no-decisions)
Championship(s):   Heavyweight, 1906–1908

Further Reading
Callis, Tracy. "Tommy Burns: 'He of the Terrible Right Hand.'" *Cyber Boxing Zone Journal*, February 2004, at http://www.cyberboxingzone.com/boxing/w01014-tc.html
Carr, Harry. "Australian Squires No Match for Burns." *Los Angeles Times*, 7/5/1907, p. II3.
McCaffery, Dan. *Tommy Burns: Canada's Unknown World Heavyweight Champion*. Toronto, Ontario: Lorimer, 2001.
Roberts, James B., and Alexander G. Skutt. *The Boxing Register: International Boxing Hall of Fame Official Record Book* (4th ed.). Ithaca, NY: McBooks Press, Inc., 2006, pp. 80–81.
"Tom Burns Beaten: Negro Wins World's Heavyweight Championship." *The Washington Post*, 12/26/1908, p. 1.
"Tommy Burns Is Now Champion." *Chicago Daily Tribune*, 2/24/1906, p. 10.

BYRD, CHRIS (1970–). Chris "Rapid Fire" Byrd is a former two-time heavyweight champion known for utilizing his superior boxing and defensive skills to frustrate and defeat many larger opponents in the ring. Born in 1970 in Flint, Michigan, Byrd followed in the footsteps of his father Joe who fought professionally.

Chris had a decorated amateur career, culminating in a silver medal at the 1992 Barcelona Olympics. He lost a decision to the skillful Cuba's Ariel Hernandez in the gold-medal match. "Fighting him was like fighting mirror," Byrd remarked after the bout.

He turned pro in 1993 and won his first 26 bouts, defeating boxers such as Jimmy Thunder, Frankie Swindell, Ross Purrity, and Bert Cooper. In 1999, he lost his first bout to the powerful **Ike Ibeabuchi** in the fifth round. He won four straight bouts before landing a title shot against World Boxing Organization (WBO) champion **Vitali Klitschko.** The taller Ukrainian dominated most of the bout with his superior size and reach, but retired in the ninth round with a hurt shoulder.

He lost the title in his first defense to Vitali's brother **Wladimir,** losing a lopsided 12-round decision. He rebounded in 2001 with a close decision win over the dangerous **David Tua.** In December 2002, he outpointed **Evander Holyfield** over 12 rounds to win the **International Boxing Federation (IBF)** heavyweight title. He successfully defended his title against Fres Oquendo, Andrew Golota, DaVarryl Williamson and Jameel McCline before losing his title to Wladimir Klitschko in 2006.

Byrd continued to fight as a heavyweight through 2007, losing to undefeated prospect Alexander Povetkin.

In 2008, he moved down to light heavyweight where he suffered a kayo loss to Shaun George. He indicated after the bout that he would retire.

Professional Record:	40-5-1
Championship(s):	WBO Heavyweight, 2000; IBF Heavyweight, 2002–2006

Further Reading

Berger, Phil. "Differing Styles Bring Winning Results." *The New York Times*, 3/2/1992, p. C7.
Brown, Clifton. "Byrd Employed Nothing Fancy To Take Title With Jab, Jab, Jab." *The New York Times*, 12/16/2002, p. D7.
Rhoden, William C. "De La Hoya Wins but Cubans dominate." *The New York Times*, 8/9/1992, p. S7.

BYONG-UK, LI (1954–). Li Byong-Uk is one of the greatest boxers ever from North Korea. Twice he represented his country in the Olympics and twice he earned medals. In the 1976 Montreal Olympics, he won a silver medal. In the semifinal round, he defeated future professional world champion **Payao Poontorat** of Thailand to advance to the final match where he lost to Jorge Hernandez of Cuba 4-1. In the 1980 Moscow Olympics, he won a bronze medal, losing to Soviet fighter Shamil Sabirov in the semifinal round.

Professional Record:	N/A
Championship(s):	N/A

CALZAGHE, JOE (1972–). Joe Calzaghe is an undefeated former super middleweight champion and one of the top pound-for-pound fighters in the world. The Welshmen possessed quick hands, a steady chin, a high work rate, and an indominatable will to win.

Born in 1972 in Hammersmith in London, England, Calzaghe grew up in Wales where he learned under the tutelage of his father, Enzo. He overcame bullies at school to become a star boxer. Calzaghe turned pro in 1993 with a bout in Cardiff, Wales.

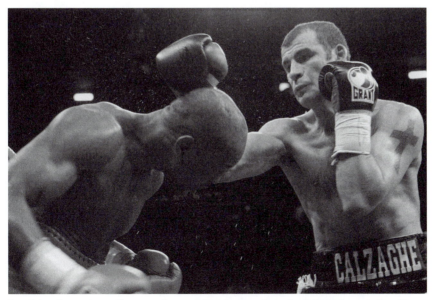

Joe Calzaghe squares off against Bernard Hopkins in their April 2008 bout in Las Vegas, Nevada. Calzaghe won a 12-round split decision. Courtesy of Chris Cozzone.

Joe Calzaghe celebrates his victory over Bernard Hopkins in April 2008. Courtesy of Chris Cozzone.

In 1997, he toppled longstanding World Boxing Organization (WBO) champion **Chris Eubank** to capture the world title—a title he never relinquished in the ring. For more than a decade, Calzaghe defended his title an astonishing 21 times, defeating the likes of Byron Mitchell, Charles Brewer, Robin Reid, and Omar Sheika. In his defining fight, Calzaghe outclassed **International Boxing Federation (IBF)** champion Jeff Lacy to capture another belt in March 2006.

Calzaghe then added another belt to his collection when he outpointed the dangerous Mikkel Kessler to add the **World Boxing Association (WBA)** championship. Calzaghe relinquished the titles in 2008 to move up in weight for a showdown with **Bernard Hopkins.** Though dropped in the first round, Calzaghe rallied and outworked Hopkins for another decision win.

In November 2008, Calzaghe defeated another legend when he easily outpointed former great **Roy Jones, Jr.**

Professional Record:	46-0
Championship(s):	WBO super middleweight, 1997–2008; IBF super middleweight, 2006; WBA super middleweight, 2007–2008

Further Reading
Calzaghe, Joe, with Brian Doogan. *No Ordinary Joe.* London: Century, 2007.
Hubbard, Alan. "The Day my Dad Called Me Chicken." *The Independent,* 6/3/2007.
McRae, Donald. "Interview Joe Calzaghe: The Welsh boxer is living his dream but it is not as he foresaw it." *The Guardian,* 4/25/2005, p. 22.
Official Web site: http://www.calzaghe.com/index.html
Rawling, John. "Calzaghe still top of the pile 10 years on." *The Irish Times,* 11/5/2007, p. 5.
Smith, Tim. "He's no ordinary Joe, Unbeaten Calzaghe unifies title." *The New York Daily News,* 11/4/2007, p. 74.

CAMACHO, HECTOR "MACHO" (1962–). Hector "Macho" Camacho was a flashy former lightweight champion known for his outrageous antics and blazing speed. Born in 1962 in Bayamon, Puerto Rico, Camacho turned pro in 1980 and won his first 38 professional bouts. He won the **World Boxing Council (WBC)** super featherweight title with an easy win over Rafael "Bazooka" Limon. In 1985, he won the WBC lightweight title with an easy decision win over Jose Luis Ramirez. Camacho's superior speed was simply too much for most of his opponents. He successfully defended his title against the tough **Edwin Rosario,** wining a split decision. In 1989, he won the World Boxing Organization (WBO) junior welterweight crown with a split decision over **Ray "Boom Boom" Mancini.** He successfully defended his title against **Vinnie Pazienza** before losing a controversial decision to Greg Haugen.

In 1992, he failed to capture the WBC lightweight title from the great **Julio Cesar Chavez,** losing a 12-round decision. He lost in two other attempts to capture the world welterweight title losing lopsided decisions to **Felix Trinidad** in 1994 and **Oscar De La Hoya** in 1997. Still, Camacho has compiled 79 wins, won several championships, and never was stopped in his pro career that spanned 25 years. He fought once in 2008, winning in the seventh round over Perry Ballard.

Record:	79-5-2
Championship(s):	WBC super featherweight, 1983–1985; WBC lightweight, 1985–1987; WBO junior welterweight, 1989–1991; 1991–1992.

Further Reading

Collins, Nigel. "Camacho's Great Escape." *The Ring* (September 1986), pp. 36–39.

Diaz, George. "Playtime Is Over; Camacho Focuses on De La Hoya Fight." *Orlando Sentinel*, 9/7/1997, p. C20.

Marder, Phil. "The Return of the 'Macho Man': Boxing's Most Exciting Star Is Back and Ready to Win His Second Title." *The Ring* (April 1985), pp. 32–33, 36–37.

Official Site: http://www.itsmachotime.com

CAMPBELL, NATE (1972–). Nate "the Galaxy Warrior" Campbell is a world lightweight champion who did not make his professional boxing debut until the relatively advanced age of 28. Born in 1972 in Jacksonville, Florida, Campbell had a tough early life; his mother was incarcerated and his father died when Nate was only 10. Shuffled through numerous foster homes, Campbell was arrested several times before reaching 18.

While working at a warehouse when he was 25, a coworker noticed Campbell shadowboxing during breaks and encouraged him to ply his trade in the boxing ring. Campbell obliged and fought amateur from 1997–1999, compiling a record of 30-6. In 2000, he turned professional and won his first 23 bouts before losing a controversial decision to **Joel Casamayor** in January 2003.

In 2004, he suffered perhaps his most embarrassing loss when he mocked his opponent Robbie Peden while ahead on the scorecards. Peden clocked him with a left hook and kayoed the overconfident Campbell. After another upset loss, Campbell's best days appeared behind him.

However, he rebuilt his career with wins over Matt Zegan and Ricky Quiles to earn a shot at champion **Juan "the Baby Bull" Diaz.** Most experts felt that the undefeated Diaz would win the fight, but Campbell pounded out a split decision victory over 12 rounds to earn the **World Boxing Association (WBA), International Boxing Federation (IBF),** and World Boxing Organization (WBO) belts. He vacated the WBA belt and then lost his other two belts when he failed to make weight for a title defense in February 2009.

Professional Record:	32-5-2
Championship(s):	WBA Lightweight, 2008–2009 ; IBF Lightweight, 2008– ; WBO lightweight, 2008–

Further Reading

Rafael, Dan. "Campbell earns three belts by split decision over Diaz." *ESPN.com*, 3/9/2008, at http://sports.espn.go.com/sports/boxing/news/story?id=3284251

Wright, Teneshia L. "Hard-knock life Campbell calls on past in ring." *Florida Times-Union*, 5/16/2007, p. D-1.

CANIZALES, ORLANDO (1965–). Orlando Canizales was a former world bantamweight champion who enjoyed a prosperous reign as **International Boxing Federation (IBF)** kingpin. Born in 1965 in Laredo, Texas, Canizales compiled a sterling amateur record of 108-12. He turned pro in 1984 in Laredo and won via a second-round kayo.

He won his first dozen bouts before dropping a decision to **Paul Gonzalez,** the former Olympic gold medalist. Canizales rebounded and in 1988 defeated Kelvin Seabrooks to win the IBF title. He defended his title 16 times against the likes of **Clarence "Bones" Adams**, Edwin Rangel, and Billy Hardy. He avenged his loss to Gonzalez by stopping him in the second round in another title defense.

Canizales moved up in weight to the super bantamweight where he was not as successful. He lost in title attempts to Wilfredo Vasquez and Junior Jones. He retired in 1999 after dropping a decision to Frank Toledo. His brother Gaby Canizales was also a world champion. Canizales will be inducted into the **International Boxing Hall of Fame** in June 2009.

Professional Record: 50-5-1
Championship(s):   IBF bantamweight, 1988–1994

Further Reading
Arias, Carlos. "Champion of Long Standing." *Orange County Register*, 9/28/1994, p. D02.
Stickney, W. H., Jr. "Canizales Eyes Sweet 16th." *The Houston Chronicle*, 10/15/1994, p. 15.
Stickney, W. H., Jr. "Canizales Could Become a Champion for the Ages." *The Houston Chronicle*, 10/9/1994, p. 33.

CANTO, MIGUEL (1949–). Miguel Canto, "El Maestro," was a ring stylist similar to his ring idol **Willie Pep**. A longtime flyweight champion, Canto used his superior boxing skills to make 14 successful defenses of his flyweight championship. Born in 1949 in Merida, Mexico, Canto turned professional in 1969 and lost his pro debut.

Canto rebounded and challenged **Betulio Gonzalez** for the vacant flyweight championship, losing a 15-round decision. In 1975, he challenged Shoji Oguma for the championship, winning a decision. He held the title until losing a close decision in 1979 to **Chan-Hee Park.** In a rematch, Canto outboxed Park in the later rounds, but the official verdict was a draw. He retired in 1982 after his third consecutive loss by knockout or technical knockout.

Professional Record: 61-9-4
Championship(s):   WBC flyweight champion, 1975–1979

Further Reading
Associated Press. "Ex-Flyweight Champ Canto Retires." *Los Angeles Times*, 10/5/1979, p. E11.
Roberts, James B., and Alexander B. Skutt. *The Boxing Register: International Boxing Hall of Fame* (4th ed.). Ithaca, NY: McBooks Press, Inc., 2006, pp. 326–329.
United Press International. "Canto in Record 14th Title Defense." *Los Angeles Times*, 2/10/1979, p. C8.

CANZONERI, TONY (1908–1959). Tony Canzoneri was the third man in boxing history to win world championships in three different divisions. Born in 1908 in Slidell, Louisiana, Canzoneri turned pro at age 16 in 1925. He captured the featherweight championship in 1927 with a win over Johnny Dundee.

He added the lightweight championship in 1930 with a first-round kayo win over Al Singer in 66 seconds. In his defining fight, he faced **Jackie "Kid" Berg** in a battle of champions, as Canzoneri risked his lightweight belt while Berg risked his junior welterweight belt. Canzoneri stopped Berg in the third round. He lost his title to **Barney Ross** in 1933. He retired in 1939 after suffering his only kayo loss to **Al "Bummy" Davis.**

The Ring magazine writer William Dettloff summed up Canzoneri the best: "Canzoneri was the kind of guy fight guys are talking about when they call someone a throwback. He fought all the time, he fought everyone around, and he could do it all—outbox faster, slicker guys and outpunch bigger, stronger guys."

Professional Record:	137-24-10
Championship(s):	Featherweight, 1927–1928; Lightweight, 1930–1933, 1935–1936; junior welterweight, 1931–1932, 1933

Further Reading

Dawson, James P. "Canzoneri Defeats Routis on Points." *The New York Times*, 11/23/1926, p. 32.
Dawson, James P. "Canzoneri Defeats Bass in Title Bout." *The New York Times*, 2/11/1928, p. 12.
Dettloff, William. "The 20 Greatest Lightweights of All Time." *The Ring* (September 2001), pp. 49–69, 57.
Roberts, James B., and Alexander B. Skutt. *The Boxing Register* (4th ed.). Ithaca, NY: McBooks Press, Inc., 2006, pp. 82–83.

CARANO, GINA (1982–). Gina Carano is a female mixed martial artist known for her powerful leg and hand strikes. She fights in the **Elite XC** stable and has showcased her skills on network television in 2008. Born in 1982 in Dallas County, Texas, Carano's father, Glenn, played quarterback for the Dallas Cowboys—"America's Team."

Carano excelled in basketball in high school before turning her attention to Muay Thai kickboxing. After graduating college in Nevada, Carano fought professionally in Muay Thai. In 2006, she turned professional in mixed martial arts. She has won six straight bouts in her career, including three straight in Elite XC bouts. Carano also has millions of fans from her role as "Crush" on American Gladiators.

Professional Record:	7-0
Championship(s):	None

Further Reading

Lang III, Roy. "Women Make Their Make in Mixed Martial Arts." *The Times* (Shreveport, LA), 2/12/2007, p. 1C.
Rodriguez, Jose. "Beauty in the beast." *The Ottawa Sun*, 5/17/2008, p. 44.

CARBAJAL, MICHAEL (1967–). Michael Carbajal was a former junior flyweight champion known for his explosive power and exciting fighting style. Many called him "Little Hands of Stone" because his style reminded many of the great **Roberto Duran.** Born in Phoenix in 1967, Carbajal began boxing at an early age and flourished as an amateur boxer. He competed in the 1988 Seoul Olympics, advancing all the way to the gold-medal match where he dropped a dubious decision to Bulgaria's Ivailo Marinov. Carbajal, like his teammate **Roy Jones, Jr.,** had to settle for a silver medal after a bad decision.

Carbajal struck gold as a professional, capturing several world titles and lasting ring glory. He made his pro debut in February 1989 against a talented opponent, **Will Grigsby,** who later became a world champion in his own right. Carbajal won a four-round decision. After winning his first 14 bouts, Carbajal challenged undefeated **International Boxing Federation (IBF)** junior flyweight champion Muangchai Kittikasem. "Little Hands of Stone" dominated the bout, dropping the champion four times en route to a seventh-round technical knockout. Carbajal defended his title five times before a unification bout with **World Boxing Council (WBC)** junior flyweight champion **Humberto Gonzalez.** The power-punching Gonzalez dropped Carbajal in two rounds and held a commanding lead when Carbajal knocked Gonzalez out with a single left hook in the seventh round. He defended his two belts twice before losing his title in a rematch with Gonzalez by a 12-round split decision. Later that year, he lost the rubber match to Gonzalez by dropping a 12-round majority decision.

In March 1996, Gonzalez won the vacant junior IBF flyweight championship with a unanimous 12-round decision victory over Melchor Cob Castro. In January 1997, he lost his title via a 12-round split decision to undefeated contender Mauriano Pastrana. Carbajal retired after losing badly to Jacob "Baby Jake" Matala in July 1997.

Carbajal returned to the ring in 1999 and won three straight bouts before facing **Jorge Arce** for the World Boxing Organization (WBO) flyweight title. Trailing badly on the scorecards, Carbajal rallied by stopping the younger man in the 11th round. It was a typical Carbajal fight, as he often pulled fights out with his tremendous punching power and never-say-die attitude. He retired for good after winning the WBO title.

Professional Record:	49-4
Championship(s):	IBF junior flyweight, 1990–1994, 1996–1997; WBC junior flyweight, 1993–1994; WBO junior flyweight, 1994, 1999

Further Reading

Friend, Tom. "Carbajal, Down Twice, Unifies the Title with Knockout." *The New York Times*, 3/14/1993, p. S4.

Gustkey, Earl. "Sweet Singer; Michael Carbajal is a Nice Guy in What Can Be a Nasty Game." *Los Angeles Times*, 3/12/1993, p. C2.

Rubin, Paul. "A Long Day's Journey." *Phoenix New Times*, 4/10/1997.

Tintle, Joseph. "Michael Carbajal Kayos Humberto Gonzalez: If This Isn't Fight of the Year, We Have a Lot to Look Forward To." *Knockout* (Summer 1994), pp. 54–56.

CARNERA, PRIMO (1906–1967). Primo Carnera was a former world heavyweight champion known for his imposing size and muscular physique years ahead of its time. Born in 1906 in Sequals, Italy, Carnera was 24 lbs. at birth. His size—6'4" and 265 pounds—was mammoth for the times and led him to the circus where he wrestled and performed feats of strength. French entrepreneur Leon See spotted Carnera and put him in the prize ring. He turned professional in 1928 and later moved to America in 1930. In his first fight on American soil, he pounded out Clayton "Big Boy" Peterson in the first round. Later that year, he won on disqualification when George Godfrey hit him low in the fifth round.

In 1933, Carnera stopped Jack Sharkey in six rounds to win the world title. He successfully defended his title against Spaniard Paulino Uzcudun. In his next defense, he lost the title to **Max Baer,** hitting the canvas 11 times before being stopped in the 11th round. After he retired from boxing, he became a professional wrestler.

Professional Record:	87-14-1
Championship(s):	Heavyweight, 1933–1934

Further Reading

Evans, Gavin. *Kings of the Ring: The History of Heavyweight Boxing.* London: Weidenfeld & Nicolson, 2005.

Mullaly, Frederic. *Primo: The Story of 'Man Mountain' Carnera.* London: Robson, 1999.

Pegler, Westbrook. "Primo Carnera, Surrounded by Managers, Lands in U.S." *Chicago Daily Tribune*, 1/1/1930, p. 49.

Pegler, Westbrook. "Primo Carnera, Italian Giant, Knocks Out Peterson in 1st Round Before 17,000." *The Washington Post*, 1/25/1930, p. 13.

Rice, Grantland. "Primo Carnera Wins on Foul in Fifth Round." *Los Angeles Times*, 6/24/1930, p. A11.

CARPENTIER, GEORGES (1894–1975). This French pugilist fought in nearly every weight division from flyweight to heavyweight in a professional career that spanned from 1908 to 1926. Born in Lens, France, in 1894, Carpentier turned professional at 14 years as a flyweight. As he grew in size, he moved up in weight classes and found his greatest lasting success at light heavyweight.

In 1920, he kayoed Battling Levinsky in the fourth round to win the championship. The next year, he challenged heavyweight kingpin **Jack Dempsey.** Carpentier took the fight to the larger champion instead of relying on his superior boxing skills. This proved his undoing as the "Manassa Mauler" stopped him in the fourth round. In 1922, he lost his light heavyweight title in a major upset to one of the truly fascinating characters in boxing history—**Battling Siki.** He retired in 1926 and later acted in movies. He authored a book titled *The Art of Boxing.*

Record:	88-14-6
Championship(s):	Light Heavyweight, 1920–1922

Further Reading

Carpentier, Georges. *The Art of Boxing.* New York: George H. Doran Company, 1926.

Carpentier, Georges. "George Carpentier, Champion Fighter of France, Tells of His Early Entrance into the Arena and His First Battle." *Los Angeles Times*, 3/21/1920, p. VII.

Roberts, James B., and Alexander B. Skutt. *The Boxing Register: International Boxing Hall of Fame Official Record Book* (4th ed.). Ithaca, NY: McBooks Press, Inc., 2006, p. 22.

CARRASCO, PEDRO (1943–2001). Pedro Carrasco was a former world lightweight champion who compiled one of the great records in boxing history. He won more than 100 bouts against only 3 defeats and was never stopped in the ring as a professional. Born in Huelva, this Spaniard who did bullfighting as a hobby turned pro in 1962 and won his first 13 bouts until a decision loss to Italian Aldo Pravisani in Italy. He then won his next 100 bouts—an incredible feat no matter whom the opponents. He captured the European lightweight title in 1967 and the European junior welterweight title in 1971.

Finally, in 1971, he received his first chance at a world title against **Mando Ramos** and won in controversial fashion. Referee Samuel Odubote awarded Carrasco the disqualification victory before the start of the 12th round because Ramos threw Carrasco to the ground at the end of the 11th. In a rematch, he lost a 15-round split decision to Ramos. The rubber match also ended in a 15-round split decision loss for Carrasco. He retired in 1972.

Professional Record:	106-3-2
Championship(s):	WBC Lightweight, 1971–1972

Further Reading

"Carrasco Not Only Looks Like a Bullfighter—He Is." *Los Angeles Times*, 2/14/1972, p. D5.

Hafner, Dan. " 'My Cleanest Fight' Mando Says of Disputed Defeat by Carrasco." *Los Angeles Times*, 11/17/1971, p. E4.

Hafner, Dan. "Carrasco Studies California Boxing Rules." *Los Angeles Times*, 2/6/1972, p. C13.

Hafner, Dan. "Ramos Forced to Go Route, Beats Carrasco on Decision." *Los Angeles Times*, 2/19/1972, p. E1.

CARTER, JIMMY (1923–1994). Jimmy Carter was a former three-time world lightweight champion known for his crowd-pleasing style and powerful left hook. Born in 1923 in Aiken, South Carolina, he lived with his grandparents in Pennsylvania before moving to New York City to rejoin his parents.

In 1943, he joined the Army and served two years. He made his professional debut in 1948 and received his first title shot three years later against heavily favored **Ike Williams.** Carter dropped Williams several times during the bout before finally finishing him off in the 14th round.

In 1952, he lost his title to Lauro Salas—a fighter he had defeated earlier in the year. Carter met Salas for the third time in that year and regained his title with a 15-round unanimous decision. In 1953, he battered Bostonian **Tommy Collins** to the canvas 10 times before Collins' corner finally threw in the town. In March 1954, he lost the title to Paddy DeMarco but regained the title later that year. He lost his title again to Wallace "Bud" Smith via a 15-round split decision. He retired in 1960 after suffering his third straight decision loss.

Professional Record: 81-31-9
Championship(s):   Lightweight, 1951–1952, 1952–1954, 1954–1955

Further Reading
Ripton, Ray. "Jimmy Carter, the Boxer, Turns Back on Fame." *Los Angeles Times*, 7/25/1976, p. WS1.
Roberts, James B., and Alexander G. Skutt. *The Boxing Register: International Boxing Hall of Fame Official Record Book* (4th ed.). Ithaca, NY: McBooks Press, Inc., 2006, pp. 334–337.
Whorton, Cal. "Carter Does His Talking With Fists." *Los Angeles Times*, 11/11/1951, p. B14.

CARTER, RUBIN (1937–). The story of Rubin "Hurricane" Carter transcends the sport of boxing. A former number 1 middleweight contender, Carter was convicted of murder in Patterson, New Jersey, and spent 20 years in jail before his ultimate release.

Born in 1937 in Clifton, New Jersey, Carter ran into trouble with the law as a juvenile. He then entered the Army, where he learned to box. He later was court-martialed and was convicted of assault; he served several years in prison. Upon his release, he turned pro in 1961.

He often showcased tremendous punching power, particularly in his left hook. He attracted attention in 1962 by stopping Florentino Fernandez, a boxer with a 31-5 record, in the first round. In 1963, he defeated the clever **George Benton** by split decision. Later that year, in his finest ring performance, he annihilated the great **Emile Griffith** in the first round.

That earned him a title shot at middleweight champion **Joey Giardello** in 1964. In a hard-fought bout, Giardello earned a 15-round decision. The next year he lost a decision to **Dick Tiger.** He still had his moments, as a first-round knockout of prospect Fate Davis showed. However, his career was in decline in 1966.

Then, his life went into decline when he and John Artis were charged and convicted of murdering three people in a bar in Patterson, New Jersey. The chief eyewitness was an admitted thief. Carter received a life sentence. Many felt he was unjustly convicted. Bob Dylan wrote and sang a hit song "Hurricane" about the unfairness of the conviction.

The New Jersey appellate courts later ordered a new trial, but Carter was convicted again at the second trial. However, his attorney successfully filed a motion for habeas corpus in federal court, collaterally attacking the racial prejudice and injustices during the state court proceedings. A federal district court judge granted Carter the petition in 1985, forcing prosecutors to retry Carter decades later or release him. Prosecutors unsuccessfully appealed and then declined to reprosecute Carter.

A hit movie *The Hurricane* starring Oscar-winning actor Denzel Washington as Carter was released in 1999.

Professional Record:　　　　　27-12-1
Championship(s):　　　　　None

Further Reading

Carter, Rubin. *The Sixteenth Round: From Number 1 Contender to #45472.* New York: Penguin Global, 1991.

Chaiton, Sam, and Terry Swinton. *Lazarus and the Hurricane: The Freeing of Rubin "Hurricane" Carter.* New York: St Martin's, 2000.

Hirsh, James S. *Hurricane: The Miraculous Journey of Rubin Carter.* Boston: Houghton Mifflin, 2000.

CASAMAYOR, JOEL (1971–). Joel Casamayor is a talented lightweight from Cuba who defected to the United States in part to fulfill his dream of becoming a world champion in professional boxing. A gifted southpaw boxer, Casamayor possesses superior boxing skills and a pugnacious attitude.

Born in 1971 in Guantanamo, Cuba, Casamayor had a decorated amateur career. He won the gold medal in the bantamweight division at the 1992 Barcelona Olympics, defeating Wayne McCullough in the gold medal match. He qualified for the 1996 Olympic Summer Games but defected to the United States.

He turned pro in 1996 and quickly established himself as a force. In 2000, he stopped undefeated champion Jong Kwon Baek to win the **World Boxing Association (WBA)** super featherweight championship. He made four successful title defenses before a unification bout with World Boxing Organization (WBO) champion Acelino Freitas. Casamayor lost a controversial, narrow decision.

The bearded Joel Casamayor takes one on the beard from Juan Manuel Marquez in their September 2008 bout. Marquez stopped Casamayor in the 11th round. Courtesy of Chris Cozzone.

In 2003 and 2004, he waged two memorable battles with the late **Diego Corrales.** Rocked in the fight, Casamayor won the first bout via sixth-round stoppage and lost a split decision in the rematch. In 2006, the two rivals fought a rubber match for the vacant **World Boxing Council (WBC)** lightweight championship. In another great battle, Casamayor prevailed by split decision.

As of this writing, he remains a force in the lightweight division. His nickname is "El Cipello" or "the Hairbrush," referring to his powerful right uppercut, which brushes his opponents' faces and causes damage. In 2008, he suffered his first loss by stoppage to **Juan Manuel Marquez** in the 10th round of their September bout.

Professional Record:	36-4-1
Championship(s):	WBA super featherweight, 2000–2002; WBC lightweight, 2006–2007

Further Reading

Bodenrader, Ted. "Campaigning for Closure: Corrales and Casamayor Have To Do It One More Time." *World Boxing* (September 2004), pp. 50–55.

Donovan, Jake. "One Win and Lightweight is Joel's Casa Again." *Boxing Scene*, 3/17/2008, at http://www.boxingscene.com/?m=show&opt=printable&id=13126

Sterngold, James. "Two Cuban Olympic Boxers Flee to the U.S." *The New York Times*, 7/1/1996, p. C1.

CASTILLO, CHUCHO (1944–). Chucho Castillo was a popular former world bantamweight champion from Mexico known for his action-packed performances and his confident attitude personified by his statemen that he was his own idol. Born in 1944 in Leon, Mexico, as Jesus Castillo Aguillera, Chucho turned pro in 1962 with a decision loss to Carlos Navarette. However, he kept learning and improving as a fighter. In 1967, he defeated Jose Medel to win the Mexican bantamweight title.

In December 1968, he faced bantamweight champion **Lionel Rose** and lost a controversial split decision. The decision caused rioting in and outside the arena, including fires and overturned cars. The actions caused Jim Deskin, former chairman of the Nevada State Athletic Commission to declare: "I think that the time has come to bar Mexican national fighters from the rings of California and Nevada." Fortunately, this was not done.

Castillo received a second world title shot—this time against **Ruben Olivares**—in 1970. He dropped Olivares in the second round but lost a unanimous decision. In a rematch later that year, he stopped Olivares on cuts in the 14th round to win the world title. He lost the title in the rubber match to Olivares, losing a unanimous decision. However, Castillo had his moments, flooring Olivares in the sixth round.

He continued to fight into 1975, retiring after two consecutive losses.

Professional Record:	46-18-2
Championship(s):	Bantamweight, 1970–1971

Further Reading

Chapin, Dwight. "Confident, Cocky Castillo Set for Forum Scrap with Pimentel." *Los Angeles Times*, 6/9/1968, p. H15.

Chapin, Dwight. "Chucho's Idol? It's Chucho, of Course!" *Los Angeles Times*, 8/26/1968, p. E4.

Hafner, Dan. "Castillo Captures Bantamweight Title." *Los Angeles Times*, 10/17/1970, p. E1.

Newhan, Ross. "Whiskey Bottle Barely Missed Rose in Riot." *Los Angeles Times*, 12/7/1968, p. C5.

CASTILLO, JOSE LUIS (1973–). Jose "El Terrible" Castillo is a former two-time world lightweight champion known for his aggressive style and action-packed fights. He engaged in

Jose Luis Castillo lands a left hook against rival Diego Corrales in their October 2005 bout. Castillo won in the fourth round to avenge an earlier defeat. Courtesy of Chris Cozzone.

Jose Luis Castillo celebrates his victory over Diego Corrales in October 2005. Courtesy of Chris Cozzone.

memorable wars with **Diego Corrales,** upset Stevie Johnston, and gave **Floyd Mayweather, Jr.** perhaps his toughest test in the ring.

Born in 1973 in Empalme, Mexico, Castillo turned pro in 1990. He won his early fights until Cesar Soto stopped him in the second round in 1993 for the Mexican featherweight title. Three fights later, Javier Jauregui stopped him in the 10th round. He won four more fights before losing to Jauregui again.

In 2000, he entered the ring as an underdog against **World Boxing Council (WBC)** champion Stevie Johnston. Castillo pressed the action and won a majority decision—a fight that *The Ring* magazine later called the "Upset of the Year." Castillo pulled out a draw in the rematch with Johnston and made two more defenses before losing a controversial decision to Floyd Mayweather, Jr. in 2002. Many ringside observers thought Castillo did enough to keep his title.

He lost a rematch with Mayweather—again by close unanimous decision. In 2004, he defeated Juan Lazcano for the vacant WBC lightweight title. He then edged the tough **Joel Casamayor** and defeated Julio Diaz before losing his title in an incredible war in May 2005 with Diego Corrales. Castillo had Corrales nearly kayoed several times during the bout but ended up losing in the 10th round. He won a rematch with Corrales, though Castillo caused controversy by not making the weight limit. In 2007, he lost badly to **Ricky Hatton.** He lost his next bout in 2008 but hopes to regain his past form in 2009 and beyond.

Professional Record: 57-9-1
Championship(s):   WBC lightweight, 2000–2002, 2004–2005

Further Reading
Doogan, Brian. "Trumping the Memories of Past Lightweight Wars Corrales-Castillo Create An Epic for the Ages." *The Ring* (October 2005), pp. 48–53.
Gutierrez, Paul. "It's a Familiar Ring to Castillo: Lightweight champion is considered underdog to Mayweather but he's used to that role." *Los Angeles Times,* 4/19/2002, p. SP 7.
Springer, Steve. "Variety of issues still weighing on Castillo." *Los Angeles Times,* 6/22/2007, p. D1.

CERDAN, MARCEL (1916–1949). France's Marcel Cerdan posted one of the most impressive records in boxing history with 107 wins and only 4 losses. He boxed even while he served in the French armed forces during World War II. He fought in Europe for most of his professional career, which began in 1934. In December 1946, he traveled to New York and defeated Georgie Abrams.

He eventually landed a title shot against the tough **Tony Zale** for the middleweight crown. Cerdan dominated the fight, winning in the 12th round. He lost his belt in 1948 to **Jake LaMotta** after dislocating his shoulder in the first round. He fought on until the 10th round before retiring. Tragically, Cerdan never got a chance to avenge the defeat, as his plane crashed on its way to the United States for the rematch against LaMotta.

Professional Record: 107-4
Championship(s):   Middleweight, 1948–1949

Further Reading
Bartlett, Charles. "Marcel Cerdan Defeats Ruadik in Stadium Battle." *The Chicago Daily Tribune,* 11/1/1947, p. 19.
Burns, Edward. "Cerdan Stops Zale in 12th; Takes Title." *Chicago Daily Tribune,* 9/22/1948, p. B1.
Dawson, James P. "World Title Bout Sought by Cerdan." *The New York Times,* 12/8/1946, p. 127.
Loiseau, Jean Claude. *Marcel Cerdan.* Paris: Flammarion, 1989.

Nichols, Joseph C. "Three Rights to Chin Decide Main Bout." *The New York Times*, 3/29/1947, p. 10.
"Williams Is Beaten By Cerdan in Paris." *The New York Times*, 7/8/1946, p. 30.

CERVANTES, ANTONIO (1945–). Antonio "Kid Pambele" Cervantes was a dominant junior welterweight champion who made 16 successful title defenses in two separate reigns. Born in Columbia in 1945, Cervantes turned pro in 1964 after only three amateur bouts. He attracted attention from boxing experts after kayoing previously unbeaten kayo artist Rodolfo Gonzalez, a ranked lightweight contender who had stopped his previous 22 opponents.

In 1971, Cervantes received his first shot at a world title, dropping a 15-round decision to "the Untouchable" **Nicolino Locche.** Cervantes received a second chance in 1972 against then-champion Alfonzo Frazer. This time Cervantes did not allow the fight to go the judges, scoring a 10th-round knockout. He enjoyed a long reign, defending his title 10 times—including a rematch win over Locche—before dropping a split decision to 17-year-old prodigy **Wilfred Benitez** in 1976.

He regained the title with a sixth-round stoppage of Carlos Gimenez. During his second reign, Cervantes made six successful title defenses before running into a buzzsaw named **Aaron Pryor** who stopped him in the fourth round. Cervantes retired in 1983 after dropping a decision to Danny Sanchez. His sterling career earned him enshrinement in the International Boxing Hall of Fame in 1998.

Record:	90-12-3
Championship(s):	WBA Junior Welterweight, 1972–1976; 1977–1980

Further Reading

Associated Press. "Cervantes Stops Locche in Tenth." *The New York Times*, 3/18/1973, p. 222.
Cady, Steve. "Cervantes Retains His Crown with Decision Over Montilla." *The New York Times*, 1/19/1979, p. A17.
Hafner, Dan. "Cervantes Ends Gonzalez's Streak." *Los Angeles Times*, 12/18/1979, p. I11.
Roberts, James B., and Alexander G. Skutt. *The Boxing Register: International Boxing Hall of Fame Register* (4th ed.). Ithaca, NY: McBooks Press, Inc., 2006, pp. 342–345.

CHACON, BOBBY (1951–). Bobby Chacon was a colorful character inside and outside of the ring who captured world titles in the featherweight and super featherweight divisions. Born in 1951 in Pacoima, California, Chacon was on probation twice before he turned 18. A promising football player in high school, he never played because of disciplinary problems. Instead, Chacon earned a reputation as a capable street fighter even though he stood only 5'3" during his youth.

He credited his positive change of life course to his young wife, Valerie, and the sport of boxing. "I was probably headed for a life of crime when she pulled me out of the gutter and got me concentrating on being a world champion," he told *The Los Angeles Times*.

He turned pro in 1972 and won his first 19 fights before losing to **Ruben Olivares** in 1973—a fighter who would defeat Chacon three times in his career. Chacon won the vacant **World Boxing Council (WBC)** featherweight title in 1974 by kayoing Alfredo Marcano in the ninth round. He lost his title in his second defense to Ruben Olivares in the second round. In November 1979, he faced the legendary **Alexis Arguello** and was stopped in the seventh round.

In December 1982, he lost to **Cornelius Boza-Edwards** in an incredible slugfest. Many believed that Chacon's title days were behind him, as his personal life and later his wife, Valerie's, suicide had exacted a terrible toll. However, in December 1982, he defeated rival Rafael "Bazooka" Limon in a decision in a highly anticipated rematch to capture the WBC junior lightweight title.

He defended the title in another war against Boza-Edwards. Chacon then moved up to lightweight to face champion **Ray "Boom Boom" Mancini** who stopped him in the third round. Chacon fought until 1988, winning all his remaining bouts but never receiving another title shot.

Professional Record: 59-7-1
Championship(s):   WBC Featherweight, 1978–1979; WBC Junior
                              Lightweight, 1982–1983

Further Reading
Florence, Mal. "Former Street Fighter: Chacon Takes Fights to Ring After Wife's Gentle Push." *Los Angeles Times*, 6/24/1973, p. F1.
Goodman, Mike. "Chacon the Fighter Wants to Be Teacher." *Los Angeles Times*, 11/15/1972, p. SF5.
Hafner, Dan. "Boxing Career Gives Bobby Chacon New Life." *Los Angeles Times*, 6/19/1972, p. E4.
Hafner, Dan. "Olivares Scores KO Over Chacon in 9th." *Los Angeles Times*, 6/24/1973, p. B1.
Hafner, Dan. "Chacon Stops Lopez in 9th Before 16,080." *Los Angeles Times*, 5/25/1974, p. C1.
Hawn, Jack. "Chacon Kos Marcano, Wins Crown." *Los Angeles Times*, 9/8/1974, p. C1.
Hawn, Jack. "Chacon's Other Life: Featherweight Champ Recalls Pre-Boxing Years." *Los Angeles Times*, 6/19/1975, p. A1.

CHAGAEV, RUSLAN (1978–). Ruslan Chagaev is the **World Boxing Association (WBA)** world heavyweight champion, upsetting 7-0' behemoth **Nikolay Valuev** to capture the title in April 2007 by a 12-round majority decision. Nicknamed "White Tyson," Chagaev possesses good power and speed.

Born in 1978 in Andijan, Uzbekistan, of the Soviet Union, Chagaev had a distinguished amateur career. He represented his native Uzbekistan in the 1996 Atlanta Olympics but lost a decision in the first round to Luan Krasniqi of Germany.

He defeated the legendary Cuban boxer **Felix Savon** at the 1997 World Amateur Boxing Championships—though he had to forfeit the title after it was discovered that he had two professional bouts.

Chagaev had fought two pro bouts in 1997 in Illinois. He then resumed his amateur career. He turned pro for good in 2001. In November 2006, he defeated former champion **John Ruiz** by split decision to earn a title shot at the giant Valuev. He then defeated Valuev by majority decision. In 2008, he successfully defended his title against Matt Skelton. Chagaev then prepared to defend his title against Valuev in a rematch but was injured in training. The WBA then stripped him of the main title and named him champion in recess.

Professional Record: 24-0-1
Championship(s):   WBA Heavyweight, 2007—2008

Further Reading
Kammerer, Roy. "Chagaev spoils Valuev's bid for Marciano's record, unification fight." *The Associated Press*, 4/15/2007.
Lewis, Ron. "Chagaev defies logic to end unbeaten run of Valuev." *The Times*, 4/16/2007, p. 57.

CHANDLER, JEFF (1956–). "Joltin" Jeff Chandler was one of the great bantamweight fighters in boxing history. Born in 1956 in Philadelphia, Chandler did not formally train in boxing until age 19. His fighting was confined to the streets in gangs. He had only two amateur fights before turning pro in 1976. In his very first fight, he drew with Mike Dowling over four rounds. He wouldn't lose again for the next seven years.

The Philadelphia native captured the title in 1980 with a stoppage of Julian Solis. He successfully defended his title nine times in 1981–1983 before dropping a 15-round decision to **Richard Sandoval** in 1984. An eye injury prompted Chandler's retirement, and unlike many former champions, he stayed retired. He was inducted into the International Boxing Hall of Fame in 2000.

Professional Record: 33-2-2
World Title(s):   WBA Bantamweight 1980–1984

Further Reading

Katz, Michael. "Small Boxer Reaches Big Time." *The New York Times*, 1/31/1981, p. 19.
Katz, Michael. "Chandler Retains His Title." *The New York Times*, 7/26/1981, p. S10.
Katz, Michael. "Chander Keeps Title, Stops Murata in 13th." *The New York Times*, 12/11/1981, p. B5.
Roberts, James B., and Alexander G. Skutt. *The Boxing Register: International Boxing Hall of Fame Official Record Book* (4th ed.). Ithaca, NY: McBooks Press, Inc., 2006, pp. 330–333.
Sharav, Ben. "Chandler 'Reassessed' After KO By Sandoval." *The Ring* (July 1984), pp. 46–48.

CHARLES, EZZARD (1921–1975). Called the "Cincinnati Cobra" for his piston-like jab and quick right cross, Ezzard Charles is best known as a former world heavyweight champion who gave **Rocky Marciano** two tough fights. But, in reality, Charles was past his prime when he fought "the Rock." His best years took place years earlier in the light heavyweight division where he dominated opponents but never received a world title shot.

Born in 1921 in Lawrenceville, Georgia, Charles moved to Cincinnati to live with his grandparents after his parents divorced. In his teens, he took to boxing and became a quick study. He won all 42 of his amateur bouts, culminating in a U.S. national championship in the middleweight division. He turned professional at age 19 and won his first 21 fights at middleweight. In 1942, he earned two decision victories over the tough **Charley Burley,** considered by many the uncrowned champion. Later that year, he won two straight decisions over **Joey Maxim.** In 1943, he lost to **Jimmy Bivins** and Lloyd Marshall.

Charles served in the military in World War II, which caused him to be inactive in the ring for 1944 and 1945. However, he returned the next year and showed his dominance at light heavyweight. He stopped Marshall in a rematch and defeated Bivins twice and the great **Archie Moore** three times. In 1948, he stopped Lee Baroudi in the 10th round. Baroudi fell into a coma and later died. Charles never recovered from the incident, fighting more cautiously the rest of his career.

After **Joe Louis** retired, Charles fought **Jersey Joe Walcott** for the vacant National Boxing Association heavyweight title in 1949. Charles won a 15-round unanimous decision. For his efforts that year he earned honors as *The Ring* magazine's "Fighter of the Year." He defended the NBA belt three times before facing a comebacking Louis in 1950. Charles won easily over 15 rounds, earning universal recognition as heavyweight champion. He defended his title four more times, including another decision win over Walcott. However, he faced Walcott for a third time in July 1951 and suffered a seventh-round knockout. He never regained the title though he tried three times— once against Walcott and twice against Marciano. In June 1952, most ringside observers thought Charles did enough to reclaim the crown against Walcott, but the three judges felt differently.

In 1954, past his prime, Charles fought Marciano valiantly twice. The first time he lost in a close unanimous decision, and the second time Marciano stopped him the eighth round. Because of money problems, he continued to fight until 1959. He died in Chicago in 1975.

Record: 97-25-1
Championship(s):   Heavyweight, 1949–1951

Further Reading

Cromie, Robert. "Ezzard Charles Knocks Out Baroudi." *Chicago Tribune*, 2/21/1948, p. A1.
Evans, Gavin. *Kings of the Ring: The History of Heavyweight Boxing*. London: Weidenfeld & Nicolson, 2005, pp. 114–117.

Hand, Jack. "Charles Whips Walcott to Win NBA Ring Title." *Los Angeles Times*, 6/23/1949, p. C1.
Parker, Roy B. "Proud Mom Tells About Her Boy, Ezzard Charles." *The Chicago Defender*, 10/21/1950, p. 17.
Sheehan, Joseph M. "'I Thought I Won,' Ezzard Declares." *The New York Times*, 6/18/1954, p. 27.
Young, Doc. "Ezzard Has the Stuff to Win—Doc." *The Chicago Defender*, 6/25/1949, p. 1.

CHAVEZ, JESUS (1972–). Jesus "El Matador" Chavez is a former super featherweight and lightweight champion known for his unique life story. Born in Mexico, Chavez crossed the Rio Grande River with his family to join his father in Chicago. He showed great promise as an amateur, compiling a record of 95-5.

However, he was arrested and convicted of armed robbery. He served more than four years in prison. When he was released, he was deported to Mexico. He entered the United States illegally and turned professional. He captured the **World Boxing Council (WBC)** super featherweight title in 2003 with a 12-round decision win over Sirimongkol Singwancha. He lost his title in his first defense in an exciting fight against **Erik Morales.** In 2005, he stopped **Leavander Johnson** to win the **International Boxing Federation (IBF)** lightweight title though his victory was bittersweet as Johnson fell into a coma and died days after the bout. Chavez lost his title in his first defense against Julio Diaz.

Professional Record:	44-4
Championship(s):	WBC super featherweight, 2003–2004; IBF lightweight, 2005–2007

Further Reading
Hirsley, Michael. "Toughest fight is outside the ring." *Chicago Tribune*, 9/18/2003, p. C1.
Katz, Michael. "Beaten Chavez Leaves with Head Up." *The New York Times*, 3/1/2004, p. D2.
Pitluck, Adam. *Standing Eight: The Inspiring Story of Jesus 'El Matador' Chavez Who Became Lightweight Champion of the World.* Cambridge, Mass.: Da Capo Books, 2006.

Jesus Chavez lives up to his nickname of "El Matador" by bulling his way through opponent Andres Ledesma. Courtesy of Chris Cozzone.

CHAVEZ, JULIO CESAR (1962–). Julio Cesar Chavez is one of the greatest fighters of his generation, a pound-for-pound great that became a national hero in his native Mexico. *The Ring* writer William Dettloff expressed it well when he wrote: "There's never been a Mexican fighter more worshipped than Chavez" (p. 80). Born in 1962 in Ciudad Obregon, Mexico, he turned professional in 1980. Chavez was known for his efficiency, chin, combination punching, and tremendous body-punching.

He won the vacant **World Boxing Association (WBA)** super featherweight title in 1984 with a victory over Mario Martinez. He successfully defended his title eight times before mov-

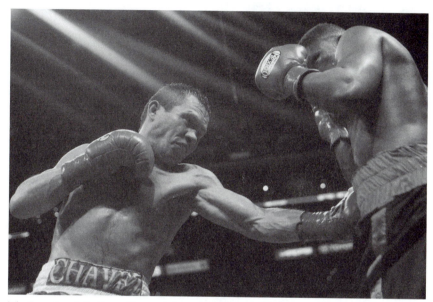

The legendary Julio Cesar Chavez delivers a punishing left hook to the body of Ivan Robinsion in their May 2005 bout. Chavez won by a unanimous decision. Courtesy of Chris Cozzone.

Julio Cesar Chavez celebrates his victory over Ivan Robinson in March 2005. Courtesy of Chris Cozzone.

Julio Cesar Chavez takes in the boxing event in Albuquerque, New Mexico, in December 2007. Chavez's son, Julio Cesar Chavez Jr., headlines the card. Courtesy of Chris Cozzone.

ing up to the lightweight division. He defeated **Edwin Rosario** in 1987 to capture the WBA lightweight belt, adding the **World Boxing Council (WBC)** belt with a win over Jose Luis Ramirez. In 1989, he won the WBC junior welterweight title by defeating **Roger Mayweather.** He added the **International Boxing Federation (IBF)** belt in 1990 with perhaps his signature win—a last-second stoppage of previously unbeaten **Meldrick Taylor.** Referee **Richard Steele** controversially stopped the bout with less than 10 seconds remaining with Taylor ahead on two of the three official cards.

In 1993, he challenged **Pernell Whitaker** for the welterweight championship. Chavez was fortunate to obtain a draw against the masterful Whitaker whose defensive skills and movement were too much for any fighter at that time. Chavez continued to reign as the king of the 140-pounders until he lost to **Oscar De La Hoya** in 1996. He lost in later title attempts to De La Hoya in 1998 and to **Kostya Tszyu** in 2000. His last fight was in 2005.

Record:	107-6-2
Championship(s):	WBC super featherweight, 1984–1987; WBA lightweight, 1987–1989; WBC lightweight, 1988–1989; WBC junior welterweight, 1989–1996; IBF junior welterweight, 1990–1991.

Further Reading

Berger, Phil. "Chavez Wins in Final Round." *The New York Times*, 3/18/1990, p. S4.

Dettloff, William. "Hail, Cesar!: Remembering the Brilliance of J.C. Superstar." *The Ring* (March 2001), pp. 76–81.

Gustkey, Earl. "Chavez Overcomes Sprained Ankle to Retain Title by Sixth Round KO." *Los Angeles Times*, 4/20/1985, p. SD_B4.

Katz, Michael. "Chavez: Too Much Talent to Hide." *The New York Times*, 7/7/1985, p. S9.

Ryan, Jeff. "Julio Cesar Chavez: The World's Best Fighter Is the Year's Best Too." *The Ring* (April 2001), pp. 34–38.

Welsh, Jack. "Julio Cesar Chavez . . . The Kid From Culiacan." *The Ring* (August 1998), pp. 30–39.

CHIONOI, CHARTCHAI (1942–). Chartchai Chionoi was a former three-time world flyweight champion and the second fighter from Thailand to capture a world championship. Born in 1942 in Bangkok, Chionoi learned boxing at age 16 and turned professional in 1959. He captured his first title in December 1966 when he stopped Walter McGowan in the ninth round. He held the title until losing to **Efren Torres** in 1969. He regained the title from Torres in 1970 and then lost it to Erbito Salaverria. He captured the title for a third time—this time the **World Boxing Association (WBA)** version—when he defeated Fritz Chervet in 1973. He held the title until losing to Susuma Hanagata in 1974.

| Professional Record: | 61-18-3 |
| Championship(s): | Flyweight, 1966–1969, 1970, WBA Flyweight, 1973 |

Further Reading

Associated Press. "Ex-Flyweight Champ Chartchai Quits." *The Washington Post*, 5/25/1971, p. D4.

Mallon, Scott. "Chartchai Chionoi: Still Going Strong." *SweetScience.com*, 8/22/2006, at http://www.thesweetscience.com/boxing-article/4249/chartchai-chionoi-still-going-strong-part/

Mallon, Scott. "Chartchai Chionoi: Family Man and Fighter." *SweetScience.com*, 8/23/2006, at http://www.thesweetscience.com/boxing-article/4253/chartchai-chionoi-family-man-fighter-part/

CHOCOLATE, KID (1910–1988). One of the greatest fighters in boxing history was a Cuban-born fighter named Eligio Sardinias Montalbo. But he made his lasting name as Kid Chocolate in New York City, where he dazzled fight fans with his incredible speed and skill. His exquisite ring skills earned him the nickname "the Cuban Bon Bon."

Born in 1910 in Cerro, Cuba, Kid Chocolate began fighting as a youth in Cuba. He went undefeated as an amateur before turning pro in Havana in 1928. He soon moved to New York City where he won his first 21 fights by knockout. In 1930, he lost to Battling Battalino for the world featherweight title. He also dropped a close decision to **Jackie "Kid" Berg** that year.

In 1931, he defeated Benny Bass to win the world junior lightweight title. He won the featherweight title by defeating Lew Feldman in 1932. He attempted to win the world lightweight title as well but lost to the tough **Tony Canzoneri.**

He retired in 1938.

| Professional Record: | 131-9-6 |
| Championship(s): | Junior lightweight, 1931–1933; featherweight, 1932–1934 |

Further Reading

Cox, Monte. "Kid Chocolate, The Cuban Bon Bon . . . 'A living, breathing boxing instruction book." *Cyber Boxing Zone Journal*, at http://coxscorner.tripod.com/chocolate.html

McArdle, Tom. "Kid Chocolate is Next Featherweight Champ." *The Chicago Defender*, 1/11/1930, p. 11.

Neil, Edward, Jr. "Kid Chocolate Winner Over Labarba." *The Washington Post*, 5/23/1929, p. 13.

Smith, Wilfrid. "Kid Chocolate Demonstrates His Title Style." *The Chicago Daily Tribune*, 8/2/1932, p. 17.

CHOI, HONG MAN (1980–). Hong Man Choi is a 7'2" Korean kickboxer who competes in kickboxing and mixed martial arts (MMA). Nicknamed the "Techno Giant," Choi has competed against the very best in K-1 and MMA. For example, he defeated K-1 superstar **Semmy Schilt** and has fought pound-for-pound the reigning MMA great **Fedor Emelianenko.**

Born in 1980, Choi suffers from agromegaly, a form of growth disorder. He has not let that stop him from competing in combat sports. He began competing in K-1 events in 2005 and has done quite well. He holds a decision win over Schilt and has defeated Akebono, **Bob Sapp, Gary Goodridge**, and Mighty Mo in his career.

Choi has been less successful in mixed martial arts. He defeated Bobby Ologun in 2006 but lost to Emelianenko via an armbar submission in December 2007 and to Mirko Cro Cop in 2008. He remains a threat to any fighter, however, due to his immense size.

Kickboxing Record:	12-5
MMA Record:	1-2
Championship(s):	None

Further Reading
Gwang-lip, Moon. "Fighter Choi Beats K-1 Champ Schilt." *Korea Times*, 6/5/2006.
Seung-Woo, Kang. "'Techno Goliath Vows Revenge Against Hard Puncher." *Korea Times*, 9/15/2007.

CHONAN, RYO "THE PIRANHA" (1976–). Ryo "the Piranha" Chonan is a gifted mixed martial artist from Japan known for his jiu-jitsu and submission skills. He is best known for his upset of **Anderson Silva** with a heel hook submission in 2004. Born in 1976 in Yamagata, Japan, Chonan made his professional mixed martial arts (MMA) debut in 2001 in Pancrease. He has fought all over the world in various promotions, including Shooto, **PRIDE,** and the **Ultimate Fighting Championships (UFC).**

He holds wins over Carlos Newton, **Hayato Sakurai,** Roan Carneiro (twice), and Daijuri Matsui. Chonan at times has been inconsistent in his MMA career, sometimes giving a spectacular performance and then other times an uninspiring effort. In his finest hour, Chonan squared off against Anderson Silva in a **PRIDE** bout in December 2004. Chonan held his own with Silva, but in the third and final round Silva began to impose his will in the stand-up. Chonan then executed his flying scissor heel hook, launching himself into the air and grabbed Silva's foot for the submission victory. It was one of the greatest individual moves in MMA history.

In 2007, Chonan fought for the first time in the UFC, losing a decision to **Karo Parisyan.** He then defeated Carneiro for the second time. In his last bout, he lost a decision to Brad Blackburn in December 2008.

Professional MMA Record:	16-8
Championship(s):	None

Further Reading
Official Web site: http://ryo-chonan.com/main.html
Zeidler, Ben. "10 Sickest Submissions of All Time." *FIGHT!*, October 2008, p. 94–97.

CHOYNSKI, JOE (1968–1943). Joseph Bartlett Choynski was one of the greatest fighters in boxing history who never won a world title. The son of a Yale graduate newspaper publisher, Choynski dropped out of high school and pursued a boxing career. A Jewish man, Choynski was unusual for a white fighter of that era in that he would face any boxer no matter what race. He turned pro in 1888 and a year later fought fellow San Fransiscan and future heavyweight champion **James "Gentleman Jim" Corbett** three times—drawing once and losing twice.

During his career, which lasted until 1904, he also faced several other heavyweight champions— **John L. Sullivan** (in an exhibition), **James J. Jeffries, Bob Fitzsimmons,** and **Jack Johnson.** He is best known for kayoing Johnson in the third round in Galveston, Texas, in 1901. Choynski later taught Johnson boxing skills while the two were jailed for participating in a mixed-race bout. He also served as a consultant for the movie *Gentleman Jim* about his former rival Corbett.

Professional Record:	50-14-6
Championship(s):	None

Further Reading
Callis, Tracy. "Joe Choynski—'Clever, Shifty, and Explosive,'" *Cyber Boxing Zone Journal*, May 2002, at
    http://www.cyberboxingzone.com/boxing/w0502-tc.htm
"Choynski Has Sport." *Chicago Daily*, 9/18/1894, p. 8.
"Joe Choynski Taken to Jail: Knocks Out Johnson in Galveston." *Los Angeles Times*, 2/26/1901, p. 5.
Roberts, James B., and Alexander B. Skutt. *The Boxing Register: International Boxing Hall of Fame Official Record Book* (4th ed.). Ithaca, NY: McBooks Press, Inc., 2006, pp. 86–87.

CHUVALO, GEORGE (1937–). George Chuvalo was a heavyweight contender from Canada who never touched the canvas in 93 professional bouts. He twice fought for the world heavyweight championship but lost to **Ernie Terrell** in 1965 and **Muhammad Ali** in 1966.

Born in 1937 in Toronto, Canada, Chuvalo became the amateur champion of Canada in 1955. He turned pro in 1956 and won his first six fights before dropping a split decision to Howard King. Two years later he kayoed King in the second round.

In 1965, he fought Terrell for the **World Boxing Association (WBA)** heavyweight championship. He lost a controversial decision. The next year he faced the real heavyweight champion—Muhammad Ali—at the peak of the champion's fistic powers. Chuvalo never took a backward step but could not cope with Ali's superior speed. He lost a unanimous decision.

He lost to **Joe Frazier** in 1967 and **George Foreman** in 1970. He defeated **Jerry Quarry, Cleveland Williams,** and Doug Jones in his career.

He initially retired in 1973 but returned in 1977 to win the Canadian heavyweight championship with a win over Earl McLeay. He made one defense and then retired for good in 1978.

Professional Record:	73-18-2
Championship(s):	None

Further Reading

Brunt, Stephen. *Facing Ali: 15 Fighters, 15 Stories.* Guilford, CT: Lyons Press, 2002, pp. 47–66.
McGowen, Deane. "Chuvalo Stops Jones at 1:28 of 11th in Garden Bout: Canadian Posts a Major Upset." *The New York Times,* 10/3/1964, p. 23.

CLARK, LAMAR (1934–2006). LaMar Clark was a former heavyweight prospect from Utah best known for winning 44 straight bouts by knockout. His early ring performances caused some to compare him to the great **Jack Dempsey,** the power-punching heavyweight champion of the 1920s. Unfortunately, Clark's record was more a product of his poor caliber of competition than actual ring greatness.

Born in 1934 in Cedar City, Utah, Clark compiled an amateur record of 25-2 before turning pro in 1958. He won his first fight via a 6-round decision and then proceeded to win 44 straight by knockout, breaking the record for consecutive knockouts held by light heavyweight "Blackjack" Billy Fox. In 1960, he suffered two straight defeats when he stepped up in competition. He first lost to Bartoli Soni of the Dominican Republic in the 9th round and then lost to former Olympic gold medalist Pete Rademacher in the 10th round. Clark retired in 1961 after losing to another former Olympic gold medalist—Cassius Marcellus Clay (**Muhammad Ali**)—in the sixth round. Clay's superior hand and foot speed were too much for the plodding Clark.

Professional Record:	45-3
Championship(s):	None

Further Reading

Associated Press. "Boxer Lamar Clark Ties Knockout Record, 43 in a Row." *The Washington Post,* 1/4/1960, p. A13.
Associated Press. "Cassius Clay KO's Clark in Second Round." *Chicago Daily Tribune,* 4/20/1961, p. F4.
Smilanich, Steve. "How Good Is Marathon Fighter Lamar Clark?" *The Chicago Defender,* 1/3/1959, p. 24.

CLEMENTI, RICH (1976–). Rich "No Love" Clementi is a hard-nosed mixed martial artist known for his superior submission skills and frequent fights. Born in 1976 in New Jersey, Clementi now lives in Louisiana. He wrestled in high school and became attracted to mixed martial arts (MMA). He spent eight years in the military.

He made his professional MMA debut in 1999, losing a decision. He made his **Ultimate Fighting Championships (UFC)** debut at UFC 41, losing to Yves Edwards. He has faced numerous top mixed martial artists, including **Din Thomas,** Roan Carnerio, and Pete Spratt.

Clementi won six fights in a row, including submission wins over **Melvin Guillard,** Anthony Johnson, and Kyle Gibbons, before losing to Gray Maynard in October 2008.

Professional MMA Record: 33-13-1
Championship(s):   None

Further Reading
Probst, Jason. "'No Love' Has Plenty of It for the Fight Game." *UFC.com*, 3/31/2007, at http://www.ufc.com/index.cfm?fa=news.detail&gid=5000
Tatar, Ben. "Interview with Mixed Martial Artist Rich 'No Love' Clementi." *CriticalBench.com*, at http://www.criticalbench.com/Rich-Clementi.htm

COBB, RANDALL "TEX" (1950–). Randall "Tex" Cobb was a heavyweight boxing contender best known for his witty sayings and iron chin. He initially began his combat career as a kickboxer, winning nine bouts before switching to professional boxing.

Cobb made his professional debut in 1977 and won his first 17 bouts, including a stoppage over feared puncher **Earnie Shavers.** He then dropped a disputed split decision to **Ken Norton** in 1980. Two years later, Cobb landed a title shot against undefeated champion **Larry Holmes.** Cobb took a beating but refused to go down, earning the respect of many for going the distance against the much more talented champion.

Cobb continued to fight until 1993, when he finally retired. During his career, he faced five former world heavyweight champions—**Michael Dokes, James "Buster" Douglas,** Holmes, Norton, and **Leon Spinks.**

Cobb was a popular movie actor as well, starring in films such as *Raising Arizona* and *The Golden Child.*

Professional Record: 43-7-1
Championship(s):   None

Further Reading
Jones, Robert F. "I'll Swing Leather, Darlin'." *Sports Illustrated*, 11/15/1982, p. 44.
Phillips, Angus. "Challenger Cobb's goal: to leave Philadelphia." *The Washington Post*, 11/24/1982, p. C5.
Slocum, Bill. "Tex Cobb still a knockout." *San Diego Union-Tribune*, 10/29/1987, p. D-1.

COETZEE, GERRIE (1955–). Gerrie Coetzee was a former world heavyweight champion from South Africa best known for his powerful right hand that earned him the nickname "the Bionic Hand." Born in 1955 in Boksburg, South Africa, Coetzee turned pro in 1974 and won his first 22 professional bouts. In 1979, he faced fellow unbeaten heavyweight "Big" John Tate in South Africa for the vacant **World Boxing Association (WBA)** heavyweight title. Tate won a unanimous decision. In 1980, he met Tate's conqueror **Mike Weaver** for another shot at the world title—again in South Africa. Coetzee built an early lead, but Weaver rallied and stopped him in the 13th round.

In 1983, Coetzee received his third chance against undefeated champion **Michael "Dynamite" Dokes.** This time Coetzee captured the crown by stopping Dokes in the 10th round. His reign was short, as he lost his title in his first defense against **Greg Page** in 1984. He initially retired after a first-round kayo loss to **Frank Bruno.** He retired for good in 1997 after a loss to **Iran Barkley.**

Professional Record: 33-6-1
Championship(s):   WBA heavyweight, 1983–1984

Further Reading
Newhan, Ross. "Coetzee Wins the Title in the 10th." *Los Angeles Times*, 9/24/1983, p. B1.

COLEMAN, MARK (1964–). Mark "the Hammer" Coleman is a mixed martial artist who used his strong wrestling background to dominate some early **Ultimate Fighting Championships (UFC)** events. He is best known for introducing the technique of "ground and pound" to mixed martial arts. This fighting technique consists of mounting an opponent and firing away power punches.

Born in Fremont, Ohio, in 1964, Coleman excelled at baseball, football, and wrestling while attending Fremont St. Joseph's High School. He earned a baseball scholarship at Miami of Ohio University. Later he transferred to Ohio State where he won the NCAA championship in wrestling in 1988. He won a gold medal at the 1991 Pan American Games. He represented the United States in the 1992 Barcelona Olympics, finishing in seventh place in freestyle wrestling. He continued to compete in wrestling with hopes of making the 1996 Olympic Team. However, he lost in the semifinals of the Olympic qualifying tournament.

However, he entered UFC 10 about a month after his disappointment in losing in the Olympic qualifier. Not only did he complete in UFC 10, but he won the tournament. He captured back-to-back UFC titles at UFC 10 and 11. At UFC 10, he defeated Moti Horenstein, **Gary "Big Daddy" Goodridge,** and **Don Frye** to win the tournament. At UFC 11, he defeated Julian Sanchez and Brian Johnston to repeat as UFC tournament champion.

In UFC 12, he defeated **Dan "the Beast" Severn** with a neck submission in the first round to win the inaugural UFC world heavyweight championship. He lost in a huge upset in his first defense at UFC 14 against kickboxer **Maurice Smith.**

He moved to **PRIDE** in 1999, fighting the best of the best. The highlight of his career in PRIDE came in the 16-man PRIDE 2000 Grand Prix finals where he won four straight matches to capture the championship and top prize of $200,000. He defeated Masaake Satake, **Igor Vovchanchyn,** Akira Shoji, and Kazuyuki Fuzaki to capture the prestigious championship. In later years, Coleman did not fare as well in PRIDE matchups against **Antonio Rodrigo Nogueira, Mirko "Cro Cop" Filopovic,** and the great **Fedor Emelianenko,** who defeated him twice with armbar submissions.

Coleman's protégé **Kevin Randleman** also became a UFC champion. In March 2008, Coleman announced that he would make a return to the Octagon in the UFC to face **Brock Lesnar.** He later had to pull out of the fight due to injury. The 44-year-old Coleman then returned to the Octagon in January 2009 to face **Mauricio "Shogun" Rua**, whom Coleman had upset in PRIDE in 2006. Coleman fought bravely but lost in the third round.

Professional MMA Record: 15-9
Championship(s):   UFC Heavyweight Champion, 1997–1998

Further Reading
Oller, Rob. "Fighting Man." *Columbus Dispatch*, 12/15/1996, p. 1E.
Wall, Jeremy. *UFC's Ultimate Warriors Top 10.* Ontario: ECW Press, 2005, pp. 129–142.
Wolfrum, Timothy. "Coleman fights his way back." *The News-Messenger*, 5/12/2000, p. 1B.

COLLINS, STEVE (1964–). "The Celtic Warrior," Steve Collins was a popular former middleweight and super middleweight champion from Ireland who compiled a career record of 32-3.

His only career losses were by decision to Mike McCallum, Reggie Johnson, and **Sumbu Ka-lambay.** Born in 1964 in Dublin, Ireland, Collins had a decorated amateur career, winning the Irish junior light-heavyweight championship in 1983.

He turned pro in 1986 by kayoing Julio Mercado in the third round. He won his first 16 bouts before challenging Mike McCallum for the **World Boxing Association (WBA)** middleweight title. Collins lost a unanimous decision. In 1992, he faced Reggie Johnson for the vacant WBA middleweight title and lost a close majority decision.

Collins won the World Boxing Organization (WBO) middleweight title in May 1994 over Chris Pyatt. He then moved up in weight and won the WBO super middleweight title from popular and longtime title holder **Chris Eubank.** He successfully defended his belt seven times. He holds two victories each over **Nigel Benn** and Eubank.

Professional Record:	34-3
Championship(s):	WBO middleweight, 1994; WBO super middleweight, 1995–1997

Further Reading
"Collins is forced to sound final bell." *The Herald* (Glasgow), 5/21/1999, p. 33.
Wiechula, Frank. "My Fire Had Gone." *The Mirror*, 10/3/1997, p. 38–39.

COLLINS, TOMMY (1929–1996). Tommy Collins was a former top featherweight and lightweight contender who was one of the most popular fighters in his heyday in the 1940s and 1950s. Born in 1929 in Boston, Collins made his pro debut in Boston in 1946 and won his first 12 bouts. In 1952, he fought the great featherweight champion **Sandy Saddler** in a nontitle bout. He dropped Saddler in the first round with a left hook but was stopped in the fifth round. It marked the first time in 143 bouts that Saddler had been knocked to the canvas. Later that year, as Saddler served in the Army, Collins stopped the great **Willie Pep** in the sixth round and then defeated Glen Flanagan for the interim featherweight title.

In April 1953, he moved up in weight to challenge lightweight champion **Jimmy Carter.** The champion floored Collins 10 times in the bout before his corner finally threw in the towel. The one-sided beating—dubbed "the Boston Massacre" by the press—caused many states to adopt a three-knockdown rule. Collins retired in 1954.

Professional Record:	60-12
Championship(s):	None

Further Reading
Eskenazi, Gerald. "Tommy Collins, 67, a Fighter Whose Beating Stirred Outcry." *The New York Times*, 6/6/1996, p. B16.

COMPUBOX. Combubox, Inc. is a New York–based company that counts punches thrown and landed for boxing bouts. Founded in the mid-1980s by Bob Canobbio and Logan Hobson, the company uses a computer program that counts punches thrown and punches landed. It further subdivides statistics based on power punches and jabs. HBO and ESPN are clients of Compubox. Originally a novelty, Compubox has become a regular staple for major boxing telecasts and has been accepted as part of the sport.

Further Reading
Canobbio, Bob, and Logan Hobson. "15 Years . . . And Counting." *KO* (February 2001), pp. 18–19.
Feour, Royce. "Local man out to become one-fight wonder." *Las Vegas Review-Journal*, 10/13/1996, p. 11C.

Katz, Michael. "Boxing Novelty: Computerizing Punches." *The New York Times*, 2/12/1985, p. B15.
Official Web site: http://www.compuboxonline.com/

CONN, BILLY (1917–1993). Billy Conn was a former light heavyweight champion who nearly toppled the great **Joe Louis** to win the heavyweight championship. Born in 1917 in Pittsburgh, Conn turned pro in 1934 and suffered a loss in his debut to Dick Woodward. He turned pro at age 16 and began as a lightweight before steadily moving up in weight. He captured the light heavyweight in 1939 with a win over Melio Bettina. He defended the title several times, including a convincing win over **Gus Lesnevich.**

In 1941, Conn relinquished the belt in order to challenge Louis in 1941. Conn used his superior speed to build an early lead heading into the 13th round. Conn made the mistake of trading with Louis in the 13ᵗʰ, and the champion felled him with a right-hand bomb. Conn won three more fights before serving in World War II. Louis defeated him easily in the 1946 rematch, and Conn retired after two wins in 1948.

Professional Record:	64-12-1
Championship(s):	Light Heavyweight, 1939–1941

Further Reading

Associated Press. "Conn Beats Lesnevich at Detroit To Keep Light-Heavyweight Title." *The New York Times*, 1/6/1940, p. 35.
Kennedy, Paul. *Billy Conn: Pittsburgh Kid.* Bloomington, IN: AuthorHouse, 2007.
O'Toole, Andrew. *Sweet William: The Life of Billy Conn.* Champaign: University of Illinois Press, 2007.

THE CONTENDER. *The Contender* is a popular reality show featuring numerous boxers living together and competing for a large sum of money. NBC broadcast Season 1 of the show, featuring celebrities Sylvester Stallone of *Rocky* fame and all-time boxing great **Sugar Ray Leonard.** Guest appearances included famed trainer **Angelo Dundee, George Foreman,** and Danny Green. It featured 16 boxers divided into the blue and yellow teams. At the end of each episode, two fighters would fight a five-round fight. The winning fighter would stay on the show, while the losing fighter was eliminated. In the finals, Sergio "the Latin Snake" Mora defeated Peter "the Pride of Providence" Manfredo for the $1 million first prize.

NBC dropped the show, but ESPN picked it up for a second season that was broadcast in 2006. The show again featured 16 boxers divided into two teams. Sugar Ray Leonard remained the main host of the show. The boxers included former world super featherweight champion Steve "Two Pounds" Forbes, Cornelius "K-9" Bundrage, Norberto Bravo, and tough journeyman Grady Brewer.

Forbes expectedly made it through to the finals with his superior boxing skills. His opponent in the finals was the surprising Brewer who entered with a mediocre record and toiled at a tire factory to support his family. Brewer defeated Forbes via a 10-round split decision in the finals to capture the $500,000 first prize.

ESPN ran a third season of *The Contender* in 2007. It again featured 16 fighters in the super middleweight (168) division, though six were eliminated during the first episode for a variety of reasons. The finals featured former super middleweight world title challenger Sakio Bika and Jaidon Covington. Both fighters hit the canvas in the first round with Bika prevailing in the seventh round in a fight-of-the-year candidate. The fourth season of *The Contender* premiered on a new television station, Versus, and features cruiserweights.

Further Reading
Carter, Bill. "Rival TV Boxing Shows Square Off in California Court." *The New York Times*, 8/18/2004,
    p. C3.
The Contender Web site: http://espncontender.secondthought.com/

CONTROVERSIAL DECISIONS (BOXING AND MIXED MARTIAL ARTS). Boxing has had its share of controversial decisions, where the judges see a fight differently than many of the boxing audience. Sometimes judges simply score fights differently based on a difference in preferences. For example, one judge may prefer the aggressive boxer who presses the action, while another judge may favor the more skillful fighter who exhibits great defense and ring generalship. One judge may favor the power-puncher who lands fewer—but harder—punches, while another judge may favor the fighter who lands more punches even if many of them are jabs.

Examples of controversial decisions include the 1976 bout between junior lightweight champion **Alfredo Escalera** and undefeated challenger **Tyrone Everett.** Most ringside observers believed that Everett lost at least 10 of the 15 rounds, but two of the three ringside judges somehow scored the bout for Everett. Unofficial HBO ringside scorer **Harold Lederman** lists it as the worst decision he has ever seen.

In 1992, middleweight champion **James "Lights Out" Toney** defended his title against unheralded challenger **Dave Tiberi** in a bout broadcast on ABC. Tiberi gave Toney all he could handle, and most thought he certainly did enough to win. However, Toney captured the decision, causing ABC commentator Alex Wallau to say that Tiberi won the bout but "a couple of incompetent people at ringside robbed him of that."

In 1999, **Lennox Lewis** seemingly outboxed **Evander Holyfield** in a battle for heavyweight supremacy. However, Judge Eugenia Williams scored the bout for Holyfield and another judge scored it even, which led to a very unpopular draw. That fight led to renewed calls for open scoring, oversight on the selection of judges and other reform proposals.

In the early part of the twentieth century, **Theodore "Tiger" Flowers** was the victim of two very unpopular decisions against Mike McTigue in 1924 and **Mickey Walker** in 1925. The bout with McTigue featured three judges who had never before judged a professional bout, and it showed. Flowers also outboxed Walker a year later but suffered a similar fate, causing the Illinois State Boxing Association to launch a full-scale investigation.

Controversial decisions also occur in mixed martial artists, as it may be even harder to score a fight in a sport with so many different fighting disciplines. Most mixed martial arts (MMA) organizations employ the **ten point must system** like professional boxing.

The different styles can lead to different verdicts, as one judge may prefer the flashy striker, while another judge may favor a fighter who continually tries for submissions.

Examples of debatable decisions in mixed martial arts include the **Kevin Randleman—Bas Rutten** fight in 2000 at **Ultimate Fighting Championships (UFC)** 20 for the heavyweight title and the **Quinton "Rampage" Jackson—Matt Lindland** fight in 2006 for the World Fighting Alliance. A more recent example was in a 2007 UFC bout between **Michael Bisping** and **Matt Hamill.** Many Octagon observers felt that Hamill won the bout, but Bisping received the decision. Still another example was the **Dan Henderson–Yuki Kondo** bout in **PRIDE** in December 2004. The judges scored a split-decision victory for Henderson, but the bout could have gone either way.

Further Reading
Crigger, Kelly. "Robbed!: Fighters Face a Tough Crossroads When an Easy Decision Becomes a Major
    Disappointment." *RealFighter*, No. 19 (2008), pp. 40–44.

Hudson, David L., Jr., and Mike Fitzgerald, Jr. "Controversial Decisions," in *Boxing's Most Wanted: The Top 10 Book of Champs, Chumps and Punch Drunk Palookas* (pp. 74–81). Alexandria, VA: Potomac Books, 2004.

Hudson, David L. Jr. "Judges Under Fire: What Can Be Done to Improve Scoring of Professional Bout." *Boxing Digest*, October 2002, pp. 62–63.

COONEY, GERRY (1956–). "Gentleman" Gerry Cooney was a former heavyweight contender best known for his 1982 loss to champion **Larry Holmes** and for his devastating left hook. Cooney compiled an undefeated record against limited opposition. He easily defeated three former top contenders well past their primes—Jimmy Young, **Ron Lyle,** and **Ken Norton.** He stopped Lyle and Norton with devastating first-round knockouts.

Born in 1956 in New York, Cooney compiled a solid amateur career that included multiple Golden Gloves titles. He turned professional in 1977 with a first-round kayo win. He won 25 straight bouts—many by knockout—before earning a title shot against Holmes.

Promoter **Don King** played on the racial aspect of the fight, emphasizing that Cooney was the "Great White Hope." While many found the racial polarizing distasteful, it probably helped lead to a great promotional success and a surprisingly (to some) competitive bout. Cooney fought a tough fight, displaying courage before succumbing via a 13th-round technical knockout. He had several points deducted for low blows, though he claimed part of the problem was Holmes' pawing on his head with his left hand.

Cooney originally retired after losing in 1987 to **Michael Spinks.** He returned to the ring against an aging, comebacking **George Foreman** but lost in the fifth round. Cooney has been very active in organizations designed to help retired boxers.

Professional Record:	28-3
World Titles:	none

Further Reading

Norman, Michael. "The Rise of Gerry Cooney." *The New York Times*, 8/9/1981, p. SM6.

Pearce, Jeremy. "Round Two: A Heavyweight Known for Resilience Wants to (Sort of) Step Back Into the Ring." *The New York Times*, 7/11/2004, p. NJ4.

Young, Dick. "Cooney a Reluctant New 'Great White Hope,'" *Chicago Tribune*, 5/28/1980, p. D2.

COOPER, HENRY (1934–). Henry Cooper was a former world heavyweight boxing contender from England known for his powerful left hook, ring courage, and propensity to bleed. Born in 1934 in South London, Cooper turned pro in 1954. Five years later in 1959, he defeated Brian London to win the British heavyweight championship. In 1963, Cooper squared off against an undefeated American heavyweight named Cassius Clay. Cooper dropped Clay with a powerful left hook, hurting the young contender. However, with extra time generated by the famous trainer **Angelo Dundee** who helped along a slight cut in Clay's glove, Clay recovered and stopped Cooper on cuts.

In 1966, Cassius Clay was now known as world heavyweight champion **Muhammad Ali,** and he gave Cooper a shot at his title. This time Ali was too much and stopped Cooper in the sixth round. Cooper kept fighting until 1971, retiring after losing a disputed decision to Joe Bugner.

In 1999, Cooper received his country's ultimate honor when Queen Elizabeth II knighted him at Buckingham Palace.

Professional Record:	40-14-1
Championship(s):	No

Further Reading
Brunt, Stephen. *Facing Ali: 15 Fighters—15 Stories*. Guilford, CT: Lyons Press, 2002, pp. 25–46.
Doogan, Brian. "Sir Henry Cooper: My Knighthood Is an Honor for the Whole Boxing Game in This County." *The Ring* (July 2001), pp. 74–79.
Edwards, Robert. *Henry Cooper: The Authorized Biography of Britain's Greatest Boxing Hero*. London: Chivers, Windsor, Paragon and Camden, 2003.

CORBETT, JAMES "GENTLEMAN JIM" (1866–1933). James J. Corbett was the second world heavyweight champion in modern boxing history. Born in San Francisco in 1866, Corbett became a bank clerk in his hometown but longed for the boxing ring. It proved to be a wise choice, as Corbett became a talented boxer. **Mike "the Professor" Donovan,** perhaps the most scientific of boxers, wrote of Corbett that "it takes an exceptionally good man to hit him anywhere."

Corbett was a well-school boxer who easily bested the brawling **John L. Sullivan** for the title in their 1892 world title match in New Orleans. He defended his title against Charlie Mitchell and the tough Tom Sharkey before losing to middleweight champion **Bob Fitzsimmons** in the 14th round. Corbett also lost in a return match with Sharkey. Corbett retired to the stage and running a restaurant. He returned to the ring once again to challenge his former sparring partner and current world champion **James J. Jeffries.** The larger Jeffries kayoed Corbett in the 23rd round.

Professional Record: 16-4-3
Championship(s): Heavyweight, 1892–1897

Further Reading
Corbett, James J. *The Roar of the Crowd: The True Tale of the Rise and Fall of a Champion*. New York: G.P. Putnam & Sons, 1925.
"Corbett Now is Champion." *The New York Times*, 9/8/1892, p. 3.
"Corbett the Conqueror." *The Washington Post*, 1/26/1894, p. 1.
Donovan, Mike. "Mike Donovan Discusses the Best Men in the Ring." *Los Angeles Times*, 2/8/1891, p. 10.
Fields, Armond. *James J. Corbett: A Biography of the Heavyweight Boxing Champion and Popular Theater Headliner*. Jefferson, N.C.: McFarland and Company, 2001.
Myler, Patrick. *Gentleman Jim Corbett: The Truth Behind a Boxing Legend*. London: Robson Books, 1998.

CORBETT III, YOUNG (1905–1993). Raffaele Capabianca Giordano was a former world welterweight champion known to the boxing world as Young Corbett III. Born in 1905 in Proteza, Italy, Giordano's family moved to Pittsburgh, Pennsylvania, and then California. He learned to box when he was 13 and turned professional the very next year at 14 in 1919. He was given his nickname by a ring announcer who refused to say his last name. The announcer dubbed him Young Corbett III because his ring style reminded him of William Rothwell who was nicknamed Young Corbett II.

Beginning in the late 1920s, Young Corbett began defeating several top-10 fighters, including Young Jack Thompson and Sammy Baker. For several years, he was considered the uncrowned welterweight champion. His punching power and southpaw stance scared away many an opponent. Finally, he received a title shot against Jackie Fields in 1933 for the welterweight title. He won a 10-round decision. He lost the title in his first defense to Jimmy McLarnin via first-round knockout. He continued to fight until 1940, splitting a pair of decisions with the young **Billy Conn** in 1937.

Record: 124-12-15
Championship(s): Welterweight, 1933

Further Reading
Edgren, Robert. "New Welter Boasts Punch and Perfect Style." *The Washington Post*, 3/12/1933, p. 16.

CORRALES, DIEGO (1977–2007). Diego "Chico" Corrales provided fight fans a lifetime of boxing excitement in his 29 years cut short by a tragic motorcycle accident in 2007. Born in 1977 in Sacramento, California, Corrales turned pro in 1996 and three years later in 1999 captured the **International Boxing Federation (IBF)** super featherweight title by defeating Roberto Garcia.

He made three successful defenses before a championship clash with **World Boxing Council (WBC)** titlist and fellow unbeaten **Floyd Mayweather, Jr.** Struggling to make weight at 130 lbs., Corrales could not handle Mayweather's superior speed and lost badly in 10 rounds. He rebounded in a major way with a 2004 victory over the tough **Joel Casamayor** and then in 2005 fought what *The Ring* magazine called an "epic for the ages" against **Jose Luis Castillo.**

Diego "Chico" Corrales prepares to do battle with Jose Luis Castillo in October 2005. Courtesy of Chris Cozzone.

In the climactic 10th round, Corrales somehow recovered from two knockdowns to stop his foe. Though he lost the rematch and later his life, Corrales remains etched in the memory of fight fans for his courageous ring wars.

Record:	40-5
Championship(s):	IBF superfeatherweight, 1999–2001; WBO super featherweight, 2004; WBO lightweight, 2004–2005; WBC lightweight, 2005.

Further Reading
Bodenrader, Ted. "Campaigning for Closure: Corrales and Casamayor Have To Do It One More Time." *World Boxing* (September 2004), pp. 50–55.
Doogan, Brian. "Corrales-Castillo Create An Epic for the Ages." *The Ring* (October 2005), pp. 48–53.
KO Interview. "Diego Corrales: 'I Had A Lot of Growing Up To Do.'" *KO* (October 2004), pp. 60–67.

CORRO, HUGO (1953–2007). Hugo Corro was a former world middleweight champion in the late 1970s who utilized superior boxing skills and good ring movement. Born in 1953 in Eusebio Bustos, Mendoza, in Argentina, Corro turned pro in 1973. He did not lose a pro bout until a 10-round decision loss in 1975 to Hugo Inocencio Saavedra—a defeat he avenged later in the year and again in a rubber match in 1976.

In 1976, he won the Argentine middleweight crown and the next year added the South American middleweight crown with a win over Antonio Alejandro Garrido. In 1978, he outboxed **Rodrigo Valdez** over 15 rounds to win the middleweight championship. He successfully defended his title over Ronnie Harris and Valdez in a rematch. He lost his title via split decision in 1979 to the rugged **Vito Antuofermo.** Corro originally retired in 1981. He made an ill-fated comeback later in the decade but retired for good in 1989.

Professional Record:	50-7-2
Championship(s):	Middleweight, 1978–1979

Further Reading
Santoliquito, Joe. "Hugo Corro, 1953–2007." *The Ring* (November 2007), p. 11.

COSELL, HOWARD (1918–1995).

Howard Cosell, born William Howard Cohen, was a famous sports broadcaster and journalist known for his pompous attitude, staccato-styled voice, and interesting exchanges with famous boxers, most notably **Muhammad Ali.** His unusual style earned him legions of admirers and detractors who either loved or hated him.

Born in 1918 in Winston Salem, North Carolina, he was reared in Brooklyn, New York. He earned an undergraduate degree from New York University and his law degree from New York University Law School. After serving in the U.S. Army Transportation Corp., Cosell practiced law. He represented sports figures such as Willie Mays in his practice.

Cosell became famous for his interviews with Ali during the 1960s and 1970s. Cosell defended Ali's antiwar stance. "What the government has done to this man is both inhuman and illegal under the Fifth and Fourteenth Amendments," Cosell intoned (Grimsley).

He later achieved more fame for broadcasting football on Monday Night Football. Cosell's distinctive voice called many great fights. For example, he covered the first bout between heavyweight champion **Joe Frazier** and challenger **George Foreman.** After Frazier was bounced to the canvas several times, Cosell bellowed: "Down Goes Frazier! Down Goes Frazier!"

Cosell quit announcing boxing matchers after calling the mismatch between heavyweight champion **Larry Holmes** and rugged challenger **Randall "Tex" Cobb** in 1982. He later said that he favored the abolition of professional boxing.

Further Reading
Grimsley, Will. "Howard Cosell: Egotist? Or Is He Fearlessly Honest?" *Los Angeles Times*, 6/20/1971, p. C4.
Kindred, Dave. *Sound and the Fury: Two Powerful Lives, One Fateful Friendship.* New York: Free Press, 2006.
Vecsey, George. "Cosell Says: 'I've Had It'" *The New York Times*, 12/6/1982, p. C4.

Miguel Cotto enters the ring to face Mohamad Abdulaev in June 2005. Cotto stopped his opponent in the 9th round. Courtesy of Chris Cozzone.

COTTO, MIGUEL (1980–).

Miguel Cotto is one of the most talented boxers in the world who has won world titles at the junior welterweight and welterweight divisions. A good boxer with excellent power, Cotto has lost only once—to the rugged **Antonio Margarito**—in his young career.

Born in 1980 in Caguas, Puerto Rico, Cotto had a sterling amateur career, representing his native country in the 2000 Sydney Olympics. He lost in the first

Miguel Cotto tags Antonio Margarito with a right hand in their July 2008 bout for welterweight supremacy. Cotto started off well but was stopped in the 11th round. Courtesy of Chris Cozzone.

round to the eventual gold medalist Mohamed Abdulaev. Cotto turned pro in 2001. In 2004, he stopped Kelson Pinto to win the World Boxing Organization (WBO) junior welterweight title. He made six successful defenses, including a win over his amateur nemesis Abdulaev before moving up in weight to the welterweight division.

He defeated Carlos Quintana to win the **World Boxing Association (WBA)** welterweight title. He successfully defended his belt three times—including wins over former champions **Zab Judah** and "Sugar" **Shane Mosley**—before losing his title to Margarito.

Professional Record:	33-1
Championship(s):	WBO junior welterweight, 2004–2006; WBA welterweight, 2006–2008, 2009

Further Reading
Official Web site: http://www.miguelcotto.com/
Smith, Tim. "Puerto Rico's Cotto rising on the icon list." *New York Daily News*, 6/7/2005.
Willis, George. "Cotto-Judah Slugfest a Bloody Masterpiece." *New York Post*, 6/11/2007, p. 57.

COTTON, EDDIE (1927–1990). Eddie Cotton was a former world-class light heavyweight contender who narrowly lost in two world title attempts. He was a fine defensive fighter with good boxing skills but also a penchant for suffering cuts. Born in Muskogee, Oklahoma, in 1927, Cotton turned pro in 1948 and fought in his hometown of Seattle, Washington. In 1961, he challenged **Harold Johnson** for the National Boxing Association (NBA) world light heavyweight title, losing a 15-round split decision.

In 1966, the 40-year-old faced **Jose Torres** for the world title again, this time suffering a close unanimous decision loss that *The Ring* magazine called "the fight of the year." Many felt that Cotton deserved the victory. *Seattle Times'* sports editor said: "Eddie may not have won the fight.

But it looked like it to nearly everybody except three men hired by the state of Nevada, where the gamblers' odds were 7-2 that Eddie wouldn't win" (Duncan). In 1967, he lost to future great **Bob Foster** and then retired after one more fight. He later served as a Washington state boxing commissioner. He died in 1990 from an infection in his blood and lungs.

Professional Record:	56-23-2
Championship(s):	None

Further Reading

Duncan, Don. "Eddie Cotton's Biggest Fight—Ex-Prizefighter's Countdown These Days Is Waiting for Beeper to Tell Him There's a Liver Ready for Transplant." *The Seattle Times*, 3/15/1990, p. A1.

COTTON, EDDIE (1947–). Eddie Cotton, not to be confused with the former light heavyweight contender, is a boxing referee best known for serving as the third man in the ring for the historic June 2002 bout between heavyweight champion **Lennox Lewis** and former champion "Iron" **Mike Tyson** held in Memphis, Tennessee.

Born in 1947 in Los Angeles, Cotton moved with his family to Paterson, New Jersey, when he was three years old. He served in the army from 1968–1971 and then moved back to New Jersey. In 1980, he began refereeing amateur bouts, and then in 1992, he made his debut as a professional boxing referee.

He has officiated many world title and other major bouts, including **Riddick Bowe**—Andrew Golota II, **Shane Mosley**—Jesse James Leija, **Fernando Vargas**—Yory Boy Campos, **Wladimir Klitschko**—Ray Austin, and Sultan Ibragimov—**Shannon Briggs**. Cotton has been used in many major heavyweight bouts, probably in part because of his size—he stands 6'5" and weighs well over 200 pounds.

Further Reading

Anderson, Dave. "The Most Important Referee." *The New York Times*, 5/29/2002, p. D1.

Ecksel, Robert. "The Third Man Eddie Cotton." *The Sweet Science*, 6/13/2005, at http://www.thesweet science.com/boxing-article/2242/third-man-eddie-cotton/

COUTURE, RANDY (1963–). Randy "the Natural" Couture is possibly the most popular fighter ever to fight in the **Ultimate Fighting Championships (UFC).** Born in Lynnwood, Washington, in 1963, Couture served in the army for several years in the mid-1980s. He then attended Oklahoma State University where he became an All-American wrestler. Twice he finished second in the NCAA championships. Upon graduation, Couture taught college wrestling at Oregon State. He began his mixed martial arts (MMA) career in 1997 and in only his fourth bout, captured the UFC heavyweight championship with an overtime decision win over **Maurice Smith.**

Couture won the UFC heavyweight title a second time in 2000 at UFC 28 with a win over **Kevin "Monster" Randleman.** He lost his title at UFC 36: Worlds Collide to **Josh Barnett.** He then lost to **Ricco Rodriguez** at UFC 39: The Warriors Return in a match for the vacant heavyweight title. Couture then dropped down to the light heavyweight division where he defeated **Chuck Liddell** and **Tito Ortiz** in consecutive events at UFC 43: Meltdown and UFC 44: Undisputed to capture the world light heavyweight title—becoming the first fighter in UFC history to win championships in two different weight classes.

Couture lost the belt in his first defense to **Vitor Belfort** at UFC 46: Supernatural, but regained the title in a rematch at UFC 49: Unfinished Business. "The Natural" lost the light heavyweight title to Liddell at UFC 52: Couture v. Liddell 2 in April 2005. In February 2006, he lost the rubber match to Liddell, and many presumed that Couture's career may be over. However, he came out of retirement to challenge Tim Sylvia for the UFC heavyweight title at UFC 68: The Uprising. In a huge upset, Couture used his superior wrestling skills to win a unanimous decision. Couture became the first man to win the UFC heavyweight title three times. He successfully defended his title at UFC 74: Respect with a win over Gabriel Gonzaga.

Couture then announced that he was leaving the UFC, leaving his career in limbo. Couture has made it known that he wants to face **Fedor Emelianenko** to settle who is the best heavyweight mixed martial artist. Couture and the UFC were embroiled in litigation over his contract status. However, Couture and the UFC resolved their differences, and in December 2008, Couture squared off against the behemoth **Brock Lesnar** for the heavyweight title. Couture lost in the second round.

Professional Record:	16-9
Championship(s):	UFC Heavyweight, 1997, 2000–2001; 2007–; UFC light heavyweight, 2003–2004, 2004–2005

Further Reading

Brown, Brad. "Randy 'the Natural' Couture Interview." *MMAWeekly.com*, 12/7/2005, at http://www.mmafighting.com/interviews/randycouture.html

Couture, Randy, with Loretta Hunt. *Becoming the Natural*. New York: Simon Spotlight Entertainment, 2008.

Craig, Donovan. "Waiting for Couture." *FIGHT!* (March 2008), pp. 76–84.

McCray, Brad. "Unretired and facing a giant." *The Oregonian*, 2/28/2007, p. E1.

Official Web site: http://www.thenatural.tv/

Wall, Jeremy. *UFC's Ultimate Warriors Top 10*. Ontario: ECW Press, 2005, pp. 95–109.

CRIBB, TOM (1781–1848). Tom Cribb was a former English champion in the early nineteenth century known for his superior skills and conditioning. Born in 1781 in Gloucester, England, Cribb worked on the wharves before turning his attention to boxing. He gained attention in 1805 when he defeated George Maddox and then Bill Richmond. In 1807, he defeated Jem Belcher in controversial fashion when Cribb's second stalled the match when his man was hurt. In an 1809 rematch, Cribb dominated Belcher to win the English heavyweight crown. In his most famous (or notorious) bout, he successfully defended his title against African American **Tom Molineaux** in 33 rounds. In the 28th round, Molineaux floored Cribb and, by some accounts, should have been awarded the victory. However, Cribb's second protested, and the fight was allowed to continue. Cribb's superior conditioning took over, and he prevailed at the end of the 33rd round. Cribb won a rematch easier, as Molineaux did not train properly. He remained the recognized English champion until he retired in 1822.

Record:	Unknown
Championship(s):	English Heavyweight, 1809–1822

Further Reading

Roberts, James B., and Alexander B. Skutt. *The Boxing Register* (4th ed.). Ithaca, NY: McBooks Press, Inc., 2006, p. 22.

CUEVAS, PIPINO (1957–). Pipino Cuevas was a former world welterweight champion known for his powerful left hook that led to 31 knockouts in his 35 career victories. He broke the jaws of several world-class opponents in his career. Born in 1957 in Mexico, Cuevas turned pro at age 14 in 1971 and suffered a second-round knockout.

Five years later—still a teenager at 19—Cuevas kayoed Angel Estrada to win the **World Boxing Association (WBA)** welterweight crown. He successfully defended his title 11 times, defeating the likes of Harold Weston, Jr., Billy Backus, and Pete Ranzany. He finally lost his title to **Thomas "the Hitman" Hearns** in 1980. Cuevas never again fought for a world title. He finally retired for good from the ring in 1989. His son Pipino Cuevas, Jr. is a young welterweight prospect.

Professional Record:	35-15
Championship(s):	WBA welterweight, 1976–1980

Further Reading
Condon, David. "That Pipino Cuevas is a tough hombre." *Chicago Tribune*, 7/29/1979, p. C1.
Hawn, Jack. "Cuevas: Quiet Man at the Top." *Los Angeles Times*, 7/31/1977, p. C16.
Hawn, Jack. "Jawbreaker Cuevas Stops Weston in 9, Retains Title." *Los Angeles Times*, 3/5/1978, p. C1.

CURRY, DONALD (1961−). Donald "Lone Star" Curry was a former world welterweight and junior middleweight champion who possessed incredible natural talent. Born in 1961 in Fort Worth, Texas, Curry was denied his chance at Olympic gold because of the U.S.A.'s boycott of the 1980 Moscow Olympics. Curry had one of the greatest records in amateur boxing history with 400 wins.

He turned pro in 1980 and in his 16th pro bout defeated Sun-Sok Hwang to win the vacant **World Boxing Association (WBA)** welterweight title. In 1984, he added the **International Boxing Federation (IBF)** belt with a win over **Marlon "the Magic Man" Starling.** He unified the division by destroying previously unbeaten **Milton "the Iceman" McCrory** in 1985 to add the **World Boxing Council (WBC)** belt to his resume. He lost his titles in an upset kayo loss to Lloyd Honeyghan.

In 1987, he lost to Mike McCallum in an attempt for the WBA junior middleweight championship. He was outboxing McCallum until felled by a left hook. Curry rebounded in 1988 with a convincing win over Gianfranco Rosi. However, he lost the title in his first defense against Rene Jacquot in France. He had two more major world title fights, losing to **Michael Nunn** in 1990 for the IBF middleweight crown and to **Terry Norris** for the WBC junior middleweight title. He retired after the Norris loss but returned to the ring in 1997. After losing to Emmett Linton, he retired for good. When Donald Curry was in his prime, there were few—if any—fighters better than he.

His brother Bruce was a former world junior welterweight champion.

Professional Record:	34-6
Championship(s):	WBA welterweight, 1983–1986; IBF welterweight, 1984–1986; WBC welterweight, 1985–1986; WBC junior middleweight, 1988–1989

Further Reading
Berger, Phil. "Reluctant Curry a Natural Fighter." *The New York Times*, 12/5/1985, p. B5.
Collins, Nigel. "Donald Curry: Sugar Ray Leonard's Successor?" *The Ring* (May 1985), pp. 16–19.
Katz, Michael. "Curry Keeps Title on Decision." *The New York Times*, 2/51984, p. S15.

CUTMEN. Cutmen are an indispensable resource to boxers and mixed martial artists competing in the ring (or a cage). They apply various substances and tools to a fighter's face to give the fighter the best possible chance of continuing even after suffering cuts and bruising on their faces. An obvious task of any cutman is to stop the flow of blood and ensure that the fighter can continue fighting. Oftentimes, a severe cut can lead to a fighter losing by technical knockout when the referee or ringside physician stops the fight.

Cutmen use a variety of substances such as adrenalin chloride (also adrenalin 1-1000), avitene, and Thromblin—coagulants—to stop the flow of blood from cuts. They also regularly use Vaseline and in-swell, a frozen piece of metal that is applied to swellings on a fighter's face.

Some of the leading cutmen are Joe Sousa, Ray Rodgers, Al Bachman, , Jacob "Stitch" Duran, and Eddie Aliano.

Further Reading

Arias, Carlos. "What is a Cutman?" *Orange County Register,* 1/3/2000, p. D13.

Davidson, Neil. "Call me Stitch; Veteran Cutman Helps Fighters keep Fighting in Boxing and MMA." *The Canadian Press,* 2/3/2007.

Rotella, Carlos. *Cut Time: An Education at the Fights.* New York: Houghton Mifflin, 2003.

Thomson, Josh. "Every boxer has a blood brother." *The Journal News,* 6/22/2005, p. 7C.

Toperoff, Sam. "Secrets of a cutman; Eddie Aliano." *Men's Health,* 8/1/1990, pp. 56–59.

CZYZ, BOBBY (1962–). Bobby Czyz was a former middleweight contender and champion at the light heavyweight and cruiserweight divisions. Born in Wanaque, New Jersey, the popular Czyz earned the nickname "the Matinee Idol" for his good looks and fine boxing skills. A promising middleweight prospect, he reeled off 20 straight wins before a unanimous decision loss to the rugged **Mustafo Hamsho.** He later moved up to the light heavyweight division and captured his first world title in 1986 with a convincing fifth-round stoppage of previously unbeaten champion **Slobodon Kacar** to win the **International Boxing Federation (IBF)** belt. He successfully defended the title three times before losing to "Prince" Charles Williams in 1987. In 1989, he failed in attempts to regain a light heavyweight belt, losing decisions to **Virgil Hill** and Williams again.

In 1991, he upset **Robert Daniels** to win the **World Boxing Council (WBC)** cruiserweight championship, capturing a 12-round split decision. He successfully defended the title twice. Later in his career, he moved up to the heavyweight division with little success. He finally retired in 1998 after losing to the much larger Corrie Sanders in two rounds. He later became a well-respected boxing analyst for SHOWTIME boxing.

Professional Record:	44-8
Championship(s):	IBF light heavyweight, 1986–1987; WBC cruiserweight, 1991–1992

Further Reading

Berger, Phil. "For Czyz, Pro Career Was Inevitable." *The New York Times,* 9/4/1986, p. D25.

Berger, Phil. "For Czyz, Lalonde Isn't Hard to Figure." *The New York Times,* 5/10/1992, p. S2.

Collins, Nigel. "Bobby Czyz: Matinee Idol Comes of Age." *The Ring* (June 1986), pp. 36–37.

Murray, Jim. "A Champion Who Doesn't Just Let Fists Do the Talking." *Los Angeles Times,* 5/12/1987, p. SP 1.

Smith, Sam. "Adversity, Foes Unable to Knock Out Czyz." *Chicago Tribune,* 10/27/1987, p. 5C.

DANIELS, ROBERT (1968–). Robert "Preacherman" Daniels is a former cruiserweight world champion who still campaigns as a heavyweight. He serves as a lay minister at his church, which earned him his catchy moniker "Preacherman." He possessed a fine left jab and good boxing skills.

Born in 1968, he turned pro at a young age in 1984. Five years later, in 1989, he faced former champion **Dwight Muhammad Qawi** for the vacant **World Boxing Association (WBA)** cruiserweight championship in France. Daniels captured split-decision victory. He successfully defended his title twice before losing a 12-round split decision to **Bobby Czyz.** He never received another shot at a world title from a major sanctioning body. In later years, Daniels moved up to the heavyweight division in search of bigger paydays. He lost to Lawrence Clay-Bey and **David Tua,** prompting him to return to his more natural weight at cruiserweight. In 2007, he still fought as a stepping stone for young prospects.

Professional Record:	49-9-1
Championship(s):	WBA cruiserweight, 1989–1991

Further Reading
Robb, Sharon. "Preacher with a Punch; Robert Daniels Can't Turn Other Cheek If He Hopes to Reap Cruiserweight Titles." *Sun Sentinel*, 6/8/2004, p. 2C.

DAVIS, AL "BUMMY" (1920–1945). Al "Bummy" Davis was a popular slugging welterweight from Brownsville, New York, who never won a world title but became a legend anyway. Born in 1920 as Albert Abraham Davidoff, Davis grew up in a tough Jewish neighborhood of Brooklyn. Davis managed to avoid the pitfalls of joining the Mob, no small feat in that day and age. Two of Davis' brothers worked as enforcers for the Mafia.

He turned pro in 1937 and fought 17 times that year, winning every fight. Many of his fights ended in knockout, as Davis possessed an extremely powerful left hook. In 1939, he stopped **Tony Canzoneri** in the third round. He did not lose until he dropped a 10-round decision to the great Lou Ambers in 1940 in his 38th professional bout. Later that year, in his most infamous bout, Davis hit **Fritzie Zivic** low about 10 times, earning a disqualification and an investigation by New York boxing officials who threatened to ban "Bummy" from the sport.

In perhaps his finest performance, he kayoed former lightweight great Bob Montgomery in the first round in 1944. He died the next year while attempting to chase down robbers of a local tavern. Though he often found himself embroiled in controversy, he died a hero.

Professional Record:	66-10-4
Championship(s):	None

Further Reading
Dawson, James P. "Referee's Action Averts Ring Riot." *The New York Times,* 11/16/1940, p. 15.
Ross, Ron. *Bummy Davis vs. Murder, Inc.: The Rise and Fall of the Jewish Mafia and an Ill-Fated Prizefighter.* New York: St. Martin's Press, 2003.

DAVIS, MARCUS (1973–). Marcus Davis is a former professional boxer who turned to mixed martial arts (MMA) and the Octagon. As a professional boxer, the Maine native compiled a record of 17-1-2 with 12 stoppages in the super middleweight division. Davis says he became bored with boxing and founded mixed martial arts more exciting. He trained in wrestling, grappling, and other necessary skills for MMA.

Davis competed on *The Ultimate Fighter* Season 2, losing to Joe Stevenson on the show and later to **Melvin Guillard** on the undercard of the season finale. However, Davis learned his lessons from his losses on the show and returned to the Octagon with six straight victories, including an improbable come-from-behind kayo of the dangerous Paul Taylor in September 2007.

In June 2008, he lost a decision to Mike Swick. However, he has rebounded with solid wins over Paul Taylor and the tough **Chris Lytle.**

Professional Boxing Record:	17-1-2
Professional MMA Record:	16-4
Championship(s):	None

Further Reading
Carlson, Mike. "Born to Fight: What You Don't Know About Marcus Davis Can Hurt You." *RealFighter,* No. 19 (2008), pp. 26–33.
Gerbasi, Thomas. "Marcus Davis' MMA Education." 10/7/2006, at http://www.ufc.com/index. cfm?fa=news.detail&gid=3485&pid=402
Hudson, David L., Jr. "Marcus Davis: 'I'm Gonna Knock Him Out!" *Fightnews.com,* 10/10/2008, at http://www.fightnewsextra.com/cc/ufc89/10-davis.htm
"Marcus Davis: I always have a puncher's chance against anyone." *FightSport,* pp. 36–37. Retrieved from http://en.wikipedia.org/wiki/Al_Bummy_Davis

DAWSON, CHAD (1982–). "Bad" Chad Dawson is a two-time light heavyweight champion whose blazing hand and foot speed has led him to an undefeated record through 2008. Already, the young champion has defeated former champions **Glen Johnson, Antonio Tarver,** and Tomasz Adamek.

Born in 1982 in Hartsville, South Carolina, Dawson moved to New Haven, Connecticut, as a child with his family. The young Dawson starred in basketball in high school. Dawson, the son of a journeyman boxer, compiled an amateur record of 67-13 before turning pro in 2001.

In 2007, he defeated Adamek by unanimous decision to win the **World Boxing Council (WBC)** light heavyweight title. He successfully defended the title three times, including a narrow decision win over the rugged Johnson. He relinquished the title and then challenged **International Boxing Federation (IBF)/International Boxing Organization (IBO)** champion Antonio Tarver in October 2008. Dawson's hand speed once again proved the difference, as he captured a unanimous decision. Dawson used to be trained by **Floyd Mayweather, Sr.** and now is trained by former light heavyweight champion **Eddie Mustafa Muhammad.**

Professional Record:	27-0
Championship(s):	WBC Light Heavyweight, 2007–2008; IBF Light Heavyweight, 2008–

Further Reading

Avila, David. "Bad Chad Dawson Too Much for Antonio Tarver." *The Sweet Science*, 10/11/2008, at http://www.thesweetscience.com/boxing-article/6266/bad-chad-dawson-too-much-antonio-tarver/

Pierpaoli, Alex. "Interview: Bad Chad Dawson goes back to school." *Doghouseboxing.com*, 3/28/2005, at http://www.doghouseboxing.com/A_Pierpaoli/Alex032805.htm

DEATHS IN THE BOXING RING. An awful reality of boxing (and other combat sports) is that sometimes ring participants die from repeated blows to their bodies, particularly their brains. Many medical groups, including the respected American Medical Association (AMA), have called for the banning of professional boxing, emphasizing that the intent of the sport is to batter your opponent into unconsciousness.

Though it is nearly impossible to confirm with certainty, reports indicate that there have been nearly 2,000 ring fatalities. Several high-profile championship fights ending in ring deaths have spurred calls from abolition to the institution of additional safety measures. Major calls to end boxing occurred after the March 1962 ring death of welterweight champion **Benny "Kid" Paret** who died four days after suffering injuries from his title defense against **Emile Griffith.** A year later, those calls escalated after popular world featherweight champion **Davey Moore** lost his life in a title defense against **Ultiminio "Sugar" Ramos.**

Another high-profile ring death occurred in November 1982 when lightweight champion **Ray "Boom Boom" Mancini** defended his title against tough South Korean challenger Duk Koo Kim. Mancini finally stopped Kim in the 14th round, but sadly the challenger never recovered. That fight caused boxing organizations to drop their championship fights from 15 rounds to 12 rounds. There have been other ring fatalities in championship bouts, including:

1947: **Sugar Ray Robinson** KO 8 Jimmy Doyle (welterweight)

1962: Emile Griffith TKO 12 Benny Paret (welterweight)

1963: Ultiminio "Sugar" Ramos KO 10 Davey Moore (featherweight)

1980: **Lupe Pintor** KO 12 Johnny Owen (**World Boxing Council [WBC]** bantamweight title)

1982: Ray Mancini TKO 14 Duk Koo Kim (WBC lightweight)

1983: Alberto Davila TKO 12 Kiki Bejines (WBC bantamweight)

1995: **Gabriel Ruelas** TKO 11 Jimmy Garcia (WBC superfeatherweight)

2005: **Jesus Chavez** TKO 11 **Leavander Johnson** (**International Boxing Federation [IBF]** super lightweight)

Numerous other proposals have been called for including the wearing of headgear, better and more extensive prefight medical testing, and better screening of potential mismatches. Others argue that death is simply an unfortunately by-product of an admittedly violent sport. The debate likely will continue as long as the sport of boxing continues.

Further Reading
Fernandez, Bernard. "When a fighter dies, his opponent suffers too." *Philadelphia Daily News*, 9/28/2005.
Springer, Steve. "When fighters die, it's part of the cost of doing business." *Los Angeles Times*, 5/1/1996, p. C3.

DEJESUS, ESTEBAN (1951–1989). Esteban DeJesus was a great lightweight champion from Puerto Rico best known for his three-fight trilogy and rivalry with the great **Roberto Duran.** Born in 1951 in Carolina, Puerto Rico, DeJesus turned pro in 1969 and won his first 20 professional bouts. In 1971, he lost a 10-round decision to Antonio Gomez. In November 1972, he scored the most famous win of his career—a 10-round unanimous decision victory over lightweight champion Duran in Madison Square Garden. He dropped Duran with a left hook in the first round and controlled most of the rounds. It was the first time in 32 fights that Duran had ever hit the canvas. Unfortunately, the fight was a nontitle affair, so DeJesus did not win a championship after that victory.

In March 1974, he faced Duran for the title. It was déjà vu in the first round, as a DeJesus left hook once again deposited Duran on the canvas. However, Duran rose and stopped DeJesus in the 11th round to retain his title. In 1975, DeJesus moved up in weight to the junior welterweight division to challenge **Antonio "Kid Pambele" Cervantes** who defeated him in a lopsided 15-round unanimous decision.

In May 1976, DeJesus captured the **World Boxing Council (WBC)** lightweight title with a 15-round decision over Guts Ishimatsu. He successfully defended his title three times before the rubber match and unification bout with Duran. In a great fight, DeJesus had his moments but fell in the 12th round. He rebounded with six straight wins before failing in another attempt at the junior welterweight title, losing to **Saoul Mamby.** In retirement he struggled with a drug problem and served time in prison for murder. He later turned his life over to religion and received a pardon after it was discovered that he had contracted the AIDS virus. In the last week of his life, he was visited by none other than Roberto Duran.

Record: 57-5
Championship(s):   WBC lightweight, 1976–1978

Further Reading
Dettloff, William. "The 20 Greatest Lightweights of All Time." *The Ring* (September 2001), pp. 49–69, 64.
McGowen, Deane. "DeJesus Triumphs in Eighth Round." *The New York Times*, 4/11/1972, p. 49.
McGowen, Deane. "DeJesus Outpoints Duran, Lightweight Titleholder." *The New York Times*, 11/18/1972, p. 45.

DE LA HOYA, OSCAR (1973–). Oscar De La Hoya, "the Golden Boy," is one of the most popular boxers ever in terms of superstar cross-over appeal. He is the biggest moneymaker in boxing today. He also is a former Olympic gold medalist and a world champion in numerous weight classes in his career, which still continues in 2008 at the time of this writing.

Born in 1973 in East Los Angeles, De La Hoya began boxing at age six and compiled an incredible amateur record, culminating in Olympic gold at the 1992 Barcelona Olympics. He turned pro later that year in 1992 with a first-round stoppage of Lamar Williams. In only his fourth fight he defeated contender Jeff Mayweather, and in his eighth fight he stopped former world featherweight champion Troy Dorsey in the first round. In his 14th pro bout, he stopped undefeated Jimmy Bredahl to win the World Boxing Organization (WBO) junior lightweight title. Later that year, he moved up in weight and crushed former world featherweight champion **Jorge Paez** in the second round to win the WBO lightweight title.

In June 1996, he moved up in weight again and soundly defeated Mexican legend **Julio Cesar Chavez** to win the **World Boxing Council (WBC)** junior welterweight title. It was only Chavez's second professional loss in 99 bouts. De La Hoya successfully defended his title against unbeaten Miguel Angel Gonzalez, winning a convincing unanimous decision.

In April 1997, he defeated welterweight kingpin **Pernell "Sweet Pea" Whitaker** by unanimous decision. He made seven successful defenses against the likes of former champion **Hector "Macho" Camacho,** Chavez (whom he soundly beat again), Wilfredo Rivera, and the dangerous Ike Quartey, whom De La Hoya dropped in the final round to ensure victory.

He finally lost in 1999 by a controversial decision to **International Boxing Federation (IBF)** welterweight titlist **Felix Trinidad.** In June 2006, he lost a split decision to fellow unbeaten fighter and former amateur rival **"Sugar" Shane Mosley.** In June 2001, he moved up in weight again and defeated Javier Castillejo over 12 rounds to win the WBC junior middleweight title. In perhaps the defining fight of his career, he stopped rival **Fernando Vargas** in the 11th round to add the **World Boxing Association (WBA)** belt to his collection in 2002.

In June 2003, he lost a second bout with Mosley over 12 rounds, though most observers felt that De La Hoya did enough to earn the victory. In 2004, he narrowly defeated Felix Sturm to

Oscar De La Hoya throws his vaunted left hook at Steve Forbes in their May 2008 bout. De La Hoya won a unanimous decision. Courtesy of Chris Cozzone.

Oscar De La Hoya is in the ring following his victory over Steve Forbes in their 2008 bout. Courtesy of Chris Cozzone.

win the WBO middleweight title. Later that year, he galliantly fought against the great **Bernard Hopkins** before falling to a body shot in the ninth round.

He returned to the ring in May 2006 with a devastating knockout of slugger **Ricardo Mayorga.** He lost his title in 2007 to the sport's reigning pound-for-pound king **Floyd Mayweather, Jr.,** though De La Hoya acquitted himself well and only lost by split decision. He planned a rematch with Mayweather in the fall of 2008, but the bout did not make. Instead, he challenged **Manny Pacquiao,** who stopped De La Hoya in the eighth round. It is still unknown whether De La Hoya will return to the ring as a pugilist.

What is known, however, is that De La Hoya has become one of boxing's leading promoters as well as fighters. In December 2001, he formed Golden Boy Promotions and employs former ring opponents Mosley and Hopkins. He remains a powerful force in the sport of boxing.

Professional Record:	38-6
Championship(s):	WBO junior lightweight, 1994; WBO lightweight, 1994–1996; WBC junior welterweight, 1996–1997; WBC welterweight, 1997–1999; WBC junior welterweight, 2001–2003, 2006–2007; WBA junior welterweight, 2002–2003; WBO middleweight, 2004

Further Reading

De La Hoya, Oscar, and Steve Springer. *American Son: My Story*. New York: HarperEntertainment, 2008.
Eskenazi, Gerald. "De La Hoya Considers His Legacy." *The New York Times*, 2/8/2002, p. D6.
Golden Boy Promotions: http://www.goldenboypromotions.com/
Friend, Tom. "Why De La Hoya Refuses to Part with His Gold." *The New York Times*, 11/25/1992, p. B11.

Kawakami, Tim. *Golden Boy: The Fame, Money and Mystery of Oscar De La Hoya.* Riverside, NJ:. Andrews McMeel Publishing, 1999.

Spousta, Tom. "Mosley and De La Hoya Renew a Boyhood Rivalry." *The New York Times,* 6/15/2000, p. D7.

DEMPSEY, JACK (1895–1983). One of the most popular fighters of all time, this former world heavyweight champion ranked in the same breath of American sports legends Babe Ruth and Red Grange during the Roaring Twenties. Born in 1895 in Manassa, Colorado, Dempsey first fought under the name "Kid Blackie." He later earned the moniker "the Manassa Mauler" for his slugging, aggressive style.

He turned professional in 1914 and suffered a first-kayo loss to Jim Flynn in 1917—a defeat he avenged in the same manner the next year. In 1918, he pounded his way through the heavyweight ranks, destroying such fine fighters as Battling Levinsky and Ed "Gunboat" Smith. His impressive string of kayo wins earned him a title shot at the giant **Jess Willard** in 1919.

Dempsey's quickness advantage and aggressive style overwhelmed the plodding Willard who was dropped seven times early in the bout. Willard bled profusely and took a beating until the referee mercifully halted the contest. Dempsey successfully defended his title several times to great fanfare and public attention. His manager **Jack Kearns** and promoter **George Lewis "Tex" Rickard** turned Dempsey into a Babe Ruth of boxing, a larger-than-life figure in sports and society.

Dempsey lived up to his billing with impressive wins against light heavyweight kingpin **Georges Carpentier** and wild Argentine slugger Luis Firpo amonst others. He finally lost his title to **Gene Tunney** in 1926. He lost the rematch in controversial fashion in the famous "Battle of the Long Count," as he dropped Tunney for more than 10 seconds but failed to go to the nearest neutral corner. He retired after the second Tunney bout.

Professional Record:	61-6-3
Championship(s):	Heavyweight, 1919–1926

Further Reading

Dempsey, Jack, and Barbara Piatelli Dempsey. *Dempsey.* New York: Harper & Row, 1977.

Fleischer, Nat. *Jack Dempsey, The Idol of Fistiana: An Intimate Narrative.* Whitefish, MT: Kessinger Publishing, 2007.

Kahn, Roger. *A Flame of Pure Fire: Jack Dempsey and The Roaring 1920s.* New York: Harcourt, 1999.

Roberts, Randy. *Jack Dempsey: The Manassa Mauler.* Champaign, IL: University of Illinois Press, 2003.

Schoor, Gene. *The Jack Dempsey Story.* New York: J. Messner, 1954.

Smith, Toby. *Kid Blackie: Jack Dempsey's Colorado Days.* Ridgway, CO: Wayfinder Press, 1987.

DEMSPEY, JACK "THE NONPAREIL" (1862–1895). Jack "the Nonpareil" Dempsey was one of the greatest boxers in history, dominating the lighter weight classes during the later part of the nineteenth century. Though most know the name "Jack Dempsey" as that of the later heavyweight champion, knowledgeable boxing experts claim that the better fighter was his namesake. His boxing greatness was shown by his nickname "the Nonpareil," meaning without equal.

Born John Edward Kelly in 1862 in Curran, Ireland, he moved at an early age to Williamsburg, New York. He turned pro in 1883 and won the welterweight championship with a win over George LaBlanche in 1889. He added the middleweight title to his resume with a win over Billy McCarthy. He lost his belt to the great middleweight champion **Bob Fitzsimmons.**

Professional Record:	50-3-8
Championship(s):	Middleweight, 1886–1891

Further Reading
Cyber Boxing Zone Profile: http://www.cyberboxingzone.com/boxing/non-jack.htm
International Boxing Hall of Fame: Profile http://www.ibhof.com/dempseyN.htm

DIAZ, JUAN (1983–). Juan "the Baby Bull" Diaz is a former world lightweight champion known for his high work rate and excellent body punching. Born in 1983 in Houston, Texas, Diaz nearly qualified for the 2000 Olympics for Mexico but was told he was too young to fight. Instead, he turned professional at age 16.

In July 2004, he outpointed Lakva Sims to win the **World Boxing Association (WBA)** lightweight championship. In April 2007, he added the World Boxing Organization (WBO) belt to his resume with a win over Brazil's **Acelino Freitas.** Then, in October he took a huge step toward unifying the titles with a convincing win over **International Boxing Federation (IBF)** titlist and rival Julio Diaz.

In March 2008, Diaz lost his titles in a surprise loss to tough contender **Nate Campbell** by split decision. Diaz attends college at the University of Houston-Downtown. He is majoring in political science and may enter politics once his ring career ends.

Professional Record:	34-1
Championship(s):	WBA Lightweight, 2004–2008; IBF lightweight, 2007–2008; WBO lightweight, 2007–2008.

Further Reading
Berkow, Ira. "Lightweight champion doesn't live for the ring." *The New York Times*, 8/8/2004, p. 1.
Donovan, Jake. "Juan Diaz: Three Titles Down, One to Go." *Boxing Scene*, 10/14/2007 at http://www.boxingscene.com/?m=show&opt=printable&id=10762
Martinez, Nancy. "Undefeated in Life; a scholar and a sportsman." *The Houston Chronicle*, 7/15/2004, p. B1.

Juan "Baby Bull" Diaz powers a left hook at Michael Katsidis. Diaz won a 12-round split decision in their September 2008 bout. Courtesy of Chris Cozzone.

Modrowski, Roman. "Classy Juan Diaz doesn't skip class; WBA/WBO lightweight champion is student at University of Houston." *Chicago Sun Times*, 9/28/2007, p. 86.

DIAZ, NICK (1983–). Nick Diaz is a talented mixed martial artist who currently fights in Elite XC but has also fought in the **Ultimate Fighting Championships (UFC), PRIDE,** the WEC, and other organizations. Born in 1983 in Stockton, California, Diaz made his mixed martial arts (MMA) debut in 2001 in the IFC. Diaz stunned the MMA world at UFC 47: It's On by kayoing the favored **Robbie Lawler** in the second round. He later lost decisions to Joe Riggs, **Sean Sherk,** Diego Sanchez, and **Karo Parisyan.** Diaz maintains that he won many of those bouts.

In February 2007, Diaz faced the legendary **Takanori Gomi** at PRIDE 33: Second Coming. Diaz submitted Gomi with a rarely used move called the **gogoplata**—where the combatant on the canvas uses his shin from a raised leg and his arm to choke out his opponent. The result was changed later to a no-contest after Diaz tested positive for marijuana. In November 2007, Diaz lost to KJ Noons in Elite XC: Renegade. Diaz's younger brother Nathan won the lightweight division on *The Ultimate Fighter 5*.

Professional MMA Record:	18-7
Championship(s):	WEC Welterweight, 2003

Further Reading
Ross, Matthew. "Don't F&ck with the Diaz Brothers." *Fight!* (February 2008), pp. 52–56.
Young, Matt. "Diaz says what he thinks." *Corpus Christi Caller-Times*, 11/8/2007, SPORTS, p. 1.

DIBELLA, LOU (1960–). Lou DiBella is a successful boxing promoter who parlayed his job as head of boxing programming at HBO. Born in Brooklyn in 1960, DiBella earned an undergraduate degree from Tufts University and a law degree from Harvard in 1985. He worked several years at the prestigious law firm Sullivan and Cromwell. In 1989, he took a job at HBO as a company lawyer. He worked 11 years at HBO, during which he launched the popular series *Boxing After Dark* in 1996.

In May 2000, he left HBO to start his own boxing firm called DiBella Entertainment. He made a splash in the industry by signing several of the 2000 Olympians from the American boxing team, including Michael Bennett, Jose Navarro, Clarence Vinson, Ricardo Williams, Dante Craig, and **Jermain Taylor.** He initially worked with middleweight great **Bernard Hopkins,** though the relationship dissolved and DiBella ended up successfully suing Hopkins for defamation. DiBella also promotes Jermain Taylor, Andre Berto, **Paulie Malignaggi,** and Curtis Stevens.

Further Reading
DiBella Entertainment: http://www.dbe1.com/about.html
Raskin, Eric. "Inside the Mind of Lou DiBella." *The Ring* (September 2006), pp. 102–107.
Woods, Michael J. "Boxing Digest Interviews Lou DiBella." *Boxing Digest* (July 2004), pp. 24–26.

DIXON, GEORGE (1870–1908). George "Little Chocolate" Dixon was the first black man to ever win a world championship in boxing history, capturing titles in the bantamweight and featherweight divisions. Born in 1870 in Halifax, Nova Scotia, he turned pro at age 16 in 1886. Four years later, he defeated Nunc Wallace in London to win the world bantamweight championship. In one of his defenses, he defeated white amateur champion Jack Skelly in a bout in New Orleans that led to racial unrest.

He added the featherweight crown in 1893 with a win over Fred Johnson. He retained the title numerous times before losing a decision to Frank Erne in 1896. He regained the title from Erne in 1897 before losing a decision to Ben Jordan in 1898. He regained the title for a third time from Dave Sullivan and held it until losing to the powerful **Terry McGovern** in 1900.

Professional Record:	65-30-48
Championship(s):	Bantamweight, 1890; Featherweight, 1891–1896, 1897–1898–1900

Further Reading

Bennett, James Gordon. "Dixon's Easy Victory." *Chicago Tribune*, 6/28/1890, p. 6.
"A Game Fighter Is He." *The Washington Post*, 3/11/1894, p. 17.
Davies, Charles E. "Passing of a Champion." *Chicago Daily Tribune*, 1/14/1900, p. 19.
"Dixon Still a Champion." *The New York Times*, 9/7/1892, p. 3.
Roberts, James B., and Alexander G. Skutt. *The Boxing Register: International Boxing Hall of Fame Official Record Book* (4th ed.). Ithaca, NY: McBooks Press, 2006, pp. 110–111.

DOKES, MICHAEL (1958–). Michael "Dynamite" Dokes was an explosive and talented heavyweight champion who failed to live up to his vast potential. Born in Akron, Ohio, in 1958, Dokes turned pro as a teenager in 1976 and showed great promise. The only blemish was a 10-round draw against Ossie Occasio in 1980, avenged with a first-round kayo in the rematch. In 1980, Dokes entered the ring undefeated and defeated **Mike Weaver** in a first-round technical knockout. Because of the quick stoppage, a rematch was ordered, and Dokes retained the title in a draw. In his next defense, he lost the title to **Gerrie Coetzee** in 1983.

Dokes never regained the title and squandered some of his career with lack of training and drug problems. He gave **Evander Holyfield** a great fight in 1989 but lost in the 10th round. In 1993, he challenged **Riddick Bowe** for the **World Boxing Council (WBC)** and **International Boxing Federation (IBF)** titles but lost spectacularly in a first-round knockout. He retired in 1997 after consecutive losses to journeyman heavyweights.

Record:	53-6-2
Championship(s):	WBA Heavyweight, 1982–1983

Further Reading

Hoffer, Richard. "Quick Win for Dokes, but a new black eye for the sport of boxing." *Los Angeles Times*, 12/11/1982, at B1.
Martinez, Michael. "Dokes To Take His Last Shot." *Chicago Tribune*, 2/7/1993, p. C9.
Shaw, Bud. "Put Down Your Dukes, Mr. Dokes." *Cleveland Plain Dealer*, 2/6/1993, p. 5F.

DONOVAN, MIKE (1847–1918). Mike Donovan's moniker describes this nineteenth-century boxer's approach to boxing—"The Professor." He possessed tremendous boxing skills that enabled him to compete against much heavier and much younger pugilists. Born in 1847 in Chicago, Donovan enlisted in the Union army and fought in the Civil War.

After the war, Donovan relocated in New Orleans where he trained under boxer Frank Kendrick. He fought many of the country's best middleweight boxers, including William McClellan, George Rooke, and **Jack "the Nonpareil" Dempsey.** Twice he fought two exhibitions with the powerful heavyweight champion **John L. Sullivan.**

His son Arthur Donovan became one of boxing's most well-known referees, and his grandson Arthur, Jr. was a great football player who made the Pro Football Hall of Fame.

Professional Record: 24-2-1
Championship(s):   Middleweight, 1878–1884

Further Reading
"Pugilism as a Fine Art." *The New York Times*, 11/26/1882, p. 5.
Roberts, James B., and Alexander B. Skutt. *The Boxing Register* (4th ed.). Ithaca, NY: McBooks Press, Inc., 2006, p. 23.

DOUGLAS, JAMES "BUSTER" (1960–). James "Buster" Douglas will always be remembered for staging perhaps the biggest upset in boxing history—a dramatic knockout win over the undefeated "Iron" **Mike Tyson** to capture the undisputed heavyweight championship of the world. Born in 1960 in Columbus, Ohio, Douglas turned pro in 1981 and won his first five fights before suffering a second-round stoppage at the hands of future heavyweight contender David Bey. In 1983, Douglas was coasting to victory over Mike "the Giant" White when he was stopped in the ninth round. In 1985, he dropped a 10-round decision to Jesse Ferguson. He rebounded with a win over **Greg Page** and put himself in position to win the heavyweight title. In 1987, he faced **Tony Tucker** for the vacant **International Boxing Federation** (**IBF**) title. Once again, Douglas squandered an early lead and was stopped in the 10th round. He rebounded with six straight wins, earning a shot at Tyson in Tokyo, Japan.

Surviving an eight-round knockdown, Douglas pulled the improbable upset, motivated in part by the recent passing of his mother. Unfortunately, Douglas could not maintain his newfound success. He entered the ring overweight in his first title defense against **Evander "the Real Deal" Holyfield** and was kayoed in the third round. He retired but returned to the ring six years later. He defeated a series of journeyman before being stopped in the first round by Lou Savarese.

Record: 38-6-1
Championship(s):   WBC, WBA and IBF Heavyweight, 1990

Further Reading
Layden, Tim. *The Last Great Fight: The Extraordinary Tale of Two Men and How One Fight Changed Their Lives.* New York: St Martin's Press, 2007.
Long, Bill, and John Johnson. *Tyson-Douglas: The Inside Story of the Upset of the Century.* Dulles, VA: Potomac Books, 2006.

DUNDEE, ANGELO (1921–). Angelo Dundee is one of the greatest boxing trainers and managers in the sport's history. He is best known for his corner work with **Muhammad Ali, Sugar Ray Leonard, Carmen Basilio, Jimmy Ellis, Willie Pastrano, Luis Rodriguez,** and **George Foreman.** Blessed with a charismatic personality, Dundee continues to engage himself with boxing fans across the globe.

Born in 1921 in Philadelphia, Pennsylvania, Dundee learned the craft of boxing at the famous Stillman's Gym. There he learned from such masters as **Ray Arcel,** Charley Goodman, and Chickie Ferrera. He is most famous for his work with Cassius Clay who later changed his name to Muhammad Ali. Dundee's best work may have been in splitting Clay's glove in his bout with

Henry Cooper who had floored Clay in the previous round. The split in the gloves gave Clay extra time to recover, and he defeated Cooper and moved closer to his shot at the heavyweight title.

Another famous Dundee moment occurred when Leonard faced **Thomas "the Hitman" Hearns** in a 1981 welterweight unification bout. His man trailing on points, Dundee urged Leonard in the corner: "You've got nine minutes. You're blowing it, son. You're blowing it. This is what separates the men from the boys. You're blowing it." Leonard proceeded to stop Hearns in the 14th round.

He later moved to Miami where his brother Chris Dundee owned a gym called Fifth Street Gym. For his lifelong contributions to the sport of boxing he was inducted into the International Boxing Hall of Fame in 1994.

Further Reading

Berger, Phil. "Dundee: Champ of Corner Men." *The New York Times*, 11/29/1981, p. SM9.

Dundee, Angelo. *My View From the Corner.* New York: McGraw Hill, Inc., 2007.

Hawn, Jack. "Dundee, Last of Breed, Heads Ring's Most Colorful Stable." *Los Angeles Times*, 5/20/1962, p. G11.

Murray, Jim. "Angelo Dundee: The Man Cassius Can't Do Without." *Los Angeles Times*, 2/5/1967, p. G1.

DURAN, ROBERTO (1951–). One of the greatest fighters in history, Roberto "Hands of Stone" Duran dominated the lightweight division for the 1970s. With an indefatigable style, this Panemanian terror literally overwhelmed opponents. In 1972, he stopped Scotland's **Ken Buchanan** in the 13th round to capture the **World Boxing Association (WBA)** lightweight crown—a title he never lost. In 1978, Duran stopped the dangerous **Esteban DeJesus**—the only man to ever defeat him at lightweight (in a nontitle bout) to capture the **World Boxing Council (WBC)** lightweight title.

In 2005, Roberto Duran looks a bit different than he did in his prime when he dominated the lightweight division in the 1970s. Courtesy of Chris Cozzone.

Roberto Duran and Mike Tyson come out to watch the big Las Vegas bout between Bernard Hopkins and Oscar De La Hoya in 2004. Courtesy of Chris Cozzone.

Duran later moved up in weight to the welterweight division, where he captured the world title in June 1980 in the historic "Brawl For It All in Montreal" with a majority decision over **Sugar Ray Leonard.** Five months later, he lost the rematch with Leonard in the infamous "No Mas" fight where Duran told the referee "no mas" (Spanish for "no more") and quit in the eighth round.

Duran redeemed himself in 1983 by winning the junior middleweight title over a game **Davey Moore.** He further added to his legacy when he gave undisputed middleweight champion **Marvelous Marvin Hagler** a tough 15-round bout in November 1983. In his next bout, **Thomas "the Hit Man" Hearns** blasted him out of the ring in two rounds.

Duran kept fighting and in February 1989 staged a memorable war with **Iran "the Blade" Barkley** to win the WBC middleweight championship. Duran kept fighting well past his prime. At age 47, he challenged William Joppy for the middleweight title and lost badly in the third round. In his last bout in July 2001, he dropped a 12-round decision to **Hector "Macho" Camacho.** *The Ring* magazine said it best in listing Duran as the greatest lightweight of all-time in 2001: "The Duran we know, the lightweight Duran, probably was the best fighter pound-for-pound for almost a decade"(p. 50).

Record: 104-15
Championship(s):   WBA Lightweight, 1972–1979; WBC Lightweight, 1978; WBC Welterweight, 1980; WBA Junior Middleweight, 1983; WBC Middleweight, 1989

Further Reading

Dettloff, William. "The 20 Greatest Lightweights of All-Time." *The Ring* (September 2001), pp. 49–69.

Giudice, Christian. *Hands of Stone: The Life and Legend of Roberto Duran.* London: Milo Books, 2006.

Heisler, Mark. "El Diablo: 'I Have Waited For This a Long Time.'" *Los Angeles Times*, 6/19/1980, p. B1.

Kimball, George. *Four Kings: Leonard, Hagler, Hearns, Duran and the Last Great Era of Boxing.* Ithaca, NY: McBooks Press, 2008.

EASTMAN, MARVIN (1971–). Marvin "the Beastman" Eastman is a skilled mixed martial artist best known for his Muay Thai kickboxing skills. Born in 1971 in Merced, California, the muscular Eastman wrestled collegiately and also played football for two years for the University of Nevada Las Vegas as a running back. He made his professional mixed martial arts (MMA) debut in June 2004 with at the King of the Cage event with a unanimous decision win over future **Ultimate Fighting Championships (UFC)** light heavyweight champion **Quinton "Rampage" Jackson.**

He has fought in numerous MMA organizations, including King of the Cage, UFC, World Extreme Fighting, and the International Fighting Organization. He has fought four times in the UFC, with a record of 1-4. In UFC 81 in February 2008, he defeated Terry Martin by unanimous decision. However, he has lost his last two bouts—to Drew McFedries and **Dennis Kang.**

Professional MMA Record:	15-9-1
Championship(s):	None

Further Reading
Official Web site: http://www.beastmantv.com/

ELLIS, JIMMY (1940–). Jimmy Ellis was a former world heavyweight champion often ignored by boxing historians because he held only a portion of the title during the time that the true champion—**Muhammad Ali**—was exiled from the sport for his draft-induction refusal. Yet, Ellis was a fine boxer with good skills who simply was not as good as the greats of his day such as Ali or **Joe Frazier.**

Born in 1940 in Louisville, Kentucky, Ellis knew Ali (then known as Cassius Clay) from an early age when both boxed under the guidance of police officer Joe Martin. Ellis even defeated Ali in an amateur bout in 1957. Ellis turned pro in 1961 as a middleweight. He won most of his bouts though he lost decisions to some of the top middleweights, men such as **Rubin "Hurricane" Carter** and **George Benton.** Clay (later Ali) often used Ellis as one of his primary sparring partners.

He moved up in weight and in the late 1960s began campaigning as a heavyweight. After Ali was stripped of the title, the **World Boxing Association (WBA)** held an elimination tournament to determine a new champion. Ellis defeated Leotis Martin, **Oscar Bonavena,** and **Jerry Quarry** to win the title in 1968. He successfully defended his title against former two-time champion **Floyd Patterson** before losing a unification bout with Frazier.

In 1971, he lost to Ali by decision and in 1973 lost in the first round to power-puncher **Earnie Shavers.** He finally retired in 1975.

Professional Record:	40-12-1
Championship(s):	WBA Heavyweight, 1968–1970

Further Reading
Anderson, Dave. "Louisville rooting for Ellis to Beat Bonavena Tomorrow." *The New York Times,* 12/1/1967, p. 60.
Anderson, Dave. "Ellis Is Not Cast in Clay's Mold." *The New York Times,* 12/4/1967, p. 91.
Hafner, Dan. "Ellis Counters With Own Counters." *Los Angeles Times,* 4/28/1968, p. I1.
Lewis, Anthony. "Ellis, Nose Broken, Retains Title." *The New York Times,* 9/15/1968, p. S1.

ELITE XC. Elite XC, or Elite Extreme Combat, is a mixed martial arts (MMA) promotion company that features regular shows broadcast on the cable station *SHOWTIME.* One of the key officials with Elite XC is its director, boxing promoter Gary Shaw. Founded in 2006, Elite XC serves as viable competition with the **Ultimate Fighting Championships (UFC)**—the most popular of MMA promotional companies. Elite XC features some of the top mixed martial artists in the world, such as **Robbie Lawler,** Renzo Gracie, **Frank Shamrock,** and others.

Elite XC gained ground when it signed a deal that allowed some of its promotions to be broadcast on CBS television. A star fighter with the company is Kevin Ferguson, better known as **Kimbo Slice**—the street brawler who achieved fame through his fights being shown on the Internet and YouTube. Other fighters fighting out of the Elite XC stable include power-punching middleweight Robbie Lawler and female fighting sensation **Gina Carano.**

Elite XC suffered a setback when the fighter it most promoted, street-fighting legend Kimbo Slice, lost badly to Seth Petruzelli in 13 seconds. The company appeared to be down for the count in the fall of 2008.

Further Reading
Arias, Carlos. "Elite XC gaining ground against mainstream UFC." *Orange County Register,* 10/25/2007.
Official Web site: http://www.elitexc.com
Pugmire, Lance. "Mixed Martial Arts' Elite XC to file bankruptcy." *Los Angeles Times,* 10/22/2008, at http://articles.latimes.com/2008/oct/22/sports/sp-mma22

EMELIANENKO, FEDOR (1976–). Fedor Emelianenko, "the Last Emperor," is considered by many to be the best and most dangerous mixed martial artist in the world. Though a heavyweight, many mixed martial arts (MMA) experts consider Fedor as the best pound-for-pound practitioner in the sport today. Though he sports a relatively unimpressive physique, Fedor possesses amazing technique, devastating power in his right hand, and an eerie-like calm in the midst of combat.

Trained in the Russian art of **sambo,** Emelianenko earned a bronze medal in 1998 in the Russian Judo Championship. Known for his "ground and pound" assault, Emelianenko has lost only one fight in MMA competition on cuts (after an illegal elbow) to Tsuyoshi Kohsaka in December 2000—a defeat he easily avenged in April 2005.

In March 2003 at **PRIDE** 25, Emelianenko upset heavyweight champion **Antonio Rodrigo Nogueira** with a convincing unanimous decision. Emelianenko showed no fear in taking the submission master to the ground and pounding him for much of the fight. Only Nogueira's granite jaw saved him from a kayo loss. Emelianenko has defeated a who's who list of great heavyweight fighters, including **Mirko "Cro Cop" Filipovic, Mark Hunt, Mark Coleman, Kevin Randleman, Matt Lindland,** and **Gary Goodridge.** Rumors continue to circulate that **Ultimate Fighting Championships (UFC)**—which purchased PRIDE FC in 2007—will bring Emelianenko to the Octagon to fight in the UFC. Most MMA fans welcome this possibility.

However, in late 2007, it was announced that Emelianenko has signed with Global-1 and would not fight in the UFC. In December 2007, he defeated Korean kickboxer **Hong Man Choi** at Yarennoka! via submission in the first round. In July 2008, Fedor showed the world why he is revered in mixed martial arts with a devastating 36-second annihilation of former UFC champion **Tim Sylvia.**

Professional MMA Record: 29-1
Championship(s):   PRIDE Heavyweight, 2003–2007

Further Reading
Arritt, Dan. "Making some noise." *The Los Angeles Times,* 7/17/2008, p. D3.
Caplan, Sam. "Who Can Beat Fedor?" *FIGHT!* (September 2007), pp. 32–35.
"Fedor Emelianenko wins in Pride Fighting Championships' U.S. Debut." *The Canadian Press,* 10/22/2006.
Official Web site: fedor.bel.ru/index_eng.shtml
Pugmire, Lance. "Face Value: Emelianenko Doesn't Reveal Much About Himself, but Opponents Have Found Out More than They Want to Know About his Ability," *Los Angeles Times,* 1/22/2009, SPORTS, p. 8.

ESCALERA, ALFREDO (1952–). Alfredo "El Salsero" Escalera was a former junior lightweight world champion from Puerto Rico known for his punishing style, quick hands, and charismatic personality. He wore elaborate-colored robes into the ring, danced to salsa music, and sometimes showcased his pet boa constrictor.

Born in 1952 in Carolina, Puerto Rico, Escalera turned pro in 1970 and suffered some tough moments early in his career. He lost his third pro bout and then in 1971 lost a decision to undefeated prospect Edwin Viruet. He rebounded, developed his skills, and earned a title shot against **World Boxing Council (WBC)** champion Kuniaki Shibata in Japan. Escalera destroyed the champion in the second round.

He successfully defended his title 10 times, including two wins over Buzzsaw Yanabe and a disputed decision over **Tyrone Everett,** before facing the legendary **Alexis Arguello** in Bayamon, Puerto Rico. In a brutal fight known as "the Bloody Battle of Bayamon," Arguello prevailed in the 13th round. Escalera lost the rematch a year later. He continued to fight, retiring in 1983 after losing a decision to Charlie "Choo Choo" Brown. His son Alfredo Escalera Jr. is a promising fighter in the cruiserweight division.

Professional Record: 53-14-3
Championship(s):   WBC junior lightweight, 1975–1978

Further Reading
Brady, Dave. "Escalera Knocks Out Beccaril in 8th." *The Washington Post,* 5/17/1977, p. D1.
Malinowski, Scoop. "Boxing Legend Profile: Alfredo Escalera." *KO Boxing 2002,* p. 71.
Ryan, Joan. "Quick Fists and 'Gritos' Keep Escalera in Boas." *The Washington Post,* 5/12/1977, p. 80.

ESCH, ERIC "BUTTERBEAN" (1968–). Eric Esch, a former Toughman competitor, is better known by his nickname "Butterbean," which describes his massive size and rotund body. While many boxing purists regard Butterbean as little more than a sideshow, he has managed to garner nearly 80 victories in his professional boxing career.

He won numerous Toughman competitions before turning professional in boxing in 1994. He called himself "the King of the Four Rounders" as he barnstormed around the country, kayo-ing hapless opponents in four-round bouts. In 2002, Esch received his biggest opportunity when he faced a 53-year-old **Larry Holmes.** The ex-champion controlled the action with his domi-nant left jab, though Butterbean went the distance and even scored a knockdown in the final round.

Butterbean also has tried his hand at professional mixed martial arts. He made his debut in mixed martial arts (MMA) at a K-1 event in 2003. He now fights more in mixed martial arts than he does in boxing. He holds victories in MMA over Wesley Correira, James Thompson, and Zuluzinho.

Professional Boxing Record:	77-7-4
Professional MMA Record:	11-7-1
Professional Kickboxing Record:	2-4
Championship(s):	None

Further Reading
Greig, Murray. "Been There, Done That; Globe-trotting boxer Eric Esch—a.k.a. Butterbean—set to shake up MMA." *Edmonton Sun,* 11/21/2007, p. S7.
Hernandez, Dylan, "Butterbean Not Just a Novelty Act in His Eyes." *San Jose Mercury News,* 7/22/2004, p. 1D.
Wade, Don. "Bean Stalk; Giant Boxer Hunts Fame, While Pounding For Fun." *Commercial Appeal,* 5/28/1999, p. D1.

ESPADAS, GUTY, JR. (1974–). Guty Espadas, Jr., is a former world featherweight champion and the son of former world champion **Guty Espadas, Sr.** The pair are the first father and son pair to win a world championship—followed by **Leon Spinks** and Cory Spinks. Born in 1974 in Merida YC, Mexico, Espadas, Jr., turned pro in 1992 and won his first 19 bouts before losing to cagey veteran Darryl Pinckney in 1996. Four years later in 2000, Espadas defeated Luisito Es-pinosa to win the vacant **World Boxing Council (WBC)** featherweight championship. He suc-cessfully defended his title once before losing via a close, unanimous decision to undefeated **Erik "El Terrible" Morales.** He initially retired after a bad loss to Rocky Juarez in 2004. He returned to the ring in 2007 and won three straight bouts in hopes of reclaiming past glory.

Professional Record:	44-7
Championship(s):	WBC featherweight, 2000–2001

Further Reading
Arias, Carlos. "Espadas Runs Winning Streak to 10 Bouts." *Orange County Register,* 8/10/1999, p. D2.
Feour, Royce. "For Espadas, boxing is true blood sport." *Las Vegas Review Journal,* 2/17/2001, p. 1C.

ESPADAS, GUTY, SR. (1954–). Guty Espadas, Sr., is a former world flyweight champion whose son by the same name later won a world title as well. Born in 1954 in Merida YC, Mexico, Espadas turned pro in 1971 and didn't lose a professional bout until his 26th bout. In 1976, he upset undefeated champion Alfonso Lopez to win the **World Boxing Association (WBA)**

flyweight belt. He successfully defended his title four times—including a rematch win over Lopez—before losing a majority 15-round decision to Venezuelan **Betulio Gonzalez** in Venezuela. He later challenged **World Boxing Council (WBC)** champion **Chan-Hee Park** in South Korea but was stopped by the power puncher in two rounds. He retired in 1984 after losing to **Payao Poontorat** for the WBC super flyweight championship.

Professional Record:	39-6-5
Championship(s):	WBA flyweight, 1976–1978

Further Reading
Hawn, Jack. "Espada Scores Kayo in 13th, Wins Flyweight Title." *Los Angeles Times*, 10/3/1976, p. C3.
Hawn, Jack. "Guty Espadas: A Heavy Hitter at 110 Pounds." *Los Angeles Times*, 11/16/1977, p. E8.
United Press International. "Espadas Wins in 7th, Keeps Title." *The New York Times*, 1/2/1977, p. 127.

EUBANK, CHRIS (1966–). One of the more interesting characters in boxing in recent times, Christopher Livingstone Eubank held the World Boxing Organization (WBO) super middleweight title from 1990–1995, successfully defending his belt 17 times before losing to **Steve Collins.** Eubank had an incredible ability to absorb punishment—and dish it out. He also held the WBO middleweight title during his impressive career. In many ways he lived up to his nickname "Simply the Best."

Born in London, England, in 1964, Eubank turned pro in 1985 and won his first 25 bouts before landing an opportunity at the vacant WBO middleweight champion against fellow unbeaten fighter Dan Sherry. Eubank prevailed in the 10th round. He made two successful defenses before moving up in weight to fight for the WBO super middleweight championship.

He won the title with a close decision win over Michael Watson that saw both fighters hit the canvas. Tragically, Watson spent 40 days in a coma and suffered permanent paralysis after the bout. Eubank then enjoyed a long reign. He nearly added the **World Boxing Council (WBC)** belt to his collection, fighting a draw with **Nigel Benn.** He finally lost his title on a close decision loss to Collins in 1995.

He retired in 1998 after two close losses to Carl Thompson for the WBO cruiserweight title. In his colorful career, Eubank defeated the likes of Graciano Rocchigiani, Nigel Benn, Thulani Malinga, and Michael Watson.

Professional Record:	45-5-2
Championship(s):	WBO middleweight, 1991; WBO super middleweight, 1991–1995

Further Reading
Eubank, Chris. *Eubank: The Autobiography.* London: McGraw-Hill, 2004.
Hawkey, Ian. "Eubank facing great weight of expectation." *The Sunday Mirror*, 10/5/1997, p. 15.
Official Web site: http://www.chriseubank.com
Sheehan, Pat. "He's back with a world title crack." *The Sun*, 10/2/1997, p. 60.

EVANS, "SUGAR" RASHAD (1979–) "Sugar" Rashad Evans continues to confound the critics with his success as a mixed martial artist. This still-undefeated fighter is the current **UFC** light heavyweight champion and former winner on the *Ultimate Fighter* **2**. Evans has used his wrestling background, speed, agility, and has developed striking skills to become one of the top mixed martial artists in the world. Born in 1979 in Niagara Falls, New York, Evans excelled at both football and wrestling in high school. He attended a community college in his hometown, where he won a national junior college wrestling championship. He then transferred to Michigan State University where he continued his wrestling career.

He turned professional in mixed martial arts in 2004 and received his big break when he earned a spot on *The Ultimate Fighter* in the heavyweight division, which he won with a win in the finals over the larger Brad Imes. After winning the season series, Evans continued his winning ways in the Octagon in the 205-pound light heavyweight division. The only blemish on his undefeated record was a draw to former champion **Tito Ortiz** in July 2007. Evans earned a title shot with a devastating one-punch knockout of another former champion, **Chuck "the Iceman" Liddell**, in September 2008. Evans then confounded the critics again with a knockout win over **Forrest Griffin** to capture the light heavyweight belt.

Professional Record: 13-0-1
Championship(s):   UFC lightheavyweight, 2008–

Further Reading
Gleason, Bucky. "Packing a Punch." *Buffalo News*, 12/27/2008, p. B1.
Official Web site: http://www.rashadevans.tv/
Rodriguez, Miguel. "Wrestler Ready to Take It to Higher Level." *Buffalo News*, 6/6/2004, p. NC5.

EVERETT, TYRONE (1953–1977). Tyrone Everett—"Ty the Fly"—was a talented southpaw boxer who should have been a world champion if not for one of the worst decisions in boxing history. Born in 1953 in Philadelphia, Everett turned pro in 1971 and amazed observers with his natural ability to avoid punches.

In the words of Nigel Collins, "The only fight he ever lost was probably fixed." On November 30, 1976, Everett faced champion **Alfredo Escalera** for the **World Boxing Council (WBC)** super featherweight title. By ringside accounts, Everett won at least 10 of the 15 rounds. However, the judges scored the bout a split-decision victory for Escalera—ironically, in Everett's hometown of Philadelphia. In 1977, Everett won two fights to ready himself for a rematch with Escalera until tragedy struck. His girlfriend shot Everett to death in May 1977.

Professional Record: 36-1
Championship(s):   None

Further Reading
Collins, Nigel. *Boxing Babylon: Behind the Shadowy World of the Prize Ring*. New York: Citadel Press, 1990.
"Tyrone Everett, Boxer, Dies of Bullet Wounds." *The New York Times*, 5/27/1977, p. 24.

FABER, URIJAH (1979–). Urijah Faber is a mixed martial artist from America who has had great success in the World Extreme Cagefighting (WEC) organization. Born in 1979 in Isla Vista, California, at home with the assistance of a midwife, Faber was raised by parents he described as "religious hippies."

Faber achieved success as a wrestler in high school. He continued wrestling at the University of California-Davis where he also earned a degree in human development, graduating with a 3.3 GPA. Upon graduation, he worked part time as a wrestling coach at his alma mater.

He turned professional in mixed martial arts (MMA) in 2003 in a Gladiator Challenge (GC) bout. He won the GC featherweight title with a convincing win over David Velasquez. In 2006, he won the WEC featherweight championship with a win over Cole Escobedo. He has compiled a record of 20-1, for years his only loss was to Tyson Griffin. Faber cemented his status as on of MMA's best with a convincing five-round decision win over former **Ultimate Fighting Championships (UFC)** champion **Jens Pulver.** However, he suffered an upset loss to Mike Brown in November 2008. He hopes to return to the pinnacle of mixed martial arts in 2009 and beyond.

Professional MMA Record:	22-2
Championship(s):	WEC featherweight, 2006—2008

Further Reading

Official Web site http://www.urijahfaber.com/

Robertson, Blair Anthony. "'California Kid' stands tall; He's a 5-foot-6 mass of muscle who drops bigger foes in a flash." *Sacramento Bee*, 1/15/2008, p. B1.

Ross, Matthew. "Urijah Faber: Why the California Kid Is Ready to Blow Up." *Fight!* (Dec. 2007), pp. 38–46.

FENECH, JEFF (1964–). Jeff Fenech was a world champion from Australia who captured titles in three different weight divisions. Some consider Fenech as the greatest boxer to ever hail from Australia. Born in 1964 in Sydney, Fenech turned pro in 1984 and captured the **International Boxing Federation (IBF)** world bantamweight championship in only his seventh pro bout against Satoshi Shingaki. In 1987, he captured the **World Boxing Council (WBC)** super bantamweight crown with a third-round stoppage of Samart Payakaroon. In 1988, he won the WBC featherweight crown with a 10th-round stoppage of Victor Callejas. He would have added a title in a fourth weight division but was awarded only a draw against the great **Azumah Nelson** for the WBC super featherweight title in 1991. He retired in 1996 after losing badly to Philip Holiday in an attempt for the IBF lightweight title. He remains a top trainer in the sport, including a stint as the trainer for former heavyweight champion **Mike Tyson.**

In June 2008, he returned to the ring in his 40s to face his old nemesis Nelson. Fenech captured a 10-round majority decision.

Professional Record:	29-3-1
Championship(s):	IBF bantamweight, 1987–1988; WBC super bantamweight, 1988; WBC featherweight, 1988–1989

Further Reading
Cowley, Michael. "Fenech has bout of humility after being voted Australia's greatest boxer." *Sydney Morning Herald*, 2/4/2003, p. 32.
Doogan, Brian. "Jeff Fenech: 'I've Worked My Ass Off To Get Where I Am Today.'" *The Ring* (August 2002), pp. 42–46.

FIGG, JAMES (1695–1734). Known as the "Father of Boxing," Figg is considered the first heavyweight champion of boxing in England. Born in 1695, Figg excelled in many sports, including fencing and swording. He later turned his attention to bare-knuckle boxing. He catapulted to fame in part because of his friendship with artist William Hogarth who called his friend the "master of the noble science of defence" (Roberts, p. 28). He later established Figg's Amphitheatre in London where he staged boxing matches. Figg spent much time teaching the art of self-defense, including his pupil George Taylor. He held well-known victories over Ned Sutton, Tom Stokes, and Bill Flanders.

Record:	Unknown
Championship(s):	English Champion, 1719–1734

Further Reading
Mee, Bob. *Bare Fists: The History of Bare-Knuckle Prize Fighting*. New York: Harper Collins Willow, 2000.
Roberts, James B., and Alexander B. Skutt. *The Boxing Register* (4th ed.). Ithaca, NY: McBooks Pressw, Inc., 2006, p. 28.

FILIPOVIC, MIRKO "CRO COP" (1974–). Mirko Filipovic is a former top kickboxer and current mixed martial arts (MMA) practitioner known for his devastating kicks. His left leg may be the single most deadly striking weapon in the entire MMA community. Fans across the world call him "Cro Cop" as he is a former Croatian police officer who served in an antiterrorism unit.

He was an accomplished amateur boxer before devoting himself to kickboxing and later mixed martial arts. In 1996, he entered a K-1 Grand Prix event and defeated Jerome Le Banner before falling to the legendary **Ernesto Hoost.** In kickboxing, he holds wins over **Remy Bonjasky, Mark Hunt,** and the goliath **Bob Sapp.** He faced the best kickboxers in the world, dropping three fights to the great Hoost.

In MMA, he fought mainly in **PRIDE** and then in the **Ultimate Fighting Championships (UFC).** He made his MMA debut in 2001 with a victory over **Kazuyuki Fujita.** In 2002, he stopped the great Japanese veteran Kazayuki Sakuraba. In 2003, he stopped **Heath Herring** and **Igor Vovchanchyn** in consecutive first-round knockouts. He later fought Brazilian jiu-jitsu master **Antonio Rodrigo Nogueira** and lost via an armbar submission in the second round.

He holds victories in MMA over **Josh Barnett, Ron Waterman, Kevin Randleman,** and **Mark Coleman.** In 2005, he gave PRIDE champion **Fedor Emelianenko** a tough bout before losing a decision.

In 2007, Cro Cop moved to the UFC. He won his first bout over Eddie Sanchez, but then suffered a devastating kayo loss against Gabriel Gonzaga in a huge upset and then a decision loss to Cheick Kongo. He left the UFC after those losses and now fights in DREAM, a Japan-based mixed martial arts organization. In his last bout, he stopped **Hong Man Choi.** Because of his unique striking ability, Cro Cop remains a fan favorite.

Professional Kickboxing Record:	16-7
Professional MMA Record:	24-6
Championship(s):	None

Further Reading
Davidson, Neil. "Cro Cop: Fighter-turned politician makes UFC debut Saturday night in Las Vegas." *The Canadian Press*, 2/2/2007.
Official Web site: http://www.mirko-crocop.com/

FITCH, JON (1978–). Jon Fitch is an exciting mixed martial artist who is one of the top welterweights in the **Ultimate Fighting Championships (UFC)** and the world. Born in 1978 in Fort Wayne, Indiana, Fitch wrestled collegiately at Purdue University where he graduated with a bachelor's in physical education. He turned professional in mixed martial arts in 2002 and lost two of his first three bouts as a light heavyweight. He made his UFC debut in October 2005 at UFC: Ultimate Fight Night 2, defeating Brock Larson. Since then, Fitch has reeled off six more victories in the Octagon, including a decision win over Diego Sanchez at UFC 76: Knockout. Though most proficient in wrestling, Fitch holds a brown belt in Brazilian jiu-jitsu. He has earned his record in the Octagon with excellent stand-up striking abilities as well as a solid ground game.

In August 2008, Fitch challenged pound-for-pound great and UFC welterweight champion **Georges St.-Pierre.** Fitch fought well but lost a unanimous five-round decision.

Professional MMA Record:	19-3
Championship(s):	None

Further Reading
Fraser, Bear. "Jon Fitch: Welterweights Beware." *FIGHT!* (February 2008), pp. 66–68.
Official Web site: http://www.fitchfighter.com/
Sievert, Steve. "Fitch Still Waiting for Big Time Test." *The Houston Chronicle*, 5/14/2007, SPORTS, p. 7.

FITZSIMMONS, BOB (1863–1917). Bob Fitzsimmons, known as "Ruby Robert," was a great boxer who held the middleweight, light heavyweight, and heavyweight championships during his long career. Born in England in 1863, his family moved to New Zealand and then Australia. Fitzsimmons showed great prowess in the hammer-throw and long distance running. Perhaps this explains Fitzsimmons remarkable power and endurance, qualities he later used to great advantage in the boxing ring.

In 1891, Fitzsimmons stopped **Jack "the Nonpareil" Dempsey** to win the middleweight title. He dropped Dempsey 13 rounds in the bout. In 1897, he defeated **James "Gentleman Jim"**

Corbett for the heavyweight title. Fitzsimmons recovered from a 6th-round knockdown to stop Corbett with a body shot—his famous solar plexus punch—in the 14th round. The *Washington Post* editorialized that Fitzsimmons was a "nervy fighter." In his first title defense, he lost to the much larger **James J. Jeffries** in the 11th round. In 1903, he decisioned George Gardner to win the newly created light heavyweight division.

Record:	54-8-7 with 17 no decisions
Championship(s):	Middleweight, 1891–1897; Light Heavyweight, 1903–1904; Heavyweight, 1897–1897.

Further Reading

"A Nervy Fighter." *The Washington Post*, 9/21/1913, p. S2.

Donovan, Mike. "Mike Donovan Discusses the Best Men in the Ring." *Los Angeles Times*, 2/8/1891, p. 10.

Webb, Dale. *Prize Fighter: The Life and Times of Bob Fitzsimmons.* Edinburgh: Mainstream Publishing, 2000.

FLEISCHER, NAT (1887–1972). Nat Fleischer was the founder of *The Ring* magazine, revered by nearly everyone in the fight game as a true devotee of the sport he loved dearly. Born in 1887 in New York City, Fleischer graduated from City College in 1908 and then pursued journalism as a career. He worked for the *New York Press* and the *Morning Sun.*

He began *The Ring* magazine's tradition of ranking boxers. He also published an annual record book that became the authoritative source. He wrote many books on boxing, including his *50 Years at Ringside, Black Dynamite: A Five Volume History of the Negro Race in Boxing,* and *Gentleman Jim: The Life Story of James J. Corbett.*

Fleischer also judged and refereed more than a thousand fights in his life.

Further Reading

Fleischer, Nat. *50 Years at Ringside.* New York: Fleet Publishing Corporation, 1958.

Fleischer, Nat. *The Heavyweight Championship: An Informal History of Heavyweight Boxing from 1719 to the Present Day* (rev. ed.). New York: G.P Putnam's Sons, 1961.

FLETCHER, FRANK (1954–). Frank "the Animal" Fletcher was never a world champion, but he thrilled millions with his nonstop, action style that led to a series of brawls. Born in 1954 in Philadelphia, the southpaw slugger turned pro in 1976 and lived up to the reputation of his city. He absorbed tremendous punishment in numerous fights, but for a period of time in the 1980s he was a top-ranked contender. He earned that status by defeating the likes of Norberto Sabater, Ernie Singletary, Tony Braxton, Clint "the Executioner" Jackson, and James "Hard Rock" Green.

Fletcher's swarming style made for great action fights, and he became a favorite on NBC, which broadcast several of his bouts, including his memorable 1982 war with Green. Fletcher's career began to turn for the downside when he lost to Wilford Scypion in 1983. A year later he suffered a terrible beating at the hands of power-punching **John "the Beast" Mugabi,** who stopped Fletcher in the fourth round. He retired in 1985 after suffering another loss to Curtis Parker. He had two brothers—Anthony and Troy—who also boxed professionally.

Professional Record:	18-6-1
Championship(s):	None

Further Reading

"How Many Wars Can One Man Survive?" *Knockout* (Summer 1994), pp. 23–25, 65.

Lidz, Frank. "Mother Fletcher." *Sports Illustrated*, 4/18/1983.

FLORIAN, KENNY (1976–). Kenny Florian is a top mixed martial artist known for his appearance on *The Ultimate Fighter* 1 and exciting bouts with Drew Fickett, Diego Sanchez, and **Sean Sherk.** Born in 1976 in Westwood, Massachusetts, Florian excelled at athletics. He earned a college scholarship playing soccer for Boston College where he graduated with a degree in communications.

He made his professional mixed martial arts (MMA) debut in 2003 and attracted the eye of the **Ultimate Fighting Championships (UFC)** in a close loss to Drew Fickett in a Combat Zone bout in 2004. Florian's skills earned him a spot on *The Ultimate Fighter 1* where he excelled, losing a narrow decision to Diego Sanchez in the finals. He rebounded with three straight wins in the UFC before losing a five-round decision to Sherk for the UFC lightweight championship. Since that loss, he has won six straight bouts at the time of this writing, including an impressive decision win over **Roger Huerta** at UFC 87 in August 2008.

Professional MMA Record: 11-3
Championship(s):   None

Further Reading
Caplan, Sam. "Five Ounces of Pain: Q & A with UFC's Kenny Florian." *cbssportsline.com*, 11/23/2007, at http://cbs.sportsline.com/mmaboxing/story/10491660/1
Official Web site: http://www.kennyflorian.com/
Pratt, Mark. "Soft-Spoken Linguist now gets his Kicks from Ultimate Fighting." *The Associated Press*, 3/17/2007.
Walker, Andrew. "Interview: Kenny Florian." *EXTREME FIGHTER* (March 2008), pp. 44–45.

FLOWERS, THEODORE (1895–1927). Theodore "Tiger" Flowers was the first African American middleweight champion who defeated the great **Harry Greb** to capture the title in 1926. Born in 1895 in Camile, Georgia, Flowers turned professional in 1918 at the age of 23. He defeated Greb in 1926 to win the world middleweight title but lost it the next year in a horrible decision to **Mickey Walker.** Many consider it to be one of the worst decisions in boxing history. His biographer Andrew Kaye writes: "The decision … united true sports fans and scribes alike in loud condemnation of the judges and referee" (p. 92). Flowers was known as "the Georgia Deacon" for his pious ways. Legend has it that he would recite a passage from Psalms upon every entrance into the ring. He died in 1927 after surgery to remove scar tissue from his eyes—ironically, the same procedure that killed Greb.

Professional Record: 115-14-16
Championship(s):   Middleweight, 1926

Further Reading
Kaye, Andrew M. *The Pussycat of Prizefighting: Tiger Flowers and the Politics of Black Celebrity.* Athens: The University of Georgia Press, 2004.
Roberts, James B., and Alexander Skutt. *The Boxing Register: International Boxing Hall of Fame Official Record Book* (4th ed.). Ithaca, NY: McBooks Press, Inc., 2006, pp. 122–123.

FOREMAN, GEORGE (1949–). "Big" George Foreman is a former two-time world heavyweight champion who has used his magnetic personality to become not only a commercial success but a cultural icon. Born in 1949 in Marshall, Texas, Foreman's family moved to Houston where he headed in the wrong direction as a juvenile. He received some direction and learned boxing after joining the Job Corps.

"Big" George Foreman attends the Juan Diaz-Michael Katsidas fight in his hometown of Houston, Texas in September 2008. Courtesy of Chris Cozzone.

Foreman captured the Olympic gold medal in 1968 and then turned pro in 1969. A human wrecking ball, Foreman pummeled his way to the heavyweight title, crushing **Joe Frazier** in two rounds to win the crown in 1973. He made two successful defenses before losing in a great upset to **Muhammad Ali** in Zaire in the **"Rumble in the Jungle."** Foreman did well early but fell into Ali's rope-a-dope tactic and punched himself out. Foreman—then a sullen man—retired from the ring in 1977 after another upset loss to Jimmy Young.

While in his dressing room from the Young loss, Foreman underwent a religious experience. He turned his life to God and became a preacher. His personality changed from a sullen, brooding brute to friendly and charismatic. He started a center for underprivileged youth and developed great speaking skills. In 1987, Foreman announced to the shock of many that he was coming back to boxing. Critics scoffed at the notion that an overweight Foreman could make an impact in the sport but he proved everyone wrong. In 1990, he stopped **Gerry Cooney** in round two, and in 1991, he fought **Evander Holyfield** 12 hard rounds for the heavyweight title. Though he lost, Foreman earned kudos for his performance. He persevered and in 1994 received another title shot against the unbeaten **Michael Moorer.** Losing badly in the 10th round, Foreman delivered a short right cross that kayoed Moorer. At 45, he became the oldest heavyweight champ in boxing history. *The Ring* magazine has called it the greatest comeback in boxing history. He retired in 1997 after a dubious decision loss to **Shannon Briggs.**

In retirement, Foreman continued to make millions on commercials and his famous Foreman grilling machines. He also served for many years as a ringside announcer for HBO. He remains a beloved figure in American society.

Professional Record:	76-5
Championship(s):	Heavyweight, 1973–1974; WBA heavyweight, 1994; IBF heavyweight, 1994–1995

Further Reading

Evans, Gavin. "Great Career Comebacks: How 10 Fighters Reinvented Themselves and Changed Boxing History." *The Ring* (October 2005), pp. 55–65.

Foreman, George, and Joel Engel. *By George: The Autobiography of George Foreman.* New York: Simon & Schuster, 2000.

Foreman, George, and Ken Abraham. *God In My Corner: A Spiritual Memoir.* Nashville, TN: Thomas Nelson, 2007.

Official Web site: http://www.georgeforeman.com

FORREST, VERNON (1971–). Vernon Forrest is a stylish boxer who has won world championships in the welterweight and junior middleweight divisions. Born in 1971 in Augusta, Georgia, Forrest had a stellar amateur career and represented the United States at the 1992 Barcelona Olympic Games. Unfortunately, he lost in the first round to Great Britain's Peter Richardson on points.

He turned pro in 1992 and received his first world title shot in 2000 against Raul Frank for the vacant **International Boxing Federation (IBF)** welterweight championship. Unfortunately, a clash of heads ended the fight as a no-contest, and Forrest had to wait another year for the rematch. He defeated Frank in the rematch to win the title by unanimous decision. In 2002, he received his big opportunity—a match against **World Boxing Council (WBC)** champion "Sugar" **Shane Mosley.** Forrest dominated over 12 rounds to win the belt and respect for the larger boxing public. He also defeated Mosley in a rematch.

In 2003, he lost his title to hard punching Nicaraguan **Ricardo Mayorga,** who stopped Forrest in the third round. He also lost a close decision in the rematch with Mayorga. Forrest regrouped and in 2007 defeated Carlos Baldomir for the **World Boxing Association (WBA)** junior middleweight title. He lost his title in 2008 to the awkward **Sergio Mora,** but regained it later that year in September with a throwback performance.

Vernon Forrest punishes Sergio Mora in their September 2008 rematch. Forrest won a lopsided unanimous decision. Courtesy of Chris Cozzone.

Professional Record: 41-3
Championship(s):   IBF welterweight, 2001–2002; WBC welterweight,
                                            2002–2003; WBA junior middleweight 2007–2008,
                                            2008–

Further Reading
Hudson, David L., Jr. "Vernon Forrest: A Champion in Search of Respect." *Fightnews.com*, 2/7/2002.
Official Web site: http://www.vernonforrest.com/
Raskin, Eric. "Vernon Forrest: He Took Out 'All The Pain And Frustration' On Mosley." *World Boxing*
    (July 2002), pp. 44–48.
Wong, Edward. "Prophetic Forrest Revelation in the Ring." *The New York Times*, 1/28/2002, p. D4.

FOSTER, BOB (1938–). Bob Foster arguably was the greatest light heavyweight champion in boxing history, dominating the division for the late 1960s and early 1970s. Possessed with tremendous power in a lanky frame, Foster dominated the 175 lb. division but could not defeat the top heavyweights. Foster won the light heavyweight title in 1968 with a fourth-round stoppage of **Dick Tiger,** earning Fighter of the Year honors that year from the Boxing Writers Association. He never lost the belt, announcing his retirement after retaining his title via 15-round draw against Jorge Victor Ahumada in September 1974. He returned to the ring in 1975 but retired in 1978 after consecutive losses. Foster failed in 1970 to capture the heavyweight title, losing in the second round to undefeated champion "Smokin'" **Joe Frazier.**

Professional record: 56-8-1
Championship(s):   Light Heavyweight, 1968–1974

Bob Foster was perhaps the greatest light heavyweight of all time. Courtesy of NewMexicoBoxing.com collection.

Further Reading
Anderson, Dave. "Foster Knocks Out Tiger in Fourth
    Round and Wins Light Heavyweight Crown."
    The New York Times, 5/25/1968, p. 39.
Brady, Dave. "Foster Adds New Toy to Collection." *The
    Washington Post*, 4/14/1969, p. D7.
Roberts, James B., and Alexander Skutt. *The Box-
    ing Register: International Boxing Hall of Fame
    Official Record Book* (4th ed.). Ithaca, NY: Mc
    Books Press, Inc., 2006, pp. 386–389.

FRANCA, HERMES (1974–). Hermes Franca is a Brazilian mixed martial artist known for his unorthodox fighting style, distinctively colored hair, and undeniable knockout power. Franca will often fight off his back, looking to catch opponents with a dizzying array of strikes from unusual angles.

Born in 1974 in Fortaleza, Brazil, Franca made his professional mixed martial arts (MMA) debut in 2001 at a HooknShoot event. He won six straight bouts before earning the attention of the **Ultimate Fighting Championships (UFC),** which signed him to fight for the first time in 2003 at UFC 42: Sudden Impact. Franca won his first two UFC bouts before losing two close decisions to Josh Thomson and Yves Edwards.

In 2006, Franca defeated Gabe Ruedinger to win the World Extreme Cagefighting's lightweight championship. That began a seven-fight win streak that included a series of submission or kayo wins over the likes of Joe Jordan and Nathan Diaz. Perhaps his most impressive win was catching Diaz in an armbar in October 2006 to successfully defend his WEC lightweight championship.

In July 2007, Franca lost a unanimous decision to **Sean Sherk** for the UFC lightweight championship—after which both fighters tested positive for steroids. Franca admitted he took the steroid Drostanolone to accelerate the healing of his ankle. He returned to the Octagon after a suspension to face Frankie Edgar. Though he lost a unanimous decision in July 2008, he showed he still possesses strong punching power and submission skills. He won his last bout in October 2008 and hopes to move up the ranks in 2009.

Professional MMA Record: 19-7
Championship(s): None

Further Reading
Bradley, Patrick. "Elbows In: UFC Lightweight Hermes Franca Crafts His Return." *FIGHT!* (August 2008), pp. 98–100.

FRANKLIN, RICH (1974–). Rich "Ace" Franklin is an American-based mixed martial artist and the former **Ultimate Fighting Championships (UFC)** middleweight champion. Born in 1974 in Cincinnati, Ohio, Franklin earned an undergraduate degree and a masters in education from the University of Cincinnati.

He turned professional in mixed martial arts (MMA) in 2000 with a win over Rob Smith at Extreme Challenge 31. In 2003, he made his UFC debut at UFC 42: Sudden Impact with a first-round stoppage of **Evan Tanner.** In June 2005, he again defeated Tanner at UFC 53: Heavy Hitters to win the middleweight championship. He successfully defended his title twice against Nathan Quarry and David Loiseau before losing via strikes in the first round to **Anderson Silva** in October 2006 at UFC 64: Unstoppable.

He rebounded with two wins in 2007 in the Octagon to earn a rematch with Silva at UFC 77: Hostile Territory. Silva again stopped Franklin via strikes—this time in the second round. Franklin rebounded with wins over Travis Lutter and **Matt Hamill**. He then lost a close decision to "Dangerous" **Dan Henderson.**

Franklin is a versatile mixed martial artist—strong in jiu-jitsu, wrestling, and Muay Thai kickboxing. In addition, Franklin possesses amazing cardio and conditioning. His only MMA losses are to Silva, the talented **Lyoto Machida,** and Henderson.

Professional MMA Record: 24-4
Championship(s): UFC Middleweight, 2005–2006

Further Reading
Chiapetta, Mike. "An Accidental Case of Superstardom: Rich Franklin Didn't Excel in Athletics Until Learning a Few Life Lessons." *FIGHT!* (October/November 2007), pp. 70–72.
Franklin, Rich "Ace," and Jon F. Merz, *The Complete Idiot's Guide to Ultimate Fighting.* Royersfield, PA: Alpha Publishing, 2007.
Official Web site: http://www.richfranklin.com/home.asp

FRAZIER, JOE (1944–). "Smokin'" Joe Frazier was a former world heavyweight champion best known for his epic rivalry with the great **Muhammad Ali.** Frazier's trademark left hook catapulted him to Olympic glory and professional greatness, but it was his courage that made him a hero to many boxing fans.

Born in 1944 in Beaumont, South Carolina, Frazier captured gold at the 1964 Tokyo Olympics after **Buster Mathis, Sr.** had to drop out because of injury. Frazier won the heavyweight championship with a convincing win over **Jimmy Ellis** in 1970. He defended the title several times, including the historic "Fight of the Century" in 1971 against Ali. The clash of the two undefeated heavyweights was one of the most significant fights in boxing history. Frazier dropped Ali in the 15th round and captured a unanimous decision victory.

He lost the title in 1973 to the mighty **George Foreman.** He lost to Ali twice—the last time in the famous **"Thrilla in Manila."** He initially retired in 1976 after losing to Foreman for the second time. He came out of retirement in 1981 but was held to a draw by journeyman Floyd "Jumbo" Cummings. Frazier's son Marvis was a heavyweight contender.

Professional Record:	32-4-1
Championship(s):	Heavyweight, 1970–1973

Further Reading

Brunt, Stephen. *Facing Ali: 15 Fighters, 15 Stories.* Guilford, Conn.: Lyons Press, 2002, pp. 101–127.

Frazier, Joe, and Phil Berger. *Smokin Joe: The Autobiography of a Heavyweight Champion of the World, Smokin' Joe Frazier.* New York: MacMillan General Reference, 1996.

Kram, Mark. *Ghosts of Manila: The Fateful Blood Feud Between Muhammad Ali and Joe Frazier.* New York: HarperCollins, 2001.

Pepe, Phil. *Come Out Smokin': Joe Frazier, The Champ Nobody Knew.* New York: Coward McCann & Geoghegan, 1972.

FRYE, DON (1965–). Don "the Predator" Frye is a former mixed martial great who won the **Ultimate Fighting Championships (UFC)** 8 tournament and the Ultimate Ultimate 96 tournament. He also boxed professionally, earned All-American honors wrestling in college, and earned legions of fans for his action style of fighting. He was a progenitor for future mixed martial artists who master many disciplines of fighting. Frye's amateur wrestling experience, professional boxing resume, and study of judo made him more well-rounded as a fighter than many of his contemporaries.

Born in Sierra Vista, Arizona, in 1965, Frye earned a wrestling scholarship to Arizona State. There, he met future UFC legend **Dan "the Beast" Severn** at Arizona State while he was a freshman and Severn was an assistant coach. Frye later transferred to Oklahoma State to continue his wrestling career. One of his teammates was **Randy "the Natural" Couture.**

Frye tried his hand as a professional boxer, compiling a record of 5-2-1. He continued to work as a firefighter.

Frye later served as a training partner for Dan Severn when "the Beast" competed in and won the Ultimate Ultimate 95 tournament in the UFC. Severn encouraged Frye that he could be a force in mixed martial arts (MMA). In 1996, Frye entered the UFC 8 tournament. He began the tournament—and his professional MMA career—with a devastating knockout of the behemoth Thomas Ramirez. Frye charged across the ring and kayoed Ramirez with a right hand. The fight ended in eight seconds—still a UFC record.

Frye then defeated Sam Adkins and **Gary "Big Daddy" Goodridge** to win the UFC 8 tournament. He then won his bout on the UFC 9 card against Amaury Bitetti before entering the

UFC 10 tournament. Frye defeated Mark Hall and Brian Johnston before losing in the finals to powerful wrestler **Mark Coleman,** who outweighed Frye by 30 pounds. Coleman pounded Frye, but "the Predator" refused to submit or quit. Referee "Big" **John McCarthy** eventually stopped the fight. Frye cemented his legendary status by winning the Ultimate Ultimate 96 tournament, defeating Goodridge, Mark Hall, and then **David "Tank" Abbott** in the finals.

For several years, Frye then competed in professional wrestling in Japan. He returned to mixed martial arts when **PRIDE** offered him a contract in 2001. In his first PRIDE bout, he won on disqualification when his opponent Gilbert Yvel held onto the ropes several times during the bout. He then defeated Cyril Abidi before finally facing **Ken Shamroc**k at PRIDE 21. Frye won a split decision over Shamrock in a major and some would say historic MMA bout given the fame of both combatants.

Frye then waged an amazing slugfest with Japanese pro wrestler Yoshohiro Takayama. Many rate the Frye–Takayama bout as one of the greatest fights of all-time.

In 2002 and 2003, Frye lost three consecutive bouts to Coleman, Goodridge, and Hidehiko Yoshida. He continues to fight sporadically in mixed martial bouts.

Professional MMA Record: 19-6-1
Championship(s):   None (but won UFC 8 Tournament and Ultimate Ultimate 96 tournament)

Further Reading
Casey, Jim. "An Ode to a Legend—Fryestache." *FIGHT!* (April 2008), pp. 88–90.
Szostak, Mike. "Fighter Doesn't Understand the Furor." *Providence Journal-Bulletin,* 6/12/1996, p. 1D.
Wall, Jeremy. *UFC's Ultimate Warriors Top 10.* Ontario: ECW Press, 2005, pp. 111–127.

FUJITA, KAZUYUKI (1970–). Kazuyuki Fujita is a Japanese-based wrestler and mixed martial artist known as "Ironhead" for his incredible ability to absorb punishment and to recuperate quickly. Born in Funabashi, Japan, Fujita competed in wrestling for many years. He represented Japan in the World Cup wrestling tournament. He also was the national champion of his country in **Greco-Roman wrestling**.

After his decorated amateur wrestling career, Fujita became a pro wrestler in 1993. After several years in the pro wrestling circuit in Japan, Fujita began as a mixed martial artist.

Fujita is best known for numerous great bouts in **PRIDE,** including an incredible fight against PRIDE heavyweight champion **Fedor Emelianenko** at PRIDE 26: Bad to the Bone. Fujita hit Emelianenko with a left hook that left the Russian great nearly out on his feet. The resourceful Fedor recovered and submitted Fujita in the first round. Fujita holds wins over **Mark Kerr, Ken Shamrock,** and **Bob Sapp** in his mixed martial arts (MMA) career.

Professional MMA Record: 15-7
Championship(s):   None

Further Reading
Clifford, R. J. "Top Ten Toughest Chins in MMA." *Tapout,* No. 24 (2008), pp. 89–91.

FULLMER, GENE (1931–). Gene Fullmer was a former two-time world middleweight champion known for his rough-and-tumble style and never-say-die attitude. Born in 1931 in West Jordan, Utah, Fullmer turned pro in 1951 and won his first 29 bouts.

In 1957, he shocked the boxing world by outpointing the legendary **Sugar Ray Robinson** to win the middleweight title. He floored Robinson in the seventh round and pressed the action against the 35-year-old champion all night to earn a unanimous decision. In their rematch, Fullmer looked good early until he was kayoed by a single left hook. Many consider that one of the greatest knockouts in boxing history. Fullmer rebounded by defeating **Carmen Basilio** to win the middleweight title in 1959 and he held the title for several years, beating such great fighters as Robinson, **Benny "Kid" Paret,** and Spider Webb. He held his title until losing to **Dick Tiger** in 1962. He retired in 1963 after another loss to Tiger.

Professional Record: 55-6-3
Championship(s):   Middleweight, 1957; 1959–1962

Further Reading
Becker, Bill. "Fullmer Stops Basilio in 14th." *The New York Times,* 8/29/1959, p. 9.
Condon, David. "Fullmer Floors Robinson; Wins Title." *Chicago Daily Tribune,* 1/3/1957, p. D1.
Roberts, James B., and Alexander B. Skutt. *The Boxing Register* (4th ed.). Ithaca, NY: McBooks Pressw, Inc., 2006, pp. 394–397.
Smith, Wilfrid. "Robinson Knocks Out Fullmer in Fifth." *Chicago Daily Tribune,* 5/2/1957, p. D1.

FUTCH, EDDIE (1911–2001). Eddie Futch was a former amateur boxer who made his claim to fame as a great trainer. Born in 1911 in Hillsdale, Mississippi, Futch moved with his family to Detroit, Michigan. He compiled an impressive amateur record of 36-3 but could not turn pro because of a heart murmur. He made his name as a trainer of numerous world champions. During his long career, he worked with six heavyweight champions—**Ken Norton, Joe Frazier, Larry Holmes, Michael Spinks, Trevor Berbick,** and **Riddick Bowe.** Futch was best known for stopping Frazier's third fight with **Muhammad Ali** in the historic **"Thrilla in Manila"** before the start of the 14th round. Futch cared more about the safety of his own fighter, as Frazier had taken much punishment from Ali in the previous round. His first world champion was Don Jordan who won the welterweight crown in 1958.

Further Reading
Eskenazi, Gerald. "Eddie Futch, Who Trained Fighters His Way, Dies at 90." *The New York Times,* 10/12/2001, p. A23.
Litsky, Frank. "Futch, 84, Imparts the Wisdom of the Ages." *The New York Times,* 7/9/1996, p. B14.

GABLE, DAN (1948–). Dan Gable is a former great collegiate wrestler who achieved even greater glory as the coach of the Iowa Hawkeyes wrestling program, which he turned into a dynasty. Born in 1948 in Waterloo, Iowa, Gable attended Iowa State University, where he compiled an 181-match winning streak until losing to Larry Owings of Washington State University in his last collegiate match.

Gable later earned a gold medal in freestyle wrestling at the 1972 Munich Games. He later coached the American freestyle wrestling teams at three different Olympic Games. Gable became the wrestling coach at the University of Iowa in 1976. His teams won 17 NCAA championships, including 9 in a row. L. Jon Wortheim says it well in his book *Blood in the Cage*: "Under Gable, the Hawkeyes would win the NCAA championships as regularly as corn would get harvested in the fall" (p. 23). He retired from coaching but later returned as an assistant coach for a couple years. He currently serves as an assistant athletic director at Iowa.

Further Reading

Distel, Dave. "Dan Gable: The King of 'Straight' Wrestling." *Los Angeles Times*, 2/26/12973, p. E4.
Distel, Dave. "Dan Gable: Wrestling Coach and True Believer." *Los Angeles Times*, 2/4/1984, p. C1.
Irving, John. "Gable, Iowa Put Stranglehold on N.C.A.A. Wrestling.," *The New York Times*, 3/18/1979, p. S6.
Wortheim, L. John. *Blood in the Cage: Mixed Martial Arts, Pat Miletich, and the Furious Rise of the UFC.* Boston: Houghton Mifflin, 2009.
Zavoral, Nolan. *A Season on the Mat: Dan Gable and the Pursuit of Perfection.* New York: Simon & Schuster, 2007.

GALAXY, KHAOSAI (1959–). One of the most dominant fighters in boxing history, Khaosai Galaxy is not a household name outside of hardcore boxing aficionados because he fought nearly his entire career in his native Thailand. Nicknamed "the Thai Tyson" for his relentless attack, he compiled an amazing record of 50-1 with 44 stoppages. The only loss for the former Muay Thai kickboxer was a 10-round decision to Sakda Saksuree in his seventh pro fight for the Thai bantamweight crown.

He won the vacant **World Boxing Association (WBA)** junior bantamweight title in November 1984 with a sixth-round kayo over Eusebio Espina. He made 19 successful defenses—16 of which did not go the distance. He retired in 1991 after a 12-round decision win over Armando Castro. Galaxy's twin brother, Khaokor, also held a world title—the first set of twins to be world champions. He was elected to the International Boxing Hall of Fame in 1999.

Professional Record: 50-1
World Title(s):   WBA junior bantamweight, 1984–1991.

Further Reading
Arias, Carlos. "Thailand's Galaxy Tops Hall Inductees." *Orange County Register*, 10/16/1999, p. D10.
"Galaxy Ruled Junior Bantamweights." *Post-Standard*, 6/10/1999, p. 5.

GALINDEZ, VICTOR (1948–1980). Argentinian Victor Galindez was a two-time light heavyweight world champion who filled the division's void after the great **Bob Foster** retired. A tough brawler, Galindez started his career slowly but steadily picked up steam.

He won the vacant **World Boxing Association (WBA)** light heavyweight title with a 13th-round stoppage of Len Hutchins in Buenos Aires in 1974. He defended his title 10 times before losing to Mike Rossman in a stunning upset in 1978. Galindez regained his title by defeating Rossman in a rematch the next year. Galindez pounded Rossman with vicious left hooks and stopped him the 10th round.

However, he lost his title to **Marvin Johnson** in his first title defense. Galindez tried his hand at the newly formed cruiserweight division but lost a 12-round decision to Jesse Burnett. He retired on the advice of doctors who cited his detached retinas in 1980. Unfortunately, Galindez did not enjoy retirement long, dying in an auto race in October 1980.

Professional record: 55-9-4
Championship(s):   WBA Light Heavyweight, 1974–1978, 1979

Further Reading
Associated Press. "Galindez Wins Title; Hutchins in Hospital." *Los Angeles Times*, 12/8/1974, p. C12.
Associated Press. "Galindez Kayoes Kates in 15th." *The Washington Post*, 5/23/1976, p. 40.
Katz, Michael. "Galindez Regains World Title." *The New York Times*, 4/15/1979, p. S1.

GANS, JOE (1874–1910). Joe Gans' nickname epitomizes his ring greatness—"Old Master." This African American pugilist captured the world lightweight championship in 1902 and held it until 1908. Born Joseph Gaines in Baltimore in 1874, he turned professional at age 17 in 1891. Gans admitted that sometimes he threw a fight in order to receive a better opportunity down the line.

He first received a world title shot against Frank Erne and lost in 1900. Two years later, Gans exacted revenge and garnered the championship with a first-round knockout. He held title until finally losing to **Battling Nelson** in 1908. Gans fought until 1909 and died the next year at age 36 of tuberculosis.

Though he faced racial discrimination, Gans managed to become a very popular fighter. *The Washington Post* wrote in 1908: "despite his color, he was a popular fighter, and won his way into the hearts of those who love the game as an able exponent of it." He also added to our cultural lexicon, according to ring historian **Bert Sugar,** who explains that after defeating Battling Nelson in their first fight, Gans telegraphed his mother with the following phrase: "Bringing Home the Bacon" (Sugar, p. 48). *The Ring* magazine listed him as the fourth greatest lightweight of all time in 2001, writing that he was "decades ahead of his time."

| Professional Record: | 123-8-10 (18 no decisions) |
| Championship(s): | Lightweight, 1902–1908 |

Further Reading

Cox, Monte D. "Joe Gans, The Old Master . . . 'He Could Lick Them All On Their Best Day!'" *Cyber Boxing Zone Journal*, September 2004, at http://coxscorner.tripod.com/gans.html

Dettloff, William. "The 20 Greatest Lightweights of All Time." *The Ring* (September 2001), pp. 49–69, 53.

"Frank Erne Out in First Round." *Chicago Daily Tribune*, 5/13/1902, p. 6.

"Gossip of Boxing: Battling Nelson Put an End to Joe Gans' Career." *The Washington Post*, 9/14/1908, p. 5.

Runyon, Damon. "Joe Gans Won't Draw Color Line." *The Chicago Defender*, 2/12/1921, p. 6.

Sugar, Bert Randolph. *Boxing's Greatest Fighters*. Guilford, Conn.: Lyons Press, 2006, pp. 46–48.

GARDNER, RULON (1971–). Rulon Gardner was an American **Greco-Roman** wrestler best known for winning the gold medal at the 2000 Sydney Olympic Games by upsetting the great Alexander Karelin—who was unbeaten in 13 years of international competition. Born in 1971 in Afton, Wyoming, Gardner attended a junior college in Idaho and then went to the University of Nebraska.

In the 2000 Olympic Games, Gardner shocked the world by capturing the gold medal by defeating the great Karelin 1-0 in the gold medal match. Gardner followed that with a bronze medal at the 2004 Olympics. Later that year, Gardner tried his hand at professional mixed martial arts by fighting in a special match against former Olympic judo champion Hidehiko Yoshido at a **PRIDE** event. Gardner, who was trained by mixed martial arts legend **Randy Couture,** captured a unanimous decision.

Gardner also had discomfort about punching and harming opponents and retired from the sport after only one bout.

| Professional MMA Record: | 1-0 |
| Championship(s): | None |

Further Reading

Couch, Greg. "Rulon really rules." *Chicago Sun-Times*, 10/20/2000, p. 141.

Stein, Joel. "Rulon Gardner; A jumbo Wyoming farm boy shocks the world, and himself, by wrangling a Russian tank." *TIME*, 10/9/2000, p. 100.

GATTI, ARTURO (1972–). Arturo "Thunder" Gatti is one of the most exciting fighters of his generation, providing fight fans with a series of memorable wars. He turned pro in 1991 and won his first world title by defeating Tracy Harris Patterson in 1995 to win the **International Boxing Federation (IBF)** super featherweight title. He defended his title several times in spectacular fashion, including knockouts of Wilson Rodriguez and **Gabriel Ruelas.** In 1998, Gatti engaged in two 10-round wars with fellow lightweight Ivan Robinson. Though he lost both fights, Gatti's warrior mentality endeared him to the boxing public.

In 2002 and 2003, he engaged in one of the most memorable trilogies in boxing history with "Irish" Micky Ward. Gatti lost the first bout but won the next two in the series, which featured two pugilists pounding each other in *Rocky* movie-style fashion. In January 2004, Gatti won the **World Boxing Council (WBC)** junior welterweight title by defeating Gianluco Branco. He successfully defended his title against Leonard Dorin and Jesse James Leija before losing badly to **Floyd Mayweather, Jr.** He rebounded in his next fight to stop the undefeated Thomas Dangaard to win the lightly-regarded International Boxing Association welterweight title. He then challenged WBC champion Carlos Baldomir but lost badly. In his last fight, he lost to former *Contender* show competitor Alfonso Gomez.

Professional Record:	40-9
Championship(s):	IBF Super Featherweight, 1995–1997; WBC Junior Welterweight, 2004–2005

Further Reading

Collins, Nigel. "Gatti Has His Ducks In a Row." *The Ring* (April 2003), pp. 28–33.

Dettloff, William. "He's Spilled His Last Drop: Now It's Time for Gatti To Say Goodbye." *The Ring* (November 2007), pp. 80–85.

Dicker, Ron. "Gatti Evens the Score with Ward." *The New York Times*, 12/24/2002, p. G14.

Donovan, Jake. "Arturo Gatti . . . Remembering the Warrior." *The Sweet Science*, 6/28/2005, at http://www.thesweetscience.com/boxing-article/2310/arturo-gatti-remembering-warrior/

Santoliquito, Joe. "Boxing Instead of Bleeding: Thunder Becomes Lightning as Gatti Revives His Career." *World Boxing* (July 2002), pp. 56–60.

Smith, Timothy W. "Gatti Leaves Little Doubt in Rematch with Patterson." *The New York Times*, 2/23/1997, p. S2.

Smith, Timothy W. "In Robinson, Gatti Finds a Warrior He Can't Beat on Desire." *The New York Times*, 8/24/1998.

Smith, Timothy W. "A Brawler Who Takes Poundings, and Dishes Them Out." *The New York Times*, 8/13/1999, p. D3.

GAVILAN, KID (1926–2003). Kid Gavilan was a flashy former world welterweight champion perhaps best known for his trademark bolo punch that he would unload on many an opponent. Boxing scribe Gavin Evans wrote in *The Ring* magazine of Gavilan: "He was not the most consistent performer, but when he felt like it, Gavilan could be dazzlingly brilliant."

Born Gerardo Gonzalez in Cuba in 1926, his managers recognized his boxing potential and took him to the United States. They dubbed him Kid Gavilan, the "Cuban Hawk."

In 1949, he challenged the great **Sugar Ray Robinson** for the world welterweight title, losing a 15-round decision. In 1951, he won the championship by defeating Johnny Bratton over 15 rounds. He successfully defended his title seven times, defeating great fighters such as Billy Graham and **Carmen Basilio.** In 1954, he challenged middleweight champion **Carl "Bobo" Olson** and lost a decision. Later that year, he lost a highly debatable decision to Johnny Saxton to lose his welterweight title. He continued to fight until 1958.

After retirement, he was forced to remain in Cuba for 10 years by the Fidel Castro–led government. He returned to the United States in 1968 and died in 2003. *The Ring* magazine recently listed him as the third greatest welterweight of all time.

Record:	107-30-6
Championship(s):	Welterweight, 1951–1954

Further Reading

Encinosa, Enrique. "Kid Gavilan: the Sparrow Hawk." *Cyber Boxing Zone Journal*, April 2003, at http://www.cyberboxingzone.com/boxing/w0403-ee.html

Evans, Gavin. "The 20 Greatest Welterweights of All Time." *The Ring* (February 2008), pp. 63–84, 66.

Goldstein, Richard. "Kid Gavilan, 77, Welterweight Champion in the Early 50's." *The New York Times*, 2/15/2003, p. A23.

Welsh, Jack. "The Cuban Hawk Still Flying High." *The Ring* (June 1986), pp. 38–43.

GIARDELLO, JOEY (1930–2008). Joey Giardello was a former world middleweight champion who won more than 100 professional bouts. While not blessed with tremendous power, Giardello made up for it with a tremendous heart, fine conditioning, aggression, and volume punching.

Born in 1930 in Brooklyn as Carmine Orlando Telleli, Giardiello moved with his family to Philadelphia where he took up boxing. He turned pro in 1948 and did not lose until his 20th pro bout. In 1952, he twice beat Billy Graham, though the second time Giardello had to sue in court to reverse the judges' verdict. Originally, the ring announcer had said Giardello was the winner but state commissioners altered the scorecard of one judge, giving the nod to Graham. He then lost to Graham in 1953. Two years later, he served three months in prison for assaulting a gas station attendant. Upon his release, he resumed his career successfully.

In 1959, he split two 10-round decisions with future middleweight champion **Dick Tiger.** In 1960, he faced **Gene Fullmer** for the middleweight championship in Bozeman, Montana. Unfortunately for Giardello the brutal fight was declared a draw. In 1963, Giardello dropped an aging **Sugar Ray Robinson** on the fourth round en route to a 10-round decision win that earned him a shot at the middleweight title against Tiger. Giardello won a unanimous decision to capture the championship at age 33 in a bout *The New York Times* declared the "the most stunning upset of the year."

He successfully defended his title by outpointing dangerous **Rubin "Hurricane" Carter.** In 1965, he lost his title to Tiger. He retired in 1967.

Professional Record:	101-25-7
Championship(s):	Middleweight, 1963–1965

Further Reading
"Action is Brutal in Montana Fight." *The New York Times,* 4/21/1960, p. 35.
"Giardello Takes Defeat to Court." *The New York Times,* 1/1/1953, p. 29.
Lipsyte, Robert. "A Dream for Joey: The King Can Do No Wrong." *The New York Times,* 12/6/1963, p. 56.
Lipsyte, Robert. "Nigerian Is Upset." *The New York Times,* 12/8/1963, p. 245.
Lipsyte, Robert. "Giardello Outpoints Carter and Retains World Middleweight Title." *The New York Times,* 12/15/1964, p. 58.
United Press International. "Sugar Ray Suffers Worst Beating from Giardello." *Los Angeles Times,* 6/25/1963, p. C1.

GIBBONS, MIKE (1887–1956). Mike "the Phantom of St. Paul" Gibbons was a great middleweight who never won a world title but still is considered one of the greatest 160 lb. fighters in history. Born in 1887 in St. Paul, Gibbons learned to box at the YMCA. He turned pro at age 19 in 1908 and quickly impressed with his fleet footwork and superior boxing skills.

He never received a shot at the world title though many considered him to be the best middleweight in the world. He fought the great **Harry Greb,** Jack Dillon, and Soldier Bartfield in his career, which spanned from 1908 to 1922. Many of his major fights ended in no-decisions as was the custom during the days before the **Walker Law.**

Professional Record:	62-3-4 (58 no decisions)
Championship(s):	None

Further Reading
Pearson, Ray. "Mike Gibbons Ranks as Boss of the Middles." *Chicago Daily Tribune,* 12/2/1917, p. A4.
Tom and Mike Gibbons Preservation Society: http://members.aol.com/_ht_a/tg3/tmgps.html

GOGOPLATA. The gogoplata is a rarely used submission in mixed martial arts (MMA) competition that results when the fighter in the guard position (on his back on the canvas) submits his opponent by choking his head with his shin and forearm. The word "gogo" is Portugese for the Adams Apple area. Heavyweight Brad Imes, **Nick Diaz,** and Shooto star **Shinya Aoki** have all successfully used this move to win professional MMA bouts. Aoki used the move to submit Joachim Hansen at a **PRIDE** event in 2006. Diaz used the gogoplata to submit **Takanori Gomi** in a PRIDE event in 2007.

Further Reading
Gurgel, Jorge. "MMA 101: The Gogoplata." *FIGHT!* (June 2008), pp. 59–61.

GOLDBERG, BENNY (1919–2001). Benny Goldberg was one of the finest fighters to never win a world championship. Born in 1919 in Warsaw, Poland, Goldberg fought most of his career out of Detroit, Michigan. He turned professional in 1937 after a fine amateur career. In 1938, he defeated future longtime bantamweight kingpin **Manuel Ortiz** three times. Goldberg finally received a shot at the world title in 1943 but lost a 15-round decision to Ortiz. He never received another world title shot.

Record:	38-2-1 (sources are not consistent in his ring record)
Championship(s):	None

Further Reading
"Benny Goldberg." *Cyberboxing Zone* at http://www.cyberboxingzone.com/boxing/goldberg-benny.htm

GOMEZ, WILFREDO (1956–). Wilfredo Gomez's nickname of "Bazooka" captured the essence of this former champion, who blasted out nearly all his opponents in a professional career that began in 1974 and ended for good in 1989. Born in Puerto Rico in 1956, Gomez turned pro with a six-round draw against Jacinto Fuentes. He rebounded with a series of kayos, including a 12-round stoppage of Dong-Kyun Yum in 1977 to win the **World Boxing Council (WBC)** junior featherweight title. He successfully defended his title 17 times. He suffered his first professional loss in August 1981 when he moved up in weight to challenge featherweight kingpin **Salvador Sanchez.** In 1984, Gomez won the WBC featherweight title by defeating Juan LaPorte. He lost in his first defense to **Azumah Nelson.** In 1985, Gomez added a third title—the **World Boxing Association (WBA)** junior lightweight title—by defeating Rocky Lockridge. He lost the title in his first defense against Alfredo Layne.

Record:	44-3-1
Championship(s):	WBC junior featherweight, 1977–1983; WBC featherweight, 1984; WBA junior lightweight, 1985–1986

Further Reading
Bazooka: The Battles of Wilfredo Gómez (2003) (film).
Farhood, Steve. "The Super Super-Bantamweights: They'll Never Be the Same Again." *Knockout* (Summer 1994), pp. 30–32, 61.
Nager, Gary. "The Bazooka Fires Back." *The Ring* (July 1984), pp. 40–43.

GOMI, TAKANORI (1978–). Takanori Gomi is a Japanese mixed martial artist who had great success in **PRIDE.** Many experts consider him to among the best, if not *the* best, lightweight in the mixed martial arts (MMA) world. Born in 1978 in Kanagawa, Japan, Gomi boxed and played baseball as a youth. He dropped out of school after failing a test and turned his attention to wrestling. The athletic Gomi quickly mastered wrestling skills and won numerous tournaments throughout Japan.

He turned pro in the MMA ranks in 1998 in the Shooto organization. He kept winning, and in December 2001, he defeated Rumina Sato to win the Shooto welterweight championship. He successfully defended his title four times before suffering his first loss to Joachim Hansen in 2003. In February 2004, he debuted in the PRIDE organization, and in his second fight he stopped Ralph Gracie in six seconds—the shortest fight in PRIDE history. Later that year, he kayoed **Jens Pulver** in the first round. In 2005, he won the PRIDE lightweight championship with a win over **Hayato Sakurai.** He initially suffered his only loss in PRIDE to **Nick Diaz** by submission, but the result was changed to a no contest after Diaz failed a post-fight drug test. Many MMA fans hope that Gomi will fight in the **Ultimate Fighting Championships (UFC),** which purchased PRIDE in 2007.

Professional MMA Record: 29-5
Championship(s):   PRIDE lightweight, 2005–2007

Further Reading
Kimura, Katie. "The Harder They Come." *The Guardian*, 4/29/2006, p. 26.
Official Web site of Takanori Gomi: http://www.t-gomi.com/

GONZALEZ, BETULIO (1949–). Betulio Gonzalez is a former three-time world flyweight champion who compiled 75 wins in his professional career. Born in Maracaibo, Venezuela, Gonzalez turned pro in 1968 and won his first 10 pro bouts before a draw.

In 1971, he challenged Japanese great Masao Ohba for the **World Boxing Association (WBA)** flyweight championship and lost a narrow 15-round decision. Later in the year, he challenged **World Boxing Council (WBC)** champion Erbito Salavarria. The fight was scored a draw, but officials later disqualified Salavarria after discovering he had been drinking sugared water between rounds. Gonzalez successfully defended his title against Socrates Batoto in 172, but lost in his second defense against Venice Borkhorsor.

In 1973, he defeated Mexican great **Miguel Canto** for the WBC flyweight championship. He successfully defended his title twice before losing a split decision to Japanese fighter Shoji Oguma in a 1974 bout in Tokyo. In 1975 and 1976, he lost split decisions to Canto in attempts to regain his championship. Finally, in 1978 Gonzalez won the title for a third time with a 15-round decision win over **Guty Espadas, Sr.** He successfully defended the title three times, including a win and a draw over old rival Oguma. He lost his belt to Luis Ibarra in 1979 and never won another world title though he received two more chances in 1981 and 1982, respectively. He finally retired in 1984.

Professional Record: 75-12-4
Championship(s):   WBA flyweight, 1972; 1973–1974; WBA flyweight, 1978–1979

Further Reading
Associated Press. "Gonzalez Keeps Flyweight Title." *Los Angeles Times*, 6/4/1972, p. C10.
Associated Press. "Gonzalez Stops Oguma and Keeps W.B.A. Title." *The New York Times*, 7/7/1979, p. 13.
United Press International. "Gonzalez Gets Nod in Disputed Fight." *The New York Times*, 11/22/1971, p. 59.

GONZALEZ, HUMBERTO (1966–). Humberto "Chiquita" Gonzalez was one of the greatest junior flyweight champions in boxing history. Born in 1966 in Nezahualcoyotl, Mexico, he turned pro in 1894 and won the Mexican junior flyweight title in 1987. In 1989, he traveled to South Korea to dethrone **World Boxing Council (WBC)** junior flyweight champion Yul-Woo Lee by unanimous decision. He successfully defended his title five times before losing to Rolando Pascua in 1990.

He recaptured the title in 1991 with a convincing win over Melchor Cob Castro. He defended his title four times before a 1993 showdown with **International Boxing Federation (IBF)** champion **Michael "Little Hands of Stone" Carbajal.** Gonzalez had an early points lead, dropping Carbajal twice. However, in the seventh round Carbajal rallied with a devastating left-hook knockout.

In 1994, Gonzalez defeated Carbajal by 12-round split decision to win the WBC and IBF belts. He successfully defended those belts three times—including another close decision win over Carbajal—before losing to **Saman Sorjaturong.**

Professional Record:	43-3
Championship(s):	WBC junior flyweight, 1989–1990, 1991–1993, 1994–1995; IBF junior flyweight, 1994–1995

Further Reading
Friend, Tom. "Carbajal, Down Twice, Unifies the Title with Knockout." *The New York Times,* 3/14/1993, p. S4.
Tintle, Joseph C. "Michael Carbajal Kayos Humberto Gonzalez." *Knockout* (Summer 1994), pp. 54–56.

GONZALEZ, PAUL (1964–). Paul Gonzalez was a former Olympic gold medalist who overcame tough circumstances in East Los Angeles to capture the top prize in amateur boxing. Born in 1964 in the Boyle Heights section of L.A., Gonzalez was shot and stabbed during his youth in what he termed *gang warfare.*

He survived with the help of police officer Al Stankle who helped Gonzalez develop his boxing skills. At the 1984 Los Angeles Summer Olympic Games, he won a gold medal in the junior flyweight division. He turned pro a year later and in his fifth pro bout defeated fellow unbeaten prospect **Orlando Canizales** in 1986 for the North American Boxing Federation flyweight title.

However, in 1990, Canizales exacted revenge by stopping Gonzalez in two rounds for Canizales' world bantamweight championship. Gonzalez retired the next year in 1991.

Professional Record:	16-4
Championship(s):	None

Further Reading
Howard-Cooper, Scott. "The Olympian From East L.A." *Los Angeles Times,* 7/26/1984, p. 12.
Ravicz, Elenita. "Boxer is a Knockout Role Model: Ex-Gang Member Talks Tough at Juvenile Court Schools." *Los Angeles Times,* 11/25/1984, p. F10.

GOODRIDGE, GARY (1966–). Gary "Big Daddy" Goodridge is a current professional kickboxer and mixed martial artist known for his imposing physique and powerful strikes. Born in 1966 in Trinidad & Tobago, Goodridge now lives and fights out of Canada. Before his professional fighting career, Goodridge was best known for his arm wrestling prowess.

He made his professional mixed martial arts (MMA) debut in explosive fashion at **Ultimate Fighting Championships (UFC)** 8 against Paul Herrera. Goodridge unloaded a series of devastating punches that ended the fight after only 13 seconds. In the next match, he stopped Jerry Bohlander in the first round before losing to **Don Frye** in the championship match. He lost to Mark Schultz at UFC 9 and eventual champion **Mark Coleman** at UFC 10.

Goodridge again made noise in the MMA world at the very first **PRIDE** event in October 1997, when he stopped former UFC tournament champion **Oleg Taktarov** in the first round. Other highlights of his MMA career including defeating **Valentijn Overeem** at PRIDE 14 in the first round and a rematch win over Frye at a 2004 PRIDE event. He has lost to **Fedor Eme-lianenko, Antonio Rodrigo Nogueira,** and **Heath Herring.** In 2008, he is scheduled to fight in the new organization YAMMA.

Goodridge began his career as a kickboxer at a K-1 event in 1999. Though he sports a losing record of 11-19, he has faced the best of the best. He has losses to champions Jerome Le Banner, **Remy Bonjasky,** and the tough Mighty Mo.

Professional Kickboxing Record:	11-20-2
Professional MMA Record:	23-19-1
Championship(s):	None

Further Reading
Official Website: http://www.garygoodridge.com.
Taflinger, Neal. "Gary Goodridge: American Fight Fans Get Reacquainted with an MMA Warhorse." *FIGHT!* (May 2008), p. 98.

GORDEAU, GERALD (1959–). Gerard Gordeau was a Dutch-based mixed martial artist best known for reaching the finals of the first **Ultimate Fighting Championships (UFC)** tournament in November 1993. Born in 1959 in Amsterdam, Gordeau was a **savate** (a form of kickboxing in France) world champion. Standing 6'5" and thin, Gordeau appeared physically overmatched in the Octagon at UFC 1 when he faced 400 lb. sumo wrestler Telia Tuli. Gordeau kicked Tuli in the face, sending one of his teeth flying and another embedded in Gordeau's foot.

Gordeau advanced to the finals by stopping Kevin Rosier in the first round as well. In the finals, Gordeau tried to stay on his feet against Brazilian jiu-jitsu master **Royce Gracie** but fell to a rear naked choke hold in the first round nearly two minutes into the bout. Gordeau returned to UFC 2 with fighters Freek Hamacker and Remco Pardoel.

Professional MMA Record:	2-2
Championship(s):	None

Further Reading
Krauss, Erich, and Brett Aita. *Brawl: A Behind-the-Scenes Look at Mixed Martial Arts Competition.* Ontario: ECW Press, 2002.
Snowden, Jonathan. *Total MMA: Inside Ultimate Fighting.* Toronto, Ontario: ECW Press, 2008.

GRACIE FAMILY. Members of the Gracie family from Brazil are the founders of Brazilian jiu-jitsu and the most celebrated family in the history of mixed martial arts. Many first learned of the Gracie family after a relatively thin man named **Royce Gracie** won three of the first **Ultimate Fighting Championships (UFC)** tournaments. But, the Gracie family has a long history.

In the early twentieth century, a Japanese jiu-jitsu champion named Mitsuyo Maeda moved to Brazil where he befriended a Brazilian man of political influence named Gastao Gracie. Gastao helped Maeda politically, and in return, Maeda imparted much of his jiu-jitsu knowledge to Gastao's son Carlos.

Carlos Gracie trained with Maeda for several years before leaving to go back to Japan. Carlos then began training other members of his family, including younger brother Helio. Helio was the smallest of the Gracie brothers, but he dedicated his life to learning and refining jiu-jitsu skills. Carlos and Helio took the knowledge they learned from the Japanese master and then added to the ancient art to form what became known as Brazilian jiu-jitsu. Carlos and Helio uttered the so-called Gracie Challenge, facing combatants from other fighting disciplines. Almost without fail, the Gracies prevailed with their superior ground-fighting techniques and submissions.

Helio's sons became the leading practitioners of Brazilian jiu-jitsu. These famous fighting brothers included **Rorion, Rickson,** Royce, and Royler.

Further Reading
Peligro, Kid. *The Gracie Way: An Illustrated History of the World's Greatest Martial Arts Family.* Montpelier, VT: Invisible Cities Press, 2003.
Snowden, Jonathan. *Total MMA: Inside Ultimate Fighting.* Toronto, Ontario: ECW Press, 2008.

GRACIE, RICKSON (1958–). Rickson Gracie may be the best fighter from the legendary Brazilian fighting family known as the Gracies. Rickson began learning jiu-jitsu from his father, Helio, at age 6 and earned his black belt at 18. In his first bout of significance, he defeated Brazilian fighter King Zulu in front of 20,000 people. He twice won the Japan Open Vale Tudo tournament in 1994 and 1995. His official mixed martial arts (MMA) record is 11-0, but reports indicate that he has won more than 400 fights in various competitions ranging from **Sambo** to judo to jiu-jitsu. Of his 11 official professional MMA bouts, Rickson won all of them by submission holds. He has been called "the Greatest Gracie."

Professional MMA Record:	11-0
Championship(s):	None (though considered best in the world)

Further Reading
Official Web site: http://www.rickson.com/
Peligro, Kid. *The Gracie Way: An Illustrated History of the World's Greatest Martial Arts Family.* Montpelier, VT: Invisible Cities Press, 2003.

GRACIE, RORION. Rorion Gracie is the oldest son of Helio Gracie and the member of the family responsible for bringing the family's fighting style to the United States and the rest of the world. He came to the United States in 1969 intent on making the fighting style profitable and marketable. After earning a law degree from Brazil, he returned to the United States in 1978 and began teaching Brazilian jiu-jistu in his garage in California.

He produced a series of tapes called *Gracies in Action* and defeated other martial arts practitioners in informal challenge matches. In 1989, he opened the Gracie Jiu-Jitsu Academy in 1989 in Torrance, California. Two of Rorion's students were Art Davie and filmmaker John Milius. The three of them planned an event originally called "War of the Worlds," which they pitched to television executive Bob Meyrowitz of Semaphore Entertainment Group. Thus, was born the **Ultimate Fighting Championships (UFC).** Rorion and Milius came up with the idea of holding mixed martial arts battles inside an eight-sided chain fence that became known as "the Octagon."

For the first event, Rorion chose his youngest brother **Royce** to participate in the event. Many believe he chose Royce because he was the least physically dominant of his brothers.

"I felt that Royce would be a very convincing example of what jiu-jitsu can do for people," he said (Krauss, 31).

Professional Record: Unknown

Further Reading
Gracie Jiu-Jitsu Academy: http://www.gracieacademy.com/
Jordan, Pat. "Bad: Rorion Gracie is willing to fight to the death to prove he's the toughest man in the West; street fighter with a standing offer for competitors." *Playboy* (September 1989).
Krauss, Erich, and Brett Aita. *Brawl: A Behind-the-Scenes Look at Mixed Martial Arts Competition.* Ontario: ECW Press, 2002.
Peligro, Kid. *The Gracie Way: An Illustrated History of the World's Greatest Martial Arts Family.* Montpelier, VT: Invisible Cities Press, 2003.

GRACIE, ROYCE (1966–). Royce Gracie was the first superstar of the **Ultimate Fighting Championships (UFC),** winning the tournament at UFC 1, UFC 2, and UFC 4. His mastery of grappling skills associated with Brazilian jiu-jitsu enabled the 180 lb. Royce to defeat much larger men, defeating them with various submission techniques. Author Jeremy Wall describes Gracie's importance in mixed martial arts as follows:

> There is an athlete at the pinnacle of every sport, an athlete whose name has become synonymous with the sport he plays due to all that he has accomplished. These athletes often end up becoming larger than the sport. In baseball there is Babe Ruth. In hockey there is Wayne Gretsky. In basketball there is Michael Jordan. And, for the UFC, there is Royce Gracie. (Wall, p. 189)

Born to the Gracie fighting family in Rio de Janeiro, Brazil, in 1966, Gracie was the sixth son of Helio Gracie. Royce grew up in Brazil but moved to the United States at age 17 to help his older brother **Rorion** in teaching mixed martial arts. Later, Rorion selected Royce to represent the family in the inaugural UFC event. Originally, **Rickson Gracie** would represent the family, but Rorion had a disagreement with him.

In November 1993, Royce displayed the superiority of Gracie jiu-jitsu by submitting boxer Art Jimmerson, shoot fighter **Ken Shamrock,** and kickboxer **Gerard Gordeau.** He repeated as champion at UFC 2, defeating karate master Minoki Ichihara, Jason DeLucia, jiu-jitsu expert Remco Pardoel, and kickboxer Patrick Smith. His four opponents lasted just over nine minutes total with Gracie and his superior ground grappling and submissions.

In UFC 3, Gracie had a tougher time in his first-round match with a virtual unknown fighter from Hawaii named Kimo Leopold. Gracie won via submission but not before Kimo's superior physical strength had taken a toll on Royce. Gracie was not able to continue in the tournament against his next scheduled opponent Harold Howard.

Gracie returned to form in UFC 4, defeating kung fu expert Ron Van Clef (who was 52 at the time of the fight), karate expert **Keith Hackney,** and wrestler **Dan "the Beast" Severn.** Severn gave Gracie his toughest fight to date, but eventually fell victim to a submission after 15 minutes.

Gracie then returned to UFC 5 in a superfight duel with Shamrock, whom he had defeated at UFC 1. The two fought to a draw after 36 minutes. Though Shamrock landed more strikes, the UFC did not have judges at that time, so the bout was declared a draw.

He returned in 2000 for the **PRIDE** Grand Prix championships, winning his first bout against former pro wrestler Nobuhiko Takada. However, Gracie faced a much tougher opponent in the second round in Japanese legend **Kazushi Sakuraba**, a man who had defeated Royce's brother Royler at an earlier PRIDE event.

No time limit was placed on the match, which was divided into 15-minute rounds. Royce and Sakuraba battled for an incredible 90 minutes. Sakuraba's leg kicks began to hurt Royce, and his corner refused to let him come out for the seventh round. Royce later lost and fought a draw with Japanese judo master Hidehiko Yoshida.

In 2006, Royce returned to the Octagon at UFC 60, losing to the much younger and stronger **Matt Hughes.** He returned in 2007 by defeating Sakuraba in a rematch of legends. He was inducted into the UFC Hall of Fame for his early domination of the event.

Professional MMA Record:	14-3-3
Championship(s):	Winner of UFC 1, 2 and 4 tournaments

Further Reading
Official Web site: http://www.roycegracie.tv/
Peligro, Kid. *The Gracie Way: An Illustrated History of the World's Greatest Martial Arts Family.* Montpelier, VT: Invisible Cities Press, 2003.
Wall, Jeremy. *UFC's Ultimate Warriors Top 10.* Ontario: ECW Press, 2005, pp. 189–213.

GRAHAM, HEROL (1958–). One of the best boxers in the modern era to never win a world title, Herol Graham displayed amazing reflexes and defensive skills, frustrating many an opponent in his fine career. The Sheffield, England, native fought three times for a world title but lost to **Mike "the Body Snatcher" McCallum, Julian Jackson,** and Charles Brewer. Graham was ahead on the scorecards against both Jackson and Brewer before succumbing to the harder punchers. Jonathan Rendell captured the essence of Graham's unique abilities in his book *This Bloody Mary Is the Last Thing I Own*:

> He was unbeaten for years, a defensive master. He was impossible to hit. His trainer only called him Bomber to confuse opponents. He'd developed his skills in working-men's clubs in the pit villages. He'd have his hands tied behind his back and challenge anyone to hit him. But no one ever had. (p. 11)

Graham turned pro in 1978 and won his first 38 bouts before finally losing a decision to **Sumbu Kalambay** in 1987. Two years later, he lost a split decision to McCallum for the **World Boxing Association (WBA)** middleweight title. In 1990, he landed his second world title shot against Jackson. He was easily winning the fight until a single left hook kayoed him and his chance at the vacant **World Boxing Council (WBC)** middleweight title in 1990. He retired in 1992 after consecutive losses to Kalambay and Frank Grant.

However, Graham returned to the ring in 1996 at the age of 37. He beat undefeated contender Chris Johnson and then **Vinnie Pazienza** to land a shot in 1998 for the **International Boxing Federation (IBF)** super middleweight title against Charles Brewer. He dropped Brewer twice before losing in the 10th round.

Professional Record:	48-6
Championship(s):	None

Further Reading
Andre, Anthony. "A Herol's Welcome: With a new wife and a new life, can super middleweight Herol Graham go the distance?" *The Voice*, 12/1/1997, p. 54.

Blerley, Stephen. "Bomber weaves in for his last raid on a world title." *The Guardian*, 11/23/1990.
Rendell, Jonathan. *This Bloody Mary Is The Last Thing I Own*. London: Faber & Faber, 1998.

GRAZIANO, ROCKY (1922–1990). Rocky Graziano was a former popular middleweight champion best known for his trilogy with **Tony Zale.** Born in 1922 in New York City, Graziano learned to box after spending time in reform school. He turned professional in 1942 and became one of the sport's most popular fighters.

Graziano attracted attention from boxing experts in 1945 with a fourth-round kayo of power-puncher **Al "Bummy" Davis** and two kayoes of Freddie "Red" Cochrane.

He challenged Zale in 1946 for the middleweight championship, losing in the sixth round in what was called "one of the great fights in fistic history." He rebounded in 1947 by kayoing Zale in their rematch in the fifth round to win the title. After the fight, he yelled: "Mama, the bad boy done it." Graziano lost the rubber match in 1948. In 1952, he challenged **Sugar Ray Robinson** for the middleweight championship but lost in the third round.

Record:	67-10-6
Championship(s):	Middleweight, 1947

Further Reading

Cuddy, Jack. "Socking Middle-Weight Gains String of KOs; 'Bummy' Davis and Arnold Among Victims." *The Washington Post*, 12/24/1945, p. 8.
Dawson, James P. "18,547 See Referee Stop Chicago Fight." *The New York Times*, 7/17/1947, p. 23.
Graziano, Rocky, with Ralph Corsel. *Somebody Down Here Likes Me Too*. New York: Stein & Day, 1981.

GREB, HARRY (1894–1926). In his short 30-year life, Harry Greb established a record that ranks him amongst the truly greatest fighters of all time. Greb overwhelmed his opponents with his ferocity, earning him the monikers "the Human Windmill" and the "Pittsburgh Windmill." Born in the Steel City in 1894, Greb turned professional in 1913. In 1922, Greb faced **Gene Tunney** for the American light heavyweight championship. Greb swarmed Tunney and took a commanding 15-round decision. It was the only loss in the future heavyweight champion's professional career. In 1923, he defeated Johnny Wilson to win the world middleweight championship. He held the title until he lost a decision to **Theodore "Tiger" Flowers** in 1926. He died later that year after a routine operation to repair facial damage.

Professional Record:	105-8-3
Championship(s):	Middleweight, 1923–1926

Further Reading

Fair, James R. *Give Him to the Angels: Story of Harry Greb*. New York: Smith & Durrell, 1946.
Paxton, Bill. *The Fearless Harry Greb: Biography of a Tragic Hero in Boxing*. Jefferson, NC: McFarland & Co., 2008.
Pearson, Ray. "Greb Captures Service Title in Close Mill." *Chicago Daily Tribune*, 7/28/1918, p. A1.
Pegler, Westbrook. "Greb Wins Light-Heavyweight Crown." *Atlanta Constitution*, 5/24/1922, p. 13.
Roberts, James B., and Alexander B. Skutt. *The Boxing Register* (4th ed.). Ithaca, NY: McBooks Press, Inc., 2006, pp. 132–133.

GRECO-ROMAN WRESTLING. Greco-Roman wrestling is a form of amateur wrestling that features upper body grappling and forbids attacks below the waist. This distinguishes Greco-Roman wrestling from the more prevalent form of wrestling—free style wrestling.

Wrestlers in Greco-Roman must engage in throws and takedowns that originate above the waist and cannot attack their opponents' legs. The sport is called "Greco-Roman" to emphasize the ancient values in the Greek and Roman combatants.

Greco-Roman wrestling emphasizes throws and body-slams. Wrestlers score points with takedowns and also for reversals, where a wrestler emerges from a defensive position into a controlling offensive position. Wrestlers can win the match if they can pin (also called a "fall") both their opponents' shoulders on the mat. Numerous mixed martial artists had Greco-Roman wrestling backgrounds, including **Randy Couture, Matt Lindland,** and **Dan "Hollywood" Henderson.** Another well-known American Greco-Roman wrestler was **Rulon Gardner,** who captured a gold medal at the 2000 Olympics and a bronze medal at the 2004 Olympics.

Further Reading
Martell, William. *Greco-Roman Wrestling.* Champaign, IL: Human Kinetics Publisher, 1993.

GRIFFIN, ERIC (1967—). Eric Griffin was a great amateur boxer in the junior flyweight division who never achieved the same level of success in the professional ranks. Born in 1967, the diminutive (5'3") Griffin had a stellar amateur career. In 1989, he won the world amateur championships by defeating Cuba's Rogelio Marcelo in the finals.

Griffin served as a co-captain of the U.S.A. boxing team for the 1992 Olympics in Barcelona. He suffered a controversial decision loss in the second round to Spaniard Rafael Lozano. Even though all the judges had Griffin ahead on their individual scorecards, amateur scoring requires three of the five judges to score the same blow for that particular punch to count. By that system, Lozano got the decision 6-5. Noted columnist Dave Anderson wrote of the disgraceful decision and scoring system: "As a result, the United States light flyweight, Eric Griffin is out of the tournament. Out even though he clearly deserved to win. Out because of a silly scoring system. Out because boxing is boxing."

Griffin turned pro after the Olympics and won his first 10 fights before having to retire against Marcos Pacheco with a dislocated shoulder in a November 1993 bout. The injury caused Griffin to lose out on his chance for the NABF light flyweight title. However, Griffin outboxed Pacheco in the rematch in March 1994 to win the regional title.

In 1997, Griffin lost to Jesus Chong for the vacant World Boxing Organization (WBO) light flyweight title. He never fought professionally again.

Professional Record:	16-4
Championship(s):	None

Further Reading
Anderson, Dave. "A Lesson in Boxing's Olympic Job Market." *The New York Times,* 8/3/1992, p. C3.
Associated Press. "Griffin Outpoints Cuban for Only U.S. Olympic Gold Medal in Moscow." *The New York Times,* 10/1/1989, p. S12.

GRIFFIN, FORREST (1978—). Forrest Griffin is a mixed martial artist best known for winning the inaugural season of *The Ultimate Fighter,* defeating Stephen Bonnar by unanimous decision in the championship bout. Born in Columbus, Ohio, in 1979, Griffin graduated high school in Evans, Georgia, and then obtained a political science degree from the University of Georgia. While attending college, he began work as a police officer.

He turned professional in 2001 on Reality Superfighting's "New Blood Conflict" card against mixed martial arts (MMA) legend **Dan Severn,** who defeated Griffin by unanimous decision.

In his second pro bout, Griffin overcame a dislocated shoulder to defeat South African Wiehan Lesh. He won seven more bouts before losing to cagey veteran **Jeremy Horn** in 2003. Griffin's career seemed to be moving slowly, and he became inactive, but he received the opportunity of a lifetime as a contestant on the inaugural season of *The Ultimate Fighter.* He won the competition with a thrilling decision win over Bonnar—considered one of the greatest modern MMA bouts ever.

He lost a split decision to former **Ultimate Fighting Championships (UFC)** light heavyweight champion **Tito Ortiz** and was knocked out by **Keith "the Dean of Mean" Jardine** in back-to-back losses in 2006. However, he rebounded with a win in 2007 over Hector Ramirez and an upset win over pound-for-pound great **Mauricio "Shogun" Rua** at UFC 76: Knockout.

Griffin has excellent stand-up skills and can absorb tremendous amounts of punishment. His win over Rua earned him a title shot at **Quinton "Rampage" Jackson** in 2008. In July 2008 at UFC 86, Griffin upset Jackson in a five-round decision to win the UFC world light heavyweight championship. In the second round, he dropped Jackson with leg strikes and then proceeded to maul him for much of the round. While he did not score a knockout or submission, Griffin weakened the dangerous striker and made the ultimate evolution from champion on *The Ultimate Fighter* to champion in the UFC. Griffin then made his first title defense against **Rashad Evans** in December 2008. Griffin controlled the first two rounds but was stopped in the third round.

Professional MMA Record: 16-5

Championship(s):   UFC light heavyweight, 2008

Further Reading
Official Web site: http://www.forrestgriffin.net/
Slutsky, Adam. "Forrest Through The Trees." *FIGHT!* (May 2008), pp. 40–50.

GRIFFITH, EMILE (1938–). Emile Griffith was a former welterweight and middleweight champion who was one of the finest fighters of his era and, arguably, of all-time. Born in 1938 in the Virgin Islands, Griffith moved to New York City with his family in 1950.

He excelled as an amateur boxer, winning all 42 of his bouts. He turned pro in 1958 in New York City. In 1961, he faced **Benny "Kid" Paret** for the welterweight title. Behind on points, Griffith rallied to score a 13th-round knockout. Later that year, he lost his title to Paret via 15-round split decision. That set up the fateful third bout between the two rivals. Paret scored an early knockdown, but Griffith rallied and in the 12th round battered Paret on the ropes, while referee Ruby Goldstein inexplicably stopped the fight too late. Paret died from brain injuries suffered during the bout.

Griffith lost his championship to **Luis Rodriguez** in 1963 but regained it in a rematch only three months later. In 1966, he successfully moved up in weight and defeated **Dick Tiger** to win the middleweight title. In 1967, he lost to **Nino Benvenuti** but regained the belt a few months later. In the rubber match, Griffith lost the belt again to Benvenuti, and he never won another world title fight. He lost in title challenges to **Jose Napoles** and twice to the great **Carlos Monzon.** He fought until 1977, retiring after losing a decision to Alan Minter.

Record: 85-24-2

Championship(s):   Welterweight, 1961, 1962–1963, 1963–1966;
Middleweight, 1966–1967, 1967–1968.

Further Reading
Conklin, William R. "Griffith Beaten on Split Verdict." *The New York Times*, 10/1/1961, p. S1.
Klores, Dan, and Ron Berger. *Ring of Fire: The Emile Griffith Story*, 2005 (documentary).
Lipsyte, Robert M. "A Title for a Fighting Choir Boy." *The New York Times*, 4/3/1961, p. 38.
McGowen, Deane. "Griffith Upsets Rodriguez, Gains Title Shot." *The New York Times*, 12/18/1960, p. S1.
Ross, Ron. *Nine . . . Ten . . . and Out!: The Two Worlds of Emile Griffith*. New York: DiBella Entertainment, 2008.
Teague, Robert L. "Griffith is Victor." *The New York Times*, 3/25/1962, p. 201.
Tuckner, Howard M. "Fear Stills the Power of a Champion." *The New York Times*, 5/8/1962, p. 48.

GRIGSBY, WILL (1971–). Will Grigsby is a former two-time world junior flyweight champion from St. Paul, Minnesota. Grigsby turned professional in 1988 and won his first fight. However, in his second pro bout he had to face former Olympian **Michael Carbajal,** who was making his pro debut. Carbajal captured a four-round decision. Following that loss, Grigsby spent nearly five years away from the ring due to managerial problems.

Undeterred, Grigsby returned to the ring in 1994. He kept winning and earned a title shot in 1998 against longtime titleholder **Ratanapol Sor Vorapin.** Grigsby won a unanimous decision. He made one successful defense before losing his belt to the great **Ricardo Lopez,** who won a unanimous decision. In 2000, he initially outpointed Nelson Dieppea to win the World Boxing Organization (WBO) junior flyweight title, but a positive test for marijuana changed that result to a no contest.

Grigsby had legal problems but reached the peak of his profession again in 2005 when he defeated Victor Burgos for the **International Boxing Federation (IBF)** junior flyweight title. He lost the title in his first defense.

Professional Record:	18-4-1
Championship(s):	IBF junior flyweight, 1998–1999; 2005–2006

Further Reading
Feour, Royce. "Grigsby fears no one in picking opponents." *Las Vegas Review-Journal*, 10/1/1999, p. 1C.
Sansevere, Bob. "Will Grigsby is a winner in the boxing world but trouble was never far behind." *St. Paul Pioneer Press*, 5/22/2005, p. B1.
Souhan, Jim. "Boxing champ Grigsby is armed with plan." *Scripps Howard News Service*, 6/21/2005.

GRIM, JOE (1881–1939). Joe Grim, born Saverio Giannone, was a boxing journeyman known for his incredible ability to absorb punishment. Though he lost nearly all of his professional bouts, Grim earned his place in boxing lore for his courage and purported saying after his bouts: "I am Joe Grim and no one can knock me out." Though he faced such greats as **Bob Fitzsimmons, Joe Gans,** Philadelphia Jack O'Brien, and **Jack Johnson,** none could kayo Grim who was known as "Iron Man" and "the Human Punching Bag."

Professional Record:	6-91-9
Championship(s):	None

Further Reading
Bearden, B. R. "Joe Grim: The Human Punching Bag Who Never Won a Fight." *Eastsideboxing*, at http://www.eastsideboxing.com/joegrim.html

GROUND AND POUND. "Ground and pound" refers to a style of fighting in mixed martial arts that involves striking an opponent on the ground. A combatant employs "ground and pound" by taking an opponent down, mounting them, and then raining down a series of punches. **Mark**

Coleman, an early **Ultimate Fighting Championships (UFC)** champion, is often credited with popularizing the "ground and pound" attack. Former **PRIDE** heavyweight champion and many experts' pound-for-pound world best **Fedor Emelianenko** has mastered the "ground and pound" technique. He utilized this technique to defeat **Antonio Rodrigo Nogueira** to win the PRIDE heavyweight title. Beginning mixed martial artists sometimes fall prey to submissions from the fighter on the bottom (in the "guard"), as the fighter on the bottom blocks a strike and then engages in an arm lock.

Further Reading
Rich Franklin, and Jon F. Merz. *The Complete Idiot's Guide To Ultimate Fighting.* New York: Alpha Books, 2007.

GUARD ("THE GUARD"). The Guard is a defensive position in mixed martial arts that enables a practitioner to defend against a striking opponent but also unveil several counter submission attacks. Popularized by **Royce Gracie** in early **Ultimate Fighting Championships (UFC)** events, the Guard "is a defensive position that allows for a series of submission holds that flow together to finish a fighter" (Shamrock, p. 55). Usually the fighter in the guard is on his back with his legs around his opponent's hips, while the opposing fighter attempts "to pass the guard" by landing strikes to his opponent or attempting various submission techniques.

There are two major types of "Guard"—closed guard and open guard. In closed guard, the fighter on the bottom has his legs tightly wrapped around the opponent sitting on top of him. The closed guard position prevents the sitting fighter to stand or to move around freely. The open guard is a more flexible position in which the fighter on the bottom may attempt to kick the opponent sitting on him or use his legs to attempt submissions. Among the most formidable proponents of "the Guard" today includes former **PRIDE** heavyweight championship and former UFC interim heavyweight titlist **Antonio Rodrigo Nogueira.**

Further Reading
Shamrock, Frank. "MMA 101: Submissions from the Guard." *Fight!* (December 2007), pp. 54–55.

GUILLARD, MELVIN (1983−). Melvin "the Young Assassin" Guillard is a talented, athletic mixed martial artist who many believe has yet to reach his full potential in the Octagon. A former star wrestler and high school football star at Bonnabel High School in Louisiana, Guillard's athleticism is unquestioned. What is questioned is his mental focus. His career has been marked by highs and lows.

A contestant on Season 2 of *The Ultimate Fighter,* Guillard was eliminated by Josh Burkman. Guillard later defeated **Marcus Davis** in *The Ultimate Fighter* finale card.

He has lost to Joe Stevenson and **Rich Clementi** by submissions but has unloaded devastating kayoes over other foes in the Octagon. If he can improve his ground game and continue his devastating striking, Guillard has a chance to be a special combat fighter.

Professional MMA Record: 21-7-2
Championship(s):   None

Further Reading
Iole, Kevin. "UFC fighter Guillard floored by Hurricane Katrina." *Las Vegas Review Journal,* 9/16/2005, p. 1C.
Official Web site: http://www.melvinguillard.tv/
Richards, Jim. "Guillard aims for return against Regan." *The Arizona Republic,* 3/7/2008, SPORTS, p. 8.

GUILLOTINE CHOKE. A guillotine choke is a popular submission move in mixed martial arts, named for its resemblance to the famous execution tool. The guillotine choke usually occurs on the ground when one fighter is leaning forward with his head facing his opponent. The opponent then places an arm around his opponent's head and then supports one arm with another. Those fighters with attacking wrestling styles of fighting have to be wary of guillotine chokes (as well as other submissions) when leaning in against opponents skilled in jiu-jitsu.

Further Reading
Rousseau, Robert. "Top 20 Submission Moves in MMA." *ExtremeProSports.Com,* at http://extremepros
    ports.com/MMA/submissions.html

GUSHIKEN, YOKO (1955–). Yoko Gushiken was a great flyweight champion from Japan who lost only one fight in his professional career. Known as "Fierce Eagle," this southpaw slugger possessed superior stamina and strong power. He turned pro in 1974 and won the **World Boxing Association (WBA)** world flyweight championship in his ninth pro bout by defeating Juan Antonio Guzman. He successfully defended his title 13 times before losing to Pedro Flores of Mexico. His manager asked the referee to stop the fight in the final stanza, as Gushiken started to take too much punishment. He retired after the bout and never fought again.

Professional record:	24-1
World Title(s):	WBA flyweight, 1976–1981

Further Reading
Associated Press. "Gushiken Triumphs." *The New York Times,* 7/30/1979, p. C6.
Associated Press. "12th Defense a Knockout for Gushiken." *The Washington Post,* 6/2/1980, p. C10.
United Press International. "Gushiken Keeps Title." *Chicago Tribune,* 5/23/1977, p. E4.

HAGLER, MARVELOUS MARVIN (1954–). Marvelous Marvin Hagler dominated the middleweight division for most of the 1980s, cementing his legacy as one of the sport's greatest at 160 lbs. The southpaw Hagler—a native of Brockton, Massachusetts—had to battle his way to the top through a slew of tough contenders—men such as **Eugene "Cyclone" Hart,** Bobby "Boogaloo" Watts, and Willie Monroe. One expert told Hagler that he had three strikes against him—he was left-handed, black, and too good.

Marvelous Marvin Hagler poses with two other great fighters—Bernard Hopkins and Oscar De La Hoya. Courtesy of Chris Cozzone.

In November 1979, Hagler seemingly defeated the tough **Vito Antuofermo** for the middle-weight title, but the judges called the bout a draw. After Antuofermo lost his title to Great Britain's Alan Minter, Hagler had to cross the Atlantic to face Minter and a hostile British crowd. Hagler dominated the bout but had to endure a bombardment of glasses from an angry mob. Famous sportswriter Red Smith wrote after Hagler's dominant performance: "Justice is not always done in this imperfect world, the meek seldom inherit the earth and the worthy are often cheated, but this time Marvin Hagler got what was coming to him" (41).

He defended his title 12 times, including a return win over Antuofermo, a victory over a tough Tony Sibson, two wins over a tough **Mustafo Hamsho,** and a thrilling third-round stoppage over **Thomas "the Hitman" Hearns,** a fight so action-packed that it has been called "the Eight Great Minutes." Hagler held his title until a 1987 showdown with the colorful **Sugar Ray Leonard**—a former Olympic gold medalist whom Hagler resented. Hagler seemingly gave away the first four rounds before steadily coming on later in the fight. Leonard flurried at the end of numerous rounds to capture a controversial split decision victory. Hagler could not believe that he lost the decision, and he never returned to the ring.

Instead, he moved to Italy where he starred in several action films. He still lives in Italy.

Professional Record: 62-3-2
Championship(s):   WBA Middleweight, 1980–1987; WBC Middleweight, 1980–1987; IBF Middleweight, 1983–1987

Further Reading
Berger, Phil. "Boxing's Angry Man." *The New York Times*, 3/22/1987, p. 222.
Dettloff, William. "The Ten Greatest Title Reigns of All-Time." *The Ring* (April 2005), pp. 65–76, 72.
Katz, Michael. "Hagler, His Dues Paid, Finally Takes Center Stage." *The New York Times*, 10/31/1983, p. C9.
Kimball, George. *Four Kings: Leonard, Hagler, Hearns, Duran and the Last Great Era of Boxing.* Ithaca, NY: McBooks Press, 2008.
Smith, Red. "Marvin Hagler Gets His Due." *The New York Times*, 9/29/1980, p. 41.

HAMED, NASEEM (1974–). "Prince" Naseem Hamed was a cocky southpaw champion in the featherweight division who dominated the division for a time in the late 1990s with his unorthodox punching style and devastating power.

Born in 1974 in Sheffeld, England, Hamed turned pro in 1992. In 1995, he stopped Steve Robinson to win the World Boxing Organization (WBO) featherweight title. In 1997, he added the **International Boxing Federation (IBF)** belt to his collection with a destruction of respected champion Tom Johnson. In 1999, he added the **World Boxing Council (WBC)** belt with an easy win over Cesar Soto. Hamed looked invincible until a 2001 showdown with Mexican great **Marco Antonio Barrera.** The tough Barrera gave Hamed a boxing lesson and embarrassed him. Hamed fought only once after that, defeating Miguel Calvo before suffering a series of legal problems.

Professional Record: 36-1
Championship(s):   WBO featherweight, 1995–2000; IBF flyweight, 1997; WBC featherweight, 1999–2000.

Further Reading
Doogan, Brian. "Naseem Hamed: The Power In His Fists Casts A Spell Over Foes and Fans." *KO* (February 2001), pp. 42–45.
Evans, Gavin. *Prince of the Ring: The Naseem Hamed Story.* London: Robson, 1998.

Goldman, Ivan. "'Prince Naseem Hamed: Primed For a Worldwide Assault." *The Ring* (October 1997), pp. 36–39, 57–58.

Pitt, Nick. *The Prince and the Prophet: The Rise of Naseem Hamed*. London: Four Walls Eight Windows, 1999.

Smith, Timothy W. "He's a Champion of Self-Promotion; Hamed Backs up His Talk with His Fists." *The New York Times*, 12/17/1997, p. C7.

HAMILL, MATT (1976–). Matt "the Hammer" Hamill is a mixed martial artist who has fought his entire professional career in the UFC. Hamill is known for his wrestling skills, physical strength and his deafness. Though born with the disability, Hamill has overcome adversity to become an inspiration to millions.

Hamill wrestled collegiately at the Rochester Institute of Technology where he won three Division III championships. In 1997 and 2001, Hamill won wrestling medals at the World Games for the Deaf or Deaflympics.

A few years later Hamill worked as a bouncer in upstate New York, a job that required him to use his wrestling skills to throw out unruly patrons. A fellow bouncer had a cousin relative who worked for the UFC. Hamill auditioned and was selected for the third season of The Ultimate Fighter. He won his first fight on the show but had to withdraw due to an injury.

Hamill then returned to the Octagon and won his first three professional bouts before dropping a controversial decision to **Michael Bisping.** Hamill won another bout before facing the much more experienced **Rich Franklin** who stopped him in the third round. Hamill has rebounded with another win and hopes to continue advancing his career.

Professional Record:	5-2
Championship(s):	None

Further Reading
Kane, Colleen. "Fighting His Way to the Top," *Cincinnati Enquirer*, 4/2/2006, p. 2C.
Official Web site: http://www.matthamill.com/
Perigard, Mark A. "Tough Guy; Matt Hamill Proves Deafness no Bar to 'Ultimate Fighter'" *Boston Herald*, 5/7/2006, p. 045.

HAMSHO, MUSTAFA (1953–). Mustafa Hamsho was a rugged middleweight contender during the 1980s who beat nearly everyone in the division except the undisputed champion **Marvelous Marvin Hagler.** Born in Syria, Hamsho literally fought nearly every day in the streets as a youngster. He came to the United States illegally in 1974 by jumping onto a Greek ship. He then lived and fought in Brooklyn, New York.

He turned professional in 1975 and lost a six-round decision to Pat Cuillo. The rugged southpaw would not lose again for six years. He defeated numerous contenders, including Wilford Scypion, Alan Minter, and Curtis Parker to earn a shot at Hagler's championship belt in 1981. Hamsho fought gamely but lost in the 11th round.

He rebounded with six straight wins, including defeats over previously unbeaten **Bobby Czyz** and former three-division champion **Wilfred Benitez.** That winning streak landed him another shot at Hagler. However, Hagler stopped him in the third round. He retired for good in 1989.

Professional Record:	44-5-2
Championship(s):	None

Further Reading

Katz, Michael. "Hamsho, a Syrian Street Fighter, Now Battling for Title Shot." *The New York Times,* 2/14/1981, p. 19.

Katz, Michael. "Hagler Stops Hamsho in 3d." *The New York Times,* 10/20/1984, p. 19.

HARADA, MASHIKO (1943–). Mashiko "Fighting" Harada was probably Japan's greatest boxer who won world championships in the flyweight and bantamweight divisions in the 1960s. Born in 1943 in Tokyo, Harada turned professional at age 16. In October 1962, he faced Thailand's **Pone Kingpetch** for the flyweight championship. The 19-year-old Harada kayoed the champion in the 11th round to capture the title. He lost the title in a rematch held in Kingpetch's hometown—Bangkok, Thailand. The Associated Press scored the bout 71-67 for Harada, but two official scorecards went for Kingpetch.

Harada later moved up in weight and challenged undefeated bantamweight champion **Eder Jofre.** Employing his trademark whirlwind attack, Harada outpointed the Brazilian legend to capture the title in 1965. He defeated Jofre by another close decision in their 1966 rematch. He held the bantamweight title until he dropped a decision to Lionel Rose in 1968. The next year, Harada moved up in weight and challenged featherweight champion Johnny Famechon in Sydney, Australia. Most ringside observers felt that Harada won the bout, but referee **Willie Pep** (who originally indicated the bout was a draw) scored the bout for the Australian champion by a single point. Even the Australian crowd booed the result. Harada retired in 1970 after he lost to Famechon in a rematch. In February 2007, Harada became president of the Japan Professional Boxing Association.

Professional Record: 55-7

Championship(s):   Flyweight, 1962–1963; Bantamweight, 1965–1968

Further Reading

Trumbull, Robert. "Harada Captures World Bantamweight Title by Outpointing Jofre." *The New York Times,* 5/19/1965, p. 55.

Trumbull, Robert. "Harada Heralds New Ring Era." *The New York Times,* 5/23/1965, p. S2.

Trumbull, Robert. "Famechon Outpoints Harada." *The New York Times,* 7/29/1969, p. 32.

HARRIS, "GYPSY" JOE (1945–1990). "Gypsy" Joe Harris was a stylish boxer from Philadelphia known for his eccentric ring style, clowning antics, and fine defensive skills. He often kept his hands extremely low and fired punches from many angles—in part because he was blind in his right eye. Harris won his first 24 professional fights, defeating the likes of Stanley "Kitten" Hayward, Curtis Cokes, and Bobby Cassidy. He lost a decision to former welterweight and middleweight champion **Emile Griffith** in 1968. Before his next fight, a ringside physician discovered Harris' blindness, and the popular Harris was forced to retire. Harris' unique style earned him the honor of gracing the cover of a June 19, 1967, cover of *Sports Illustrated*—the only nonheavyweight boxer who never won a world championship to earn such an honor.

Professional Record: 24-1

Championship(s):   None

Further Reading

"Gypsy Joe Harris." *Cyber Boxing Zone Encyclopedia* at http://www.cyberboxingzone.com/boxing/harris-gj.htm

Smith, Greg. "Gypsy Joe Harris: Career (and Life) Interrupted." *The Sweet Science,* 7/29/2005, at http://www.thesweetscience.com/boxing-article/2432/gypsy-joe-harris-career-life-interrupted/

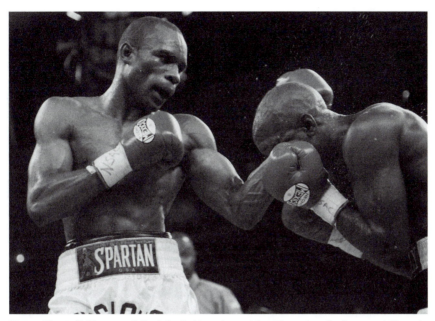

Vivian Harris (left) successfully defends his welterweight title against Soulemayne M'baye in July 2003. Courtesy of Chris Cozzone.

HARRIS, VIVIAN (1978−). "Vicious" Vivian Harris is a lanky former junior welterweight champion who usually provides fans an action fight. Born in 1978 in Georgetown, Guyana, to boxing promoter Herman Harris, Vivian was exposed to boxing at an early age. His older brother Wayne once fought for the junior middleweight title. He left Guyana at age 15 for Brooklyn. He turned professional in 1997 and won his first 16 pro fights before dropping a decision to Ray Oliveira. In 2002, he defeated Diosbelys Hurtado to win the **World Boxing Association (WBA)** junior welterweight title. He made three successful defenses before losing to Carlos Maussa in 2005. In 2007, he lost to **Junior Witter** in an attempt for the **World Boxing Council (WBC)** junior welterweight title. He rebounded with a win in 2008 and hopes to fight for a world title again in the near future.

Record:	29-3-1
Championship(s):	WBA junior welterweight, 2002–2005

Further Reading
Stradley, Don. "'Vicious' Vivian Harris: He's One of Those Guys Nobody Wants to Fight." *The Ring* (April 2005), pp. 52–56.

HARRISON, AUDLEY (1971−). Audley Harrison was the Olympic gold medalist in the super heavyweight division at the 2000 Sydney Games and Great Britain's hope for a successor to the great **Lennox Lewis** as the future world heavyweight champion. Born in 1971 in London England, Harrison ran into trouble as a youngster and was expelled from the Northwood Hills school for bullying. He later received a prison sentence of 32 months. He entered prison at age 17 and came out at 19.

Upon his release, he learned to box and graduated from Brunel University. He became an excellent amateur boxer, utilizing his superior height (6'6") and weight (250 pounds) to his

Audley Harrison towers above opponent Jason Barnett in their April 2008 bout. Harrison won in the fifth round. Courtesy of Chris Cozzone.

advantage. In the 2000 Olympic Games, he defeated Italian Paulo Vidoz in the semifinals and Muktarkhan Dildabekov of Kazakhstan in the finals to win the gold.

He turned pro in 2001 and initially performed quite well. He won his first 19 professional bouts until a December 2005 loss to Danny Williams and then a loss to Dominick Guinn in his next bout. He rebounded with two quick wins—including a rematch with Williams. However, his career plummeted in 2007 when he suffered a third-round technical knockout loss to Michael Sprott and a decision loss to unheralded Martin Rogan in 2008. It remains to be seen whether Harrison can rebound and revive his professional career.

Professional record:	23-4
Championship(s):	None

Further Reading

Doogan, Brian. "British Olympic Champ Audley Harrison: Is He the Next Lennox Lewis—Or The New Frank Bruno?" *The Ring* (March 2001), pp. 42–45.

Harrison, Audley. *Audley Harrison: Realising the Dream.* London: Andre Deutsch, 2001.

Official Web site: http://www.audleyharrison.com

HART, EUGENE "CYCLONE" (1951–). Eugene "Cyclone" Hart was a Philadelphia-based middleweight with a left hook that could render opponents unconscious with a single blow. In his 30 professional victories, Hart garnered 28 knockouts, many of which he displayed at the famous Blue Horizon.. He began his career with 19 straight knockouts and then captured a 10-round decision over veteran Don Fullmer. Trained by the legendary Cus D'Amato—best known as the trainer of heavyweight champions **Floyd Patterson** and **Mike Tyson**—Hart was susceptible of being knocked out himself. He lost eight fights by knockout in his career, including a first-round loss to fellow Philadelphia middle Bobby Watts. Hart lost to future champions **Vito Antuofermo, Marvelous Marvin Hagler,** and **Eddie Mustafa Muhammad** in his pro career, which spanned from 1969–1982.

| Record: | 30-9-1 (one no-contest) |
| Championships: | None |

Further Reading
Cushman, Tom. "A sad lament for Philly's forgotten heroes, all mostly forgotten." *San Diego Union-Tribune*, 2/16/1985, p. B-1.

HART, MARVIN (1876–1931). Marvin Hart was one of the most unlikely and undistinguished heavyweight champions. He initially campaigned at light heavyweight, losing in a world title shot to George Gardner. When **James J. Jeffries** retired as the undefeated world champion, he selected Hart and light heavyweight boxer Jack Root to fight to determine his successor. Hart was selected because in 1905, he surprisingly won a 20-round decision over **Jack Johnson.** Hart entered the ring as the underdog because Root had defeated him years earlier at light heavyweight. However, Root improved as a fighter when he moved up to the heavyweight division. Root opened up an early lead and dropped Hart in the seventh round. However, the man known as the "Fightin' Kentuckian" kept attacking and wore down his smaller opponent. Hart lost the title in his first defense against **Tommy Burns** by decision.

| Professional Record: | 31-9-7 (1 no-decision) |
| Championship(s): | Heavyweight, 1905–1906 |

Further Reading
Siler, George. "Siler's Talk of the Ring: Marvin Hart's Victory Over Root Due to Strength." *Chicago Daily Tribune*, 7/9/1905, p. A4.
Siler, George. "Marvin Hart Not Taken Seriously as Champion." *Chicago Daily Tribune*, 7/16/1905, p. A4.
Sullivan, John L. "Hart As Champion Criticised." *The Washington Post*, 7/23/1905, p. S4.

HATTON, RICKY (1978–). Ricky "Hitman" Hatton is one of boxing's most exciting fighters. The pride of Manchester, England, Hatton employs an aggressive, take-no-prisoners style of fighting that can make for great action fights. However, to some fans Hatton has engaged in excessive holding and clinching. Born in 1978 in Stockport, England, he turned pro in 1997 and has yet to lose a professional fight. In 2005, he upset **Kostya Tszyu** to win the **International Boxing Federation (IBF)** junior welterweight title, stopping the champion in the 11th round. He added the **World Boxing Association (WBA)** belt with a victory over Carlos Maussa.

In May 2006, Hatton moved up in weight to challenge WBA welterweight titlist Luis Collazo. Hatton dropped Collazo in the first round but then struggled to hold on for a close decision win. In January 2007, he defeated Juan Urango to win the IBF junior welterweight title over 12 rounds. Later in the year he destroyed former world champion **Jose Luis Castillo** in the fourth round.

Hatton's rise culminated in a showdown in December 2007 with boxing's pound-for-pound kingpin **Floyd Mayweather, Jr.** Though he fought bravely, Mayweather's speed proved too much and Hatton lost in the 10th round. Since his first professional loss, he has rebounded with wins over **Juan Lazcano** and **Paulie Malignaggi**.

| Record: | 45-1 |
| Championship(s): | IBF junior welterweight, 2005–2006, 2007; WBA junior welterweight, 2005–2006; WBA welterweight, 2006 |

Ricky "the Hitman" Hatton (left) battles Juan Urango in their January 2007 bout. Hatton won a unanimous decision. Courtesy of Chris Cozzone.

Further Reading

Doogan, Brian. "Hatton's Defeat of Tszyu Thrills a Nation." *The Ring* (October 2005), pp. 42–47.
Doogan, Brian. "Fighter of the Year Ricky Hatton." *The Ring* (April 2006), pp. 34–39.
Hatton, Ricky. *The Hitman: My Story.* London: Ebury Press, 2007.

HAZZARD, LARRY. Larry Hazzard was one of boxing's top referees in the 1980s and served as the chairman of the New Jersey boxing commission for 22 years. Born in Newark, Hazzard was a successful amateur boxer in the Golden Gloves. He later earned an undergraduate and masters degree in education from Montclair State.

In 1967, Hazzard began working as a referee of amateur bouts. In the 1970s, he began refereeing professional bouts. In the 1980s, he became one of the sport's top referees, serving as the third man in the ring for such world-title bouts as **Sean O'Grady—Hilmer Kenty, Marvelous Marvin Hagler**—William "Caveman" Lee, **Michael Spinks—Dwight Muhammad Qawi,** Michael Spinks—David Sears, Jimmy Paul—Harry Arroyo, **Pernell Whitaker—James "Buddy" McGirt,** and **Riddick Bowe**—Jesse Ferguson.

In 1985, he became the state's boxing commissioner and was known for ruling with a firm—but fair—hand. He served in that position for 22 years until his controversial removal in November 2007. The official line was that "it was just time for a change." In January 2008, Hazzard filed a lawsuit against state officials over his discharge.

Further Reading

McClure, Sandy. "Boxing world: N.J. chief's a champ Hazzard described as tough, fair man who's improved fight conditions." *Asbury Park Press*, 11/9/2003, p. A15.
Roberts, Penni. "He's No Hazzard to Boxing." *The Philadelphia Tribune*, 9/29/1995, p. 5.
Searcy, Jay. "Boxing's Larry Hazzard Plays It By the Book." *The Philadelphia Inquirer*, 3/24/1998.

HEARNS, THOMAS (1958–). One of the most exciting champions ever, Thomas "the Hitman" Hearns captured world championships in five different weight divisions, though his two most famous bouts were losses to contemporaries **Sugar Ray Leonard** and **Marvelous Marvin Hagler.** He burst onto the scene as a lanky power-puncher in the welterweight division, decimating opponents usually within the first few rounds. He won the **World Boxing Association (WBA)** welterweight title in August 1980 with a second-round stoppage of Mexico's **Pipino Cuevas.** In September 1981, he lost in the 14th round to Sugar Ray Leonard in a unification bout. Ahead on the scorecards, Hearns weakened in the later rounds—perhaps due in part to the difficulty he had making weight at the 147 lb. welterweight division. Years later in 1989, Hearns gained a measure of revenge by dropping Leonard twice though the judges scored the bout a draw.

Thomas Hearns is ringside in Las Vegas, Nevada, watching his son Ronald fight and win in October 2004. Courtesy of Chris Cozzone.

Hearns rebounded in December 1982 by outpointing the slick **Wilfred Benitez** to win the **World Boxing Council (WBC)** junior middleweight title. In April 1985, Hearns squared off against undisputed middleweight kingpin Marvelous Marvin Hagler in what became "the Eight Great Minutes." Hearns landed numerous bombs in the first round, opening a gash on Hagler's forehead, but the middleweight champion stopped Hearns with a vicious attack in the third round.

Hearns later added titles in the junior middleweight, middleweight, light heavyweight, and cruiserweight divisions. In June 1991, he outboxed the undefeated **Virgil Hill** to capture the world light heavyweight title for the second time. Hearns continues to flirt with more bouts. In 2006, he defeated Shannon Landbergh. His son Ronald is a promising young fighter.

Professional Record:	61-5-1
Championship(s):	WBA Welterweight, 1980–1981; WBC junior middleweight, 1982–1986; WBC middleweight, 1987–1988; WBO super middleweight, 1988–1990; WBC Light Heavyweight, 1987; WBA Light Heavyweight, 1991–1992

Further Reading

Feinstein, John. "Thomas Hearns: The Hit Man." *The Washington Post*, 8/5/1981, p. D1.
Hoffer, Richard. "Detroit Has One Winner: Boxer Tommy Hearns." *Los Angeles Times*, 8/1/1980, p. D1.

Kimball, George. *Four Kings: Leonard, Hagler, Hearns, Duran and the Last Great Era of Boxing.* Ithaca, NY: McBooks Press, 2008.
Verdi, Bob. "Hearns pulverizes Cuevas in 2." *Chicago Tribune*, 8/3/1980, p. C1.

HEINZ, W. C. (1915–2008). W. C. Heinz was a leading American journalist, biographer, and novelist who covered boxing for numerous publications during his distinguished career. Born in 1915 in Mount Vernon, New York, Heinz graduated from Middlebury College in 1937 where he served as sports editor of the school newspaper.

He later worked for the *New York Sun* and often wrote pieces on boxing. He also contributed articles to the leading boxing magazine *The Ring* on a freelance basis. He wrote profiles of **Al "Bummy" Davis, Rocky Graziano, Rocky Marciano, Joe Louis, Sugar Ray Robinson,** and many other leading pugilists.

In 1958, he published his first novel, *The Professional*, about a middleweight contender. He later wrote regularly for *Sports Illustrated.* He was inducted into the International Boxing Hall of Fame in 2004. He also edited *The Fireside Book of Boxing*, published in 1961.

Further Reading

Heinz, W. C., ed. *The Fireside Book of Boxing.* New York: Simon & Schuster, 1961.
Schudel, Matt. "W.C. Heinz, 93; He Broke New Ground in Journalism." *The Washington Post*, 3/5/2008, p. B07.

HENDERSON, DAN "HOLLYWOOD" (1970–). Dan Henderson was the former welterweight and middleweight champion of **PRIDE**, holding both belts simultaneously—the only man to accomplish such a feat. Henderson has world-class wrestling skills, evidenced by his participation in the 1992 and 1996 Olympic Games in **Greco-Roman wrestling**.

Born in 1970 in Apple Valley, California, Henderson wrestled at Cal State Fullerton and Arizona State University. After college, Henderson continued to compete in wrestling on an international basis, including the 1992 and 1996 Olympics. He made his professional mixed martial arts (MMA) debut in 1997 at the Brazil Open. The next year he entered the Octagon and defeated Allan Goes and Carlos Newton at **Ultimate Fighting Championships (UFC)** 17: Redemption to win the UFC's first middleweight tournament.

In 2000, he made his debut in PRIDE at PRIDE 12: Cold Fury, losing a unanimous decision to **Wanderlei Silva.** He later defeated Silva at PRIDE 33: The Second Coming to win the PRIDE middleweight title. He also holds wins over Renzo Gracie, **Vitor Belfort,** and Murilo Bustamante. He is 1-1 against the great **Antonio Rodrigo Nogueira,** despite a significant weight disadvantage. He lost to **Quinton "Rampage" Jackson** via unanimous decision in a light heavyweight unification bout in September 2007 at UFC 75: Champion v. Champion. In 2008, Henderson challenged **Anderson Silva** for the UFC middleweight championship, but he lost in the second round via a **guillotine choke**. Later in the year, Henderson rebounded with a solid win over dangerous submission specialist Rousimar Pulhares. In 2009, Henderson defeated **Rich Franklin** via split decision to earn a spot as a coach on an upcoming season of **The Ultimate Fighter** and a future match against **Michael "the Count" Bisping.**

Professional MMA Record:	23-7
Championship(s):	PRIDE Welterweight Champion, 2005–2007; PRIDE middleweight, 2007

Further Reading

Duggan, Dan. "Ultimate Fighting Championship, Henderson down for it." *The Boston Herald*, 2/24/2008, p. b25.

Hudson, David L. "'Dangerous' Dan Henderson looks to get back on winning track." *Fightnews.com*, 8/27/08, at http://www.fightnewsextra.com/cc/ufc88/14-henderson.htm.

"In my mind, I'm the best." *FightSport* (August 2007), pp. 78–81.

Official Web site: http://www.thenatural.tv/

Ross, Matthew. "Hendo's Moment of Truth: 'Dangerous' Dan says he's the Man to beat Anderson Silva." *FIGHT!* (March 2008), pp. 38–46.

HERRING, HEATH (1978-). Heath "the Texas Crazy Horse" is a mixed martial arts (MMA) heavyweight who has competed in **PRIDE** and the **Ultimate Fighting Championships (UFC)** for many years. Born in 1978 in Amarillo, Texas, Herring made his mixed martial arts debut in 1997. In 2000, he made his debut at PRIDE 9 with a win over Willie Peeters. In 2001, he defeated **Mark "the Smashing Machine" Kerr** with a stoppage in the second round.

Herring has fought a who's who list of MMA world-class fighters including **Antonio Rodrigo Nogueira** (3 times), **Fedor Emelianenko, Vitor Belfort, Evan Tanner** (twice), and **Igor Vovchanchyn.** In 2008, he upset Cheick Kongo at UFC 82: Pride of a Champion via a split decision. Then, he faced the behemoth **Brock Lesnar** and lost a unanimous decision.

Professional MMA Record:	28-14
Championship(s):	None

Further Reading

Official Web site: http://www.heath-herring.com/

Wagner, Adam. "Nothing new: MMAmania.com exclusive interview with Heath Herring." *MMAMania.com*, 8/4/2008, at http://mmamania.com/2008/08/04/nothing-new-mmamaniacom-exclusive-ufc-87-interview-with-heath-herring/

HILL, VIRGIL (1964-). Virgil "Quicksilver" Hill was a former Olympic medalist, longtime champion in the light heavyweight division, and a two-time champ in the cruiserweight division. Born in 1964 in Clinton, Missouri, his family moved to North Dakota when he was a youngster. He captured a silver medal at the 1984 Los Angeles Olympics, losing a disputed 3-2 decision to South Korean Shin Joon-Sup in the finals.

He turned pro in 1984 and in 1987 defeated Leslie Stewart to win the **World Boxing Association (WBA)** light heavyweight title. He successfully defended his title 10 times before falling victim to an aging **Thomas "the Hitman" Hearns** in 1991.

Hill rebounded to recapture the vacant WBA belt by defeating Frank Tate in 1992. He made 10 successful defenses before losing to undefeated German Dariusz Michalczweski in a unification bout. In 2000, he shocked the boxing world with a devastating first-round stoppage of **International Boxing Federation (IBF)** cruiserweight champion **Fabrice Tiozzo.** He lost the title in his first defense against Jean Marc Mormeck. In 2006, he won the WBA cruiserweight title with a 12-round decision win over undefeated Valery Brudov. He lost the title in 2007 to Filat Arslan.

Professional Record:	50-7
Championship(s):	WBA light heavyweight, 1987–1991; 1992–1997; IBF light heavyweight, 1996–1997; WBA cruiserweight, 2000–2002; 2006–2007

Further Reading
Drodz, Jonathan. "An Interview with Virgil Hill." *East Side Boxing*, 9/11/2006, at http://www.eastsideboxing.com/news.php?p=8809&more=1
Feinstein, John. "Hill Feels Rotten as U.S. Loser." *The Washington Post*, 8/12/1984, p. C10.
Gildea, William. "Unbeaten Hill Defends Against Ex-Hit Man." *The Washington Post*, 6/2/1991, p. C10.

HINTON, JEMAL (1969–). Jemal Hinton was a world-class super bantamweight who retired from boxing before he ever fought for a world championship. Born in 1969 in District Heights, Maryland, Hinton was a decorated amateur boxer. In 1988, he won the U.S. Amateur boxing championships with a decision win over Kennedy McKinney. However, Hinton failed to make the Olympic team, losing to McKinney in the Olympic Trials. McKinney went on to capture a gold medal at the Seoul Olympics. He turned pro later that year and won 22 straight bouts. However, Hinton retired unexpectedly in 1992. Many speculated he retired for religious reasons to concentrate on his Muslim faith.

Professional Record:	22-0
Championship(s):	None

Further Reading
Most, Doug. "He's E.T. in Boxing Trunks." *The Washington Post*, 12/13/1989, p. C2.

HOLMES, LARRY (1949–). Larry Holmes dominated the heavyweight division for at least seven years with a terrific jab, quick right cross, and fine defensive skills. He struggled throughout his career to escape the shadow of **Muhammad Ali** and once famously opined: "I have not received my just due." Despite this, Holmes was one of the great heavyweights of all time and richly deserved his 2008 induction into the **International Boxing Hall of Fame.**

Born in 1949 in Cuthbert, Georgia, he made his home in Easton, Pennsylvania, which earned him the moniker "the Easton Assassin." A former sparring partner of Ali, Holmes turned pro in 1973 with a decision win over Rodell Dupree. In 1975, he defeated Rodney Bobick, and in 1976, he defeated the very tough Roy Williams. In 1978, he overcame a split in his trunks to easily outpoint dangerous powerpuncher **Earnie Shavers** to earn a shot at the world heavyweight title.

Holmes captured the **World Boxing Council (WBC)** title with a 15-round split decision win over **Ken Norton.** Holmes won in a thriller, overcoming a torn bicep muscle and winning the last round. He defended his title 19 times, sometimes rising off the canvas to finish his foes. Perhaps his signature win was a 13th-round stoppage of power-puncher **Gerry Cooney.** He held the title until 1985 when he lost a close decision to **Michael Spinks.** Many thought Holmes won the rematch, but the judges awarded Spinks a split decision victory. Holmes failed in two other attempts to regain the crown, losing to **Mike Tyson** in 1988 and **Evander Holyfield** in 1992. His last fight was a 2002 decision win over Eric "**Butterbean**" Esch at age 52.

Record:	69-6
Championship(s):	WBC heavyweight, 1978–1985; IBF heavyweight, 1983–1985

Further Reading
Brunt, Stephen. *Facing Ali: 15 Fighters, 15 Stories.* Guilford, CT: Lyons Press, 2002, pp. 279–298.
Dettloff, William. "The Ten Greatest Title Reigns of All-Time." *The Ring* (April 2005), pp. 65–76, 74.

Holmes, Larry, with Phil Berger. *Larry Holmes: Against the Odds.* New York: St. Martin's Press, 1998.
Morgenstein, Gary. "Larry Holmes Wins the WBC Heavyweight Championship!" *Knockout* (Summer 1994), pp. 10–13.
Official Web site: http://www.larryholmes.com

HOLYFIELD, EVANDER (1962–). Evander "the Real Deal" Holyfield is a former four-time world heavyweight champion who, in his 40s, continues in his quest to capture a fourth title. Born in 1962 in Atmore, Alabama, Holyfield moved with his family as a youngster to Atlanta, Georgia, which remains his home. He impressed observers at the 1984 Los Angeles Olympics but had to settle for a bronze medal after hitting New Zealand's Kevin Barry on the break and suffering a disqualification.

He turned pro in 1984 and two years later challenged **Dwight Muhammad Qawi** for the **World Boxing Association (WBA)** cruiserweight championship. Holyfield captured a 15-round split decision in one of the toughest bouts of his career. He added the **International Boxing Federation (IBF)** belt in 1987 with an easy win over Ricky Parker. He unified the division in 1988 by defeating Carlos DeLeon for the **World Boxing Council (WBC)** belt.

Holyfield then moved to the heavyweight division. In 1990, he demolished **James "Buster" Douglas** to win the world title. He defended the title several times before losing a 12-round unanimous decision to undefeated challenger **Riddick "Big Daddy" Bowe.** He regained the title in 1993 with a 12-round majority decision over Bowe but lost it in his first defense to **Michael Moorer** in 1994. In November 1996, he won the heavyweight crown for the third time with a dramatic upset of **Mike Tyson.** In the infamous rematch, Holyfield prevailed after Tyson was

Evander Holyfield is in the ring to face Lou Savarese in their June 2007 bout. Courtesy of Chris Cozzone./FightWire Images.

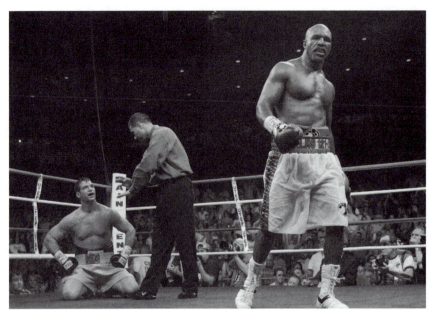

"The Real Deal" Evander Holyfield shows Lou Savarese he still has plenty of punch. Holyfield won a unanimous decision in their June 2007 bout. Courtesy of Chris Cozzone./FightWire Images.

disqualified for biting Holyfield's ear twice. In November 1999, he lost the title by decision to **Lennox Lewis.** He regained the title for a fourth time with a decision win over **John Ruiz.** In a rematch, he lost to Ruiz. Several times—most recently in 2008 against **Nikolai Valuev**—he has tried to capture the heavyweight title for the fifth time but has not succeeded. Whether he ever wins the title again, Holyfield has lived up to his nickname "the Real Deal."

Professional Record:	42-10-2
Championship(s):	WBC cruiserweight, 1986–1988; IBF cruiserweight, 1987–1988; WBA cruiserweight, 1988; Heavyweight, 1990–1992; WBA and IBF heavyweight, 1993–1994; WBC heavyweight, 1996–1999; IBF heavyweight, 1997–1999; WBA heavyweight, 2000–2001

Further Reading

Gustskey, Earl. "Holyfield Stopped by 4-Letter Word." *Los Angeles Times*, 8/10/1984, p. L1.

KO Interview. "Evander Holyfield: 'I'm Not A Quitter,'" *KO* (February 2001), pp. 52–59.

Holyfield, Evander, and Bernard Holyfield. *Holyfield: The Humble Warrior.* Nashville, TN: Thomas Nelson, 1996.

Holyfield, Evander, with Lee Guenfeld. *Becoming Holyfield: A Fighter's Journey.* New York: Simon & Schuster, 2008.

Kluck, Ted A. *Facing Tyson: 15 Fighters, 15 Stories.* Guilford, CT: Lyons Press, 2006, pp. 169–185.

Thomas, James J. *The Holyfield Way: What I Learned Courage, Perseverance and the Bizarre World of Boxing.* Champaign, IL: Sports Publishing LLC, 2005.

HOOST, ERNESTO (1965–). Ernesto "Mr. Perfect" Hoost is a former world champion kickboxer who won many titles in K-1. A native of Holland, Hoost began boxing at age 15. He discovered Thai boxing shortly thereafter and developed his skills. Many consider him to be one of the greatest fighters in K-1 history. He won the K-1 World Grand Prix Championship in 1997, 1999, 2000, and 2002. He won 98 fights in his illustrious career, which ended with his retirement in 2006. During his career he defeated a virtual who's who of great kickboxers, including **Andy Hug, Remy Bonjasky, Mirko "Cro Cop" Filipovic,** and **Michael McDonald.**

Professional Kickboxing Record:	98-19-1
Championship(s):	IKBF light heavyweight title, 1990; K-1 World Grand Prix Champion, 1997, 1999, 2000 and 2002

Further Reading
K-1 Profile of Ernesto Hoost: http://www.k-1.co.jp/k-1gp/fighter/ernesto_hoost.htm
Official Web site of Ernesto Hoost: http://www.ernestohoost.nl/

HOPKINS, BERNARD (1965–). Bernard "the Executioner" Hopkins remains one of boxing's finest pound-for-pound practitioners even at the age of 43 in 2009. The longest reigning middleweight of all-time, Hopkins is a masterful all-around boxer who rates among the greats of all time.

Born in 1965 in Philadelphia, Hopkins turned pro in 1988 at light heavyweight and dropped a four-round decision to Clinton Mitchell. He moved down in weight and began his winning ways. He didn't lose again until a 1993 decision loss to **Roy Jones, Jr.,** for the **International Boxing Federation (IBF)** middleweight title. In 1994, he failed to capture the middleweight title—only managing a draw against champion Segundo Mercado.

He won the rematch in 1995 and then made 20 successful title defenses before finally losing the title in a disputed decision to **Jermain Taylor** in 2005. His signature win was his 2001 domination of previously unbeaten **Felix Trinidad** in 2001. Hopkins lost another disputed decision to Taylor in 2006, and many boxing experts thought he was done. He proved the critics

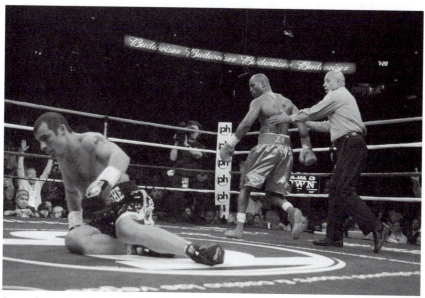

Bernard Hopkins drops Joe Calzaghe in the first round of their April 2008 bout. However, Calzaghe rose and won a 12-round split decision. Courtesy of Chris Cozzone.

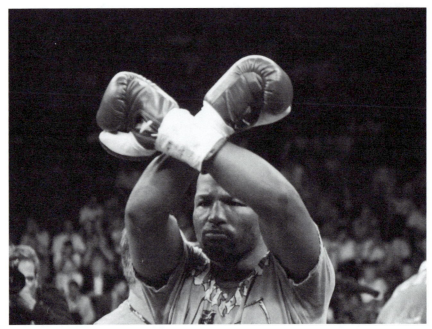

Bernard Hopkins gives a symbolic gesture that he is ready for battle against Joe Calzaghe. Courtesy of Chris Cozzone.

Bernard Hopkins needed all his defensive skills when facing a much younger Jermain Taylor in their July 2005 bout. Hopkins lost his middleweight title by a 12-round split decision. Courtesy of Chris Cozzone.

wrong, dominating light heavyweight kingpin **Antonio Tarver** in a 2006 clash. In 2007, he defeated fellow pound-for-pound great **Ronald "Winky" Wright** over 12 tough rounds. In 2008, he dropped a decision to the unbeaten **Joe Calzaghe.** However, Hopkins again shocked the boxing public with a dominating 12-round win over middleweight kingpin Kelly Pavlik in a display that boxing scribe Tim Smith called "a performance for the ages." *The Ring* senior writer William Dettloff rates Hopkins' 10-year middleweight reign as the second greatest title reign in boxing history behind only the great **Joe Louis** (67).

At times in his career, Hopkins has been a rebel, preferring to do things his way—even if that means ruffling feathers and becoming his own worst enemy. For instance, he lost more than $600,000 in libel damages to his former promoter **Lou DiBella,** seemingly being his own worst enemy. However, Hopkins has rebounded professionally both in and outside the ring. Not only does he continue to amaze observers in the ring at an advanced age, but he seems to work well for Golden Boy Promotions and former opponent **Oscar De La Hoya.**

Record:	49-4-1
Championship(s):	IBF middleweight, 1995–2005; WBC middleweight, 2001–2005; WBA middleweight, 2001–2005.

Further Reading

Collins, Nigel. "Bernard Hopkins' Upset of Winky Wright: A Simple Case of Mind Over Matter." *The Ring* (November 2007), pp. 36–42.

Dettloff, William. "The 10 Greatest Title Reigns of All-Time." *The Ring* (April 2005), pp. 65–76.

Donovan, Jake. "Still Waiting for Bernard Hopkins to Grow Old?" *The Sweet Science*, 7/15/2005, at http://www.thesweetscience.com/boxing-article/2375/still-waiting-bernard-hopkins-grow-old/

Raskin, Eric. "Boxing's Biggest Factor: Can Hopkins Recover From His Self-Inflicted Wounds?" *KO Magazine* (July 2003), pp. 30–35.

Santoliquito, Joe. "Hopkins' Throwback Night in Jersey: The New Light Heavyweight Champion Honors the Legends—and Himself." *The Ring Extra* (October 2006), pp. 26–32.

Smith, Tim. "Hopkins Turned Back Time while Turning Away Pavlik's Challenge," ESPN.com, 10/19/2008, at http://sports.espn.go.com/sports/boxing/news/story?id=3651918

"*The Ring* Interview: Bernard Hopkins: 'I Need A Major Threat, Where If I Don't Win, I'm Dead.' " *The Ring* (March 2007), pp. 96–101.

HOPSON, ED (1971–). Ed Hopson, or "Fast Eddie," was a 5'4" southpaw sparkplug of a fighter who won a world super featherweight championship. Born in 1971 in St. Louis, Missouri, Hopson nearly made the 1988 U.S. Olympic team as a teenager. A then 17-year-old Hopson lost a disputed decision to Kelcie Banks for the coveted spot.

He turned pro in 1989 and won his first 25 fights before landing a fight against fellow unbeaten prospect Moises Pedroza for the vacant **International Boxing Federation (IBF)** super featherweight championship in April 1995. Hopson's blazing speed proved too much, and he prevailed in the seventh round. However, Hopson lost his belt in his first defense to Tracy Harris Patterson. He initially retired after losing to journeyman Santos Lopez.

He returned to the ring in 1998, winning three straight bouts against limited opposition.

Professional Record:	30-2
Championship(s):	IBF super featherweight, 1995

Further Reading

Berger, Phil. "Boxer Is Making Name for Himself." *The New York Times*, 7/11/1988, p. C7.

Berger, Phil. "Popular Featherweight Loses." *The New York Times*, 7/'17/1988, p. S4.

HORN, JEREMY (1975–). Jeremy Horn is a rare professional mixed martial artist, as he may have had more professional bouts than any other mixed martial arts (MMA) combatant in the professional ranks. He has fought more than 100 times, compiling 88 victories. A jiu-jitsu specialist, Horn has won 49 bouts by submissions.

Born in 1975 in Omaha, Nebraska, Horn began his professional MMA career in 1996. In 1998, he challenged **Frank Shamrock** for the **Ultimate Fighting Championships (UFC)** middleweight title but lost in the second round. He is well known for handing **Chuck "the Iceman" Liddell** his first MMA loss in 1999. However, Horn lost to Liddell in a 2005 rematch, which was for Liddlell's UFC light heavyweight title. Horn also has wins over **Forrest Griffin,** Josh Burkman, and Vernon White.

Professional MMA Record:	80-19-5 (sources differ on his record)
Championship(s):	None

Further Reading

Iole, Kevin. "Confident Horn can't see Liddell retaining title." *Las Vegas Review-Journal*, 8/19/2005, p. 9C.
Iole, Kevin. "Liddell retains UFC crown." *Las Vegas Review-Journal*, 8/21/2005, p. 7C.

HUERTA, ROGER (1983–). Roger "El Matador" Huerta is a top contender in the **Ultimate Fighting Championships' (UFC)** lightweight division known for his all-around skills, frequent fights in the Octagon, and his cover appearance on *Sports Illustrated* in 2007. Born in 1983 in Los Angeles, California, Huerta began his professional mixed martial arts (MMA) career in 2003 in Extreme Combat.

Huerta progressed to the UFC, making his debut in September 2006 with a win over Jason Dent. In 2007, he fought and won five bouts in the UFC with wins over John Halverson, Leonard Garcia, Doug Evans, Alberto Crane, and Clay Guida. Huerta showed great heart in overcoming devastating strikes from Guida and submit his dangerous foe by a rear naked choke hold in the third round.

In his last bout, Huerta lost a decision to the talented **Kenny Florian.** Huerta hopes to rebound from his defeat and win a championship in the near future.

Professional MMA Record:	25-2
Championship(s):	None

Further Reading

Arritt, Dan. "Roger Huerta, abandoned as a child, finds peace and encouragement en route to MMA fame." *Los Angeles Times*, 8/8/2008, at http://www.latimes.com/sports/la-spw-ufc9-2008aug09,0,744876.story
Taflinger, Neal. "Don Caballero: El Matador Takes the Bull by the Horns." *FIGHT!* (August 2008), pp. 42–52.

HUG, ANDY (1964–2000). Andy Hug was a former world kickboxing champion in K-1 who earned the nickname "the Blue-Eyed Samurai" from the Japanese martial arts fans. He was known for his powerful spinning back kick and his vaunted axe kick. An axe kick is one where a fighter raises his leg above his opponent and then chops down with his heel.

Born in 1964 in Wohlen, Switzerland, Hug started learning karate at age 10. He became the champion of his country in karate and later won several European tournaments. He achieved international acclaim after winning the K-1 World Grand Prix championship in 1996. He held two wins over **Ernesto "Mr. Perfect" Hoost** and a win each over **Mirko "Cro Cop" Filopovic** and **Maurice Smith.** He won his last fight in July 2000. He died the next month at the age of 35 of leukemia.

Professional Kickboxing Record:	37-9-1
Championship(s):	K-1 World Grand Prix Champion, 1996

Further Reading

Official Web site: http://www.andyhug.com/

Tezuka, Mako. "Thousands gather to mourn the death of a K-1 samurai." *The Nikkei Weekly* (Japan), 9/4/2000.

HUGHES, MATT (1973—). Matt Hughes is one of the greatest mixed martial artists of all time and a long-time **Ultimate Fighting Championships (UFC)** welterweight champion. He is known for his superb conditioning, physical strength, and superior wrestling skills. Born in 1973 in Hillsboro, Illinois, Matt and his twin brother, Mark, competed in football and wrestling in high school.

Matt won back-to-back state high school wrestling championships, earning a scholarship to Southwestern Illinois College in Bellevue, Illinois. He competed there one year before transferring to Lincoln College. After a year at Lincoln, he then competed two years at Eastern Illinois University, earning All-American honors.

He later met Monte Cox and started competing in minor-league mixed martial arts (MMA) fight promotions in 1998. He won his first three bouts before losing on a choke hold to the more experienced Dennis Hallman. He then won 18 more bouts—fighting in different countries and in different organizations until finally landing a rematch against Hallman in the UFC at UFC 29: Defense of the Belts. Unfortunately for Hughes, he suffered another submission loss to his nemesis.

In November 2001, Hughes landed the chance to face UFC welterweight champion Carlos Newton—the man who had defeated Hughes' long-time trainer and mentor **Pat Miletich** of Miletich Fighting Systems. Newton started strongly, but Hughes kayoed him with a tremendous slam in the second round. He successfully defended his UFC belt against **Hayato Sakurai,** Newton, Gil Castillo, **Sean Sherk,** and **Frank Trigg.**

Hughes lost his belt at UFC 46: Supernatural to the talented **B. J. "the Prodigy" Penn** by rear naked choke. However, he recaptured his UFC belt at UFC 50: War of 04 with a submission of the gifted **Georges St.-Pierre.** He defended his title against Trigg, and then defeated the legendary **Royce Gracie,** who made an ill-fated comeback. Hughes then exacted revenge on B. J. Penn.

Hughes lost his belt in November 2006 via strikes to Georges St.-Pierre. He rebounded with a decision win over the tough **Chris Lytle** but then lost a rubber match to the more athletic St.-Pierre. He suffered a second setback in 2008 when he lost to a bigger Thiago Alves in England at UFC 85: Bedlam. Hughes hopes to land a match against rival **Matt Serra,** whom he coached against in *The Ultimate Fighter* 5 and a fighter whom he dislikes.

In 2007, Hughes left Team Miletich and longtime trainer Pat Miletich to form his own Team Hughes. He works with **Robbie Lawler, Jeremy Horn,** and several other top MMA fighters.

Professional MMA Record: 43-7

Championship(s):   UFC Welterweight, 2001–2004, 2004–2006

Further Reading

Hughes, Matt, with Michael Malice. *Made in America: The Most Dominant Champion in UFC History.* New York: Simon Spotlight Entertainment, 2008.

Official Web site: http://www.matt-hughes.com

HUNT, MARK (1974—). Mark Hunt is a Samoan mixed martial artist from New Zealand who first made his mark in the world of combat sports with his kickboxing prowess. Born in

1974 in South Auckland, New Zealand, Hunt turned pro as a kickboxer in 1999. He competed in numerous bouts in K-1, the premier kickboxing organization in the world. He defeated such fighters as Jerome Le Banner (though he lost to Le Banner several times), Hiromi Amada, and **Gary Goodridge.**

In 2004, Hunt shifted his attention to mixed martial arts, debuting in **PRIDE** with a loss to Hidehiko Yoshida. Hunt then scored five straight victories, including wins over legendary fighters **Wanderlei Silva** and **Mirko "Cro Cop" Filopovic.** In 2007, he lost to perhaps the two top heavyweights in PRIDE—**Josh Barnett** and champion **Fedor Emelianenko.** He gave the great Fedor trouble in their encounter before losing via a kimura. In 2007, **Ultimate Fighting Championships (UFC)** President **Dana White** announced that Hunt was under contract with his organization.

Professional MMA Record:	5-5
Professional Kickboxing Record:	29-12
Championship(s):	None

Further Reading
Clifford, R. J. "Top Ten Toughest Chins in MMA." *Tapout,* No. 24 (2008), pp. 89–91.
Rogue, Boa. "Mark Hunt Returns!: 'The Hammer Talks Schilt and Fedor." *Rogue Magazine,* 3/12/2008, at http://www.roguemag.com/index.php?option=com_content&task=view&id=231&Itemid=86

I

IBEABUCHI, IKE (1973–). Ike "the President" Ibeabuchi never lost a professional boxing match but lost badly outside the ring. Born in 1973 in Nigeria, Ibeabuchi turned pro in 1994. He captured the attention of boxing experts when he outpointed the power-punching phenom **David Tua** in 1997 on HBO. In his last fight in 1999, Ibeabuchi became the first man to defeat future heavyweight champion **Chris Byrd** with a convincing fifth-round stoppage. Ibeabuchi looked like he would become the next dominant heavyweight champion. However, in 2001, he pleaded guilty to attempted sexual assault and battery. He remains incarcerated in a Nevada prison at the time of this writing. He did obtain an associate's degree while in prison and hopes to one day resume boxing upon his release.

Professional Record: 20-0
Championship(s):   None

Further Reading

Mladinich, Robert. "Ike 'the President' Ibeabuchi: A New Heavyweight Candidate." *The Ring* (November 1997), pp. 22–24, 57–58.
Watkins, Calvin. "Fighting Himself: Former Dallas boxer goes from rising star to jailed rape suspect amid bizarre behavior." *The Dallas Morning News*, 12/18/2000, p. 10B.

INOUE, ENSON (1967–). Enson Inoue was a famous American mixed martial artist known for his incredible ability to withstand punishment and diehard refusal to submit even in the face of a stone-cold submission hold or repeated strikes.

Born in 1967, Inoue turned professional in mixed martial arts (MMA) in 1995 with four straight wins. In October 1998, he submitted **Randy "the Natural" Couture** with an armbar, handing Couture the first loss of his professional MMA career. But Inoue is best known for his never-say-die attitude even in the face of near-death. He lost to **Igor Vovchanchyn** when his corner threw in the towel. He suffered a broken jaw, a ruptured eardrum, and brain swelling. Against the Brazilian jiu-jitsu master **Antonio Rodrigo Nogueira** at **PRIDE** 19, Inoue refused to tap out and was left unconscious by his opponent rather than submit. His last mixed martial arts bout was in 2004.

Professional MMA Record:	11-8
Championship(s):	None

Further Reading
Campany, Jerry. "Inoue a Relentless Fighter." *The Honolulu Star-Bulletin,* 4/16/2004.
Official Web site: http://www.enson-inoue.com/

INTERNATIONAL BOXING FEDERATION (IBF). The International Boxing Federation (IBF) is one of the three major sanctioning bodies in professional boxing along with the **World Boxing Association (WBA)** and the **World Boxing Council (WBC).** It is the only one of the big three organizations that is based in the United States; its headquarters are in New Jersey.

The IBF formed in the 1980s after Bob Lee, an official with the U.S. Boxing Association (USBA), failed to win the presidency of the WBA. Lee and others then formed the IBF.

The organization gained near-immediate credibility when heavyweight champion **Larry Holmes** became its first heavyweight champion.

The IBF suffered a black eye when Bob Lee faced a litany of charges stemming from a multiyear FBI investigation and charges that he took bribes from promoters. In August 2000, a federal jury acquitted Lee of most of the more serious racketeering charges but did convict him of a few charges, including tax evasion. Lee was convicted on only 6 of more than 30 charges. Lee agreed to a lifetime ban from boxing. In 2004, a federal judge ended federal monitoring of the organization.

The IBF rebounded well from that scandal. It elected Hiawatha Knight, former boxing commissioner in Michigan, as its president in 2000—the first woman ever elected chairperson of a major boxing organization. After Knight left, another woman, Marian Muhammad, took over as president. It remains a leading and respected sanctioning body in professional boxing.

Further Reading
Fernandez, Bernard. "Reputation-rehab-is-ex-IBF-boss-toughest-fight." *Philadelphia Daily News,* 4/13/2006.
Gold, Jeffrey. "Judge ends federal monitoring of boxing organization." *Associated Press,* 9/29/2004.
International Boxing Federation: http://www.ibf-usba-boxing.com/

INTERNATIONAL BOXING ORGANIZATION (IBO). The International Boxing Organization (IBO) is a Florida-based sanctioning body known for its independent, computerized rankings and excellent reputation. The IBO was founded in 1993. However, the organization did not receive a higher profile until Ed Levine, a former world-class boxing judge, attorney, and official with the World Boxing Organization (WBO), came to the IBO. Levine still serves as the IBO's president.

The IBO is best known for its independence and computerized ranking system. As it states in one of its editorials: "Our mandate from the beginning—recognizing the corruption and cronyism and payoffs that have proliferated in the sport—has been to create a fair ratings system for boxing."

Formed in 1993, the IBO crowns champions in virtually all weight classes. Many prominent, world-class fighters have captured IBO championships, including heavyweight **Lennox Lewis,** light heavyweight **Antonio Tarver,** light heavyweight **Roy Jones, Jr.,** and welterweight

Floyd Mayweather, Jr. Current IBO champions include heavyweight **Wladimir Klitschko** and junior welterweight **Ricky "the Hitman" Hatton.**

Further Reading

Feour, Royce. "Minor organization seeks major changes." *Las Vegas Review-Journal*, 12/1/2001, p. 3C.

Grahame, Ewing. "IBO Can Be Ed of the Class; Levine Out to Restore Faith." *Daily Record*, 1/25/2000, p. 40.

International Boxing Organization: http://www.iboboxing.com

IBO Editorial. "The IBO Computerized Rankings." http://www.iboboxing.com/ibo_computerized_ratings.html

INTERNATIONAL FIGHT LEAGUE (IFL). The International Fight League (IFL) was a mixed martial arts (MMA) organization best known for its team-style aspect. The brainchild of Jay Larkin, a longtime executive of Showtime, the IFL employs past MMA greats to serve as coaches of different squads. The IFL, which began in 2006, originally featured several city-based teams, including the Quad-City Silverbacks, the New York Pitbulls, and the Nevada Lions.

For 2008, the IFL employs team "camps" that revolve around famous mixed martial arts training facilities, such as Team Quest, Xtreme Couture, Miletech Fighting Systems, Midwest Combat, Team Tompkins, American Top Team, Renzo Gracie Jiu-Jitsu, and the Lion's Den. Each camp has a coach and fighters in six different weight classes—145, 155, 170, 185, 205, and 265. MMA legend **Bas Rutten** served as the IFL's Vice President of Fighter Operations.

However, in July 2008, the IFL ceased to exist as it was bought by Zuffa, the parent company of the **UFC.**

Further Reading

Falzon, Andrew. "Big Changes in the International Fight League." *FIGHT!* (April 2008), pp. 36–37.

Official Web site: http://www.ifl.tv/

ISHIDA, MITSUHIRO (1978–). Mitsuhiro Ishida is a Japanese-based wrestler and mixed martial artist who is known for his incredible aerobic conditioning. He has compiled an exceptional professional mixed martial arts (MMA) record of 16-4-1. He turned pro at a Shooto event in 2001, losing to Daisuke Sugie by decision. He rebounded with four straight wins before a draw with Naoki Matsushika.

In April 2006, he made his debut in **PRIDE,** defeating Paul Rodriguez with a guillotine choke. He won three more bouts in PRIDE before losing to the vaunted **Takanori Gomi.** In his last bout at Yarennaka in December 31, 2007, he defeated the then-unbeaten Gilbert Melendez.

Professional MMA Record:	17-4-1
Championship(s):	Shooto champion, 2006–2007

Further Reading

PRIDE profile of Mitsuhiro Ishida: http://www.pridefc.com/pride2005/index.php?mainpage=fighters&fID=334

JACK, BEAU (1921–2000). Beau Jack was one of the most exciting fighters in boxing history, headlining more cards at Madison Square Garden than any other fighter. He fought with an all-out energy that endeared him to the fistic public. Born in 1921 in Augusta, Georgia, as Sidney Walker, he got his name "Beau Jack" from one of his grandmothers. He earned a living as a youngster shining shoes and caddying at the famous Augusta National Golf Club. The great golfer Bobby Jones helped fund Jack's boxing career, which took him to New York City. He made his professional debut in 1939 in Aiken, South Carolina, but hooked up with New York City publicity man Chuck Wergeles, who placed Jack on the big stage. In December 1942, he stopped Tippy Larkin in the third round to win the NBA lightweight crown. He lost the title to rival **Bob Montgomery** in 1943 but regained it later that year in a fight *The New York Times* described as an event where "a great little fighter came back to the heights" (Dawson). He also lost several times to fellow Hall of Famer **Ike Williams.** Jack finally retired for good from the ring in 1955.

Professional Record:	83-24-5
Championship(s):	Lightweight, 1942–1943, 1943

Further Reading

Burley, Dan. "Beau Jack's 'Rags to Riches' Rise." *Chicago Daily Defender*, 5/25/1959, p. 9.

Daley, Arthur. "Beau Jack with Conversational Overtones." *The New York Times*, 2/5/1943, p. 24.

Dawson, James. "Beau Jack Regains Ring Title by Outpointing Montgomery." *The New York Times*, 11/20/1943, p. 17.

Goldstein, Richard. "Beau Jack, 78, Lightweight Boxing Champion in the 1940's." *The New York Times*, 2/12/2000, p. B8.

Moses, Alvin. "Twilight Hour Looms for Beau Jack, Once an Idol." *The Chicago Defender*, 7/31/1948, p. 10.

JACKSON, JULIAN (1960–). One of boxing's best one-punch kayo artists, Julian "the Hawk" Jackson captured 49 of his 55 professional victories via knockout. He captured world titles in the junior middleweight and middleweight divisions, winning his first title in 1987 with a third-round stoppage of Korea's In Chul Baek. He decimated the talented **Terry Norris** in the second round in perhaps his career-best performance.

He won the **World Boxing Council (WBC)** world middleweight title in 1990 with a single punch over the talented boxer **Herol Graham** in the fourth round. Graham had outboxed Jackson easily for the first three rounds before running into a monstrous right hand that left Graham on the canvas for five minutes. Jackson lost his belt to the power-punching **Gerald McClellan.** He retired after suffering two straight defeats in 1998.

Professional Record:	55-6
Championship(s):	WBA Junior Middleweight, 1987–1990; WBC Middleweight, 1990–1993, 1995

Further Reading

Borges, Ron. "Jackson Claims Crown." *The Boston Globe*, 3/18/1995, p. 77.

Matthews, Wallace. "Jackson Drops Minton with Three Strong Rights." *Newsday*, 9/15/1991, SPORTS, p. 11.

JACKSON, PETER (1861–1901). Peter Jackson was a great heavyweight fighter denied a shot at the world heavyweight title because he was black. Born in St. Croix, Virgin Islands, and reared in Australia, Jackson traveled the world defeating many of the best boxers of the day. For much of the 1890s, he was known as the Coloured Heavyweight champion after besting George Godfrey.

World champion **John L. Sullivan** refused to face Jackson, wishing to avoid the humiliation of losing to a black man. In 1891, Jackson battled to a 61-round-draw against future champion **James "Gentleman Jim" Corbett.** Ironically, Corbett also refused to defend his title against Jackson when he lifted the title from Sullivan. Years later, Corbett would write that Jackson was "the greatest fighter I have ever seen." Sportswriter Harvey Woodruff wrote of Jackson: "As a fighter in the ring and a clean living fellow outside the ring, he was admired by fistic followers of all races."

The inscription on his tombstone says it best: "This was a man."

Professional Record:	45-4-5
Championship(s):	None

Further Reading

Davies, Charles E. "Peter Jackson Is In Hard Lines." *Chicago Daily Tribune*, 11/6/1899, p. 9.

Hales, A. G. *Black Prince Peter: The Romantic Career of Peter Jackson.* New York: Wright & Brown, 1931.

"Jackson Is Here: Colored Fighter Says He Will Box Any of Them." *Chicago Daily Tribune*, 9/19/1897, p. 5.

"Jackson Wants to Fight Slavin." *The Chicago Daily Tribune*, 11/10/1891, p. 7.

Woodruff, Harvey. "Louis Patterns His Career After Peter Jackson." *Chicago Daily Tribune*, 6/23/1935, p. A4.

JACKSON, QUINTON "RAMPAGE" (1978–). Quinton "Rampage" Jackson is one of the most exciting and explosive mixed martial artist fighters in the world. Known for his trademark howl, powerful strikes, and massive body slams, Jackson has competed at the highest levels of both **PRIDE** FC and the **Ultimate Fighting Championships (UFC),** facing and defeating many of the toughest fighters in the world.

Born in 1978 in Memphis, Tennessee, Jackson earned all-state honors as a star wrestler at Raleigh Egypt High School. He later wrestled in junior college before fighting in mixed martial arts (MMA). He turned pro in 1999, making a name for himself in several Gladiator Challenge events.

He earned respect in the MMA world in his PRIDE debut in PRIDE 15, putting up a tremendous fight in a losing effort to the vaunted Kazushi Sakuraba in July 2001. Jackson, known for his powerful body slams and kayo power in his hands, also possesses strong wrestling skills. He knocked out **Chuck "the Iceman" Liddell** twice—once in a PRIDE fight in 2003 and then in a much-anticipated rematch at UFC 71: Liddell v. Jackson. In the second bout, Jackson kayoed Liddell with a counter right hand, ending the bout in under two minutes. He successfully defended his belt against **Dan "Hollywood" Henderson,** winning a unanimous decision at UFC 75: Champion v. Champion. Jackson's nemesis earlier in his career has been Muay Thai master **Wanderlei Silva** who stopped Jackson in PRIDE bouts in 2003 and 2004 with brutal knees to the head.

In July 2008, Jackson lost his championship to his opposing coach on *The Ultimate Fighter 7* show, **Forrest Griffin.** Jackson lost a unanimous five-round decision, though many believed the fight was much closer than the official scorecards. Jackson's life seemed to unravel after the defeat, as he was arrested for reckless driving and hit and run.

However, Jackson rebounded in a major way in December 2008 by knocking out his old nemesis Silva with a brutal left hook.

Professional MMA Record: 29-7
Championship(s):   UFC light heavyweight, 2007–2008

Further Reading

Davidson, Neil. "Ready to live up to his nickname; Rampage Jackson prepares to take down superstar Chuck Liddell again." *Edmonton Journal,* 5/25/2007, p. C2.
Official Web site: http://www.allrampage.com
Pugmire, Lance. "'Rampage rollout: Jackson, whose nickname says it all, is set to establish himself in Ultimate Fighting circles." *Los Angeles Times,* 2/3/2007, p. D11.
Ross, Matthew. "Rising Son: Quinton Jackson and Juanito Ibarra Took A Chance on Each Other—How It's Paid off Inside and Out of the Cage." *FIGHT!* (July 2008), pp. 42–52.

JARDINE, KEITH (1975–). Keith "the Dean of Mean" Jardine is a popular mixed martial artist who competes in the **Ultimate Fighting Championships (UFC).** Born in 1975, Jardine excelled in wrestling and football as a youngster. He attended Pierce College in Los Angeles and then New Mexico Highlands University. He fought professionally as a kickboxer and a boxer. He compiled a record of 3-0-1 as a professional boxer, fighting in 2003 and 2004.

He made his professional mixed martial arts (MMA) debut in 2001, defeating Amir Rahnavardi at a Gladiator Challenge event. His big break came in 2005 when he was selected as a participant on *The Ultimate Fighter 2,* where he lost in the semifinals to **Rashad Evans.** Jardine's aggressive style has endeared him to the fans. In December 2006, he defeated **Forrest Griffin** via kayo. He lost in 2007 in a first-round knockout to virtual unknown **Houston Alexander.** However, he rebounded in a major way in his next bout by defeating **Chuck "the Iceman" Liddell** by split decision.

Unfortunately for Jardine, his career took another roller coaster turn when **Wanderlei Silva** destroyed him in less than 40 seconds in June 2008 at UFC 84. He rebounded from that devastating loss with a decision win over Brandon Vera in 2008.

Professional MMA Record: 14-4-1
Championship(s):   None

Further Reading

Davidson, Neil. "Keith (the dean of mean) Jardine wants everybody to be a mean one." *The Canadian Press*, 5/23/2008.

Official Web site: http://meanjardine.net

JEFFRIES, JAMES J. (1875–1953). James J. Jeffries dominated the heavyweight division for several years, retiring as an unbeaten champion. He is best known for coming out of retirement to challenge unsuccessfully **Jack Johnson** in what many called the "Fight of the Century."

A large man at 6′2″ and over 200 pounds, Jeffries won the heavyweight title in 1899 by knocking out the smaller champion **Bob Fitzsimmons.** Jeffries successfully defended his title six times against Tom Sharkey, Jack Finnegan, former champion **James "Gentleman Jim" Corbett,** Gus Ruhlin, Fitzsimmons, and Jack Monroe. He retired in 1905, claiming that he had defeated "all logical challengers." This conveniently ignored several top black fighters. Jeffries returned to the ring in 1908 to attempt to wrest the title from Jack Johnson, the first black world champion. Johnson easily defeated Jeffries and stopped him in the 15th round. Jeffries returned to retirement and his alfalfa farm.

Professional Record:	19-1-2
Championship:	Heavyweight, 1899–1905

Further Reading

Callis, Tracy. "Jim Jeffries … 'Warhouse of Yesteryear,'" *Cyber Boxing Zone Journal*, February 2001, at http://www.cyberboxingzone.com/boxing/w4x-tc.htm

Corbett, James. "Jeffries Greatest Fighter." *The New York Times*, 4/24/1910, p. S2.

Jeffries, James J. "Big Fight Is on Tonight." *Chicago Daily*, 11/3/1899, p. 4.

"Jeffries An Easy Winner." *Los Angeles Times*, 8/15/1903, p. A1.

"Jeffries a Kingpin." *Los Angeles Times*, 6/10/1899, p. 3.

Fullerton, Hugh. *Two Fisted Jeff: Life Story of James J. Jeffries World's Greatest Heavyweight Champion.* Chicago: Consolidated Book Publishers, 1929.

Naughton, W. W. "Big Fighters Meet Tonight: Fitzsimmons and Jeffries Are Ready for Contest at Coney Island." *Chicago Daily*, 6/9/1899, p. 4.

Naughton, W. W. "Johnson Rends Jeff to Pieces in 15 Rounds." *The Washington Post*, 7/5/1910, p. 1.

Nicholson, Kelly Richard. *A Man Among Men: The Life and Ring Battles of Jim Jeffries, Heavyweight Champion of the World.* Draper, UT: Homeward Bound Publishing, 2002.

Oliver, Grey. "Glimpse at Private Life of Jeffries." *Los Angeles Times*, 1/10/1909, p. VII.

JENNUM, STEVE (1964–). Steve Jennum is a mixed martial artist best known for his unlikely victory in the third **Ultimate Fighting Championships (UFC)** tournament—UFC 3. Jennum, a Nebraska-based police officer, entered the UFC 3 as an alternate. The eight-man tournament was supposed to showcase a finale between two-time defending champion **Royce Gracie** and **Ken Shamrock.** True to form, Gracie and Shamrock won their opening round bouts—Gracie over Kimo Leopoldo and Shamrock over Felix Lee Mitchell.

However, Gracie and Shamrock dropped out. Gracie dropped out due to injury, while Shamrock refused to fight once he realized he would not have the opportunity to avenge his loss to Gracie at UFC 2. For the finale, Harold Howard faced the alternate Jennum. Howard placed Jennum in a guillotine choke, but Jennum escaped. The two fighters then went toe-to-toe standing up, trading punches. Jennum took Howard down and then pounded him—in a move later called "ground and pound." Jennum won the fight at 1:46 of the first round, becoming the most unlikely of UFC champions.

Jennum returned to the Octagon at UFC 4. He won his opening round match against boxer Milton Bowen. However, Jennum could not advance further due to injury. He also fought in the original Ultimate Ultimate tournament, losing to **David "Tank" Abbott.**

Professional MMA Record: 2-3
Championship(s):   UFC 3 Winner

Further Reading
Gentry, Clyde. *No Holds Barred: Ultimate Fighting and the Martial Arts Revolution.* London: Milo Books, 2002.

JOHANSSON, INGEMAR (1932–2009). Ingemar Johansson was a former world heavyweight champion best known for his exciting trilogy of fights with **Floyd Patterson.** Born in 1932 in Gothenburg, Sweden, Johnansson represented his country in the 1952 Helsinki Olympics. He made it to the gold medal match against American heavyweight Ed "Big Ed" Sanders. Sanders' size must have intimidated Johansson, for the Swede—in the words of a *Los Angeles Times* columnist—"turned in the greatest retreat since the Allies swept through Germany in World War II." The referee disqualified Johansson for running away from his opponent in the ring, though Ingemar claimed that he was merely trying to tire Sanders out for a third-round attack. Initially deprived of his medal, he later received it 30 years later.

Johansson turned pro in 1952 and won his first 21 professional bouts before facing Patterson for the world heavyweight title in June 1959. In his greatest performance, Johansson unleashed his powerful right hand and dropped Patterson seven times in the third round before referee Ruby Goldstein stopped the bout. Patterson won the rematch via a fifth-round stoppage. In the rubber match held in 1961, Johansson nearly regained his title in the first round, dropping Patterson twice. However, Patterson recovered, knocked Johansson down near the end of the round, and prevailed in the sixth round. Johansson won four more bouts but retired in 1963.

Professional Record: 26-2
Championship(s):   Heavyweight, 1959–1960

Further Reading
Distel, Dave. "Old Foes Revive a Marathon Rivalry." *Los Angeles Times,* 4/26/1983, p. SD_B1.
Johansson, Ingemar. *Seconds Out of the Ring.* London: Sportsmens Book Club, 1961.
Nichols, Joseph C. "Patterson Knocks Out Johansson in 5th; First to Regain the Heavyweight Title." *The New York Times,* 6/21/1960, p. 1.
Smith, Wilfrid. "Johansson New Champion." *Chicago Daily Tribune,* 6/27/1959, p. 1.
Zimmerman, Paul. "Five U.S. Fighters Triumph." *The Los Angeles Times,* 8/3/1952, p. B9.

JOFRE, EDER (1936–). Eder Jofre was a great bantamweight and featherweight world champion from Brazil who lost only two fights in his entire career. A pure boxer who could bang, Jofre was considered one of the sport's pound-for-pound best during his heyday as bantamweight kingpin. Born in 1936 in Sao Paulo, his father taught Jofre how to box at age 3. Jofre represented Brazil in the 1956 Melbourne Olympics but lost in the quarterfinals. He turned professional the next year, fighting his first 11 bouts in Sao Paulo.

In 1960, he defeated Eloy Sanchez for the NBA bantamweight title and then achieved worldwide recognition as bantamweight champion by stopping Piero Rollo in the 10th round. He held the title until losing a close decision to **Mashiko "Fighting" Harada** in 1965. After losing to Harada by another close decision in a rematch, he retired.

Jofre returned to the ring in 1969 and kept winning. In 1973, he defeated Jose Legra by decision to win the featherweight championship. He successfully defended his title against fellow future Hall of Famer **Vincente Saldivar** later that year. He was stripped in 1974 for failing to defend his title but did not lose in the ring. He retired in 1976 after defeating top-10 contender Octavio Gomez at age 40.

Professional Record:	72-2-4
Championship(s):	Bantamweight, 1961–1965; WBC Featherweight, 1973–1974

Further Reading

Cuoco, Dan. "Eder Jofre—The Second Best Pound-for-Pound Fighter in Boxing History." *Cyber Boxing Zone Journal*, July 2000, at http://www.cyberboxingzone.com/boxing/box7-00.htm

Roberts, James B., and Alexander B. Skutt. *The Boxing Register* (4th ed.). Ithaca, NY: McBooks Press, Inc., 2006, pp. 450–453.

Sares, Ted. "Eder Jofre: The Greatest Fighter Who Fought Under the Radar." *Eastsideboxing*, 5/25/2007, at http://www.eastsideboxing.com/news.php?p=11082&more=1

Smith, Dan. "Jofre, 24, in Training 21 Years—and Looks It." *Los Angeles Times*, 8/16/1960, p. C3.

JOHN, CHRIS (1979–). Chris John is a world featherweight boxing champion—the third from his native country of Indonesia. In addition to being a world-class boxer, John excels at wushu—a sport that blends gymnastics and martial arts. Blessed with excellent speed and quickness, John also possesses an excellent chin.

Born in 1979 in Jakarta, John first boxed as an amateur when he was 15. His father, a former boxer, taught him the basics of the sport. He turned professional in 1998. In 2003, he won the **World Boxing Association's (WBA)** interim featherweight title by defeating Oscar Leon. He cemented his hold on the belt with a decision win over former champion Derrick "Smoke" Gainer in 2005. In March 2006, he stunned many boxing experts by outboxing **Juan Manuel Marquez** over 12 rounds to retain his title. He remains the champion and hopes to unify the division.

Professional Record:	42-0-2
Championship(s):	WBA featherweight, 2003–

Further Reading

"Chris John Calm in the Face of Fierce Opposition." *Jakarta Post*, 1/26/2008.

JOHNSON, GLEN (1969–). Glen "the Road Warrior" Johnson is a former world light heavyweight champion who still remains one of the best fighters in his division though he is close to 40 years of age. Born in 1969 in Jamaica, Johnson turned pro in 1993 and won his first 32 bouts before facing middleweight champion **Bernard "the Executioner" Hopkins.**

Hopkins stopped Johnson in the 11th round—the only time Johnson has ever been stopped his entire career. Johnson continued to persevere, despite losing some questionable decisions through the years. In 1999, he lost a controversial decision to **International Boxing Federation (IBF)** super middleweight champion **Sven Ottke.**

In 2004, Johnson's career took off when he decisioned Clinton Woods to win the vacant IBF light heavyweight crown. In his first defense he shockingly kayoed the great **Roy Jones, Jr.** Then, later that year, he won a split decision over **Antonio Tarver**—considered by many the best light heavyweight in the world.

Johnson continues to chase his dream of winning a world title. Many thought he should have won the **World Boxing Council (WBC)** title, but instead he lost a close decision to undefeated **Chad Dawson.**

Professional Record:	48-12-2
Championship(s):	IBF light heavyweight, 2004

Further Reading

Donovan, Jake. "Glen Johnson: 2004's Fighter of the Year Still Fights for Respect." *The Sweet Science,* 6/17/2005, at http://www.thesweetscience.com/boxing-article/2265/glen-johnson-2004-fighter-year-still-fights-respect/

Doogan, Brian. "No Glencoffe Breaks For This Light Heavy." *World Boxing* (September 2004), pp. 62–65.

Parrish, Gary. "Win changes Johnson's world." *The Commercial Appeal,* 5/3/2005, p. C1.

Glen Johnson proudly displays his IBO world belt that he won by defeating favored Antonio Tarver in December 2004. Courtesy of Chris Cozzone.

JOHNSON, HAROLD (1928–). Harold Johnson was a former world light heavyweight champion known for his fine boxing skills and superior defensive abilities. Born in 1928 in Manayunk, Pennsylvania, Johnson joined the Navy at age 15 and learned to box in the service. Following his service, he turned pro in 1946. He won his first 24 bouts before losing a decision to **Archie Moore**—who would defeat Johnson in four of five bouts.

In 1954, Johnson challenged Moore for the world light heavyweight title. Johnson dropped Moore in the 10th but fell in the 14th round of a great bout. In 1961, Johnson won the NBA light heavyweight title and then later that year won the vacant world light heavyweight title with a decision win over Doug Jones. He successfully defended the title once before losing a 15-round split decision to **Willie Pastrano** in 1962. He fought infrequently after losing the title and retired for good in 1971 after losing to Herschel Jacobs.

Johnson's career had its moments of controversy, such as his inexplicable loss in 1955 to Julio Mederos in the second round, when he fell to the ground. Drugs were found in Johnson's system though he claimed he never took such substances knowingly. He later passed a lie-detector test and resumed boxing.

Professional Record:	76-11
Championship(s):	Light Heavyweight, 1961–1962

Further Reading

Livingston, Charles J. "When It Rains It Pours Trouble for Jinxed Boxer, Harold Johnson." *The Chicago Defender,* 6/11/1955, p. 10.

Roberts, James B., and Alexander G. Skutt. *The Boxing Register: International Boxing Hall of Fame Register* (4th ed.). Ithaca, NY: McBooks Press, Inc., 2006, pp. 458–461.

The one and only Jack Johnson. Courtesy of New MexicoBoxing.com collection

JOHNSON, JACK (1878–1946). Arthur John Johnson made history as the first black heavyweight champion who refused to allow white society to tell him how to behave. Instead Johnson lived by his own rules, marrying white women, flouting societal conventions, and taunting opponents. Aside from his chaotic personal life, Johnson at his peak was one of the best boxers in history. He possessed great defensive skills in addition to powerful punches. He held the title for seven years, finally losing to the giant **Jess Willard** in Havana, Cuba, in 1915. But, Johnson was more than a boxer—he was a cultural icon or anti-icon.

Born in Galveston, Texas, in 1878, Johnson improved as a boxer, learning lessons from the tough Jewish boxer **Joe Choynski,** who had kayoed him in the third round with a blow to the temple. The two were thrown in jail for engaging in an illegal boxing match, and apparently Choynski schooled Johnson on tricks of the trade.

Johnson defeated Denver Ed Martin in 1903 to win the Coloured world heavyweight title. A few years later, Johnson traveled the world attempting to persuade champion **Tommy Burns** to give him a title shot. To his credit (and a large payday), Burns agreed, and Johnson won the title in 1908 in Sydney. Johnson dominated the division for years with his toughest battles outside the ring against law enforcement who charged him with violating the Mann Act—for transporting a woman across state lines for immoral purposes. The reason for the charge was that Johnson openly cavorted with white women. In his most famous fight, Johnson defeated former champion **James J. Jeffries** in the fight of the century. He lost his title to the much larger Willard in 1915 and never received another title shot.

Professional Record:	82-14-11 (20 no-decisions)
Championship:	Heavyweight, 1908–1915

Further Reading

Farr, Finis. *Black Champion: The Life and Times of Jack Johnson.* New York: Charles Scribner's Sons, 1964.

Hietala, Thomas. *Jack Johnson, Joe Louis and the Struggle for Racial Equality.* New York: ME Sharpe, 2002.

Johnson, Jack. *My Life and Battles,* ed. Chris Rivers. Westport, CT: Praeger, 2007.

Kent, Graeme. *The Great White Hopes: The Quest to Defeat Jack Johnson.* Gloucester, England: Sutton Publishing, 2005.

Roberts, Randy. *Papa Jack: Jack Johnson and the Era of White Hopes.* New York: Free Press, 1985.

Ward, Geoffrey. *Unforgiveable Blackness: The Rise and Fall of Jack Johnson.* New York: Alfred A. Knopf, 2004.

Wells, Jeff. *Boxing Day: The Fight That Changed the World.* New York: HarperCollins, 2000.

JOHNSON, LEAVANDER (1969–2005). Leavander Johnson was a former lightweight champion who died after the first defense of his belt in 2005. Born in 1969 in New Jersey, Johnson turned pro in 1989. In 1994, he challenged Miguel Angel Gonzalez for the **World Boxing**

Tragic Defeat! Jesus Chavez lands another punch on Leavander Johnson in their fateful September 2005 bout for Johnson's IBF lightweight title. The bout was finally stopped in the 11th round and Johnson later died from injuries suffered in the ring. Courtesy of Chris Cozzone.

Council (WBC) lightweight title and lost in the eighth round. In 1997, he lost to Orzebeck Nazarov in his second attempt at a major title—the **World Boxing Association (WBA)** lightweight belt. In 2003, he lost to Javier Jauregui in a bout for the vacant **International Boxing Federation (IBF)** title. Finally, on his fourth try, Johnson won a major world championship by defeating Stephano Zoff for the IBF championship. In his first fateful defense, he met the tough **Jesus Chavez.** Johnson was hurt in the second round with a big left hook but continued to fight. Chavez battered him in the 11th round when the fight was stopped. Unfortunately, Johnson sustained brain injuries, fell into a coma, and died six days later.

Record: 34-5-2
Championship(s):   IBF lightweight, 2005

Further Reading
Stradley, Don. "Anguished Cries After Johnson Death." *The Ring* (February 2006), pp. 62–67.

JOHNSON, MARK (1971–). Mark "Too Sharp" Johnson is a former world flyweight and super flyweight champion known for his excellent boxing skills. Born in 1971 in Washington, D.C., Johnson turned pro in 1990. Though he lost his second pro bout by decision, Johnson quickly rose through the ranks. In 1996, he decimated Francisco Tejedor in the first round to capture the vacant **International Boxing Federation (IBF)** flyweight championship. He made seven successful defenses, never losing the belt in the ring.

Instead, Johnson moved up in weight in 1999 and faced **Ratanapol Sor Vorapin** for the vacant IBF super flyweight championship. Johnson won a unanimous 12-round decision. He later moved up to bantamweight but suffered two losses to **Rafael Marquez.** In 2003, Johnson rebounded to outpoint undefeated Fernando Montiel for the World Boxing Organization (WBO) super flyweight title. He lost the title in 2004 to Ivan Hernandez. He last fought in 2006, losing by kayo.

Professional Record:	44-5
Championship(s):	IBF flyweight, 1996–1999; IBF super flyweight, 1999–2000; WBO super flyweight, 2003–2004

Further Reading
Whitehead, Johnnie. "Can 'Too Sharp' Johnson Put It Together Again?" *The Ring* (July 2001), pp. 80–83.

JOHNSON, MARVIN (1954–). Marvin Johnson was the first man to win the world light heavyweight championship three times. A rugged southpaw, Johnson earned a bronze medal at the 1972 Munich Olympic Games in the middleweight division. The Indianapolis native turned pro after the Olympics.

He won his first 15 pro fights before losing to fellow prospect and future champion **Matthew Saad Muhammad** in the 12th and final round. Johnson won the vacant **World Boxing Council (WBC)** title in 1978 with a 10th-round stoppage of Mate Parlov in Italy. It was the first time that Pavlov had ever been stopped in his pro career.

Johnson lost the title in his first defense to Saad Muhammad in a brutal war. Johnson received another title shot in 1979 and made the most of it by upsetting **Victor Galindez** to earn the **World Boxing Association (WBA)** crown. The fight was in the balance in the 11th round when Johnson kayoed the favored Argentinian champion with a brutal left hook. He lost the title in his first defense to **Eddie Mustafa Muhammad.** Johnson regained the title a third time by stopping Leslie Stewart on cuts in the seventh round to win the WBA crown. After one successful defense, Johnson lost the belt to Stewart in their rematch. He retired after that fight.

Professional Record:	43-6
Championship(s):	WBC Light Heavyweight, 1978; WBA Light Heavyweight, 1979–1980, 1986–1987

Further Reading
Associated Press. "Johnson Stops Pavlov in 10th." *Los Angeles Times,* 12/3/1978, p. C7.
Smith, Sam. "Johnson Adds 3d Light Heavy Title." *Chicago Tribune,* 2/10/1986, p. 5C.

JONES, ROY, JR. (1969–). For many years Roy Jones, Jr., reigned supreme as boxing's pound-for-pound king, utilizing uncanny hand and foot speed to bedevil opponents and boxing purists alike. Born in 1969 in Pensacola, Florida, Jones won a silver medal at the 1988 Seoul Olympics, though only an outright robbery of a decision deprived him of the gold. He was named the Games' outstanding boxer even though he did not get the gold medal.

He turned pro in 1989 and captured the vacant **International Boxing Federation (IBF)** middleweight title with a unanimous 12-round decision over future great **Bernard Hopkins.** In 1994, he won the IBF super middleweight title with a dominant performance over James Toney. His dominance in the mid-1990s was obvious. Once, he defended his title against challenger Eric Lucas and then played in a minor pro basketball league game on the same evening.

Roy Jones Jr. exults in his defeat of heavyweight champion John Ruiz in March 2003. Courtesy of Chris Cozzone.

In 1996, he outpointed veteran Mike McCallum to win the **World Boxing Council (WBC)** light heavyweight title. In 1997, he suffered the first loss of his career when he hit Montell Griffin when the challenger was on the canvas. He rebounded with a devastating first-round knockout in the rematch to regain his title.

He unified the light heavyweight title and made numerous title defenses until 2003 when he accomplished the unthinkable—moving up in weight and defeating a heavyweight champion. He outpointed **John Ruiz** to capture the championship. Unfortunately for Jones, his career went into decline as he dropped weight and resumed fighting as a light heavyweight. He suffered back-to-back kayo losses to **Antonio Tarver** and **Glen Johnson** in 2004. In 2005, he lost the rubber match with Tarver (whom he had defeated in their first fight) for his third straight loss. Jones then won three fights in a row before challenging unbeaten **Joe Calzaghe**. Unfortunately for Jones, Calzaghe dominated him over 12 rounds in their 2008 encounter. Jones says he will continue fighting in 2009. He remains active and hopes to regain his past glory.

Professional Record:	52-5
Championship(s):	IBF middleweight, 1993–1994; IBF super middleweight, 1994–1996; WBC light heavyweight, 1996–1997, 1997–2003; WBA and IBF light heavyweight, 1997–2003; WBA heavyweight, 2003

Further Reading

Anderson, Dave. "Roy Jones Jr. Still Fighting For the Gold." *The New York Times*, 3/22/1989, p. B9.

Eskenazi, Gerald. "Jones Does Double Duty in Ring and On Court." *The New York Times*, 6/16/1994, p. S6.

Fernandez, Bernard. "Time's Running Out On Roy: Soon It'll Be Too Late To Prove His Greatness." *KO* (February 2001), pp. 36–40.

Privman, Jay. "Pound for Pound, It's Jones Over Toney in Easy Decision." *The New York Times*, 11/19/1994, p. 33.

Smith, Timothy W., Jr. "Remember Roy Jones? Virgil Hill Is Likely To." *The New York Times*, 4/26/1998, p. SP7.

JUDAH, ZAB (1977–). Zab "Super" Judah is a talented southpaw boxer who has won world championships in the junior welterweight and welterweight divisions. Blessed with incredible hand speed, Judah once graced boxing's pound-for-pound top 10 lists though he has at times self-destructed.

Born in 1977 in Brooklyn, Judah turned pro in 1996 at age 18. He won his first world championship in 2000 when he defeated Jan-Piet Bergman to capture the **International Boxing Federation (IBF)** junior welterweight championship. He made five successful defenses, often in dominating fashion, before facing fellow junior welterweight title holder **Kostya Tszyu.** Unfortunately for Judah, Tszyu bombed him out in the second round. Then, Judah attacked referee Jay Nady, earning himself a suspension from the Nevada Boxing Commission.

He rebounded in 2003 with a decision win over Demarcus "Chop Chop" Corley to win the World Boxing Organization (WBO) junior welterweight title. In 2004, he lost a decision to Cory Spinks in an attempt to win the welterweight championship. The next year, Judah gained revenge by stopping Spinks in the ninth round to win three world championship belts at welterweight. In 2006, he lost his IBF title to Carlos Baldomir in a major upset. Later in 2006, he gave pound-for-pound king **Floyd Mayweather, Jr.,** a tough fight but lost a unanimous decision.

In 2007, he failed to capture the **World Boxing Association (WBA)** welterweight title and lost in a spectacular fight against undefeated **Miguel Cotto.** In 2008, Judah fought well but lost to the tough Ghanian fighter Joshua Clottey. Judah still hopes to regain his championship form in 2008 and beyond. He is trained by his father, Yoel Judah, a former kickboxing champion.

Zab Judah looks amazed that he lost the decision to Joshua Clottey in their August 2008 bout. Courtesy of Chris Cozzone.

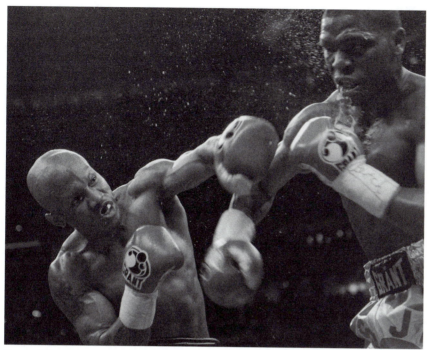

Rematch Revenge—Zab Judah pounds Cory Spinks and reclaims his title in their February 2005 rematch. Courtesy of Chris Cozzone.

Professional Record:	37-6
Championship(s):	IBF junior welterweight, 2000–2001; WBO junior welterweight, 2003–2004; WBC welterweight, 2005–2006; IBF welterweight, 2005–2006; WBA welterweight, 2005–2006

Further Reading
Donovan, Jake. "Zab Judah's Last Chance at Lasting Impression." *The Sweet Science*, 1/14/2005, at http://www.thesweetscience.com/boxing-article/1557/zab-judah-last-chance-lasting-impression/
McNeil, Franklin. "Dad's wise words packed a punch with Judah." *The Star-Ledger*, 2/20/2005, p. 13.

JUDGING OF BOXING BOUTS. The art of judging a professional boxing match is an inexact science, though most rounds are quite easy to score in favor of a particular pugilist. Most organizations or states mandate that judges score bouts on the following factors: clean punching, effective aggressiveness, ring generalship, and defense. By far the most important factor is clean, effective punching. The boxer who consistently lands clean blows to his opponent's head and body should capture the round. Difficulties come in determining how to measure quantity of punches versus quality of punches. Another difficulty is that some judges seemingly prefer different styles. Some judges favor fighters who are aggressive and throw many punches over a more selective counterpuncher who lands a higher percentage but lands fewer blows.

Most boxing bouts today are judged under the **ten point must system**—where the winner of a round receives 10 points, and the loser generally receives 9. Even rounds are disfavored under the 10-point must system. Other systems of judging include the 5-point system and the round system. Under the 5-point system, the winner of a round receives 5 points. Under the round system, the boxer who wins the most rounds wins.

In most boxing matches, the judges' scores are unknown to everyone until the fight is over. A person with the supervising commission and sanctioning body at ringside tabulates the scores. The ring announcer then informs the audience and the pugilists the official verdict. In a reform effort, some sanctioning bodies and jurisdictions have employed "open scoring" where the official scorecards are read at the end of certain rounds. Many criticize open scoring for taking away the suspense of who won a close bout.

Unfortunately, boxing sometimes suffers from what is termed "hometown" decisions where judges seemingly favor the hometown fighter over the out-of-town fighter. Sometimes this happens on a national level where judges seemingly vote for the fighter of their country. Fortunately, most well-trained ring officials rise above partisan concerns and score fights fairly.

Further Reading

Collins, Nigel. "Are Bad Decisions Killing Boxing?" *The Ring* (August 1988), pp. 14–15.

Donovan, Jake. "Scoring Discrepancies—Suspect or Subjective?" *Fightbeat*, 9/10/2007, at http://fightbeat. com/article_detail.php?AT=161

Hudson, David L. Jr. "Judges Under Fire: What Can Be Done to Improve the Scoring of Professional Bout," *Boxing Digest*, October 2002, pp. 62–63.

Layden, Tim. "Boxing Judges: On the Ropes." *Newsday*, 5/13/1990, p. 32.

Odd, Gilbert. *Debatable Decisions*. London: Nicholson & Watson, 1953.

JUDGING OF MMA BOUTS. Many mixed martial arts (MMA) bouts end in knockout, technical knockout, or submission. However, others go to the scorecards just like professional boxing. In most bouts a clear winner can be identified by even the untrained eye, as one combatant has clearly inflicted greater damage on another.

However, some bouts are extremely difficult to score and lead to controversial results. Some judges may prefer the aggressive striker; other judges may prefer the fighter who attempts more submissions; while other judges may prefer fighters who put their opponent on their back with superior wrestling skills.

Most MMA organizations employ the **ten point must system**—the same system used widely in professional boxing. Under the 10-point must system, the winner receives 10 points, and the loser of the round generally receives 9 points. If a fighter dominates a round, he may win a round by a 10-8 or 10-7 score.

Often, the scoring of an MMA bout will depend on where the majority of the fighting in a round takes place. For example, if the bulk of a fight is fought standing up, the more effective striker likely will carry the round. However, if the bulk of the round is fought on the ground, the more effective grappler or the fighter who attempts more submissions likely will carry the round.

There have been many prominent fights that have ended with controversial or debatable decisions, such as **Bas Rutten–Kevin Randleman** (1999), **Matt Hamill–Michael Bisping** (2007) or **Forrest Griffin–Rampage Jackson** (2008).

Further Reading

Crigger, Kelly. "Robbed!: Fighters Face A Tough Crossroads When an Easy Decision Becomes a Major Disappointment." *Real Fighter*, pp. 40–44.

Davidson, Neil. "Mixed martial arts scorecard." *The Canadian Press*, 7/2/2007.

KACAR, SLOBODAN (1957–). Slobodan Kacar was a decorated amateur boxer from Yugoslavia who went to win a world championship in the professional ranks before his retirement in 1986. Born in 1957 in Belgrade, Kacar compiled an amazing amateur record of 241-9, culminating in a gold medal at the 1980 Moscow Olympics in the light heavyweight division. He turned professional in 1983 and earned a shot in December 1985 at the vacant **International Boxing Federation (IBF)** light heavyweight championship against former champion **Eddie Mustafa Muhammad.** Kacar won a 15-round split decision to take the title. He lost the title in his first defense against American **Bobby Czyz.** He retired in 1987 after an embarrassing second-round loss to journeyman Blaine Logsdon.

Professional Record:	22-2
Championship(s):	IBF light heavyweight, 1985–1986

Further Reading
Moran, Malcolm. "A Champion in Any Language." *The New York Times,* 9/4/1986, p. D25.

KALULE, AYUB (1954–). Ayub Kalule was the first fighter to win a world championship from the country of Uganda. A slick southpaw boxer, Kalule won the first 36 bouts of his professional career before losing to **Sugar Ray Leonard.** Born in 1954 in Uganda, Kalule won an amateur world championship in 1974 and turned pro in 1976. Kalule had moved to Denmark where he fought nearly all of his matches.

In 1979, he traveled to Japan to face undefeated **World Boxing Association (WBA)** junior middleweight champion Masashi Kudo. Kalule used his superior boxing skills to capture a unanimous 15-round decision. He successfully defended his title four times before losing to Leonard in 1981 via a ninth-round technical knockout. In 1982, he lost to **Davey Moore** in another attempt at the WBA title. He retired in 1986 after losing to **Herol Graham.**

Professional Record:	46-4
Championship(s):	WBA junior middleweight, 1979–1981

Further Reading
Katz, Michael. "Kalule and Baez Known Only as the 'Opponents.'" *The New York Times*, 6/24/1981, p. B12.
Shapiro, Leonard. "Kalule Left Alone to Ponder Fate as Card's Forgotten Man." *The Washington Post*, 6/24/1981, p. D3.

KALAMBAY, SUMBU (1954−). Sumbu Kalambay is a former world junior middleweight champion born in Zaire who fought out of Italy. Born in 1954, Kalambay turned pro in 1980 after sporting an impressive amateur record of 90-5. He challenged **Iran Barkley** in 1987 for the vacant **World Boxing Association (WBA)** middleweight championship, winning a unanimous decision. In his first defense, Kalambay upset Hall-of-Famer Mike McCallum by a close unanimous decision in 1988. He gathered further momentum with wins over Robbie Sims and Doug DeWitt before being stripped of his title for facing **International Boxing Federation (IBF)** titlist **Michael Nunn.**

It got worse for Kalambay, as Nunn kayoed him in the first round with one of the greatest kayos in modern times. In 1991, Kalambay challenged McCallum for the WBA middleweight title but lost a split decision. He retired in 1993 after losing to Chris Pyatt for the World Boxing Organization (WBO) middleweight title.

Professional Record:	57-6-1
Championship(s):	WBA middleweight, 1987–1989

Further Reading
Gustkey, Earl. "Kalambay is Fighting for Name Recognition." *Los Angeles Times*, 3/25/1989, p. III-1.

KAPLAN, HANK (1919–2007). Hank Kaplan was a widely respected boxing historian known for his encyclopedic knowledge of the sport he loved. Born in 1919 in Brooklyn, Kaplan attended fights as a youngster and fought in the amateurs as a middleweight. He had one professional fight, which he won. In the 1950s and 1960s, he served as a publicist for **Angelo Dundee** and Chris Dundee. In later years, he served as a historian for *Sports Illustrated*, HBO, Showtime, and ESPN. In 1989, he helped established the International Boxing Hall of Fame, serving on its nominating committee for many years.

Further Reading
Schudel, Matt. "Esteemed Boxing Historian Hank Kaplan." *The Washington Post*, 112/16/2007, at http://www.washingtonpost.com/wp-dyn/content/article/2007/12/15/AR2007121501821.html

KEARNS, JACK (1882–1963). Jack "Doc" Kearns was one of the greatest managers in boxing history—best known for his expert handling of the popular heavyweight champion **Jack Dempsey.** Born in 1882, Kearns grew up in the state of Washington and later moved to San Francisco in the early twentieth century when that city was a boxing mecca.

Kearns began managing and promoting fights. In 1917, he met Dempsey and later became his manager. Kearns was responsible for boxing's first million-dollar gate when Dempsey defended his title against the popular French light heavyweight champion **Georges Carpentier.**

In the 1940s, Kearns began promoting fights in Chicago. Through the years he managed many great boxers, including **Abe Attell, Benny Leonard,** Jackie Fields, Joey Maxim, **Archie Moore,** and **Mickey Walker.**

The Associated Press said it best when writing Kearns' obituary in 1963: "Kearns' career was so fantastic that a Hollywood movie writer would blush if he had to put it all down on paper. No one would believe it."

Further Reading

Associated Press. "Kearns Dies; Managed Champs." *Chicago Tribune*, 7/8/1963, p. C1.

Chamberlain, Charles. " 'Doc' Kearns Now Promotes at Old Chicago Coliseum." *The Washington Post*, 4/26/1944, p. 13.

Dyer, Braven. "Age No Handicap to Jack Kearns." *Los Angeles Times*, 4/17/1959, p. C1.

Kearns, Jack 'Doc,' and Oscar Fraley. *The Million Dollar Gate.* New York: The MacMillan Co., 1966.

KENTY, HILMER (1955–). Hilmer Kenty was a former world lightweight champion and the first fighter that Hall-of-Fame trainer **Emanuel Steward** guided to a world championship. Standing nearly six feet tall, Kenty possessed a long, accurate jab and a sharp right hand. Born in 1955 in Austin, Texas, he later located to Michigan, where he began working with Steward as an amateur.

He turned pro in 1977 and won his first 16 bouts before challenging Ernesto Espana for the **World Boxing Association (WBA)** lightweight championship. Though he entered the bout as a 5-1 underdog, Kenty overcame a first-round knockdown to prevail in the ninth round. He made three successful defenses before losing a 15-round unanimous decision to **Sean O'Grady** in 1982. He suffered a detached retina after that bout but returned to the ring. He suffered a second loss to Roberto Elizondo when he told the referee he could not come out for the third round because of stomach cramps. He rebounded to win several fights in a row but retired in 1984.

Professional Record:	29-2
Championship(s):	WBA Lightweight, 1980–1982

Further Reading

Katz, Michael. "Kenty and Hearns Triumph." *The New York Times*, 3/3/1980, p. C3.

Katz, Michael. "Kenty Sees Defense Against Oh as 'Easy.'" *The New York Times*, 8/1/1980, p. A19.

KERR, MARK (1968–). Marr "the Titan" Kerr is a mixed martial artist also known as "the Smashing Machine." Born in 1968 in Toledo, Ohio, Kerr excelled at wrestling at an early age. He wrestled collegiately for Syracuse University, winning the 1992 NCAA Championships at 190 lbs with a win over **Randy "the Natural" Couture.** Kerr then turned to mixed martial arts (MMA) as a way to make money.

He dominated the **Ultimate Fighting Championships (UFC),** capturing heavyweight tournaments at UFC 14: Showdown and UFC 15: Raging Rumble. In the finals of both events, Kerr won in the first round. In 1998, Kerr moved to **PRIDE,** where he became a huge star. He did not lose in his first six matches in PRIDE. In 2003, a documentary was released titled *The Smashing Machine: The Life and Times of Mark Kerr.* It showed Kerr's struggles with painkillers and fighting. After losing to **Heath Herring** in PRIDE 15 in 2001, Kerr took a long layoff. He returned to MMA in 2004, losing to Yoshihisa Yamamoto. In 2007, Kerr successfully returned and won a match in the World Cage Fighting Organization.

However, his comeback stalled in 2008 with consecutive losses to fellow former UFC veteran **Oleg Taktarov** and Tracy Willis.

Professional MMA Record:	15-10
Championship(s):	Won UFC 14 and 15 Tournaments

Further Reading

Gentry, Clyde. *No Holds Barred: Ultimate Fighting and The Martial Arts Revolution.* London: Milo Books, 2005.

Hayes, Marcus. "Reversal of Fortune Wrestler Mark Kerr Breaks Free of His Past to Pursue Richer Goals." *The Post-Standard*, 8/26/1994, p. D1.

KETCHEL, STANLEY (1886–1910). Known as "the Michigan Assassin," Stanislaus Kaicel terrorized the middleweight division—and much larger men—in the early twentieth century under the name Stanley Ketchel. Most accounts read that Ketchel was born in 1886 in Grand Rapids, Michigan, though Ketchel sometimes claimed he was born in 1887 in Butte, Montana.

Ketchel eschewed boxing technique for brawling power. He claimed no formal boxing training but won fights on sheer aggression and power. He captured the vacant middleweight championship in 1908 with a first-round demotion of Mike Sullivan. He lost his title to Billy Papke in September 1908 but regained the title by savagely beating Papke over 11 rounds in their November 1908 rematch. In 1909, Ketchel challenged world heavyweight champion **Jack Johnson** and acquitted himself well. He floored Johnson in the 12th round, enraging the larger man. Johnson proceeded to quickly regain his feet and knock Ketchel cold. Ketchel may well have accomplished greater ring glory but died at the age of 24—shot by Walter Dipley (also known as Walter Hurtz), who thought Ketchel tried to steal his lady. In his excellent book *Boxing Babylon*, Nigel Collins writes: "Due to Ketchel's fabled prowess and violent death at age twenty-four, interest in him has remained high throughout the ensuing decades. For years after the shooting, writers, historians and fans made pilgrimages to the scene of his bloody demise" (p. 34). Famed *New York Times* sportswriter Arthur Daley said it best: "His career was meteoric in every sense of the word, a blazing flash across the fistic heavens—and then extinction."

Professional Record:	52-4-4
Championship(s):	Middleweight, 1908; 1908–1910 (won, lost and regained the title in 1908)

Further Reading
Blake, James Carlos. *The Killings of Stanley Ketchel: A Novel.* New York: HarperCollins, 2005.
Collins, Nigel. *Boxing Babylon.* New York: Citadel Press, 1990.
Daley, Arthur. "The Life and Times of Stanley Ketchel." *The New York Times*, 10/25/1946, p. 40.

KIM, JI-WON (1959–). Ji-Won Kim was a former super bantamweight world champion who was one of the few pugilists to retire undefeated in the professional ranks. Born in 1959, Kim turned pro in 1982. In 1985, he kayoed Seung Il Sun in the 10th round of a very close fight to capture the **International Boxing Federation (IBF)** super bantamweight title. He successfully defended his title four times before retiring in 1986.

Professional Record:	16-0-2
Championship(s):	IBF super bantamweight, 1985–1986

Further Reading
Hudson, David L., Jr., and Mike Fitzgerald. *Boxing's Most Wanted: The Top Ten Book of Champs, Chumps and Punch-Drunk Palookas.* Alexandria, VA: Potomac Books, 2003.

KIM, KI SOO (1939–1997). Ki Soo Kim was the first world champion from South Korea in the history of professional boxing. Born in 1939 in Buk Chong, South Korea, Kim represented his country at the 1960 Rome Olympics, where he lost in the second round to eventual gold medalist **Nino Benvenuti** in the second round.

He turned pro in 1961, and five years later in 1966, he gained the ultimate revenge when he outpointed Benvenuti over 15 rounds to capture a split decision victory and the world junior middleweight championship. An Italian judge voted for Benvenuti, but a Korean judge and an American referee sided with Kim. President Chung He Park was in attendance and congratulated Kim after his upset victory.

The southpaw Kim successfully defended both the **World Boxing Association** (**WBA**) and **World Boxing Council** (**WBC**) belts with decision wins over Stan Harrington and **Freddie Little.** He lost his title via a controversial split decision to Italian Sandro Mazzinghi in Milan in 1968. He retired in 1969 after a pair of fights with Hisao Minami.

Professional Record: 33-2-2
Championship(s):   WBA and WBC junior middleweight, 1965–1968

Further Reading
"Kim Ki-Soo of Korea Takes Junior Middleweight Crown from Benvenuti." *The New York Times*, 6/26/1966, p. S2.

KIMURA, MASAHIKO (1917–1993). Masahiko Kimura was a famous Japanese judo expert who dominated opponents with superior technique and fighting prowess. He did not lose a judo match for 13 years in a row. He later turned to professional wrestling and challenge matches worldwide to earn more money. In his most famous match, he defeated Brazilian jiu-jitsu expert Helio Gracie by a famous arm lock, which led to a broken elbow for the courageous Gracie. Kimura's technique was respected enough that the arm lock is called a "Kimura."

Further Reading
Chen, Jim, and Theodore Chen. "Masahiko Kimura: The Man Who Defeated Helio Gracie." http://www. judoinfo.com/kimura.htm

KING, DON (1931–). Don King is a controversial, flamboyant, Hall-of-Fame boxing promoter who has produced some of the greatest fights in boxing history, including the **"Rumble in the Jungle"** between **Muhammad Ali** and **George Foreman;** the **"Thrilla in Manila"** between Muhammad Ali and **Joe Frazier;** and "The Brawl in Montreal" between **Sugar Ray Leonard** and **Roberto Duran.** He is also well known for his distinctive hairstyle, his mantra of "Only in America," and his legal battles.

Born in 1931 in Cleveland, Ohio, King eventually began running numbers—an illegal gambling operation. He attended college for a year but dropped out. During his pre-boxing career, King killed two men: in 1954, though it was deemed self-defense; and in 1966, when he beat to death a man named Sam Garrett who refused to pay a gambling debt. A jury convicted him of second-degree murder, but a judge reduced the charge to manslaughter. King served four years in an Ohio prison. He later received a pardon.

In 1972, King met Muhammad Ali through singer Lloyd Price. King convinced Ali to box an exhibition for a benefit King ran for the Forest City Hospital in Cleveland, Ohio. He later promoted many of Ali's biggest fights. King's greatest achievement was convincing the ruler of Zaire to put up millions of dollars to host the George Foreman—Muhammad Ali heavyweight championship fight in Kinshasa, Zaire, called "the Rumble in the Jungle."

King has survived numerous federal investigations and 1984 federal income tax charges. After his 1985 acquittal on tax evasion charges, King flew the jurors to London for a heavyweight title fight he was promoting. He also avoided conviction on insurance fraud charges. A number of his former fighters have sued King through the years, including Muhammad Ali, **Tim Witherspoon,** and **Terry Norris.** Many other fighters have contended that King bilked them out of purses. He once told a group of Harvard Law School students: "I've been in more courtrooms than you."

Perhaps his greatest testament was his 1997 induction into the International Boxing Hall of Fame. As King himself once said: "I have revolutionized boxing."

Further Reading
Diaz, George. "Time to Crown Him." *The Orlando Sentinel*, 6/15/1997, p. C18.
Gildea, William. "And, in This Corner, The King of Flair and Sizzle." *The Washington Post*, 4/30/1976, p. B1.
Newfield, Jack. *Only in America: The Life and Crimes of Don King*. New York: William Morrow, 1995.
Official Web site of Don King Productions: http://www.donking.com
Smith, Red. "King of the Ring." *The New York Times*, 9/28/1975, p. 234.
Stickney, W. H., Jr. "King of promoters earns Hall pass." *Houston Chronicle*, 1/19/1997.

KINGPETCH, PONE (1935–1982). Pone Kingpetch, also known as Mana Sridokbuab, was the first boxer from Thailand to win a world title. He also was the first person from anywhere to win the flyweight champion on multiple occasions. Born in 1935, Kingpetch turned professional in 1954. Six years later, he challenged champion **Pascual Perez** of Argentina for the world flyweight championship. Kingpetch won a split decision, as Judge Nat Fleischer (editor of *The Ring* magazine) cast the deciding vote 146-140 for Kingpetch. A Thai judge and Argentinian referee had scored it for the countrymen. Kingpetch kayoed Perez in a rematch to cement his hold on the title.

In 1962, he lost his title to **Mashiko "Fighting" Harada** of Japan, but the next year he regained the title from Harada in a rematch. He became the first two-time flyweight champion. In 1963, he lost his title via a first-round knockout to another Japanese fighter, Hiroyuki Ebihara. In the 1964 rematch, Kingpetch won a split decision to capture the title for the third time. He lost the belt to Salvatore Burruni in 1965 and retired in 1966. He died in 1982 at the age of 47.

Professional Record: 28-7
Championship(s):   Flyweight, 1960–1962, 1963, 1964–1965

Further Reading
Associated Press. "Kingpetch Takes Split Decision and Regains Flyweight Crown." *The New York Times*, 1/24/1964, p. 31.
Associated Press. "Thai Fighter Beats Perez in Title Bout." *Chicago Daily Tribune*, 4/17/1960, p. A4.

KLITSCHKO, VITALI (1971–). The elder of the two Klitschko champions, Dr. Vitali "Ironfist" Klitschko was considered the best heavyweight in the world following his unexpected retirement in the spring of 2006. Born in 1971 in the Belovodsk settlement of Kyrghyzstan, Klitschko moved with his family to Ukraine in 1985.

He was a former professional kickboxer before he turned to boxing. He turned pro in 1996 and won the World Boxing Organization (WBO) heavyweight title with an easy win over Herbie Hide in 1999. He successfully defended his title twice before retiring against **Chris Byrd** due to a shoulder injury. Critics castigated Klitschko because he was far ahead on the scorecards at the time of his retirement.

He rebounded with five straight wins before challenging **Lennox Lewis** for the heavyweight title in June 2003. Klitschko fared well in the early rounds, but the fight was stopped because of a cut over Klitschko's eye. After Lewis retired, Klitschko captured the **World Boxing Council (WBC)** title with a convincing win over Corrie Sanders, who had defeated Vitali's younger brother **Wladimir.** He successfully defended his title against Danny Williams and then, after a string of injuries, announced his retirement. He announced he was returning to the ring in 2007, but injuries delayed his return until 2008. In October 2008, he dominated Samuel Peter to win the WBC heavyweight title. He obtained his Ph.D. in 2000.

Vitali Klitschko proudly displays his Ring Championship belt in September 2004. Courtesy of Chris Cozzone.

Record: 36-2
Championship(s):   WBO Heavyweight, 1999–2000; WBC Heavyweight, 2004–2006; WBC Heavyweight, 2008–

Further Reading

Anderson, Dave. "The Brothers Klitschko: From Kiev With Gloves." *The New York Times*, 6/25/2002, p. D4.
Goldman, Ivan. "Dr. Klitschko: The Perfect Band-Aid For The Heavyweight Division." *KO* (October 2004), pp. 22–27.
Hudson, David L., Jr. "Klitschko: I was wronged by the Doctor!" *Fightnews*, 6/25/2003.
Katz, Michael. "Brothers Are Ready to Rumble and Charm." *The New York Times*, 12/4/2002, p. D2.
Raskin, Eric. "Klitschko's Sudden Retirement." *The Ring* (March 2006), pp. 32–35.
Woolever, Phil. "All in the Family: Vitali Victorious." *Boxing Digest* (July 2004), pp. 12–14.

KLITSCHKO, WLADIMIR (1976−). Wladimir Klitschko, the younger brother of **Vitali,** is a world heavyweight boxing champion blessed with incredible physical gifts, tremendous power, and a suspect chin. Many boxing experts regard him as the best heavyweight in the world over the last two years. Born in Kazakhstan in 1976, Klitschko won a gold medal at the 1996 Atlanta Olympics with a decision over Paea Wolfgramm.

He turned pro later that year and won his first 24 bouts before suffering a late-round kayo loss to tough journeyman Ross Purrity. Klitsckho had a big lead in the fight but fatigued in the later rounds. In 2000, he defeated **Chris Byrd** by a lopsided unanimous decision to win the World Boxing Organization (WBO) heavyweight championship. He made five successful defenses before a shocking second-round loss to Corrie Sanders in 2003. In 2004, he suffered another devastating kayo loss to **Lamon Brewster** for the vacant WBO title. Klitsckho dominated Brewer in the early rounds only to tire and suffer a kayo loss in the fifth round.

In 2006, Klitschko revived his career with another decisive win over Byrd to win the **International Boxing Federation (IBF)** heavyweight title. He has made six successful title defenses, including a rematch win over Brewster. Guided by expert trainer **Emanuel Steward,** Klitschko hopes to unify the heavyweight title.

Wladimir Klitschko survives a dangerous DaVarryl Williamson in October 2004. Klitschko overcame a knockdown and nasty cut to win. Courtesy of Chris Cozzone.

Professional Record:	52-3
Championship(s):	WBO Heavyweight, 2000–2003; IBF Heavyweight, 2006–

Further Reading

Anderson, Dave. "The Brothers Klitschko: From Kiev With Gloves." *The New York Times*, 6/25/2002, p. D4.

George, Thomas. "Mercer Is the Next Hurdle As Klitschko Chases Lewis." *The New York Times*, 6/29/2002, p. D3.

Katz, Michael. "Brothers Are Ready to Rumble and Charm." *The New York Times*, 12/4/2002, p. D2.

Stradley, Don. "Klitschko Spreads His Powerful Message: A Charitable Man . . . Just Not in the Ring." *The Ring* (March 2007), pp. 46–51.

Whitehead, Johnnie. "Wladimir Klitschko: Is He The Next Great Heavyweight?" *KO Boxing 2002*, pp. 22–26.

LAGUNA, ISMAEL (1943–). Ismael "El Tigre Colonese" Laguna was a former two-time world lightweight champion from Panama known for his great jab, awkward style, and great chin. Laguna never hit the canvas in his 75 professional bouts. Born in 1943 in Colon City, Laguna turned pro in 1960 and won his first 27 bouts before losing a decision to Antonio Herrera. In 1965, Laguna outboxed the great **Carlos Ortiz** to win the world lightweight title. In his first defense he lost the title to Ortiz in a rematch. He won the championship for the second time by stopping **Mando Ramos** in the ninth round. Laguna made one successful defense before losing to **Ken Buchanan.**

He retired in 1971 after losing a rematch to Buchanan. He was inducted into the International Boxing Hall of Fame in 2001.

Professional Record:	65-9-1
Championship(s):	Lightweight, 1965, 1970

Further Reading

Dettloff, William. "The 20 Greatest Lightweights of All Time." *The Ring* (September 2001), pp. 49–69, 67.

Roberts, James B., and Alexander G. Skutt. *The Boxing Register: International Boxing Hall of Fame Official Record Book* (4th ed.). Ithaca, NY: McBooks Press, Inc., 2006, pp. 462–465.

LAMOTTA, JAKE (1921–). Jake LaMotta, the "Raging Bull," was a fierce middleweight champion known for his incredible resiliency and attacking style. Born in 1921 in the Bronx, LaMotta turned pro in 1941 and quickly moved up the middleweight ranks. In 1943, he became the first fighter to ever defeat the legendary **Sugar Ray Robinson**—though Robinson won five of their six meetings. LaMotta won the middleweight championship in his first, long overdue title shot against **Marcel Cerdan** in 1949. Overcoming a hurt left hand, LaMotta mauled Cerdan around the ring and showed superior strength and punching power. He successfully defended the title twice—including a dramatic 15th-round come-from-behind kayo of Laurent Dauthille—before losing it to his nemesis Robinson in 1951.

LaMotta was a controversial figure in boxing, admitting to U.S. Senate investigators in 1960 that he threw a fight with Billy Fox in 1947. Fox stopped LaMotta in the fourth round in a performance that caused New York boxing officials to ban LaMotta for a time. LaMotta said that he threw the fight in order to receive a title shot.

He retired in 1954 after losing to Billy Kilgore. LaMotta's life story was brought to life vividly by actor Robert De Niro, who won an Oscar in 1983 for his portrayal of LaMotta in the critically acclaimed movie *Raging Bull*.

Professional Record:	83-19-4
Championship(s):	Middleweight, 1949–1951

Further Reading

Associated Press. "LaMotta Flattens Dauthille in 15th Round to Save Title." *Los Angeles Times*, 9/14/1950, p. C1.

Dawson, James P. "LaMotta Wins Title by Knockout as Cerdan Is Unable to Answer Bell for 10th." *The New York Times*, 6/17/1949, p. 31.

LaMotta, Jake, with Joseph Carter and Peter Savage. *Raging Bull: My Story*. New York: Da Capo Press, 1997.

Smith, Red. "LaMotta Just a Hard Man to Deck." *The Washington Post*, 2/1/1951, p. 16.

United Press International. "LaMotta Confesses He Threw 47 Garden Bout With Billy Fox." *The New York Times*, 6/15/1980, p. 1.

LANE, MILLS (1936–). Mills Lane was a popular referee known for his no-nonsense style, effective control of the ring, and his catch phrase "Let's Get It On." Born in Atlanta, Georgia, in 1936, Lane boxed in college at the University of Nevada, Reno, and in the amateurs. He nearly made the 1960 U.S. Olympic team, losing to Phil Baldwin in the Olympic Trials. He later turned pro, compiling a record of 10-1. His only loss was in his professional debut. However, Lane traded in his boxing trunks for a bow tie when he became a referee in 1964.

Lane refereed some of the most significant bouts in boxing history, including: **Evander Holyfield—Mike Tyson** II, **Riddick Bowe**—Evander Holyfield II, and **Lennox Lewis—Oliver McCall** II. All three of those heavyweight bouts were memorable for odd events. In the Holyfield—Tyson rematch, Tyson bit off part of Holyfield's ear, forcing Lane to disqualify Tyson. In the second bout between Holyfield and Bowe, a paraglider landed in the ring during the middle of the fight, causing a nearly 30-minute delay. Finally, the Lennox Lewis—Oliver McCall rematch forced Lane to disqualify McCall after McCall had an emotional breakdown in the ring.

Lane also worked the **Larry Holmes—Ken Norton** classic in 1978 and a 1980 battle between **Salvador Sanchez** and **Danny "Little Red" Lopez.** He first used his catchy "Let's Get It On" phrase before the Holmes—**Gerry Cooney** fight in 1982. He trademarked the phrase in 1998.

Lane was known for his no-nonsense approach in the ring. He was a lawyer and a judge, serving as district attorney in Washoe County, Nevada, and later a district judge from 1991–1998. He earned the nickname "Maximum Mills" for his tough sentencing on criminals. He later parlayed his popularity into a popular judge show called "Judge Mills Lane." Lane also got into promoting boxing shows with Tony Holden. He suffered a stroke in March 2002, leaving him partially paralyzed.

Further Reading

Gustkey, Earl. "Mills Lane is a No-Nonsense Judge." *The Washington Post*, 6/29/1991, p. G6A.

Hudson, David L., Jr. "Mills Lane: 'Getting it On' with Promoting!" *Fightnews*, 12/18/2001.

Lane, Mills, with Jedwin Smith. *Let's Get It On*. New York: Crown Publications, 1998.

LANGFORD, SAM (1883–1956). Sam Langford, "the Boston Tar Baby," was one of the greatest fighters in boxing history who was denied an opportunity at a world title because of racial discrimination. Born in 1883 in Nova Scotia in Canada, Langford later moved to Boston where he met drugstore owner Joe Woodman, who became his manager.

Langford, who stood only 5'6" inches tall, possessed a powerful chest and long reach for a man his height. Famed sportswriter Arthur Daley described his physique the best when he wrote: "The legendary Boston Tar Baby was fistic freak because he was only 5 feet 6½ inches tall and never weighed more than 165 pounds. But he met anyone who would fight him during his twenty-two years in the ring and size was unimportant."

He also possessed power and tremendous boxing skills that he refined through hundreds of bouts, more than 600 according to some reports. He turned pro in 1902 at the age of 19 and fought until he was 43 years old in every weight division, from welterweight to heavyweight. During the course of his career he often faced men who outweighed him by 30 pounds.

In 1906, he lost a 15-round decision to future heavyweight champion **Jack Johnson,** who later refused to give Langford a title shot when he became heavyweight champion. Langford destroyed former light heavyweight champion Philadelphia Jack O'Brien in 1911. Many white fighters were scared to face Langford. Years later, the great heavyweight champion **Jack Dempsey** admitted he feared the fistic prowess of Langford. This forced Langford to accept fights against larger African American opponents such as Joe Jeannette, Sam McVey, and **Harry Wills.**

Professional Record:	167-38-37
Championship(s):	None

Further Reading

Cuddy, Jack. "Dempsey Admits Being Afraid To Fight Langford." *Chicago Daily Defender,* 5/11/1960, p. A22.

Daley, Arthur. "The Boston Tar Baby." *The New York Times,* 1/13/1956, p. 27.

Moyle, Clay. *Sam Langford: Boxing's Greatest Uncrowned Champion.* Seattle, Wash.: Bennett & Hastings, 2008.

Sloan, Alex J. "Sam Langford Is The Best Fighter." *Los Angeles Times,* 6/27/1911, p. III2.

Young, Fay. "Sam Langford—The Ring's Wonder Man: 'Boston Tar Baby' Fought Them All; Gans to Johnson." *The Chicago Defender,* 3/5/1949, p. 14.

LAWLER, ROBBIE (1982–). "Ruthless" Robbie Lawler is a mixed martial artist who held the **Elite XC** middleweight championship. Born in 1982 in San Diego, California, Lawler possesses an aggressive, attacking style and is a very adept wrestler. He turned professional in 2001 with a win over Jason Reed at Extreme Challenge 39.

In 2002, he began fighting in the **Ultimate Fighting Championships (UFC),** winning his first three bouts before losing to Pete Spratt at UFC 42: Sudden Impact, to **Nick Diaz** at UFC 47: It's On, and to **Evan Tanner** at UFC 50: The War of 04. Since the loss to Tanner, Lawler has won seven of his last eight bouts, including three straight bouts in 2007. Lawler learned for years at the hands of former UFC great **Pat Miletich.** In 2007, he joined another former Miletich protégé, **Matt Hughes,** in becoming a part of Team Hughes.

In 2008, Lawler fought two exciting fights against Scott Smith for the Elite XC middleweight championship. The first fight ended prematurely and was declared a no-contest after Lawler inadvertently poked Smith in the eye. In the rematch held in July 2008, Lawler kayoed Smith in an entertaining bout. He remains a fan favorite because of his attacking style and proclivity to stand and trade bombs with his opponents.

Professional MMA Record: 18-4

Championship(s):   Elite XC Middleweight, 2007—2008 (organization in
                                  financial trouble; Lawler never lost title)

Further Reading
Hull, Billy. "It's Showtime for Robbie Lawler and Elite XC." *The Honolulu Star Bulletin*, 9/14/2007.
Morinaga, Dayton. "Lawler will let his hands do talking tomorrow against Rua." *The Honolulu Advertiser*,
    9/14/2007, p. 1D.

LE, CUNG (1972–). Cung Le is a talented mixed martial artist best known for his mastery of
the Chinese combat sport San Shou and his impressive array of striking skills with his legs. Born
in 1972 in South Vietnam, Le later emigrated to California and made Long Beach home.

Le fought in Tae Kwon Do tournaments until discovering San Shou in 1994. He compiled
a record of 17-0 in San Shou with 12 stoppages, but he failed to gain widespread acceptance
from the American mixed martial arts (MMA) community until he started his MMA career
in 2006 with Strikeforce. Le has dominated his opponents since his MMA debut, winning all
six fights by knockout. In 2008, he stopped the legendary **Frank Shamrock** to win the Strikeforce Middleweight title. Shamrock had to retire after a series of Le kicks broke Shamrock's
right arm.

Professional MMA Record: 6-0

Championship(s):   Strikeforce Middleweight, 2008—

Further Reading
Lynch, Ann Marie. "The Making of a Superstar: Cung Le Has Officially Arrived." *FIGHT!* (July 2008),
    pp. 78–79.
Official Web site: http://www.cungle.com/
Walker, Andrew. "Cung Le." *Extreme Fighter* (March 2008), pp. 24–25.

LEBEN, CHRIS (1980–). Chris "the Crippler" Leben is a mixed martial artist who currently
thrills fans of the **Ultimate Fighting Championships (UFC)** with his freewheeling, brawling
style. Reared in Portland, Oregon, Leben took boxing lessons as a youth and then wrestled in
high school.

A few years later he ventured into a mixed martial arts gym and fell in love with the sport. He
made his professional MMA debut in 2002 at the Full Contact Fighting Federation's (FCFF)
Rumble at the Roseland 4 with a win over Justin Terherst. He won nine straight fights before
finally losing to veteran Joe Doerksen at Freestyle Fighting Championships 9 in May 2004.

His big break came when he was selected as a member of the inaugural season of **The Ultimate Fighter,** which showed several sides of Leben's personality and character. It showed Leben
get drunk, urinate on a fellow fighter's pillow, and break a window. But the show also showed
Leben's all-action fighting style.

In April 2005, he defeated Jason Thacker in the Octagon at UFC Ultimate Fighter Finale.
He then won a series of bouts on UFC Fight Nights before finally losing to the talented **Anderson "Spider" Silva** in June 2006. He continues to fight in the UFC, defeating Alessio Sakara and
recently losing to **Michael Bisping**.

Professional MMA Record: 18-5

Championship(s):   None

Further Reading
Dhoot, Jatinder. "Fire and Intensity: A Few Surprising Moments with Chris Leben." *Elite Fighter* (March 2008), pp. 82–83.
Official Web site: http://www.chrisleben.com/

LEDERMAN, HAROLD (1940–). Harold Lederman is known to boxing fans throughout the world as "HBO's Unofficial Ringside Scorer." A former world-class boxing judge, Lederman now gives his "unofficial" scoring from ringside and assists Jim Lampley and the other members of the HBO team with some insights into judging and boxing rules.

Born in 1940 in the Bronx, Lederman attended Columbia University and later became a practicing pharmacist. He earned his judge's license in the 1960s and started judging fights. His first world title fight was the **World Boxing Association (WBA)** lightweight title clash between **Ismael Laguna** and **Ken Buchanan** in 1971. He judged many landmark boxing bouts, including **Muhammad Ali—Ken Norton** III (1976)**, Larry Holmes—Mike Weaver** I (1979), **Lupe Pintor—Wilfredo Gomez** (1982), **Evander Holyfield—Dwight Muhammad Qawi** (1986), and **Michael Spinks—Gerry Cooney** (1987).

He began working for HBO in 1986 and remains a staple of the network's boxing coverage. His daughter Julie is now a well-known boxing judge in her own right. Harold Lederman is known as one of the truly good individuals in the sport.

Further Reading
Hoffarth, Tom. "Lederman Leads with His Shrill." *The Daily News of Los Angeles*, 5/4/2007, p. S4.
Hudson, David L., Jr. "Harold Lederman speaks out on career; controversial decisions." *Fightnews.com*, 12/5/2001.

LEONARD, BENNY (1896–1947). With apologies to **Roberto Duran,** many boxing experts consider Benny Leonard the greatest lightweight in boxing history. Born Benjamin Leiner in 1896, Leonard learned to fight on the streets of New York, earning him the nickname the Ghetto Wizard. He turned professional in 1911 at age 15. It proved an inauspicious debut as Mickey Finnegan stopped him in the third round. Leonard rebounded and challenged for the lightweight championship in 1917. He stopped Freddie Welsh in the ninth round to capture the belt in a brilliant performance.

He held the title until his retirement in 1925, defeating the likes of Lew Tender, Johnny Dundee, and Charlie White. In 1922, he nearly captured the welterweight title. He dropped champion **Jack Britton** but was disqualified for hitting his opponent while he was down. Leonard returned to the ring in 1931 and won 16 straight fights. He retired in 1932 after losing to **Jimmy McLarnin.** Leonard remained in the ring as a referee for several years. He died in 1947 at the age of 51, while refereeing a bout between Mario Ramos and Bobby Williams. William Dettloff concludes: "The depth and width of Leonard's work is what makes him a true ring immortal and, pound-for-pound, one of the greatest fighters ever. Irrefutably" (p. 51).

Record:	85-5-1 (121 no decisions)
Championship(s):	Lightweight, 1917–1925

Further Reading
Associated Press. "Welsh Hardly Wins a Round." *Los Angeles Times*, 4/1/1916, p. I1.
"Benny Leonard Dies Refereeing Fight." *Chicago Daily Tribune*, 4/19/1947, p. 17.
Dettloff, William. "The 20 Greatest Lightweights of All-Time." *The Ring* (September 2001), pp. 49–69, 51.
Jemison, Dick. "Benny Leonard Beats Jack Britton." *The Atlanta Constitution*, 6/26/1918, p. 12.

LEONARD, SUGAR RAY (1956–). Sugar Ray Leonard was one of boxing's most popular superstars. A former Olympic gold medalist, Leonard became a media darling and bona fide all-time boxing great who defeated fellow greats **Wilfred Benitez, Roberto Duran, Thomas "Hitman" Hearns,** and **Marvelous Marvin Hagler** in his illustrious career.

Born Ray Charles Leonard in Wilmington, North Carolina, in 1956, Leonard struck gold at the 1976 Montreal Olympic Games with teammates **Leo Randolph,** Howard Davis, Jr., **Leon Spinks,** and **Michael Spinks.** He turned pro to great fanfare in 1977 and did not disappoint. In 1979, he challenged the great Benitez for the welterweight championship. He stopped Benitez in the final round to capture the belt. In 1980, he lost his first professional fight—a narrow decision loss to Duran in a fight fittingly billed as "the Brawl for It All in Montreal." Leonard regained the title from Duran later that year in a fight infamously known as "No Mas" (Spanish for "no more"). Leonard's superior boxing and showboating upset Duran, who quit on his stool.

Leonard unified the welterweight title with a dramatic, come-from-behind kayo of Hearns in the 14th round. He initially retired in 1982 with a detached retina. He returned in 1984 for one fight against Kevin Howard—a ninth-round TKO. He retired again and then made perhaps his most spectacular comeback—a 1987 12-round decision win over the favored Hagler for the world middleweight title. He added the **World Boxing Council (WBC)** super middleweight and light heavyweight belts with a stoppage of Donny LaLonde in 1988. In other comebacks, he was less successful, losing badly to **Terry Norris** in 1991 and to **Hector "Macho" Camacho** in 1997.

In retirement, Leonard formed his own promotional company and helps to produce the popular boxing reality television series, *The Contender.*

Professional Record:	36-3-1
Championship(s):	WBC welterweight, 1979–1980; 1980–1981; WBA junior middleweight, 1981; WBC middleweight, 1987; WBC super middleweight, 1988–1990; WBC light heavyweight, 1988

Sugar Ray Leonard promotes one of his boxing shows in Albuquerque, New Mexico, in 2003. Courtesy of Chris Cozzone.

Further Reading
Goldstein, Alan. *A Fistful of Sugar: The Sugar Ray Leonard Story*. New York: Coward, McCann & Geoghegan, 1981.
Haskins, James. *Sugar Ray Leonard*. London: Robson Books, 1989.
Hudson, David L., Jr. "Interview: Sugar Ray Leonard." *Fightnews.com*, 12/25/2001.
Kimball, George. *Four Kings: Leonard, Hagler, Hearns, Duran and the Last Great Era of Boxing*. Ithaca, NY: McBooks Press, 2008.
Nack, William. "Comeback for the Ages." *Sports Illustrated*, 4/13/1987, pp. 18–25.
Newhan, Ross. "The Selling of Sugar Ray: The Gold He's Going for Tonight Could Make the Gold He Won in 76 Look Like a Trinket." *Los Angeles Times*, 11/30/1979, p. OC_ B1.
Roberts, James B., and Alexander G. Skutt. *The Boxing Register: International Boxing Hall of Fame Register* (4th ed.). Ithaca, NY: McBooks Press, Inc., 2006, pp. 470–475.

LESNAR, BROCK (1977–). Brock Lesnar is a former collegiate and professional wrestling star who had made a remarkably successful transition to mixed martial arts in a short amount of time. Lesnar excelled at wrestling as a youngster, earning a scholarship. He wrestled for two years at Bismarck State College in North Dakota and then for two years at the University of Minnesota. In 2000, he won the NCAA heavyweight championship.

After college, Lesnar turned to professional wrestling with the World Wrestling Federation (WWF), which later became World Wrestling Entertainment (WWE). In 2007, Lesnar fought his first mixed martial arts event in K-1 against former Olympic judo silver medalist Min Soo Kim. The mammoth Lesnar overwhelmed Kim in just more than a minute. In February, Lesnar made his debut in the Octagon at **Ultimate Fighting Championships (UFC)** 81 against former heavyweight champion and submission specialist **Frank Mir.** Lesnar dominated the opening minute of the fighting, taking Mir to the ground and pounding him with heavy shots. However, Mir submitted Lesnar with a knee bar.

Lesnar returned to the Octagon with more experience and an even greater focus at UFC 87, where he pounded **Heath Herring** over three rounds to win a lopsided decision. In November 2008, Lesnar dominated all-time great **Randy Couture** for the UFC heavyweight crown. He is expected to face Mir in a highly anticipated rematch in 2009.

Professional MMA Record:	3-1
Championship(s):	UFC Heavyweight, 2008–

Further Reading
Avila, David A. "Lesnar can Fight for Real." *The Press Enterprise*, 11/16/2008, p. B15.
Davidson, Neil. "Brock Lesnar: His First True Test Awaits." *Fight!* (February 2008), pp. 36–44.
Hudson, David L., Jr. "This Is a True Test for Me!" *Fightnews*, 2/4/2008 at http://www.fightnewsextra.com/cc/ufc81/10.htm
Malinowski, Scoop. "Talkin' MMA with Brock Lesnar," MMAMemories.com, 7/15/2008, at http://www.mmamemories.com/interviews/talkin-mma-with-brock-lesnar/

LESNEVICH, GUS (1915–1964). Gus Lesnevich was a former world light heavyweight champion who held the title for more than six years. Born in 1915 in Cliffside Park, New Jersey, Lesnevich turned pro in 1934 and won his first 10 bouts before a split decision loss to Jackie Aldare—a defeat he avenged twice.

He suffered a beating at the hands of Freddie Steele in November 1936 and then lost to **Young Corbett III** in 1937. He rebounded with a series of wins before challenging champion **Billy Conn** twice, in 1939 and 1940. He lost unanimous decisions in both encounters. After Conn retired, Lesnevich was awarded the National Boxing Association (NBA) world light heavyweight championship in 1941. He solidified his status and added the New York State Athletic Commission light heavyweight crown with a 15-round split decision win over Tami Mauriello. He then served his country in the U.S. Coast Guard.

Many thought his career was over, but Lesnevich resumed his fighting after completion of his service. In 1946, he defeated **Freddie Mills** to retain his title. Later that year, however, he suffered a bad loss to Bruce Woodcock in 1946, as the unheralded British fighter kayoed Lesnevich for the 10-count. However, Lesnevich rebounded in a major way in 1947 with a win over previously unbeaten Billy Fox, a first-round kayo of Melio Bettina, and two wins over old rival Mauriello. For his efforts, *The Ring* magazine awarded Lesnevich Fighter of the Year honors.

He lost his title in 1948 by decision to Freddie Mills in London. He retired in August 1948 after an unsuccessful attempt at lifting the world heavyweight title from the talented **Ezzard Charles.** He later refereed bouts in New York and New Jersey. He died in 1964 at the age of 49.

Professional Record:	59-14-5
Championship(s):	Light Heavyweight, 1941–1948

Further Reading
Associated Press. "Gus Lesnevich, Boxer, 49, Dies; Was Light Heavyweight Champ." *The New York Times,* 2/29/1964, p. 21.
Smith, Wilfrid. "Mills Dethrones Lesnevich in 15 Rounds." *Chicago Daily Tribune,* 7/27/1948, p. A1.

LEWIS, LENNOX (1965–). Lennox Lewis was a dominant heavyweight champion who avenged the only two professional losses he suffered in his professional career. Born in 1965 in London, he moved with his family to Canada when he was 12. He represented Canada in the 1984 and the 1988 Olympics in the super heavyweight division. At the 1984 Los Angeles Olympics, he lost a controversial decision to Tyrell Biggs and did not medal. However, at the 1988 Seoul Olympics, he won the gold medal with a second-round stoppage of **Riddick Bowe.**

He turned professional in 1989. Four years later, he stopped Donovan "Razor" Ruddock in 1992 in a title eliminator and, shortly after, was declared **World Boxing Council (WBC)** heavyweight champion after champion Bowe refused to fight him. He successfully defended his title several times before a shocking kayo loss to **Oliver McCall** in 1994. He recaptured the WBC title in 1997 by stopping McCall. He beat the best heavyweights for several years, including a decision win over **Evander Holyfield.** In the first clash of the champions, Lewis outboxed Holyfield but was awarded only a draw—a decision so controversial that led to many calls to reform the judging of professional boxing matches.

Lewis successfully defended the titles for several years, defeating many top heavyweights, such as the dangerous **David Tua.** He held the crown until another shocking kayo loss in 2001 to **Hasim Rahman.** Once again, Lewis redeemed himself by kayoing Rahman later that year. He successfully defended his title against **Mike Tyson** and **Vitali Klitschko** and then retired in 2003.

Lewis now serves as an expert commentator for HBO boxing telecasts. He appears content in retirement and will be inducted into the **International Boxing Hall of Fame** in June 2009.

Professional Record:	41-2-1
Championship(s):	WBC Heavyweight, 1992–1994, 1997–2001; 2001–2003; WBA Heavyweight, 2000; IBF Heavyweight, 1999–2001, 2001–2002

Further Reading

Dubin, Josh. "World Heavyweight Champion, and Not Just of Boxing." *Boxing Digest* (April 2004), pp. 36–45.

Eskenazi, Gerald. "Lennox Lewis Is Man on a Mission." *The New York Times*, 5/6/1994, p. B14.

Kluck, Ted A. *Facing Tyson: 15 Fighters, 15 Stories*. Guilford, Conn.: Lyons Press, 2006.

Lewis, Lennox. *Lennox Lewis: The Autobiography of the WBC Heavyweight Champion of the World*. London: Faber & Faber, 1994.

Martinez, Michael. "Lewis Looks Beyond the Trash Can." *The New York Times*, 12/17/1992, p. B31.

Smith, Timothy W. "Lewis Is the Champion No One Really Knows." *The New York Times*, 10/1/1997, p. C1.

Smith, Timothy W. "Let the Disputes Begin." *The New York Times*, 3/14/1999, p. SP1.

LEWIS, TED (1894–1970). Ted "Kid" Lewis was one of the greatest welterweights in the early twentieth century. He is often known as being the first fighter to wear a mouthpiece in the boxing ring. Lewis' dentist—former fighter Jack Marsh—designed the piece for Lewis in 1913. Lewis is also well known for his long rivalry with American champion **Jack Britton.** The pair fought 20 bouts, and they often exchanged the world welterweight championship.

Born in 1894 in London, England, as Gershon Mendeloff, Lewis turned professional in 1909 when he was just 14 years old. He captured the English flyweight title in October 1913.

In 1915, he outpointed Britton to win the world welterweight championship. He became the first fighter from Great Britain to win a world title on American soil. He lost the title to Britton the next year. Lewis regained the title in 1917 from Britton and held the belt until 1919 when he lost to Britton again. Lewis retired in 1929 at the age of 36.

Professional Record: 173-30-14 (65 no decisions)
Championship(s):   Welterweight, 1915–1916, 1917–1919

Further Reading

Associated Press. "Kid Lewis Leaves Ring, In Clash with Referee." *The New York Times*, 12/18/1928, p. 44.

Evans, Gavin. "The 20 Greatest Welterweights of All Time." *The Ring* (February 2008), pp. 63–84, 77.

Merry, Robert. "Kid Lewis, Ring Great, Dies at 76." *Chicago Tribune*, 10/21/1970, p. C1.

"Ted Kid Lewis Is Victor." *The New York Times*, 5/25/1917, p. 8.

LIDDELL, CHUCK (1969–). Chuck "the Iceman" Liddell is a former **Ultimate Fighting Championships (UFC)** light heavyweight champion who was the most feared and famous fighter in the UFC for years. Known for his powerful striking ability, Liddell owns two kayo victories each over **Randy Couture** and **Tito Ortiz.**

Born in 1969 in Santa Barbara, California, Liddell studied karate as a youngster. He learned the disciplines of Kenpo and Koei-Kan. He also wrestled collegiately at Cal Poly San Luis Obispo. Liddell performed well as a kickboxer, winning a national championship and compiling a 10-2 record.

Liddell made his debut in professional mixed martial arts (MMA) at UFC 17 in 1998 with a win over Noe Hernandez. In his second bout, he lost to the much-more experienced **Jeremy Horn** via an arm triangle choke. He then won 10 straight bouts before suffering his second career loss to Couture at UFC 43.

He has lost only six times—once to Couture, once to Jeremy Horn (which he avenged), twice to **Quinton "Rampage" Jackson,** a narrow decision loss to **Keith Jardine,** and a kayo loss to **Rashad Evans.** He is best known for his trilogy with Couture. Liddell lost the first match at

UFC 43 in June 2003 but rebounded with wins in 2005 and 2006 at UFC 52 and UFC 57, respectively.

In December 2007, "the Iceman" rebounded with a great performance against **Wanderlei Silva,** dominating the Brazilian striker for much of the bout. After the huge win, Liddell appeared back on the fast track for another title but got derailed with another shocking kayo loss—this time to Rashad Evans in September 2008.

Liddell often fights with his hands down at his side. His best weapon may be his right hand bombs, though his karate background enables him to inflict damage with his kicks as well. Liddell also possesses an exceptional defense against those who try to take him to the ground. He remains one of the most popular MMA fighters in the world.

Professional MMA Record: 21-7

Championship(s):   UFC Light Heavyweight, 2005–2007

Further Reading
Arias, Carlos. "Star power out in force; mixed martial arts; Chuck Liddell has become the face of the popular UFC, and his appeal is paying off for the growing sport." *The Orange County Register,* 5/26/2007, p. C1.
Glazer, Jay. "The Real Chuck Liddell." *FIGHT!* (September 2008), pp. 40–50.
Liddell, Chuck, with Chad Millman. *Iceman: My Fighting Life.* New York: Dutton, 2008.
Official Web site: http://www.icemanmma.com

LINARES, JORGE (1982–). Jorge Linares is an undefeated world featherweight champion who has the potential to be one of boxing's biggest stars in the next few years. Born in 1982 in Barinas, Venezuela, Linares compiled a sterling amateur career record of 89-5. He then turned pro in 2002 in Japan where he resides.

In July 2007, he defeated the more experienced Oscar Larios—a former super bantamweight world champion—via a 10th-round stoppage to win the **World Boxing Council (WBC)** featherweight title. He s made one successful defense before moving up in weight to defeat Whyber Garcia to win the World Boxing Association (WBA) super featherweight title.. Some boxing experts have compared Linares to the great **Alexis Arguello.**

Professional Record: 26-0

Championship(s):   WBC featherweight, 2007—2008; WBA super featherweight, 2008

Further Reading
Avila, David. "Calling him the next Arguello." *The Press-Enterprise,* 12/11/2007, p. C08.

LINDLAND, MATT (1970–). Matt "the Law" Lindland is a mixed martial artist and a former Olympic medalist in **Greco-Roman wrestling.** Born in 1970, Lindland learned wrestling as a teenager. He quickly developed his skills, earning a wrestling scholarship at the University of Nebraska. He later served as an assistant wrestling coach while he continued wrestling nationally and internationally.

In 2000, Lindland lost a controversial match to Keith Seiracki. Lindland eventually sued, as the U.S. Wrestling Association had placed Seiracki on the Olympic team even though an arbitrator had ruled that Lindland had the right to a rematch. Lindland claimed that Seiracki had tripped him during the match. Lindland won an intense battle in the federal courts, earning him the moniker "the Law." He then won the ordered rematch with Seiracki in decisive fashion by an 8-0 score. He made the most of his second opportunity and earned a silver medal at the 2000

Sydney Olympics in **Greco-Roman wrestling** in the 167 pound division. He won his first three matches but then fell to Russia's Mourat Kardanov in the final.

Lindland nearly captured the gold medal at the 2001 Greco-Roman World Championships but lost to Georgia's (the former Soviet republic) Mukhran Vakhtangadze 2-1 at the end of overtime.

He made his mixed martial arts (MMA) debut while still wrestling in 1997. After his Olympic success, he made his **Ultimate Fighting Championships (UFC)** debut at UFC 29: Defense of the Belts with a win over Yoji Anjo in the first round. He followed that up with consecutive victories over Phil Baroni at UFC 34: High Voltage and over **Pat Miletich** at UFC 36: Worlds Collide. He lost to Murilo Bustamante at UFC 37: High Impact for the UFC middleweight championship.

Lindland has never been afraid to step up from his best weight of 185 lbs. to challenge bigger men. In 2006, he faced **Quinton "Rampage" Jackson** and lost a split decision at the World Fighting Alliance—King of the Streets. Even more impressive, he challenged heavyweight king **Fedor Emelianenko** in April 2007 at Bodog's Clash of the Nations. Lindland took Fedor down with his wrestling skills, but Fedor prevailed with an armbar submission in the first round.

Lindland resumed his career on July 19 at an event promoted by **Affliction,** defeating Fabio Negao. In his second bout, however, Lindland suffered a devastating kayo defeat to **Vitor Belfort** seconds into the bout.

Lindland serves as a coach of Team Quest (an MMA group he cofounded with MMA legend **Randy Couture**). Lindland also harbors political ambitions, evidenced by his campaign for a spot in the Oregon House of Representatives.

Professional MMA Record: 21-6
Championship(s):   None

Further Reading

Caplan, Sam. "5 Oz. Exclusive Q & A with Matt Lindland." 4/30/2008, at http://fiveouncesofpain.
    com/2008/04/30/5-oz-exlusive-interview-matt-lindland-talks-about-his-political-campaign-
    questions-the-direction-of-the-ifl-and-vents-about-the-mma-media/
Crouse, Karen. "Lindland's Legacy Will Be Grasp of Law." *The Daily News of Los Angeles*, 9/27/2000.
Dhoot, Jatinder. "Fighting For Respect." *Ultimate Grappling* (April 2008), pp. 50–54, 124.
Sesker, Craig. "Lindland eyes gold before end of career." *Omaha World Herald*, 12/4/2001, p. 5C.

LISTON, SONNY (1932–1971). Charles "Sonny" Liston was a former world heavyweight champion known for his pulverizing punching power, menacing glare, and unfortunate demise. Born in 1932 in Johnson Township, Arkansas, Liston was the 12th of 13 children. His father beat him regularly. By age 13, Liston ran away from home to escape the brutality of his home life.

When he was a teenager, Liston robbed a gas station, landing him in prison. A Catholic priest discovered Liston's boxing prowess and helped him to gain early parole. After a brief amateur career, he turned pro in 1953.

He won his first seven fights before dropping an eight-round split decision to Marty Marshall in 1954. He avenged the defeat to Marshall in 1955 and again in 1956. He was sent to prison again in 1956 after a parole violation and was prohibited from boxing in 1957.

He returned to the ring in 1958 and began to climb the heavyweight ranks. He destroyed **Cleveland Williams** twice and kayoed contender Roy Harris in the first round. He then destroyed the tough Zora Folley in the third round in 1960.

These wins moved him to the precipice of the heavyweight crown, but he could not receive a title shot. Instead, he became known as the "uncrowned champion." Finally, in 1962, champion **Floyd Patterson** gave Liston his long-overdue title shot. Liston destroyed Patterson in the first round. He then kayoed Patterson in the first round again in their 1963 rematch. At this time, many boxing experts viewed Liston as an indestructible force. However, many openly rooted against Liston, viewing him as the epitome of all that is wrong with boxing.

However, in 1964, Liston lost to a young, brash heavyweight named Cassius Clay—who later changed his name to **Muhammad Ali.** Clay's speed bothered Liston, and the champion retired in his corner, claiming a shoulder injury.

In 1965, Ali defeated Liston in the first round rematch with what some called a "phantom" punch. Ali landed an uppercut, but some experts claim that the punch would not have been strong enough to kayo Liston.

Liston won 14 straight bouts from 1966–1969 until he faced prospect Leotis Martin. Leading comfortably on the scorecards, Martin landed a devastating right hand that kayoed Liston. Liston fought only one more bout, defeating **Chuck Wepner.**

In 1971, Liston died under suspicious circumstances. Though the official cause of death was a drug overdose, some remain convinced that Liston was the victim of foul play.

Professional Record: 50-4
Championship(s):   Heavyweight, 1962–1964

Further Reading
Steen, Rob. *Sonny Boy: The Life and Strife of Sonny Liston.* London: Methuen, 1993.
Tosches, Nick. *The Devil and Sonny Liston.* New York: Little Brown and Company, 2000.
Young, A. S. *"Doc", The Champ Nobody Wanted.* Chicago: Johnson, 1963.

LITTLE, FREDDIE (1936–). Freddie Little was a former world junior middleweight champion who had to overcome some of the strangest decisions in boxing history to obtain his just due. Born in 1936 in Picayune, Mississippi, Little turned pro in 1957 in a bout held in the Coliseum Arena in New Orleans.

He won his first 11 bouts before losing to Norris Burse in 1958—a defeat he avenged the next year. He rebounded from his first loss to win 11 more fights before dropping a decision to **George Benton** in 1960. Little, who doubled as a schoolteacher in Chicago for much of his fighting career, moved up the rankings, but his career was harmed by inactivity. He didn't lose a bout in either 1962 or 1964.

He lost a 12-round split decision to Eddie Pace in 1966 but defeated Pace later that year. Finally, in October 1967, Little traveled to South Korea to face **Ki Soo Kim** for the world junior middleweight championship. Little dropped Kim in the 11th round but lost a controversial split decision. The Korean judge scored the bout 72-68 in favor of Kim, the Korean referee scored the bout 72-69 for Kim, and the American judge scored Little the winner 75-64. Joe Kiernan, Little's manager, expressed outrage after the decision: "No wonder Kim does not want to fight outside Korea. This is the lousiest decision I ever have seen."

In 1968, Little traveled to Rome, Italy, to face junior middleweight champion Sandro Mazzinghi. Little dominated the action, and the ringside physician proclaimed that Mazzinghi was unfit to continue after the end of the eighth round. German referee Herbert Tomser stopped the bout and declared the fight a "no contest" for inexplicable reasons. The referee claimed that European rules require the bout to be declared a no contest when one fighter cannot continue before the fight is halfway over. The referee could not explain the completion of eight rounds qualified as half of a 15-round bout.

Little said the only reason he thought the fight was stopped was "I just kept knocking him around." Kiernan was more vocal: "I am going to protest this to every boxing board in the world. We were royally robbed in Korea [referring to the decision in the Kim fight] and this is an international scandal."

Governing boxing officials ordered a rematch within 90 days. Mazzinghi failed to come to contract terms. Little then met Philadelphia contender Stanley "Kitten" Hayward for the vacant world title. Little outboxed Hayward over 15 rounds to win the world title he should have won two years earlier. He made three successful defenses before losing a close unanimous decision to Carmelo Bossi in Italy. Little retired after three straight wins in 1972.

Professional Record: 38-6 (1 no contest)
Championship(s):   Junior middleweight, 1968–1970

Further Reading
Associated Press. "Kim Wins Disputed Decision To Retain Boxing Title." *The New York Times*, 10/4/1967, p. 58.
Associated Press. "Title Match Ruled No Contest; U.S. Boxer Is Denied a Victory." *The New York Times*, 10/26/1968, p. 48.
Associated Press. "Little Wins Vacant Title By Decision." *The Washington Post*, 3/18/1969, p. D1.

LOCCHE, NICOLINO (1939–2005). Known as "El Intocable" or "the Untouchable," Nicolino Locche of Argentina routinely outboxed opponents to compile an astounding record of 117 wins against only 4 defeats. His defense enabled him to score points while avoiding punishment. He incorporated showmanship into his ring arsenal, routinely mocking opponents while making them miss. He allegedly even smoked cigarettes between rounds in some fights. He turned pro in 1958 but didn't earn his first world title shot until 1968. He stopped Takeshi Fuji in the 10th round to capture the **World Boxing Association (WBA)** junior welterweight title. He made five successful defenses before losing a decision to Panama's Alfonso "Peppermint" Frazer. He tried to regain his title but lost to champion **Antonio Cervantes.** He retired in 1976 after a 10-round win over Ricardo Molina.

Record: 117-4-14
Championship(s):   WBA junior welterweight, 1968–1972

Further Reading
Associated Press. "Locche of Argentina Stops Fuji in 10th to Win 140 lb. Title." *The New York Times*, 12/13/1968, p. 69.
Davison, Phil. "Obituary: Nicolino Locche; 'Untouchable' Boxer." *The Independent*, 11/12/2005, p. 27.
Roberts, James B., and Alexander G. Skutt. *The Boxing Register: International Boxing Hall of Fame Register* (4th ed.). Ithaca, NY: McBooks Press, Inc., 2006, pp. 480–483.

LOI, DUILIO (1929–2008). Italian Duilio Loi was the second world champion in the junior welterweight division, though many consider him the greatest fighter in the history of the 140 lb. division. Born in Trieste, Italy, in 1929, he turned professional in 1948. In his career, he compiled an amazing record of 115 wins and only 3 defeats—all decision losses.

In 1952, he lost a 15-round decision to hometown champion Jorgen Johansen in Copenhagen, Denmark, for the European lightweight title. He captured the title in a 1954 rematch. For many years, he defended that European title before finally receiving the chance to challenge

Carlos Ortiz for the recently created junior welterweight title. Ortiz won a 15-round split decision. However, three months later, Loi won the title in a rematch. He held the title until losing a 15-round decision to **Eddie Perkins** in September 1962. He regained the title in a December 1962 rematch and then retired.

Record:	115-3-8
Championship(s):	Junior Welterweight, 1960–1962

Further Reading
"Ortiz Retains Ring Title, Beats Loi on Split Decision." *Los Angeles Times*, 6/16/1960, p. C1.
Roberts, James B., and Alexander G. Skutt. *The Boxing Register: International Boxing Hall of Fame Register* (4th ed.). Ithaca, NY: McBooks Press, Inc., 2006, pp. 484–487.

LOPEZ, DANNY (1952–). Danny "Little Red" Lopez was a former world featherweight champion known for his punching power, exciting style, and ability to absorb punishment. Born in 1952 on a Utah reservation, Lopez turned pro in 1971 and kept winning until he lost to the talented **Bobby Chacon** in 1974. It proved to be a rough patch in Lopez's career as he lost two of his next three bouts as well.

However, Lopez rebounded in 1976 with a solid win over prospect **Sean O'Grady** and later that year defeated David Kotey by unanimous decision to win the **World Boxing Council (WBC)** featherweight title. He successfully defended his title seven times, including a memorable 1979 war with **Mike Ayala.** Lopez lost his title to the great **Salvador Sanchez** in 1980. He retired after losing a rematch with Sanchez. He made an ill-fated comeback in 1992 but retired for good after losing.

Professional Record:	47-6
Championship(s):	WBC featherweight, 1976–1980

Further Reading
Farhood, Steven. "Danny Lopez: A Great Champion." *Knockout* (Summer 1994), pp. 14–16.
Hafner, Dan. "Chacon Stops Lopez in 9th Before 16,080." *Los Angeles Times*, 5/25/1974, p. C1.

LOPEZ, RICARDO (1966–). Ricardo "Finito" Lopez may have been a small man, but he looms large in boxing history. The Mexican star reigned for nine years as the kingpin of the strawweight division. Born in 1966 in Mexico City, he turned pro in 1995 and never lost a professional fight. He captured the **World Boxing Council (WBC)** strawweight belt in 1990 with a win over Hideyuki Ohashi in Tokyo. He made 21 successful defenses of his crown, including a draw and split-decision win over the tough **Rosendo Alvarez.** In 1999, he moved up in weight and won the **International Boxing Federation (IBF)** junior flyweight title from **Will Grigsby.** He made two successful defenses and then retired in 2001. *The Ring* senior writer William Dettloff rates Lopez's strawweight dominance as the sixth-greatest title reign in boxing history.

Record:	50-0-1
Championship(s):	WBC strawweight, 1990–1998; IBF junior flyweight, 1999–2001

Further Reading
Dettloff, William. "The Ten Greatest Title Reigns of All-Time." *The Ring* (April 2005), pp. 65–76, 71.
Williams, Bruce. "Don't Quit Ricardo!" *KO* (May 1995), pp. 24–27, 53.

LOUGHRAN, TOMMY (1902–1982). Tommy Loughran was a former light heavyweight champion who possessed a great left jab. Born in 1902 in Philadelphia, Pennsylvania, Loughran turned pro in 1919 and fought a series of bouts with the great **Harry Greb.** In 1927, he defeated Mike McTigue to win the world light heavyweight crown. He successfully defended the title five times over the next two years before relinquishing the title in a quest for heavyweight glory. He prevailed over future heavyweight champions **James J. Braddock, Max Baer,** and Jack Sharkey, but lost in his one title shot to **Primo Carnera.** Though outweighed by 86 pounds, Loughran went the distance. He retired in 1937.

Professional Record: 94-23-9 (45 no decisions)
Championship(s): 1927–1929

Further Reading

Dawson, James P. "Braddock Is Beaten by Tommy Loughran." *The New York Times*, 7/19/1929, p. 22.
Loughran, Tommy. "Tommy Loughran Advises Spanish American Boxers." *Los Angeles Times*, 2/9/1928, p. B3.
Roberts, James B., and Alexander G. Skutt. *The Boxing Register: International Boxing Hall of Fame Register* (4th ed.). Ithaca, NY: McBooks Press, 2006, pp. 172–173.
"Tommy Loughran Beats Carpentier." *The New York Times*, 6/18/1926, p. 17.

LOUIS, JOE (1914–1981). "The Brown Bomber," Joe Louis held the world heavyweight championship for 12 years—longer than any fighter in history. In fact, Louis' reign from 1937–1949 represents the longest title reign for any division in boxing history. Born in Alabama, Louis' family migrated northward to Detroit, Michigan. After success as an amateur, Louis turned pro in 1934 under the watchful guidance of managers Julian Black and John Roxborough. They cautioned Louis—as an African American man in segregated America—to conduct himself in a gentlemanly fashion the opposite of **Jack Johnson.** For example, they warned Louis to never gloat over a fallen opponent—particularly a white opponent. Instead, Louis' handlers urged him to follow the example of **Peter Jackson,** a great black heavyweight in the late nineteenth century admired by nearly all boxing fans but denied a shot at the title because of race prejudice.

He won 27 straight bouts until veteran **Max Schmeling** knocked him out in June 1936 in the 12th round. Louis rebounded with seven straight victories, landing a title shot against champion **James J. Braddock**—"the Cinderella Man." Though he suffered a knockdown in the first round, Louis rebounded to pummel Braddock in an eighth-round stoppage.

Louis proceeded to defend his title 25 times before retiring after twice defeating **Jersey Joe Walcott** in 1947 and 1948. His most significant fight—billed as a "fight of the century"—was his June 1938 rematch with Schmeling. The fact that Schmeling hailed from Germany (though he did not support Hitler) during the eve of World War II and Adolf Hitler's quest for world domination also heightened tension for this highly anticipated rematch. Louis decimated Schmeling in the first round, elevating this African American man to U.S. hero. Famed sportswriter Jimmy Cannon famously said Louis was "a credit to his race—the human race."

Louis came out of retirement to challenge **Ezzard Charles** to regain his championship. Charles easily outpointed him over 15 rounds. He won eight straight bouts before facing undefeated contender **Rocky Marciano,** who overwhelmed the faded ex-champion in eight rounds. Marciano allegedly cried in his locker room after beating up on his former idol. Louis struggled with tax difficulties and drug problems in later life but remained beloved by the boxing and sporting worlds. He was indeed a "credit to his race."

Record:	68-3
Championship(s):	Heavyweight Champion, 1937–1949.

Further Reading
Bak, Richard. *Joe Louis: The Great Black Hope.* New York: Da Capo Press, 1998.
Barrow, Joe Louis, Jr., and Barbara Munder. *Joe Louis: 50 Years An American Hero.* New York: McGraw Hill, 1988.
Hietala, Thomas R. *The Fight of the Century: Jack Johnson, Joe Louis and the Struggle for Racial Equality.* Armonk, NY: M.E. Sharpe, 2002.
Woodruff, Harvey. "Louis Patterns His Career After Peter Jackson." *Chicago Daily Tribune,* 6/23/1935, p. A4.
Young, Frank A. "Is Joe Louis The Greatest Fighter of All Time." *The Chicago Defender,* 2/18/1939, p. 13.

LYLE, RON (1941–). Ron Lyle was a former heavyweight contender known for his powerful punch and rise from personal demons. Born in 1941 in Dayton, Ohio, Lyle ran into trouble with the law as a teenager. Convicted of second-degree murder, he served seven-and-a-half years in prison, where he learned how to box. In prison, he survived a terrible knifing, which nearly led to his death.

After obtaining parole, Lyle went to a boxing gym in Colorado and boxed for a couple years in the amateur ranks. He made his professional debut in 1969 at the age of 29. He won his first 19 bouts, 17 by knockout. In his 20th bout, he faced **Jerry Quarry,** who outboxed him for 12 rounds. In May 1975, Lyle received a shot at world heavyweight champion **Muhammad Ali,** who stopped Lyle in the 11th round.

Later in 1975, Lyle faced murderous puncher **Earnie Shavers.** Lyle survived a second-round knockdown to stop Shavers in the sixth round. Then, in 1976, Lyle faced **George Foreman.** In a war for the ages, Lyle and Foreman battered each other before Foreman kayoed Lyle in the fifth round. He kept fighting until suffering a brutal first-round kayo loss to **Gerry Cooney.**

Years later, in 1995—inspired by his old rival Foreman—Lyle made a comeback while in his 50s. He won four straight fights against nondescript opposition before calling it quits for good.

Professional Record:	44-7-1
Championship(s):	None

Further Reading
Berkwitt, Brad. *Boxing Interviews of a Lifetime.* Bloomington, IN: 1st Books, 2002, pp. 235–245.
Brunt, Stephen. *Facing Ali: 15 Fighters, 15 Stories.* Guilford, CT: Lyons Press, 2002, pp. 231–243.
Dettloff, William. "George Foreman KO 5 Ron Lyle." *The Ring* (November 2007), pp. 52–53.
Gordon, Randy. "Foreman-Lyle: The 'Superbrawl in Las Vegas." *Knockout* (Summer 1994), pp. 6–9, 60–61.

LYNCH, BENNY (1913–1946). Benny Lynch was a former world flyweight champion who was the first man from Scotland to win such an honor in the ring. Born in 1913 in Clydesdale, Lynch turned pro at age 18 in 1931. He defeated Jackie Brown in 1935 to win the NBA and International Boxing Union championships. Then, he captured the world flyweight championship in 1937 with a win over Small Montana. He never lost his belt in the ring but later moved up to the bantamweight division. He retired in 1938 after suffering the only kayo loss of his career to Aurel Toma.

Professional Record:	83-13-15
Championship(s):	1937–1938

Further Reading
Roberts, James B., and Alexander G. Skutt. *The Boxing Register: International Boxing Hall of Fame Register* (4th ed.). Ithaca, NY: McBooks Press, 2006, pp. 174–175.

LYTLE, CHRIS (1974–). Chris "Lights Out" Lytle is a mixed martial artist with a wrestling background, strong boxing skills, and an aggressive style that makes for exciting fights. Born in 1974 in Indianapolis, Indiana, Lytle wrestled for Southport High School.

Lytle made his professional mixed martial arts (MMA) debut in 1999 with a win over Bo Hershberger in Neutral Grounds 10. He fought in Pancrease, HOOK-n-SHOOT, Extreme Challenge, and Cage Rage events, among others. In 2002, he lost a decision to **Nick Diaz** in a Warriors Challenge event.

In 2000, he made his **Ultimate Fighting Championships (UFC)** debut at UFC 28: High Stakes, losing a decision to Ben Earwood. He didn't return to the Octagon until UFC 45: Revolution, losing a decision to **Robbie Lawler.** He rebounded the next year with wins at UFC 47: It's On over Tiki Ghosn and UFC 49: Unfinished Business over Ronald Jhun. Lytle got a major break when he was selected as a participant for *The Ultimate Fighter 4,* which showcased veteran fighters who had never won a title. Lytle surprised experts by making it to the finals by defeating Pete Spratt and **Din Thomas.** In the finals, Lytle lost a split decision to **Matt "the Terror" Serra.** The decision was questionable, as Lytle certainly performed better when the two fighters were on their feet.

The exposure from the show landed Lytle another fight in the Octagon against the legendary **Matt Hughes** at UFC 68. Hughes controlled the action with his wrestling and earned a unanimous decision. Lytle continues to earn more fans with his exciting style. At UFC 81: Breaking Point, he earned "Knockout of the Night" honors with a first-round stoppage of Kyle Bradley. At UFC 89, he earned "Fight of the Night" honors for his thrilling win over Paul Taylor.

Lytle has never submitted in a mixed martial arts bout. He has been stopped only twice—to Thiago Alves and Joe Riggs—due to cuts.

Lytle also showed great promise in the boxing ring, even though he had no amateur experience. He turned professional in 2002 and compiled a respectable record of 13-1-1. In his last boxing match, he stopped a talented Philadelphia fighter named Omar Pittman in the seventh round.

Professional MMA Record:	26-17-5
Professional Boxing Record:	13-1-1

Further Reading
Dorsey, Patrick. "Fight craze; Mixed martial arts quickly becoming most popular combat sport." *The Indianapolis Star,* 8/11/2007, p. 1.
Emanuel, Bob. "Serra to meet Lytle in Saturday's Ultimate Fighter 4: The Comeback finale." *The Miami Herald,* 11/9/2006.

MACHIDA, LYOTO (1978–). Lyoto "the Dragon" Machida is a talented Brazilian-based mixed martial artist well-versed in karate, jiu-jitsu, and wrestling. Born in 1978 in Salvador, Brazil, Machida learned karate at age 4, garnering a black belt at age 13.

Machida turned pro in 2003 and by early 2008 has yet to lose a mixed martial arts (MMA) bout. He has defeated **Rich Franklin, B. J. Penn,** and most recently Rameau Thierry Sokoudjou at **Ultimate Fighting Championships (UFC)** 79: Nemesis. Machida has also excelled in K-1-MMA events, defeating both **Michael McDonald** and Sam Greco. In May 2008, Machida defeated former UFC light heavyweight champion **Tito Ortiz** by unanimous decision. He remains on the short list for a shot at the light heavyweight championship.

Professional MMA Record: 14-0
Championship(s):   None

Further Reading
Ross, Matthew. "Enter the Dragon: Lyoto Machida has been preparing for this moment his entire life." *FIGHT!* (June 2008), pp. 66–70.

MALIGNAGGI, PAULIE (1980–). Paulie, the "Magic Man" Malignaggi is a slick boxer who won a world championship in the junior welterweight division. Born in 1980 in New York City, Malignaggi had a fine amateur career, culminating in winning the 2001 National Amateur Championships.

He turned pro in June 2001 and won his first 21 bouts before challenging unbeaten champion **Miguel Cotto** for the World Boxing Organization (WBO) junior welterweight championship. Malignaggi showed great courage in lasting the full 12 rounds with the powerful Cotto. He managed to survive the distance even though he suffered a brutal beating that including a broken cheekbone. He did display fine boxing skills during parts of the bout.

He rebounded in June 2007, winning a lopsided decision over Lovemore N'dou to capture the **International Boxing Federation (IBF)** junior welterweight crown. Malignaggi was simply too slick for N'dou. At the time of this writing, Malignaggi has made two successful defenses of his crown against a very tough Herman Ngoudjo and a split-decision victory in a rematch with N'dou.

Malignaggi is a very talented boxer but seems to suffer with fragile hands, as he has suffered injuries to them after several bouts. In November 2008 he squared off against **Ricky "the Hitman" Hatton** and lost in the eleventh round.

Professional Record: 25-2
Championship(s):   IBF junior welterweight, 2007–2008

Further Reading
Donovan, Jake. "Wait Til This Year: Malignaggi Seeks Magical 08." *Boxing Scene*, 1/1/2008, at http://www.boxingscene.com/?m=show&opt=printable&id=11875
Official Web site: http://www.paulmalignaggi.com.
Raskin, Eric. "Do You Believe in 'Magic'?" *The Ring* (November 2007), pp. 94–101.
Santoliquito, Joe. "The Ring Interview: Paulie Malignaggi: No Pain in the Ring Is Greater Than What I'd Gone Through Personally." *The Ring* (October 2008), pp. 48–59.
Stewart, Don. "Malignaggi Learns A Lesson: The Magic Man Should Have No Illusions About His Power." *The Ring* (May 2008), pp. 50–55.

MAMBY, SAOUL (1947–). Saoul Mamby is a former world junior welterweight champion known for his defensive skills and incredible longevity in a ring career that had him fighting in his 40s and 50s. Born in 1947 in the Bronx, Mamby turned pro in 1969 and earned the nickname "Sweet Saoul" for his defensive skills.

In 1977, he traveled to Thailand to face **World Boxing Council (WBC)** junior welterweight champion **Saensak Muangsurin.** The referee had Mamby ahead by seven points—147-140—but judges from Thailand and Hong Kong ruled in favor of the hometown fighter. Mamby persevered and in 1980 defeated Sang Hyun Kim for the WBC title. He retained his title five times, including a win over **Esteban DeJesus,** before suffering a questionable 15-round split decision loss to Leroy Haley.

He lost another questionable decision to Haley in 1983 and then a decision in 1984 to Billy Costello in attempts to regain his world title. He never received a world title shot but continued to fight at an advanced age in the 1990s. He even fought once in 2008 at 60 years old, losing a 10-round decision.

Professional Record: 45-34-6
Championship(s):   WBC junior welterweight, 1980–1982

Further Reading
Katz, Michael. "Mamby: Hard-Luck Champion." *The New York Times*, 7/6/1980, p. S4.

MANCINI, RAY (1961–). Ray "Boom Boom" Mancini was a popular former world lightweight champion known for his aggressive fighting style and ebullient personality. Born as Raymond Michael Mancino in 1961 in Youngstown, Ohio, Mancini learned boxing from his father Lenny, himself a professional boxer.

The young Ray had a lifelong goal of winning a world title in large part for his father, a contender whose title dreams were dashed by his drafting into World War II. Ray Mancini turned pro in 1979 and won his first 20 bouts, including an impressive decision win over the tough **Jose** Luis Ramirez. That landed Mancini a shot at the **World Boxing Council (WBC)** world lightweight title against the legendary **Alexis Arguello** in 1981. Mancini's aggressive style gave Arguello some trouble, but the champion stopped the game challenger in the 14th round.

In 1982, Mancini challenged Art Frias for the **World Boxing Association (WBA)** world lightweight title. In an action-packed opening round, Mancini's power proved too much. He won in impressive fashion in the first round. He made a successful defense against Ernesto Espana before his fateful fight against South Korean fighter Duk Koo Kim. Mancini battered the courageous Kim until the fight was finally stopped in the 14th round. Kim died days later from brain injuries suffered in the bout.

Kim's death greatly affected Mancini, but he did make two more successful defenses against Orlando Romero and **Bobby Chacon**. In 1984, he lost his title to the tough **Livingstone Bramble** in 1984. He lost a close rematch to Bramble in 1985 and then retired. He made a comeback in 1989 to fight **Hector "Macho" Camacho** and lost a close decision. He then made one more comeback in 1992 and lost badly to Greg Haugen.

He remains a beloved figure in boxing. A movie was made about his life titled *The Heart of a Champion: The Ray Mancini Story*.

Professional Record:	29-5
Championship(s):	WBA lightweight, 1982–1984

Further Reading
Anderson, Dave. "Legacy of a Father." *The New York Times*, 7/12/1982, p. C6.
Anderson, Dave. "Mancini Reacts to More Tragedy." *The New York Times*, 2/3/1983, p. B11.
Katz, Michael. "Arguello Stops Mancini in 14." *The New York Times*, 10/4/1981, p. S3.
Medwid, Steve. "Ray Mancini: Will Boom-Boom Be Able to Convert Another Bad Break Into Good Fortune." *The Ring* (June 1983), pp. 18–23.
Verdi, Bob. "Boxer Seeking Poetic Justice." *Chicago Daily Tribune*, 4/3/1981, p. C1.
Welsh, Jack. "Bye-Bye 'Boom Boom." *The Ring* (May 1985), pp. 32–39.

MARCIANO, ROCKY (1923–1969). Rocky Marciano remains the only undefeated world heavyweight champion in boxing history. He possessed an iron jaw, power in both hands and, most of all, an indomitable will to win. One of his biographers, Russell Sullivan, accurately referred to his impact as "the Rock of His Time." Born 1923 in Brockton, Massachusetts, as Rocco Francis Marcegiano, Marciano's early athletic interests were in baseball. "The Brockton Blockbuster" turned pro in 1947 under the expert tutelage of manager Al Weill and trainer Charley Goldman.

He won his first 16 fights by knockout before a 10-round decision over Don Mogard. In 1951, he beat former champion **Joe Louis** via eight-round knockout. Marciano was upset for his fallen idol, evening crying in the dressing room after defeating a past-his-prime Louis. In 1952, he fought **Jersey Joe Walcott** for the heavyweight crown, kayoing the champion with his devastating right hand—a punch he called his "Susie Q."—in the 13th round. Marciano absorbed great punishment in several of his fights but always managed to inflict more on his opponents.

He successfully defended his title six times against Walcott, Roland La Starza, **Ezzard Charles** (twice), Don Cockell, and **Archie Moore**. Marciano possessed an iron jaw, indefatigable energy, and incredible punching power.

Record:	49-0
Championship(s):	Heavyweight, 1952–1955

Further Reading
Breit, Harvey. "A Lamb in Lion's Clothing." *The New York Times*, 9/20/1953, p. SM24.
Callis, Tracy. "Rocky Marciano—'The Hardest One-Punch Slugger.'" *Cyber Boxing Zone Journal*, October 2000, at http://www.cyberboxingzone.com/boxing/wail1000_tracy.htm

Mayes, Harold. *Rocky Marciano.* London: Panther Books, 1956.
"Rocky Remembered: A Tribute to the Only Undefeated Heavyweight Champion in Boxing History." *The Ring Double* (2005, v. 6), pp. 69−130.
Skehan, Everett. *Rocky Marciano: Biography of a first son.* New York: Houghton Mifflin, 1977.
Sullivan, Russell. *Rocky Marciano: The Rock of His Times.* Champagne: University of Illinois Press, 2002.

MARGARITO, ANTONIO (1978−). Antonio Margarito is a rugged world welterweight champion from Mexico known for his aggressive, all-out attacks in the ring. A fan favorite, Margarito also comes to fight and pressures his opponents into fighting his style of a fight.

Born in 1978 in Torrance, California, Margarito moved to Tijuana at an early age. He turned pro in his native city in 1994 and gradually worked his way into the attention of Bob Arum's Top Rank promotions.

In 2002, he defeated the tough (and favored) Antonio Diaz to win the vacant World Boxing Organization (WBO) welterweight championship—a title he held for nearly five years before finally losing a close decision to Paul "the Punisher" Williams in 2007. In 2004, Margarito moved up in weight to challenge Daniel Santos for the WBO junior middleweight title. After Margarito suffered a bout-ending cut from a headbutt, the fight went to the scorecards and he lost a split decision.

Undeterred, Margarito continued his dominance at 147 lbs., including impressive wins over the highly touted Kermit Cintron and the tough Joshua Clottey. After his loss to Williams, Margarito defeated Cintron in a rematch to win the **International Boxing Federation (IBF)** welterweight crown. In July 2008, he staked his claim as the number one welterweight in the world by handing **World Boxing Association (WBA)** champion **Miguel Cotto** his first loss in an entertaining bout. Some experts believe that former pound-for-pound great **Floyd Mayweather, Jr.,** assiduously avoided facing Margarito in the boxing ring. However, Margarito's

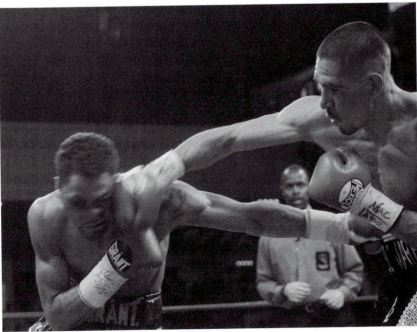

Antonio Margarito unleashes damage on Kermit Cintron in their April 2005 bout. Margarito won in the fifth round. Courtesy of Chris Cozzone.

Antonio Margarito stops Miguel Cotto in their epic June 2008 battle for welterweight supremacy. Courtesy of Chris Cozzone.

mystique took a devastating blow in January 2009 when he was beaten badly by **"Sugar" Shane Mosley.**

Professional Record: 37-6
Championship(s):   WBO welterweight, 2002—

Further Reading
Baxter, Kevin. "Margarito pummels title out of Cotto." *Los Angeles Times*, 7/27/2008, p. D1.
Official Web site: http://www.antoniomargarito.com/antoniomargaritoenglishversion.htm

MARQUEZ, JUAN MANUEL (1973–). Juan Manuel Marquez is a Mexican-born world champion in the featherweight and super featherweight divisions. Blessed with great boxing skills and a powerful punch, Juan Manuel is the older brother of the equally gifted **Rafael Marquez**—himself a two-division titlist.

Born in 1973 in Mexico City, Juan Manuel turned pro in 1993 and suffered a disqualification loss in his pro debut. In 1999, he lost a decision to then-unbeaten featherweight champion **Freddie Norwood.** However, Marquez rebounded and in 2003 defeated **Manuel Medina** to capture the **International Boxing Federation (IBF)** featherweight title. He added the **World Boxing Association (WBA)** belt with a destruction of Derrick "Smoke" Gainer later in the year.

In 2004, he successfully defended his title with a controversial draw against the Philippine sensation **Manny Pacquiao.** Marquez survived three-first round knockdowns and pulled himself back into the fight. He held a featherweight title until losing to Chris John in 2006.

He rebounded in a major way in March 2007 with a convincing decision win over **Marco Antonio Barrera.** He then defeated the dangerous Rocky Juarez in his first defense. He lost a narrow decision to Pacquiao in a rematch but rebounded with a stoppage of the dangerous **Joel Casamayor** in a lightweight showdown.

Juan Manuel Marquez celebrates his July 2007 victory over Marco Antonio Barrera. Courtesy of Chris Cozzone./FightWire Images.

Juan Manuel Marquez trades punches with Joel Casamayor in their September 2008 bout. Courtesy of Chris Cozzone.

Juan Manuel Marquez raises his hand in triumph as he stops Joel Casamayor in the 11th round of their September 2008 fight. Courtesy of Chris Cozzone.

Juan Manuel Marquez lands a nice right hand against Manny Pacquaio in their March 2008 bout. Marquez dropped a 12-round split decision. Courtesy of Chris Cozzone.

Juan Manuel Marquez celebrates after his grueling March 2008 bout against Manny Pacquiao. Unfortunately for Marquez, he lost a split decision. Courtesy of Chris Cozzone.

Professional Record:	49-4-1
Championship(s):	IBF featherweight, 2003–2005; WBA featherweight, 2003–2005; WBO featherweight, 2006–2007; WBC super featherweight, 2007–

Further Reading
Goldman, Ivan. "Now That Marquez Has Beaten Barrera . . . Will Politics Rob Us of a Dream Rematch with Pac-Man?" *The Ring* (July 2007), pp. 32–37.

MARQUEZ, RAFAEL (1975–). Rafael Marquez is a Mexican-born world champion in the bantamweight and super bantamweight divisions known for his tremendous power. He is the younger brother of **Juan Manuel Marquez**—a world champion in the featherweight and super featherweight divisions.

Born in 1975 in Mexico City, Rafael turned pro in 1995 against contender Victor Rabaneles—a veteran of more than 50 fights. As a result, Marquez opened his career with a loss. He continued to plug away, though he suffered two more losses early in his career.

He first made his mark as a pro with a close decision win in 2001 over longtime flyweight kingpin **Mark "Too Sharp" Johnson** who until then had lost only 1 bout in more than 40 pro fights. Marquez convincingly captured the rematch, stopping Johnson in the eighth round.

In February 2003, he stopped previously unbeaten Tim Austin to capture the **International Boxing Federation (IBF)** bantamweight title. Marquez successfully defended his title seven times before he moved up in weight to challenge **Israel Vazquez** for the **World Boxing Council (WBC)** super bantamweight title. He broke Vazquez's nose en route to stopping him in the seventh round. He lost to Vazquez in a rematch and then in February 2008 lost the rubber match with his rival by split decision. He remains a highly marketable boxer and probably a future world champion again.

Rafael Marquez (left) and Israel Vasquez trade bombs in their March 2007 bout. Marquez won this fight in the eighth round. Courtesy of Chris Cozzone.

Rafael Marquez celebrates his successful title defense against Mauricio Pastrana in November 2004. Courtesy of Chris Cozzone.

Professional Record:	37-5
Championship(s):	IBF bantamweight, 2003–2007; WBC super bantamweight, 2007

Further Reading
Goldman, Eddie. "Why Can't They All Be Like Vazquez and Marquez?" *Tapout*, No. 24 (2008), p. 31.
Goldman, Ivan. "Junior Feather Champion Rafael Marquez: Can His Marketability Catch Up To His Talent." *The Ring* (July 2007), pp. 38–43.

MARSH, TERRY (1958−). Most fight fans will not recall the name of British fighter Terry Marsh, but he deserves inclusion in this encyclopedia for being one of the precious few championship boxers to retire undefeated. Born in Stepney, England, in 1958, Marsh turned professional in 1981. He won his first six fights and then fought a draw with Lloyd Christie. Marsh continued his winning ways, capturing the European junior welterweight title in 1985. In 1987, he stopped Joe Manley to win the **International Boxing Federation (IBF)** junior welterweight title. He successfully defended his title once against Akio Kameda and then retired because of epilepsy. In 1989, Marsh's life took an even stranger turn, as he was charged with attempted murder for the shooting of his former promoter **Frank Warren.** A jury acquitted Marsh.

Record:	26-0-1
Championship(s):	IBF junior welterweight, 1987

Further Reading
Marsh, Terry. *Undefeated: My Story.* London: Terry Marsh Publishing, 2005.

MARTIN, CHRISTY (1968−). Christy "the Coalminers' Daughter" Martin was the first women to earn significant money fighting as a professional boxer. She possesses an aggressive style and powerful left hook with a less-than-stellar defense. These elements combine to give her a very crowd-pleasing style and garnered her a *Sports Illustrated* cover.

Christy Martin (right) struggles with opponent Holly Holm in their September 2005 bout. Courtesy of Chris Cozzone.

Christy Martin gets a pep talk and counsel from her trainer and husband Jim Martin during her September 2005 bout with Holly Holm. Courtesy of Chris Cozzone.

Born Christy Salters in 1968 in Bluestem, West Virginia, Martin earned all-state honors in basketball in high school and earned a scholarship to Concord College in Athens, West Virginia. Her freshman year she entered a tough woman competition, won three bouts, and collected $1,000. She later won two more times before graduating in three years with honors.

She later met and married Jim Martin, a boxing trainer from Bristol, Tennessee. She turned pro under her husband's guidance in 1989 with a five-round draw. She later split a pair of bouts with Andrea Deshong. She became known internationally after signing with promoter **Don King** and appearing on the undercard of the **Mike Tyson—Frank Bruno** title fight in 1996 against Deidre Gogarty, which she won by six-round decision.

She continued to land high-profile fights, including a 2002 win over fellow female star Mia St. John over 10 rounds. In 2003, she faced a much-heavier and younger **Laila Ali** who stopped her in four rounds. She last fought in June 2007 in West Virginia.

Professional Record: 47-5-2

Further Reading
Berg, Aimee. "This Fighter is Making Fans of Her Skeptics." *The New York Times*, 3/17/1996, p. S2.
Official Web site: http://www.christymartin.com/
Nieves, Ellen. "A Boxer in a Hurry." *The New York Times*, 11/3/1996, p. SM38.

MATHIS, BUSTER, SR. (1943–1995). Buster Mathis, Sr., was a former heavyweight contender known for his unusually quick movements, especially for a man of his prodigious girth. Though he weighed nearly 300 pounds, Mathis possessed extremely quick hands. Born in 1943 in Sledge, Mississippi, he moved to Michigan as a youngster.

Mathis had a decorated amateur career, culminating in his earning a spot on the 1964 Olympic team. He defeated **Joe Frazier** by unanimous decision to win the spot to represent his country in the Tokyo Olympics. However, an untimely injury forced him to withdraw, allowing Frazier the opportunity to go instead, where he captured Olympic gold.

He turned pro in 1965 and won his first 23 bouts before facing his former amateur rival Frazier for the heavyweight title in 1968. Mathis performed well in the early round but tired as the fight progressed. Frazier stopped him in the 11th round. He rebounded with six straight wins before losing consecutive decisions to **Jerry Quarry** and the great **Muhammad Ali.** He retired in 1972 after suffering a second-round kayo loss to undefeated contender **Ron Lyle.**

Mathis' son, Buster Mathis, Jr., also became a heavyweight contender. Mathis, Sr., died in 1995 of heart failure at the age of 51.

Professional Record: 30-4
Championship(s):   None

Further Reading
Litsky, Frank. "Boxer Weak and Scared as a Boy." *The New York Times*, 5/18/1964, p. 40.
Litsky, Frank. "In This Corner, Weighing 290 . . ." *The New York Times*, 8/17/1965, p. 27.
Litsky, Frank. "Buster Mathis, Heavyweight Fighter, Dies at 51." *The New York Times*, 9/8/1995, p. B9.
United Press International. "298-Pounder Too Fast for Foe in Ring Finals." *Los Angeles Times*, 5/21/1964,
        p. B3.

MAYORGA, RICARDO (1973–). Ricardo Mayorga is a colorful, controversial former world champion in the welterweight and junior middleweight divisions known for his tremendous power and unorthodox actions—such as smoking in the ring after a victory. Born in 1973 in Managua, Nicaragua, Mayorga turned pro in 1993 and suffered a loss in his professional debut.

He rebounded and eventually earned a title shot against **World Boxing Association (WBA)** welterweight champion Andrew "Six Heads" Lewis. Their first bout ended in a no-contest after an unintentional clash of heads, but Mayorga dominated the rematch to win his first world title in 2002. He added the **World Boxing Council (WBC)** belt with a surprising domination of **Vernon Forrest** in 2003. He lost his title to the slick Cory Spinks in 2003.

El Matador! Ricardo Mayorga looks at the referee who refuses to call a knockdown when his opponent Vernon Forrest was pushed to the floor. Mayorga won a 12-round decision in the July 2003 rematch. Courtesy of Chris Cozzone.

In 2004, he lost to **Felix Trinidad,** but in 2005, he defeated Michele Piccirillo to win the vacant WBC junior middleweight title. Unfortunately for "El Matador," he lost his title in 2006 to **Oscar De La Hoya** in a comeback fight for "the Golden Boy." In 2007, he defeated **Fernando Vargas** in a crossroads bout but lost to **Shane Mosley** in 2008.

Professional Record: 29-7-1

Championship(s):   WBA welterweight, 2002–2003; WBC welterweight, 2003; WBC junior middleweight, 2005–2006

Further Reading

Argeris, Steve. "Mayorga's Truly Unorthodox Style; In Ring and Out, Fighter Does Things a Little—Make That a Lot—Differently." *The Washington Post*, 12/11/2003, p. D10.

Wertheim, L. Jon, and Luis Fernando Liosa. "He Drinks, He Smokes, He Wins; Welterweight Champion Ricardo Mayorga, a reckless fighter with an unruly lifestyle, is boxing's hottest ticket." *Sports Illustrated*, 12/8/2003, p. 70.

MAYWEATHER, FLOYD, JR. (1977–). "Pretty Boy" Floyd Mayweather, Jr., is an extremely talented professional boxer viewed by many as the sport's pound-for-pound best. Blessed with incredible hand and foot speed, Mayweather's skills have led him to championships in five different weight divisions. Born in 1977 in Grand Rapids, Michigan, Mayweather earned a bronze medal at the 1996 Olympics after losing a very controversial decision to Bulgarian Serafim Todorov.

He turned pro in 1996 and has never lost. In 1998, he won his first world title—the **World Boxing Council (WBC)** super featherweight crown—by defeating Genaro Hernandez in the eighth round. He made eight successful defenses of his crown before moving up to the lightweight division. In 2002, he won a 12-round decision over **Jose Luis Castillo** to win the WBC lightweight title. In 2005, he added the WBC junior welterweight crown with an easy win over **Arturo Gatti.** He fought once in 2006, capturing the WBC welterweight title with an easy decision win over Carlos Baldimir. Then, in a 2007 mega-fight, he defeated **Oscar De La Hoya** by split decision to win the WBC junior middleweight title. Later in the year, he dominated unbeaten challenger **Ricky Hatton** to cement his standing as boxing's pound-for-pound best. In 2008, Mayweather announced his retirement from the sport.

Professional Record: 38-0

Championship(s):   WBC super featherweight, 1998–2002; WBC lightweight, 2002–2004; WBC junior welterweight, 2005–2006; IBF junior welterweight, 2006; WBC welterweight, 2006–; WBC junior middleweight, 2007

Further Reading

Berkow, Ira. "Lessons From in the Ring and Inside the Prison Cell." *The New York Times*, 3/24/1998, p. C5.

Donovan, Jake. "Floyd Mayweather Jr. Still Searching for Superstardom." *The Sweet Science*, 1/20/2005, at http://www.thesweetscience.com/boxing-article/1579/floyd-mayweather-still-searching-super stardom/

Donovan, Jake. "Mayweather: Undefeated and the Undisputed Best." *Boxing Scene*, 12/10/2007 at http://www.boxingscene.com/?m=show&opt=printable&id=11637

Johnson, Chuck. "Mayweather born to be champion: Fighter comes from boxing family, works way to top." *USA TODAY*, 9/26/2006, p. 3C.

Katz, Mike. "Father and Son Trade Jabs in Buildup for Fight." *The New York Times*, 4/19/2003, p. S2.

Mayo, David. "The Floyd Gates Open: Now It's Time For Opponents To Ask 'Pretty Boy' For A Date." *The Ring* (August 2006), pp. 42–47.

Official Web site of Floyd Mayweather, Jr.: http://www.floydmayweather.net/

Raskin, Eric. "Too Much Pretty Boy, Not Enough Gritty Boy: New Welter King Mayweather Leaves Us Wondering if Perfection Is Enough." *The Ring* (March 2007), pp. 30–35.

MAYWEATHER, FLOYD, SR. (1952−). Floyd Mayweather, Sr., is a former welterweight king, the father of pound-for-pound great **Floyd Mayweather, Jr.,** and one of the top trainers in boxing. He may be best known for his tense relationship with his talented son. Born in 1952 in the Bronx, Mayweather displayed great skills as an amateur.

He turned pro in 1974 and won 16 of his first 17 bouts heading into a 1978 showdown with former Olympic gold medalist **Sugar Ray Leonard.** Mayweather was stopped in the 10th round. He rebounded with four straight wins before losing to another undefeated prospect, **Marlon "the Magic Man" Starling.** He finally retired in 1990 with a record of 29-5. He never received a world title shot.

He later received a prison sentence for drug dealing, which caused him to miss his son's meteoric rise in the amateur and pro ranks. Upon his release, Floyd, Sr., guided his son to the world super featherweight championship in 1998. For that, the elder Mayweather received Trainer of the Year honors from the Boxing Writers Association. However, the two squabbled and for years were not on speaking terms.

Despite the estrangement from his son, Mayweather, Sr., has had a successful career as a trainer. He has worked with many world champions, including **Oscar De La Hoya,** Juan Guzman, **Laila Ali,** and **Ricky Hatton.** He is known for his flashy dressing and poetry before fights. For example, in the days before the De La Hoya—**Fernando Vargas** fight, Mayweather unveiled poetry he composed that praised his fighter De La Hoya and degraded Vargas. A sample stanza included:

Floyd Mayweather Jr. suffers a low blow from Zab Judah in their April 2006 bout. Floyd won a 12-round unanimous decision. Courtesy of Chris Cozzone.

Mr. Wanna Be Ferocious Vargas
You say you don't like De La Hoya
But you will soon feel the Real McCoy
When you are touched by the Golden
Boy . . .
You don't have the mindset to compete in
the ring
Jealousy and drama is all that you bring.
Your skills are nothing
You're all about bluffing.

Professional Record: 29-6-1
Championship(s):   None

Further Reading

Berkow, Ira. "Lessons From in the Ring and Inside the Prison Cell." *The New York Times*, 3/24/1998, p. C5.

Feour, Royce. "Mayweathers prove to be successful combination." *Las Vegas Review-Journal*, 5/18/1999, p. 1C.

Hudson, David L., Jr. "Floyd Mayweather Sr.: 'It Should Be An Easy Fight.'" *Fightnews*, 9/5/2002.

Springer, Steve. "Mayweathers Rift Beyond Repair." *Los Angeles Times*, 1/13/2001, p. D9.

Floyd Mayweather Jr. celebrates with promoter Bob Arum after his win over Zab Judah. Courtesy of Chris Cozzone.

MAYWEATHER, ROGER (1961–).

Though now known mainly for training his nephew—the talented **Floyd Mayweather, Jr.**—Roger Mayweather was a former world champion in his own right. Nicknamed "the Black Mamba," Mayweather had a quick left jab and powerful right cross that he used to capture two world titles. Born in Grand Rapids, Michigan, in 1961, Mayweather turned pro in 1981 and won his first 14 fights before challenging Samuel Serrano for the **World Boxing Association (WBA)** super featherweight title in 1983. The young Mayweather dominated the champion, winning via an eighth-round technical knockout. He defended his title twice before Rocky Lockridge kayoed him in the first round. Mayweather rebounded in 1987, winning the **World Boxing Council (WBC)** junior welterweight title with a victory over Rene Arredondo. He successfully defended his title four times before losing to the great **Julio Cesar Chavez.** He failed in two later attempts to win the **International Boxing Federation (IBF)** junior welterweight crown, losing to Rafael Pineda and **Kostya Tszyu.**

Mayweather trains his nephew Floyd, Jr., who has been recognized for many years as boxing's pound-for-pound best fighter. Mayweather became embroiled in controversy in April 2006 when he charged into the ring after **Zab Judah** hit Floyd, Jr., with a blatant low blow. Mayweather received a one-year suspension from the Nevada State Athletic Commission.

Professional Record: 59-13
Championship(s):   WBA super featherweight, 1983–1984; WBC junior welterweight, 1987–1989

Further Reading

Hoffer, Richard. "He Sees the Light." *Los Angeles Times*, 7/8/1984, p. E16.

MCAULIFFE, JACK (1866–1937). Jack McAuliffe was a world lightweight champion during the bare knuckle days of boxing. Born in Cork, Ireland, in 1866, McAuliffe won the world title in 1886 from Billy Frazier and held it until 1894. He never lost a professional bout, though he did fight in the era of no-decisions.

He won the lightweight title in 1886, held it for eight years, and retired undefeated. In his most famous bout, he fought a draw with British champion Jem Carney that lasted more than 70 rounds. Because of his ring dominance and diminutive stature, McAuliffe was called "the Napoleon of the Ring."

Professional Record: 30-0-5

Championship(s): Lightweight, 1886–1894

Further Reading

Callis, Tracy. "Jack McAuliffe . . . 'Quick as Greased Lightning.'" *Cyber Boxing Zone Journal*, May 2001, at http://www.cyberboxingzone.com/boxing/w5x-tc.htm

CyberBoxing Zone on Jack McAuliffe: http://www.cyberboxingzone.com/boxing/mcaul.htm

Dettloff, William. "The 20 Greatest Lightweights of All Time." *The Ring* (September 2001), pp. 49–69, 66.

MCCALL, OLIVER (1965–). Oliver "the Atomic Bull" McCall is a former world heavyweight champion known for his iron chin, powerful punch, and at-times strange behavior. He is best known for his one-punch knockout of **Lennox Lewis** in 1994 to win the **World Boxing Council (WBC)** heavyweight championship and then his bizarre behavior that led to his disqualification loss to Lewis in their 1997 rematch.

Born in 1965 in Chicago, McCall turned pro in 1985. He lost his second pro bout by decision. In 1989 and 1990, he lost decisions to fellow prospect **James "Buster" Douglas** and Orlin Norris. He rebounded in 1991 with wins over future champion Bruce Seldon and Jesse Ferguson.

However, in 1992 he lost a decision to Tony Tucker in an attempt for the NABF heavyweight title. Two years later, McCall entered the ring as a heavy underdog against WBC world heavyweight champion Lennox Lewis. However, in the second round, "the Atomic Bull" unloaded a devastating right hand that kayoed the champion. He made one successful defense against former champion **Larry Holmes** before losing his title in 1995 to **Frank Bruno.**

His career unraveled when he faced Lewis for the vacant WBC title in 1987. Lewis controlled the early rounds with his jab and then McCall seemingly had a mental breakdown. He started crying in the ring and refused to engage Lewis. Upon his disqualification, McCall had to start from scratch.

He won 13 straight fights from 1997–2004 against largely nondescript opposition, though in 2001, he kayoed former world heavyweight challenger Henry Akinwande in the 10th and final round. In 2004, he lost a decision to DaVarryl Williamson. He continued to fight in 2007, last losing a decision to former cruiserweight champion Juan Carlos Gomez.

Professional Record: 51-9

Championship(s): WBC heavyweight, 1994–1995

Further Reading

Clarity, James F. "Lewis Halted in 2 Rounds by McCall." *The New York Times*, 9/25/1994, p. S1.

Eskenazi, Gerald. "McCall is a Titleholder Obscured by Ex-Champions." *The New York Times*, 4/6/1995, p. B15.

Eskenazi, Gerald. "McCall Tries to Explain Bizarre Actions." *The New York Times*, 2/9/1997, p. 334.

Santoliquito, Joe. "From Champ to Crackhead to Contender: Can Oliver McCall Make It All The Way Back?" *KO Boxing 2002*, pp. 28–32.

MCCARTHY, JOHN (1962–). "Big" John McCarthy is the most well-known referee in the history of mixed martial arts. He served as the primary referee in the **Ultimate Fighting Championships (UFC)** nearly from its inception until his retirement in December 2007. He began refereeing in the Octagon at UFC 2 and has been a fixture ever since. McCarthy, who is a Los Angeles police officer, stands 6′4″ tall and weighs more than 250 pounds, earning him his nickname "Big John." McCarthy is best known for his phrase that he bellowed out to each fighter in the Octagon—"Are you Ready? Let's get it on!" McCarthy retired to become the analyst for the Fight Network. He also serves as a regular contributor to *Fight!* Magazine. Fortunately, for mixed martial arts fans, McCarthy has returned to officiating, refereeing the recent bout between **Fedor Emelianenko** and **Andrei Arlovski.**

Further Reading
Kreutzer, Robert. "In the Octagon, cop urges fighters on." *The Press-Enterprise*, 5/16/1996, p. B1.
Official Web site: http://www.bigjohnmccarthy.com

MCCLELLAN, GERALD (1967–). Gerald "the G-Man" McClellan was a devastating puncher who captured versions of the world middleweight title twice in the early 1990s by outgunning dangerous sluggers **John "the Beast" Mugabi** and **Julian Jackson.** Born in 1967 in Freeport, Illinois, McClellan first laced up a pair of boxing gloves when he was only eight years old. His family moved to Wisconsin, where McClellan performed well in the amateur ranks. He nearly made the U.S. Olympic team in 1988.

He turned pro in 1988 and won his first 10 bouts before a decision loss to Dennis Milton. In 1991, he entered the ring as a heavy underdog to Mugabi. However, McClellan devastated Mugabi and stopped him in the first round to win the World Boxing Organization (WBO) middleweight title.

McClellan successfully defended his title three times before moving to the super middleweight division to challenge Great Britain's **Nigel "the Dark Destroyer" Benn.** McClellan knocked Benn out of the ring in the first round and nearly stopped Benn in the eighth round. However, the warrior Benn rebounded to stop McClellan in the 10th round. Tragically, McClellan suffered debilitating head injuries from which he has never recovered. He remains unable to care for himself—a tragic tale of boxing's dangers.

Professional Record:	34-3
Championship(s):	WBO middleweight, 1991–1992; WBC middleweight, 1993–1994

Further Reading
Berkow, Ira. "A Boxer's Darkness: Damaged McClellan Has Poignant Battles With Everyday Life." *The New York Times*, 11/12/1995, p. S1.
Donovan, Jake. "Gerald McClellan: A Fallen Warrior in Need of Forgiveness and Support." *The Sweet Science*, 2/24/2005, at http://www.thesweetscience.com/boxing-article/1730/gerald-mcclellan-fallen-warrior-need-forgiveness-support/

MCCOY, CHARLES (1872–1940). Charles "Kid" McCoy was one of the most unique figures in boxing history. He became the first southpaw to win a world title. He was known for the "corkscrew" punch—in which he turned his fist upon impact to inflict greater damage. He also was known on occasion to give less than his best effort in the ring. Once, after McCoy gave a good account of himself in the ring, a sportswriter said he had seen "the Real McCoy."

Born in 1872 in Indiana as Norman Selby, McCoy ran away from home as a youth and turned pro as a boxer in 1891 at age 17. Only five years later he defeated welterweight champion **Tommy Ryan** in a nontitle bout. The next year he defeated **"Mysterious" Billy Smith.**

In 1897, he defeated Dan Creedon for the world middleweight title. He then moved up in weight and challenged top light heavyweights and heavyweights. In 1903, he lost to Jack Root for the vacant world light heavyweight championship. He retired in 1916.

In 1924, McCoy was convicted of manslaughter for killing a woman with whom he lived. He served seven years in prison. He committed suicide in 1940.

Professional Record:	86-6-6
Championship(s):	Middleweight, 1897

Further Reading
Callis, Tracy. "Kid McCoy . . . 'Dr. Jekyll and Mr. Hyde,'" *Cyber Boxing Zone Journal*, January 2000, at http://www.cyberboxingzone.com/boxing/box1-00.htm
Cantwell, Robert. *The Real McCoy: The Life and Times of Norman Selby.* New York: Auerbach Publishers, 1971.
Strauss, Darin. *The Real McCoy.* New York: Plume Books, 2002.

MCCRORY, MILTON (1962–). Milton "the Ice Man" McCrory was a former world welterweight champion known for his powerful punch and lanky frame. He drew comparisons to fellow Detroit native and former welterweight kingpin **Thomas "the Hitman" Hearns.** McCrory's first love was baseball, but his father steered him to compete in boxing.

McCrory turned pro in 1980 and won his first five fights by knockout in the first round. He won his first 20 bouts before fighting a 12-round draw with Colin Jones. In the rematch, McCrory survived the last two rounds to earn a split decision victory and the **World Boxing Council (WBC)** title. He successfully defended his title four times before losing in a unification bout with fellow unbeaten welterweight champion **Donald "the Cobra" Curry.**

In 1987, McCrory unsuccessfully challenged **World Boxing Association (WBA)** junior welterweight champion **Mike McCallum.** He retired in 1990 with a career record of 35-4-1. His late younger brother Steve McCrory was a former Olympic gold medalist and professional world title challenger.

Professional Record:	35-4-1
Championship(s):	WBC welterweight, 1983–1985

Further Reading
Gammon, Clive. "A crown for the (n)iceman." *Sports Illustrated*, 8/22/1983, p. 68.
Girard, Fred. "Champion gives up ring for family life." *The Detroit News*, 2/12/2001.

MCCRORY, TAMDAN (1986–). Tamdan "the Barn Cat" McCrory is a lean mixed martial artist who, though he stands 6′4″ tall, fights in the **Ultimate Fighting Championships' (UFC)** 170 lb. weight division. Born in 1986 in Ithaca, New York, McCrory turned pro in mixed martial arts (MMA) in 2006 at an event held by the World Fighting League. He kept winning fights, earning a shot in the UFC against veteran Pete Spratt at UFC Fight Night 10 in June 2007.

In his debut in the Octagon, McCrory impressed observers and stopped the much more experienced Spratt in the second round. McCrory lost his first MMA fight at UFC 78: Validation to Japanese legend Aakihiro Gono via an armbar submission. McCrory temporarily put his fighting plans on hold, concentrating on obtaining his college degree from State University of New York at Cortland.

Professional MMA Record:	10-1
Championship(s):	None

Further Reading

Constable, Derek. "Barn Cat Unleashed: Welterweight Tamdan McCrory, Ready to Make his Mark in the UFC, is a Warrior of Unmatched Intensity." *Ultimate Grappling* (April 2008), pp. 72–73.

Davidson, Neil. "Tamdan McCrory looks to make mark at UFC against Pride veteran Akihiro Gomo." *The Canadian Press*, 11/13/2007.

MCCULLOUGH, WAYNE (1970–). Wayne "the Pocket Rocket" McCullough is a former world bantamweight champion known for his high-volume punch output and his iron chin. Born in 1970 in Belfast, Northern Ireland, McCullough had a remarkable amateur career. He represented Ireland in both the 1988 Seoul and 1992 Barcelona Olympics. He fought in the 1988 Olympics as a light flyweight, losing on points in the second round to Canada's Scotty Olson. In 1992, he fought in the bantamweight division and captured a silver medal. He lost the gold-medal match to fellow future professional champion **Joel Casamayor** of Cuba.

McCullough turned pro in 1993 and quickly advanced up the ranks. In July 1995, he defeated Japan's Yasuei Yakushiji to win the **World Boxing Council (WBC)** world bantamweight title. He made two successful defenses before moving up in weight. In 1997, he lost a split decision in an attempt to lift the WBC super bantamweight title from **Daniel Zaragoza.** In 1998, he lost a unanimous decision to then-unbeaten superstar "Prince" **Naseem Hamed** for the World Boxing Organization (WBO) featherweight title. In 1999, he lost a unanimous decision to **Erik Morales** for the WBC featherweight title. In both the Hamed and Morales bouts, McCullough absorbed tremendous amounts of punishment but went the distance.

Controversy surrounded McCullough after it was discovered by medical examiners that he had a cyst on his brain. British boxing authorities refused for a time to allow him to fight. Later medical testing seemingly showed that the cyst was not in a dangerous location, and he was granted a license in Nevada. In 2005, McCullough lost two straight bouts to Oscar Larios for the WBC super bantamweight title. He planned on returning to the ring in 2007, but his opponent failed to make weight. He hopes to make his return in 2008.

Professional Record:	27-6
Championship(s):	WBC bantamweight, 1995–1996

Further Reading

Crossan, Brenda. "The Rocket's journey is still not complete." *Irish News*, 11/23/2005, p. 70.

Doogan, Brian. "'I'm Not Dead: The Nightmare Is Over For Wayne McCullough." *World Boxing* (July 2002), pp. 62–66.

Donovan, Jake. "Wayne McCullough's Last Chance at Boxing Gold." *The Sweet Science*, 2/9/2005, at http://www.thesweetscience.com/boxing-article/1670/wayne-mccullough-last-chance-boxing-gold/

McCullough, Wayne. *Pocket Rocket: Don't Quit, The Autobiography of Wayne McCullough*. London: Mainstream Publishing, 2005.

Official Web site: http://www.pocketrocketbox.com

MCDONALD, MICHAEL (1965–). Michael McDonald is a Canadian-born kickboxer who achieved great success in K-1. Born in 1965 in Birmingham, England, McDonald became introduced to Muay Thai kickboxing as a teenager. In 1996, he started fighting in K-1 and has won several major tournaments. Known as "the Black Sniper," McDonald has won the K-1 Grand

Prix North American championship in 2002 and 2004. He holds wins over **Mirko "Cro Cop" Filipovic, Rick Roufus, Marvin Eastman,** and Dewey Cooper.

Professional Kickboxing Record:	52-20
Championship(s):	Numerous North American kickboxing titles

Further Reading
Official Web site: http://www.blacksniper.com

MCFARLAND, PACKEY (1888–1936). Chicago's Patrick "Packey" McFarland lost only 1 bout in more than 100 bouts but never received a shot at a world championship. He campaigned at lightweight for much of his career, which spanned from 1904 to 1915. Thirty-four of his bouts were classified as no-decisions, as he fought in the Frawley Law era when many fights that went the distance resulted in no one declared a winner.

Born in 1888 in Chicago, Illinois, McFarland fought in the Chicago stockyards as a youth. This earned him the nickname "the Pride of the Stockyards." He turned pro at age 16 in 1904. He lost his professional debut to a fighter named Dusty Miller. He didn't lose again for several years.

Longtime lightweight champion **Battling Nelson** would never give McFarland a title shot. McFarland often preferred to outbox his opponents rather than risk injury going for a knockout. Sportswriter Robert Edgren called him "the cleverest fighter of all time." Once when a referee in Boston called one of McFarland's fights a draw, McFarland knocked the referee cold, causing a near riot. He is best known for his three fights against Freddie Welsh.

Record:	64-1-5 (34 no decisions)
Championship(s):	None

Further Reading
Edgren, Robert. "McFarland Called Cleverest Fighter of All Time." *The Washington Post*, 2/4/1934, p. M17.
Roberts, James B., and Alexander G. Skutt. *The Boxing Register: International Boxing Hall of Fame Official Record Book* (4th ed.). Ithaca, NY: McBooks Press, Inc., 2006, pp. 184–185.

MCGIRT, JAMES "BUDDY" (1964–). James "Buddy" McGirt is known today as one of boxing's top trainers, handling such champions as **Antonio Tarver, Paulie Malignaggi,** and **Arturo Gatti.** However, Buddy McGirt was a great boxer in his own right, a skilled practitioner of the Sweet Science who captured world titles in both the junior welterweight and welterweight divisions.

Born in 1964 in Brentwood, New York, McGirt turned pro in 1982 and did not lose in his first 29 pro bouts, going 28-0-1. In his 30th bout, he met fellow unbeaten prospect Frankie Warren and lost a 10-round decision in 1986. McGirt got sweet revenge two years later when he stopped Warren in the 12th round to win the vacant **International Boxing Federation (IBF)** junior welterweight title. He successfully defended the title once against Howard Davis, Jr., before losing his title to undefeated **Meldrick Taylor,** who stopped him in the 12th round.

McGirt rebounded to win the **World Boxing Council (WBC)** welterweight title with a 12-round unanimous decision win over the heavily favored **Simon Brown.** McGirt successfully defended his title twice before losing to the great **Pernell Whitaker.** He lost a rematch to Whitaker—his last shot at a world title. He finally retired in 1997.

He has been even more successful as a trainer, earning the Boxing Writers Association of America Trainer of the Year award in 2002. He also oversees the career of his son James "Buddy" McGirt, Jr.

Professional Record: 73-6-1

Championship(s):   IBF junior welterweight, 1988; WBC welterweight, 1991–1993

Further Reading
Berger, Phil. "A Masterpiece by McGirt." *The New York Times*, 12/1/1991, Section 8, p. 6.
Samples, Scott. "A father, a son, a legacy." *The Stuart News*, 1/17/2004, p. C1.

MCGOVERN, TERRY (1880–1908). "Terrible" Terry McGovern was a former world bantamweight and featherweight champion known for his aggressive style and powerful punches. Born in 1880 in Johnstown, Pennsylvania, he turned professional in 1897 at age 17.

Two years later, he crushed bantamweight champion Tom (Pedlar) Palmer in the first round to win the world title. He then won the featherweight championship over a past-his-prime **George Dixon** in 1900. McGovern also kayoed lightweight champion Frank Erne in the third round though it was a nontitle bout. He lost his featherweight championship in 1901 to Young Corbett. He retired in 1908 and died later that year while refereeing bouts at an Army camp.

Professional Record: 60-4-4

Championship(s):   Bantamweight, 1899–1900; Featherweight, 1900–1901

Further Reading
"McGovern Conquers Dixon." *The New York Times*, 1/10/1900, p. 2.
"McGovern Easily Whipped Palmer." *The Atlanta Constitution*, 9/13/1899, p. 6.
Roberts, James B., and Alexander G. Skutt. *The Boxing Register: International Boxing Hall of Fame Register* (4th ed.). Ithaca, N.Y.: McBooks Press, 2006. pp. 186–187.
Siler, George. "Terry Meets An Equal At Last." *Chicago Daily Tribune*, 12/1/1901, p. 17.

MCGUIGAN, BARRY (1960–). Ireland's Barry McGuigan shocked the boxing world by dethroning longtime featherweight kingpin **Eusebio Pedroza** in 1985. Born in 1960 as Finbar Patrick McGuigan, he turned professional in 1981. He moved through the ranks with only one defeat in his third pro bout. At the time he faced Pedroza, the champion had made 19 successful defenses of his crown. But McGuigan easily captured the crown, winning the fight by large margins on the scorecards. He successfully defended the title twice before losing a close decision to Stevie Cruz in a fight-of-the-year battle. He never received another shot at the title and retired after losing on cuts to Jim McDonnell in 1989.

Record: 32-3

Championship(s):   WBA featherweight, 1985–1986

Further Reading
Collins, Nigel. "Barry's Back in the USA." *The Ring* (June 1986), pp. 6–7.
Magowan, Jack. "Sir Finbar Patrick McGuigan?" *The Ring* (December 1985), pp. 6–9.
McGuigan, Barry, Gerry Callan and Harry Mullan. *Barry McGuigan: The Untold Story.* London: Arrow Books, 1992.
Sheridan, Jim. *Leave the Fighting to McGuigan: The Official Biography of Barry McGuigan.* New York: Penguin Books, 1986.

MCINTOSH, HUGH (1876–1942). Hugh D. McIntosh was an Australian-based entrepreneur who ventured into boxing as a promoter and manager at various times during his career. He is best known for promoting the heavyweight title bout between champion **Tommy Burns** and challenger **Jack Johnson** in Sydney, Australia, in 1908. Born in Sydney in 1876, McIntosh owned a newspaper, tended bar, and operated a physical fitness club. He made a good bit of money from the Burns—Johnson fight and from the film rights to the fight, which he showcased in the United States. He later staged bouts in London and Paris.

Further Reading
Kent, Graeme. *The Great White Hopes: The Quest to Defeat Jack Johnson.* Sutton Publishing, 2005.

MCLARNIN, JIMMY (1907–2004). Jimmy "Baby Face" McLarnin was a former two-time world welterweight champion. Born in County Down, Ireland, in 1907, McLarnin turned professional in 1923. In 1928, he lost a close decision to Sammy Mandell in an attempt for the lightweight championship.

In 1933, he defeated **Young Corbett III** to win the welterweight title. He then fought a trilogy of great bouts with **Barney Ross**—losing two of the three in competitive bouts. In 1936, he retired after defeating top contenders and former champions **Tony Canzoneri** and Lou Ambers. McLarnin lived into his 90s and died in 2004.

Professional Record:	62-11-3
Championship(s):	Welterweight, 1933–1934, 1934–1935

Further Reading
Evans, Gavin. "The 20 Greatest Welterweights of All Time." *The Ring,* pp. 63–84, 79.
Murray, Jim. "They Almost Never Laid A Glove on Him." *Los Angeles Times,* 12/27/1987, p. SP1.
Roberts, James B., and Alexander G. Skutt. *The Boxing Register: International Boxing Hall of Fame Register* (4th ed.). Ithaca, N.Y.: McBooks Press, 2006, pp. 188–189.

MEDICAL DANGERS OF BOXING AND MIXED MARTIAL ARTS. It seems obvious that repeated blows to a boxer's head would have harmful health effects. Detached retinas, punch-drunk syndrome, and pugilistic dementia are just a few injuries that appear to occur with greater frequency in former boxers. The great **Muhammad Ali,** for example, suffers from Parkinson's Syndrome.

Many former boxers have suffered from a variety of head injuries, probably caused in part from taking too many punches. In 1928, pathologist Harrison Martland used the term "punch drunk" to describe a condition suffered by many boxers.

In 1983, the American Medical Association published studies and editorials in its *Journal of the American Medical Association* (JAMA) about the harmful effects of boxing. "Boxing seems to me to be less sport than it is cockfighting; boxing is an obscenity," wrote Dr. George D. Lundberg, editor of JAMA. He concluded that "boxing should not be sanctioned in any civilized society."

The Journal showed studies showing common occurrences of developing brain damage in boxers, particularly those who had a significant number of professional bouts. Such findings caused many medical associations in different countries to call for the abolition of boxing.

However, others—including Dr. Max M. Novich, the founder of the Association of Ringside Physicians—contended that the evidence of harm was overblown and, in fact, not proven. "The fact is that boxing is a relatively safe sport, even though some modifications of its rules are needed to make it safer still."

Many physician groups—including the American Academy of Neurology—contend that boxing should be banned. Surgeon General E. Everett Koop attempted to remove boxing from the Olympics, citing its negative health impacts.

Yet, other doctors maintain that the medical dangers of boxing can be minimized to an acceptable degree. Dr. Barry Jordan, who served as the medical director of the New York State Athletic Association until 1995 and the editor of the book *The Medical Aspects of Boxing*, contends that frequent brain scans and eye exams can reduce medical problems.

MMA Safety

As for mixed martial arts, there is a commonly held belief that it is more dangerous than boxing as the participants wear only five-ounce gloves and can use their elbows and knees to crush their opponents' faces. However, a 2006 study published in Johns Hopkins University's *Journal of Sports Science and Medicine*, finds evidence that mixed martial arts is actually safer than boxing. The study points out that "sports involving grappling have demonstrated much lower rates of injury" and that "knockout rates are lower in MMA competitions than boxing." The study points out that many MMA fights end with a fighter tapping out when submitted by their opponent.

Further Reading

Bledsoe, Gregory, et al. "Incidence of Injury in Professional Mixed Martial Arts Competitions." *Journal of Sports Science and Medicine*, 2006, at http://www.jssm.org/combat/1/18/v5combat-18.pdf

Clancy, Frank. "The Bitter Science: Head blows from boxing can cause dementia and Alzheimer's. Can the same chronic brain injury also lead to Parkinson's?" *Neurology Now* (March–April 2008), pp. 24–25. http://www.aan.com/elibrary/neurologynow/?event=home.showArticle&id=ovid.com:/bib/ovftdb/01222928-200602020-00005

Jordan, Barry D., ed. *Medical Aspects of Boxing*. Ann Arbor, M.I.: CRC Press, 1992.

Kotulak, Richard. "Ban Boxing: AMA Journal." *The Chicago Tribune*, 1/14/1983, p. D1.

Nagler, Barney. "Boxing: There's Good and Bad, But the Fights Must Go On." *The New York Times*, 2/6/1983, p. S2.

Novich, Max M. "A.M.A. Journal Jumps the Bell on Boxing." Letter to the Editor, *The New York Times*, 2/22/1983, p. A18.

Rosenthal, Elizabeth. "Rebel Neurologists Say Boxing Can Be Safe." *The New York Times*, 5/22/1990, p. C1.

MEDINA, MANUEL (1971–). Manuel "Mantecas" Medina is a five-time world featherweight champion who refuses to leave the upper echelons of the division. His nickname "Mantecas," or "Smooth," says it all, as this slick boxer has befuddled opponents for a long time in the 126 lb. division. Born in 1971 in Tijuana, Mexico, Medina turned pro in 1985 at age 14. In 1991, he earned a title shot at **International Boxing Federation (IBF)** champion Troy Dorsey. Medina won a unanimous decision to capture his first world title.

He made four successful defenses before losing his title via a 12-round split decision to Tom Johnson in France. He won his second world title in 1995 when he defeated Alejandro Gonzalez for the **World Boxing Council (WBC)** featherweight title. He lost the title in his first defense.

Three years later, he won his third featherweight title by defeating Hector Lizarraga by a lopsided unanimous decision. He successfully defended his title against a tough Victor Polo before losing a narrow decision to Paul Ingle. In 2001, he won his fourth world featherweight title by upsetting Frankie Toledo. He lost the title in a very close decision to **Johnny Tapia.**

Many felt that Medina was no longer a top contender, but he proved the critics wrong by upsetting Scott Harrison in 2003 to win the World Boxing Organization (WBO) featherweight title. He lost the title to Harrison in a rematch but continues to seek a sixth world title.

Professional Record: 67-15-1
Championship(s):   IBF featherweight, 1991–1993, 1998–1999,
                         2001–2002; WBC featherweight, 1995; WBO
                         featherweight, 2003

Further Reading
Raskin, Eric. "Four-Time Featherweight Titlist Manuel Medina: Being Just Good Enough is Great For
     Him." *KO Boxing 2002*, pp. 60–64.

MENDOZA, DANIEL (1763–1836). Daniel Mendoza was an early boxing champion
from the late eighteenth century who revolutionized boxing and became the first Jewish champion of the sport. He was known for his exceptional defensive skills, first showcasing the sport
as a science rather than a brawling affair. Born in 1763 or 1764 in London, Mendoza first
fought in 1784 against a much larger man named Harry the Coalheaver. Mendoza won in a
long bout.

Though he stood only 5'7" and weighed 160 pounds, Mendoza's superior boxing technique
enabled him to regularly outbox much larger foes in the ring. He defeated Richard Humphries
in two of three bouts. He also defeated Sam "the Bath Butcher" Martin and Bill Warr.

He was recognized as champion of England from 1791 until his defeat in 1795 to John Jackson. He last fought at the age of 41 in 1806 with a victory over Henry Lee. Nat Fleischer wrote
that "Mendoza established himself as the most skillful boxer of his day" (p. 17).

Professional Record: Unknown
Championship(s):   English champion (Heavyweight, 1791–1795

Further Reading
Fleischer, Nat. "Daniel Mendoza and His Contributions," in *The Heavyweight Championships: An Informal
     History of Heavyweight Boxing from 1719 to the Present Day* (rev. ed.). New York: GP Putnam's Sons,
     1961, pp. 13–22.
Magriel, Paul, ed. *The Memoirs of the Life of Daniel Mendoza*. London: B T Batsford Ltd., 1951.
Ribalow, Harold Uriel. *Fighter from Whitechapel: The Story of Daniel Mendoza*. London: Farrar, Straus and
     Cudahy, 1962.

MERCANTE, ARTHUR, SR. (1920–). Arthur Mercante, Sr., is arguably boxing's greatest
referee—serving as the third man in the ring for six different decades. He is perhaps best known
for officiating the first fight between **Muhammad Ali** and **Joe Frazier**—the so-called Fight of
the Century.

Born in 1920 in Brockton, Massachusetts, Mercante participated in the New York Golden
Gloves as an amateur but never fought professionally. Instead, he went into the U.S. Navy. After
he left the Navy in 1946, he worked as a boxing instructor at West Point, the U.S. Military
Academy.

He then began refereeing professional bouts in 1954. In 1959, he refereed the second bout
between heavyweight champion **Ingemar Johansson** and former champion **Floyd Patterson.**
From 1959–2001, Mercante became a fixture in major world title bouts. Among his most
famous bouts include: Muhammad Ali—Joe Frazier I, Muhammad Ali—**Ken Norton** III,
Wilfredo Gomez—Lupe Pintor, Mike Tyson—Tony Tubbs, and **Roy Jones, Jr.**—Montell
Griffin II.

Mercante's last world title bout was in 2001 when **Ricardo Lopez** defeated Zolani Petelo in
Madison Square Garden.

Further Reading
Mercante, Arthur, with Phil Guarnieri. *Inside the Ropes*. Ithaca, NY: McBooks Press, 2006.

MERCER, RAY (1961–). "Merciless" Ray Mercer is a former world heavyweight boxing champion and Olympic gold medalist known for his iron chin, powerful punching, and longevity in the sport. Born in 1961 in Jacksonville, Florida, Mercer served in the U.S. Army in the 1980s, where he excelled in amateur boxing. His amateur status culminated in earning a spot on the 1988 U.S.A. boxing team for the Seoul Olympics in the heavyweight division. Mercer crushed the opposition, including a first-round kayo of South Korea's Baik Hyun-Man.

He turned pro later that year and compiled an impressive winning streak. In 1991, he faced Italy's Francisco Damiani for the World Boxing Organization (WBO) heavyweight crown. Down badly on points, Mercer kayoed Damiani with a left uppercut that broke his nose. He successfully defended his title against unbeaten prospect **Tommy "the Duke" Morrison,** with a brutal fifth-round kayo—once again while he was behind on points.

He relinquished the title after the Morrison fight and then suffered a disappointing loss in 1992 to aging, former champion **Larry Holmes** over 12 rounds. He allowed Holmes to dictate the pace for most of the bout. In 1993, he suffered the most embarrassing loss of his career—a decision loss to journeyman Jesse Ferguson in which Mercer allegedly tried to bribe Ferguson during the bout. He faced criminal charges for bribery but was acquitted.

He remained a tough contender, losing close decisions to heavyweight greats **Evander Holyfield** and **Lennox Lewis** in 1995 and 1996, respectively. In 2002, he challenged **Wladimir Klitschko** for the WBO championship but lost badly. He still remains active, losing a fight to prospect Derrick Rossy in January 2008.

Mercer has not confined his combat-sports activity to the boxing ring. He has fought numerous kickboxing bouts in K-1 and also fought a mixed martial arts bout against street-fighting legend **Kimbo Slice** in 2007. He lost to Slice via a **guillotine choke** in the first round.

Professional Record:	35-7-1
Championship(s):	WBO heavyweight, 1991

Further Reading
Ostler, Scott. "Mercer Just May Be Sowing the Seeds for a High-Paying Career." *The Los Angeles Times,*
    11/29/1988, p. 6.
Thomas, Robert McG. "Jury Finds Mercer is Not Guilty in Ferguson Bout Bribery Case." *The New York
    Times,* 3/30/1994, p. B15.
Official Web site: http://www.raymercer.com

MESI, JOE (1973–). "Baby" Joe Mesi is an undefeated heavyweight contender who is extremely popular in his native Buffalo. Though he has never lost a professional bout, some consider Mesi a dangerous risk because he allegedly suffered bleeding in his brain following a close decision win over former world cruiserweight champion Vassily Jirov in 2004.

Mesi turned pro in 1997 under the guidance of his father, Jack. Mesi progressed slowly, fighting limited opposition, but he kept winning. In 2003, he stepped up in competition and shined with consecutive first-round kayos of fringe contenders Robert Davis and DaVarryl Williamson. He then defeated former world title challenger Monte Barrett in a tough 10-round majority decision before narrowly defeating Jirov in 2004.

Mesi returned to the ring in 2006 and has won seven fights in a row entering 2008. He hopes to land a title shot in the near future. Mesi has an interesting career outside of the ring, as he ran as a Democrat for a New York State Senate seat. He won the Democratic primary but lost in the general election to his Republican opponent.

Professional Record:	36-0
Championship(s):	None

Further Reading

Greenhill, Mike. "The Morrison, Mesi Comebacks: An Extra Element of Danger." *The Ring* (July 2007), pp. 86–91.

Smith, Tim. "Still In His Blood: Mesi's Comeback from Brain Injury Sparks Controversy." *Daily News,* 3/26/2006, p. 90.

MILETICH, PAT (1968—). Pat Miletich is a leading trainer of mixed martial arts (MMA) fighters and a former champion in the **Ultimate Fighting Championships (UFC)** lightweight and welterweight divisions. Born in 1968 in Davenport, Iowa, Miletich began wrestling at age 6. He wrestled in junior college but had to leave school for financial reasons.

He later turned to mixed martial arts, beginning his professional career in 1995. In 1998, he won the UFC's lightweight tournament at UFC 16: Battle of the Bayou with a submission win over Chris Brennan. The UFC abandoned the lightweight division for the welterweight title, and Miletich became the organization's first welterweight champion in 1998 with a win over Mikey Burnett. He lost his title to Carlos Newton in 2001 at UFC 31: Locked and Loaded via a move called the bulldog choke. In 2002, he lost in a UFC bout against tough wrestler **Matt Lindland.** He then retired from the ring and focused on training.

The Miletich Fighting Systems is one of the most successful training camps in the MMA world. L. Jon Wertheim writes that "prospects are attracted to Miletich's gym like iron filings to a magnet" (p. 16). Not only prospects, but also world-champion-caliber mixed martial artists seek out the sage advice and training of Miletich, who has trained such top fighters as **Matt Hughes, Tim Sylvia, Robbie Lawler,** and **Jens Pulver.**

Professional MMA Record:	28-7-2
Championship(s):	UFC Welterweight, 1998–2001

Further Reading

Craig, Donovan. "Pat Miletich: Inside the World of the MFS Elite." *Fight!* (December 2007), pp. 82–88.

Official Web site: http://www.mfselite.com/

Wertheim, L. Jon. *Blood in the Cage: Mixed Martial Arts, Pat Miletich and the Furious Rise of the UFC.* Boston: Houghton Mifflin, 2009.

MILLER, FREDDIE (1911–L962). Freddie Miller was a former world featherweight champion and one of the greatest southpaws in history. Born in 1911 in Cincinnati, Miller turned pro at age 16 and had 75 pro bouts by age 18. He lost a decision to Battling Battalino in his first attempt at a world title in 1931. Three years later, he won the championship with a win over Nel Tarleton. He successfully defended his title five times before losing to rival Petey Sarron. He retired at age 28 after suffering the only stoppage loss of his career to Herschel Joiner.

Professional Record:	208-28-7
Championship(s):	Featherweight, 1934–1936

Further Reading

Roberts, James B., and Alexander G. Skutt. *The Boxing Register: International Boxing Hall of Fame Register* (4th ed.). Ithaca, NY: McBooks Press, 2006, pp. 192–193.

MILLS, FREDDIE (1919–1965). "Fearless" Freddie Mills was a former world light heavyweight champion from Great Britain known for his courageous ring battles. Born in 1919 in Bournemouth, Mills turned pro in 1936, at 17 years of age. In 1942, he stopped Len Harvey in the second round to win the British Commonwealth light heavyweight title. In 1946, he challenged **Gus Lesnevich** for the world light heavyweight title, losing in the 10th round.

Mills exacted revenge as a heavy underdog in July 1948 when he dropped Lesnevich twice en route to a unanimous 15-round decision to win the world light heavyweight title. He lost the title to Joey Maxim in 1950 and never fought again. Many times during his career Mills challenged heavyweights, giving away more than 20 pounds in weight. In retirement, Mills acted and ran a nightclub called Freddie Mills Nite Spot. In 1965, he died from what was ruled a self-inflicted gunshot wound.

Professional Record: 76-18-7
Championship(s):   Light Heavyweight, 1948–1950

Further Reading
Associated Press. "Death of Freddie Mills Called a Suicide." *The Washington Post,* 7/26/1965, p. C1.
Smith, Wilfred. "Mills Dethrones Lesnevich in 15 Rounds." *Chicago Daily Tribune,* 7/27/1948, p. A1.

MIR, FRANK (1979–). Frank Mir is the former world **Ultimate Fighting Championships** (UFC) heavyweight champion known for his mastery of submissions. He holds black belts in both Kenpo Karate and Brazilian jiu-jitsu. He won the UFC title in spectacular fashion, breaking champion **Tim Sylvia**'s right forearm in a submission armlock only 50 seconds into the fight. He lost his title because he was unable to defend it after a bad motorcycle accident, which kept him out of the Octagon for more than a year and a half. He lost in his first fight back to Marcia Cruz. In 2006, he also lost to Brandon Vera, but rebounded with a win in 2007 over Antoni Hardnonk. His nickname is "the Baddest Man on the Planet."

Mir cemented his stature in the mixed martial arts (MMA) world by submitting the goliath **Brock Lesnar** with a knee lock in the first round of their 2008 encounter. Mir appeared in the eighth season of **The Ultimate Fighter** where he coached opposite then-UFC heavyweight champion **Antonio Rodrigo Nogueira.** In December 2008, Mir shocked many in the MMA world by dominating Nogueira with a much-improved stand-up game. He stopped Nogueira in the second round.

Mir also doubles as an expert color commentator for World Extreme Cagefighting matches.

Professional MMA Record: 12-3
Championship(s):   UFC Heavyweight, 2004–2005

Further Reading
Davidson, Neil. "Lesnar brought back to earth by Mir." *The Toronto Sun,* 2/3/2008, p. SP28.
Hill, Adam. "Mir earns Oscar-like victory." *Las Vegas Review-Journal,* 2/3/2008, p. 1C.
Iole, Kevin. "Mir finally gets serious." *Las Vegas Review-Journal,* 10/31/2006, p. 2C.
Official Web site of Frank Mir: http://www.frankmir.com/
Vontz, Andrew. "Full Circle." *Real Fighter,* No. 20 (2008), pp. 22–28.

MOLINEAUX, TOM (1784–1818). Former slave Tom Molineaux earned his freedom from master Algernon Molineaux due to his fistic prowess. Born in 1784 in Georgetown, Maryland, Tom Molineaux was reared on a Virginia plantation. He often engaged in bouts with slaves of other plantation owners. Before one of his bouts, Algernon promised he would set Tom free if he won the bout. Algernon kept his word and freed his former slave. Molineaux set sail for England to pursue boxing. Trained by Bill Richmond, Molineaux declared he could defeat any fighter. He defeated Bill Burrows in England before challenging the champion **Tom Cribb.** Molineaux should have been declared the winner when he dropped Cribb for more than 30 seconds in the 28th round. However, Cribb's second cried foul, and the fight was allowed to continue. Molineaux trained badly for the rematch and was stopped in the 11th round. He died in Ireland at the age of 34.

Record: Unknown
Championship(s):   None

Further Reading
Fraser, George McDonald. *Black Ajax*. New York: Carroll & Graf, 1999.
Roberts, James B., and Alexander B. Skutt. *The Boxing Register* (4th ed.). Ithaca, NY: McBooks Press, Inc., 2006, p. 37.

MONDAY, KENNY (1961–). Kenny Monday is one of the most decorated amateur freestyle wrestlers in history. If he was born a bit later, he probably would have been one of the best mixed martial artists as well, given his immense physical strength, agility, and athletic ability.

Born in 1961 in Tulsa, Oklahoma, Monday wrestled at Oklahoma State University, where he won a NCAA championship in 1984. He won Olympic Gold at the 1988 Seoul Olympics by defeating Soviet great Adlan Varaev in overtime. He then won a silver medal at the 1992 Barcelona Olympics. He also competed in the 1996 Atlantic Olympics, finishing sixth.

In 1997, Monday competed in his first and only mixed martial arts bout, stopping John Lewis in the second round in an Extreme Challenge bout. In 2001, he was inducted into the National Wrestling Hall of Fame.

Professional MMA Record: 1-0
Championship(s):   None

Further Reading
Gildea, William. "With Victory, Monday's No. 1." *The Washington Post*, 10/1/1988, p. D1.
Tramel, Jimmie. "Pushed to succeed Monday remembers those who helped him achieve wrestling greatness." *Tulsa World*, 6/2/2001.

MONTANEZ, PEDRO (1914–1996). Pedro Montanez was one of the greatest fighters from Puerto Rico and one of the greatest fighters to never win a world title. Born in 1914 in Cayey, Puerto Rico, Montanez turned pro in 1931 and two years later captured his country's lightweight title. His growing ring prowess caused some to dub him the "**Joe Louis** of the lightweights." In April 1937, he defeated lightweight champion Lou Ambers in a 10-round nontitle bout. Later that year, he faced Ambers for the world lightweight title and lost a controversial 15-round decision.

In 1940, Montanez challenged **Henry Armstrong** for the world welterweight title. Though Montanez scored well in the second round, the rest of the bout featured an onslaught by Armstrong who dropped Montanez three times—the first times that the Puerto Rican warrior had ever hit the canvas.

He retired in 1940 with an impressive career record of 92-7-4. He was inducted posthumously into the International Boxing Hall of Fame in 2007.

Professional Record: 92-7-4
Championship(s):   None

Further Reading

Cuddy, Jack. "Armstrong Stops Montanez in Ninth to Retain Crown." *Los Angeles Times,* 1/25/1940, p. A9.

"Is Montanez Joe Louis of the Lights." *The Chicago Defender,* 2/22/1936, p. 13.

Nichols, Joseph C. "18,000 See Montanez Win Unanimous Decision Over Ambers in Non-Title Bout." *The New York Times,* 4/6/1937, p. 27.

MONTGOMERY, BOB (1919–1998). Bob Montgomery was one of the toughest light-weights to ever lace up a pair of gloves. He fought in his prime in the 1940s against the likes of fellow Hall-of-Famers **Beau Jack** and **Ike Williams.** He was known for his aggressive style and brutal body-punching attack.

Born in 1919 in Sumter, South Carolina, Montgomery moved to Philadelphia as a teenager where he took to boxing. He turned pro in 1938 and fought frequently. In 1940, he dropped a pair of decisions to Sammy Angott and Lew Jenkins. In May 1943, Montgomery faced Jack for the first of their four meetings for the New York world lightweight championship. Montgomery won a 15-round decision. He lost the title in a rematch to Jack later that year.

He regained the title from Jack in 1944. In 1947, Montgomery faced Williams for the National Boxing Association (NBA) world lightweight title. In a see-saw affair Williams prevailed by knockout in the seventh round. Montgomery retired in 1950 after several decision losses. He later promoted boxing at the legendary Blue Horizon in Philadelphia.

Record: 75-19-3
Championship(s):   New York World Lightweight, 1943, 1944–1947.

Further Reading

Cuddy, Jack. "Montgomery Whips Jenkins." *Los Angeles Times,* 5/17/1941, p. 9.

Mastro, Frank. "Montgomery Knocks Out Day in First Round of Stadium Bout." *Chicago Daily Tribune,* 10/11/1941, p. 19.

Roberts, James B., and Alexander G. Skutt. *The Boxing Register: International Boxing Hall of Fame Official Record Book* (4th ed.). Ithaca, NY: McBooks Press, Inc., 2006, pp. 510–513.

MONZON, CARLOS (1942–1985). Carlos Monzon of Argentina is considered one of the greatest middleweight champions of all-time. Born in Santa Fe, Argentina, in 1942, Monzon turned pro in 1963. He lost three fights in his first two years as a professional. He would never lose again.

In 1970, he traveled to Rome to face **Nino Benvenuti** for the middleweight title. He stopped Benvenuti in the 12th round. He then successfully defended his title 14 times until his retirement in 1977. He defeated the likes of **Emile Griffith, Bennie Briscoe, Jose Napoles,** and Rodrigo Valdez. In his last fight, he came off the canvas in the second round to win a 15-round decision over Valdez. *The Ring* senior writer William Dettloff rates Monzon's middleweight reign as the fourth greatest in boxing history. Life outside the ring was tougher on the champion. In 1988, he was found guilty of murdering his lover. In 1995, while returning to prison from a furlough, he died in a car accident.

Record: 87-3-9
Championship(s):   1970–1977

Further Reading
Associated Press. "Monzon Keeps Middleweight Title by Outpointing Briscoe." *The New York Times*, 11/12/1972, p. S26.
Dettloff, William. "The Ten Greatest Title Reigns of All Time." *The Ring* (April 2005), pp. 65–76, 69.
Katz, Michael. "Monzon Retains Title, Stops Benvenuti in 3d." *The New York Times*, 5/9/1971, p. S1.
Roberts, James B., and Alexander G. Skutt. *The Boxing Register: International Boxing Hall of Fame Register* (4th ed.). Ithaca, NY: McBooks Press, Inc., 2006, pp. 514–517.

MOORE, ARCHIE (1913–1998). Archie "the Mongoose" Moore was one of the greatest fighters and punchers in boxing history known for his longevity, power, and incredible boxing savvy. The longtime light-heavyweight champion, Moore recorded more knockouts than any fighter in the history of the sport. *The Ring* magazine's William Dettloff writes: "He was at once a meticulous genius and an explosive puncher—the rarest combination" (p. 19).

Born in 1913 in Mississippi, Moore turned pro in 1936. For years, he was denied a shot at the light heavyweight title because of race. However, he finally received his chance in 1952 against champion Joey Maxim. Moore dominated the fight en route to a 15-round decision. He kept the title until 1962, including a memorable defense against Frenchman Yvon Durelle, who knocked Moore down four times before succumbing in the 11th round.

Moore attempted to win the heavyweight title in 1955 against undefeated **Rocky Marciano.** He surprised Marciano in the first round with a knockdown but fell to the champion in the ninth round. In 1956, he fought undefeated **Floyd Patterson** for the heavyweight crown but lost in the fifth round. In 1962, he faced a brash youngster named Cassius Clay and lost in the fourth round. He is the only man to have fought both Rocky Marciano and **Muhammad Ali** (then Cassius Clay) in the professional ranks.

Record:	184-24-10
Championship(s):	Light Heavyweight, 1952–1962

Further Reading
Dettlof, William. *The Ring Yearbook 2003: 100 Greatest Punchers of All-Time*, 2003, pp. 18–19.
Fitzgerald, Mike. *The Ageless Warrior: The Life of Boxing Legend Archie Moore*. Champaign, IL.: Sports Publishing LLC, 2004.
Milstein, Gilbert. "In This Corner, At Long Last, Archie Moore!" *The New York Times*, 9/11/1955, p. SM26.
Roberts, James B., and Alexander G. Skutt. *The Boxing Register: International Boxing Hall of Fame Register* (4th ed.). Ithaca, NY: McBooks Press, Inc., 2006, pp. 518–523.

MOORE, DAVEY (1933–1963). Former featherweight champion Davey Moore—known as "the Springfield Rifle"—stands at the centerpiece of one of boxing's most well-known tragedies. Born in 1933 in Lexington, Kentucky, Moore turned pro in 1953 and captured the world featherweight title in 1959 with a win over **Hogan "Kid" Bassey.**

He successfully defended his title five times—including a rematch win over Kid Bassey—until his fateful encounter with young challenger **Ultiminio "Sugar" Ramos.** Moore battled courageously with the younger Ramos but fell in the 10th round. His head hit the bottom rope, later causing a fatal brain injury. After the bout, Moore appeared fine and even gave an interview in which he asked for a rematch. However, he later fell into a coma and died four days later. The televised bout and Moore's death led to many calls to ban boxing. It also ensured Moore a permanent place in American culture, as popular folk singer-songwriter Bob Dylan penned his famous song—"Who Killed Davey Moore."

Professional Record: 59-7-1
Championship(s):   Featherweight, 1959–1963

Further Reading

Kahn, Alex. "Davey Moore Captures Title from Kid Bassey." *The Chicago Defender*, 3/28/1959, p. 24.

St. Amant, Joe. "Davey Moore Eyes Brown, Becerra: Seeks Big Money Bouts After Bassey Triumph." *The Chicago Defender*, 8/29/1959, p. 24.

United Press International. "Autopsy Shows '1 in a Million' Brain Injury Fatal to Moore." *Chicago Tribune*, 3/26/1963, p. B1.

MOORE, DAVEY (1959–1988). There is something eerie about the name "Davey Moore" and tragedy. This Davey Moore was a former junior middleweight champion from the Bronx who captured a world title in only his ninth pro bout. Born in 1959 in the Bronx, Moore had a fine amateur career and made the 1980 U.S. Olympic team that was to go to Moscow.

After the boycott, Moore turned pro in 1981 and defeated Tidashi Mihari in the sixth round to win the **World Boxing Association (WBA)** junior middleweight title. He successfully defended the title three times before losing to the legendary **Roberto Duran,** who punished him over eight rounds. He lost in 1986 in an attempt to regain his title. While planning a comeback, he died in 1988 when he fell under his moving Jeep and was crushed to death.

Professional Record: 18-5
Championship(s):   WBA junior middleweight, 1982–1983

Further Reading

Katz, Michael. "Bronx Boxer Goes Long Way Quickly." *The New York Times*, 2/13/1982, p. 19.

Katz, Michael. "Davey Moore on Edge in Hometown." *The New York Times*, 6/15/1983, p. B15.

MOORER, MICHAEL (1967–). Michael Moorer was a former world light heavyweight and heavyweight champion who holds the distinction as the first southpaw to capture the heavyweight crown. Born in 1967 in Pittsburgh, Moorer turned pro in 1988 and won his first 26 professional bouts by knockout. In only his 12th pro bout, he knocked out Ramzi Hassan to win the inaugural World Boxing Organization (WBO) light heavyweight belt. He successfully defended that title nine times before moving up to the heavyweight division in 1991.

In 1992, he defeated Bert Cooper in a wild slugfest to capture the WBO heavyweight title. Two years later, he upset **Evander Holyfield** by majority decision—overcoming a second-round knockdown—to win the more prestigious **World Boxing Association (WBA)** and **International Boxing Federation (IBF)** heavyweight title belts. Unfortunately for Moorer, he lost those belts in his first defense against 45-year-old **George Foreman.** Holding a sizeable lead, Moorer got careless, and Foreman kayoed him in the 10th round. In 1996, he captured the IBF belt with a split-decision win over Axel Schultz. He successfully defended the title twice before losing in a rematch to Holyfield. He retired after the loss and did not return to the ring until 2000. He still fights as of the time of this writing, hoping to land another shot at heavyweight glory.

Professional Record: 52-4-1
Championship(s):   WBO light heavyweight, 1988–1991; WBO
                                          Heavyweight, 1992–1993; WBA and IBF
                                          Heavyweight, 1994; IBF Heavyweight, 1996–1997

Further Reading

Berger, Phil. "Moorer is a Knockout in Victory over Cooper." *The New York Times*, 5/17/1992, p. S11.

Eskenazi, Gerald. "Can Master of Menace Master His Talents?" *The New York Times*, 4/20/1994, p. B17.
Singer, Eric. "A Perfect One-Two—Atlas: Too Demanding, Moorer: Too Unyielding." *The Ring* (March 1997), pp. 19–21, 69–71.

MORALES, ERIK (1976–). Erik "El Terrible" Morales was one of boxing's brightest stars during the 1990s, known for his tremendous punching power, skills, and heart. This Mexican warrior won world championships in three different weight divisions—super bantamweight, featherweight, and super featherweight. He engaged in one of the most memorable boxing trilogies with Mexican rival **Marco Antonio Barrera.**

Born in 1976 in Tijuana, Morales turned pro in 1993. He dominated his opponents and received his first world title shot in 1997 against aging **World Boxing Council (WBC)** super bantamweight champion **Daniel Zaragoza.** Morales stopped Zaragosa in the 11th round. He successfully defended his title eight times, his last defense a 12-round split decision victory over Barrera for which he added the World Boxing Organization (WBO) crown.

After the Barrera victory in 2000, Morales moved up to the 126 lb. featherweight division, defeating **Guty Espadas, Jr.,** for the WBC title in 2001. He successfully defended that title once before losing a 12-round decision to Barrera in a 2002 rematch. He regained the WBC title later that year by defeating **Paulie Ayala.** In 2004, he defeated **Jesus Chavez** to win the WBC super featherweight championship, holding that belt until a loss to Barrera in their rubber match. He rebounded in a major way by outpointing **Manny Pacquiao** in 2005 to recapture the WBC belt. However, he later lost his last four fights—one to Zahir Raheem, two to Pacquiao, and a narrow 12-round loss to David Diaz in 2007 for the WBC lightweight title. He announced his retirement after that loss.

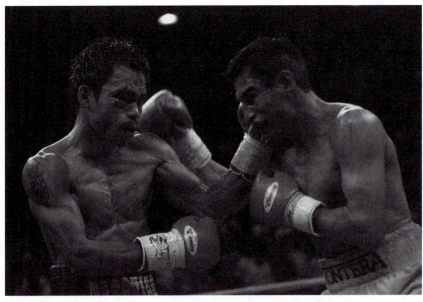

What a War! Manny Pacquaio and Erik Morales trade blows in their March 2005 bout. Morales won a close unanimous decision. Courtesy of Chris Cozzone.

| Professional Record: | 48-6 |
| Championship(s): | WBC super bantamweight, 1997–2000; WBO super bantamweight, 2000; WBC featherweight, 2001–2002; 2002–2003; WBC super featherweight, 2004; IBF super featherweight, 2004. |

Further Reading

Katz, Michael. "Morales Tops Ayala and Wins W.B.C. Title." *The New York Times*, 11/17/2002, p. H5.

Katz, Michael. "For Morales and Barrera, National Pride is the Prize." *The New York Times*, 6/22/2002, p. D4.

Katz, Michael. "Morales Beats Injured Chavez for Junior Lightweight Title." *The New York Times*, 2/29/2004, p. SP6.

MORRISON, TOMMY (1969–). Tommy "the Duke" Morrison is a former world heavyweight champion known for his powerful left hook, weak chin, imposing physique, and contraction of the HIV virus (which Morrison disputes). Born in 1969 in Jay, Oklahoma, Morrison turned pro in November 1988 and overpowered a series of lesser opponents.

In 1990, he starred as "Tommy Gunn" in the movie *Rocky V* opposite Sylvester Stallone. He won his first 28 bouts before facing World Boxing Organization (WBO) heavyweight champion "Merciless" **Ray Mercer.** Morrison won several early rounds but suffered a devastating kayo loss in the fifth round. He rebounded with several wins, including a courageous 1992 win over tough Joe Hipp, a bout in which Morrison overcame a broken jaw to stop Hipp in the ninth round. In 1993, he outboxed **George Foreman** over 12 rounds to win a unanimous decision for the WBO championship in the finest performance of his career. He made one successful defense before suffering a huge first-round upset loss to unheralded Michael Bentt.

Morrison once again rebounded with a series of wins, including a tough 1995 stoppage of the dangerous Donovan "Razor" Ruddock, which saw Morrison climb off the canvas to win in the sixth round. That performance earned him a shot at world heavyweight champion **Lennox Lewis,** who overwhelmed Morrison in over six rounds.

His career and life took a detour when, in 1996, he reportedly tested positive for the HIV virus in tests for the Nevada Athletic Commission. He fought once more in Japan against a journeyman opponent before retiring that year. Morrison suffered a series of legal scrapes, which included a prison stint. He got his life back together and apparently believed the test was a false positive. Allegedly, he had a test in Arizona that showed him to be HIV-negative. In 2007, he returned to the boxing ring with a win over John Castle. In 2008, he fought once in Mexico, winning in the third round. He may fight again in 2009 and beyond.

| Professional Record: | 48-3-1 |
| Championship(s): | WBO championship, 1993 |

Further Reading

Farine, Michael. "The reel thing? Rocky V co-star Morrison looks to become a real contender." *The Washington Times*, 3/17/1992, p. D3.

Greenhill, Mike. "The Morrison, Mesi Comebacks: An Extra Element of Danger." *The Ring* (July 2007), pp. 86–91.

Official Web site: http://www.tommymorrison.net

MOSLEY, SHANE (1971–). "Sugar" Shane Mosley is one of the most exciting fighters in boxing of the 1990s and early 2000s. Born in 1971 in Pomono, California, Mosley turned pro in 1993 and captured the **International Boxing Federation (IBF)** lightweight title with a 12-round decision win over undefeated champion Philip Holiday.

He successfully defended his title eight times before moving up in weight to challenge former amateur rival **Oscar De La Hoya** for the **World Boxing Council (WBC)** welterweight title. In a thrilling bout, Mosley captured a 12-round split decision. He successfully defended his title three times before losing to **Vernon Forrest** in 2002. After losing to Forrest in the rematch, many felt that Mosley's best days were behind him. He rebounded in a major way with a disputed decision over De La Hoya to win the WBC and **World Boxing Association (WBA)** junior middleweight titles. He lost the title in his first defense to the underrated **Ronald "Winky" Wright.** After losing to Wright in a rematch, Mosley revived his career with two wins over former champion **Fernando Vargas.** In 2007, he lost a narrow decision to the undefeated **Miguel Cotto** for the welterweight title. In 2008, he stopped **Ricardo Mayorga** in the final seconds of their 12-round bout. In January 2009, Mosley turned in a brilliant performance in defeating the feared **Antonio Margarito** to win the WBA welterweight title.

Record: 46-5
Championship(s):   IBF lightweight, 1997–2000; WBC welterweight,
                                   2000–2002; WBC and WBA junior middleweight,
                                   2003; WBA welterweight, 2009–.

Further Reading
Katz, Michael. "Mosley Wants to Be King of the Hill." *The New York Times*, 2/5/2003, p. D4.
KO Interview. "Shane Mosley: 'I'm Still One of the Three Sugars.'" *KO Magazine* (July 2003), pp. 48–57.
Official Web site: http://www.sugarshanemosley.com/
Spousta, Tom. "Mosley and De La Hoya Renew a Boyhood Rivalry." *The New York Times*, 6/15/2000, p. D7.

MUANGSURIN, SAENSAK (1950–).
Saensak Muangsurin holds the record for winning a world title in the fewest number of bouts. This native of Phetchabun, Thailand, fought for a world title in only his third professional bout against Perico Fernandez in 1975. The southpaw Muangsurin won the **World Boxing Council (WBC)** junior welterweight title in the third round. He lost his title via disqualification to Miguel Velasquez in 1976. However, he regained the title in a rematch with Velasquez and successfully defended his belt seven times before losing to Sang-Hyun Kim in 1978. He retired in 1981.

Record: 14-6
Championship(s):   WBC junior welterweight, 1975–1976; 1976–1978

Further Reading
Hudson, David L., Jr., and Mike Fitzgerald, Jr. *Boxing's Most Wanted: The Top 10 Book of Champs, Chumps and Punch-Drunk Palookas.* Alexandria, VA: Potomac Books, 2003.

MUAY THAI.
Muay Thai, or Thai boxing, is a form of standup fighting popularized in Thailand in which combatants utilize their hands, knees, elbows, and feet. A trademark move in Thai boxing is the knee strike, a powerful blow that can debilitate an opponent quickly. The bulk of the debilitating blows are delivered from the clinch, where both opponents are locked together and attempt to deliver elbow, knee, and other types of strikes. It is the national sport of Thailand.

Many top mixed martial artists have employed Muay Thai skills effectively in full mixed martial arts (MMA) competitions. Notable Muay Thai–skilled fighters include **Anderson Silva, Wanderlei Silva,** and **Mauricio "Shogun" Rua.** Similar to boxing, Muay Thai fighters fight in many different weight classes. The fighters use either 10, 8, or 6-ounce gloves.

Further Reading
Sheridan, Sam. *A Fighter's Heart: One Man's Journey Through the World of Fighting.* New York: Atlantic Monthly Press, 2007.
Thai Boxing Association of the United States: http://www.thaiboxing.com/

MUGABI, JOHN (1960−). John "the Beast" Mugabi was a former junior middleweight champion known for his ferocious punching power. Born in 1960 in Kampala, Uganda, Mugabi compiled an outstanding amateur record, culminating in a silver medal in the welterweight division at the 1980 Moscow Olympics. He turned professional in 1980 and won his first 25 professional bouts before a March 1986 showdown with middleweight champion **Marvelous Marvin Hagler.** Mugabi nearly closed Hagler's right eye and landed some hard shots, but Hagler prevailed in the 11th-round slugfest. In his next bout, Mugabi faced Duane Thomas for the vacant **World Boxing Council (WBC)** junior middleweight title. Perhaps still feeling the harmful effects of the Hagler fight, Mugabi lost in the third round. After his second consecutive loss for a world title, Mugabi won eight straight fights before landing another a shot at the WBC junior middleweight title. This time Mugabi's power overwhelmed Rene Jacquot in the first round. He lost his title in his first defense—a first-round kayo loss to "Terrible" **Terry Norris.** In 1991, **Gerald McClellan** kayoed Mugabi in the first round in another world title fight. He retired after that devastating loss, but returned to the ring five years later. He finally called it quits in 1999 after a loss to Glen Kelly.

Professional Record:	42-7-1
Championship(s):	1989–1990

Further Reading
Welsh, Jack. "Night of Knockouts: Hagler Hedges on Hearns Rematch After Taming the Beast." *The Ring* (May 1986), pp. 6–10.

MUSTAFA MUHAMMAD, EDDIE (1952−). Eddie Mustafa Muhammad was a former world light heavyweight champion who now works as a lead trainer in the sport that brought him fame. Born in 1952 in Brooklyn, New York as Eddie Gregory, he turned pro in 1972 after a successful amateur career.

In 1977, he lost in his first attempt at a world title, losing a 15-round decision to **Victor Galindez.** However, Muhammad (then still known as Gregory) showed great heart in coming off the mat in the fifth round. In 1980, Gregory defeated **Marvin Johnson** to win the World Boxing Association (WBA) light heavyweight title. Once he became champion he changed his name for religious reasons. He made two successful defenses before losing his title to undefeated prospect and future great **Michael Spinks** in 1981. He nearly gained another world title in 1985, losing a close decision to **Slobodon Kacar** in Italy. Mustafa Muhammad retired in 1988.

Mustafa Muhammad has achieved great success as a boxing trainer after his career ended. He has trained **Iran Barkley**, Danny Romero, and **James Toney**. He now works with many great young fighters, including **Chad Dawson.**

Professional Record:	50-8-1
Championship(s):	WBA Light Heavyweight, 1980–1981

Further Reading
Brady, Dave. "Gregory Whips Johnson in 11, Wins WBA Title," *The Washington Post*, 4/1/1980, p. E6.
Heisler, Mark. "Muhammad Is Living the Good Life," *Los Angeles Times*, 11/23/1980, p. SD, B20.
Katz, Michael. "Mustafa Muhammad Keeps Title," *The New York Times*, 7/21/1980, p. C4.

NAPOLES, JOSE (1940–). Jose Napoles lived up to his nickname of "Mantequilla" (Spanish for "butter") because this stylist was smooth as butter in the boxing ring. Born in 1940 in Cuba, Naples displayed great talent as a amateur boxer, winning an astonishing 158 bouts against only 1 defeat. He turned pro in 1958 and fought his first 19 fights in Havana, winning 18.

In 1962, he fled his native country to Mexico after dictator Fidel Castro banned professional boxing. In 1969, he challenged Curtis Cokes for the world welterweight title, winning in the 13th round. He successfully defended his title three times before losing to Billy Backus in 1970. He regained the title from Backus in their 1971 rematch. He successfully defended his title 10 times during his second reign before losing to John Stracey in 1975. He retired after the loss and never fought again. In 1974, he moved up in weight and challenged champion **Carlos Monzon.** The middleweight Monzon stopped him in the seventh round.

Record:	78-7
Championship(s):	Welterweight, 1969–1970, 1971–1975

Further Reading
Hafner, Dan. "Napoles, Last Cuban Champ, Rated Greatest." *Los Angeles Times*, 8/15/1971, p. C10.
Roberts, James B., and Alexander G. Skutt. *The Boxing Register: International Boxing Hall of Fame Register* (4th ed.). Ithaca, NY: McBooks Press, Inc., 2006, pp. 524–527.

NELSON, AZUMAH (1958–). Nicknamed "the Professor," this longtime champion from Ghana failed to receive proper recognition for his ring greatness. *New York Times* boxing writer Tim Smith called this boxer from Ghana "the best boxer nobody knows."

Born in 1958 in Accra, Ghana, Nelson turned pro in 1979 and won his first 13 bouts. In his 14th fight he challenged the great **Salvador Sanchez** for the **World Boxing Council (WBC)** featherweight title and lost in the final round in 1982. Undeterred, Nelson learned more of his craft and in 1984 challenged another legend, **Wilfredo Gomez.** Nelson captured the title with an 11th-round knockout. He successfully defended his title six times before moving up in weight to fight Mario Martinez for the vacant WBC junior lightweight belt. He won a 12-round decision and defended his title 10 times.

In 1990, he challenged **Pernell "Sweet Pea" Whitaker** for the lightweight championship and lost a lopsided 12-round decision. However, Nelson kept his junior lightweight championship until a 1994 decision loss to Jesse James Leija. In 1995, he regained the title with a dominant performance over **Gabriel Ruelas.** He lost his title to Genaro Hernandez in 1997 and retired in 1998 after another loss to Leija. Ten years later, in 2008, he returned to the ring against fellow former great **Jeff Fenech** and lost a decision. He remains active in politics in his native Ghana. In 2004, Nelson was inducted into the International Boxing Hall of Fame.

Record:	39-6-2
Championship(s):	WBC featherweight, 1984–1988; WBC junior lightweight, 1988–1994, 1995–1997

Further Reading

Roberts, James B., and Alexander G. Skutt. *The Boxing Register: International Boxing Hall of Fame Register* (4th ed.). Ithaca, N.Y.: McBooks Press, Inc., 2006, pp. 528–531.

Smith, Timothy W. "The Best Boxer Nobody Knows; After 19 Years, the Career of a Ghanian Legend Nears an End." *The New York Times,* 7/11/1998, at http://query.nytimes.com/gst/fullpage.html?res=9902EED81431F932A25754C0A96E958260

NELSON, BATTLING (1882–1954). Oscar Matthew Nielson, better known to the world as Battling Nelson, was a rugged former two-time world lightweight champion in the early twentieth century known for his relentless attacks in the ring and incredible ability to absorb punishment. As ring historian Tracy Callis writes: "Oscar 'Battling' Nelson was one of the roughest, toughest men to ever enter the ring, no doubt about it."

Born in 1882 in Copenhagen, Denmark, Nelson moved with his family as an infant and grew up in Chicago. He turned pro in 1896 at age 14, kayoing his opponent in the first round. In 1904, he lost a decision to Jimmy Britt for the world lightweight title. However, in a rematch the next year, he exacted revenge and captured the title. He lost the title to the talented **Joe Gans** in 1906 in the 42nd round.

He regained the title from Gans in 1908 with a 17th-round kayo. He held the title until losing to Al Wolgast in the 40th round in 1910. He finally retired in 1917 after losing to Freddie Welsh.

Professional Record:	59-19-19 (33 no decisions)
Championship(s):	Lightweight, 1905–1906, 1908–1910

Further Reading

Associated Press. "Battling Nelson, One of the Greatest Lightweight Champions, Dies at 71." *The Washington Post,* 2/8/1954, p. 8.

Callis, Tracy. "Battling Nelson: Always Battered, Seldom Beaten." *The Cyber Boxing Zone Journal,* February 2006, at http://www.cyberboxingzone.com/boxing/0106-callis.html

Roberts, James B., and Alexander G. Skutt. *The Boxing Register: The International Boxing Hall of Fame Official Record Book.* Ithaca, N.Y.: McBooks Press, Inc., 2006, pp. 198–199.

NEWFIELD, JACK (1938–2004). Jack Newfield was a famous American journalist best known in boxing circles for his fine exposé on promoter **Don King** titled *Only in America: The Life and Crimes of Don King.* He also produced a documentary on King titled *Don King: Unauthorized.* In his well-received essay on boxing for *The Nation* titled "The Shame of Boxing," Newfield called for a "Bill of Rights" for boxers, including the creation of a national commission, the elimination of the international sanctioning bodies, a pension system, and the organization of a labor union for fighters.

Further Reading

Newfield, Jack. *Only in America: The Life and Crimes of Don King.* New York: William Morrow & Co., 1995.

Newfield, Jack. "The Shame of Boxing." *The Nation,* 11/12/2001, available at http://www.thenation.com/docprint.mhtml?i=20011112&s=newfield

NOGUEIRA, ANTONIO RODRIGO (1976–). The Brazilian Nogueira—also known by the nickname "Minotauro"—is the former **PRIDE** heavyweight champion and a master of submissions known for his iron grip and mastery of Brazilian Jiu-Jitsu. Born in 1976 in Vitoria de Conquista, Brazil, in 1976, Antonio and his twin brother, Antonio Rogerio, learned martial arts at an early age. He started learning judo at age 5. At age 11, a neighbor accidentally backed his truck into Nogueira. The accident left him in a coma for four days. Nogueira says the near-fatal accident helped him to develop a strong mental will to survive and succeed in life.

He started learning jiu-jitsu at age 14. He turned pro in mixed martial arts (MMA) in 1999 in World Extreme Fighting with a win over David Dodd. He later won the RINGS—King of Kings championship in February 2001 with three wins in the same evening over Volk Han, Hiromitsu Kanehara, and **Valentijn Overeem.** In July 2001, he made his debut in PRIDE with a win over **Gary Goodridge.**

Nogueira is best known for his exploits in PRIDE, where he defeated numerous top fighters, including: **Mirko "Cro Cop" Filipovic, Dan "Hollywood" Henderson, Mark Coleman,** and Goodridge. He held the championship for several years before losing a unanimous decision to **Fedor Emelianenko.**

He gained a legion of fans when he took punishment from K-1's behemoth **Bob Sapp** but rallied to win by an armbar submission. He won the PRIDE heavyweight championship in 2001 with a win over **Heath Herring.** He held the title until a March 2003 loss to Emelianenko.

Nogueira, whose twin brother Antonio Rogerio is active in MMA, made his **Ultimate Fighting Championships (UFC)** debut in UFC 73 with a unanimous decision win over Heath Herring. In February 2007, he submitted former two-time UFC heavyweight champion **Tim Sylvia** after taking serious punishment to capture the UFC's interim heavyweight championship. But in December 2008, Nogueria looked sluggish and lost badly to former UFC heavyweight champion **Frank Mir.** Nogueira certainly will try to rebound in 2009 and beyond, as his warrior spirit is unquestioned.

Professional MMA Record:	31-5-1
Championship(s):	PRIDE Heavyweight, 2001–2003; Interim UFC Heavyweight, 2008

Further Reading

Botter, Jeremy. "Antonio Rodrigo Nogueira: A Legendary Heart," BleacherReport.com, 9/16/2008, at http://bleacherreport.com/articles/58210-antonio-rodrigo-nogueira-a-legendary-heart

Habib, Hal. "Indomitable: ADJ—Impossible to Subdue." *Palm Beach Post,* 5/6/2008, p. 1C.

Robb, Sharon. "Early Struggles Fuel Nogueira's Career." *Sun-Sentinel,* 5/15/2008, p. 1C.

Sportak, Randy. "Twin bill for fighting brothers." *Calgary Sun,* 2/1/2008, p. SP12.

NORRIS, TERRY (1967–). "Terrible" Terry Norris was one of the finest junior middleweight champions in the 154 lb. division. Born in 1967 in Lubbock, Texas, he turned to boxing after an early interest in baseball. He turned pro in 1986 and three years later challenged power-punching **Julian Jackson** for the junior middleweight championship. Norris dominated the first stanza but succumbed to the champion's power in the second round.

Norris received another title shot in 1990 against power-punching **John "the Beast" Mugabi.** This time Norris captured the title with a blistering first-round kayo. He successfully defended his title 10 times, including an easy decision win over the comebacking **Sugar Ray Leonard** and a convincing win over former welterweight and junior middleweight champion **Donald Curry.**

He lost his belt in 1993 via fourth-round kayo to **Simon Brown.** He regained the title with a rematch victory over Brown in 1994. In a strange trilogy, Norris lost his title to Luis Santana on a foul after he dropped the challenger with a shot to the back of the head. In their second bout, Norris once again lost on a disqualification, this time kayoing Santana with a shot after the belt. In both fights, Santana obtained the victory though he left the ring on a stretcher. In their third encounter, Norris finally regained the belt with a second-round kayo in 1995. He added the **World Boxing Council (WBC)** belt with a 12-round decision win over Paul Vaden. He held the title until 1997 when he lost to underdog Keith Mullings. He retired in 1998 after failing to regain his title from Laurent Boudouani. Terry's brother Orlin was a former world cruiserweight champion.

Record:	47-9
Championship(s):	WBC junior middleweight, 1990–1993, 1994, 1995–1997; IBF junior middleweight, 1995–1997.

Further Reading
Berger, Phil. "Norris Proves How Easy It Is to Spot a 'Champ.'" *The New York Times*, 6/3/1991, p. C2.
Berger, Phil. "Psst! Norris Is No Longer Just a Stealth Fighter." *The New York Times*, 9/26/1992, p. 32.
Katz, Michael. "A Sad Victory, Norris Says As Baton is Passed." *The Washington Post*, 2/11/1991, p. B4.
Roberts, James B., and Alexander G. Skutt. *The Boxing Register: International Boxing Hall of Fame Register* (4th ed.). Ithaca, NY: McBooks Press, Inc., 2006, pp. 532–535.

NORTON, KEN (1943–). Ken Norton was a former world heavyweight champion best known for his trilogy of fights against the great **Muhammad Ali** and his classic battle with **Larry Holmes.** A fine athlete in track & field and football, Norton turned to boxing when he entered the Marine Corp.

He turned professional in 1967, garnering 16 straight victories before losing to Jose Luis Garcia. He returned with 13 straight victories heading into his biggest fight as a heavy underdog to Ali. The southpaw Norton broke Ali's jaw en route to a stunning 12-round split decision victory. After dropping a close decision to Ali in a rematch, Norton landed a title shot against the formidable **George Foreman** in Venezuela. Foreman annihilated Norton in two rounds in their 1974 bout. Norton rebounded with wins over the tough **Jerry Quarry** and his former nemesis Garcia.

In 1976, Norton received a second title shot, dropping another disputed decision to Ali. In 1977, the **World Boxing Council (WBC)** awarded Norton the title after **Leon Spinks** chose to fight Ali in a rematch rather than face Norton, who was the #1 contender. In Norton's first defense, he fought a 15-round war with Larry Holmes, dropping a split decision. His career plummeted after that great fight, as he was kayoed in the first round by both **Earnie Shavers** and **Gerry Cooney.**

During his boxing days, Norton also dabbled in action, securing title roles in the films about the horrors of plantation life in *Mandingo* and *Drum*. His son Ken Norton, Jr., became an all-pro linebacker in the National Football League.

Professional record:	43-7-1
Championship(s):	WBC Heavyweight, 1977–1978

Further Reading

Brunt, Stephen. *Facing Ali: 15 Fighters, 15 Stories*. Guilford, Conn.: Lyons Press, 2002, pp. 165–183.

Christon, Lawrence. "Ken Norton Meets the Challenges." *Los Angeles Times*, 6/4/1978, p. T102.

Norton, Ken, with Marshall Terrill and Mike Fitzgerald. *Going the Distance: The Ken Norton Story*. Champaign, IL: Sports Publishing, 2000.

NORWOOD, FREDDIE (1970–). Freddie Norwood was a talented former two-time featherweight world champion who had great ring skills but often was his own worst enemy. Born in 1970 in St. Louis, Missouri, he turned pro in 1989 and continued to win. Nicknamed "Lil Hagler" for his facial resemblance to the great middleweight champion, Norwood displayed great boxing skills, excellent defense, and deceptive power.

In 1998, he finally received a world title shot against Antonio Cermeno in Puerto Rico. Norwood dominated the bout, winning a unanimous 12-round decision. He made two successful defenses before being stripped for failing to make weight in 1998. The next year he regained the title with a split decision victory over Cermeno. In his second reign, Norwood made three successful defenses, including a decision win over **Juan Manuel Marquez.** He lost his title in controversial fashion to Derrick Gainer, as Gainer appeared to stop Norwood with a very low blow.

Norwood retired after the loss. He returned to the ring in 2006 and won his first four bouts. In 2007, he was disqualified for low blows against Johnnie Edwards. His career may be over after another loss to Nelson in 2008.

Professional Record:	42-3-1
Championship(s):	WBA featherweight, 1998–1999; 1999–2000

Further Reading

Wheatley, Tom. "Norwood Has Taken a Hard Route to a Title and Now First Defense." *St. Louis Post-Dispatch*, 6/11/1998, p. D6.

Whitehead, Johnnie. "Derrick Gainer Finally Wins The Title: With Some Help From Roy Jones, Freddie Norwood & The Referee." *KO* (February 2001), pp. 30–34.

NUNN, MICHAEL (1958–). Michael "Second to" Nunn was a talented former world champion who held titles in the middleweight and super middleweight division. Blessed with blazing speed and excellent punching power, Nunn had the potential to be one of the sport's all-time greats. Though he had an excellent career, many believe he did not live up to his vast potential.

Born in 1958 in Davenport, Iowa, he turned pro in 1984 and had to wait four years before his first world title opportunity. He made the most of it in 1988 with a ninth-round stoppage of unbeaten champion Frank Tate. He successfully defended his title five times against the likes of Juan Roldan, **Iran Barkley, Donald Curry,** and **Sumbu Kalambay,** whom he flattened in the first round.

He lost his title in a hometown defense against unheralded James Toney. Nunn, leading heavily on the scorecards, was kayoed in the 11th round. He rebounded in 1992 by defeating Victor

Cordoba to win the **World Boxing Association (WBA)** super middleweight title. He successfully defended this title four times before losing a split decision to Steve Little.

In 1998, he lost a split decision to Italy's Graciano Rocchigiani in an attempt for the vacant **World Boxing Council (WBC)** light heavyweight championship. His last fight was in 2002. He has suffered from legal problems and is serving a prison term for drugs.

Professional Record:	58-4
Championship(s):	IBF middleweight, 1988–1991; WBA super middleweight, 1992–1994

Further Reading

Klein, Frederick C. "Nunn Flattens Kalambay." *Wall Street Journal*, 3/27/1989, p. A8.
Stravinsky, John. "The Boxer The Champs Won't Fight." *The New York Times*, 8/13/1989, p. SM32.

O'GRADY, SEAN (1959–). Sean O'Grady was a former world lightweight champion who posted more than 80 professional victories in his professional career that started when he was still in high school. Born in 1959 in Oklahoma City, O'Grady began boxing at age 6 under the tutelage of his father Pat. He turned professional in 1975 and won 73 of his first 74 bouts—often fighting several times per month. In 1980, he challenged Jim Watt for the **World Boxing Council (WBC)** lightweight title and lost on cuts in the final round.

The next year he defeated **Hilmer Kenty** for the **World Boxing Association (WBA)** lightweight title by a lopsided unanimous decision. The WBA stripped O'Grady of the belt for failing to defend against the number 1 contender. He retired in 1983 after losing to John Verdersosa. In retirement, O'Grady became a respected boxing announcer for USA network's Tuesday night fights for years.

Professional Record:	81-5
Championship(s):	W BA lightweight, 1981

Further Reading
Hawn, Jack. "Another Knockout for Sean O'Grady." *Los Angeles Times*, 4/16/1978, p. D6.
Ostler, Scott. "Sanchez and Time Take Their Toll on Lopez." *Los Angeles Times*, 6/22/1980, p. D1.

OLIVARES, RUBEN (1947–). Ruben Olivares arguably was the hardest punching bantamweight and featherweight champion of all-time. William Dettloff of *The Ring* writes: "Olivares' left hook was the bantamweight equivalent of Joe Frazier's and then some. . . . He had that screaming left hook, and it terrorized the bantamweight and featherweight division for a good ten years" (p. 34). His power earned him the nickname "Senor Nocaut" or "Mr. Knockout."

Born 1947 in Mexico City, Olivares turned professional in 1965 and won his first 23 fights by knockout before settling for a 10-round decision over Felipe Gonzalez. In 1969, he won the world bantamweight title with a fifth-round kayo over **Lionel Rose.** He successfully defended his title twice before losing to **Chucho Castillo** in 1970. He regained the title in a 1971 rematch and defended the title twice before losing to Rafael Herrera in 1972. In 1974, he won the vacant **World Boxing Association (WBA)** featherweight crown with a seventh-round stoppage of Zensuke Utagawa. He lost the title to the great **Alexis Arguello** in the 13th round later that year. Olivares won his last title in 1975—the **World Boxing Council (WBC)** featherweight title—with one of his greatest performances. He demolished **Bobby Chacon** in two rounds. He lost the title in his first defense against David Kotey. In 1979, he failed in one final attempt at a world championship, losing to **Eusebio Pedroza.** If Olivares had trained more and partied less, his Hall-of-Fame career may have been even better. But his amazing punching power earned him enshrinement in the International Boxing Hall of Fame in 1991.

Record:	88-13-3
Championship(s):	Bantamweight, 1969–1970; WBA featherweight, 1974; WBC featherweight, 1975.

Further Reading

Dettlof, William. *The Ring Yearbook 2003: 100 Greatest Punchers of All-Time* Ambler, P.A.: London Publishing. 2003, pp. 34-35.

Hafner, Dan. "Olivares: His Wit Is as Quick as His Fists." *Los Angeles Times*, 8/17/1969, p. C2.

Hafner, Dan. "Olivares: A Swinger In and Out of the Ring." *Los Angeles Times*, 3/29/1970, p. C8.

Hafner, Dan. "Olivares Seeks New Boxing Life in Bout." *Los Angeles Times*, 11/3/1972, p. D7.

Roberts, James B., and Alexander G. Skutt. *The Boxing Register: International Boxing Hall of Fame Register* (4th ed.). Ithaca, NY: McBooks Press, Inc., 2006, pp. 540–543.

OLIVO, JOEY (1958–). Joey Olivo was a former junior flyweight world champion from the United States who won his championships after nine years of professional boxing. Born in 1958 in San Fernando, California, Olivo began boxing at age 10.

He turned pro in 1976 at age 18 and won his first 22 bouts before dropping a decision to the much-more experienced Martin Vargas—a veteran of more than 60 bouts and three-time world challenger for the flyweight championship. Olivo rebounded and in 1981 challenged **Hilario Zapata** for the **World Boxing Council (WBC)** junior flyweight championship, losing in the 13th round. Olivo's manager contended that Olivo was sick during the fight, losing seven pounds off his diminutive 104-pound body during the bout.

In March 1985, Olivo defeated Francisco Quiroz for the **World Boxing Association (WBA)** junior lightweight title. He made one successful defense before suffering a split-decision to South Korean **Myung-Woo Yuh.** He retired in 1989 after three consecutive losses.

Professional Record:	31-8
Championship(s):	WBA junior flyweight, 1985

Further Reading

Hoffer, Richard. "Joey Olivo: In a Division Where the Purses Are Just as Light as the Fighters, He's Persevered to Become WBA's Junior-Flyweight Champion." *Los Angeles Times*, 5/14/1985, p. B1.

United Press International. "Zapata Keeps Title, Stops Olivo in 13th." *Los Angeles Times*, 2/9/1981, p. D5.

OLSON, CARL "BOBO" (1928–2002). Carl "Bobo" Olson was a former middleweight champion who fought professional for 22 years from 1944 to 1966. The son of a Swedish immigrant who moved to Hawaii, Olson was known as "the Hawaiian Swede." He turned pro at age 16 and fought his first three fights in his birth place of Honolulu. He first challenged for the middleweight crown in 1952 against the great **Sugar Ray Robinson** and lost a 15-round decision. In 1953, he won the vacant title with a 15-round decision over Randy Turpin. He successfully retained his title three times with wins over **Kid Gavilan,** Rocky Castellani, and Pierre Langlois. He failed in his bid for the world light heavyweight title, losing to **Archie Moore,** and then lost his middleweight championship to Robinson in 1955. He tried once more for the title in 1956, but Robinson beat him badly again. He retired in 1966 after losing to Don Fullmer.

Record:	99-16-2
Championship(s):	Middleweight, 1953–1955

Further Reading

Goldstein, Richard. "Bobo Olson, 73, Boxing Champion in the 1950's." *The New York Times*, 1/19/2002, p. A20.

Muller, Ed. "Little man with a BIG dream." *The Washington Post*, 6/19/1955, p. AW16.

Newland, Russ. "Robinson Retains Title by Decision." *Los Angeles Times*, 3/14/1952, p. C1.

Roberts, James B., and Alexander G. Skutt. *The Boxing Register: International Boxing Hall of Fame Register* (4th ed.). Ithaca, NY: McBooks Press, Inc., 2006, pp. 544–549.

OPEN SCORING. Open scoring refers to a system in which the judges' scorecards are announced during a fight. This contrasts with the customary method of announcing the verdict after the completion of the bout. Proponents of the system argue that open scoring will reduce the number of incompetent or corrupt scorecards, similar to the rationale used for open meetings laws. Critics counter that open scoring takes away the suspense factor for the fans and could lead to fighters in the scoring lead fighting too cautiously.

In April 1999—in the wake of the scandalous draw in the **Lennox Lewis—Evander Holyfield** bout—open scoring was used in three championship bouts held in Washington D.C.: **Mark Johnson**—Ratanachai Vorapin for the IBC junior bantamweight title, Keith Holmes—Hacine Cherifi for the **World Boxing Council (WBC)** middleweight title, and Sharmba Mitchell—Reggie Green for the **World Boxing Association (WBA)** super lightweight title.

Both the WBA and WBC have used open scoring in some of their bouts. For 12-round title fights, the judges' scorecards are often announced at the end of the fourth and eighth rounds. An example was the November 2006 bout for the WBC middleweight title between champion **Jermain Taylor** and challenger **Kassim Ouma.** In 2007, promoter **Don King** announced that he is in favor of open scoring.

Further Reading

Litke, Jim. "How to save boxing and earn Don King's undying gratitude." *Associated Press*, 8/23/2007.

Smith, Timothy. "Open Scoring Is Used in 3 Championship Bouts." *The New York Times*, 4/25/1999, p. 365.

ORTIZ, CARLOS (1936–). Carlos Ortiz was a great champion from Puerto Rico who won world titles in the junior welterweight and lightweight divisions. Born in Ponce in 1936, Ortiz moved to New York when he was 9. Raised in a tough neighborhood in the Lower East Side, Ortiz learned to fight to survive. "I couldn't go to school or even to the corner candy store without getting beat up by the other kids," Ortiz told a *Los Angeles Times* reporter. "One day I just got tired of taking those beatings, so I enrolled in a boxing class at the neighborhood boys' club." The bullies began leaving Ortiz alone, and he moved on his way to his destiny as a great fighter.

Ortiz turned professional in 1955 and won his first 20 fights. In 1959, he won the vacant junior welterweight title with a 10-round decision win over nemesis Kenny Lane, who had defeated Ortiz a year earlier. He retained the title twice before losing a controversial decision in Milan to Italian **Duilio Loi** in 1960.

He captured the lightweight championship with a lopsided 15-round decision over **Joe Brown** and held the belt until a 1965 decision loss to **Ismael Laguna.** Ortiz regained the title in a rematch and held the title until another disputed decision to Carlos Teo Cruz in Cruz's hometown in the Dominican Republic. Ortiz retired in 1969 but returned in 1971 and 1972. He won nine straight bouts before losing to **Ken Buchanan** in the sixth round.

Record:	61-7-1
Championship(s):	junior welterweight, 1959–1960, lightweight, 1962–1965, 1965–1968

Further Reading

Allen, Johnny. "Ortiz Shocked by Easy Victory." *Los Angeles Times*, 4/22/1962, p. C6.
Finch, Frank. "Here's the Pitch: Ortiz Fought for Survival." *Los Angeles Times*, 1/31/1960, p. D2.
Florence, Mal. "Ortiz Remains Undefeated With Unanimous Decision." *Los Angeles Times*, 10/28/1956, p. C10.
Roberts, James B., and Alexander G. Skutt. *The Boxing Register: International Boxing Hall of Fame Register* (4th ed.). Ithaca, NY: McBooks Press, Inc., 2006, pp. 544–549.
United Press International. "Pick Carlos Ortiz 'Fighter of Year.' " *Chicago Daily Defender*, 11/29/1967, p. 28.
Whorton, Cal. "Ortiz Collects TKO in Seventh Over Filippo." *Los Angeles Times*, 4/10/1957, p. C1.

ORTIZ, MANUEL (1916–1970). Manuel Ortiz was a longtime bantamweight champion who made 20 successful defenses of his bantamweight title during his two reigns. Born in 1916 in Corona, California, Ortiz turned pro in 1938 and lost his pro debut to **Benny Goldberg.** He lost to Goldberg twice more during 1938.

However, Ortiz rapidly improved and received a shot against Lou Salica for the world bantamweight title. Ortiz won a 12-round decision and proceeded to dominate the division for five years. In 1943, he defended his title an amazing eight times—including a decision win over his nemesis Goldberg. He finally lost his belt in 1947 with a decision loss to Harold Dade. Ortiz regained the title from Dade in a rematch two months later. He retained the title until a 1950 decision loss to Vic Toweel. He retired in 1955 after a loss to Enrique Esqueda. He died in 1970.

Record:	96-29-3
Championship(s):	Bantamweight, 1942–1947, 1947–1950

Further Reading

Lowry, Paul. "Ortiz Captures Title from Salica." *Los Angeles Times*, 8/8/1942, p. 11.
Roberts, James B., and Alexander G. Skutt. *The Boxing Register: International Boxing Hall of Fame Register* (4th ed.). Ithaca, NY: McBooks Press, Inc., 2006, pp. 554–557.
Singer, Jack. "Ortiz Bows to Oriental." *Los Angeles Times*, 11/9/1938, p. 21.

ORTIZ, TITO (1975–). Tito Ortiz, the "Huntington Beach Bad Boy," is a former **Ultimate Fighting Championships (UFC)** world light heavyweight champion who continues to fight in the sport, attracting attention wherever he fights. Born in 1975 in Huntington Beach, California, Ortiz overcame a very tough childhood that included his parents addicted to heroin. He engaged in petty crime and juvenile detention but found a bit of salvation in high school wrestling, where he showed great promise.

After high school, he wrestled at the junior college level for Golden West College, winning a state championship. He then competed for California State Bakersfield.

In 1996, he began serving as a training or sparring partner with **David "Tank" Abbott**—who also hailed from Huntington Beach. Ortiz turned pro in mixed martial arts (MMA) in 1997 and quickly developed into an emerging star. In only his sixth MMA professional fight, he challenged the legendary **Frank Shamrock** for the UFC middleweight title, losing in the fourth round.

He won the UFC title in 2000 at UFC 25 with a decision win over **Wanderlei "the Axe Murderer" Silva.** After the bout, Ortiz displayed a T-shirt bearing the message: "I just killed the Axe Murderer." The brash Ortiz often will display t-shirts with provocative messages after defeating an opponent. For example, after he defeated **Ken Shamrock** for the third time at UFC 60, he wore a shirt with the message: "Punishing Him into Retirement."

After defeating Silva to win the title, he successfully defended his belt against Yuki Kondo, **Evan Tanner,** Elvis Sinosic, Vladimir Matyushenko, and **Ken Shamrock**. He lost his title to **Randy "the Natural" Couture** at UFC 44: Undisputed. He lost in his next fight to former trainer partner **Chuck "the Iceman" Liddell.**

Ortiz then won five fights in a row, including a win over the dangerous **Vitor Belfort** and two more over Ken Shamrock. He then lost a rematch to Liddell at UFC 66: Liddell v. Ortiz.

Ortiz also is known for making waves outside the ring, such as his romance with former porn star Jenna Jameson. He has lost twice to former friend Chuck "the Iceman" Liddell. He holds victories over Ken Shamrock, Vitor Belfort, **Forrest Griffin,** Wanderlei Silva, and Guy Metzger in his career.

In perhaps his last fight in the Octagon, Ortiz lost a decision to **Lyoto Machida** in May 2008 at UFC 84: Ill Will.

Professional MMA Record:	15-6
Championship(s):	UFC Light Heavyweight, 2000–2003

Further Reading

Hudson, David L., Jr. "Tito:11 Years of Blood, Sweat and Tears in the Octagon." *Fightnews,* 5/16/08, at http://www.fightnewsextra.com/cc/ufc84/10_ortiz.htm

Iole, Kevin. "Ortiz plans to do talking with fists, feet vs. Belfort." *Las Vegas Review-Journal,* 2/5/2005, p. 9C.

Official Web site of Tito Ortiz: http://www.titoortiz.com/

Ortiz, Tito, with Marc Shapiro. *This Is Gonna Hurt: The Life of a Mixed Martial Arts Champion.* New York: Simon Spotlight Entertainment, 2008.

Walls, Jeremy. *UFC's Ultimate Warriors Top 10.* Ontario: ECW Press, 2005.

OTTKE, SVEN (1967–). Sven "Phantom" Ottke was a stylish German boxer known for his fine defensive skills and reluctance to fight outside his home country. While some criticized his decision to remain in Germany, no one can argue with his unblemished professional record of 34-0. Born in Berlin-Spandau, Ottke turned pro in 1997 after a lengthy amateur career in which he won more than 280 bouts and competed in three Olympics (1988, 1992, and 1996). He turned pro in 1997 and in his 13th pro bout captured a split decision victory over Charles Brewer in 1998 to win the **International Boxing Federation (IBF)** super middleweight championship. He successfully defended his title 21 times and added the **World Boxing Association (WBA)** belt with a split decision win over Byron Mitchell in 2003. His last bout was in 2004. One of his more impressive wins was his knockout of the brash Anthony Mundine in December 2001. Ottke is planning to return to the ring in late 2008 or 2009.

Professional Record:	34-0
Championship(s):	IBF super middleweight, 1998–2005; WBA super middleweight, 2003–2004

Further Reading
Doogan, Brian. "A Tale of Two Retirements: Ottke and Paz: Different Routes to the Same Finish Line." *KO* (October 2004), pp. 48–52.
Knish, Joey. "If Sven Ottke Fell in the Boxing Forest, Would He Make a Sound?" *The Sweet Science,* 3/30/2004, at http://www.thesweetscience.com/boxing-article/344/sven-ottke-fell-boxing-forest-would-make-sound/

OUMA, KASSIM (1978–). Kassim "the Dream" Ouma turned a nightmarish early life into a dream by capturing the world junior middleweight championship. Born in Kampala, Uganda, in 1978, Ouma had to fight in the Uganda army when he was only 7 or 8 years old. He boxed in an amateur boxing program in the military and defected to the United States at age 19.

He turned professional in 1998 and won his first nine bouts before losing to Augustin Silva. He returned on another winning streak that culminated in a 2004 win over Verno Phillips to win the **International Boxing Federation (IBF)** junior middleweight championship. He successfully defended his title against fellow African Kofi Jantuah before losing a decision to Roman Karmazin. In 2006, he lost a decision to IBF middleweight champion **Jermain Taylor.** He lost two more fights after that title loss, though he hopes to regain his winning ways. A documentary has been made about his amazing life.

Kassim Ouma celebrates his world championship after defeating Verno Phillips in October 2004 to win the IBF junior middleweight title. Courtesy of Chris Cozzone.

Professional Record:	25-5-1
Championship(s):	IBF junior middleweight, 2004–2005

Further Reading
Donovan, Jake. "The Dream Becomes a Network Nightmare: What More Can Be Asked of Kassim Ouma?" *The Sweet Science,* 5/26/2005, at http://www.thesweetscience.com/boxing-article/2142/dream-becomes-network-nightmare-more-asked-kassim-ouma/
Donovan, Jake. "The War at 154: Ouma and Jantuah Ready to Battle." *The Sweet Science,* 1/27/2005, at http://www.thesweetscience.com/boxing-article/1613/war-154-ouma-jantuah-ready-battle/
Gilken, Rochelle E. B. "Rough Dream." *Palm Beach Post,* 11/1/2007, p. 1C.

OVEREEM, ALISTAIR (1980–). Alistair Overeem is a Dutch-based mixed martial artist who possesses dangerous striking skills. Trained extensively in Muay Thai kickboxing, Overeem has earned his nickname "the Demolition Man" with his dangerous hand, leg, and knee strikes. His weakness is the ground game. Born in 1980 in Ultrecht, Netherlands, Overeem turned pro in mixed martial arts (MMA) in 1999. In 2002, he made his debut in **PRIDE,** dispatching Yusuke Immamura in only 43 seconds. In 2003, he entered the PRIDE grand prix middleweight tournament, losing to **Chuck "the Iceman" Liddell.**

He owns two wins over **Vitor Belfort,** a win over **Igor Vovchanchyn,** and most recently a submission win over **Paul "the Headhunter" Buentello** for the vacant Strikeforce heavyweight title. His brother **Valentijn** is also a well-known mixed martial artist.

Professional MMA Record:	29-11
Professional Kickboxing Record:	2-1
Championship(s):	Strike Force Heavyweight, 2007—

Further Reading
Official Web site: http://www.alistairovereem.com/

OVEREEM, VALENTIJN (1976–). Valentijn Overeem is a Dutch-based mixed martial artist and the brother of **Alistair.** He began his mixed martial arts career in 1996 with a win over Tjerk Vermanen. He literally has faced a virtual "who's who" of great mixed martial artists in his long career. His best performance was a submission win over **Randy "the Natural" Couture** in 2001 at the King of Kings 2000 Final. Overeem submitted Couture with a **guillotine choke.**

During his career, he has faced the likes of **Antonio Rodrigo Nogueira, Gary Goodridge, Igor Vovchanchyn,** Gilbert Yvel, and Renato Sobral. Interestingly, Overeem has fought in **PRIDE** but has never fought in the **Ultimate Fighting Championships (UFC).**

Professional MMA Record:	26-22
Championship(s):	None

Further Reading
Sherdog Fight Preview: http://www.sherdog.com/fighter/Valentijn-Overeem-466

PACQUIAO, MANNY (1978–). Manny "Pacman" Pacquiao is one of boxing's best current pound-for-pound fighters in addition to being one of the sport's most popular and exciting champions. The southpaw Pacquiao fights with great energy and possesses tremendous power, particularly for a fighter in the smaller weight divisions.

Manny Pacquiao tags Marco Antonio Barrera in their second bout held in October 2007. Pacquiao won a unanimous decision. Courtesy of Chris Cozzone.

Manny Pacquiao dominates David Diaz to add a lightweight title to his collection in June 2008. Courtesy of Chris Cozzone.

Manny Pacquiao lands a lead right hook on Juan Manuel Marquez in their 2004 bout, which ended in a controversial draw. Courtesy of Chris Cozzone.

Born in 1978 in Kibawe, this Filipino sensation turned professional in 1995 at the age of 16. In December 1998, he defeated Chatchai Sasakul to win the **World Boxing Council (WBC)** flyweight title. Unfortunately, Pacquiao had trouble making weight in the 112-pound division and failed to make weight for his second title defense against **Medgoen Singsurat.** He also lost to Singsurat in the ring, losing in the third round.

Pacquiao rebounded in a major way in June 2001 as a late challenger for heavily favored **International Boxing Federation (IBF)** super bantamweight champion Lehlo Ledwaba. Pacquiao dominated the champion and stopped him in the sixth round. In December 2003, he became a worldwide sensation with a dominant victory over pound-for-pound great **Marco Antonio Barrera.** Pacquiao stopped Barrera in the 11th round after dropping him several times. In his next fight, he dropped **Juan Manuel Marquez** three times in the first round but managed only a draw after one judge mistakenly scored the first round to him 10-8 instead of the customary 10-7 (see entry on **Ten Point Must System**).

In March 2005, he lost a close decision to **Erik Morales** over 12 rounds for the vacant WBC international super featherweight title. He gained sweet revenge and the title in a January 2006 bout, stopping Morales in the 10th round. He has since won return bouts with both Morales and Barrera. In March 2008, he defeated his other rival Marquez by split decision. In June 2008, Pacquiao dominated David Diaz to add the WBC lightweight title to his list of conquests. In December 2008, Pacquaio became boxing's unofficial pound-for-pound best in the world when he dominated the larger **Oscar De La Hoya.**

Professional Record:	46-3-2
Championship(s):	WBC flyweight, 1998–1998; IBF super bantamweight, 2001–2004; WBC super featherweight, 2005–2008 ; WBC lightweight, 2008–

Further Reading

Detloff, William. "Best in the World?: Pac-Man's Closing in on Pretty Boy." *The Ring* (March 2007), pp. 38–44.

Official Web site: http://mannypacquiao.ph/

Santoloquito, Joe. "The Pacquaio-Marquez Feud: All We Can Do Is Pray For a Third Fight." *The Ring* (July 2008), pp. 30–36.

PAEZ, JORGE (1965–). Jorge "Maromero" Paez was a former world featherweight champion known for his clowning tactics, outrageous ring entrances, and unique personality. Born in Colima, Mexico, in 1965, Paez was born into a family of circus performers. Paez traveled with his family in the circus as an acrobat, juggler, and a clown. He carried such talents into his ring entrances and even his ring performances.

He turned pro in 1987 and earned a world title the next year against undefeated **International Boxing Federation (IBF)** featherweight champion Calvin Grove. Paez dropped Grove three times in the final round to win a close, unanimous decision. He successfully defended his title eight times, adding the World Boxing Organization (WBO) belt after a split decision win over Espinoza in 1990. Two times he defended his title against former kickboxer Troy Dorsey, eking out a split decision win and a controversial draw.

In 1991, he moved up in weight to challenge undefeated and undisputed lightweight champion **Pernell Whitaker.** Paez's defense abilities at times seemed to frustrate Whitaker, but Paez lost a unanimous decision. In 1993, he lost to Freddie Pendleton in an attempt for the IBF lightweight crown. The next year he lost badly to undefeated **Oscar De La Hoya** for the vacant WBO lightweight crown. Paez continued to fight with less success and even fought a bout as late as 2007.

His son Jorge Paez, Jr., is a promising young junior welterweight.

Professional Record:	**79-14-5**
Championship(s):	IBF featherweight, 1988–1990; WBO featherweight, 1990

Further Reading
Arias, Carlos. "Send in the Clown: Former featherweight champion Jorge Paez takes his circus act back to the ring." *Orange County Register*, 5/2/1996, p. D02.
Berger, Phil. "Paez is More Than Just Eccentric." *The New York Times*, 12/13/1989, p. D24.
Gustkey, Earl. "Paez Might Still Be a Clown, But Now He Has a Serious Side." *Los Angeles Times*, 5/15/1993, p. C4.

PAGE, GREG (1958–). Greg Page was a former world heavyweight champion who possessed fine boxing skills but never quite reached his potential. Born in 1958 in Louisville, Kentucky, Page reminded some of **Muhammad Ali** as an amateur because of his fine jab and quick hands. He compiled a record of 90–11 as an amateur, owing victories over **John Tate, Tony Tubbs,** and Marvin Stinson.

He turned pro in 1979 and won his first 18 bouts until dropping a decision to future champion **Trevor Berbick.** The high point of his career came in December 1984 when he traveled to South Africa to upset **Gerrie Coetzee** to win the **World Boxing Association (WBA)** heavyweight title. Page seemingly could not handle success, as he lost the belt in his first title defense to Tony Tubbs. He retired from the ring in 1993 but made a comeback in 1996, compiling numerous victories against lesser opposition.

Tragedy struck in March 2001 when he faced tough journeyman Dale Crowe in Kentucky. He suffered permanent injuries from the fight and remains in a wheelchair.

Professional Record:	58-17-1
Championship(s):	WBA Heavyweight, 1984–1985

Further Reading
Adams, Jim. "Greg Page in the Fight of His Life." *The Courier-Journal* (Louisville, KY), 6/21/2005, p. 4K.
Blewett, Bert. "Coetzee Clobbered: Greg Page Wins WBA Title Amidst a Whirlwind of Controversy." *The Ring* (February 1985), pp. 32–37.
Diaz, George. "Former boxer won't give up." *Orlando Sentinel*, 10/21/2003, p. D1.

PALOMINO, CARLOS (1949–). Carlos Palomino was a former world welterweight champion known as one of the truly good guys in the sport. Born in 1949 in San Luis, Mexico, Palomino moved to New Mexico with his family when he was 10 years old. He had a fine amateur boxing career, earning all-Army honors and winning a national AAU championship in 1972.

He turned professional that year with a win in Los Angeles. In 1976, he traveled the Atlantic Ocean to face British champion John Stracey for the world welterweight title. In an upset, he stopped Stracey in the 12th round. He successfully defended his title seven times before losing a decision to the crafty prodigy **Wilfred Benitez** in 1979. Later that year, he lost a 10-round decision to the great **Roberto Duran.** He retired after that defeat but returned to the ring many years later in 1997. He won four straight bouts before losing a decision to Wilfredo Rivera in 1998. Palomino is a college graduate, earning a degree from Long Beach State University, and currently acts in movies and television shows.

Record: 31-4-3
Championship(s):   Welterweight, 1976–1979

Further Reading
Gustkey, Earl. "Palomino: The Fighter Wins Hearts of Kids." *Los Angeles Times*, 9/11/1975, p. F11.
Hawn, Jack. "Palomino Kicks Like Army Mule." *Los Angeles Times*, 7/13/1975, p. C13.
Hawn, Jack. "Palomino's Lightning Hit Twice." *Los Angeles Times*, 6/19/1977, p. P14.
Roberts, James B., and Alexander G. Skutt. *The Boxing Register: International Boxing Hall of Fame Register* (4th ed.). Ithaca, NY: McBooks Press, Inc., 2006, pp. 558–561.

PAPP, LASZLO (1926–2003). Laszlo Papp was one of the greatest amateur boxers in boxing history who turned pro at the age of 31 and never lost a professional fight. Sadly, he never received a world title shot in the professional ranks. Born in 1926 in Angyafold, Hungary, Papp first achieved world recognition by winning a gold medal at the 1948 London Olympics in the middleweight division. He won gold medals as a light middleweight in the 1952 and 1956 Olympics, becoming the first fighter to win three Olympic gold medals. In the gold medal match at the 1956 Olympics, he defeated future professional champion **Jose Torres.**

In 1957, at the advanced age of 31, Papp turned professional. He never lost a professional fight and had two draws—one to a French fighter in Paris and one to an Italian pugilist in Milan. He won the European middleweight title in 1962 with a seventh-round stoppage of Christian Christensen. He retained the title six times and retired in 1964. Just as he was about to receive a world title bout in 1965, he was ordered back to Hungary. The government prohibited him from receiving his long-overdue shot at a professional world title. The government's action could not, however, diminish Papp's ring greatness.

Record: 27-0-2
Championship(s):   None

Further Reading
Daley, Robert. "Years Close In on Laszlo Papp." *The New York Times*, 2/21/1961, p. 43.
Daley, Robert. "Budapest Fight is Papp's Dream." *The New York Times*, 3/23/1963, p. 14.
Roberts, James B., and Alexander G. Skutt. *The Boxing Register: International Boxing Hall of Fame Register* (4th ed.). Ithaca, NY: McBooks Press, Inc., 2006, pp. 562–565.
Searcy, Jay. "Old Ring Hero Gets Hungarian Sendoff." *The New York Times*, 12/10/1974, p. 59.

PARET, BENNY (1937–1962). Benny "Kid" Paret was a former two-time world welterweight champion whose name evokes memories of tragedy—he died from injuries he suffered in his third bout with rival **Emile Griffith.** Despite his tragic death, Paret's story was a remarkable one in that he managed to rise out of poverty in his native Cuba to become a world champion.

Born in 1937 in Santa Clara, Cuba, Paret was one of eight children. He picked in the sugar cane fields for meager money. He turned pro in 1954 in Santa Clara and won his first 13 bouts. Manuel Alfaro brought Paret to the United States after the youngster showed great promise as an amateur and as a rising pro.

In May 1960, he defeated Don Jordan over 15 rounds to win the world welterweight championship. He made one successful defense before losing to Griffith in the 13th round in April 1961. However, he regained the title from Griffith in August 1961 with a 15-round split decision.

Three months later, Paret attempted to lift the middleweight title from the heavier **Gene Fullmer.** Paret fought courageously but succumbed in the 10th round. He took tremendous punishment in the bout. That set the stage for his infamous rubber match with his heated rival Griffith in March 1962. Paret fought well but Griffith's greater power proved the difference. In the fateful 12th round, Griffith battered Paret senseless on the ropes, while referee Ruby Goldstein inexplicably refused to stop the action until it was too late. Paret slipped into a coma and died 10 days later.

Professional Record:	35-12-3
Championship(s):	Welterweight, 1960–1961, 1961–1962

Further Reading
Conklin, William R. "Griffith Beaten on Split Verdict." *The New York Times*, 10/1/1961, p. S1.
Lipsyte, Robert M. "The Story of Benny (Kid) Paret: From $4 a Day to the World Title." *The New York Times*, 4/3/1962, p. 47.
Shapiro, Michael. "Paret Tragedy: A Shared Burden." *The New York Times*, 3/23/1983, p. B9.

PARK, CHAN-HEE (1957–). Chan-Hee Park was a former two-time world flyweight champion from South Korea. Born in 1957 in Pusan, he represented his country at the 1976 Montreal Olympics. He won his first two rounds over fighters from Morocco and Turkey but then lost to eventual light flyweight gold medalist Jorge Hernandez from Cuba. He turned professional in 1977 and in his 11th pro bout defeated long-time flyweight kingpin **Miguel Canto** for the **World Boxing Council (WBC)** flyweight championship. He successfully defended the title five times—including a draw against Canto—before losing a split decision to Japanese fighter Shoji Oguma in 1980. He received two more world title shots at Oguma but lost two disputed decisions. He retired in 1982.

Professional Record:	17-4-1
World Championship(s):	WBC flyweight, 1979–1980

Further Reading
Associated Press. "Oguma Outpoints Korean, Retains Flyweight Crown." *The New York Times*, 10/19/1980, Section 5, p. 6.

PARNASSUS, GEORGE (1897–1975). George Parnassus was a stellar boxing promoter, matchmaker, and manager best known for helping form the **World Boxing Council (WBC)** and for staging great fights in the West Coast area. Born in 1897 in Methone, Greece, Parnassus emigrated to the United States in 1915, finding work as a waiter and dishwasher. He later owned a restaurant in Phoenix, Arizona, that happened to be located across from a boxing gym.

He managed many great Mexican fighters, including **Juan Zurita,** Enrique Bolanos, and **Jose Beccera.** He later moved into promoting fights in the Los Angeles area with Aileen Eaton. Though Parnassus and Eaton later split professionally, they copromoted major bouts such as a 1957 clash between Alphonse Halimi and Raton Macias and the 1958 bout between **Hogan "Kid" Bassey** and Pajarito Moreno. Parnassus later promoted numerous world title fights at the Forum, which opened in December 1967. He shared mightily in profits with Forum owner Jack Kent Cooke. Parnassus promoted numerous fights involving popular Mexican fighters **Ruben Olivares, Chucho Castillo,** and **Vincente Saldivar.**

Further Reading

Newhan, Ross. "Parnassus: He'll Ring Up a Record." *Los Angeles Times*, 12/12/1969, p. G8.

Newhan, Ross. "Complex Greek." *Los Angeles Times*, 12/5/1968, p. C1.

Walker, Turnley. "George Parnassus, A Figthers' Friend, Is Home Again." *Los Angeles Times*, 11/23/1969, p. A63.

PASTRANO, WILLIE (1935–1997). Willie Pastrano was a smooth-boxing light heavy-weight champion known for his active jab and fine defense. Born in 1935 in New Orleans, Loui-siana, Pastrano overcame childhood bullying and early obesity by diligently practicing boxing in the gym. He turned pro at age 15 in 1951. In 1952, his manager sent him to Miami Beach to train with **Angelo Dundee.** The Pastrano–Dundee partnership worked great, as Pastrano dili-gently applied Dundee's excellent training principles. In 1963, Pastrano finally received a world title shot and made the most of it. He decisioned **Harold Johnson** over 15 rounds to capture the title. He retained the title twice before losing in 1965 to **Jose Torres.** He never fought again. He died in 1997.

Record:	63-13-8
Championship(s):	Light Heavyweight, 1963–1965

Further Reading

McGowan, Deane. "Pastrano Stops Peralta in Sixth and Retains Light Heavyweight Title." *The New York Times*, 4/11/1964, p. 20.

Roberts, James B., and Alexander G. Skutt. *The Boxing Register: International Boxing Hall of Fame Register* (4th ed.). Ithaca, NY: McBooks Press, Inc., 2006, pp. 566–569.

PATTERSON, FLOYD (1935–2006). Floyd Patterson was the first two-time world heavy-weight champion and former Olympic gold medalist known for his fine defensive skills, speed, and overall good nature. Born in 1935 in Waco, North Carolina, Patterson moved to New York with his family. Legendary trainer Cus D'Amato discovered Patterson and taught him his famous peek-a-boo defense. Patterson won gold as a middleweight at the 1952 Olympics in Helsinki.

Patterson turned pro in 1952 and won his first 12 fights before dropping an 8-round decision to future champion Joey Maxim. In 1956, Patterson defeated Tommy Jackson to earn a shot at **Archie Moore** for the world heavyweight title. Patterson captured the belt by stopping Moore in the fifth round. He successfully defended his title four times before a shocking kayo loss to **Ingemar Johansson.** Patterson regained the title from Johansson in 1960 and won the rubber match in 1961. He lost his title to the ferocious **Sonny Liston** by first-round kayo in 1962. He suffered another first-round embarrassment to the powerful Liston in 1963. Patterson failed in two more attempts at a world title to **Muhammad Ali** in 1965 and **Jimmy Ellis** in 1968. He retired in 1972 after another loss to Ali. In retirement, he later served as chairman of the New York State Athletic Commission. He died in 2006.

Record:	55-8-1
Championship(s):	Heavyweight, 1956–1959; 1960–1962

Further Reading

Levy, Alan H. *Floyd Patterson: A Biography.* Jefferson, North Carolina: McFarland & Company, 2008.

Patterson, Floyd, and Milton Gross. *Victory Over Myself.* Scholastic Book Services, 1966.

Roberts, James B., and Alexander G. Skutt. *The Boxing Register: International Boxing Hall of Fame Register* (4th ed.). Ithaca, NY: McBooks Press, Inc., 2006, pp. 570–573.

Ryan, Jeff. "A Credit to His Grace." *The Ring Extra* (October 2006), pp. 16–17.

PAUL, MELVIN (1960–). Melvin Paul was a great U.S. amateur boxer denied his chance at Olympic gold because of the U.S. boycott of the 1980 Moscow Olympics. In his stellar amateur career, Paul compiled a record of 222-32, including a 1978 national AAU championship. The 5'4" dynamo turned pro in 1980 and won his first 16 bouts before dropping a 10-round decision to **Hector "Macho" Camacho.**

In 1984, he faced Charlie "Choo Choo" Brown for the vacant **International Boxing Federation (IBF)** lightweight title. Paul dropped Brown in the 15th and final round but lost a split decision. "I really beat Choo Choo Brown," Paul said years later. Many ringside experts agreed with his assessment. Paul continued fighting professionally until 1986 when he lost in the first round to Walter Sims.

Professional Record:	21-8
Championship(s):	None

Further Reading
Smith, Jimmy. "'Boxing Saved Me,' So Says Melvin Paul, Who Beat the Streets to Become One of Boxing's Best Lightweights." *New Orleans Times-Picayune*, 12/21/1993, p. D2.

PAVLIK, KELLY (1982–). Kelly "the Ghost" Pavlik is the undisputed middleweight champion of the world who was unbeaten in his first 34 professional bouts. Born in 1982 in Youngstown, Ohio, Pavlik had an outstanding amateur career but lost to an older **Jermain Taylor** in the Olympic Trials.

Pavlik turned pro in 2000 under the promotional banner of Top Rank and under the guidance of his longtime trainer Jack Loew. Moved slowly, Pavlik continued to progress as a professional. In July 2006, he turned heads with a convincing win over former junior middleweight champion Bronco McKart.

Kelly Pavlik and Jermain Taylor stare each other down before their February 2008 rematch. Courtesy of Chris Cozzone.

Kelly Pavlik, the middleweight champion, looks confident and comfortable in his Affliction t-shirt. Courtesy of Chris Cozzone.

Kelly Pavlik has his hand raised after defeating Ross Thompson in November 2004. Courtesy of Chris Cozzone.

In 2007, he upset powerpuncher Edison Miranda, blasting his opponent out in the seventh round to earn a shot against amateur nemesis Jermain Taylor for the middleweight title. Pavlik survived a terrible second round and slowly imposed his will with his superior physical conditioning and punishing right cross. He shocked the boxing public with a seventh-round stoppage of Taylor. In February 2008, he proved his title win was no fluke by outpointing Taylor in a nontitle bout rematch. In October 2008, Pavlik squared off against the legendary **Bernard Hopkins** in a nontitle bout at the catch weigh of 170 lbs. Pavlik looked uncharacteristically sluggish and lost a lopsided 12-round decision.

Professional Record:	35-1
Championship(s):	WBC Middleweight, 2007–;
	WBO Middleweight, 2007–

Further Reading

Dettloff, William. "A Superstar is Born: Pavlik Revs Up the Engine That Drives the Sport." *The Ring* (February 2008), pp. 38–45.
Official Web site: http://www.teampavlik.com/
Raskin, Eric. "Which Weigh Should He Go?" *The Ring* (Fall 2008), pp. 36–42.

PAZIENZA, VINNY (1962–). Vinny Pazienza was a colorful former brawler who won world titles at lightweight and junior middleweight in a career that spanned more than 20 years. Born in 1962 in Cranston, Rhode Island, Pazienza turned pro in 1983 with a fight in Atlantic City, New Jersey.

He attracted the attention of the boxing world in 1985 with consecutive wins over Jeff Bumphus and **Melvin Paul.** In June 1987, he challenged undefeated champion Greg Haugen for the **International Boxing Federation (IBF)** lightweight title, which he won via unanimous decision. However, in the rematch the next year he lost a decision to Haugen.

In 1988, he challenged **World Boxing Council (WBC)** junior welterweight champion **Roger "the Black Mamba" Mayweather** but lost a 12-round decision. Two years later he lost a close decision to **Hector "Macho" Camacho** for the World Boxing Organization (WBO) junior welterweight title. In 1991, he moved up two weight divisions to face undefeated **World Boxing Association (WBA)** junior middleweight champion Gilbert Dele. In a surprise, Pazienza stopped the champion in the 10th round, earning the belt and later *The Ring* magazine's 1991 Comeback Fighter of the Year award. Unfortunately, tragedy struck Pazienza as a terrible car accident left him with a broken neck.

However, Paz not only recovered but returned to the ring. He then won nine more consecutive bouts before challenging **Roy Jones, Jr.**—the middleweight champion who was then universally recognized as the best pound-for-pound fighter in the world. Jones overwhelmed the Pazmanian Devil over six rounds.

In 1996, he stopped undefeated Dana Rosenblatt in a fight of bitter regional rivals. Rosenblatt won the first three rounds before a powerful overhand right hurt him badly. Paz not only stopped Rosenblatt but hit referee Tony Orlando who intervened to stop the fight.

Paz continued to fight several more years, even earning a shot in 2002 at the WBC super middleweight crown against Eric Lucas. Paz fought gamely but lost a 12-round decision. Paz was known for his high-energy, powerful left hook, and charismatic personality.

Professional Record:	50-10
Championship(s):	IBF lightweight, 1987–1988; WBA junior
	middleweight, 1991–1992

Further Reading

Caduto, Tommy Jon. *Fight or Die: The Vinny Paz Story*. Guilford, CT: The Lyons Press, 2009.

Looney, Douglas S. "The Paz That Refreshes." *Sports Illustrated*, 6/1/1987, p. 62.

Smith, Martha. "In His Corner Island's Vinny Pazienz, Super-Middleweight Boxing Champion, Prepares for The Fight of His Life—and a Career Beyond the Ring." *Providence Journal-Bulletin*, 6/8/1995, p. 6M.

PEARL, DAVEY (1918–2006). Davey Pearl was a referee who officiated 70 world title bouts, including such luminaries as **Muhammad Ali—Leon Spinks** I, **Sugar Ray Leonard—Thomas Hearns** I, and **Marvelous Marvin Hagler—Vito Antuofermo** II. Though he stood only 5'4" tall and weighed less than 130 pounds, Pearl commanded respect from boxers of all sizes. He was close friends with billionaire Howard Hughes and with former heavyweight champion **Sonny Liston.** "For a man of his size, he was one of the top referees in the history of the sport," said Marc Ratner, executive director of the Nevada Athletic Commission. "The fighters respected him" (Feour).

Pearl began his career in boxing as a judge and then started refereeing. For many years he could not land a title bout in part because of his small stature. After more than 10 years, he finally landed his first title fight.

Further Reading

Feour, Royce. "Small size belies Pearl's imprint on Las Vegas." *Review Journal*, 5/27/2006, at http://www.reviewjournal.com/lvrj_home/2006/Mar-27-Mon-2006/sports/6563189.html

Lindenmann, Barry. "Davey Pearl Interview." *Cyber Boxing Zone* at http://cyberboxingzone.com/boxing/pearl.htm

PEDROZA, EUSEBIO (1953–). Eusebio Pedroza was a longtime featherweight champion known for his good boxing skills, fine jab, and penchant for ignoring some of the **Queensbury Rules** when necessary. Born in 1953 in Panama City, Pedroza turned pro in 1973 as a bantamweight. In 1976, he challenged Mexico's **Alfonso Zamora** for the world bantamweight title. Zamora brutally kayoed him in the second round. In 1978, Pedroza moved up in weight to the featherweight division and kept winning.

He won the **World Boxing Association (WBA)** title that year with a 13th-round stoppage of Cecilio Lastra. He then proceeded to successfully defend his title 19 times before finally losing to **Barry McGuigan** in 1985. Some of his defenses were controversial, including a split-decision win over Juan Laporte in 1992, a draw with Bernard Taylor in 1982, and a split-decision win over Rocky Lockridge in 1983. Pedroza initially retired after losing to Edgar Castro in 1986 but returned to the ring in 1991. He won three straight before losing to Mauro Gutierrez in 1992. In his native Panama, he served in Congress.

Record:	42-6-1
Championship(s):	WBA featherweight, 1978–1985

Further Reading

Dettloff, William. "The Ten Greatest Title Reigns of All-Time." *The Ring* (April 2005), pp. 65–76, 73.

Roberts, James B., and Alexander G. Skutt. *The Boxing Register: International Boxing Hall of Fame Register* (4th ed.). Ithaca, NY: McBooks Press, Inc., 2006, pp. 570–573.

PENN, B. J. (1978–). B. J. Penn, known as "the Prodigy," is one of the most skilled pound-for-pound mixed martial artists in the world. Born in 1978 in Hawaii, Penn began training in

Brazilian jiu-jitsu at age 17 under Ralph Gracie. Only three years later, he won a gold medal in the black belt division of the Mundial World Championships in Brazil. He earned the moniker "the Prodigy" for the rapidity with which he mastered jiu-jitsu and other martial art disciplines.

Managed by his older brother J. D., B. J. began his professional career in mixed martial arts (MMA) in 2001, defeating Joey Gilbert in the **Ultimate Fighting Championships (UFC)** 31: Locked and Loaded. He won his next two UFC bouts before losing a majority decision to **Jens Pulver** for the UFC world lightweight championship at UFC 35: Throwdown.

He rebounded with several major MMA wins, including a submission win over the talented **Takanori Gomi** at Rumble on the Rock 4, a decision win over **Matt Serra** in UFC 39: The Warriors Return, and then a shocking submission of **Matt Hughes** at UFC 46: Supernatural to win the UFC welterweight championship. He left the UFC to fight in several K-1 bouts in 2004 and 2005.

Penn returned to the UFC in 2006, losing a split decision to the talented **Georges St.-Pierre** at UFC 58: USA v. Canada. In his only bout of 2007, he avenged his earlier loss to Jens Pulver with a rear naked choke submission win at the Ultimate 5 Finale. In early 2008, he defeated Joe Stephenson for the UFC lightweight championship. He then dismantled former champion **Sean Sherk** in May 2008, showing superior striking skills.

Professional MMA Record:	13-5-1
Championship(s):	UFC Welterweight, 2004;
	UFC Lightweight, 2008–

Further Reading

Davidson, Neil. "The Prodigy looks to add to MMA legacy by winning title in second weight class." *The Canadian Press*, 1/18/2008.

Morinaga, Dayton. "Penn wants to pulverize rival." *The Honolulu Advertiser*, 4/2/2007, p. 1D.

Official Web site: http://www.bjpenn.com/2008/

Penn, B. J., with Glen Cordozo and Erich Krauss. *Mixed Martial Arts: The Book of Knowledge*. Auberry, CA. Victory Belt Publishing, 2007.

Sheridan, Sam. "A Force of Nature: The Evolution of B.J. Benn." *FIGHT!* (October/November 2007), pp. 32–40.

PEP, WILLIE (1922–2006). Willie Pep may have been the greatest pure boxer in boxing history. Many experts consider him to be the equivalent of a Michaelangelo in the ring, an artist of the utmost excellence. Others called him the finest defensive fighter in the history of the sport. Born Guiglermo Papaleo in 1922 in Middletown, Connecticut, he became known to the world with his anglicized name of Willie Pep. He turned pro in 1940 and won the world featherweight title in 1942 with a decision victory over **Albert "Chalky" Wright.**

He lost a nontitle bout to lightweight Sammy Angott but continued his amazing winning ways until he fought **Sandy Saddler** in 1948. Pep lost his title but regained it in 1949 with a masterful boxing display that lived up to his moniker "Will O Wisp." Sportswriter Bill Gallo wrote years later: "For 15 rounds he put on the greatest exhibition of boxing any fan would ever see." He could not solve Saddler's physical advantages of superior height and reach and lost two more fights to his rival and fellow hall-of-famer. He retired in 1959 but returned in 1965, winning nine straight fights until a 1966 loss to Calvin Woodland. He later served as the boxing inspector for his home state of Connecticut.

Record:	230-11-1
Championship(s):	Featherweight, 1942–1948, 1949–1950

Further Reading
Gallo, Bill. "Pep Had Will to Win." *Daily News*, 11/29/2006, p. 88.
Hughes, Brian. *Willie Pep: The Will o' the Wisp*. Manchester, England: Collyhurst and Hughes, 1997.
Pep, Willie, with Robert Sacchi. *Willie Pep Remembers*. New York: F. Fell Publishers, 1973.
Roberts, James B., and Alexander G. Skutt. *The Boxing Register: International Boxing Hall of Fame Register* (4th ed.). Ithaca, N.Y.: McBooks Press, Inc., 2006, pp. 578–583.

PEREZ, PASCUAL (1926–1977). Pascual Perez was a dominant flyweight champion and the first Argentine to win a world boxing championship. Though he stood less than 5 feet tall, Perez looms large in boxing history. Born in 1926 in Mendoza, Perez took to boxing despite family opposition. He captured a gold medal at the 1948 Olympic Games, but did not turn professional until 1952. In July 1954, he fought a 10-round, nontitle draw with champion Yoshio Shirai. Several months later, the two met in Tokyo for a world title bout. Perez dropped Shirai in the 12th and won a 15-round decision to win the championship by unanimous decision. He made nine successful defenses over the next few years before finally losing his belt by decision to **Pone Kingpetch** in 1960. He continued fighting until 1964 when he retired after suffering two straight technical knockout losses.

Professional Record:	84-7-1
Championship(s):	Flyweight, 1954–1960

Further Reading
Associated Press. "Argentine Takes 15-Round Verdict." *The New York Times*, 11/27/1954, p. 9.
Roberts, James B. and Alexander G. Skutt. *The Boxing Register: International Boxing Hall of Fame Register* (4th ed.). Ithaca, NY: McBooks Press, Inc., 2006, pp. 584–587.

PERKINS, EDDIE (1937–). Eddie Perkins was a former two-time world junior welterweight champion who fought professionally from 1956 to 1975. Born in Clarksdale, Mississippi, in 1937, Perkins turned pro in 1956 and received his first title shot in 1961 against Italian great **Duilio Loi** for the **World Boxing Association (WBA)** title. Loi retained the title after the bout in Milan was declared a draw. Perkins received another chance against Loi in Italy and this time won the title by unanimous decision. Perkins showed great skill and perseverance in overcoming two knockdowns to gain the title. He lost the title in a rubber match against Loi—another close decision. "I had what you call a raw deal," Perkins remarked of the decision.

Perkins received another shot at the title against champion Roberto Cruz in Manila, Philippines, in 1963 to capture the WBA and **World Boxing Council (WBC)** titles. Perkins dominated the action and won a unanimous decision. He held the title until he dropped a controversial 15-round split decision to Venezuelan Carlos Hernandez in Caracas, Venezuela. "I won all 15 rounds," Perkins said. He continued to fight until 1975, retiring after four straight decision losses. The great **Henry Armstrong** refereed the fight, and he scored the fight easily for Perkins, but he was overruled by two Venezuelan judges.

In 2008, Perkins was inducted into the International Boxing Hall of Fame.

Record:	75-20-2
Championship(s):	WBA junior welterweight, 1962; 1963–1965;
	WBC junior welterweight, 1963–1965

Further Reading
"Eddie Perkins, Wearing Tag 'I Was Robbed,' Okay Manila." *Chicago Daily Defender*, 6/10/1963, p. 22.
Markus, Robert. "Rioting Eddie Ends Exile." *Chicago Tribune*, 2/12/1970, p. D3.

PHILLIPS, VINCE (1963–). Vince Phillips is a former world junior welterweight champion best known for his upset of **Kostya Tszyu.** Born in 1963 in Pensacola, Florida, Phillips turned pro in 1990 and won his first 28 professional bouts before losing to the tough Anthony Jones in 1993. During this time, Phillips battled drug addiction—a disease that slowed his progress as a fighter. Three years later, Phillips challenged unbeaten welterweight champion Ike Quartey for the **International Boxing Federation (IBF)** welterweight title, losing in three rounds.

Phillips wisely dropped back down to the junior welterweight division and hit paydirt with a shocking kayo win over Tszyu in 1997. He made three successful defenses before losing to Terron Millett in 1999. He never received another world title shot and has now become a stepping stone for younger contenders.

In 2003, Phillips tried his hand at kickboxing in K-1 but lost badly to Masato.

Professional Record:	48-12-1
Championship(s):	IBF junior welterweight, 1997–1999

Further Reading
Maloney, Ed. "Vince Phillips: The Man Who Zapped Tsyzu Can't Get Any Higher." *The Ring* (October 1997), pp. 28–31, 59–61.

PICAL, ELLYAS (1960–). Ellyas "the Exocet" Pical is a former three-time world super flyweight champion and the first man from Indonesia to ever win a world boxing championship. Born in 1960 in Sapura, Pical turned pro in 1982 and only three years later kayoed China's Ju Do Chun in May 1985 to win the **International Boxing Federation (IBF)** super flyweight title.

He made one successful defense before dropping a 15-round split decision to Cesar Polanco in 1986. He regained the title in their rematch by stopping him with a body punch. Once again he made one successful defense before losing to the great **Khaosai Galaxy** in an abortive attempt to win the great Thai's **World Boxing Association (WBA)** belt. After the fight, the IBF stripped Pical of his title.

Undeterred, Pical regained his title for the third time with a split decision win over Tae-Il Chang in 1988. During his third reign, he made three successful defenses before losing to Juan Polo Perez.

In 2005, he was arrested for allegedly selling illegal drugs. After serving less than a year in jail, he was released.

Professional Record:	20-5-1
Championship(s):	IBF superflyweight, 1985–1986, 1987, 1987–1989

Further Reading
"Sports News: Pical Retains Title." *Associated Press,* 2/20/1988.

PINTOR, LUPE (1955–). Lupe Pintor was a tough former world champion in the bantamweight and super bantamweight divisions. Born in 1955 in Caujimalpa, Mexico, Pintor survived a tough childhood that for a time including living on the streets.

He turned pro in 1974. Five years later, in 1979, he earned a controversial 15-round split decision over **Carlos Zarate** to win the **World Boxing Council (WBC)** bantamweight. He made eight successful defenses, including a win over Scotsman Johnny Owen, who later died from injuries suffered during the bout.

In 1982, Pintor moved up in weight to challenge **Wilfredo Gomez** but lost in the 14th round. He won the super bantamweight title in 1985 with a win over Juan Meza but lost it in his first defense. He retired after the loss. He made a comeback many years later with no success.

Professional Record: 56-14-2
Championship(s):   WBC bantamweight, 1979–1982;
                                   WBC super bantamweight, 1985–1986

Further Reading
Broadbent, Rick. *The Big If: The Life and Death of Johnny Owen.* London: MacMillan, 2006.
Farhood, Steve. "The Super Super-Bantamweights: They'll Never Be the Same Again." *Knockout* (Summer 1994), pp. 30–32, 61.
Harris, Lee. "Boxer in Coma 6 Weeks After Knockout Dies." *Los Angeles Times,* 11/4/1980, p. A5.
Hoffer, Richard. "Zarate Is Upset After He's Upset." *Los Angeles Times,* 6/4/1979, p. B1.

POONTORAT, PAYAO (1954–2006). Payao Poontorat was a former super flyweight champion from Thailand who also became his country's first Olympic medalist in boxing with a bronze medal at the 1976 Montreal Games. Born in 1954 in Bangsapan, Thailand, he defeated fighters from Romania, the Soviet Union, and Hungary before losing to North Korean **Li Byung-Uk** in the finals of the light flyweight division.

He turned professional in 1981 and captured the **World Boxing Council (WBC)** super flyweight championship in only his 9th bout with a 12-round split decision win over Rafael Orono in 1983. He successfully defended his title once before losing a split decision to **Jiro Watanabe** in a 1984 fight in Tokyo. He retired in 1985.

After retirement, Poontorat later entered politics, earning a seat in Parliament. He died in 2006 from Amyotrophic Lateral Sclerosis (ALS).

Professional Record: 10-4-1
Championship(s):   WBC super flyweight, 1983–1984

Further Reading
Associated Press. "Thailand Boxer Wins Title." *The New York Times,* 11/28/1983, p. C4.

PRIDE. The Pride Fighting Championships was a premier mixed martial arts (MMA) organization based in Japan that boasted many of the top fighters in the world. Given its stable of top mixed martial artists and huge crowds, many aficionados of the sport considered PRIDE to be the best MMA organization in the world—on a par or even better than the **Ultimate Fighting Championships (UFC).** However, the UFC proved to be the better organized group, and it eventually purchased PRIDE in March 2007.

Despite such an ending, for nearly 10 years PRIDE provided some of the best fights in the world. **Antonio Rodrigo Nogueira, Fedor Emelianenko, Quinton "Rampage" Jackson, Dan "Hollywood" Henderson, Mirko "Cro Cop" Filopovic,** and **Anderson Silva** were just some of this era's top mixed martial artists who competed in PRIDE events.

Founded by Yukino Kanda, PRIDE held its first event in October 1997 at the Tokyo Dome in front of more than 40,000 fans. The first card was headlined by a "bout of the century" between **Rickson Gracie** and Japanese wrestler Nobuhiko Takada, which Gracie won. PRIDE prided itself on obtaining the services of the top mixed martial artists in the world.

PRIDE rules differed from that of the UFC in that the first round of PRIDE was 10 minutes long. PRIDE fights last three rounds—even for championship fights—rather than the five rounds for UFC title bouts. In addition, PRIDE allowed fighters to use knee and leg strikes to an opponent on the mat. PRIDE held its competitions in a 16-foot ring as opposed to the 32-foot octagon used in the UFC. PRIDE also disallowed the use of elbow strikes. Another aspect of PRIDE was that the referee could issue yellow cards to fighters who were not pushing the action and fighting. Yellow cards led to a reduction in the fighter's purses and often spurred on the action to an even higher pitch. Despite its huge commercial successes, PRIDE suffered setbacks. In 2003, PRIDE president Naoto Morishita committed suicide. In 2007, the organization was purchased by the UFC.

Further Reading
Gobetz, Mitch, and Todd Martin. "PRIDE Report Card." *FIGHT!* (June 2008), pp. 31–33.
Mezaros, Jeff. "PRIDE." *Extreme Fighter* (March 2008), pp. 32–33.
Official Web site: http://www.pridefc.com/pride2005/index_new_temp.php
Snowden, Jonathan. *Total MMA: Inside Ultimate Fighting.* Toronto: ECW Press, 2008.

PROFESSIONAL BOXING SAFETY ACT OF 1996. The Professional Boxing Safety Act of 1996 was a significant federal law that provided regulation and safety measures to the sport of boxing. Introduced by Senator John McCain, the measure was passed in large measure to protect the safety of journeyman boxers. Under the law, boxers must present a federal I.D. card to participate in a state-licensed boxing bout. The boxer then becomes listed in a boxing registry.

The law requires boxing commissions to report the results of fights and requires that such bouts be regulated by state commissions. It further required that those states without boxing commissioners must involve another state's boxing commission to oversee the event. The measure was passed in part to prevent boxers kayoed recently in one state from crossing interstate lines and participating in another bout in another state without adequate recovery time.

The great Aaron Pryor worked the corner of his son Aaron Pryor Jr. in an August 2006 bout in Las Vegas, Nevada. His son won a split decision. Courtesy of Chris Cozzone.

Further Reading
Anderson, Dave. "Finally! Federal Law for Boxing." *The New York Times*, 6/29/1997, p. S1.
Howard, Kelley C. "Regulating the Sport of Boxing—Congress Throws the First Punch with the Professional Boxing Safety Act." *Seton Hall Journal of Sports* 7 (1997), pp. 103–127.

PRYOR, AARON (1955–). Aaron "the Hawk" Pryor was a whirling dervish of a junior welterweight who overwhelmed his opponents with style reminiscent of "Hammering" **Henry Armstrong.** Born in 1955 in Cincinnati, Pryor compiled an outstanding amateur career but lost to Howard Davis, Jr., in the box-offs for the 1976 Montreal Olympics. Pryor turned professional in 1976 and in 1980 defeated the legendary **Antonio "Kid Pambele" Cervantes** to win the junior welterweight title. He successfully defended his title eight times, including two classic wars over fellow Hall-of-Famer **Alexis Arguello.** Pryor retired undefeated in 1985. He came back in 1987 and suffered the only loss of his professional career to Bobby Joe Young. He finally retired for good in 1990.

Professional Record: 39-1
Championship(s):   Junior Welterweight, 1980–1985

Further Reading
Countis, Rick. "Aaron Pryor: A Place Among the Superstars." *Knockout* (Summer 1994), pp. 26–29.
Terrill, Marshall. *The Flight of the Hawk: The Aaron Pryor Story.* Sun Lakes, AR: Book World, 1996.

PULVER, JENS (1974–). Jens "Little Evil" Pulver is one of the best fighters in the lower weight classes in mixed martial arts (MMA). Born in 1974 in Sunnyside, Washington, Pulver overcame a tough background and abusive father to excel in wrestling. Pulver won three straight state wrestling championships at Tahoma High School, losing only one match in his last three years. Upon graduation, he later wrestled for Highland Community College and Boise State University before an injury ended his amateur career.

He made his professional MMA debut in 1999 at the **Bas Rutten** Invitational. After five fights, he made his **Ultimate Fighting Championships (UFC)** debut at UFC 22: There Can Be Only One Champion drawing against Alfonzo Alcarez. In UFC 30: Battle on the Boardwalk, he defeated Carol Uno to become the UFC's inaugural lightweight champion, which had a weight limit of 155 lbs. He then successfully defended his title against Dennis Hallman and **B. J. "the Prodigy" Penn.** Pulver was the first man to defeat Penn in mixed martial arts.

Pulver vacated his title and later fought in both Shooto and **PRIDE** events. He lost to the legendary Japanese fighter **Takanori Gomi** by kayo in 2004. He returned to the UFC in 2006, losing to Joe Lauzon. Pulver starred on *The Ultimate Fighter* 5 as a coach against his rival Penn. At the conclusion of the season, at *The Ultimate Fighter* 5 Finale, Penn submitted Pulver with a rear naked choke in the second round.

Pulver rebounded to win his first fight in the World Extreme Cagefighting (WEC) organization, which is owned by Zuffa (the company that owns the UFC). Pulver lost a unanimous decision to WEC star **Urijah Faber** in 2008.

Professional MMA Record: 21-10-1
Professional Boxing Record: 4-0
Championship(s):   UFC Lightweight, 2001–2002

Further Reading
Davidson, Neil. "Jens Pulver: From the ultimate survivor to the Ultimate Fighter." *The Canadian Press,*
    10/25/2007.
MacKinnon, Timothy J. "Jens Pulver: A New Introduction." *FIGHT!* (June 2008), pp. 44–54.
MacKinnon, Timothy J. *Jens Pulver and the Wednesday Group That Will Change the World.* Bloomington,
    IN: iUniverse, 2007.
Official Web site: http://www.jenspulver.com/
Pulver, Jens, with Erick Krauss. *Little Evil. One Ultimate Fighter's Rise to the Top.* Ontario: ECW Press,
    2003.
Ringer, Sandy. "Once is Quite Enough for Pulver—Two-Time State Champion Vows to Bounce Back from
    Upset Loss." *The Seattle Times,* 1/12/1993, p. D4.

QAWI, DWIGHT MUHAMMAD (1953–). Dwight Muhammad Qawi was a rugged former light heavyweight and cruiserweight champion known for his relentless attacking style that more than made up for his short stature. Though he stood less than 5'7", he loomed large over the 175 lb. and 190 lb. divisions.

Born in 1953 in Baltimore, Maryland, Dwight Braxton moved with his family to Camden, New Jersey. One of 13 children, Braxton had a tough childhood, spending time in reform schools. At 19, he attempted to rob a liquor store, earning a prison sentence at Rahway State Prison.

After serving five and a half years, Braxton turned pro in 1978. He managed only a 1-1-1 record in his first three bouts. He progressed rapidly, including a 10-round decision over top contender **James Scott**—ironically, an inmate at Rahway State Prison who was allowed to box at the prison. Braxton did not like Scott when the two were inmates in Rahway, and he proceeded to win a 10-round decision victory.

That victory landed Braxton a shot at popular **World Boxing Council (WBC)** light heavyweight champion **Matthew Saad Muhammad.** Braxton punished Saad Muhammad, stopping the champion in the 10th round. Braxton also changed his name to Dwight Muhammad Qawi for religious reasons. He made three successful title defenses before losing his title in a unification bout with **World Boxing Association (WBA)** champion **Michael Spinks.**

In 1985, Qawi won the WBC cruiserweight championship by defeating Piet Crous in South Africa. He made one successful defense against former heavyweight champion **Leon Spinks** before losing his title to **Evander Holyfield.**

He then lost to a comebacking **George Foreman.** Qawi did not fare as well when he moved up to the heavyweight division. In November 1989, he fought **Robert Daniels** for the vacant WBC cruiserweight title but lost a 12-round decision. He finally retired for good in 1998.

Professional Record:	41-11-1
Championship(s):	WBC light heavyweight, 1981–1983; WBC cruiserweight, 1985–1986

Further Reading

Associated Press. "Qawi, a/k/a Braxton: Under Any Name, He's Still Champ," *Los Angeles Times*, 11/21/1982, p. D20.

Katz, Michael. "Braxton 'Amazed' at His Prowess." *The New York Times*, 8/9/1982, p. C9.

Katz, Michael. "Braxton vs. Scott: A Rahway Grudge." *The New York Times*, 9/3/1981, p. D20.

Katz, Michael. "A Champion's Rocky Road." *The New York Times*, 3/10/1982, p. B9.

Roberts, James B., and Alexander G. Skutt. *The Boxing Register: International Boxing Hall of Fame Official Record Book* (4th ed.). Ithaca, NY: McBooks Press, Inc., 2006, pp. 592–595.

QUARRY, JERRY (1945–1999). Jerry Quarry was a former top-flight heavyweight contender who never captured the world title but defeated many great heavyweights in his day. Born in 1945 in Bakersfield, California, he first put on a pair of boxing gloves at age 3. He fought in the amateurs until turning pro in 1965. He won his first 12 fights before a draw with Tony Doyle. He didn't lose until dropping a decision in 1966 to tough veteran Eddie Machen.

In 1967, Quarry made his move, earning a draw and a victory over former two-time world champ **Floyd Patterson.** In April 1968, he lost a majority decision to **Jimmy Ellis** for the vacant **World Boxing Association (WBA)** world heavyweight title. In 1969, he challenged **Joe Frazier** for the heavyweight title but lost on cuts in the eighth round.

He never received another world title shot but continued to remain a top contender for much of the 1970s. He lost twice to **Muhammad Ali.** In fact, he was Ali's first opponent after his exile for the Vietnam draft controversy. In one of his finest outings, Quarry kayoed **Earnie Shavers** in the first round in 1974. He initially retired after losing to **Ken Norton** in 1975 but made a few comebacks. His last fight was a six-round loss to Ron Cramer when Quarry was 47 years old.

He died in 1999 from dementia pugilistica. He was the best of the Quarry boxing brothers; Mike and Bobby Quarry never scaled the same heights.

Professional Record:	53-9-4
Championship(s):	None

Further Reading

Allen, Jerry. "Promoters Line Up for Jerry Quarry." *Los Angeles Times*, 4/17/1966, p. H9.

Distel, Dave. "Jerry Quarry: A Fistic Enigma." *Los Angeles Times*, 6/16/1972, p. F1.

Finch, Frank. "Quarry Calls Frazier Chicken, Mathis a Bum." *Los Angeles Times*, 1/6/1968, p. A1.

Flaherty, Joe. "The Ups and Downs of Jerry Quarry." *Los Angeles Times*, 6/15/1969, p. M1.

Goldstein, Richard. "Jerry Quarry, 53, Boxer Battered by Years in Ring, Dies." *The New York Times*, 1/5/1999, p. A15.

Hamilton, Tom. "Jerry Quarry Lets Boxing Have It on the Chin." *Los Angeles Times*, 4/12/1979, p. OC_B13.

QUEENSBERRY RULES. The Queensberry Rules are considered modern boxing's leading rules and regulations. Named after its patron, John Sholto Douglas—otherwise known as the Marquis of Queensbury—the rules were written by John Graham Chambers. The rules provided for three-minute rounds with a minute rest in between, boxing gloves, and a ring near the size of 24-square feet. The rules also provided for what constituted a legal knockdown in the sport.

Further Reading

Cyber Boxing Zone Encyclopedia. "Marquis of Queensberry Rules Governing Contests for Endurance (1865)," at http://www.cyberboxingzone.com/boxing/q-rules.htm

RAHMAN, HASIM (1972–). Hasim "the Rock" Rahman is a former world heavyweight champion and current contender whose career has been plagued with inconsistent performances. Born in Baltimore in 1972, Rahman turned professional and won his first 29 bouts. In 1998, he faced fellow contender **David Tua.** Rahman dominated the action with his superior reach and boxing skills, leading easily on all three scorecards. Tua hurt Rahman with a devastating punch

Hasim Rahman eats a right hand from Oleg Maskaev in their August 2006 bout. Rahman lost in the final round. Courtesy of Chris Cozzone.

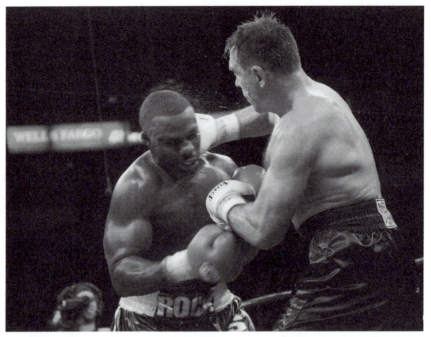

Rahman does battle with his nemesis Maskaev in their August 2006 bout. Courtesy of Chris Cozzone.

Hasim Rahmn looks ready to go to battle with Oleg Maskaev in their August 2006 bout. Rahman lost in the final round. Courtesy of Chris Cozzone.

after the bell of the ninth round. Rahman could not recover, and Tua finished him off in the next round. In March 1999, the pattern reemerged, as Rahman outboxed Oleg Maskaev until a single right hand knocked him through the ropes and out in the eighth round.

Rahman rebounded in April 2001 with a shocking upset of **Lennox Lewis,** kayoing the champion with a single right hand bomb in the fifth round in Brakman, South Africa, to win the world championship. It was one of the biggest upsets in boxing history, as Lewis had dominated the heavyweight division for several years. Rahman lost the title in a rematch later that calendar year. In 2005, he won the **World Boxing Council (WBC)** title with a win over Monte Barrett but lost the belt to his nemesis Maskaev in a final-round kayo in 2006. He rebounded in 2007 with several straight wins, but lost to **Wladimir Klitschko** in another attempt at regaining the heavyweight title.

Professional Record: 45-7-2

World Championship(s):   WBC Heavyweight, 2001, 2005–2006.

Further Reading

Murphy, John. "Rahman revels in title: 'That's How You Fight,'" *The Baltimore Sun*, 4/23/2001, p. 1D.

Satterfield, Lem and Mike Klingaman. "Punches Land Close to Home; For Rahmans, a Life of Blood, Sweat and Fears." *The Baltimore Sun*, 8/6/2006, p. 1D.

The Ring Exclusive. "Heavyweight King Hasim Rahman." *The Ring* (September 2001), pp. 28–32, 88–89.

RAMOS, MANDO (1945–2008). Mando Ramos was a boxing prodigy who twice won the world lightweight championship. If he had better discipline outside the ring, he may have accomplished even more. Ramos had more trouble battling alcohol then he did ring opponents. Born in 1948 in Long Beach, California, Ramos turned pro in 1965 and won his first 17 bouts. In 1968, he challenged Carlos "Teo" Cruz for the world lightweight title and lost a close unanimous decision. The next year the 20-year-old Ramos defeated Cruz to capture the championship. He lost his title to Ishmael Laguna in 1970. Two years later, he won the title again with a decision over **Pedro Carrasco**. He lost the title later in 1972 and never fought for a world title again. He retired in 1975. He passed away in 2008 at the age of 59.

Professional Record: 37-11-1

Championship(s):   Lightweight, 1969–1970; WBA lightweight 1972

Further Reading

Hafner, Dan. "Mando Ramos: Always on the Ropes." *Los Angeles Times*, 12/26/1973, p. C1.

RAMOS, ULTIMINIO "SUGAR" (1941–). Ultiminio "Sugar" Ramos was a featherweight champion known for his powerful right hand and for a horrible tragedy that occurred to one of his opponents. Born in 1941 in Mantanzas, Cuba, Ramos lived life early. He married at age 12, fathered a child at age 14 and divorced at age 15.

He turned pro in 1957 in Havana. In 1963, he challenged champion **Davey Moore** for the featherweight championship. In the 10th round, Ramos drilled Moore with a series of punches that dropped the champion. On his way to the canvas, Moore's head hit the bottom rope. Moore rose at the count of three but could not come out for the next round. He spoke with reporters after the fight but then fell into a coma from which he never awoke. Ramos wept when he learned the fate of his opponent. He defended the title several times before falling to **Vincente Saldivar** in September 1964. In 1966 and 1967, he challenged **Carlos Ortiz** for the lightweight title but lost badly both times. He finally retired in 1972.

Professional Record: 55-7-4

Championship(s):   Featherweight, 1963–1964

Further Reading

Hafner, Dan. "Sugar Ramos: A Lot of Living in 28 Years." *Los Angeles Times*, 3/22/1970, p. C13.

Roberts, James B., and Alexander G. Skutt. *The Boxing Register: International Boxing Hall of Fame Register* (4th ed.). Ithaca, NY: McBooks Press, Inc., 2006, pp. 596–599.

RANDLEMAN, KEVIN (1971–). Kevin "the Monster" Randleman is an explosive mixed martial artist known for his incredible strength and athleticism, wrestling skills, and unpredictability. Born in 1971 in Sandusky, Ohio, Randleman was a star wrestler for Ohio State University, twice winning the NCAA championships in 1992 and 1993. He began his mixed martial arts (MMA) career in 1996 at the Universal Vale Tudo competition in Brazil under the guidance of **Mark Coleman.** Randleman moved to the **Ultimate Fighting Championships (UFC)** in 1999, challenging the great **Bas Rutten** for the vacant heavyweight championship at UFC 20: Battle for the Gold. He lost a split decision despite having Rutten on the ground for the majority of the match.

In his next bout, he faced Pete Williams at UFC 23: Ultimate Japan 2 for the UFC heavyweight title following Rutten's retirement. Randleman won a unanimous decision to win the belt. He successfully defended his title at UFC 26: Ultimate Field of Dreams with a win over the dangerous and then undefeated **Pedro Rizzo.** He lost his title to the great **Randy Couture** at UFC 28: High Stakes. Randleman then had a successful run in **PRIDE,** defeating Renato Sobral, Kenichi Yamamoto, and Murilo Rua. He suffered his first loss in PRIDE at PRIDE 25: Body Blow to **Quinton "Rampage" Jackson.** In April 2004, at PRIDE Shockwave 2004, Randleman scored the greatest win of his career with a devastating first-round kayo over the favored **Mirko "Cro Cop" Filopovic.** It is still considered one of the most brutal knockouts in MMA history. Randleman later suffered losses to **Fedor Emelianenko, Ron Waterman,** Mirko "Cro Cop" (in a rematch), and **Mauricio "Shogun" Rua.** He has battled health problems since 2007.

Professional Record:	17-12
Championship(s):	UFC Heavyweight, 1999–2000

Further Reading
Official Web site: http://www.kevinrandleman.com/

RANDOLPH, LEO (1958−). Leo Randolph won the highest honors as both an amateur and professional boxer, capturing gold at the 1976 Montreal Olympics along with higher profile teammates **Sugar Ray Leonard, Leon Spinks,** and **Michael Spinks.** He also garnered a world championship in the professional ranks in 1980. Born in 1958 in Tacoma, Washington, Randolph pulled the shocker of the Olympic Games when he upset favored Cuban boxer Ramon Duvalon to win the gold medal. He turned professional in 1978 and earned a title shot against **World Boxing Association (WBA)** super bantamweight champion Ricardo Cardona in 1980. Cardona dropped Randolph in the fifth round and bloodied the challenger, but Randolph rallied in the later rounds and stopped Cardona in the 15th round. He lost the title in his first defense to Sergio Victor Palma. Randolph retired after that loss.

Professional Record:	17-2
World Championship:	WBA super bantamweight, 1980

Further Reading
Associated Press. "Randolph Wins Title." *The New York Times,* 5/5/1980, p. C2.

REID, DAVID (1973−). For many years in his boxing career, David Reid lived up to his nickname "the American Dream." Blessed with incredible hand speed, Reid had an impressive amateur career, which included a gold medal in the junior middleweight division at the 1996 Olympics in Atlanta. Entering the gold-medal round, Reid faced the Cuban world champion Alfredo Duvergel. In the third and final round, Duvergel had a commanding lead. Duvergel had hurt Reid in the second round, and the American had to take a standing eight-count. However, "the American Dream" landed the most dramatic punch in the history of U.S.A. Olympic boxing, kayoing the Cuban great and capturing the U.S. Boxing team's only gold medal.

Reid turned pro the next year, making his debut against an undefeated pugilist with 10 victories. Reid won that bout and in only his fifth pro bout he easily defeated former world welterweight champion Jorge Vaca. In his 12th pro bout, he outpointed Laurent Boudouani to win the

World Boxing Association (WBA) junior middleweight title. He successfully defended his title twice before facing the undefeated **Felix Trinidad**—the longtime welterweight champion who was moving up in weight. Reid dropped Trinidad in the third round and looked to be on his way to the biggest win of his young boxing career. However, Trinidad recovered and pounded Reid over 12 rounds. Reid suffered a detached retina from the beating and never was the same fighter. He retired in 2001 after losing to unheralded Sam Hill.

Professional Record:	17-2
Championship(s):	WBA junior middleweight, 1999–2000

Further Reading

Collins, Nigel. "David Reid: Yesterday, Today, & Tomorrow." *The Ring* (January 1997), pp. 35–37, 54–55.

Smith, Timothy. "Trinidad Takes Control to Win Decision Over Reid." *The New York Times*, 3/4/2000, p. D1.

Wise, Mike. "Victory for Reid Arrives with a Single Punch." *The New York Times*, 8/5/1996, p. C1.

RICKARD, GEORGE LEWIS "TEX" (1870–1929). George Lewis "Tex" Rickard was one of sports' great promoters known for owning the New York Rangers hockey team and for promoting several world title bouts involving popular heavyweight champion **Jack Dempsey.** Born in 1871 in Missouri, Rickard made a fortune chasing gold in Alaska and Nevada before turning his attention to boxing.

He became boxing's greatest promoter, staging bouts between **Joe Gans** and **Battling Nelson.** He also promoted several of Jack Dempsey's bouts, including his historic clashes with **Jess Willard** and **Georges Carpentier.** He later made Madison Square Garden into the premier boxing venue in the country. It became known as "The House That Tex Built." Upon his death the Associated Press referred to him as "the Czar of Boxing."

Further Reading

Associated Press. "Tex Rickard, Greatest Promoter, Dies at Miami." *The Atlanta Constitution*, 1/7/1929, p. 1.

Rickard, Tex. "Tex Rickard Starts Story of Champions." *The Atlanta Constitution*, 1/20/1924, p. C4.

Samuels, Charles. *The Magnificent Rube: The Life and Gaudy Times of Tex Rickard.* New York: McGraw Hill, 1957.

Williams, Harry A. "Tex Rickard Crafty and Cunning Promoter." *The New York Times*, 1/14/1916, p. III3.

RIJKER, LUCIA (1967–). Lucia Rijker was one of the greatest female boxing champions ever. A former kickboxing champion, Rijker never lost a professional boxing bout in 17 contests. Born in 1967 in Amsterdam, Rijker enjoyed great success as a professional kickboxer, winning all 36 of her bouts, including 25 by knockout.

In 1996, she made her debut as a boxer, stopping her opponent in the first round. She fought professionally until 2004, never coming close to losing a fight. In 2005, she signed a deal to face longtime nemesis **Christy Martin,** but Rijker suffered an injury in training, and the fight had to be canceled. Many experts believe she is the finest female boxer ever, though she never was tested in the ring given her superior skills.

Rijker achieved fame for the documentary about her titled *Shadow Boxers* and, particularly, for her role as "Bille the Blue Bear" in the hit movie *Million Dollar Baby*, starring Hilary Swank and directed by Clint Eastwood. She currently stars on the Showtime hit series *The L-Word.*

Professional Boxing Record:	17-0
Professional Kickboxing Record:	36-0

Further Reading
Official Web site: http://www.luciarijker.net/
Petrakis, John. "'Shadow Boxers' Showcases A Stylist." *The Chicago Tribune*, 12/29/2000, at C-1.
Plaschke, Bill. "One in a Million." *Los Angeles Times*, 7/10/2005, p. D1.

RIZZO, PEDRO (1974–). Pedro "the Rock" Rizzo is a Brazilian-based mixed martial artist known for his excellent striking ability. Born in 1974 in Rio de Janeiro, Rizzo turned pro in 1996 and two years later made a successful debut at the **Ultimate Fighting Championships (UFC)** Brazil with a first-round kayo of **David "Tank" Abbott.** Rizzo had a great year in the Octagon in 1999; he won consecutive bouts against **Mark Coleman,** Tra Telligman, and Tsuyoshi Kohsaka. Those wins led Rizzo to a bout with **Kevin "the Monster" Randleman** for the UFC heavyweight championship. He lost a decision over five rounds.

He rebounded with wins over UFC legend **Dan Severn** and the behemoth **Josh Barnett.** Those wins landed Rizzo another shot at the UFC heavyweight title against **Randy "the Natural" Couture.** Rizzo again lost a decision. In a rematch at UFC 34: High Voltage, he again lost to Couture. In September 2007, he defeated Jeff Monson to win the heavyweight championship in the Undisputed Arena Fighting Championships. In 2008, he lost via kayo to Barnett in a long-awaited rematch promoted by **Affliction.**

Professional MMA Record: 16-8
Championship(s):   None

Further Reading
Blaze, Joe. "Pedro 'the Rock' Rizzo Interview." *MMAWeekly.com*, 11/14/2003, at http://www.mmaringreport.com/text-interviews/text-interviews/pedro-the-rock-rizzo-interview.html

ROACH, FREDDIE (1960–). "Fast" Freddie Roach was a former welterweight contender who has made a more significant impact on the sport of boxing as a trainer. Born in Dedham, Massachusetts, in 1960, Roach learned to box when he was very young. After a successful amateur career, he turned pro in 1978 and won his first 10 fights. He frequently fought on ESPN during his heyday. Roach could not scale the upper echelons of the division, losing to such fighters as **Hector "Macho" Camacho, Bobby Chacon,** Greg Haugen, and Darryl Tyson. He finally retired in 1986 with a record of 39-13. He worked as a trainer under his former mentor **Eddie Futch.** The first world champion Roach handled was **Virgil Hill,** a light heavyweight and cruiserweight champion. Through the years, Roach has worked with numerous top-flight fighters, including **Oscar De La Hoya, Mike Tyson,** James Toney, and **Manny Pacquiao.** Roach also worked with mixed martial artist **Andrei Arlovski** for his bout with **Fedor Emelianenko** and plans to guide Arlovski's professional boxing career.

Professional Record: 39-13
Championship(s):   None

Further Reading
Feour, Royce. "Trainer Roach was once an exciting boxer." *Las Vegas Review-Journal*, 1/19/2006, p. 7C.
Lidz, Frank. "Loyalty and Honesty? In the Ring?: Believe it. Freddie Roach is one of the hottest trainers in the game because his fighters know they can trust him." *Sports Illustrated*, 6/7/2004, p. Z9.

ROBINSON, SUGAR RAY (1921–1989). Pound-for-pound, most boxing experts agree that the greatest fighter in boxing history was Sugar Ray Robinson. A skilled boxer with fine

Expert trainer Freddie Roach poses with his prize pupil Manny Pacquiao after a victory over Erik Morales in November 2006. Courtesy of Chris Cozzone.

defensive skills, Robinson also possessed one-punch kayo power. Many considered him the perfect fighter in his prime. Born Walker Smith, Jr., in Detroit, Michigan, in 1921, he learned boxing as a youngster at the same location where his early idol **Joe Louis** did. When he first fought as an amateur, he used the boxing card of another fighter named Ray Robinson. The rest, as they say, was history, as it became clear that Ray Robinson was sweeter than "Sugar" in the boxing ring.

After a successful amateur career, he turned professional in 1940 and kept winning. He earned victories over **Sammy Angott, Jake LaMotta,** and **Fritzie Zivic.** His only loss in his first 100 fights was a decision loss to LaMotta in their second of five meetings. In 1946, he finally received a title shot and defeated Tommy Bell to win the world welterweight title. In his first defense, he stopped Jimmy Doyle, who later died as a result of injuries from the bout. He never lost his welterweight championship but later moved up in weight to the middleweight division.

He captured the middleweight belt for the first time with a stoppage of LaMotta. He then won and lost the title on several more occasions, earning the middleweight title five different times. He had storied rivalries with such fighters as **Gene Fullmer, Carmen Basilio,** and Randy Turpin.

He nearly added the light heavyweight belt in 1952 when he outboxed Joey Maxim for 13 rounds but fell victim to the New York summer heat and was stopped in the 14th round. He finally retired from the ring at age 44 in 1965.

Robinson also introduced the modern concept of an entourage, as he traveled with a voice coach, masseur, and others. He often traveled in a pink Cadillac and owned several businesses in Harlem. He was a unique individual and a unique fighter.

Professional Record: 173-19-6
Championship(s):   Welterweight, 1946–1951; Middleweight, 1951,
                                1951–1952, 1955–1957, 1958–1960.

Further Reading
Boyd, Herb, with Ray Robinson II. *Pound for Pound: A Biography of Sugar Ray Robinson*. New York: Amistad Press, 2006.
Robinson, Sugar Ray, and Dave Anderson. *Sugar Ray*. New York: Viking Press, 1970.
Shropshire, Kenneth. *Being Sugar Ray: The Life of Sugar Ray Robinson, America's Greatest Boxer and First Celebrity Athlete*. New York: Basic Civitas Book, 2007.
Smith, Wilfrid. "Robinson Knocks Out Fullmer in Fifth." *Chicago Daily Tribune*, 5/2/1957, p. D1.

RODGERS, MIKE (1970–). Michael David Rodgers, or Mike Rodgers, was a cult legend on the Tennessee boxing circuit where he campaigned under the nickname of "the Honkytonk Hitman." Born in 1970 in Arkansas, Rodgers compiled more than 150 wins as an amateur under the expert tutelage of his father Ray Rodgers—a leader in amateur boxing and a leading cutman in professional boxing.

However, Rodgers's main passion for much of his life was music and he traveled the Southeast in the pursuit of a country music career. Rodgers did not box for more than eight years after the conclusion of his amateur career until in 1997, he traveled to Nashville, "Music City," in hopes of furthering his music career. Homeless and in need of money, Rodgers learned that promoter Jimmy Adams was holding regular shows at the Music Mix Factory. The matchmaker did not know of Rodgers' amateur background. Instead, they threw him in the ring as an opponent. In his first pro fight in 1997, he entered the ring in a pair of tennis shoes, swimming trunks, and his cowboy hat. Somebody in the crowd yelled, "Who are you? The Honkytonk Hitman?" The legend of the Honky Tonk Hitman had begun.

Rodgers fought professionally until 2002. In his last bout, he defeated Art Jimmerson—Royce Gracie's first opponent in mixed martial arts in the UFC—for the World Boxing Federation's (WBF) super cruiserweight championship.

Professional Record:	25-2
Championship(s):	No major championships

Further Reading
Hudson, David. "The Legend of the Honky Tonk Hitman: Mike Rodgers," *Boxing Digest*, July 2002, p. 41.
Kuharsky, Paul. "Sweet Chin Music," *The Tennessean*, 8/9/2001, p. 1C.

RODRIGUEZ, LUIS (1937–1996). Luis Rodriguez was a great welterweight champion in the 1960s best known for his rivalry with **Emile Griffith.** Born in 1937 in Camaguey, Cuba, Rodriguez turned pro in 1956 and later traveled to Miami Beach, Florida, to work with **Angelo Dundee.** In 1963, he defeated Griffith by a 15-round unanimous decision to win the welterweight crown. He lost the title in his first defense in a rematch to Griffith by a controversial split decision. In 1964, he lost another split decision to Griffith for the title. He later moved up in weight to the middleweight division and challenged **Nino Benvenuti** for the title. He outboxed Benvenuti for much of the bout, but lost in the 11th round. He kept fighting until 1972.

Professional Record:	107-13
Championship(s):	Welterweight, 1963

Further Reading
Allen, John. "It's Unanimous: Rodriguez Too Much for Carter." *Los Angeles Times*, 8/27/1965, p. B1.
Allison, Granville, Jr. "Rodriguez Foils Critics." *The Chicago Defender*, 2/27/1960, p. 24.
De La Vega, John. "Rodriguez Modest, but Confident Boxer." *Los Angeles Times*, 4/3/1960, p. H5.

Roberts, James B., and Alexander G. Skutt. *The Boxing Register: International Boxing Hall of Fame Register* (4th ed.). Ithaca, NY: McBooks Press, Inc., 2006, pp. 608–611.

RODRIGUEZ, RICCO (1977–). Ricco "Suave" Rodriguez is a former **Ultimate Fighting Championships (UFC)** heavyweight champion who has competed in **PRIDE, Elite XC,** World Extreme Challenge, YAMMA, and many others. Born in 1977 in San Jose, California, Rodriguez grew up in New York. He excelled as a wrestler in high school. Upon graduation, he moved back to California where he studied extensively in Brazilian jiu-jitsu.

He turned pro in 1999 and won his first three fights before losing to Bobby Hoffman at SuperBrawl 13 in September 1999. He then won six straight bouts, including wins over **Gary "Big Daddy" Goodridge** and **Paul Buentello.** That earned him a bout in the Octagon against **Andrei Arlovski** at UFC 32. Rodriguez stopped Arlovski in the third round.

He then defeated Pete Williams, Jeff Monson, and Tyushosi Kohsaka in consecutive UFC bouts. This landed Rodriguez a fight against **Randy "the Natural" Couture** for the vacant UFC heavyweight championship. Rodriguez submitted Couture in the fifth and final round to win the title.

He lost the title in his first defense against **Tim Sylvia.** In his next two bouts, he lost a disputed decision to **Antonio Rodrigo Nogueira** in a PRIDE bout and then to Pedro Rizzo in the UFC. His career never again reached its championship level when he defeated Couture.

Mike "the Honkytonk Hitman" Rodgers proudly displays his World Boxing Federation (WBF) super cruiserweight championship, which he won in October 2002. Courtesy of Mike Rodgers.

He took some time away from mixed martial arts (MMA), including a well-publicized role in the reality television show *Celebrity Rehab*. He currently fights under the YAMMA Pit Fighting banner and hopes to regain his past glory.

Professional MMA Record: 32-9
Championship(s):   UFC Heavyweight, 2002–2003

Further Reading
Frazer, Bear. "Where Are They Now? Ricco Rodriguez." *FIGHT!* (October–November 2007), pp. 58–59.
Frias, Daniel. "Ricco ready for the next chapter." *Press Telegram*, 7/21/2006, at http://www.presstelegram.com/mixedmartialarts/ci_4077061

ROGAN, JOE (1967–). Joe Rogan is a popular comedian and television personality who serves as the color commentator for **Ultimate Fighting Championships (UFC)** events. Born in Bridgewater, New Jersey, in 1967, Rogan holds a black belt in jiu-jitsu and has studied various martial arts disciplines, including kung fu, Kempo karate, and Muay Thai. At 19, he captured the U.S. Open lightweight Tae Kwon Do championship. In 1996, he began work as an interviewer for the UFC and in 2002 became the color commentator. He still interviews fighters in the Octagon after their bouts.

Further Reading
Official Web site: http://www.joerogan.net
Walker, Andrew. "The UFC's Ultimate Commentator: Joe Rogan." *Extreme Fighter* (March 2008),
    pp. 20–23.

ROMAN, GILBERTO (1961–1990). Gilberto Roman was a two-time super flyweight world champion who may have added a third belt if not for a deadly auto accident that took his life in 1990. Born in 1961 in Mexicali, BC, Mexico, Roman represented his country at the 1980 Moscow Olympics. He lost in the second round of the flyweight competition to Bulgarian Peter Lessov, the eventual gold medalist.

Roman turned pro in 1981 and won his first 10 bouts before a disqualification loss. He then pulled off 22 more wins before another disqualification loss. In 1986, he faced longtime super flyweight champion **Jiro Watanabe.** Roman won a 12-round unanimous decision to capture the title. He successfully defended the title six times before losing on cuts to Santos Benigno Laciar in the 11th round. At the time of the stoppage, Roman was ahead on the scorecards.

In 1988, he recaptured the title with a decisive decision win over undefeated Sugar Baby Rojas. He successfully defended the title five times including a win over Laciar before losing to Nana Konadu in 1989. His last fight was a 1990 loss to Sung-Kil Moon for the **World Boxing Council (WBC)** belt. He died in an auto accident later that year.

Professional Record:	54-6-1
Championship(s):	WBC super flyweight, 1986–1987; 1988–1989

Further Reading
Associated Press. "Gilberto Roman, 29, Ex-Boxing Champion." *The New York Times*, 6/30/1990, p. 29.
Gustkey, Earl. "Roman Downed in Fourth But Wins Fight at Forum." *Los Angeles Times*, 6/6/1989, p. SP 2.
Springer, Steve. "Roman Retains His WBC Super Flyweight Title." *Los Angeles Times*, 9/13/1989, p. SP 6.

ROSARIO, EDWIN (1963–1997). Edwin "El Chapo" Rosario was one of the best fighters of the 1980s and early 1990s who was a dominant force in the lightweight division. Unfortunately, Rosario's ring greatness was offset by a drug problem that eventually cost him his life at only 34 years of age. Born in 1963 in Toa Baja, Puerto Rico, Rosario turned to boxing before he was a teenager. He attracted the attention of trainer Manny Siaco, who trained former lightweight great **Esteban DeJesus.**

He turned professional in 1979 with a victory in the Dominican Republic. He kept winning and earned a shot at the vacant **World Boxing Council (WBC)** lightweight title in 1983 with a 12-round decision win over Jose Luis Ramirez. In his third title defense, he faced Ramirez in a rematch. He dropped Ramirez in the first two rounds but lost on a technical knockout in the fourth round—the first loss of his professional career. In 1986, he lost a split decision to **Hector "Macho" Camacho** in an attempt to regain his title. Later that year, however, he crushed the tough **Livingstone Bramble** to win the **World Boxing Association (WBA)** lightweight title.

He lost his title to the great **Julio Cesar Chavez** in 1987 but regained it for the third time with a sixth-round knockout of Anthony Jones in 1988. He later won the WBA junior welterweight title in 1991 but lost it in his first title defense. He stopped fighting for several years while he battled drug problems. He returned to the ring in 1997 and won five straight fights before dying.

Professional Record: 47-6
Championship(s):   WBC lightweight, 1983–1984; WBA lightweight,
                              1986–1987; WBA junior welterweight, 1991–1992

Further Reading

Collins, Nigel. "Camacho's Great Escape." *The Ring* (September 1986), pp. 36–39.
Katz, Michael. "Rosario, 18, Seems Headed for a Title." *The New York Times*, 6/23/1981, p. A22.
Waters, Mike. "Way Overdue: Long-Overlooked Lightweight is Honored Posthumously." *Post-Standard*,
    6/12/2006.

ROSE, LIONEL (1948–). Lionel Rose became the first Aboriginal to win a world boxing title in 1970 when he captured the world bantamweight title. Born in 1948 in Jackson's Track Victoria, Australia, Rose learned to box from his father, Roy, who used to fight all comers at local fairs and carnivals. Unfortunately, Roy died of a heart attack when young Lionel was 14. The next year, Lionel captured an Australian flyweight amateur title at age 15.

He turned pro in 1964 and in 1968 upset **Mashiko "Fighting" Harada** in Tokyo, Japan, to win the world bantamweight championship. He dropped the champion near the end of the ninth round and used his height and reach advantages deftly to win a unanimous decision. He successfully defended his title three times—including narrow wins over Takao Sakurai and **Chucho Castillo.** Rose's split decision victory over Castillo in Los Angeles caused a riot at the Forum in Los Angeles, including fires and a barrage of bottles hurled into the ring.

Rose lost his title to Mexican power puncher **Ruben Olivares** in 1969. In 1971, Rose nearly captured the **World Boxing Council (WBC)** super featherweight title, losing a close decision to Yoshiaki Numata. He finally retired in 1976.

Professional Record: 42-11
Championship(s):   Bantamweight, 1968–1969

Further Reading

Farris, Rick. "A Walkabout With Lionel Rose." *Cyber Boxing Zone Journal*, Febuary 2000, at http://www.
    cyberboxingzone.com/boxing/box2-htm
Newhan, Ross. "Whiskey Bottle Barely Missed Rose in Riot." *Los Angeles Times*, 12/7/1968, p. C5.
Trengrove, Alan. "Rose Fights Way Out of Despair of Australian Bush to Bantamweight Title." *The New
    York Times*, 8/18/1968, p. S4.
Trumble, Robert. "Aussie Aboriginal Upsets Harada." *The New York Times*, 2/28/1968, p. 56.
Trumble, Robert. "Rose Floored by Sakurai in 2d, But Keeps Bantamweight Title." *The New York Times*,
    7/3/1968, p. 41.
United Press International. "Rose Whips Harada, Takes Bantam Crown." *Chicago Daily Defender*,
    2/28/1968, p. 29.

ROSEMBLOOM, MAXIE (1903–1976). Maxie Rosembloom was a sweet-boxing former light heavyweight champion who won more than 200 professional bouts in his career, which spanned from 1923–1936. Born in 1903 in Harlem, Rosembloom turned pro in 1923 and baffled opponents from the beginning with his exceptional defensive skills.

In 1930, he defeated Jimmy Slattery to win the light heavyweight championship. He held the title until losing a decision to Bob Olin in 1934. During the course of his career, he defeated such great fighters as **Mickey "the Toy Bulldog" Walker,** John Henry Lewis (whom he also lost to), and future heavyweight champion **James J. Braddock.**

Upon retirement, Rosembloom had a successful career in film, radio, and business.

| Professional Record: | 210-38-26 (23 no decisions) |
| Championship(s): | Light Heavyweight, 1930–1934 |

Further Reading
Rosenbloom, Maxie. "Ouch, That Hurt." *The Atlanta Constitution*, 1/27/1930, p. 8.
Tomasson, Robert E. "Maxie Rosenbloom Dead; Boxer and Actor was 71." *The New York Times*, 3/8/1976, p. 27.

ROSS, BARNEY (1909–1967). Barney Ross was a former three-division world champion recognized by boxing experts as one of the greatest fighters in the history of the sport. Born in 1909 in New York City, Beryl David Rosofsky grew up in Chicago in a Jewish family. He took the ring name Barney Ross, and the rest was history. He turned professional in 1929 and by 1933 had won world championships in the lightweight, junior welterweight, and welterweight divisions. He defeated a "who's who" list of great fighters, including **Tony Canzoneri, Jimmy McLarnin,** and Billy Petrolle. His greatest rivalry was with fellow Hall-of-Famer McLarnin. From 1934–1935, the two fought three 15-round decisions with Ross taking two of them. Ross retired in 1938 after losing badly to **Henry Armstrong** for the welterweight title. Despite taking great punishment, Ross refused to hit the canvas. He lost only four fights in his entire career and was never stopped.

Professional Record:	72-4-3
Championship(s):	Lightweight, 1933–1935; junior welterweight,
	1933–1935; welterweight, 1933–1938.

Further Reading
Century, Douglas. *Barney Ross*. New York: Schocken, 2006.
Evans, Gavin. "The 20 Greatest Welterweights of All Time." *The Ring* (February 2008), pp. 63–84, 78.
Ross, Barney, and Martin Abramson. *No Man Stands Alone: The True Story of Barney Ross*. New York: Lippincoff, 1957.

ROUFUS, RICK (1967–). Rick Roufus is an American kickboxing legend who dominated the International Kickboxing Federation in the early 1990s. Born in 1967 in Milwaukee, Wisconsin, Roufus was nicknamed "the Jet" for his prowess with his hands and feet. In the early 1990s, Roufus switched his attention to professional boxing. He compiled a record of 13-5-1. He returned to kickboxing in the late 1990s, winning another world championship in the International Kickboxing Federation (IFF).

In 1997, he began fighting in K-1 competitions, compiling a career record of 9-5. He defeated Jeff Ford, Akebono, and the great **Maurice Smith.** However, he lost to **Michael McDonald,** Jerome Le Banner, and Carter Williams. In February 2008, he made his mixed martial arts (MMA) debut at a Strikeforce event against old rival Maurice Smith, who defeated him via a kimura in the first round., Roufus continues in MMA bouts with mixed results.

Professional Boxing Record:	13-5-1
Professional Kickboxing Record:	57-7
Professional MMA Record:	4-5

Further Reading
Brown, Ben. "Kick boxer gets leg up on competition," *USA TODAY*, 12/14/1992, p. 1C.
Official Web site: http://www.roufuskickboxingcenter.com/
Zurkowsky, Herb. "Roufus dominates Theriault in posting unanimous decision." *The Gazette* (Montreal, Quebec), 3/27/1994, p. D5.

RUA, MAURICIO "SHOGUN" (1981–). Mauricio "Shogun" Rua is a Brazilian-based mixed martial artist known for his command of various styles of fighting from Brazilian Jiu-Jitsu to Muay Thai to wrestling and boxing. Born in 1981 in Curitiba, Brazil, Rua made his professional mixed martial arts (MMA) debut in August 2003 by winning three straight bouts to capture the championship at the Meca World Vale Tudo competition.

Later that year, he moved to **PRIDE** and reeled off a series of impressive wins. Many of his wins came from his deadly kicking strikes, earning him recognition as the top light heavyweight in the world. He defeated such notables as **Quinton "Rampage" Jackson,** Ricardo Arona, **Antonio Rogerio Nogueira,** and **Kevin Randleman.** After the **Ultimate Fighting Championships** (**UFC**) purchased PRIDE, Rua made his long-awaited UFC debut against **Forrest Griffin** at UFC 76: Knockout. To the surprise of many, Griffin dominated Rua and appeared in much better condition. He stopped Rua with a rear naked choke in the third round. Injuries kept Rua out of competition until 2009 when he returned to the Octagon to defeat 44-year-old **Mark Coleman**—a former UFC champion who had defeated Rua in PRIDE in 2006. . . His older brother Murilio is also an accomplished mixed martial artist.

Professional MMA Record: 17-3
Championship(s):   PRIDE 2005 Grand Prix tournament

Further Reading
Official Web site: http://www.mauricioshogun.com.br/2007/

RUAS, MARCO (1961–). Marco Ruas was a Brazilian-based mixed martial artist and the winner of the **Ultimate Fighting Championships (UFC)** 7: The Brawl in Buffalo. Born in 1961, Ruas is a versatile combat veteran well-versed in Muay Thai, grappling, and submission skills.

He entered UFC 7 as something of an unknown. He won three consecutive bouts with first-round stoppages against Larry Cureton, Remco Pardoel, and the massive Paul Varelans to capture the championship. He returned to the Octagon for the Ultimate Ultimate 95—a competition of former UFC winners and finalists. He lost a decision to **Oleg Taktarov.** Ruas later lost to former UFC champion **Maurice Smith** at UFC 21: Return of the Champions in 1999. In 2007, he lost to his rival Smith at an **International Fight League (IFL)** event in Chicago.

Professional MMA Record: 8-4-2
Championship(s):   None

Further Reading
Krauss, Erich, and Brett Aita. *Brawl: A Behind-the-Scenes Look at Mixed Martial Arts Competition.* Ontario: ECW Press, 2002.

RUELAS, GABRIEL (1970–). Gabriel Ruelas is a former super featherweight champion known for his dangerous punching power and popular appeal. Born in 1970 in Jalisco, Mexico, Gabriel and his brother Rafael moved to California in their younger days. Legend has it that they stumbled upon prominent boxing manager Joe Goosen's boxing gym selling candy door-to-door. They pestered Goosen to teach them to box and history was made.

Gabriel and Rafael beat the odds and both became world champions. Gabriel turned pro in 1988 and won his first 21 bouts before injuring his elbow against Jeff Franklin in 1990. In 1993, he lost an unpopular majority decision to **Azumah Nelson** for the **World Boxing Council (WBC)** super featherweight championship.

He rebounded with five straight wins, landing himself another title shot—this time against undefeated champion Jesse James Leija. Gabriel dominated and won a unanimous decision. He made two successful defenses, including an 11th-round technical knockout of Jimmy Garcia, who died two weeks later. Gabriel was never the same fighter after the Garcia tragedy.

He lost his title to Azumah Nelson in a listless performance in 1995. He later faced **Arturo "Thunder" Gatti** for the **International Boxing Federation (IBF)** super featherweight title. Gabriel had Gatti badly hurt in the fourth and fifth rounds, but Gatti rallied and stopped Gabriel in the fifth round.

Gabriel fought on but never achieved the same level of success. He retired in 2003 after losing to Courtney Burton.

Professional Record: 49-7

Championship(s):   WBA super featherweight, 2000–2001

Further Reading

Friend, Tom. "A Heart-Rending Vigil After Tragedy in the Ring." *The New York Times*, 5/19/1995, p. B7.

Hudson, David L., Jr. "Gabriel Ruelas: 'Boxing Gave Me Everything I Have. It Has Made Me Who I Am.'" *Fightnews.com*, 6/26/2002.

Martinez, Richard. "Boxing's Brothers in Arms—Rafael and Gabriel Ruelas literally are a rags-to-riches tandem." *San Antonio Express-News*, 4/28/1996, p. 1C.

RUELAS, RAFAEL (1971–). Rafael Ruelas was a former lightweight champion and the younger brother of former super featherweight champion **Gabriel.** Born in 1971 in Mexico, Gabriel and Rafael moved to California while they were youngsters. They met prominent boxing trainer and manager Joe Gooseen and begged him to teach them the sport. The rest became an incredible rags-to-riches story.

Rafael turned pro in 1989 and won his first 27 bouts before a controversial loss to Mauro Gutierrez. Rafael rebounded with quality wins over **Jorge Paez** and Darryl Tyson. In 1994, he overcame a first-round knockdown to outpoint Freddie Pendleton to win the **International Boxing Federation (IBF)** lightweight championship. He made two successful title defenses before losing badly to undefeated challenger **Oscar De La Hoya** in the second round.

Rafael fought on and retired in 1999.

Professional Record: 53-4

Championship(s):   IBF lightweight, 1994–1995

Further Reading

Martinez, Richard. "Boxing's Brothers in Arms—Rafael and Gabriel Ruelas literally are a rags-to-riches tandem." *San Antonio Express-News*, 4/28/1996, p. 1C.

RUIZ, JOHN (1972–). John "the Quiet Man" Ruiz is a former two-time world heavyweight champion who was disrespected by the critics but managed to plod, grab, and clutch his way to the top of the division. Though many criticize his style, Ruiz possesses a good jab, good conditioning, and a strong will. Born in 1972 in Methuen, Massachusetts, Ruiz turned pro in 1992. In 1996, he faced fellow heavyweight prospect **David Tua** and suffered a brutal kayo beating in only 19 seconds. Because of this dismal defeat, many thought that Ruiz would never seriously contend for heavyweight supremacy.

However, Ruiz kept battling, and in 2000, he faced **Evander Holyfield** for the vacant heavyweight championship. Though many observers thought Ruiz deserved the nod, Holyfield won

John Ruiz looks ready to inflict some damage on Roy Jones Jr. during their March 2003 bout. However, Jones proved too elusive and Ruiz lost a 12-round decision. Courtesy of Chris Cozzone.

the decision. In 2001, Ruiz dominated the champion to win a unanimous decision in the rematch. He successfully defended his title twice before losing to **Roy Jones, Jr.**

Once again, Ruiz rebounded and in 2004 defeated Fres Oquendo to recapture the **World Boxing Association (WBA)** belt. He lost his title via a disputed decision to **Nikolai Valuev.** He fought once in 2007 and obtained a victory. In 2008, he lost another close decision to Valuev in another attempt for the WBA championship.

Professional Record: 43-8-1

Championship(s):   WBA Heavyweight, 2001–2003; 2004–2005

Further Reading

Bodenrader, Ted. "John Ruiz Wins His Five-Year Marathon." *The Ring* (July 2001), pp. 56–60.

Stickney, W. H., Jr. "Ruiz Making Strikes on Road to Redemption." *The Houston Chronicle*, 8/11/2004, SPORTS, p. 4.

Watkins, Calvin. "Ruiz achieves a Latino first; Heavyweight title was goal." *Dallas Morning News*, 3/5/2001, p. 13B.

"RUMBLE IN THE JUNGLE." The "Rumble in the Jungle" was the name given to the historic world heavyweight title fight held in Kinshasa, Zaire, in 1974 between champion **George Foreman** and former champion **Muhammad Ali.** Boxing promoter **Don King** convinced Zaire president Mobutu Sese Seko to host the historic bout.

Foreman entered as a huge favorite, as he was younger, undefeated, and by far the more powerful puncher. Most assumed that Ali was far past his prime of the 1960s. Ali, however, employed his famous "Rope-a-Dope" strategy, laying on the ropes and letting Foreman wail away at him. Foreman punched himself out, and gradually Ali began to sting Foreman with quick countershots. Ali prevailed in the eighth round to regain the heavyweight crown.

Further Reading
Mailer, Norman. *The Fight.* New York: Vintage, 1997 (originally published in 1975).

RUTTEN, BAS (1965–). Bas Rutten is a former **Ultimate Fighting Championships (UFC)** heavyweight champion and well-known color commentator and mixed martial arts (MMA) instructor.

He captured the UFC world heavyweight champions at UFC 20 with a close decision victory over **Kevin "the Monster" Randleman.** Rutten made his name in the Pancrease competitions in the early 1990s, earning himself the title "King of Pancrease" or champion three different times.

Rutten's background in Muay Thai kickboxing made him a feared competitor, capable of taking an opponent out with his legs as well as his hands. He retired from MMA in 1999 after suffering knee and bicep injuries. In retirement, he served as commentator for many **PRIDE** cards, as well as starring in several movies and television shows. In 2006, Rutten returned to fight in the World Fighting Alliance against Ruben Villareal. Rutten won in the first round, stopping Villareal with leg strikes.

Rutten currently trains street fighting phenom **Kimbo Slice** until the fall of 2008.

Professional MMA Record:	28-4-1
Championship(s):	UFC Heavyweight, 1999; King of Pancrease

Further Reading
Gentry, Clyde. "Bas Rutten—the Flying Gentleman," in *No Holds Barred: Ultimate Fighting and the Martial Arts Revolution.* Preston, England: Milo Books, Ltd, 2002. pp. 275–279.
Official Web site: http://www.basrutten.tv/

RYAN, TOMMY (1870–1948). Tommy Ryan was a former welterweight and middleweight champion who lost only three bouts in his entire professional career, which spanned 20 years from 1887 to 1907. Born Joseph Youngs in 1870 in Redwood, New York, Ryan turned pro in 1887. In 1891, he won the welterweight title and later legitimized it by defeating **Mysterious Billy Smith** in 1894, who had questioned Ryan's claim to the title.

In 1898, Ryan defeated Jack Bonner for the middleweight championship—a title he held until he retired in 1906. He returned to the ring in 1907 but never fought for another world title. Many consider him as one of the all-time great fighters.

Professional Record:	86-3-6
Championship(s):	Welterweight, 1891–1898; Middleweight, 1898–1906

Further Reading
"Brutal Fist Fight." *The Washington Post,* 10/6/1890, p. 1.
Evans, Gavin. "The 20 Greatest Welterweights of All Time." *The Ring* (February 2008), pp. 63–84, 71.
"Ryan Wins the Fight." *Chicago Tribune,* 2/18/1891, p. 2.

SAAD MUHAMMAD, MATTHEW (1954–). A movie should be made about the life and career of former light heavyweight champion Matthew Saad Muhammad. Born Maxwell Antonio Loach in Philadelphia, Catholic nuns cared for the orphaned 4-year-old. Given the name Matthew Franklin after the Biblical saint Matthew, he turned his life from rags to riches in the boxing ring. It took him years to find out that his original birth name was Maxwell Loach.

In April 1979, Franklin overcame cuts over both eyes to stop champion **Marvin Johnson** in a classic war that became Saad Muhammad's trademark. Adopting his Muslim name after winning the title, Saad Muhammad successfully defended his title nine times against a solid array of challengers.

In July 1980, he absorbed tremendous punishment against the tough Yaqui Lopez before staging a furious rally to stop his opponent in the 14th round. He lost his title to Dwight Braxton (later **Dwight Muhammad Qawi**) in December 1981. The punishment he received took a terrible toll on his career, as he never could reclaim his past glory and fought too long, losing many fights in the later stages before finally retiring for good in 1992. His career ledger of 39-16-3 does not do justice to one of the bravest warriors in the history of the sport.

Professional Record:	39-16-3
Championship(s):	WBC Heavyweight, 1979–1981

Further Reading
Associated Press. "Bloodied Franklin Wins Title." *The Washington Post*, 4/23/1979, p. D9.
Fernandez, Bernard. "Saad Muhammad Goes Into Hall in 1st Round." *Philadelphia Daily News*, 1/14/1998, p. 83.
McGowen, Deane. "Saad Muhammad Wins By Decision." *The New York Times*, 8/19/1979, p. S8.

SADDLER, SANDY (1926–2001). Sandy Saddler was a great featherweight champion best known for beating **Willie Pep** in three of their four bouts. A long, lanky puncher, Saddler's superior power overwhelmed most men his size. He also possessed an incredible chin, not suffering a single knockdown until his 143rd pro bout.

Born in Boston, Saddler's family moved to Harlem. He turned professional at 17 and suffered a third-round knockout in his second pro bout. In October 1948, he won the featherweight title by stopping Pep in the fourth round with a devastating left hook. *The New York Times* reporter covering the bout called it "one of the biggest ring upsets of the year."

He lost his title in the rematch to Pep the next year. However, he regained the title in 1950 by stopping Pep in the eighth round after Pep dislocated a shoulder. In their final meeting, Saddler won in a foul-plagued affair that caused the New York boxing commission to revoke Pep's license and suspend Saddler. He also won the vacant junior lightweight title in 1949 by decisioning Orlando Zulueta over 10 rounds. He continued to hold his featherweight title until his forced retirement in 1957 due to eye injuries suffered in an automobile accident. In later years, Saddler trained fighters, including **George Foreman.**

Record:	144-16-2
Championship(s):	Featherweight, 1948–1949; 1950–1957; Junior Lightweight, 1949–1950

Further Reading

Dawson, James P. "Pep, Shoulder Injured, Loses Featherweight Title to Saddler in Eighth Round." *The New York Times*, 9/9/1950, p. 12.

Eskenazi, Gerald. "Sandy Saddler, Boxing Champion, Dies at 75." *The New York Times*, 9/22/2001, p. A12.

Nichols, Joseph C. "Saddler Wins World Featherweight Title by Knocking Out Pep in 4th Round." *The New York Times*, 10/30/1948, p. 18.

SAKURAI, HAYATO (1975–). Hayato Sakurai is a Japanese mixed martial artist who had great success in the Shooto, **PRIDE**, and DEEP organizations. Born in 1975 in Ibaraki Prefecture, Japan, Sakurai studied and trained in kickboxing, judo, and wrestling. This well-rounded mixed martial artist first developed a fan following when he turned professional in 1996 in a Shooto match. In May 1998, he won the Shooto middleweight title with a decision win over Jutaro Nakaro. He successfully defended his title numerous times, including wins over such notable opponents as **Frank Trigg**, Marcelo Aguiar, and Ronny Rivano. He finally lost his title in August 2001 to **Anderson "Spider" Silva.**

In March 2002, he challenged **Ultimate Fighting Championships (UFC)** welterweight champion **Matt Hughes** at UFC 35: When Worlds Collide but lost in the fourth round. From 2003–2007, Sakurai fought mostly in PRIDE with great success. Among his victims were **Jens Pulver** and Mac Danzig. He last fought in December 2007, defeating Hidehiko Hasegawa.

Professional MMA Record:	34-8-2
Championship(s):	Shooto Middleweight, 1998–2001

Further Reading

Official Web site: http://www.machweb.jp/

SALDIVAR, VINCENTE (1943–1985). Vincente Saldivar was a featherweight champion known as "Zurdo de Oro" or "Lefty of Gold." A rugged southpaw, Saldivar possessed good power in both hands and often employed a relentless attack to wear down his opponents. Born in 1943 in Mexico City, he represented Mexico in the 1960 Olympics.

The next year he turned professional, earning a title shot three years later against **Ultiminio "Sugar" Ramos.** Saldivar stopped the champion in the 12th round to capture the crown. He successfully defended the title seven times before retiring at age 24. He returned to the ring two years later and in 1970 recaptured the featherweight title with a win over Johnny Famechon. He lost the title in his first defense against Kuniaki Shibata. He retired in 1973 after a failed attempt against **Eder Jofre** for the title.

Professional Record: 38-3
Championship(s):   Featherweight, 1964–1967, 1970

Further Reading

Associated Press. "Saldivar Retains Title, Whips Seki." *Los Angeles Times*, 8/8/1966, p. B4.

Roberts, James B., and Alexander G. Skutt. *The Boxing Register: International Boxing Hall of Fame Register* (4th ed.). Ithaca, NY: McBooks Press, Inc., 2006, pp. 626–629.

SAMBO. Sambo is a Russian combat sport that is a combination of judo and wrestling. It literally means self-defense without weapons. The Russian military trains its members in sambo as a great form of self-defense and battle technique. There are different versions of sambo, including sport sambo, self-defense sambo, and combat sambo. Combat sambo differs from the other forms, as its participants utilize all strikes and throws. It more closely approximates the fighting one sees in mixed martial arts bouts.

Sambo has been a competitive sport in the Soviet Union since 1938. **Oleg Taktarov, Andrei Arlovski,** and the great **Fedor Emelianenko** were sambo champions before they ventured into international mixed martial art matches. Emelianenko still competes regularly in sambo competitions.

Further Reading

Perez-Mazzola, Vince. "Outside the Big 4." *FIGHT!* (April 2008), pp. 54–56.

SANCHEZ, SALVADOR (1959–1982). Killed in his prime in a car accident, Salvador Sanchez still managed to box his way to a hall-of-fame career in his 23 years. Born in Mexico in 1959, he turned pro in 1975 and won 18 straight bouts before losing a 12-round decision to Antonio Becerra for the vacant Mexican bantamweight title. He would never lose again in the ring.

Sanchez won the **World Boxing Council (WBC)** featherweight title by stopping popular champion **Danny "Little Red" Lopez** in the 14th round. He defended his title nine times, defeating the likes of Juan LaPorte, **Wilfredo Gomez,** and **Azumah Nelson.** In August 1982, while in training camp to fight LaPorte again, Sanchez crashed his Porsche and died.

Record: 44-1-1
Championship(s):   WBC featherweight, 1980–1982

Further Reading

Berkow, Ira. "Sanchez Accepts Award with Gusto." *The New York Times*, 1/13/1987, p. B13.

Hoffer, Richard. "Sanchez Retains His Title, Beats Gomez on TKO in 8th." *Los Angeles Times*, 8/22/1981, p. B1.

Riding, Alan. "Sanchez: The 100 Percent Boxer." *The New York Times*, 7/19/1982, p. 1 C1.

SANDOVAL, RICHIE (1960–). Richie Sandoval is a former world bantamweight champion best known for upsetting the hall-of-fame champion "Joltin'" Jeff Chandler to win the crown. He had a stellar amateur career, compiling a record of 156-12. He sought an Olympic goal medal in the Moscow Olympics but was denied when President Jimmy Carter boycotted the games. He turned pro in 1980 and kept winning. He won the title from Chandler in 1984 with a 15th-round stoppage. He knocked Chandler down in the 11th round—the first time the champion had ever hit the canvas. Sandoval successfully defended his title twice before losing to Gaby Canizales in 1986. Canizales pounded Sandoval, dropping him three times in the seventh round. Sandoval fell into a coma. He later recovered but could never fight again.

Record:	29-1
Championship(s):	WBA Bantamweight, 1984–1986

Further Reading
Coats, Christopher. "Richie Sandoval: Former Champion." *The Ring* (July 1986), pp. 10–12.

SAPP, BOB (1974–). Bob "the Beast" Sapp is a behemoth, muscle-bound fighter who fights in K-1. Born in 1974, in Colorado Springs, Sapp attended the University of Washington on a football scholarship. A star offensive lineman, Sapp was drafted in the NFL's third round and played sparingly for four seasons. He defeated former Chicago Bears star William "the Refrigerator" Perry in a toughman competition.

That caused fight promoters in Japan to believe they could make a star out of Sapp. He initially fought in **PRIDE** twice, defeating Yoshihisa Yamamoto and Kiyoshi Tamura in 2001. Sapp fought more bouts as a kickboxer in K-1, defeating the legendary **Ernesto Hoost** twice. He lost to **Remy Bonjasky.** His best performance was at the K-1 Grand Prix in 2005, where he defeated three straight Japanese fighters to capture the championship. He still competes in mixed martial arts bouts, fighting bouts for Strikeforce and K-1 Dynamite in 2008. He also still performs in professional wrestling where he remains hugely popular.

Professional MMA Record:	**10**-3-1
Professional Kickboxing:	10-7
Championship(s):	None

Further Reading
Cummings, Roy. "The Other Sapp." *Tampa Tribune,* 6/18/2003, SPORTS, p. 1.
Kelley, Steve. "What About Bob?" *The Seattle Times,* 2/13/2008, p. E1.

SAVON, FELIX (1967–). Felix Savon is a former three-time Olympic gold medalist who captured top honors at the 1992, 1996, and 2000 Olympic Games. Born in 1967 in San Vicente, Savon compiled an amazing amateur record of 362-21. During his illustrious career, the 6'6" Savon won six world championships and was universally considered the finest amateur boxer of his era.

He defeated David Izon to win gold at the 1992 Barcelona Games, David Defiagbon to win the 1996 Atlanta Games, and Sultan Ibragimov to win in Sydney. He once kayoed **Shannon Briggs.** The great boxing writer Hugh McIlvanney wrote of Savon after witnessing the Cuban captured his third gold medal: "[he] used yet another Olympic boxing final as a declaration of the superiority he has been ramming home to the rest of the world's amateur heavyweights since the middle of the 1980s." He retired at age 33 after the Sydney 2000 Olympic Games and now coaches boxers in his native country.

Amateur Record:	362-21
Championship(s):	Olympic gold in 1992, 1996 and 2000.

Further Reading
Janofsky, Michael. "A Punching Patriot From Cuba: IN a Time of Change, Boxer Defends His Nation's System." *The New York Times,* 8/3/1990, p. A20.

Moran, Malcolm. "Savon of Cuba Dominates Bent." *The New York Times*, 8/21/1987, p. B16.
McIlvanney, Hugh. "Savon cruises home to golden treble." *The Sunday Times*, 10/1/2000, p. 4.

SAVATE. Savate, or French kickboxing, is a form of kickboxing in which combatants wear gloves and are only allowed to use their hands and feet as weapons. Unlike Muay Thai boxing, savateurs are not allowed to use their elbows, shins, and elbows as striking weapons. Savate is a French word that means "old boot." The 1924 Paris Olympics featured savate as a demonstration sport.

Savate may have originated in the seventeenth century when French sailors encountered Asia, where they saw many martial arts practitioners. The sailors took home some of their knowledge and combined it with a then-existing form of street-fighting in Paris.

Savate first became popular or legitimate in the nineteenth century from the efforts and abilities of a French prizefighter named Michel Casseux and his student Charles Lecour. It has often been described as fencing with the use of hands and feet.

Gerard Gordeau was a former savate champion who used his considerable skills in that fighting discipline to reach the championship round of the first **Ultimate Fighting Championships** before submitting to the great **Royce Gracie.**

Further Reading

MacKenzie, Mark. "Inner-City Kicks: It Was Invented by Thieves on the Mean Streets of 19th Century Paris." *Independent on Sunday* (London), 5/22/2005, p. 10.
North American Savate Sport Association: http://sportsavate.org/sv/html/website/WebSite_19/m_main.jsp?id=19&

SCHILT, SEMMY (1973–). Semmy Schilt is a 6′11″ Dutch-based kickboxer and mixed martial artist known for his dominance in kickboxing. He won the K-1 Grand Prix tournament an unprecedented three times in a row in 2005–2007.

Born in 1973 in Rotterdam, Netherlands, Schilt first began learning karate at age eight. He won the Daido Juku world championships in Japan and then competed in mixed martial arts in a Pancrease event in 1996. He split a pair of fights with Guy Mezger, Yuki Kondo, and Masakatsu Funaki. In 2001, he made his debut in the Octagon, kayoing Pete Williams in the second round. In his second **Ultimate Fighting Championships (UFC)** fight, he lost to the powerful **Josh Barnett.**

After the UFC bouts, he moved to **PRIDE** and won his first three straight bouts. He then lost to **Fedor Emelianenko, Antonio Rodrigo Nogueira,** and Barnett.

In 2002, Schilt made his debut in K-1 and in his second bout fought to a draw with **Ernesto "Mr. Perfect" Hoost.** He has lost only three times in K-1 to Alexey Ignashov, Peter Aerts, and **Hong Man Choi.** He has defeated the best of the best, including **Remy Bonjasky** twice, Hoost twice, **Michael McDonald,** and Jerome Le Banner twice. In the 2007 K-1 Grand Prix, he defeated Glaube Feitosa, Jerome Le Banner, and Peter Aerts.

Given his dominance at the recent K-1 Grand Prix events, some are now ranking Schilt at or near the list of kickboxing greats.

Professional Kickboxing Record:	28-4-1
Professional MMA Record:	26-14-1
Championship(s):	Kickboxing Championships—2005–2007 K-1

Further Reading

Iole, Kevin. "Dutchman Schilt aims to tower over competition at K-1." *Las Vegas Review-Journal*, 4/29/2006, p. 8C.

"Sammy Schilt: If I prepare 100% I have a good chance against Fedor." *FightSport* (April 2008), pp. 38–39.

"Striker of the Year: Wild bunch for one belt." *FightSport* (February 2008), pp. 80–85.

SCHMELING, MAX (1905–2005). Max Schmeling was a former world heavyweight champion best known for his powerful right hand and for being the first man to defeat the great **Joe Louis** in a professional prizefight. Born in 1905 in Klein Luckrow, Germany, Schmeling turned pro in 1924 and fought for several years as a light heavyweight.

In 1928, he defeated Franz Diener for the German heavyweight title. In June 1930, he won the world heavyweight championship via disqualification after Jack Sharkey hit him with a low blow. He successfully defended his title against **William Lawrence "Young" Stribling** before losing a controversial decision in the rematch to Sharkey. After the fight, Schemeling's manager Joe Jacobs famously said: "We wuz robbed."

In 1933 and 1934, he suffered back-to-back losses to **Max Baer** and Steve Hamas. Many felt that Schmeling was past his prime and would never seriously contend for a championship. However, he revived his career in June 1936 with a stunning 12th-round stoppage of undefeated prospect and future heavyweight great Joe Louis. In June 1938, Louis stopped him in the first round in their rematch. He initially retired in 1939 but made an abortive comeback in the late 1940s after World War II.

In his post-fight career, Schmeling became a very successful businessman. For many years, Schmeling's name was besmirched because he was used by Nazi dictator Adolf Hitler as an example of German power—particularly after his surprise victory over Louis. However, Schmeling was not a supporter of Nazism, and he actually helped two Jewish youths escape Germany. In later years, he also helped Joe Louis. He died in 2004 at the age of 99.

Professional Record:	56-10-4
Championship(s):	Heavyweight, 1930–1931

Further Reading

Erenberg, Lewis. *The Greatest Fight of Our Generation: Louis v. Schmeling.* New York: Oxford University Press, 2005.

Margolick, David. *Beyond Glory: Joe Louis v. Max Schmeling, and a World on the Brink.* New York: Vintage, 2005.

Myler, Patrick. *Ring of Hate: Joe Louis v. Max Schmeling: The Fight of the Century.* New York: Arcade Publishing, 2006.

Schmeling, Max, and George Von Der Lippe. *Max Schmeling: An Autobiography.* Santa Monica, CA: Bonus Books, 1998.

SCOTT, JAMES (1947–). James Scott was a top light heavyweight contender of the 1970s and early 1980s who amazingly fought several high-profile, televised bouts while incarcerated at Rahway State Prison in New Jersey. Scott turned pro in 1974 and won his first 11 bouts, fighting in Miami Beach, Florida. He then did not fight for several years because he was imprisoned in Rahway for armed robbery and murder. Scott was convicted in 1981 after an eight-day trial in which he was represented by famed defense attorney William Kuntsler.

He fought and defeated several top contenders while in Rahway, including future or former champions **Eddie Mustafa Muhammad** and Richie Yates. By the end of 1979, many speculated that Scott was the best light heavyweight in the world, and many clamored for him to receive a title shot. However, he lost his next fight in 1980—a decision loss to Jerry "the Bull" Martin. He lost another decision in 1981 to future champion Dwight Braxton (who later changed his name to **Dwight Muhammad Qawi**). His career ended because a new warden would not allow Scott to fight professionally anymore.

Professional Record: 19-2-1
Championship(s): None

Further Reading

Associated Press. "Scott is Found Guilty of Murder, Faces Life." *The New York Times*, 2/5/1981, p. B7.
Hudson, David L., Jr., and Mike Fitzgerald, Jr. *Boxing's Most Wanted: The Top Ten Book of Champs, Chumps and Punch Drunk Palookas.* Alexandria, VA: Potomac Books, 2003.
Schenerman, Beth. "Inmate Sets Sights on Boxing Title." *The New York Times*, 12/17/1978, p. NJ31.

SERRA, MATT (1974–). Matt "the Terror" Serra is an American mixed martial artist who holds a black belt in Brazilian jiu-jitsu. He was the first American to earn a black belt under legendary instructor Renzo Gracie. He turned professional in mixed martial arts (MMA) in 1999 and first fought in the **Ultimate Fighting Championships (UFC)** at UFC 31: Locked and Loaded, losing to Shonie Carter, who connected on a spinning backfist.

His career received a revival from his participation in *The Ultimate Fighter* 4: *The Comeback*, which featured a series of UFC veterans who had yet to win a world championship. On the show, Serra defeated Pete Spratt and Carter to reach the finals against **Chris Lytle,** whom he defeated by split decision. The victory earned him a shot at UFC welterweight champion **Georges St.-Pierre,** the prohibitive favorite.

Surprisingly, Serra kayoed St.-Pierre in the first round to win the championship. He was set to defend his title in December 2007 against heated rival **Matt Hughes**—his opposing coach in *The Ultimate Fighter 5*—but Serra suffered a back injury in training. He lost his title in a rematch with St.-Pierre in April 2008, losing via strikes in the second round.

Professional MMA Record: 9-5
Championship(s): UFC welterweight, 2007–2008

Further Reading

Hall, Joe. "Matt Serra: Living in the Moment." *FIGHT!* (September 2007), pp. 26–31.
Official Web site: http://www.serrajitsu.com/

SEVERN, DAN (1954–). Dan "the Beast" Severn was a dominant American wrestler who achieved great success during the early days of the **Ultimate Fighting Championships (UFC)**. Born in 1954 in Michigan, Severn attended college on a wrestling scholarship at Arizona State University where he earned All-American honors three years in a row. Upon graduation, he continued to compete in wrestling on an international basis, capturing top honors at the 1977 World Championship, the 1986 Pan-An Games, and the 1986 World Cup (Wall, p. 80).

Severn entered mixed martial arts in 1994 at UFC 4: Revenge of the Warriors. He defeated Antony Macias and Marcus Bossett to advance to the finals to the face the legendary **Royce Gracie.** Severn outweighed Gracie by more than 70 pounds and put Gracie on his back. However, the submission master stopped Severn with a triangle choke more than 15 minutes into the fight.

Severn returned to the Octagon in 1995 as the featured fighter at UFC 5: The Return of the Beast. He defeated Joe Charles, **Oleg Taktarov,** and Dave Beneteau to win the championship. Severn lost to rival **Ken Shamrock** at UFC 6: Clash of the Titans in a match billed as a "superfight." Severn continued his dominance at the UFC Ultimate Ultimate in 1995, defeating Paul Varelans, **David "Tank" Abbott,** and Oleg Taktarov to capture another championship.

He returned again to the Octagon in UFC 9: Motor City Madness in 1996 in a rematch against Shamrock. This time "the Beast" prevailed in a decision. Severn fought in other mixed martial arts (MMA) matches around the world. He returned to the UFC in 1997 at UFC 12: Judgment Day, facing **Mark Coleman** for the UFC heavyweight championship. Coleman choked Severn out three minutes into the bout. Severn then fought in **PRIDE** against Kimo, a bout that ended in a draw after 30 minutes. Severn has continued to compete in various MMA organizations. In November 2007, he won a decision over Don Richard at a King of the Cage event.

Professional MMA Record: 86-15-7

Championship(s):   UFC 5 Tournament winner and winner of Ultimate Ultimate 95 tournament

Further Reading
Marvez, Alex. "At the Top of His Game, Severn Branches Out." *The Sun Herald,* 1/28/2004, p. 42.
Morse, Lee. "The Beast has left mark on combat sports." *The Flint Journal,* 11/31/2006, p. C3.
Wall, Jeremy. *UFC Ultimate Warriors Top 10.* Ontario: ECW Press, 2005, pp. 79–94.
Zartman, Josh. "Severn Still Proving He's the Beast." *The Ottawa Sun,* 8/20/2000, p. 34.

SHAIN, EVA (1917–1999). Eva Shain was the first woman to ever judge a world professional boxing match when she served as one of the three judges for **Muhammad Ali's** defense of his crown against **Earnie Shavers.** A native of Jersey City, Shain initially despised boxing, but her husband Frank—later a prominent ring announcer—insisted that she go to shows with him. She later developed an appreciation for the sport and began judging amateur bouts in the 1960s. In 1975, she received her license from the state of New York to judge professional bouts. Two years later, she served as one of the judges for the Ali—Shavers match. She judged more than 50 world title bouts and thousands of professional bouts during her career. "It wasn't the idea of being a trailblazer," she said when asked about being the first woman to judge a world title bout. "It was something I wanted to do. It was a challenge."

Further Reading
Goldstein, Richard. "Eva Shain, 81, a Pioneering Boxing Judge." *The New York Times,* 8/23/1999, p. B9.
Williams, Lena. "Ring Hater Becomes Judge." *The New York Times,* 7/25/1976, p. 138.

SHAMROCK, FRANK (1972–). Frank Shamrock was in many ways the ultimate progenitor of modern mixed martial artists with his focus on superb conditioning, mastery of multiple disciplines, and absolute dedication to his craft.

Born Frank Alisio Juarez in 1972 in Santa Monica, California, this mixed martial arts legend took the last name Shamrock in honor of his foster father, Bob, who helped Frank from his haven for troubled youth in California. Bob officially adopted Frank when he was 21.

Frank learned mixed martial arts (MMA) from his foster brother Ken at Ken's training school called The Lion's Den. Frank made his debut—as his brother before him—in Pancrease winning a decision against the legendary **Bas Rutten.** He continued to fight in Pancrease, losing two return bouts with Rutten and winning many others. He fought such greats as Manabu Yamada, Katsunomi Inagaki, Masakatsu Funaki, and Minori Suzuki.

In January 1997, Shamrock faced Jon Lober at Super Brawl 3 in Hawaii, losing a split decision. He then fought Tsuyoshi Kohsaka in RINGS, winning a decision. He then defeated **Enson Inoue** in a Shooto competition.

In December 1997 at **Ultimate Fighting Championships (UFC)** Japan, Shamrock first competed in the Octagon, defeating Kevin Jackson in 16 seconds via an armbar to become the organization's first middleweight champion. He never lost that title in the Octagon, making several successful defenses against Igor Zinoviev, **Jeremy Horn,** John Lober, and the much larger **Tito Ortiz.** Shamrock destroyed Zinoviev in 22 seconds, slamming his opponent so hard that he suffered a broken collarbone and fractured vertebra. Shamrock submitted Horn—himself a submission master. He battered Lober, avenging an earlier defeat. The Ortiz bout was a tough one for Shamrock, as he faced a younger, stronger opponent. Ortiz dominated much of the first three rounds, but Shamrock's amazing conditioning carried him to victory in the fourth round. Shamrock retired from the UFC having never lost in five career bouts.

He returned to MMA, fighting in other organizations. In June 2007, he defeated rival Phil Baroni to win the **Elite XC** Strikeforce Middleweight title. He regularly writes for *Fight! Magazine* and remains active in the MMA world. In 2008, he lost to kung-fu and san shou expert **Cung Le.**

Professional MMA Record: 23-9-2
Championship(s):   Strikeforce Middleweight, 2007–2008; UFC Light Heavyweight, 1997–1999

Further Reading

Official Web site of Frank Shamrock: http://www.frankshamrock.com
Herman, Gary. "Q & A with EliteXC and Strikeforce fighter Frank Shamrock." *Cbssportsline.com*, 3/24/2008, at http://www.sportsline.com/print/mmaboxing/story/10734736
Walker, Andrew. "Frank Shamrock: Still 'the Legend.'" *Extreme Fighter* (March 2008), p. 48–50.
Walls, Jeremy. *UFC's Ultimate Warriors Top 10.* Ontario: ECW Press, 2005, pp. 143–158.

SHAMROCK, KEN (1964–). Ken Shamrock was an all-time mixed martial arts (MMA) great who is enshrined in the **Ultimate Fighting Championships (UFC)** Hall of Fame. Blessed with a muscular physique and excellent submission skills, Shamrock was one of the early stars of the UFC. Born Kenneth Wayne Kilpatrick in Macon, Georgia, in 1964, Ken later changed his last name to Shamrock in honor of his foster father, Bob Shamrock, who helped Ken survive a troubled childhood at the Shamrock Ranch, a haven for troubled youth in Susanville, California.

Shamrock excelled in wrestling in high school, though he suffered a serious neck injury. After high school, Shamrock competed in several Toughman events. He then turned to pro wrestling on the advice of Bob Shamrock.

Shamrock was an accomplished wrestler and turned to pro wrestling. He began his mixed martial arts career in September 1993 in Pancrease—an early hybrid of wrestling and full-contact mixed martial arts. Shamrock then competed in the first UFC tournament.

In his first match, he defeated kickboxer Patrick Smith, but in his next match he was choked to submission by eventual winner **Royce Gracie.** In 1994, Shamrock competed in UFC 3, winning his first two matches, but he pulled out of the finals when he saw that he could not face Gracie in a rematch. He returned to Pancrease in dominating fashion. Shamrock eventually received a return match with Gracie at UFC 5 and fought the Brazilian to a 36-minute draw. Later, in UFC 6: Clash of the Titans, Shamrock submitted **Dan Severn** in just over two minutes with a **guillotine choke** to win the organization's first ever "Superfight."

Shamrock returned to UFC 7 in a Superfight with Russian **sambo** expert and UFC 6 champion **Oleg Taktarov.** The two fought to a relatively uneventful draw. However, Shamrock returned to UFC 8 in a superfight with Kimo. Shamrock submitted his opponent just over four minutes into the bout with a kneebar.

Shamrock then fought a rematch with Severn at UFC 9. The two legends fought a boring fight that ended in a decision in Severn's favor. Shamrock then competed at the Ultimate Ultimate 96 tournament of champions. He choked out Brian Johnston in the first round but suffered a broken hand in the process that forced his withdrawal.

He left MMA in 1997 and returned to pro wrestling. From 1997–1999, he competed in the World Wrestling Federation (WWF) under his nickname that originally came during his UFC days, "the World's Most Dangerous Man."

Shamrock eventually returned to MMA—specifically **PRIDE**—in 2000 but with less success. He defeated Alexander Otsuka in his first PRIDE bout but lost to **Kazuyuki Fujita** badly in his next bout.

He later fought in the UFC in 2002 against the brash **Tito Ortiz** for the UFC light heavyweight title. Shamrock lost but returned to the Octagon twice more against Ortiz in major box office draws. He lost the last two bouts to Ortiz and failed to make it out of the first round. Even though he was overwhelmed by the younger Ortiz, to many mixed martial arts fans he remains "the World's Most Dangerous Man."

Professional MMA Record:	26-13-2
Championship(s):	UFC Superfight title, 1995–1996; King of Pancrease, 1994

Further Reading

Official Web site: http://www.kenshamrock.com/

Shamrock, Ken, with Richard Hanner and Calixtro Romias. *Inside the Lion's Den: The Life and Submission Fighting System of Ken Shamrock.* North Clarendon, VT: Tuttle Publishing, 1998.

Shamrock, Ken, and Erich Krauss. *Beyond the Lion's Den.* North Clarendon, VT: Tuttle Publishing, 2005.

Walls, Jeremy. *UFC's Ultimate Warriors Top 10.* Ontario: ECW Press, 2005, pp. 159–188.

SHAVERS, EARNIE (1945-). Earnie Shavers was a heavyweight contender in the 1970s known for his devastating power that catapulted him to 68 knockouts in 74 professional wins. He possessed a right hand bomb that decapitated many opponents. He felled heavyweight champions **Jimmy Ellis** and **Ken Norton** in the first round. Unfortunately, he failed in his two attempts at the world championship—losing a close decision to **Muhammad Ali** and a technical knockout loss to **Larry Holmes.**

Born in Garland, Alabama, in 1945, his family moved to Ohio where Shavers turned to boxing. He turned pro in 1969 and began kayoing opponents with frightening regularity. At one point in his career, he felled 27 opponents in a row. Shavers did not have the greatest chin, which let him down in other fights. He suffered kayo losses to **Jerry Quarry, Ron Lyle,** Bernardo Mercardo, and **Randall "Tex" Cobb.** In 1979, Shavers nearly captured the heavyweight crown when he faced Holmes. Down on points, Shavers threw a right-hand bomb that dropped Holmes. To his credit, the champion somehow rose from the canvas and later stopped Shavers. Earnie initially retired in 1983 but returned to the ring in his 50s in 1995. He retired after suffering a kayo loss to journeyman Brian Yates.

Professional Record:	74-14-1
Championship(s):	None

Further Reading

Brunt, Stephen. *Facing Ali: 15 Fighters, 15 Stories.* Guilford, CT: Lyons Press, 2002, pp. 263–277.

Keese, Parton. "Right By Shavers Stops Ellis in 2:39." *The New York Times,* 6/19/1973, p. 45.

Shavers, Earnie, with Mike Fitzgerald and Marshall Terrill. *Welcome to the Big Time.* Champaign, IL: Sports Publishing L.L.C, 2002.

SHERK, SEAN (1973–). Sean "the Muscle Shark" Sherk is a muscle-bound former lightweight champion of the **Ultimate Fighting Championships (UFC)** known for his powerful wrestling techniques and for his incredible record. Born in 1973 in St. Francis, Minnesota, Sherk began wrestling at age seven.

He began his mixed martial arts (MMA) career in 1999 with a win in an Ultimate Wrestling event. Through the years, Sherk has fought in numerous fighting organizations, including: Extreme Challenge, King of the Cage, Pancrase, TKO, Extreme Challenge, The Ultimate Fighting Championship, and Pride Bushido. In 2000 and 2001, he won bouts against judo specialist **Karo Parisyan.** In 2003, he suffered the first loss of his career—a five-round unanimous decision loss to **Matt Hughes** at UFC 42: Sudden Impact.

He suffered only the second loss of his career in November 2005 to the talented **Georges St.-Pierre.** Sherk rebounded and in October 2006 defeated **Kenny Florian** to win the UFC world lightweight championship. In his first defense, he defeated **Hermes Franca** by decision, but controversy ensued after post-fight test results revealed steroid use by both fighters. Sherk was suspended, though he maintained his innocence. He later passed a couple blood tests, adding credence to his claims.

In 2008, Sherk resumed his career against lightweight champion **B. J. Penn.** Sherk fought courageously but lost in the third round at UFC 84: Ill Will.

Professional MMA Record: 33-3-1
Championship(s):   UFC Lightweight, 2006–2007

Further Reading

Herman, Gary. "Q & A with Former Lightweight Champion Sean Sherk." *CBSSports.com*, 5/15/2008, at http://www.sportsline.com/mmaboxing/story/10826877/1
Official Web site: http://seansherk.com
Shapiro, Eric. "Exclusive Interview with UFC Lightweight Champ Sean Sherk." *Five Ounces of Pain*, 10/22/2007, at http://fiveouncesofpain.com/2007/10/22/exclusive-interview-with-ufc-lightweight-champion-sean-sherk/
Walker, Andrew. "Sean Sherk: 'Shark' Attack." *Extreme Fighter!* (March 2008), pp. 18–19.

SIKI, BATTLING (1897–1925). Arguably the most fascinating character in boxing history, Battling Siki lived a truth-is-stranger-than fiction life both in and out of the ring. Born in 1897 in Saint Louis, Senegal, as Louis Mbarick Fall, he moved to France as a teenager and began his professional boxing career. He later joined the French army. He received medals for his bravery in battle.

After the war, he resumed his boxing career with a vengeance. In 1922, he shocked the boxing world with an upset kayo win over **Georges Carpentier** to win the world light heavyweight title. After winning the title, Siki enjoyed the high life, even walking his pet tiger down the streets of Paris. He lost his title on St. Patrick's Day in 1923 to Irishman Mike McTigue in Dublin on a controversial decision. His ring career went into decline, and he was murdered on the streets of New York City in 1925.

Professional Record: 64-25-5
Championship(s):   Light Heavyweight, 1922–1923

Further Reading

Benson, Peter. *Battling Siki: A Tale of Ring Fixes, Race, and Murder in the 1920s.* Little Rock: University of Arkansas Press, 2006.
Skene, Don. "Battling Siki Knocks Out Georges Carpentier." *Chicago Daily Tribune*, 9/25/1922, p. 1.

SILER, GEORGE (1846–1908). George Siler was a noted sportswriter and boxing referee admired for his knowledge of the sport and ring integrity. The *Chicago Tribune* wrote of him in 1896: "Professional pugilists and their backers respect him as a referee who understands the fighting game thoroughly and one who may always be depended to give a square and impartial decision." Born in New York City in 1846, Siler boxed as a kid and fought many noted pugilists in his day. He later worked at a wholesale furniture house and on an iron pier before becoming a boxing instructor in Chicago. As a boxing instructor, he met many newspaper reporters and helped them with their stories. He then began writing sports stories and later turned to sports writing full time as a writer and editor for the *Chicago Tribune*. Siler also began refereeing bouts and quickly developed a fine reputation as an impartial ring arbiter. He refereed many historic bouts, including **Joe Gans—Battling Nelson** for the lightweight championship, **Bob Fitzsimmons—James "Gentleman Jim" Corbett** for the heavyweight championship, and **James J. Jeffries**—Bob Fitzsimmons for the heavyweight title.

Further Reading
"He Knows the Game." *Chicago Daily Tribune*, 1/26/1896, p. 41.

SILVA, ANDERSON (1975–). Anderson Silva is a **Ultimate Fighting Championships (UFC)** middleweight champion famous for his devastating knee strikes. Trained in Muay Thai kickboxing, Silva is arguably the most feared striker in mixed martial arts (MMA). He also has a black belt in Brazilian jiu-jitsu, training under the legendary **Antonio Rodrigo Nogueira.** He kayoed **Rich Franklin** with a knee strike to the head to win the UFC middleweight title in October 2006 at UFC 74: Unstoppable. He later dominated Franklin in a rematch at UFC 77: Hostile Territory to solidify his hold on the title.

He has fought in several MMA organizations, including Mecca, Shooto, Cage Rage, **PRIDE**, and the UFC. He began his MMA career in 2000 and in August 2001 defeated **Hayato Sakurai** to the win the Shooto middleweight title. In 2002, he moved to PRIDE where he won two straight fights before a surprising submission loss to Japanese fighter **Daiju Takase** via a triangle choke at PRIDE 26: Bad to the Bone. He also lost via submission to **Ryo Chonan** via a flying scissors heel hook that may be one of the greatest moves in MMA history.

However, Silva's career began to skyrocket after joining the UFC in 2006. In his first bout he destroyed brawler Chris Leben in less than a minute. He has followed that up with five more victories in the Octagon. At UFC 82: Pride of a Champion, he submitted "Dangerous" **Dan Henderson** in the second round to retain his middleweight championship. He cemented his status with a quick devastation of James Irwin in his first move to the 205 lb. light heavyweight division in July 2008. In many experts' eyes, he sits atop the mixed martial arts as the best pound-for-pound fighter in the world.

He also is 1-0 as a professional boxer, stopping his opponent in the second round.

Professional MMA Record: 23-4
Championship(s):   Cage Rage Middleweight, 2004; UFC Middleweight, 2006—

Further Reading
Official Web site: http://www.spidersilva.com
Hachat, Josh. "Silva on another level." *The Newark Advocate*, 3/4/2008, p. 1.
Mink, Ryan. "Triumphant Silva is Running Out of Foes." *The Washington Post*, 3/2/2008, p. D5.
Murgel, Ricardo. "Fighter Profile: Anderson Silva: A Look at One of the Middle-Weight Division's Most Feared Fighters." *FIGHT!* (October–November 2007), pp. 74–76.
Pugmire, Lance. "The Man to Beat." *Los Angeles Times*, 3/1/2008, at SP6.

SILVA, THIAGO (1982–). Thiago Silva is a once-beaten light heavyweight who currently fights in the **Ultimate Fighting Championships (UFC)**. Born in Sao Paulo, Brazil, Silva trains in Brazilian jiu-jitsu and Muay Thai kickboxing. He turned professional in 2005 with a win in a Predator FC event.

In May 2007, he made his UFC debut at UFC 71: Liddell v. Jackson with a first-round win over James Irwin. He later won matches at UFC 75: Champion v. Champion against Tomasz Drwal and UFC 78: Validation against the feared **Houston Alexander.** In 2009, he lost to fellow unbeaten Lyoto Machida.

Professional Record:	13-1
Championship(s):	None

Further Reading
UFC Profile of Thiago Silva: http://www.ufc.com/index.cfm?fa=fighter.detail&pid=634

SILVA, WANDERLEI (1976–). Wanderlei "the Axe Murderer" Silva is one of the most popular mixed martial artists in the history of the sport. He is known for his love of fighting, all-out aggressive style, and devastating striking ability. Perhaps his most feared weapons are his knees, as the Brazilian is a master at Muay Thai. Twice he has kayoed **Quinton "Rampage" Jackson** with such knee strikes. Three times he crushed Japanese legend Kazushi "The Gracie Hunter" Sakuraba.

Born in 1976 in Curitiba, Brazil, Silva turned professional in 1996 in several Vale Tudo ("anything goes") events in his native country. In 1999, he began fighting in the Japan-based **PRIDE** organization, though he did fight in the **Ultimate Fighting Championships (UFC)** a couple of times as well.

He made his name in PRIDE by defeating such fighters as Guy Metzger, Sakuraba, Hidehiko Yoshida, and many others. He first served notice that he was a force to be reckoned with when he destroyed Sakuraba in March 2001 at PRIDE 13: Collision Course.

He won the PRIDE Grand Prix middleweight tournament by defeating Sakuraba in November 2001. Silva never backs down from anyone and often has fought much bigger opponents, including heavyweights **Mirko "Cro Cop" Filipovic** (twice), **Mark Hunt,** and **Kazuyuki Fujita.**

After the UFC purchased PRIDE, he moved to the United States and began fighting in the Octagon. He lost to **Chuck Liddell** in December 2007 at PRIDE 79: Nemesis but rebounded in a major way with a 36-second destruction of **Keith "the Dean of Mean" Jardine** at UFC 84: Ill Will. In December 2008, he suffered a one-punch kayo loss to Jackson in their third bout.

Professional MMA Record:	32-9-1
Championship(s):	PRIDE Middleweight, 2001–2007

Further Reading
Kalstein, Dave. "Wanderlei Silva Has Got Your Back," *FIGHT!* (January 2009), p. 42–50.
Official Web site: http://www.wanderleisilva.com.br/
Rodriguez, Jose. "Silva Alive 'N' Kicking." *The Calgary Sun,* 12/22/2007, p. SP4.

SINGSURAT, MEDGOEN (1978–). Medgoen Singsurat is a former world flyweight champion best known for his third-round stoppage of future pound-for-pound great **Manny Pacquiao** in 1999. Born in 1978 in Roi-Et, Thailand, Singsurat turned pro in 1997 in Chumpon. He won his first 18 fights before challenging Pacquiao for the **World Boxing Council (WBC)**

flyweight title. Amazingly, Singsurat stopped Pacquiao in the third round. He successfully defended his title once before losing to unbeaten challenger Malcolm "Eagle Eye" Tunacao in May 2000.

Singsurat has never received another world title shot, though he did capture the vacant WBC Asian Boxing Council super flyweight title in 2003 with a win over Afren Bulala. He remains an active boxer, fighting eight times in 2007 and six times in 2008.

Professional Record: 59-5
Championship(s):   WBC flyweight, 1999–2000

Further Reading
"Pacquaio Has Soared After Thai Defeat," *Bangkok Post*, 12/11/2008.
"Thai Champ Retains WBC Title," Agence France Presse, 2/25/2000.

SITHBANPRACHAN, PICHIT (1966–). Pichit Sithbanprachan was a former world flyweight champion who never lost a professional bout, though he never fought outside his native Thailand. Born in 1966, he turned professional in 1990 and won all 24 of his professional bouts. He captured the **International Boxing Federation (IBF)** flyweight title with a third-round kayo over Rodolfo Blanco. He held the title until initially retiring in 1994 after a split-decision victory over Jose Luis Zepeda. He came back for one fight in 1996 and two bouts in 2000.

Professional Record: 24-0
Championship(s):   IBF flyweight, 1992–1994

Further Reading
Hudson, David L., and Mike Fitzgerald, Jr. *Boxing's Most Wanted: The Top Ten Book of Champs, Chumps and Punch-Drunk Palookas.* Alexandria, VA: Brassey's, 2003.

MMA fighter Kimbo Slice attends a boxing event in Nevada in May 2008. Courtesy of Chris Cozzone.

SLICE, KIMBO (1974–). Kimbo Slice is the nickname of Kevin Ferguson, a former street fighter turned mixed martial artist. Born in 1974 in Miami, Florida, Ferguson was a football star in high school and later briefly attended the University of Miami on an academic scholarship.

Slice became well known after several of his fights were shown over the Internet. He won all but one of the bouts, usually pounding his opponents with powerful blows. His one loss was a brutal affair with Sean Gannon, a Boston-based police officer who controversially used a knee strike to the head to disable Slice.

In June 2007, Slice made his professional mixed martial arts (MMA) debut in Cage Fury Fighting Championships 5 against former world heavyweight boxing champion **Ray Mercer.** To the surprise of some, Slice stopped Mercer in the first round with a **guillotine choke** in a bout that was officially billed as an exhibition. In November 2007, he kayoed Bo Cattrall in 19 seconds in **Elite XC: Renegade.** In February 2008, he destroyed former **Ultimate Fighting Championships (UFC)** legendary street brawler **David "Tank" Abbott** in 43 seconds. Slice then made his prime-time television debut in May 2008 against James "the Colossus" Thompson. Slice prevailed in the third round but showed some definite holes in his ground game, particularly in the second round. Slice was exposed even more in his next bout against former UFC fighter Seth Petrezulli, who stopped him in 14 seconds.

Slice has trained with former Pancrease and martial arts legend **Bas Rutten.**

Professional MMA Record:	3-1
Championship(s):	None

Further Reading

Bush, Terry E. "The Great Kimbo Slice Debate: Is Kimbo Slice Good or Bad for the Sport?" *FIGHT!* (June 2008), pp. 36–37.

Official Web site: http://www.kimboslice.org

Thorpe, Mark. "Miami slice: the fabled backyard brawls of Kimbo Slice created an Internet legend. Will that reputation survive the professional fury of the MMA cage?" *Muscle & Fitness*, 3/1/2008, pp. 122–130.

Varsallone, Jim. "Slice of Life." *The Miami Herald*, 2/19/2008.

Woods, Michael. "Slice set to make EliteXC debut against Cantrell." *ESPN.com*, 11/10/2007, at http://sports.espn.go.com/extra/mma/news/story?id=3101253

SMITH, BILLY (1871–1937). "Mysterious" Billy Smith was a former world welterweight champion known for his rough style of fighting and disregard for the Marquis of Queensbury rules of boxing. Born in 1871 in either Nova Scotia, Canada, or Eastport, Maine, Smith began his professional boxing career in San Francisco in 1891.

He won the welterweight championship in 1892 with a knockout of Danny Needham. He lost his title in 1894 to **Tommy Ryan.** He regained the title in 1898 with a win over William Matthews. He lost his title to James "Rube" Ferns by disqualification. Amazingly, Smith had dropped Ferns 15 times during the bout but lost on a foul. He finally retired in 1915.

Famous promoter **Jack "Doc" Kearns** said of Smith: "If you fought Smith, it was always a mystery what he would do next—rub his laces across your eyes, butt you or hit you in the balls" (Kent, p. 58). He will be finally inducted posthumously into the International Boxing Hall of Fame in June 2009.

Professional Record:	Unknown
Championship(s):	Welterweight, 1892–1894, 1898–1900

Further Reading

Cyber Boxing Zone profile of Smith: http://www.cyberboxingzone.com/boxing/smith-mb.htm

Kent, Graeme. The *Great White Hopes: The Quest to Defeat Jack Johnson*. Gloucester, England: Sutton Publishing, 2005.

Schutte, William. *Mysterious Billy Smith: The Dirtiest Fighter of All Time*. Author, 1996.

Solloway, Steve. "Mysterious Billy Smith's Career—and Story—are Worthy of Hall," *Portland Press Herald*, 12/11/2008, at http://pressherald.mainetoday.com/story.php?id=226902&ac=

SMITH, JAMES "BONECRUSHER" (1953–). James "Bonecrusher" Smith was a former world heavyweight champion known for his sledgehammer right hand. Born in 1953 in Magnolia, North Carolina, Smith attended and graduated from Shaw College. Smith played basketball in high school and college rather than take up boxing. He served in the military and then worked as a prison guard. He did not take up boxing until he was 28.

He turned pro in 1981 and lost to experienced former amateur champion James "Broad Ax" Broad. However, Smith developed, defeating undefeated prospects Rickey Parker and Chris

McDonald. In 1984, in only his 16th pro fight, he challenged undefeated champion **Larry Holmes** for the **International Boxing Federation (IBF)** title. Smith lost in the 12th round but acquitted himself quite well in the ring.

In 1986, he knocked out former heavyweight champion **Mike Weaver** in the first round. Later that year, Smith shocked the boxing world by kayoing **"Terrible" Tim Witherspoon** in the first round for the **World Boxing Association (WBA)** heavyweight championship. He lost his championship in a unification bout with **World Boxing Council (WBC)** champion **Mike Tyson**. Smith lost a lopsided 12-round decision.

He continued fighting but became relegated to journeyman status. He dropped a 10-round decision to Levi Billups in 1991. He also lost decisions to **Greg Page, Michael Moorer,** and Axel Schultz. He finally retired in 1999 after losing a rematch to Larry Holmes in a battle of 40-something heavyweights.

Professional Record:	44-17-1
Championship(s):	WBA heavyweight, 1986–1987

Further Reading

Berger, Phil. "Bonecrusher Smith: An Unlikely Route to Boxing Summitt." *The New York Times*, 3/2/1987, p. C4.

Kluck, Ted A. *Facing Tyson: 15 Fighters, 15 Stories*. Guilford, CT: Lyons Press, 2006.

SMITH, LONNIE (1962–). "Lightning" Lonnie Smith was a former junior welterweight champion known for his speed and defensive skills who fought for nearly 20 years as a professional. Smith turned pro in 1980 and compiled an impressive record against nondescript opposition. In 1985, he faced undefeated **World Boxing Council (WBC)** champion Billy Costello. Most ringside observers believed Costello would win easily. However, Smith recovered from a first-round knockdown to batter the champion over eight rounds. Unfortunately, Smith could not maintain the momentum, losing the title in his first defense against Rene Arredondo. In 1991, he challenged **Julio Cesar Chavez** for the junior welterweight championship, losing a 12-round decision. His last fight was a 10-round decision loss to Diosbelys Hurtado.

Record:	45-6-2
Championship(s):	WBC junior welterweight, 1985–1986

Further Reading

O'Brian, Joseph D. "Lighting Strikes: An inside look at Lonnie Smith." *The Ring* (November 1985), pp. 6–8.

SMITH, MAURICE (1961–). Maurice Smith is a former kickboxer and mixed martial artist known for his great striking ability with his hands and feet. He won multiple world kickboxing championships in the 1980s before turning his attention to mixed martial arts (MMA) in the 1990s. As a kickboxer, he went nine straight years without a defeat.

Born in 1961 in Seattle, Smith attended West Seattle High School where he excelled in football and gymnastics. He first became interested in martial arts as a kid after watching the Bruce Lee movie *The Chinese Connection*.

Smith made his kickboxing debut in 1980 at age 18. He fought the best kickboxers of the day, including Don "the Dragon" Wilson, Tony Morelli, and Travis Everett. Smith won several kickboxing titles through the years.

In 1993, he participated in the inaugural event of K-1, a Japan-based kickboxing promotion company that featured elements of kickboxing, karate, and Muay Thai. Smith defeated

Toshiyuki Atokawa before losing to the legendary **Ernesto "Mr. Perfect" Hoost,** perhaps the greatest kickboxer of all time.

Smith also fought in Pancrease, gaining experience in mixed martial arts. He lost to **Ken Shamrock** and **Bas Rutten** because those fighters had greater MMA experience and were more versatile. Smith gradually learned more ground fighting skills, which he used to his advantage in an Extreme Fighting bout against Kazunari Murakami. Smith kayoed Murakami in a bout that gave notice that Smith could compete at the higher levels of mixed martial arts.

The pinnacle of his MMA career came in 1997 when he upset feared wrestler and "ground and pound" practitioner **Mark "the Hammer" Coleman** by unanimous decision in 1997 at **Ultimate Fighting Championships (UFC)** 14 to win the UFC heavyweight championship. Smith had trained hard for the bout with **Frank Shamrock,** learning much about grappling techniques.

In his first title defense, he stopped **David "Tank" Abbott.** He lost his UFC belt to **Randy Couture** via unanimous decision. He then lost in the UFC to the athletic **Kevin Randleman,** a gifted wrestler and protégé of Coleman. Smith initially retired in 2000 after losing to Renato Sobral. However, in 2007, he returned to the MMA professional ranks with a technical knockout of **Marco Ruas** in the **International Fight League (IFL).** In February 2008, he submitted fellow kickboxer **Rick "the Jet" Roufus** via a kimura in a Strikeforce event.

Professional MMA Record:	12-13
Kickboxing Record:	63-11-4
Championship(s):	UFC Heavyweight, 1997; World Kicking Boxing Association, 1983

Further Reading
O'Neil, Danny. "Maurice Smith can't subdue competitive drive." *Seattle Times,* 2/22/2008.
Wall, Jeremy. *UFC's Ultimate Warriors Top 10.* Ontario: ECW Press, 2005, pp. 43–61.

SORJATURONG, SAMAN (1968–). Saman Sorjaturong was a former world junior flyweight champion from Thailand known for his late start in boxing, punching power, and ability to come back in his bouts. Born in 1968 in northeast Thailand, Sorjaturong took up boxing until his early 20s—an advanced age for a boxer. He turned pro in 1989 and in 1993 faced **Ricardo Lopez** for the **World Boxing Council (WBC)** strawweight (or minimumweight) world championship. The much-more experienced Lopez stopped Sorjaturong in the second round.

He rebounded and in 1995 defeated **Humberto Gonzalez** to win the WBC and **International Boxing Federation (IBF)** junior flyweight titles in an amazing bout that *The Ring* magazine called the "fight of the year." Sorjaturong came off the canvas twice to defeat the great champion. He defended his WBC belt 10 times until finally losing to Korea's Yo-Sam Choi in 1999. He retired in 2005 after losing to Koki Kameda.

Professional Record:	46-8-1
Championship(s):	WBC junior flyweight, 1995–1999; IBF junior flyweight, 1995–1996

Further Reading
Tongpituk, Sudrudee Saundra. "Bang the Gong Sorjaturong: In Thailand, Saman's The Man." *The Ring* (October 1997), pp. 40–42, 57–58.

SPADAFORA, PAUL (1975–). Paul Spadafora is a former world lightweight champion whose great boxing skills have at times been overshadowed by his out-of-the-ring legal troubles. Born in 1975 in Pittsburgh, Spadafora turned pro in 1995 and kept winning.

In 1999, he outpointed Israel Cardona over 12 rounds to win the **International Boxing Federation (IBF)** lightweight title. He made seven successful defenses of his title, including a decision win over Angel Manfredy, a decision over Victoriana Sosa, and a draw with Leonard Dorin. In the Sosa and Dorin fights, Spadafora showed great resolve in coming back from adversity to salvage his title belt.

He relinquished his belt to move up in weight. Unfortunately, Spadafora's life spiraled out of control outside the ring. He shot his girlfriend in the chest in 2003 and later served 13 months in jail. He won one fight in 2008 and hopes to end his legal troubles and reclaim his past ring glory.

Professional Record:	41-0-1
Championship(s):	IBF lightweight, 1999–2003

Further Reading

Harlan, Chico. "Paul Spadafora; Now He's Engaged in the Fight of His Life." *Pittsburgh Post-Gazette*, 2/27/2005, p. A1.

Lidz, Frank. "Staying power; though lacking a knockout punch, lightweight Paul Spadafora thrives on guile and determination." *Sports Illustrated*, 5/26/2003.

"10 Questions: Paul Spadafora." *KO: Boxing 2002*, pp. 12–15.

SPERRY, MARIO (1966–). Mario "the Zen Machine" Sperry is a Brazilian-based mixed martial artist known for his mastery of Brazilian jiu-jitsu and his training of such greats as **Antonio Rodrigo Nogueira** and Ricardo Arona. A pupil of Carlson Gracie, Sperry dominated the Brazilian Jiu-Jitsu world championships, defeating Royler Gracie in 1998. He won the Abu Dhabi Contest, a prestigious tournament created by the former president of the United Arab Emirates.

He made his professional mixed martial arts (MMA) debut in 1995, winning his first two matches before losing to Igor Zinoviev at an Extreme Fighting event. In 2001, he made his debut with **PRIDE** at PRIDE 17: Championship Chaos with a submission win over dangerous Russian striker **Igor Vovchanchyn.** In his most recent fight, he defeated Lee Hasdell at Cage Rage 22: Hard as Hell in July 2007. Sperry's nickname is "the Zen Master" for his seemingly imperturbability even in tough combat situations.

He currently serves as a coach in the **International Fight League (IFL).** He hopes to create a strong team in the IFL and continuing working in the MMA world.

Professional MMA Record:	13-4
Championship(s):	None

Further Reading

De Camargo, Franco. "The Zen Machine: Mario Sperry Won't Promise a Championship with His New IFL Team But He Will Make One Guarantee." *Ultimate Grappling* (April 2008), pp. 90–95.

Official Web site: http://members.aol.com/zenmario/

SPINKS, LEON (1953–). Leon "Neon" Spinks is best known for winning the world heavyweight championship in only his eighth professional bout with a decision over **Muhammad Ali.** Born in 1953, Spinks and his brother **Michael** captured Olympic gold in the Montreal Olympics—Leon at light heavyweight and Michael at middleweight.

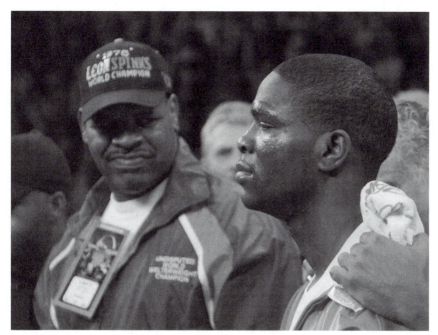

Leon Spinks looks on as a proud father as his son Cory prepares to do battle with Zab Judah in February 2005. Courtesy of Chris Cozzone.

Leon turned professional in 1977 and fought a 10-round draw with contender Scott LeDoux in his sixth pro bout. Handpicked as an easy defense for Ali, Spinks shocked the world by winning the title in a split decision. Unfortunately, Spinks could not handle success; his training habits suffered, and he lost the rematch badly by unanimous decision. In 1981, he challenged **Larry Holmes** for the **World Boxing Council (WBC)** heavyweight title but lost in the third round. He finally retired in 1995 after a decision loss to Fred Houpe. His brother Michael was a great light heavyweight champion who also won the heavyweight title, and his son Cory captured world titles in the welterweight and junior middleweight divisions. Though he won Olympic gold and the world heavyweight championship, many view Leon as a tragic figure in boxing.

Professional Record:	26-17-3
Championship(s):	Olympic Gold, 1976; WBA Heavyweight Championship, 1978

Further Reading
Doogan, Brian. "Rocky the road; The big interview; Leon Spinks." *The Sunday Times*, 10/1/2006, p. 16.
Katz, Michael. "Leon Spinks in Search of Himself and Title." *The New York Times*, 6/8/1981, p. C1.

SPINKS, MICHAEL (1956–). Michael Spinks, one of the greatest light heavyweight champions in boxing history, is best known for moving up in weight and capturing the world heavyweight title. Born in 1956 in St. Louis, Missouri, Michael and his brother Leon were members of the famous 1976 U.S. Olympic team that won five gold medals at the Montreal Games. Michael won gold in the middleweight division, while Leon captured gold at light heavyweight.

Michael turned pro in 1977 and won 16 straight fights before facing **World Boxing Association (WBA)** light heavyweight champ **Eddie Mustafa Muhammad**. Spinks earned a unanimous decision victory. He unified the light heavyweight title by adding the **World Boxing Council (WBC)** belt with a 15-round decision over Dwight Braxton (**Dwight Muhammad Qawi**). Spinks never lost as a light heavyweight, using his superior boxing skills and his powerful right cross known as the "Spinks Jinx."

In 1985, Spinks moved up in weight and challenged heavyweight champion **Larry Holmes.** He frustrated Holmes and won a 15-round unanimous decision. Never before had a light heavyweight successfully moved up in weight to capture the heavyweight title. Spinks also won a rematch in a debatable 15-round split decision. He lost his title in 91 seconds to a young destructive force named **Mike Tyson.** Spinks retired after the Tyson fight—the only loss of his professional career.

Record:	31-1
Championship(s):	WBA light heavyweight, 1981–1985; WBC light heavyweight, 1983–1985; IBF Heavyweight, 1985–1988

Further Reading
Blackburn, Doug. "Michael Spinks Eyes a Duel with History." *The Ring* (July 1984), pp. 22–27.
Hoffer, Richard. "Spinks Wrestles Title Away from Mustafa." *Los Angeles Times*, 7/19/1981, p. B1.
Hoffer, Richard. "Michael Spinks Adds WBC Title to His WBA Title." *Los Angeles Times*, 3/19/1983, p. B1.
Katz, Michael. "Michael Spinks Wins by Knockout." *The New York Times*, 2/25/1980, p. C25.
Welsh, Jack. "There's Always a First Time." *The Ring* (December 1985), pp. 32–39.

STARLING, MARLON (1959–). Marlon "the Magic Man" Starling was a former world welterweight champion and stylish boxing technician. Born in 1959 in Hartford, Connecticut, Starling grew up in a section of Hartford known as "the Brickyard." However, he had a stable family environment, graduated high school, and devoted himself to amateur boxing. He was a fine amateur but missed an opportunity for the 1976 Montreal Olympics because he suffered a wrist injury.

He turned pro in 1979 and won his 25 bouts before losing a 12-round split decision to fellow unbeaten prospect and future champ **Donald Curry** for a regional title in 1982. Two years later, he challenged Curry for the **World Boxing Association (WBA)** and **International Boxing Federation (IBF)** welterweight titles but lost a close unanimous decision.

In August 1987, he upset undefeated champion **Mark Breland** to win the WBA welterweight title after trailing badly on the scorecards. He dropped Breland with a left hook in the 11th round and captured the title. He successfully defended his title five times before finally losing his belt by close decision to Maurice Blocker in 1990. He also lost a majority decision to middleweight champion **Michael Nunn** in his previous fight. Starling retired at age 32 after losing to Blocker, citing age and increasing difficulty making the welterweight limit.

Professional Record:	45-6-1
Championship(s):	WBA Welterweight, 1987–1990

Further Reading
Alfano, Peter. "Breland Stopped by Starling." *The New York Times*, 8/23/1987, Section 5, p. 1.
Murray, Jim. "His Aim is to Avoid Getting Hit." *Los Angeles Times*, 7/1/1988, p. 1.

STEVENSON, TEOFILO (1952–). Cuban heavyweight Teofilo Stevenson is considered one of the greatest amateur boxers in the history of the sport. This heavyweight with a sledgehammer of a right hand won Olympic gold medals at the 1972 Munich Games, the 1976 Montreal Games, and the 1980 Moscow Games. He may have captured more gold medals, but Cuba boycotted the 1984 Los Angeles Games and refused to attend the 1988 Seoul Games because North Korea was not allowed to cosponsor the event.

Born in 1952, Stevenson first attracted attention in his country when he won the national heavyweight crown at age 17. He pummeled American Duane Bobick in the quarterfinals on his way to capturing his first gold medal. In 1976, he devastated future world heavyweight champion John Tate in the semifinals on his way to gold in Montreal. Tate referred to Stevenson's jab as a "steering wheel." In 1980, he outpointed Soviet boxer Pyotr Zaev to win his third consecutive gold medal.

Speculation abounded whether Stevenson would leave Cuba and launch a professional career. Despite the efforts of leading promoters **Don King, Bob Arum,** and others, Stevenson remained in Cuba as an amateur. He later served as an advisor to Cuba's national boxing program.

Amateur Record:	302-22
Championship(s):	Olympic Gold in 1972, 1976 and 1980

Further Reading

Amdur, Neil. "Stevenson Wins 3d Boxing Gold." *The New York Times,* 8/3/1980, p. S1.
Brubaker, Bill. "A Boxer To Whom Money Didn't Talk." *The Washington Post,* 2/21/1986, p. A1.
Gustkey, Earl. "Teofilo Can No Longer Retreat to Quiet Corner." *Los Angeles Times,* 7/28/1983, p. D1.

STEELE, RICHARD (1944–). Richard Steele is a boxing and mixed martial arts (MMA) promoter and former boxing promoter who is best known as a world-class boxing referee. Born in 1944, Steele boxed in the Marines as an amateur and later as a professional in the light heavyweight division. He compiled a 16-4 record before retiring in 1970.

Steele became a referee a couple years later and went on to serve as the third man in the ring for more than 160 world title bouts. In 1976, he refereed a **Carlos Zarate** bantamweight title defense against Paul Ferreri. Among his most famous bouts were **Meldrick Taylor—Julio Cesar Chavez** I (1990), **Aaron Pryor—Alexis Arguello** II (1983), **Ray Mancini—Bobby Chacon** (1984), and **Marvelous Marvin Hagler—Thomas Hearns** (1985).

Steele became embroiled in controversy after he stopped the Chavez—Taylor bout in the 12th and final round with only seconds remaining in the bout. Steele's stoppage in favor of Chavez denied Taylor, who was only a few seconds away from a decision win. Steele retired as a referee in 2001 to become a promoter and matchmaker. However, Steele returned to the ring in 2005 as a referee. He remains a respected figure in boxing circles.

Further Reading

Newman, Sean. "Richard Steele Speaks to Doghouse Boxing—'It Feels Great to B e Back!" 5/29/2005 at
　　http://www.doghouseboxing.com/Newman/Newman052905.htm
Official Web site: http://www.steeleboxing.com

STEWARD, EMANUEL (1944–). Emanuel Steward is a world-class boxing trainer and manager known for working with many great boxing champions, including **Thomas "the Hitman" Hearns, Lennox Lewis,** and **Wladimir Klitschko.** Born in 1944 in West Virginia, Steward moved in his youth to Detroit, Michigan, where he became an amateur boxer. He compiled an impressive record as an amateur but did not turn professional. Instead, he worked as an electrician for Detroit Edison. He gave up his electrician job to serve as head boxing trainer in the city's recreation department. He worked out of the city-run recreation center known as the Kronk (named after city councilman John F. Kronk). Steward became famous for developing many fine boxers at the Kronk Gym. Steward had his first world champion when **Hilmer Kenty** defeated Ernesto Espana in 1980 to win the **World Boxing Council (WBC)** lightweight title. The Kronk Gym became famous in the 1980s as a haven for great boxing talent. Steward has trained innumerable world champions, including James Toney, **Michael Moorer, Oscar De La Hoya,** Mike McCallum, and **Milton McCrory.**

Further Reading
Hoffer, Richard. "The Kronk Gym: Even Tougher on the Inside than the Outside." *Los Angeles Times,* 2/20/1985, p. OC_B1.
Katz, Michael. "The Kronk: Detroit Boxing Assembly Line." *The New York Times,* 3/2/1980, p. S3.

ST.-PIERRE, GEORGES (1981–). Georges "Rush" St.-Pierre—better known by his initials GSP—is arguably the most talented mixed martial artist pound-for-pound. He possesses an amazing degree of athleticism, superior striking skills, and a gifted ground game. Born in 1981 in Saint-Isidore, Quebec, St.-Pierre learned karate at age six. He later studied Brazilian jiu-jitsu, wrestling, and boxing.

He turned pro in 2002 with a win over Ivan Menjivar and then fought several fights under the promotion of the Ultimate Combat Challenge (UCC)—a mixed martial arts (MMA) group based in Canada. His winning streak in UCC bouts attracted the attention of the **Ultimate Fighting Championships (UFC)** which landed St.-Pierre at UFC 46: Supernatural against the talented **Karo Parisyan.** St.-Pierre dominated and won a three-round unanimous decision.

He then defeated Jay Hieron to earn a shot at longtime UFC welterweight champion **Matt Hughes.** St.-Pierre appeared to be doing well early but got careless and lost via an armbar submission. He rebounded with three straight wins over **Sean Sherk, Frank Trigg,** and **B. J. "the Prodigy" Penn** to earn a rematch with Hughes. He dominated Hughes in the rematch, stopping him on strikes in the second round.

In April 2007, he suffered only his second loss to unheralded and huge underdog **Matt "the Terror" Serra.** St.-Pierre rebounded with a convincing decision win over the tough wrestler Josh Koscheck. He then dominated Matt Hughes in a rubber match to earn a rematch against Serra. St.-Pierre annihilated Serra in the second round to regain his UFC title. In 2009, he dominated Penn in a rematch.

Professional MMA Record:	18-2
Championship(s):	UFC Welterweight, 2006–2007, 2008–

Further Reading
Davidson, Neil. "Montreal fighter has bad intentions as he goes after UFC title." *The Canadian Press,* 10/6/2006.
Davidson, Neil. "The Real GSP: Remaking a Champion." *FIGHT!* (April 2008), pp. 42–50.
Rodriguez, Jose. "The New St. Pierre." *The Edmonton Sun,* 8/18/2007, p. S22.
"The Party is Over." *FightSport* (April 2008), pp. 48–51.

STRIBLING, WILLIAM LAWRENCE "YOUNG" (1904–1933). William Lawrence "Young" Stribling was a power-punching light heavyweight who recorded 125 knockouts in his career and more than 220 wins in a career cut short by a tragic motorcycle accident. Born in 1904 in Bainbridge, Georgia, Stribling turned pro in 1921 as a featherweight.

In 1923, he fought Mike McTigue for the world light heavyweight crown but came away with a draw. The two battled in Columbus, Georgia. After 10 rounds, referee Harry Ertle called the match a draw. The referee then changed the decision in favor of Stribling for several hours before once again changing his mind and calling the bout a draw.

In 1926, he lost a 15-round decision to Pete Berlenbach in his second attempt at a world light heavyweight championship. In 1931, he challenged heavyweight champion **Max Schmeling** for the world title, falling in the 15th round after a gallant effort. Stribling defeated the clever **Maxie Rosenbloom** by decision in 1933. The next month he died in the fatal motorcycle accident.

Professional Record: 256-16-14
Championship(s):   None

Further Reading
Allen, John. "Stribling Boosts Light Heavyweight Class." *The Atlanta Constitution*, 1/6/1924, p. B6.
Associated Press. "McTigue Gets Draw After Riotous Bout." *The New York Times*, 10/5/1923, p. 15.
Gould, Alan J. "Champion Triumphs: Schmeling Stops Bill Stribling." *Los Angeles Times*, 7/4/1931, p. 1.
Newman, Harry. "Berlenbach Beats Stribling and Retains Title." *Chicago Daily Tribune*, 6/11/1926, p. 25.

STRICKLAND, REGGIE (1968–). Reggie Strickland has had one of the most remarkable careers in boxing history—though not for the reasons that the champions and contenders included in this encyclopedia. Strickland deserves inclusion—much like the older journeyman Joe Grim—for his remarkable longevity as a cagey journeyman who had enough defensive skills to lose decisions month after month and week after week. The *Miami Herald* referred to him as "the most enterprising bum in boxing." Strickland lost more than 260 bouts in his professional career that began in 1987 with a four-round decision loss.

Strickland, along with his brother Jerry, were paid to come into a prospect's hometown and lose fights. The remarkable thing is that Strickland possesses decent boxing skills and perhaps could have even been a contender. "If I had trained better, I could have been a contender," he told this author in 2002. Instead, he chose to become the ultimate opponent. His unusual place in boxing has earned him front-page coverage in the *New York Times* and profiles on ESPN and HBO's *Real Sports with Bryant Gumbel*.

In his career, Strickland sometimes used different names—Reggie Raglin and Reggie Buse. In 1997, he once had a fight in Tennessee one night and a fight in Missouri the very next day. He lost both fights by decision. He suffered a head injury in a car accident, which forced his retirement from boxing in 2005. Strickland still works in the sport as a matchmaker. Legend has it that one day at a local mixed martial events in Indiana (before the state regulated the sport), a fighter had to withdraw and a local promoter needed someone to fill in at the last minute. Strickland stepped in and kayoed his opponent—something he did not often do in his boxing career.

Professional Record: 66-276-16 (sources disagree)
Championships: None

Further Reading
Alesia, Mark. "Local Man Makes a Living as Boxing's Biggest Loser." *The Indianapolis Star*, 10/17/2004, p. 10C.
Diaz, George. "Meet Reggie Strickland, Professional Loser." *The Orlando Sentinel*, 8/11/2003, p. D1.
Hudson, David. "Reggie Strickland: The Most Active Pro." *Boxing Digest*, August 2002, p. 25.
Johnson, Kirk. "Boxing in the Shadows." *The New York Times*, 6/1/1998, p. A1.
Rodriguez, Ken. "Some Loser: Strickland Prospers as Bum." *The Miami Herald*, 7/19/1998, p. 7C.

SUGAR, BERT (1936–). Bert Sugar is a famous boxing writer known for his prolific authorship of boxing books, his trademark cigar and hat, and his quick wit. For many years he was editor and publisher of the boxing magazines *Boxing Illustrated* and *The Ring*.

Born in 1936 in Washington, D.C., Sugar fought Golden Gloves as a youth and then for the University of Maryland. He referred to himself as the "great white hopeless" for his lack of ring skills.

He earned a law degree and an M.B.A. from the University of Michigan. He passed the District of Columbia bar exam but realized he did not want to practice law. He worked in the advertising business for a decade before moving into sportswriting. In 1969, he purchased *Boxing Illustrated*. Ten years later, in 1979, he bought *The Ring* magazine.

Sugar has written numerous boxing books through the years, including: *Boxing's Greatest Fighters* (2006) and *The Great Fights: A Pictorial History of Boxing* (1981).

Further Reading

Jorgenson, Eric. "The Bert Sugar Interview." *Cyber Boxing Zone Journal*, May 2001, at http://www.cyber boxingzone.com/w52x-ej.htm

Sugar, Bert Randolph. *Boxing's Greatest Fighters*. Guilford, CT: Lyons Press, 2006.

Sugar, Bert Randolph, and the Editors of *Ring* Magazine. *The Great Fights: A Pictorial History of Boxing's Greatest Bouts*. New York: Rutledge Press, 1981.

SULLIVAN, JOHN L. (1858–1918). John L. Sullivan, the "Boston Strong Boy," reigned as boxing's premier bare knuckle champion in the late nineteenth century and served as boxing's first champion under modern rules, which required gloves. He allegedly honed his prowess with his hands by challenging men in barrooms, boldly proclaiming: "I can lick any son of a bitch in the house."

In 1880, Sullivan began to attract attention as a serious boxer when he roughed up Mike Donovan, a technical fighter known as "the Professor" who later served as a trainer for President Theodore Roosevelt. Two years later, he battered Paddy Ryan and stopped him in the ninth round. *The Washington Post* described his performance: "From the start, Sullivan acted on the offensive, attacking his opponent with a violence almost amounting to ferocity."

Sullivan earned widespread recognition as world champion in July 1889 when he defeated Jake Kilrain in Mississippi in a bareknuckle fight. Sullivan refused to defend his title against black men, harboring regrettable racial sentiments reflected during his time. For instance, he refused to face George Godfrey and later **Peter Jackson,** stating: "I will not fight a negro. I never have and never shall" (Isenberg, p. 293). In 1892, Sullivan lost his title to **James "Gentleman Jim" Corbett** in a match conducted under the **Queensberry Rules.** Corbett stopped Sullivan in the 21st round.

Professional Record:	38-1-1 (not all sources agree)
Championship(s):	Heavyweight Championship, 1889–1892

Further Reading

Dibble, Roy F. *John L. Sullivan: An Intimate Narrative*. Boston: Little, Brown, and Company, 1925.

Isenberg, Michael. *John L. Sullivan and His America*. Urbana: University of Illinois Press, 1988.

Pollack, Adam J. *John L. Sullivan: The Career of the First Gloved Heavyweight Champion*. Jefferson, NC: McFarland Press, 2006.

"Sullivan Wins Easily." *The Washington Post*, 2/8/1882, p. 1.

SUMO WRESTLING. Sumo wrestling is a competitive form of wrestling where wrestlers attempt to force one another outside of a circle. The wrestler who forces his opponent outside the circle or forces his opponent to touch the ground with anything other than his feet wins the match. Sumo wrestling is most popular in Japan where sumo wrestlers can compete professionally.

Sumo wrestling has taken place in Japan regularly at least since the early seventeenth century in a time frame called the Edo period. The very best sumo wrestlers are treated like royalty in

Japan, similar to a top National Football League or National Basketball Association player in the United States. The very best sumo wrestlers are in a category called yokozuna.

Some sumo wrestlers have tried their hand at mixed martial arts—though with little success. For example, Akebono was a superstar sumo wrestler but fared poorly in mixed martial arts and kickboxing, losing to **Don Frye, Royce Gracie, Bob Sapp,** and **Hong Man Choi.**

Another example was Emanuel Yarborough, a massive amateur sumo wrestling champion who fought in the early **Ultimate Fighting Championships (UFC).** He lost badly to Keith Hackney at UFC 3 and then lost to **Daiju Takase**—a man whom he outweighed by more than 400 pounds.

Further Reading

Cameron, Deborah. "Big in Japan; Super Sport." *Sydney Morning Herald*, 1/21/2006, p. 52.

Onishi, Norimitsu, "Japan's ancient art struggles to stay in form." *The International Herald Tribune*, 10/21/2007, p. 2.

SYLVIA, TIM (1976–). Tim Sylvia, called "The Maine-iac" because he hails from the state of Maine and fights like a maniac, is a former two-time world **Ultimate Fighting Championships (UFC)** heavyweight champion. Standing 6'8", Sylvia dominates many of his fights with his imposing size and striking ability. His excellent take-down defense prevents many of his opponents from managing to take him out of his vaunted striking attack.

He won the UFC title for the first time in 2003 with a first-round stoppage of **Ricco Rodriguez.** He defeated Gan McGhee in a title defense but lost the title after he tested positive for an anabolic steroid after the bout. He lost to **Frank Mir** and **Andrei Arlovski** via submission in two subsequent attempts to regain the title. He earned his second championship and a measure of revenge when he stopped Arlovski in 2006. He defeated Arlovski in their rubber match and added another title defense before losing to **Randy "the Natural" Couture** in March 2007.

In March 2008, Sylvia used his strong stand-up attack to pound **Antonio Rodrigo Nogueira** for much of their fight until the Brazilian jiu-jistu master submitted Sylvia in the third round. Sylvia had finished his UFC contract and moved on to a showdown with pound-for-pound great **Fedor Emelianenko** in a July 2008 event promoted by **Affliction.** Many expected Sylvia's height and reach to pose at least a challenge for the great Fedor. However, Fedor overwhelmed Sylvia and submitted him in a mere 36 seconds.

Professional Record: 24-5

Championship(s):   UFC Heavyweight, 2003–2005; 2006–2007

Further Reading

Davidson, Neil. "UFC heavyweight champion Tim (The Maine-iac) Sylvia says bring it on." *The Canadian Press*, 2/21/2007.

Official Web site: http://www.tim-sylvia.com/

Pugmire, Lance. "UFC Fight is Pumping Ire; After Turning off Fans, 6 foot 8 Heavyweight Champion Tim Sylvia has his Reputation on the Line in a Title Fight Against the Popular Couture." *Los Angeles Times*, 3/3/2007, p. D3.

TAKASE, DAIJU (1978–). Daiju Takase is a Japanese-based mixed martial artist best known for his submission skills. Though he has lost more than he has won in his mixed martial arts (MMA) career, Takase has pulled off some amazing victories. In his MMA debut at **PRIDE** 3, the 180 lb.-Takase stunned the world by stopping 600 lb. sumo wrestler Emmanuel Yarbrough with strikes in 1998. Then, in his greatest triumph, Takase faced dangerous striker **Anderson Silva** at PRIDE 26: Bad to the Bone. Most expected Silva to kayo Takase with his feared kicks, knee strikes, or punches. Instead, Takase submitted Silva with a triangle choke in the first round. He also holds wins over Chris Brennan and Carlos Newton in his career.

Professional MMA Record:	7-11-1
Championship(s):	None

Further Reading
PRIDE profile: http://www.pridefc.com/pride2005/index.php?mainpage=fighters&fID=164

TAKTAROV, OLEG (1967–). Oleg Taktarov is a Russian-based mixed martial artist best known for his strong performances in the early days of the **Ultimate Fighting Championships (UFC).** A practitioner well-versed in sambo and judo, Taktarov began his mixed martial arts (MMA) career in 1993.

In 1995, he competed in UFC 5, winning his first match before falling to **Dan "The Beast" Severn.** Taktarov returned to UFC 6, defeating Dave Beneteau, Anthony Macias, and **David "Tank" Abbott** to win the title.

He competed in the initial **PRIDE** event in 2000, losing via kayo to the powerful **Gary Goodridge.** Taktarov initially retired in 1998 from MMA and focused on his acting career. He has starred in numerous movies, including *15 Minutes*, *Bad Boys II*, and *Air Force One*. However, in 2007, he returned to the ring. In 2008, he defeated **Mark Kerr.**

Professional MMA Record:	11-5-2
Championship(s):	UFC 6 Tournament

Further Reading
Gentry, Clyde. *No Holds Barred: Ultimate Fighting and the Martial Arts Revolution*. Preston, England: Milo Books, 2005.
Official Web site: http://www.olegt.com/

TANNER, EVAN (1971–2008). Evan Tanner was a former American-based mixed martial artist who lived on his own terms. Born in 1971 in Amarillo, Texas, Tanner excelled in high school wrestling in Texas, winning a state championship.

He began his professional mixed martial arts (MMA) career in 1997 with three wins in the same night, including a win over **Paul Buentello.** In 2001, he challenged **Tito Ortiz** for the **Ultimate Fighting Championships (UFC)** light heavyweight title but lost in just more than 30 seconds into the bout. In 2005, he won the UFC middleweight title with a win over David Terrell. He lost the title in his first defense against **Rich Franklin.**

Tanner initially retired in 2006 but returned to the Octagon in 2008. In September 2008, he ventured out into the desert in California for an adventure. Tragically, he died of heat exhaustion.

Professional MMA Record: 32-8
Championship(s):   UFC Middleweight, 2005

Further Reading
Gerbasi, Thomas. "Evan Tanner's Greatest UFC Moments." *UFC.com*, 9/10/2008, at http://www.ufc.com/index.cfm?fa=news.detail&gid=14457
Iole, Kevin. "Evan Tanner Follows His Own Path." *Yahoo.com*, 2/27/2008, at http://sports.yahoo.com/mma/news?slug=ki-tanner022708&prov=yhoo&type=lgns

TAPIA, JOHNNY (1967–). Johnny Tapia is a popular former champion of several lower weight classes known for his great boxing skills and an out-of-control life outside the ring that he calls "Mi Vida Loco" (Spanish for "my crazy life"). Born in 1967 in Albuquerque, New Mexico, Tapia's mother was murdered when he was 8 years old. He turned to boxing at age 11 and

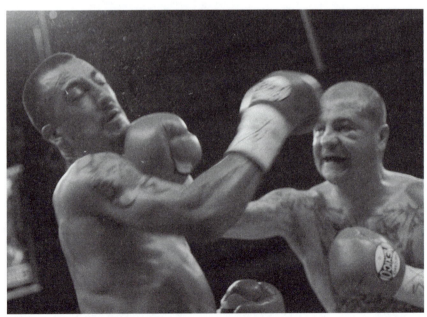

Johnny Tapia lands a beautiful right hand on Frankie Archuletta in their March 2005 bout. Tapia won a unanimous decision. Courtesy of Chris Cozzone.

ran with a gang as a youngster. He turned professional in 1988 with a six-round draw. Tapia did not lose until his 49th professional bout against **Paulie Ayala** by decision.

In 1991, Tapia's boxing license was revoked after he tested positive for cocaine for the third time in a year. He did not fight in the years 1991–1993. In 1994, he defeated Henry Martinez to win the World Boxing Organization (WBO) super flyweight title. He continued to defend his belt and then added the **International Boxing Federation (IBF)** title with perhaps the finest performance of his career—a convincing decision win over hometown rival Danny Romero in 1997. He won the **World Boxing Association (WBA)** bantamweight title with a decision win over Nana Konadu. He then lost his title to Ayala in a close decision. He also lost a disputed decision to Ayala in 2000. He rebounded to win the IBF featherweight title with a decision over **Manuel Medina.** He lost his next bout to the great **Marco Antonio Barrera,** and then his career went downhill, though he continues to fight.

Record:	56-5-2
Championship(s):	WBO super flyweight, 1994–1998; IBF super flyweight, 1997–1998; WBA Bantamweight, 1998–1999; WBO super bantamweight, 2000; IBF featherweight, 2002.

Further Reading
KO Interview. "Johnny Tapia: 'Boxing Got Me Out of a Lot of Trouble.'" *KO Magazine* (July 1995), pp. 42–48.
Tapia, Johnny. *Mi Vida Loca: The Crazy Life of Johnny Tapia.* Los Angeles: Volt Press, 2006.

TARVER, ANTONIO (1968–). Antonio "the Magic Man" Tarver is a former world light heavyweight champion who is best known for being the first man to kayo the great **Roy Jones, Jr.** Born in 1968 in Orlando, Florida, Tarver had a battle with drugs shortly after high school. However, he recovered to have a very decorated amateur career record of 158-8. His career culminated in a bronze medal at the 1996 Olympic Games in Atlanta. He lost in the semifinal round to eventual gold medal winner Vassily Jirov by decision.

Antonio Tarver looks like he is in a battle with Glen Johnson in their December 2004 bout. Tarver lost a close decision. Courtesy of Chris Cozzone.

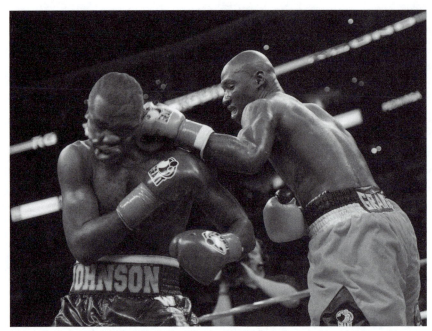

Antonio Tarver lands a good left hand against rival Glen Johnson in their December 2004 bout. Tarver lost a close decision. Courtesy of Chris Cozzone.

Tarver turned pro in 1997 and won his first 16 bouts before an upset loss to fellow unbeaten contender Eric Harding in 2000. In April 2003, he defeated Montell Griffin to win the vacant **World Boxing Council (WBC)** and **International Boxing Federation (IBF)** world light heavyweight titles. In his next bout, he lost a disputed decision to Roy Jones, Jr. In the rematch, Tarver exacted his revenge with a second-round knockout. Tarver famously exuded confidence before the bout, speaking into the microphone in the ring instructions to Jones, asking whether Roy had any excuses tonight.

Tarver lost his title via split decision to the rugged **Glen Johnson** but defeated Johnson in a rematch for the **International Boxing Organization (IBO)** championship in June 2005. In October 2005, he defeated Jones by decision in their rubber match. Tarver then took some time off from the ring to star in the latest *Rocky* movie opposite Sylvester Stallone in the character role of "Mason Dixon." Tarver earned rave reviews for his cinematic performance but not for his next performance in the ring, where he looked lethargic in losing to former middleweight champion **Bernard Hopkins** in June 2006.

Tarver rebounded with two wins in 2007 and then regained the IBF light heavyweight title with a decision win over Clinton Woods. He lost the title to undefeated "Bad" **Chad Dawson** in October 2008.

Professional Record:	27-5
Championship(s):	WBC light heavyweight, 2003, 2004; IBF light heavyweight, 2003; WBA light heavyweight, 2004

Further Reading

Diaz, George. "A Portrait of Perseverance: Taking the Hard Road Through Life Has Helped Make Orlando's Antonio Tarver a World Champion." *Orlando Sentinel*, 12/18/2004, p. D12.

Official Web site: http://www.antonio-tarver.com/

Stewart, Don. "Tarver Regains the Light Heavyweight Championship." *The Ring* (Vol. 5, 2005), pp. 32–37.

TAYLOR, JERMAIN (1978–). Jermain "Bad Intentions" Taylor is a former undisputed middleweight champion and the man who finally lifted the crown from longtime division kingpin **Bernard Hopkins.** Born in 1978 in Little Rock, Arkansas, Taylor had a fine amateur career under the tutelage of his trainer Ozell Nelson. He won a bronze medal at the 2000 Sydney Olympics, losing to Yermakhan Ibraimov in the semifinal round.

He turned pro under the watchful eye of Nelson and lead trainer Pat Burns in 2001. He kept winning and in 2005 challenged Hopkins for the middleweight championship. Taylor entered as a solid underdog but performed well in the early rounds. He won a controversial split decision, surviving some tough moments in the later rounds. He then defeated Hopkins via another close decision in the rematch. After the Hopkins fights, Taylor dropped Burns as his lead trainer and hired **Emanuel Steward,** though Nelson always remained in the corner.

In 2006, he fought to a draw against **Ronald "Winky" Wright** and then defeated former champions **Kassim Ouma** and Cory Spinks. In 2007, Taylor lost his title in a classic slugout with undefeated challenger **Kelly Pavlik.** Taylor had Pavlik badly hurt in the second round but could not finish the resilient Pavlik, who rallied to win in the seventh round. Taylor lost a rematch in a nontitle bout in February 2008. He then dropped Steward as his trainer and father-figure Nelson took lead duties. Taylor rebounded in November 2008 with a strong performance against Jeff Lacy as a super middleweight and hopes to gain another world championship in 2009.

Jermain Taylor looks unmarked and happy after defeating Raul Marquez in their 2004 bout. Courtesy of Chris Cozzone.

Professional Record:	28-2-1
Championship(s):	IBF Middleweight, 2005; WBA Middleweight, 2005; WBC Middleweight, 2005–2007; WBO Middleweight, 2005–2007

Further Reading

Mayo, David. "The $50 Question: Is Jermain Taylor Really a Pay-Per-View Fighter?" *The Ring* (April 2006), pp. 26–31.

Official Web site: http://jermaintaylor.com/

Pugmire, Lance. "Taylor knows about knockout blows." *Los Angeles Times,* 2/15/2008, p. D8.

Sandomir, Richard. "Taylor Has a Polished Jab for an Aging Hopkins." *The New York Times,* 7/14/2005, p. D1.

TAYLOR, MELDRICK (1966–). Meldrick "TNT" Taylor was one of boxing's brightest stars in the late 1980s and early 1990s. A former Olympic gold medalist and world champion in two divisions, Taylor was blessed with incredible hand and foot speed. Born in 1966 in Philadelphia, Pennsylvania, Taylor made the 1984 Los Angeles Olympic team at age 17. He dominated the opposition on the way to winning his gold medal in the featherweight division. He either stopped or shut out every opponent on his march to Olympic stardom.

He turned pro in 1984 and four years later won his first world title with a 12-round stoppage of the talented **James "Buddy" McGirt.** Taylor successfully defended his title twice before a mega-unification fight with the great **Julio Cesar Chavez.** Taylor fought brilliantly but took a lot of punishment, heading into the final round. Taylor had the fight in hand on two of the three official scorecards, but referee **Richard Steele** stopped the bout with two seconds left, as Chavez battered Taylor in the corner.

He rebounded the next year and defeated Aaron Davis to win the **World Boxing Association (WBA)** welterweight title. He successfully defended the title twice before suffering an upset loss to Christano Espano. Before his loss to Espano, he made an ill-advised move up in weight to the junior middleweight division and lost badly to **Terry Norris.**

Taylor never seemingly recovered from those back-to-back losses, and his skills deteriorated. His last fight was in 2002.

Professional Record:	38-8-1
Championship(s):	IBF junior welterweight, 1988–1990; WBA welterweight, 1991–1992

Further Reading
Berger, Phil. "Counting on Talent is Hard to Count Out." *The New York Times*, 5/5/1992, p. B5.
Berger, Phil. "Taylor Stops McGirt in 12 For I.B.F. Title." *The New York Times*, 9/4/1988, p. S11.
Berger, Phil. "Taylor Pounds Davis to Take Title." *The New York Times*, 1/20/1991, p. S9.
Wise, Mike. "Taylor and Chavez: Old Soldiers Who Keep Fighting." *The New York Times*, 9/17/1994, p. 31.

TEN POINT MUST SYSTEM. The ten point must system describes the generally prevailing method of scoring or judging boxing bouts. The major sanctioning bodies in boxing employ this system for scoring bouts. Under the ten point must system, the winner of each round receives 10 points, while the loser generally receives 9 points. If the winning fighter scores a knockdown or inflicts significant damage and dominates the round, that boxer generally takes the round 10-8. A boxer who wins a round while scoring two knockdowns usually wins the round 10-7.

The ten point must system has been in use in some locations since the 1930s. When first introduced, many criticized it as an inferior system to the rounds scoring system—where fights were scored based on number of rounds won. For example, if a fighter won 6 rounds in a 10-round fight and his opponent captured 4, the score would be 6-4. The system had its critics, including *Washington Post* writer Lewis F. Atchison who wrote in 1938: "The 10 point must system is a distinctly collegiate method of scoring a boxing bout, and not trustworthy in a prize fight. It is time the 10-point system were thrown out together, and a straight-forward round for round judging basis installed."

The ten point must system is also used by many mixed martial arts (MMA) organizations, including the **Ultimate Fighting Championships (UFC).** The scoring system there is arguably even more nuanced because there are more elements to consider in MMA than in boxing.

In October 2007, the **World Boxing Association (WBA)** announced that it would consider a change to the current ten point must system by calling for a half-point system modification. Under this system, the winning boxer would garner 10 points, while the losing boxer could earn up to 9.5 points. The WBA will experiment with the half-point modification before determining its future.

Further Reading
Atchison, Lewis F. "The Punch Line." *The Washington Post*, 10/18/1938, p. X19.
Layden, Tim. "Boxing Judges: On the Ropes." *Newsday*, 5/13/1990, p. 28.

TERRELL, ERNIE (1939–). Ernie Terrell was a former world heavyweight champion best known for his height (6'6"), reach, and loss to **Muhammad Ali.** Born in 1939 in Belzoni, Mississippi, Terrell turned pro in 1957. He went 18-2 in his first 20 bouts, both losses by split decision to Johnny Gray.

In 1962, Terrell suffered his first stoppage loss at the hands of **Cleveland "Big Cat" Williams.** However, in 1963, Terrell avenged the loss to Williams with a decision win, vaulting him into national prominence as a future threat in the heavyweight division.

In 1965, Terrell won the vacant **World Boxing Association (WBA)** heavyweight title with a decision win over tough contender Eddie Machen. He successfully defended his title twice with decision wins over **George Chuvalo** and Doug Jones. In 1967, he lost his title to Muhammad Ali via a lopsided 15-round decision. After Ali's exile, Terrell participated in a tournament process to determine the new champion but lost to Thad Spencer. Terrell retired in 1973 after consecutive losses to **Chuck Wepner** and Jeff Merritt.

Following his retirement, Terrell continued to perform with his jazz band and later promoted boxing matches.

Professional record: 45-9
Championship(s):   WBA Heavyweight, 1965–1967

Further Reading
Lipsyte, Robert. "Jabbing and Running Terrell Scores Unanimous Decision Over Chuvalo." *The New York Times*, 11/2/1965, p. 39.
Lipsyte, Robert. "Terrell Outpoints Jones to Retain W.B.A. Title in Dull, Rough Fight." *The New York Times*, 6/29/1966, p. 52.
Lipsyte, Robert. "Ernie Terrell, the Champion, Wants to be Known as 'The' Champion." *The New York Times*, 10/29/1965, p. 55.
Markus, Robert. "Sunlight or Shadow for Ernie Terrell." *Chicago Tribune*, 2/4/1967, p. E3.
Smith, Sam. "The ring leader: In this corner, wearing a 3-piece suit and a worried look . . . Ernie Terrell." *Chicago Tribune*, 2/12/1984, p. H16.

THOMAS, DIN (1976–). Din Thomas is an American mixed martial artist who has competed in the **Ultimate Fighting Championships (UFC)** and several other mixed martial arts (MMA) organizations since his professional debut in 1998. He competed on *The Ultimate Fighter 4,* advancing past two bouts before dropping a decision to fellow veteran **Chris Lytle.** Born in 1976 in Delaware, Thomas became well-versed in boxing and Brazilian jiu-jitsu.

He holds wins over many great MMA artists, including **Matt Serra, Rich Clementi, Jens Pulver,** and Clay Guida. In his first UFC match in 2003, he lost to **B. J. "the Prodigy" Penn.** He teaches mixed martial arts at his academy in Port St. Lucie, Florida. He was arrested in 2007 for "felony prohibited competitions," but the district attorney's office declined to file formal charges.

Professional MMA Record: 22-8
Championship(s):   None

Further Reading
Taflinger, Neal. "Smoker." *FIGHT!* (March 2008), pp. 94–96.

THOMAS, PINKLON (1958–). Pinklon Thomas was a former world heavyweight champion known for his powerful and quick left jab and his pink boxing trunks. Born in 1958 in Pontiac, Michigan, Thomas overcame an early drug addiction and turned pro in 1978 after only a few amateur fights. His natural talent and devastating jab carried him to a 24-0-1 record entering the biggest fight of his career against "Terrible" **Tim Witherspoon, the World Boxing Council (WBC)** heavyweight champion.

Thomas outboxed Witherspoon to win the title. He successfully defended his title against former champion **Mike Weaver.** In his second defense he lost a close decision to **Trevor Berbick.** In 1987, he challenged champion **Mike Tyson** but lost in the sixth round. His career plummeted after that defeat, as he piled up losses to **Evander Holyfield, Riddick Bowe,** and **Tommy Morrison.** He finally retired in 1993.

Professional Record: 43-7-1
Championship(s):   WBC heavyweight, 1984–1986

Further Reading
Kluck, Ted A. *Facing Tyson: 15 Fighters, 15 Stories.* Guilford, Conn.: Lyons Press, 2006, pp. 87–107.
O'Brian, Joseph D. "In Search Of A Champion." *The Ring* (January 1986), pp. 32–39.

"THRILLA IN MANILA." This famous 1975 boxing match held near the city of Manila in the Philippines featured the rubber match between heavyweight rivals **Muhammad Ali** and **Joe Frazier.** The bout featured Ali as undisputed champion defending his title against former champion Frazier—the first man to ever defeat Ali. The famous moniker for the fight came from Ali who promoted the fight with his typically outrageous braggadocio, including that he would whip Frazier in that "chilla, killa, thrilla in Manila with a gorilla." The fight did not disappoint the 25,000 fans at the Philippines Coliseum and the millions of fans who watched the event around the world. Ali prevailed via a 14th-round TKO after Frazier's trainer **Eddie Futch** refused to let his man come out for the final round. Many boxing experts consider it one of the greatest fights of all time. *The Ring* magazine called it the fight of the year for 1975.

Further Reading
Sugar, Bert Randolph, and the Editors of *Ring* Magazine. *The Great Fights: A Pictorial History of Boxing's Greatest Bouts.* New York: Rutledge Press, 1981.
UPI. "Ali builds up his 'act' for Frazier." *Chicago Defender,* 7/23/1975, p. 26.

TIBERI, DAVE (1966–). Dave Tiberi was a former middleweight contender best known for his championship bout with **International Boxing Federation (IBF)** champion James Toney that led to a controversial split decision victory for Toney. The decision led to federal hearings on boxing chaired by Senator William Roth from Tiberi's home state of Delaware.

Born in 1966 in New Castle, Delaware, Tiberi was the youngest of 14 children with a lifelong goal of becoming a boxing champion. He turned pro at age 18 and built a 21-3-3 record before challenging Toney for the IBF title. Most thought the little-known Sunday school teacher from Delaware would be cannon fodder for the undefeated champion. They were wrong.

Tiberi pressured Toney the entire fight, throwing more punches and apparently landing more as well. However, two of the three judges scored Toney the winner, causing ABC boxing analyst Alex Wallau to declare it the most "disgusting decision" he had ever seen. Donald Trump, whose hotel hosted the fight, wrote: "While your opponent is laid out practically dead, you're here standing up. I think it's disgusting what happened in boxing."

Tiberi never fought again. He testified later that year before a Senate committee on problems with boxing. He testified about his experiences in the sport and said that "federal regulation is long overdue."

Professional Record: 22-3-3
Championship(s):   None

Further Reading

Berger, Phil. "Toney Wins by Decision But Gets a Real Workout." *The New York Times*, 2/9/1992, p. S13.

Ercole, Andy, and Ed Oconowicz. *Tiberi: The Uncrowned Champion*. Wilmington, Del.: Jared Co., 1992.

Senate Subcommittee Hearing. "Corruption in Professional Boxing." S. Hrg. 102–1013, August 11–12, 1982.

TIGER, DICK (1929–1971). Dick Tiger was a great former champion who won world titles in the middleweight and light heavyweight divisions. Born in 1929 in Nigeria, Tiger moved to London. He turned pro in 1952 and fought most of his early fights in his native country. In 1962, he defeated **Gene Fullmer** for the NBA middleweight title. He kept the title until a 15-round decision loss to **Joey Giardello.** He regained the title in a rematch in 1965. He lost his belt to **Emile Griffith** in 1966 but later that year won the light heavyweight title from **Jose Torres.** He successfully defended his title twice before losing to **Bob Foster.** He retired in 1971 and died later that year of cancer.

Record:	59-19-3
Championship(s):	NBA middleweight, 1962–1963; Middleweight, 1963, 1965–1966; Light Heavyweight, 1966–1968

Further Reading

Ifaturoti, Adeamola, "25 Years After His Death . . . Dick Tiger Remains a Champion." *The Ring* (January 1997), pp. 32–33, 62–64.

Makinde, Adeyinka. *Dick Tiger: The Life and Times of a Boxing Immortal.* Tarentum, PA: Word Association Publishers, 2005.

Roberts, James B., and Alexander G. Skutt. *The Boxing Register: International Boxing Hall of Fame Register* (4th ed.). Ithaca, NY: McBooks Press, Inc., 2006, pp. 642–645.

TIOZZO, FABRICE (1969–). Fabrice Tiozzo is a former world light heavyweight and cruiserweight champion whose only professional blemishes are two losses to **Virgil Hill.** Born in 1969 in St. Denis, Franck, Tiozzo was part of a fighting family that included brothers Christophe—a former super middleweight champion—and Franck, a heavyweight.

Fabrice turned pro in 1988 and first challenged for a world title in 1993 against **World Boxing Council (WBC)** light heavyweight champ Virgil Hill. Tiozzo lost a split decision over 12 rounds. He captured his first world title in 1995 with a win over the great **Mike McCallum** over 12 rounds. He successfully defended his title twice before moving up in weight to challenge **World Boxing Association (WBA)** cruiserweight champion Nate Miller. Tiozzo won a 12-round decision to win the title in 1991. He successfully defended the title four times before a shocking first-round kayo loss to his nemesis Hill. He resurrected his career by capturing the WBA light heavyweight title in 2004 with a win over Silvio Branco and a defense against Dariusz Michelczewski. Tiozzo became the first man to ever stop Michelczewski.

Professional Record:	48-2
Championship(s):	WBC light heavyweight, 1995–1997; WBA cruiserweight, 1997–2000; WBA light heavyweight, 2004–2006

Further Reading

Dahlberg, Tim. "Tiozzo Wins Cruiserweight Title on Holyfield-Moorer undercard." *Associated Press*, 11/9/1997.

"Tiozzo Beats Branco to Clinch WBA Light-Heavyweight Title." *Associated Press*, 3/20/2004.

TORRES, EFREN (1943–). Efren Torres was a former flyweight champion from Mexico who won the title on this third attempt. Known as "El Alacron" or "the Scorpion," Torres was an exciting slugger who would get quite emotional in the ring. Born in 1943 in Guadalajara, Mexico, Torres turned professional in 1961. He gained attention in 1963 when he kayoed former flyweight great **Pascual Perez** in the third round. In 1966, he failed to capture the **World Boxing Association (WBA)** flyweight title, losing a close decision to Horacio Enrique Accavallo. In 1968, he was stopped in the 13th round by **World Boxing Council (WBC)** flyweight champion **Chartchai Chionoi.** The third time was the charm for Torres, as he stopped Chionoi in the eighth round to win the WBC title in February 1969. He lost the title to Chionoi in the rubber match in a 1970 match in Bangkok. Torres retired from the ring in 1972.

Professional Record:	52-9-1
Championship(s):	WBC Flyweight, 1969–1970

Further Reading
Associated Press. "Chartchai Takes Flyweight Title." *The New York Times*, 3/21/1970, p. 52.
Hafner, Dan. "Champ Soundly Outpointed." *Los Angeles Times*, 6/20/1969, p. C1.

TORRES, JOSE (1936–2009). Jose Torres was a former Olympic medalist, world light heavyweight champion, boxing author, New York State Athletic Chairman, and President of the World Boxing Organization (WBO). Born in 1936 in Puerto Rico, Torres won a silver medal at the 1956 Melbourne Olympics, losing to the great **Laszlo Papp** in the final round.

He turned pro in 1958 and earned victories over middleweight contenders Randy Sandy and Don Fullmer. In 1965, he finally received a title shot against **Willie Pastrano** for the light heavyweight title. Torres stopped Pastrano in the ninth round.

He successfully defended his title three times before losing to the great **Dick Tiger**—the former middleweight kingpin—on a close decision. In a rematch, he lost another decision to Tiger. He retired in 1969.

Managed by Cus D'Amato, Torres received exposure to the great trainer's promising protégé **Mike Tyson.** Torres wrote a book about Tyson titled *Fire and Fear: The Inside Story of Mike Tyson* and later a biography of **Muhammad Ali** titled *Sting Like a Bee: The Muhammad Ali Story.* Given his serving as commissioner on the New York State Athletic Commission and serving as head of the WBO, the International Boxing Hall of Fame was amply justified in calling Torres "boxing's renaissance man." When he passed away in 2009, boxing lost one of its great champions and ambassadors.

Professional Record:	41-3-1
Championship(s):	Light heavyweight, 1965–1966

Further Reading
Kimball, George. "Torres, master of pugilism, prose and politics." *The Irish Times*, 1/22/2009, SPORTS, p. 26.
Torres, Jose. *Fire and Fear: The Inside Story of Mike Tyson.* New York: Warner Books, 1990.
Torres, Jose. *Sting Like a Bee: The Muhammad Ali Story.* New York: McGraw Hill, 2001.

TRIANGLE CHOKE. The triangle choke is one of the more popular and effective submission moves in mixed martial arts. It is called the triangle choke because the legs of the fighter employing the hold will often form a triangle. Normally, the triangle choke is applied by the combatant on the ground in the **guard.** The fighter wraps his legs around the fighter above him and squeezes his opponent's arm and neck in such a manner as to constrict the flow of blood to the head.

Further Reading
"Triangle choke hold for mixed martial arts," MMAWeekly.com, 1/23/2007, at http://www.mma training.com/triangle-choke/

TRIGG, FRANK (1972–). Frank "Twinkle Toes" Trigg is a top American mixed martial artist known for his rivalries with **Matt Hughes,** Dennis Hallman, and **Robbie Lawler.** Born Dewey Franklin Trigg in 1972 in Rochester, New York, Trigg attended high school in New York before moving to Oklahoma to attend college.

Trigg excelled at wrestling at Oklahoma and nearly made the 2000 Olympic team. He turned pro as a mixed martial artist in 1997 and won his first seven bouts, including a win over Fabiano Iha at **PRIDE** 8. In 2002, he submitted the tough Dennis Hallman in a fight. He made his **Ultimate Fighting Championships (UFC)** debut in November 2003, losing to Matt Hughes in the first round. He then defeated Hallman in another UFC fight and landed a rematch with Hughes. Once again, Hughes choked him out for a victory. He then lost to **Georges St.-Pierre** in his next UFC bout.

Trigg continued to fight, winning a fight promoted by HDNet over Edwin DeWees. He remains a top personality in the mixed martial arts (MMA) world. He is a successful businessman, establishing a clothing company called Triggonomics in 2003.

Professional MMA Record:	18-6
Championship(s):	None

Further Reading
Caplan, Sam. "Frank Trigg Interview." *Five Ounces of Pain,* 12/10/2007, at http://fiveouncesofpain. com/2007/12/10/frank-trigg-talks-zuffa-hdnet-fights-m-1-global-mayhem-and-more-in-new-5-oz-interview/
Official Web site: http://www.triggonomics.com/

TRINIDAD, FELIX (1973–). Felix "Tito" Trinidad was one of the great welterweight champions who never lost at 147 lbs. His boxing skills and powerful left hook were too much for the opposition. Born in 1973 in Cupey Alto, Puerto Rico, Trinidad turned professional in 1990 and in 1993 captured the **International Boxing Federation (IBF)** welterweight crown with a convincing third-round kayo over the more experienced Maurice Blocker. He successfully defended his title 16 times, often rising from early knockdowns to kayo his foes. His last defense was a unification triumph over fellow unbeaten welter champ **Oscar De La Hoya** in a debatable decision win for Trinidad in 1999.

After the De La Hoya win, Trinidad moved up to the junior middleweight division and captured the **World Boxing Association (WBA)** crown with a win over **David Reid.** He added the IBF belt in a thrilling win over **Fernando Vargas** in 2000. He then conquered William Joppy to win the WBA middleweight crown to set up a showdown with IBF and **World Boxing Council (WBC)** champion **Bernard Hopkins.** Trinidad lost for the first time in his career. He retired in 2002 and did not return to the ring until 2004. He lost in 2005 to **Ronald "Winky" Wright.** Again, Trinidad retired but came out of retirement in 2008 and lost a decision to **Roy Jones, Jr.** in 2008.

Professional Record:	42-3
Championship(s):	IBF welterweight, 1993–1999; WBC welterweight, 1999; WBA junior middleweight, 2000–2001; IBF junior middleweight, 2000–2001; WBA middleweight, 2001

Further Reading
Anderson, Dave. "Behind Trinidad's Knockout Punch, There Is His Father's Steady Hand." *The New York Times*, 5/7/2001, p. D1.
Brown, Clifton. "Trinidad Adds To His Reputation." *The New York Times*, 12/4/2000, p. D10.
Smith, Timothy W. "Trinidad Scores Stunning Upset in a Decision vs. De La Hoya." *The New York Times*, 9/19/1999, p. SP1.

TSZYU, KOSTYA (1969–). The Russian-born Kostya Tszyu emigrated to Australia and became known as "the Thunder from Down Under." He moved to Australia from his native Siberia in 1991 after winning a world amateur championship. He dominated the junior welterweight division for many years beginning in the mid-1990s. He turned professional in 1992 and won his first world title, the **International Boxing Federation (IBF)** junior welterweight crown, in 1995 with a win over Jake Rodriguez. He successfully defended his title five times before losing by knockout to **Vince Phillips** in 1997.

In 1999, he defeated Miguel Angel Gonzalez to win the **World Boxing Council (WBC)** junior welterweight title. He added the **World Boxing Association (WBA)** belt in 2000 by defeating Sharmba Mitchell. In 2001, he unified the title by winning the IBF with the signature win of his career—a second-round knockout of previously unbeaten **Zab Judah.** He held at least one world title belt until 2005 when he lost in Manchester, England, to **Ricky "the Hitman" Hatton.** He has not fought since the Hatton fight.

Record:	31-2
Championship(s):	IBF Junior Welterweight, 1995–1997, 2001–2005; WBC junior welterweight, 1999–2003; WBA junior welterweight, 2001–2003.

Kostya Tszyu drops Zab Judah en route to a 2nd-round stoppage and junior welterweight supremacy in their 2001 bout. Courtesy of Chris Cozzone.

Kostya Tszyu looks ready to battle Sharmba Mitchell in their rematch in November 2004. Tszyu was ready, as he stopped Mitchell in three rounds. Courtesy of Chris Cozzone.

Photo 84: Kostya Tszyu inflicts more punishment on Sharmba Mitchell during their November 2004 bout, which Tszyu won in three rounds. Courtesy of Chris Cozzone.

Further Reading

Collins, Nigel. "The Persistent Presence of Kostya Tszyu." *KO Magazine* (July 2003), pp. 24–27.

Donovan, Jake. "Lord of the Ring: Kostya Tszyu Stops Mitchell in Three." *The Sweet Science*, 11/6/2004, at http://www.thesweetscience.com/boxing-article/1299/lord-ring-kostya-tszyu-stops-mitchell-three/

Evans, Gavin. "The Metamorphosis of a Near-Perfect Fighter." *The Ring* (April 2005), pp. 32–37.

"KO Interview: Kostya Tszyu: 'My Finish Line Is Still Out Of Sight." *KO* (August 2002), pp. 48–57.

Tszyu, Kostya. *Kostya: My Story*. Sydney: ABC Books, 2003.

TUA, DAVID (1973–). David "Tuaman" Tua is a squat, power-punching Samoan heavyweight from New Zealand known for his great chin and incredible one-punch kayo power. Most famously, Tua kayoed future world heavyweight champion **John Ruiz** in only 19 seconds in 1996. During his professional career, Tua has kayoed several other former world heavyweight champions, including **Hasim Rahman,** Oleg Maskaev, and **Michael Moorer.** Unfortunately, Tua failed in his one shot at the world championship, losing a lopsided decision to undisputed champion **Lennox Lewis** in 2000.

Before he turned pro, Tua earned a bronze medal at the 1992 Olympics, dropping a semifinal round decision to David Izon—another Tua knockout victory in the professional ranks. During his pro career, Tua has never been stopped, losing decisions to Lewis, **Chris Byrd,** and **Ike Ibeabuchi.** He continues to fight, seeking a world title.

Professional Record:	49-3-1
Championship(s):	None

Further Reading

Anderson, Dave. "Tua is Looking to Make a Name for Himself, At Last." *The New York Times*, 11/10/2000, p. D6.

Fernandez, Bernard. "Tua opening eyes again after dispatching Moorer." *Philadelphia Daily News*, 8/19/2002, p. 88.

Smith, Tim. "He's Learned One or Tua Things." *Daily News*, 7/26/2006, p. 127.

Taylor, Phil. "The Unraveling of David Tua's Camp." *The New Zealand Herald*, 3/6/2004.

TUBBS, TONY (1958–). Tony Tubbs was a former world heavyweight champion known for his portly size, quick hands, and good skills. Born in 1958 in Cincinnati, Ohio, Tubbs had an impressive amateur career. He turned pro in 1980 and won his first 20 bouts before challenging former amateur nemesis **Greg Page** for the **World Boxing Association (WBA)** championship in 1985. Tubbs boxed expertly and won a clear unanimous decision. The revenge was sweet for Tubbs, as Page had broken his nose in the amateurs. "Those were my amateur days. This was the pros," Tubbs said after winning the heavyweight title.

Unfortunately, Tubbs seemingly couldn't handle success, and he lost the title in his first defense against "Terrible" **Tim Witherspoon.** He rebounded to win three straight bouts to land a title shot against **Mike Tyson** for the heavyweight title in Tokyo, Japan. Tyson's power proved too much, and Tubbs fell in the second round.

In August 1993, he lost in the first round to Jimmy Ellis in a low point in his career. However, later that year he entered a "People's Choice One Night Heavyweight Tournament." The competition featured 16 boxers facing off in 3-round bouts. Tubbs defeated Willie Jackson, Tyrell Biggs, Jose Ribalta, and Daniel Dancuta to capture the title.

Legal troubles kept Tubbs out of the ring for several years, but he mounted a comeback in 2002. He last fought in 2006.

Professional Record:	47-10
Championship(s):	WBA Heavyweight, 1985–1986

Further Reading

Associated Press. "Tubbs Surprises Page, Takes WBA Title." *Los Angeles Times*, 4/30/1985, p. SP 3.

Kluck, Ted A. *Facing Tyson: 15 Fighters, 15 Stories.* Guilford, CT: Lyons Press, 2006, pp. 133–147.

TUNNEY, GENE (1897–1978). James Joseph "Gene" Tunney was a former world heavyweight champion best known for twice defeating the popular slugger **Jack Dempsey.** He lost only one fight in his professional career to **Harry Greb**—a defeat that Tunney avenged more than once. Born in 1897 in New York, Tunney took to boxing as a teenager. He turned pro in 1915 but interrupted his career to join the Marines and serve in World War I. After his military service, Tunney returned to the ring in 1918. He fought as a light heavyweight for much of his career but later moved up to the heavyweight ranks.

In 1926, "the Fighting Marine" challenged Dempsey for the heavyweight title. A heavy underdog, Tunney stunned the champion in the first round and outboxed him to capture the title. In the highly anticipated rematch at Soldier Field in Chicago, Tunney once again outboxed Dempsey in the early rounds. However, Dempsey dropped Tunney in the seventh round. Dempsey failed to go to a neutral corner, giving Tunney additional time to gather his senses. Because Tunney was on the canvas for more than 10 seconds, the rematch is called "the Battle of the Long Count." In reality, the referee's actions were proper, as Illinois rules provided that the count would not start until the standing fighter moved to a neutral corner. Tunney beat the official count and won another decision by a wide margin. Tunney defended his title against Tom Heeney and then retired. Tunney prospered as a businessman in retirement.

Record:	61-1-1 (19 no decisions and one no contest)
Championship(s):	Heavyweight, 1926–1928

Further Reading

Cavanaugh, Jack. *Tunney: Boxing's Brainiest Champ and His Upset of the Great Jack Dempsey.* New York: Ballentine Books, 2006.

Edgren, Robert. "Gene Tunney, New Type of Boxer, Has Eye on Jack Dempsey's Crown." *Chicago Daily Tribune*, 4/30/1922, p. A3.

Jarett, John. *Gene Tunney: The Golden Guy Who Licked Jack Dempsey Twice.* London: Robson Books, 2003.

TYSON, MIKE (1966–). Mike Tyson was a former two-time world heavyweight champion and the youngest man to ever capture the crown jewel of boxing. In his prime in the mid to late 1980s, Tyson was a fearsome combination of speed and power—dominating and unifying the division.

Born in 1966 in Brooklyn, New York, he grew up in tough circumstances and learned to box in reform school. A trainer there introduced Tyson to famed boxing manager Cus D'Amato who recognized the youth's immense potential in the ring. Tyson compiled a 24-3 record as an amateur and won a National Junior Olympics title. He was considered a favorite to make the U.S.A. 1984 Olympic team but lost two decisions to Henry Tillman.

He turned pro in 1985 and began decimating the opposition. In November 1986, he stopped **Trevor Berbick** in two rounds to win the **World Boxing Council (WBC)** heavyweight title, winning the belt at only 20 years of age. By age 22, he had unified the division—defeating **James**

Mike Tyson watches the Antonio Tarver–Glen Johnson fight in December 2004. Courtesy of Chris Cozzone.

"**Bonecrusher**" **Smith** to win the **World Boxing Association (WBA)** title and Tony Tucker later that year to win the **International Boxing Federation (IBF)** title.

At the peak of his powers, he destroyed previously unbeaten **Michael Spinks** in the first round to retain his belts. He lost his championships in a shocking upset loss to **James "Buster" Douglas** over 10 rounds in Tokyo, Japan. Tyson's chaotic personal life had begun to affect the prodigy in the ring.

Tyson did not fight for several years in the early 1990s due to an Indiana rape conviction. He returned to the ring in 1995 and proceeded to dominate the opposition again. In March 1996, he stopped **Frank Bruno** in the third round to win the WBC heavyweight title. In his next bout, he overwhelmed Bruce Seldon in the first round to win the WBA belt. He had once again established himself as the king of the heavyweight division.

However, in November 1996, he suffered his second professional loss to **Evander Holyfield** in the 11th round. In June 1997, he faced Holyfield in a rematch. Upset over headbutts from his opponent, Tyson bit Holyfield's ear and suffered a disqualification. In several other bouts, Tyson's conduct became the source of extreme controversy. He tried to break Francois Botha's arm in the ring and hit Orin Norris while he was on the ground.

In June 2002, he faced **Lennox Lewis** for the WBC and IBF heavyweight belts. He won the first round but after that began to take a beating from the much taller and bigger Lewis. He retired from the ring for good after losing to Kevin McBride.

Boxing experts disagree over where Tyson ranks in the history of the sport. His protractors emphasize his early, dominant years and his unification of the belts. They also point to the ease of his victories. Detractors point to the sorry state of the division when Tyson was king. They also reason that once the Tyson mystique was exposed, he was never the same fighter. Whatever the case, it is indisputable that Tyson was one of the most captivating athletes (for good or bad) that the world has ever known.

Professional Record:	50-6
Championship(s):	WBC heavyweight, 1986–1990, 1996–1997; WBA, 1987–1990, 1996; IBF heavyweight, 1987–1990

Further Reading

Heller, Peter. *Bad Intentions: The Mike Tyson Story*. New York: Da Capo Press, 1995.

Hoffer, Richard. "All the Rage." *Sports Illustrated*, 5/20/2002, pp. 34–41.

Kluck, Ted A. *Facing Tyson: Fifteen Fighters, Fifteen Stories*. Guilford, CT: Lyons Press, 2006.

O'Connor, Daniel, ed. *Iron Mike: A Mike Tyson Reader*. New York: Da Capo Press, 2002.

Torres, Jose. *Fire and Fear: The Inside Story of Mike Tyson*. New York: Warner Books, 1989.

THE ULTIMATE FIGHTER™. *The Ultimate Fighter* is a television reality series produced by the **Ultimate Fighting Championships** (**UFC**) that has attracted scores of new fans to mixed martial arts (MMA). Debuting on SPIKE TV in January 2005, the show has—at the time of this writing—completed its eighth season.

It features a group of hopeful mixed martial artists competing for top honors and a UFC contract to fight in the big time. The show's format features fighters divided into two teams or camps with each camp led by a coach, who is a famous UFC fighter. For example, season one featured eight middleweights and eight light heavyweights. Half were coached by **Randy Couture** and the other half were coached by **Chuck "the Iceman" Liddell.**

At the season's conclusion, the two coaches usually fight each other. So, after season one, Couture and Liddell had one of their three historic matches. The season one winners were Diego Sanchez at middleweight and **Forrest Griffin** at light heavyweight. The season two winners were Joe Stevenson at middleweight and Rashad Evans at light heavyweight. Season three winners were Kendall Grove at middleweight and **Michael Bisping** at light heavyweight.

Season four marked a change in the show. Instead of featuring aspiring mixed martial artists who had never set foot in the Octagon, season four consisted of fighters in the welterweight and middleweight divisions who had competed in the UFC but had never won a title. This season also didn't feature a rivalry between two lead coaches, but several prominent UFC fighters served as trainers and/or advisers. The season four winners were **Matt Serra** at welterweight and Travis Lutter at middleweight. The winners then had title shots at the existing UFC champions. Serra capitalized on his opportunity by stunning **Georges St.-Pierre** and winning the UFC welterweight championship. Lutter failed in his title shot, coming in overweight and then losing to middleweight champion **Anderson Silva.**

Season five changed format again, as it had 16 fighters from one weight class—lightweight. Nate Diaz emerged as the winner. Season six featured only welterweights, and Mac Danzig emerged triumphant. Past coaches of *The Ultimate Fighter* have included—in addition to

Couture and Liddell: **Matt Hughes, Rich Franklin, Tito Ortiz, Ken Shamrock, Jens Pulver, B. J. Penn,** and **Quinton "Rampage" Jackson.**

Further Reading

Baker, Bob. "Reality Television Without Fake Smiles." *The New York Times*, 8/21/2005, p. 28.
Casey, Jim. "The Magnificent Seven: A Look at The Ultimate Fighter's Best and Brightest." *FIGHT!* (August 2008), pp. 68–70.
Official Web site: http://www.spike.com/show/22307
Slutsky, Adam. "The Ultimate Fighter Season 7." *FIGHT!* (May 2008), pp. 76–79.

ULTIMATE FIGHTING CHAMPIONSHIPS™ (UFC). The Ultimate Fighting Championships, or UFC, is the premier mixed martial arts (MMA) organization in the world. Formed in 1993 by Arthur Davie and John Milius, the UFC originally had few rules, though it held its matches in an eight-sided cage known as the "Octagon." The original shows were broadcast by Semaphore Entertainment Group (SEG). Michael Abramson of SEG came up with the name that stuck—Ultimate Fighting Championships.

Davie and Milius set up the idea of UFC matches with a member of the legendary fighting family in Brazil—the Gracies—particularly **Rorion Gracie.** In November 1993, the UFC held UFC 1, featuring eight fighters from different fighting disciplines. The event was won by one of Rorion's younger brothers, **Royce Gracie.** Royce's successful tournament championship runs at UFC 1, UFC 2, and UFC 4 showed the world the effectiveness of the Gracie jiu-jitsu fighting system. He easily defeated boxers, kickboxers, karate specialists, kung-fu practitioners, and even wrestlers.

In 1995, SEG purchased UFC. In the early days of the UFC, there were very few rules, no weight classes, and no judges. The lack of rules created many critics, including U.S. Senator John McCain, who famously referred to the UFC on the Senate floor in 1996 as "human cockfighting."

A positive turning point occurred when, in January 2001, **Dana White,** Frank Fertitta, and Lorenzo Fertitta—through their corporate entity Zuffa, LLC—purchased the UFC for $2 million. White provided the public charisma and day-to-day leadership, while the Fertittas provided the monetary backing and primary ownership. Under Zuffa's (Italian for "fight") ownership, the UFC changed dramatically. Fights were now held with weight classes and rounds. Most UFC matches consist of three 5-minute rounds, and championship matches consist of five 5-minute rounds.

The UFC's popularity escalated even more when it launched its own reality television series called *The Ultimate Fighter,* which featured more than a dozen mixed martial artists living together and competing for a top-flight UFC contract. *Spike TV* broadcast the show, and it became an instant hit. The UFC has gained acceptance in more than half of the states and holds events around the world. White's stated goal is to take the UFC global. The UFC has staged events in Canada, Great Britain, and Japan. It looks to stage events in Mexico, Europe, and elsewhere.

The UFC's profitability inspired *Forbes* magazine to call it "the Ultimate Cash Machine"; its estimated value is more than $2 billion. The UFC has purchased several of its former competitors, including most notably its Japan-based rival **PRIDE.** Even in the face of more competition, the UFC remains the premier mixed martial arts organization in the world.

Further Reading

McCarthy, "Big" John. "The Beginning: John McCarthy on the first UFC." *FIGHT!* (October–November 2007), pp. 64–65.
Miller, Matthew. "Ultimate Cash Machine." *Forbes*, 5/12/2008, pp. 80–84.
Official Web site: http://www.ufc.com
Werthem, L. Jon. "The New Main Event." *Sports Illustrated*, 5/28/2007, pp. 52–60.

VALUEV, NIKOLAY (1973–). Nikolay Valuev, at 7′0″, is the tallest man ever to win a world boxing championship. Born in St. Petersburg, Russia, Valuev turned professional in 1993 and won his first 46 fights. He captured the **World Boxing Association (WBA)** crown by decisioning **John Ruiz** in December 2005 over 12 rounds. He then successfully defended his title three times before losing a 12-round majority decision to fellow Russian **Ruslan Chagaev.**

Though ponderous, Valuev possesses a good, stiff jab and surprising stamina. Since his title loss, Valuev looked impressive in defeating former champion Sergei Lyakhovich. In August 2008, he regained the WBA title with a decision win over Ruiz. In December 2008, he defended his title with a controversial decision win over **Evander Holyfield.**

Professional record:	50-1
World Title:	WBA Heavyweight, 2005–2007, 2008–

Further Reading

Donovan, Jake. "Shall We Embrace the Chase of Nikolai Valuev." *Boxing Scene,* 4/2/2007, at http://www.boxingscene.com/?m=show&opt=printable&id=8034

Donovan, Jake. "Valuev Dominates, Eyes Chagaev Rematch." *Boxing Scene,* 2/16/2008, at http://www.boxingscene.com/?m=show&opt=printable&id=12647

VARGAS, FERNANDO (1977–). "Ferocious" Fernando Vargas was a talented former junior middleweight champion known for his crowd-pleasing style and warrior attitude. Born in 1977 in Oxnard, California, Vargas represented his country in the 1996 Atlanta Olympic Games. Though he lost in the second round, Main Events signed him and actively promoted him in the professional ranks.

He turned pro in 1997 and in his 15th pro bout he defeated Yory Boy Campos for the **International Boxing Federation (IBF)** junior middleweight title. He made five successful defenses, including wins over **Ronald "Winky" Wright** and Ike "Bazooka" Quartey—before facing **World Boxing Association (WBA)** champion **Felix "Tito" Trinidad** in a blockbuster bout. In a brutal fight that saw both fighters hit the canvas, Trinidad prevailed in the 12th round.

In 2001, Vargas won the WBA junior welterweight title with a win over Jose Alfredo Flores. He lost the title in his first defense against longtime nemesis **Oscar De La Hoya.** In another thrilling affair, De La Hoya stopped Vargas in the 11th round. Vargas never received another world title shot. He lost his last three fights—two to "Sugar" **Shane Mosley** in 2006 and one to **Ricardo Mayorga** in 2007.

Professional Record:	26-5
Championship(s):	IBF junior middleweight, 1998–2001; WBA junior middleweight, 2001–2002

Further Reading
Brown, Clifton. "Vargas Has a Lot of Fight in Him." *The New York Times*, 12/1/2000, p. D1.
Official Website: http://www.fernandovargas.com/intro. html
Smith, Timothy W. "Will Vargas Be Up to the Challenge?" *The New York Times*, 12/11/1998, p. D4.
Whitehead, Johnnie. "Fernando Vargas' Internal Battle: If He Can't Win It, He Can't Beat Trinidad." *KO* (February 2001), pp. 24–28.

VAZQUEZ, ISRAEL (1977–). Israel Vazquez is a power-punching super bantamweight champion best known for his incredible trilogy with rival **Rafael Marquez.** Born in 1977 in Mexico City, Vazquez turned pro in 1995 with three straight first-round knockouts. In 2002, he received a major opportunity against Oscar Larios for the interim **World Boxing Council (WBC)** super bantamweight title. In a great battle, Vazquez lost in the 12th and final round.

He received a second chance in 2004 with a win over Jose Luis Valbuena to win the vacant **International Boxing Federation (IBF)** super bantamweight title. In December 2005, he exacted revenge against Larios by overwhelming his foe in the third round to win the WBC title. He made two successful defenses before losing to Rafael Marquez in July 2007. He rebounded in August 2007 by stopping Marquez in another slugfest. Finally, in March 2008, he won the rubber match over his rival with a 12-round split decision victory.

Israel Vasquez batters Rafael Marquez in their third fight in March 2008. Vasquez won a split decision. Courtesy of Chris Cozzone.

Professional Record: 43-4

Championship(s):   IBF super bantamweight, 2004–2005; WBC super bantamweight, 2005–2007, 2007

Further Readi ng

Goldman, Eddie. "Why Can't They All Be Like Vazquez and Marquez?" *Tapout*, No. 24 (2008), p. 31.

Goldman, Ivan. "Junior Featherweight Champion Israel Vazquez: Will His Paycheck Ever Match His Ability?" *The Ring* (April 2006), pp. 72–77.

Marks of Battle! Israel Vasquez exults after winning a split decision in his third bout with Rafael Marquez in March 2008. Courtesy of Chris Cozzone.

VILLA, PANCHO (1901–1925). Pancho Villa was a former great flyweight champion who never lost his belt in the ring but instead died tragically at age 24 of an infection from a throat cavity. Born in 1901 in the Philippines as Francisco Guilledo, Villa got his name from manager Frank Churchill, who named him after the great Mexican bandit. He possessed amazing speed and power, which enabled him to overwhelm the vast majority of his ring opponents.

Villa turned pro in 1919 and three years later won the American flyweight title with a convincing win over Johnny Buff. He dropped Buff twice in the 10th round and won in the 11th. The next year, Villa defeated the great **Jimmy Wilde** to win the world flyweight title. He successfully defended his title four times before his unfortunate infection.

Professional Record: 73-5-4

Championship(s):   Flyweight, 1923–1925

Further Reading

Edgren, Robert. "New Flyweight Champion is Real Scrapper." *The Atlanta Constitution*, 10/18/1922, p. C2.

"Jimmy Wilde Flattened Out by Pancho Villa." *Los Angeles Times*, 6/19/1923, p. III1.

"New Flyweight Champ." *The Chicago Daily Tribune*, 9/15/1922, p. 16.

Pegler, Westbrook. "Pancho Villa Easy Winner." *The Atlanta Constitution*, 11/17/1922, p. 8.

Roberts, James B., and Alexander G. Skutt. *The Boxing Register: International Boxing Hall of Fame Register* (4th ed.). Ithaca, NY: McBooks Press, Inc., 2006, pp. 234–235.

VILLAFLOR, BEN (1952–). Ben Villaflor was a two-time world champion who won his first world championship at age 19. Born in 1952 in Negros, Philippines, the southpaw Villaflor turned pro at age 14 in 1966. In 1972, he decisioned Alfredo Marcano to win the **World Boxing Association (WBA)** super featherweight title. He set a record for being the youngest fighter to ever win a world title—a record later broken by 17-year-old **Wilfred Benitez** in 1976. He lost his title in 1973 to Kuniaki Shibata. Later that year, he crushed Shibata in the first round to recapture his title. He successfully defended it five times before losing to Samuel Serrano in 1976.

Professional Record: 54-8-7

Championship(s):   WBA super featherweight, 1972–1973; 1973–1976

Further Reading

Associated Press. "Villaflor, 19, Youngest to Win Boxing Title." *The New York Times*, 4/27/1972, p. 54.

VORAPIN, RATANAPOL SOR (1974–). Thailand's Ratanapol Sor Vorapin is a former strawweight champion best known for his long stranglehold on the **International Boxing Federation (IBF)** championship. Born in 1974 Dankoonthod, Vorapin turned professional in 1990. Two years later he defeated Manny Meltor to win the IBF strawweight (or minimumweight) title. He successfully defended his title 19 times before finally losing to South African Zelani Petelo. Vorapin failed in two subsequent attempts to capture a world title in the junior flyweight division, losing to **Will Grigsby** in 1998 and the great **Ricardo Lopez** in 2000. He initially retired after the loss to Lopez but returned to the ring in 2005. He has won 13 straight bouts and hopes to regain a world championship. His younger brother Ratanachai is a former bantamweight champion.

Professional Record: 51-6-1

Championship(s):   IBF strawweight, 1992–1997

Further Reading

Hudson, David L., Jr., and Mike Fitzgerald, Jr. *Boxing's Most Wanted: The Top 10 Book of Champs, Chumps and Punch-Drunk Palookas.* Alexandria, VA: Potomac Books, 2003.

VOVCHANCHYN, IGOR (1973–). Igor "Ice Cold" Vovchanchyn is a former Russian kickboxing great who also compiled an impressive record in mixed martial arts (MMA). His kickboxing skills enabled him to become one of the most feared strikers in MMA history. He was known as "Ice Cold" because he possessed the power to knock opponents out cold.

Ratanachai Sor Vorapin attacks the body of Johnny Gonzalez in their October 2005 bout for the IBO bantamweight title. Vorapin loses in the seventh round. Courtesy of Chris Cozzone.

Born in 1973, he turned pro in MMA in 1995 with a series of wins in various promotions including the International Fighting Championships in Russia and mixed martial arts events in the Ukraine. He made his debut in **PRIDE** at PRIDE 4 with a first-round knockout of **Gary "Big Daddy" Goodridge.** In the PRIDE Grand Prix Finals 2000, he defeated Japanese legend Kazushi Sakuraba before losing in the next round to **Mark Coleman.**

He defeated **Mark "the Smashing Machine" Kerr** at PRIDE 12: Cold Fury. He has faced a litany of MMA greats, including **Mirko "Cro Cop" Filopovic, Quinton "Rampage" Jackson, Heath Herring,** and **Mario Sperry.**

Professional MMA Record: 45-9-1
Championship(s):   None

Further Reading
PRIDE profile: http://www.pridefc.com/pride2005/index.php?mainpage=fighters&fID=172

WALCOTT, JERSEY JOE (1914–1994). Jersey Joe Walcott was a former world heavyweight champion known for his clever ring skills and deceptive power. Born in 1914 in New Jersey as Arnold Raymond Cream, he adopted the ring name of Jersey Joe Walcott in honor of his father's favorite fighter (his father was from Barbados—the home of the Original Joe Walcott).

He turned pro in 1930 and fought regularly as a light heavyweight. He lost two fights to Joey Maxim and dropped several other decisions. No one expected that he might become heavyweight champion of the world. However, in 1947, he received a title shot from **Joe Louis** and shocked the world. He dropped Louis in the first and fourth rounds but lost a 15-round split decision. Most experts felt he was robbed. In the rematch, Louis kayoed Walcott in the 11th round.

In 1949, he lost in his third attempt for a title, dropping a decision to **Ezzard Charles.** In his fourth attempt, he lost again to Charles in 1951 but gained revenge later that year, defeating Charles to become the then-oldest man to capture the heavyweight title at age 37 (a record later broken by **George Foreman** at age 45 in 1994). Walcott lost his title in 1952 when he faced unbeaten contender **Rocky Marciano.** Ahead on the scorecards headed into the 13th round, Marciano kayoed Walcott with a picture-perfect right hand. After losing badly to Marciano in the rematch, Walcott retired. He refereed bouts, including the infamous rematch between **Muhammad Ali** and **Sonny Liston** in 1965. In the 1970s and 1980s, he served as Chairman of the New Jersey's State Athletic Commission.

Professional Record: 53-18-1
Championship(s):   Heavyweight, 1951–1952

Further Reading
Hand, Jack. "Walcott Retains Heavyweight Title." *Los Angeles Times*, 6/6/1952, p. C1.
Sher, Jack. "Jersey Joe Walcott: Boxing's 'Forgotten Man' Remembered." *The Ring* (June 1983), pp. 72–84.
Young, Fay. "Through the Years." *Chicago Defender*, 12/20/1947, p. 6.
Ward, Gene. "A Punch and a Prayer." *Chicago Daily Tribune*, 7/25/1951, p. C2.

WALCOTT, JOE ("THE ORIGINAL") (1873–1935). Heavyweight champion **Jersey Joe Walcott** took that name because of the greatness of a short welterweight champion in the late nineteenth and early twentieth century named Joe Walcott, a man they called "the Barbados Demon." Born in 1873 in the British West Indies, Walcott spent much time in Barbados. He came to Boston in 1887 and turned pro a few years later.

He won the welterweight championship in 1901 with a fifth-round kayo of Jim "Ruby" Ferns. He held the title until a 1904 loss to the Dixie Kid. Standing only 5'2", he possessed long and powerful arms that allowed him to dominate most opponents his size. For that reason, he regularly fought men much bigger. In 1900, he kayoed heavyweight contender **Joe Choynski.** He fought heavyweight Fred Russell who outweighed him by more than 100 pounds and dropped the big man in the first round and should have earned more than the official draw. "Boxing observers at the turn of the century referred to Walcott as a sawed-off Hercules" (Sugar, p. 83).

Professional Record:	69-23-18 (21 no decisions)
Championship(s):	Welterweight, 1901–1904

Further Reading
Associated Press. "David and Goliath of the Prize Ring." *Los Angeles Times*, 4/5/1902, p. 5.
Evans, Gavin. "The 20 Greatest Welterweights of All Time." *The Ring* (February 2008), pp. 63–84, 72.
Sugar, Bert Randolph. *Boxing's Greatest Fighters.* Guilford, CT: Lyons Press, 2006.

WALKER LAW. The Walker Law, named after its legislative sponsor Senator James J. Walker, was a New York law passed in 1920 that legalized and regulated the sport of boxing in the state. "I believe the Legislature is ready to enact sane boxing legislation," Walker said after the measure passed initial committee review in the state senate in March 1920. Among its provisions, the Walker Law called for the creation of a state boxing commission. The initial commission members were former fire commissioner Joseph J. Johnson, lawyer Edward W. Ditmars, and Walter J. Hooke, a key member of the Army, Navy, and Civilian Board of Boxing.

The law provided comprehensive regulations for the sport, including a 15-round limit for major bouts and weight classes. It also provided that professional bouts that went the distance would no longer be classified as no-decisions (as they were in many locales), but instead, ring officials would declare the winner of the bout.

Further Reading
"Johnson, Ditmars and Hooke Named: Governor Appoints Them as Members of Boxing Commission under Walker Law." *The New York Times*, 8/13/1920, p. 17.
"Walker Bill Gets Favorable Report: Senate Committee Submits Boxing Measure for Final Action by 9 to 2 Vote." *The New York Times*, 3/10/1920.

WALKER, MICKEY (1901–1981). Mickey "the Toy Bulldog" Walker was former welterweight and middleweight champion who fought with ferocity—often against men that outweighed him. Born in 1901 in Elizabeth, New Jersey, as Edward Patrick Walker, he turned professional in 1919.

In 1922, he defeated **Jack Britton** to win the welterweight title. He defended his title four times before attempting to defeat **Harry Greb** for the middleweight title. Walker lost that fight though he gave away weight during the fight. He returned to defend his title two more times before losing to Pete Latzo.

In 1926, he won the middleweight title from **Theodore "Tiger" Flowers** in a disputed decision. He nearly added the light heavyweight title to his ledger, losing decisions to champions **Tommy Loughran** and **Maxie Rosenbloom.** Sometimes, Walker even fought heavyweights, including a loss to future heavyweight champion **Max Schmeling.**

Professional Record:	93-19-4
Championship(s):	Welterweight, 1922–1926; Middleweight, 1926–1931

Further Reading
Evans, Gavin. "The 20 Greatest Welterweights of All Time." *The Ring* (February 2008), pp. 63–84, 75.
Roberts, James B., and Alexander G. Skutt. *The Boxing Register: International Boxing Hall of Fame Register* (4th ed.). Ithaca, NY: McBooks Press, Inc., 2006, pp. 658–661.

WARREN, FRANK (1952–). Frank Warren is a London-based manager and promoter who has parlayed himself into one of boxing's premier powers. Born in 1952 in London, Warren began promoting shows in London in 1980. He has managed many great fighters, including "Prince" **Naseem Hamed, Nigel Benn, Joe Calzaghe,** and **Ricky Hatton.** He founded London Theatre, owning it until he sold it in 1996.

Warren nearly lost his life in 1989 after being shot outside a nightclub. His former fighter, **Terry Marsh**—a former junior welterweight champion—was charged with murder but acquitted. Warren testified in court that he did not see his assailant. Warren rebounded and promoted the sport through a deal with SKY network. He remains one of the sport's top promoters.

Further Reading
Doogan, Brian. "After Going Bankrupt, Getting Shot, and Standing Up to Mike Tyson . . . Promoter Frank Warren Is Back on Top." *The Ring Extra* (August 2006), pp. 70–75.
Holt, Oliver. "Tyson's a Tough Guy but if He'd Punched Me a Couple of Years Earlier I'd Have Hit Him Over the Head with a Lump of Wood; Frank Warren Exclusive 25 Years in the Hardest Game of Them All." *The Mirror*, 12/3/2005, pp. 56–57.

WATANABE, JIRO (1955–). Jiro Watanabe was one of the greatest professional boxers ever from the country of Japan and a feared force in the super flyweight division for much of the 1980s. Born in 1955 in Osaka, the southpaw turned pro in 1979. In only his 11th pro fight, he challenged South Korean Chul Ho Kim for the **World Boxing Association (WBA)** super flyweight championship. He lost a disputed decision in a bout held in Seoul.

He rebounded and in 1982 easily decisioned Rafael Pedroza to win the WBA title. Watanabe successfully defended his WBA belt six times. He then signed to face **World Boxing Council (WBC)** champion **Payao Poontorat.** Unfortunately, the WBA stripped Watanabe of his belt for signing the unification bout. Watanabe defeated Poontorat by split decision over 12 rounds to capture the WBC belt in 1984. He successfully defended the WBC belt four times before losing a decision to **Gilberto Roman** in 1986. He retired after that loss. Unfortunately, he has faced legal troubles in his post-fighting career.

Professional Record:	26-2
Championship(s):	WBA super flyweight, 1982–1984; WBC super flyweight, 1984–1986

Further Reading
Associated Press. "Watanabe Retains Title." *The Washington Post*, 11/12/1982, p. D4.
"Roman Takes Title from Watanabe." *San Diego News-Tribune*, 3/31/1986, p. C7.

WATERMAN, RON (1965−). Ron Waterman is a muscle-bound mixed martial artist who also dabbled in professional wrestling. A former Division II All-American wrestler at the University of Northern California, Waterman then became a high school football and wrestling coach in Colorado.

Waterman began his mixed martial arts (MMA) career in 1999 at the **Bas Rutten** Invitational, winning three straight bouts to win the competition. After those three victories, Waterman entered the Octagon at the **Ultimate Fighting Championships (UFC)** 20: Battle for the Gold. He stopped Chris Condo in the first round. He left MMA competition to perform as a professional wrestler with World Wrestling Entertainment. Waterman then also succeeded in **PRIDE,** defeating **Valentijn Overeem** in the first round at PRIDE 24: Cold Fury 3. He has fought in Pancrease, bodog, World Extreme Cagefighting, and others. He holds a victory over former UFC heavyweight champion **Kevin Randleman.** Waterman is a member of Team IMPACT, an organization of athletes who profess their dedication to Jesus Christ and spread his gospel.

Professional MMA Record:	15-6-2
Championship(s):	None

Further Reading

Meachum, Brandon. "Muscle Ministry Ron Waterman lives in two worlds: the violent arena of ultimate fighting and the worldwide public stage of Christian evangelism." *The Denver Post,* 8/7/2006, p. D-01.

Official Web site of Ron Waterman: http://ronwaterman.com/

WEAVER, MIKE (1952−). Mike "Hercules" Weaver was a most unlikely heavyweight champion best known for the dramatic way in which he captured the title. Born in 1952 in Gatesville, Texas, Weaver boxed in the military. He turned pro in 1972 and lost his first two professional fights to Howard Smith. After his first 10 fights, he had a mediocre record of 5-5. However, Weaver began to improve his skills and rose in the ranks. In 1978, he dropped consecutive decisions to Stan Ward and Leroy Jones.

Weaver then won five straight bouts, including a rematch victory over Ward. That propelled him into a shot at **Larry Holmes** for the **World Boxing Council (WBC)** heavyweight title. Weaver made a strong showing, hurting the champion on several occasions. However, Holmes rallied and stopped Weaver in the 12th round. The next year, Weaver earned a shot at another undefeated champion—**World Boxing Association (WBA)** kingpin "Big" John Tate who many regarded as the future of the division. Tate dominated the action for most of the bout, heading into the final round with a commanding lead. Forty-five seconds left in the bout, Weaver landed a devastating left hook that knocked Tate unconscious. It was one of the most stunning and widely replayed knockouts in boxing history. Weaver successfully defended his title against power-punching **Gerrie Coetzee** and James "Quick" Tillis. He lost his title in controversial fashion to **Michael "Dynamite" Dokes** in the first round. In a rematch, Weaver managed a draw but could not reclaim his belt. In 1985, Weaver received his last shot at a heavyweight title against WBC titlist **Pinklon Thomas.** In a good action fight, Thomas won in the eighth round.

Record:	41-18-1
Championship(s):	WBA Heavyweight, 1980–1982

Further Reading

Katz, Michael. "Weaver Unfazed at Being Underdog." *The New York Times,* 3/27/1980, p. B13.

Katz, Michael. "One Last Chance for Mike Weaver." *The New York Times,* 6/15/1985, p. 21.

Landsbaum, Mike. "Mike Weaver Basks in Limelight at Last." *Los Angeles Times*, 4/24/1980, p. SG1.
Rollow, Cooper. "Weaver hook snags Tate title." *Chicago Tribune*, 4/1/1980, p. D1.

WEPNER, CHUCK (1939–). Chuck Wepner—better known as the Bayonne Brawler or
Bayonne Bleeder—was a tough heavyweight contender best known for his courageous challenge
to champion **Muhammad Ali** in 1975. Wepner's gutsy performance inspired Sylvester Stallone to create the Oscar-winning movie *Rocky*. The lead character, Rocky Balboa—played by
Stallone—was based at least in part on Wepner.

Born in 1939 in Bayonne, New Jersey, Wepner boxed while serving in the Marines. He turned
professional in 1964. He lost consecutive bouts to Bob Stallings and **Buster Mathis** in 1965 and
1966. In 1969, he lost consecutive bouts to Jose Roman and behemoth contender **George Foreman.** The next year he lost to former heavyweight champion **Sonny Liston.**

Beginning in 1972, he won eight straight fights, including a win over former world champion
Ernie Terrell. That winning streak landed him a title shot against the great Ali. In the ninth
round, Wepner knocked Ali down—at least according to referee Tony Perez. Ali stopped Wepner in the 15th round.

He retired in 1978 after losing to Scott Frank.

Professional Record:	35-14-2
Championship(s):	None

Further Reading
Brunt, Stephen. *Facing Ali: 15 Fighters, 15 Stories*. Guilford, CT: Lyons Press, 2002, pp. 209–229.
Condon, David. "Wepner Has a Dream—Does He Have a Prayer?" *Chicago Tribune*, 3/12/1975, p. E3.
Official Web site: http://wepner.homestead.com/

WHITAKER, PERNELL (1964–). Pernell "Sweet Pea" Whitaker was one of the finest defensive fighters of all time, a master boxer who won multiple world championships with his
superior boxing skills. Born in 1964 in Norfolk, Virginia, Whitaker had an extensive amateur
career, culminating in a gold medal at the 1984 Los Angeles Olympics.

He turned professional in 1984 and earned his first world title shot in 1988 against **Jose** Luis
Ramirez for the lightweight championship. To most ringside observers, Whitaker outboxed the
tough champion, but two of the three judges awarded the bout to Ramirez. The next year, Whitaker stopped Greg Haugen to win the **International Boxing Federation (IBF)** lightweight
championship. He added the **World Boxing Council (WBC)** belt in 1989 when he outclassed
Ramirez in a rematch. In 1990, he unified the belts with a victory over Juan Nazario. In 1992, he
captured the IBF junior welterweight title with a decision win over Rafael Pineda.

The next year, he won the WBC welterweight title with a win over **James "Buddy" McGirt.**
In 1995, he won the **World Boxing Association (WBA)** junior middleweight belt with a win
over Julio Cesar Vasquez. He continued to hold his welterweight title until 1997 when he lost
a close decision to **Oscar De La Hoya.** He retired in 2001. After some drug-related problems,
Whitaker has come back strong as a boxing trainer.

Professional Record:	40-4-1
Championship(s):	IBF Lightweight, 1989–1992; WBC lightweight, 1989–1992; WBA lightweight, 1990–1992; IBF junior welterweight, 1992–1993; WBC welterweight, 1993–1997; WBA junior middleweight, 1995

Further Reading
Borges, Ron. "Willing and Still Able: Can Pernell Whitaker Tame the Young Lions?" *The Ring* (January 1997), pp. 38–39, 55–57.
Dettloff, William. "The 20 Greatest Lightweights of All Time." *The Ring* (September 2001), pp. 49–69, 52.
Evans, Gavin. "The 20 Greatest Welterweights of All Time." *The Ring* (February 2008), pp. 63–84, 82.
Sugar, Bert Randolph, "Pernell Whitaker: The Undefined Champion." *ESPN.com*, 3/26/2007, at http://sports.espn.go.com/sports/boxing/news/story?id=2786103

WHITE, DANA (1969–). Dana White is the colorful and charismatic president of the **Ultimate Fighting Championships (UFC)**—the premier mixed martial arts (MMA) organization in the world. White is known for his business savvy, tireless energy, and ability to throw a barb at rivals or foes. Born in 1969 in Manchester, Connecticut, White entered college but dropped out after a couple of years. He worked as a bellhop in Boston but eventually moved to boxing to pursue his dream of making money in the business. He eventually opened three boxing gyms in Las Vegas and served as a manager for light heavyweight contender Derrick Harmon, who challenged **Roy Jones, Jr.**, for the world light heavyweight title.

White later managed UFC fighters **Tito Ortiz** and **Chuck Liddell.** During these times, he negotiated with then-UFC President Bob Meyrowitz. In 2001, he learned that Meyrowitz and his company Semaphore Entertainment Group (SEG) were looking to sell the UFC. White told his friends, casino owners Frank and Lorenzo Fertitta, and the Fertitta brothers purchased the UFC for $2 million and set up a company, Zuffa, LLC, to run the UFC. The Fertitta brothers installed White as UFC President, gave him 10 percent of the company, and the rest is history. A tireless worker and effective promoter, White has been a key figure in the amazing growth of the UFC and MMA in general.

Further Reading
Walker, Andrew. "Follow the Leader!: UFC President Dana White." *Extreme Fighter* (March 2008), pp. 10–15.
Werthem, L. Jon. "The New Main Event." *Sports Illustrated*, 5/28/2007, pp. 52–60.

WILDE, JIMMY (1892–1969). The Welsh-born Jimmy Wilde was perhaps the greatest flyweight champion in boxing history. Though a scrawny man, this 5'2" dynamo packed dynamite in his right hand. *The Ring* magazine listed this flyweight as the second greatest puncher of all-time in their *Ring Yearbook 2003: 100 Greatest Punchers of All-Time*—behind only heavyweight **Joe Louis.** His power caused some to dub him "the Ghost with a Hammer in His Hand," "The Ghost with a Sledgehammer," or "the Mighty Atom."

Wilde allegedly floored men twice his size at carnivals in Wales. He began boxing in 1908, weighing less than 80 pounds. He turned professional in 1911 and proceeded to win his first 61 bouts. He captured the world flyweight championship in 1916—the first year that such a title was recognized in America—with an 11th-round stoppage of Frankie Di Melfi, better known as Young Zulu Kid, in London. He held the flyweight championship until losing to the great **Pancho Villa** in 1923 in New York. B. F. Steinel wrote for *The Chicago Tribune* about Wilde: "This game little Welshman has everything that a fighter should possess. England has had many boxers of whom she is proud. But none compare with little Jimmy when it comes to being an idol. He is simply worshipped by British fight fans." At his funeral, former world champion **Gene Tunney** called Wilde "the greatest fighter I ever saw."

Record:	131-3-2
Championship(s):	Flyweight, 1916–1923

Further Reading

The Ring Magazine. *The Ring Yearbook 2003: 100 Greatest Punchers of All-Time.* 2003.

Steinel, B. F. "Wilde Rated as Greatest Little Fighter of All Time." *The Chicago Tribune,* 12/1/1919, p. 22.

WILLARD, JESS (1881–1968). Jess Willard, the "Pottawatomie Giant," was a former world heavyweight champion best known for lifting the title from **Jack Johnson** in Havana, Cuba, in 1915. Born in 1881 in St. Clere, Kansas, Willard grew up on his stepfather's cowboy ranch. Nearly 6′7″ tall, Willard turned pro in 1911 and lost his pro debut via disqualification.

He rebounded to win several fights in a row before quitting in the fifth round against Joe Cox. In 1913, Willard kayoed a journeyman fighter named William "Bull" Young who died the following day. Willard, his promoter, and his manager were all charged with manslaughter, but later the charges were dropped. Eventually, Willard emerged as the "White Hope" able to challenge Jack Johnson, who had successfully beat back many challengers during his long title reign.

Finally, in 1915, Johnson defended his title against Willard. The aging Johnson fared well in the early rounds, and through 20 rounds the fight was about even. However, the poorly conditioned champion began to tire, and Willard continually pressed his reach advantage and superior conditioning. He stopped Johnson in the 26th round.

Willard successfully defended his title once against Frank Moran until losing badly to **Jack Dempsey** in 1919. He retired but returned to the ring in 1923. After winning one bout, he faced Luis Firpo in a "Battle of the Giants." After losing to Firpo, he retired for good.

Professional Record:	26-6-1
Championship(s):	Heavyweight, 1915–1919

Further Reading

Harris, L. David. "Jess Willard Revisited: A Nostalgic Look At A Forgotten Champ. *The Ring* (March 1997), pp. 68–73.

Kent, Graeme. *The Great White Hopes: The Quest to Defeat Jack Johnson.* Stroud, Gloucestershire, UK: Sutton Publishing, 2005.

WILLIAMS, CLEVELAND (1933–1999). Cleveland "Big Cat" Williams was a former top heavyweight contender in the late 1950s and 1960s who could never beat the very best fighters of his era. Williams possessed tremendous power in his tall frame but lost to both **Sonny Liston** and **Muhammad Ali** (then Cassius Clay).

Born in 1933 in Griffin, Georgia, Williams fought out of Houston, Texas. He made his professional debut in 1951 and won his first 27 fights before an upset loss to unheralded Sylvester Jones. In 1959 and 1960, he lost badly to the powerful Liston. In 1963, he lost a split decision to **Ernie Terrell.**

Williams nearly lost his life in 1964 after being shot by a Texas state trooper, but he survived a five-hour operation and returned to the boxing ring in 1966. He won three straight bouts before facing the talented Ali, who stopped him in the third round. Williams finally retired in 1972.

Professional Record:	78-13-1
Championship(s):	None

Further Reading

Lewis, Mike. "Cleveland Williams; a Boxer Brought Low by Cassius Clay—and a Bullet." *The Guardian,* 9/28/1999, p. 22.

United Press International. "Heavyweight Contender Williams Shot in Scuffle with Patrolman." *The Washington Post*, 11/30/1964, p. B1.

WILLIAMS, HOLMAN (1915–1967). Holman Williams was one of the greatest boxers to never win a world title. In the words of boxing historian Harry Otty, he was "one of the most historically neglected fighters of all time."

Born in 1915 in Pensacola, Florida, Williams moved with his family to Michigan, where he began a fine amateur career. He nearly made the team for the 1932 Olympics. He turned professional as a featherweight later that year. He never received a world title shot, but he boxed many of the best fighters of his day. He defeated **Charley Burley** in 1939, Lloyd Marshall in 1943, and **Archie Moore** in 1945.

Eddie Futch once said that he would rather watch Holman Williams shadowbox than watch other boxers fight in the ring.

Professional Record:	145-30-11
Championship(s):	None

Further Reading

Otty, Harry. "Holman Williams Belongs in the Hall of Fame." *Cyber Boxing Zone Journal*, July 2006, at http://cyberboxingzone.com/boxing/0001-otty.html

Webster, John. "Holman Williams Is Robbed in Philadelphia." *The Chicago Defender*, 8/21/1943, p. 21.

WILLIAMS, IKE (1923–1994). Ike Williams was a former world lightweight champion who was a great boxer-puncher. Born in 1923 in Brunswick, Georgia, Isiah Williams turned professional in 1940 with a decision win over Carmine Fatta in New Brunswick, New Jersey. He compiled a less than impressive 5-2-1 record in his first eight bouts. However, Williams continued to show great improvement in the ring. For example, he won all 12 of his bouts in 1942. Even more impressive, he won all 19 of his bouts in 1943.

That long winning streak led Williams to a showdown with future rival Bob Montgomery, who stopped Williams in the 12th round in an action bout in Philadelphia. Undeterred, Williams returned to the ring and destroyed **Juan Zurita** in the second round to win the National Boxing Association (NBA) lightweight title.

He won the world championship and avenged an earlier defeat from his rival Bob Montgomery with a sixth-round knockout in August 1947. He retained the title until a 1951 loss to **Jimmy Carter.** He fought until 1955 when he lost consecutive fights to **Beau Jack.** Williams was managed by mobster Frank "Blinkie" Palermo. Williams later admitted to a Senate committee headed by Senator Estes Kefauver that he carried other fighters on orders from Palermo.

Professional Record:	126-24-5
Championship(s):	Lightweight, 1947–1951

Further Reading

Associated Press. "Ike Williams Stop Zurita in Second Round." *Chicago Daily Tribune*, 4/19/1945, p. 27.

Dettloff, William. "The 20 Greatest Lightweights of All Time." *The Ring* (September 2001), pp. 49–69, 54.

Roberts, James B., and Alexander G. Skutt. *The Boxing Register: International Boxing Hall of Fame Register* (4th ed.). Ithaca, NY: McBooks Press, Inc., 2006, pp. 658–661.

WILLS, HARRY (1889–1958). Harry "the Black Panther" Wills was a tough African American heavyweight who never received a world title shot due to race. Born in 1889, in New Orleans,

Louisiana, Wills turned pro in 1910. He used his size and power to overwhelm many opponents during his career. He stood 6′4″ and weighed more than 220 pounds.

He became the "Colored Heavyweight Champion" in 1918 with a decision win over rival **Sam Langford.** Wills should have received a world title shot from champion **Jack Dempsey,** but he never got his shot. Instead, he had to fight other top black fighters, such as Langford, whom he fought an amazing 19 times. He also faced Sam McVey and Joe Jeanette many times. Wills stopped Ed "Gunboat" Smith in the first round. In 1919, Wills retained his "Colored Heavyweight Championship" by defeating the likes of Langford, Joe Jeanette, and other top fighters. He continued to fight but could never receive a world title shot. His career in the ring went downhill after losing to future champion **Jack Sharkey** in 1926. He fought his last fight in 1932.

Professional Record:	65-8-2 (sources not consistent on Wills' record)
Championship(s):	None

Further Reading
Fullerton, Hugh. "Boxing Expert Declares Wills Should Have Tilt with Dempsey." *Los Angeles Times,* 9/4/1922, p. II 14.
Rohde, Bob. "Poor Stable Boy To Star of Ring, Story of Wills." *Chicago Daily Tribune,* 3/9/1922, p. A3.
"Wills Ices Fred Fulton." *The New York Times,* 7/27/1920, p. III 1.

WINSTONE, HOWARD (1939–2000). Howard "the Welsh Wizard" Winstone was a former world featherweight champion who overcame the loss of the tops of three fingers on his right hand at age 17 to have a successful career. Born in 1939 in Methyr Tydfil, Wales, Winstone had a decorated amateur career, including a gold medal in the Commonwealth Games.

He turned pro in 1959 and won his first 34 bouts before suffering a second-round stoppage loss to American Leroy Jeffrey. He rebounded and kept winning with his superior boxing skills.

In 1965, he fought the great **Vincente Saldivar** for the world featherweight title. Saldivar won a 15-round decision. In 1967, he faced Saldivar in Wales and lost a razor-thin decision. His performance garnered him a third bout against Saldivar, but he lost again. After his nemesis Saldivar retired, Winstone faced Mitsunori Seki for the vacant **World Boxing Council (WBC)** featherweight title in January 1968. Winstone stopped Seki in the ninth round to capture the title. He lost the title to Jose Legra in his first defense in 1968.

Professional Record:	61-6
Championship(s):	WBC featherweight, 1968

Further Reading
Jones, Ken. "Winstone's Genius Turned Boxing Into Art and Glorified Tradition of Merthyr Heroes." *The Independent,* 10/9/2000, p. 6.

WITHERSPOON, TIM (1957–). "Terrible" Tim Witherspoon was a former two-time world heavyweight champion known for his powerful left hook, excellent defense, less-than-stellar conditioning, and all-around superior skills. Born in 1957 in Philadelphia, Pennsylvania, Witherspoon turned pro in 1979 and won his first 15 bouts. In only his 16th bout, he challenged undefeated champion **Larry Holmes** for the world title in 1983. An 11-2 underdog, Witherspoon nearly captured the belt, losing a split decision. Many ringside observers thought he won the bout. Holmes said after the bout: "The judges gave me the bout" (Katz).

Undeterred, he captured the **World Boxing Council (WBC)** title in 1984 with a decision win over **Greg Page.** He lost the title in his first defense to **Pinklon Thomas.** In 1986, he won the **World Boxing Association (WBA)** heavyweight title with a decision win over unbeaten **Tony Tubbs.** He successfully defended his title against **Frank Bruno** but then lost via a devastating first-round kayo loss **to James "Bonecrusher" Smith.**

He never received another world title shot, though he fought all the way until 2003. Witherspoon was known for suing famous promoter **Don King,** contending that King and his son Carl King had taken too much of his money. King later settled the lawsuit with Witherspoon.

Professional Record: 55-13-1
Championship(s):   WBC Heavyweight, 1984; WBA Heavyweight, 1986

Further Reading
Berger, Phil. "Witherspoon Captures Crown." *The New York Times,* 1/18/1986, p. 47.
Eskenazi, Gerald. "Witherspoon Gets Back to Battles in the Ring." *The New York Times,* 1/9/1996, p. 45.
Katz, Michael. "Witherspoon Suffers First Loss." *The New York Times,* 5/21/1983, p. 33.

WITTER, JUNIOR (1974–). Junior "the Hitter" Witter is a talented junior welterweight champion whose quickness, elusiveness, and defensive skills have made him an avoided foe by many of the division's bigger names. Born in 1974 in Bradford, Yorkshire, in the United Kingdom, Witter turned pro in 1997 under the tutelage of top trainer Brendan Ingle, who seemingly specializes in working with unorthodox, talented boxers.

Witter fought to a draw in his professional debut against an 8-1 Cameron Raeside but then went on a long winning streak. In June 2000, he finally received a world title shot against **International Boxing Federation (IBF)** junior welterweight champion **Zab Judah** in a matchup of undefeated boxers. Judah's seeming power advantage proved to be the difference in the unanimous decision victory.

Witter rebounded from his lone professional loss with a long series of wins. Finally, in June 2006, he faced Demarcus "Chop Chop" Corley for the vacant **World Boxing Council (WBC)** junior welterweight title. Witter won a convincing unanimous decision. He s successfully defended his title twice, including a stoppage of dangerous former champion **Vivian Harris,** before losing to unheralded (but unbeaten) challenger Timothy Bradley in 2008.

Professional Record: 37-2-1
Championship(s):   WBC junior welterweight, 2006–2008

Further Reading
Donovan, Jake. "Witter Starches Harris in Seven." *Boxing Scene,* 9/7/2007, at http://www.boxingscene.
     com/?m=show&opt=printable&id=10233
Doogan, Brian. "WBC Titleholder Junior Witter: The One Man Hatton Refuses to Fight." *The Ring* (February 2008), pp. 92–99.

WOMACK, RICKEY (1961–2002). Rickey Womack was a talented boxer with a troubled past that he could not overcome. Born in 1961 in Jackson, Tennessee, he relocated with his mother and siblings in Detroit after his father shot her. A turbulent home life led to Womack being declared a ward of the state. He went to jail for armed robbery as a teenager. On his release, he returned to boxing and showed great promise as an amateur.

He captured the 1984 Olympic trials by beating **Evander Holyfield.** However, he lost out on a spot on the Olympic team because he lost twice to Holyfield in the Olympic box-offs. Denied a chance at a gold medal, Womack turned pro under the guidance of legendary manager/trainer **Emanuel Steward.** All looked great for Womack, as he won 10 straight bouts in 1984 and 1985. Then, Womack was arrested and charged with attempted murder and armed robbery. He served 16 years in prison. Amazingly, upon his release, he returned to the ring and won four straight bouts in 2001. However, he could not defeat his demons and committed suicide in January 2002.

Professional Record:	14-0
Championship(s):	None

Further Reading
Berger, Phil. "Paths That Crossed in the Ring." *The New York Times*, 2/8/1987, p. S1.

WONGJONGKAM, PONGSAKLEK (1977–). Thailand's Pongsaklek Wongjongkam is one of the most—if not the most—dominant flyweight champions in boxing history. Born in Nakhon Ratchasima in 1977, Wongjongkam turned pro in 1994. He lost two early fights to journeyman Jerry Pahayahay. He didn't lose again for more than 50 bouts.

In March 2001, he destroyed Malcolm Tunacao in the first round to win the **World Boxing Council (WBC)** flyweight championship. Over the next 6 years, he made 17 successful title defenses, including a devastating 34-second knockout of Japan's Daisuke Naito. The southpaw Wongjongkam is known for his aggressive attack, body punching, and solid chin. He finally lost his title in July 2007 by a close unanimous decision to Naito in Japan. In March 2008, he fought a 12-round draw with Naito. He still hopes to regain his title and continues to fight.

Professional Record:	70-3-1
Championship(s):	WBC flyweight, 2001–2007

Further Reading
"The Reign Is Over." *The Nation* (Thailand), 7/19/2007.
"Pongsaklek is new world champion." *Bangkok News*, 3/3/2001.

WORLD BOXING ASSOCIATION (WBA). One of the leading sanctioning bodies in boxing, the World Boxing Association (WBA) came into being in 1962 as the world successor to the National Boxing Association (NBA), which was centered exclusively in the United States. Many believed that boxing needed a universal and globally-based boxing organization that would truly recognize the best fighters in the world.

In December 1962, the state of California applied for membership in the WBA, saying that it believed the goals of the WBA were better than the goals of the old NBA.

Many critics of boxing contend that the WBA and other sanctioning bodies have only led to a decline in popularity of the sport. The WBA achieved headlines for stripping title recognition from heavyweight champion Cassius Clay (later **Muhammad Ali**) in September 1964 for agreeing to a rematch with former champion **Sonny Liston.** In 1976, Jose Cordero of Puerto Rico and others at the WBA convention gave less control to each individual state in the United States, making it a more globally-based organization.

Its current president is Gilberto Mendoza.

Further Reading
Associated Press. "World Boxing Association Kills Controversial Proposal." *The New York Times*, 8/21/1966, p. 193.
Klein, Frederick. "Why Boxing Now Has Two Heavyweight Champs." *Wall Street Journal*, 4/4/1978, p. 22.
Official Web site: http://www.wbaonline.com

Roberts, James B., and Alexander G. Skutt. "Who Rules? Boxing's Governing Bodies," in *The Boxing Register: International Boxing Hall of Fame Official Record Book*. Ithaca, NY: McBooks Press, Inc., 2006, pp. 48–51.

United Press International. "California Seeks to Join World Boxing Group." *The New York Times*, 12/20/1962, p. 16.

WORLD BOXING COUNCIL (WBC). The World Boxing Council (WBC) is one of the major sanctioning bodies in boxing. Its championships are considered among the top four in boxing along with the **World Boxing Association (WBA),** the **International Boxing Federation (IBF),** and the World Boxing Organization (WBO).

The WBC was formed in Mexico in February 1963 partly in response to the formation the year before of the WBA. Under the WBA, individual states in the United States had as much voting power as other countries. Many believed this to be unfair, including promoter **George Parnassus.** Representatives from 11 countries, including the United States, met in Mexico City to form the organization. For much of the 1960s, '70s, and '80s, the WBC and WBA were the only two major sanctioning bodies in boxing.

Since 1976, the WBC's president has been Jose Sulaiman, who formerly was the organization's secretary. He has had a long career in boxing. At times the WBC and Sulaiman have been criticized for a close relationship with controversial boxing promoter **Don King.** However, the WBC remains a leading boxing organization.

Further Reading
Hawn, Jack. "Boxing Solomon." *Los Angeles Times*, 1/17/1977, p. D1.

Official Web site: http://www.wbcboxing.com

Roberts, James B., and Alexander G. Skutt. "Who Rules? Boxing's Governing Bodies," in *The Boxing Register: International Boxing Hall of Fame Official Record Book*. Ithaca, NY: McBooks Press, Inc. 2006, pp. 48–51.

WORLD BOXING ORGANIZATION (WBO). The World Boxing Organization is one of professional boxing's major sanctioning bodies. Formed in 1988 in Puerto Rico, it is often considered the fourth most important organization behind the **World Boxing Council** (WBC), the **World Boxing Association** (WBA), and the **International Boxing Federation** (IBF). The WBO was formed in 1988 after many delegates of the WBA were upset by the direction of the organization. "The **WBO** is a result of the **WBA** gone bad," said one leading official of the WBO in 1994. (Borges, 1988). The WBO's current president is Francisco Varcarcel.

Further Reading
Borges, Ron. "Fledging WBO has a fight on its hands." *The Boston Globe*, 11/5/1988, p. 40.

Official Web site: http://www.wbo-int.com/

Roberts, James B., and Alexander G. Skutt. "Who Rules? Boxing's Governing Bodies." in *The Boxing Register: International Boxing Hall of Fame Official Record Book* (pp. 48–51). Ithaca, NY: McBooks Press, Inc., 2006.

WRIGHT, ALBERT "CHALKY" (1912–1957). Albert "Chalky" Wright was a former world featherweight champion who compiled more than 160 career victories in a professional career that spanned 20 years. Many dispute when Wright was born, though official sources list his birth in 1912 in Durango, Mexico. After his father abandoned the family, his mother moved the family to Los Angeles.

Wright turned pro in 1928 and fought for 12 years before receiving a title shot. For many years his manager Eddie Walker described him as the "uncrowned champion." During his early years he often served as a sparring partner for other great fighters, such as **Barney Ross** and **Henry Armstrong.** He also often had to move up in weight to find suitable opposition. Wright was the chauffeur for the legendary actress Mae West.

In September 1941, he stopped Joey Archibald in the 11th round to win the world featherweight title. He lost his title to the great **Willie Pep,** who decisioned Wright over 15 rounds. He received another title shot in 1944—against Pep. Wright fought well, but Pep's masterful boxing skills and younger age prevailed. Wright retired in 1948 after a kayo loss. He died in 1957 after suffering a heart attack in the bathtub.

Professional Record: 160-43-16
Championship(s):   Featherweight, 1941–1942

Further Reading
Daley, Arthur. "The Right Slant on Wright." *The New York Times*, 6/4/1943, p. 26.
Hailey, Al. "Chalky Wright to Fight on Conn Card." *The Washington Post*, 2/26/1941, p. 21.
Roberts, James B., and Alexander G. Skutt. *The Boxing Register: International Boxing Hall of Fame Register* (4th ed.). Ithaca, NY: McBooks Press, Inc., 2006, pp. 662–667.
Whorton, Cal. "Chalky Wright Scores T.K.O. Over Lemos." *Los Angeles Times*, 2/4/1942, p. 15.

WRIGHT, RONALD "WINKY" (1971−). Ronald "Winky" Wright is a stylish, southpaw boxer known for his slick skills, outstanding jab, and excellent defensive skills. Born in 1971 in Washington, D.C., his mother moved him to St. Petersburg, Florida, at an early age. He came into contact with trainer Dan Birmingham, who became his trainer his entire career. Wright turned pro in 1990 and won his first 25 bouts. He traveled to France to face Julio Cesar Vasquez for the **World Boxing Association (WBA)** junior middleweight title. Wright lost a unanimous decision.

Wright captured the World Boxing Organization (WBO) title in 1996 with a decision win over Bronco McKart—one of three victories Wright would hold over McKart. He defended

Ronald "Winky" Wright does battle with the great Bernard Hopkins. Wright lost a unanimous decision in July 2007. Courtesy of Chris Cozzone..

that title several times before a close decision loss to undefeated Nambian fighter Harry Simon in South Africa. Wright then lost another decision to "Ferocious" **Fernando Vargas.**

In 2001, Wright defeated Robert Frazier for the vacant **International Boxing Federation (IBF)** junior middleweight title. He added the **World Boxing Council (WBC)** and WBA belts in a unification victory over **"Sugar" Shane Mosley**—Wright's signature win as he "turned the jab into a brush and painting a masterpiece," according to boxing writer Michael Katz. After defeating Mosley in a rematch, Wright moved up to middleweight and dispatched **Felix Trinidad.** In 2006, he faced middleweight champion **Jermain Taylor.** Many thought he did enough to win, but he only managed a draw. In 2007, he fought once—losing a decision to **Bernard Hopkins.**

Professional Record:	51-4-1
Championship(s):	WBO junior middleweight, 1996–1998; IBF junior middleweight, 2001–2004; WBA junior middleweight, 2004–2005; WBC junior middleweight, 2004–2005

Further Reading

Donovan, Jake. "Winky Wright's Long Road to the Top." *The Sweet Science*, 11/19/2004, at http://www.thesweetscience.com/boxing-article/1355/winky-wright-long-road-top/

Donovan, Jake. "Winky Ready for Wright of Passage." *The Sweet Science*, 5/12/2005, at http://www.thesweetscience.com/boxing-article/2056/winky-ready-wright-passage/

Fernandez, Bernard. "Winky Beats Mosley . . . But Does He Have The Wright Stuff to Cash In?" *World Boxing* (September 2004), pp. 44–49.

Katz, Michael. "Wright, the Underdog, Defeats Mosley." *The New York Times*, 3/14/2004, p. SP8.

Katz, Michael. "Wright is Wondering What's Next." *The New York Times*, 3/15/2004, p. D10.

Wilson, Jon. "Working on the Wright Stuff." *St. Petersburg Times*, 7/7/1994, p. 1C.

YUH, MYUNG-WOO (1964–). South Korea's Myung-Woo Yuh should be in the International Boxing Hall of Fame, as this dominant junior flyweight champion made 17 successful defenses of his crown and held the belt from 1985 until 1991. Born in Seoul in 1964, Yuh turned pro in 1982 and captured the title three years later with a decision win over **Joey Olivo.** He held the title until a 1991 split decision loss to Japanese fighter Hiroki Ioka in Tokyo. Yuh regained the title in a rematch, made one more defense, and then retired. He finished his career with a record of 38-1.

Professional Record:	38-1
Championship(s):	WBA junior flyweight, 1985–1991, 1991–1993

Further Reading
Hudson, David L., Jr., and Mike Fitzgerald. *Boxing's Most Wanted: The Top 10 Book of Champs, Chumps and Punch Drunk Palookas.* Alexandria, VA: Potomac Books, 2003.

ZALE, TONY (1913–1997). Tony Zale, the so-called "Man of Steel," was an iron-jawed former middleweight champion of the world known for his ability to absorb punishment and still come back to win. Born in 1913 in Gary, Indiana, as Tony Zaleski, he later shortened his name to Zale. He turned professional in 1934 rather than work in the steel mills. After an impressive amateur record of 87-9, Zale turned pro in 1934.

He struggled a bit in his first year as a pro, at one point losing three straight decisions. He also lost three straight bouts in 1935—not the stuff that boxing legends are made of. However, Zale steadily improved as a boxer and in 1940 defeated Al Hostak for the National Boxing Association (NBA) middleweight title. According to the Associated Press, he "methodically mowed down" Hostak.

In 1941, he won the middleweight championship with a win over Georgie Abrams. He then served in World War II in the Navy. He resumed defending his title in 1946, defeating **Rocky Graziano** in a slugging classic. He lost to Graziano in 1947 but regained the title from his rival in 1948 as a 34-year-old challenger. In the second bout, Zale pummeled Graziano in the second round and knocked him down in the third round, but Graziano rallied to stop Zale in the fifth round. However, in the rubber match, Zale knocked Graziano out in the third round.

Many boxing experts consider the Zale—Graziano trilogy as the greatest in boxing history. In two of those bouts, Zale showed his incredible resiliency and amazing ability to come back after absorbing punishment. He retired after losing his title to **Marcel Cerdan** later in 1948.

Professional Record: 67-18-2
Championship(s):   Middleweight, 1941–1947, 1948

Further Reading
Associated Press. "Zale Takes Title, Stopping Hostak." *The New York Times*, 7/20/1940, p. 11.
Burns, Edward. "Cerdan Stops Zale in 12th; Takes Title." *Chicago Daily Tribune*, 9/22/1948, p. B1.
Dawson, James P. "18,547 See Referee Stop Chicago Fight." *The New York Times*, 7/17/1947, p. 23.
Povich, Shirley. "Tony Floors Rocky Three Other Times." *The Washington Post*, 6/11/1948, p. B3.

Roberts, James B., and Alexander G. Skutt. *The Boxing Register: International Boxing Hall of Fame Register* (4th ed.). Ithaca, NY: McBooks Press, Inc., 2006, pp. 668–671.

ZAMORA, ALFONSO (1954–). Alfonso Zamora was a power-punching former bantamweight champion who won all but one of his professional victories by knockout. *The Ring* magazine said that "Zamora could knock down a wall with his right hand" (p. 106). Born in 1954 in Mexico, Zamora captured a silver medal at the 1972 Munich Olympics. Zamora became a sensation at the tournament after stopping two opponents en route to the semifinals. He dropped a unanimous decision to Cuba's Orlando Martinez Romero in the gold-medal match.

Zamora turned professional after the Olympics and began racking up kayo victories. He captured the **World Boxing Association (WBA)** bantamweight championship in March 1975 with a third-round knockout over Soo Hwan Hong. He made five successful defenses of his title, including an impressive third-round stoppage over future featherweight kingpin **Eusebio Pedroza.** In April 1975, Zamora squared off against **World Boxing Council (WBC)** bantamweight champion **Carlos Zarate** in a 10-round nontitle bout. Expectations for the clash between the two undefeated warriors were fulfilled in a bout known as the "Battle of the Champions and "the Battle of the Zs." Zamora buckled Zarate's knees in the first round and captured the opening stanza. Zarate may have been aided when a young man wearing shorts and a t-shirt jumped in the ring. Zarate's superior boxing skills took over, and he finished Zamora in the fourth round, knocking him down three times.

Zamora never seemed the same after losing the biggest fight of his pro career, losing his title in his next fight to the unheralded Jorge Lujan. He rebounded in 1978 with a stoppage of contender and future champion **Alberto "Richie" Sandoval.** He retired in 1980, losing two of his last three fights.

Record:	33-5
Championship(s):	WBA Bantamweight, 1975–1977

Further Reading

Dettlof, William. *The Ring Yearbook 2003: 100 Greatest Punchers of All-Time.* Ambler, PA: London Publishing, 2003, pp. 106–107.
Hawn, Jack. "Father Stops Zamora but Zarate Does It First." *Los Angeles Times,* 4/24/1977, p. C1.

ZAPATA, HILARIO (1958–). Hilario Zapata was a former two-time world junior flyweight champion and a flyweight champion from Panama known for his stylish boxing skills. Born in 1958 in Panama City, he turned pro in 1977. In his 12th pro bout, he defeated Shigeo Nakejima in Tokyo, Japan, over 15 rounds to win the **World Boxing Council (WBC)** junior flyweight title in 1980. He made eight successful defenses—including a win over American **Joey Olivo**—before losing to Amado Ursua in two rounds in 1982.

Later, in 1982, he defeated Tadashi Tomori to recapture his WBC belt. This reign he made two successful defenses before losing to Jung-Koo Chang in 1983. In 1984, he traveled to Argentina to face Santos Benigno Laciar for the **World Boxing Association (WBA)** flyweight title and lost a close unanimous decision. He captured the championship in 1985 with a win over Alonzo Gonzalez. He made five successful defenses before losing in 1987 to undefeated Fidel Bassa. He retired in 1993 after an unsuccessful attempt for the WBC super flyweight title, losing to Sung-Kil Moon.

Professional Record:	43-10-1
Championship(s):	WBC junior flyweight, 1980–1982; 1982–1983; WBA flyweight, 1985–1987

Further Reading
Associated Press. "Zapata Keeps Title, Stops Olivo in 13th." *Los Angeles Times*, 2/9/1981, p. D5.

ZARAGOZA, DANIEL (1957–). Daniel Zaragoza was a former world bantamweight and junior featherweight champion known for his ability to change styles and overcome adversity in the ring. Born in 1957 in Mexico City, Zaragoza was part of a boxing family. His older brother Agustin represented Mexico in the 1968 Olympics. Daniel followed in his older brother's footsteps when he also represented Mexico at the 1980 Moscow Olympics, losing in the quarterfinals to Ghana's Michael Anthony.

He turned pro in 1980 and fought for 17 years, capturing world titles on four different occasions—once at bantamweight and three times at junior featherweight. He won his first world title in 1985 with a win over Freddie Jackson for the **World Boxing Council (WBC)** bantamweight title. He lost the title in his first defense against Miguel Lora.

Zaragoza moved up to the junior featherweight division where he had his greatest success. In 1988, he dominated the legendary **Carlos Zarate** to win the WBC junior featherweight title. He made five successful defenses before losing to Paul Banke in 1990. He regained the title in 1991 with a win over Kiyoshi Hatanaka over 12 rounds in Japan. He made two successful defenses before losing to France's Thierry Jacob in Calais, France, over 12 rounds.

After two unsuccessful attempts at winning another world title against Tracy Harris Patterson in 1992 and 1993, many boxing experts believed Zaragoza would never climb the mountain again. However, in November 1995, he defeated Hector Acero Sanchez over 12 rounds to win the junior featherweight title for the third time. He made four successful defenses—including a win over the popular **Wayne McCullough** at age 39—before finally losing his title to undefeated **Erik Morales** in 1997. Zaragoza—always prone to cuts—wisely retired after that bout. He earned enshrinement into the International Boxing Hall of Fame in 2004.

Professional Record: 55-8-3
Championship(s):   WBC bantamweight, 1985–1986; WBC junior feather-
                               weight, 1988–1990, 1991–1992, 1995–1997

Further Reading
Kimball, George. "McCullough Taught Lesson." *The Guardian*, 1/13/1997, p. 20.
O'Hara, Dennis. "Mexican Shatters Wayne's World." *Belfast News Letter*, 1/13/1997, SPORTS, p. 22.
Roberts, James B., and Alexander G. Skutt. *The Boxing Register: International Boxing Hall of Fame Register* (4th ed.). Ithaca, N.Y.: McBooks Press, Inc., 2006, pp. 672–675.

ZARATE, CARLOS (1951–). Carlos Zarate was one of the greatest—perhaps the greatest—bantamweight champions of all time. He compiled a record of 66-4 with 63 knockouts. Born in 1951 in Tepito, Mexico, Zarate turned professional at age 18. He racked up 39 straight wins before receiving his title shot against **World Boxing Council (WBC)** champion Rodolfo Martinez. Zarate won in the ninth round. He made nine successful defenses of his crown, but his most impressive victory came in a nontitle clash with **World Boxing Association (WBA)** champion and fellow countryman **Alfonzo Zamora.** Zarate won in impressive fashion, stopping Zamora in the fourth round.

Zarate suffered his first professional loss while still bantamweight champion when he moved up in weight to challenge super bantamweight champion **Wilfredo Gomez.** Zarate entered the October 1978 bout as a 2-1 favorite but was stopped in the fifth round. The next year, Zarate lost his bantamweight title in a controversial decision to **Lupe Pintor.** Zarate dropped Pintor in the fourth round but lost the title by split decision. He retired after the loss but returned to the ring seven years later in 1986. He won 12 straight bouts against modest competition before landing consecutive shots for the WBC junior featherweight title, losing to **Jeff Fenech** and **Daniel Zaragoza.** After being stopped by Zaragoza, Zarate retired for good in 1988.

Record:	66-4
Championship(s):	WBC Bantamweight, 1976–1979

Further Reading
Hawn, Jack. "Champion Zarate is a Cut Above Davila." *Los Angeles Times*, 2/26/1978, p. C1.
Hoffer, Richard. "Zarate is Upset After He's Upset." *Los Angeles Times*, 6/4/1979, p. B1.
Roberts, James B., and Alexander G. Skutt. *The Boxing Register: International Boxing Hall of Fame Register* (4th ed.). Ithaca, NY: McBooks Press, Inc., 2006, pp. 676–679.

ZIVIC, FRITZIE (1913–1984). Fritzie Zivic was a rough-and-tough former welterweight champion known for his many fights and his willingness to engage in all tactics—legal and illegal—in the ring. Born in Lawrenceville, Pennsylvania, Zivic was part of a fighting family of five boxing brothers.

He turned pro in 1931 in Pittsburgh. He won the world welterweight title in 1940 by defeating the legendary **Henry Armstrong** over 15 rounds. A 4-1 underdog, Zivic battered Armstrong for much of the fight and floored him in the final round. Zivic defeated Armstrong in a rematch, but lost his title to Freddie Cochrane in 1941. He never received another world title shot but fought many former world champions throughout his career, including **Sugar Ray Robinson, Jake LaMotta, Bob Montgomery,** Lew Jenkins, and **Beau Jack.** He finally retired in 1949.

Professional Record:	157-65-10
Championship(s):	Welterweight, 1940–1941

Further Reading
Cuddy, Jack. "Armstrong Loses Ring Title to Fritzie Zivic." *Los Angeles Times*, 10/5/1940, p. 11.
Dawson, James P. "Referee's Action Averts Ring Riot." *The New York Times*, 11/16/1940, p. 15.
Richman, Milton. "A Career of Ifs and Butts." *Los Angeles Times*, 5/26/1976, p. F2.

ZURITA, JUAN (1917–2000). Juan Zurita was a former world lightweight champion from Mexico who compiled more than 120 professional victories in a career that spanned from 1932 to 1945. Born in Guadalajara, Mexico, in 1917, he turned pro as a young teenager in 1932 and won his first 17 bouts.

In 1936, he was stopped for the first time by the legendary **Henry Armstrong** in the fourth round. He won the Mexican lightweight title in 1938 by defeating Joe Conde. In 1942, he fought Armstrong a second time but suffered a similar fate as the first fight. In 1944, he finally received a world title and made the most of it with a decision win over Sammy Angott. He lost his championship to the great **Ike Williams** in 1945. He retired after the Williams fight.

Professional Record:	121-23-1
Championship(s):	NBA Lightweight, 1944–1945

Further Reading
Lowry, Paul. "Zurita Whips Lemos in Easy Style." *Los Angeles Times*, 7/25/1942, p. 11.
Lowry, Paul. "Zurita Dethrones Angott in Dull Tilt." *Los Angeles Times*, 3/9/1944, p. A10.
Whorton, Cal. "Wright Faces Tough Foe in Zurita." *Los Angeles Times*, 3/24/1942, p. 20.

TIMELINE

648 B.C.   Pankration, an ancient combat sport often viewed as a progenitor of modern mixed martial arts, is introduced at the Olympic Games.

408 B.C.   Polydamus, one of the celebrated pankrationists, wins the Olympics.

23 B.C.   The first recorded sumo wrestling bouts occur in Japan. Sumo bouts probably took place much earlier, but this is the first event recorded in history.

1578   A major sumo wrestling tournament of more than 1,500 competitors is held by Oba Nobunaga.

1719   James Figg is recognized as England's first boxing champion. He held the title until 1740.

1743   Jack Broughton, the "Father of Boxing," adopts boxing's first set of rules (called Broughton's Rules) to govern the sport of boxing. Broughton adopts these rules after one of his opponents, George Stevenson, dies in the ring.

1794   Daniel Mendoza becomes the first Jewish man to win a boxing championship when he captured England's title.

1825   Miguel Casseux opens the first training school in France for the practice of the martial art discipline savate.

1838   The London Prize Ring Rules are adopted, replacing Broughton's Rules.

1867   The Queensbury Rules are adopted, providing a new set of rules governing the sport of boxing.

1882   John L. Sullivan, "the Boston Strongboy," becomes the bareknuckle heavyweight champion.

            Jigoro Kano founds the martial arts discipline that is known as modern judo.

1888   George Dixon becomes the first black man to win any world boxing title by capturing the bantamweight title.

1892   Sullivan defends his heavyweight title against James "Gentleman Jim" Corbett in the first bout fought under the Queensbury Rules. Corbett wins the bout and becomes champion.

1899	Bob Fitzsimmons win the world light heavyweight champion and becomes the first man to win world titles in three different weight classes. He had previously won the middleweight title in 1891 and the heavyweight crown in 1897.
1904	Boxing is a recognized sporting event at the Modern Olympic Games in St. Louis, Missouri.
1908	Jack Johnson wins the heavyweight championship from Tommy Burns to become the first African American heavyweight champion.
1914	Al McCoy becomes the first southpaw to win a world boxing title when he defeated George Chip in the first round.
1919	Jack Dempsey knocks out Jess Williard to win the heavyweight championship.
1920	New York passes the Walker Law, which establishes more stringent rules on professional boxing.
1921	A group of state athletic commissions meet and form the National Boxing Association (NBA).
	In July, Jack Dempsey's successful heavyweight title defense against Georges Carpentier in Jersey City, New Jersey, generates boxing's first million-dollar gate.
1922	Battling Siki upsets Georges Carpentier to win the world light heavyweight championship.
1925	Carlos Gracie, along with his younger brother Helio, open their first jiu-jitsu academy in Rio de Janeiro, Brazil.
1927	In September, former champion Jack Dempsey fails to regain his title from champion Gene Tunney in a fight known as "the Battle of the Long Count." In the seventh round, Dempsey floored Tunney but forgot to go the neutral corner for the referee's count to begin. That gave Tunney extra time to recuperate and defend his title.
1935	James J. Braddock, dubbed "Cinderella Man" by writer Damon Runyon, becomes one of the sport's unlikeliest heavyweight champion by defeating heavily favored Max Baer.
1937	Joe Louis wins the world heavyweight title by defeating Braddock.
1938	Sambo is recognized as an official sport in the Soviet Union.
	Henry Armstrong holds the featherweight, lightweight, and welterweight titles simultaneously.
1955	Masahiko Kimura defeats Brazilian jiu-jitsu expert Helio Gracie in a celebrated match in Brazil witnessed by more than 20,000 people. Kimura broke Gracie's arm in a shoulder lock, but Gracie refused to submit. Gracie's brother had to throw in the towel to end the bout.
1956:	Lazlo Papp becomes the first man to win gold medals at three consecutive Olympic Games.
	Rocky Marciano retires from boxing as the undefeated heavyweight champion.
1958	Sugar Ray Robinson becomes the first man to win a world title in the same weight class five times.
1960	A confident young man named Cassius Marcellus Clay wins a gold medal in the light-heavyweight division at the Rome Olympics.
1962	Emile Griffith defeats Benny "Kid" Paret to regain his welterweight world title. Griffith pummels Paret with more than 20 unanswered blows before referee Ruby Goldstein finally halts the bout. Paret later dies from injuries suffered in the bout. The televised bout led to many calls to ban boxing.

The National Boxing Association (NBA) changes its name to the World Boxing Association (WBA).

1963   The World Boxing Council (WBC) is formed.

1964   Cassius Marcellus Clay, Jr. (Muhammad Ali) wins the world heavyweight champion from Sonny Liston.

1971   In January, former heavyweight champion Sonny Liston is found dead. Many still believe his death—ruled a suicide—involved foul play. It still remains shrouded in secrecy.

In the "Fight of the Century" in March, undefeated heavyweight champion Joe Frazier defeats former champion Muhammad Ali by a 15-round decision to retain his title.

In April, the United States Supreme Court reverses the conviction of Ali (Cassius Clay) for refusing induction into the United States Army.

1974   Muhammad Ali regains the world heavyweight title by defeating George Foreman in Kinshasa, Zaire, in a bout known as the "Rumble in the Jungle."

1975   Ali successfully defends his title against his nemesis Joe Frazier in a bout in the Philippines called the "Thrilla in Manila."

1976   Wilfred Benitez becomes the youngest man to ever win a world boxing title when at the age of 17 he defeated Antonio "Kid Pambele" Cervantes to win the world junior welterweight championship.

Five American boxers—Howard Davis, Ray Leonard, Leo Randolph, Leon Spinks, and Michael Spinks—capture gold medals at the Montreal Olympic Games.

1978   In September, Muhammad Ali outpoints Leon Spinks over 15 rounds to regain his heavyweight title and become the first man to win the crown for the third time.

1980   In June, Roberto "Hands of Stone" Duran defeats previously unbeaten Sugar Ray Leonard at "the Brawl in Montreal" to win Leonard's welterweight title.

At the Moscow Olympics (boycotted by the United States), Cuban heavyweight Teofilo Stevenson wins a gold medal, at his third consecutive Olympics.

In November, Sugar Ray Leonard gained revenge when he made Duran infamously say *"no mas"* (no more) toward the end of the eighth round. Up to that point, Leonard had outboxed and taunted Duran during the bout.

1982   In November, popular lightweight champion Ray "Boom Boom" Mancini successfully defends his title against South Korean challenger Duk Koo Kim. The courageous Kim was stopped in the 14th round but never regained consciousness. He died a few days after the bout. His death caused the sanctioning bodies to reduce championship fights from 15 rounds to 12 rounds.

1985   The International Boxing Federation (IBF) is founded in New Jersey.

Michael Spinks, the former light heavyweight champion, pulls off a shocker by defeating heavyweight champion Larry Holmes.

1986   In November, Mike Tyson defeats WBC heavyweight champion Trevor Berbick to win the title and—at age 20—become the youngest heavyweight champion in history.

1988   A group of former WBA members splinter off and form a new boxing sanctioning body in Puerto Rico known as the World Boxing Organization (WBO).

1990   A 42-1 underdog named James "Buster" Douglas shocks the world by defeating undefeated heavyweight champion Mike Tyson to win the title.

1993	The Ultimate Fighting Championships (UFC) is formed and holds its first tournament in Colorado. The event was won by Brazilian jiu-jitsu expert Royce Gracie.
1994	In March, Royce Gracie wins the second UFC tournament by defeating Minoki Ichihara, Jason Delucia, Remco Pardoel, and Patrick Smith (in the finals).
	In September, an unlikely winner emerged from UFC 3, as alternate Steve Jennum defeated Harold Howard for the title. Royce Gracie had to withdraw from the tournament before his semifinal match against Harold Howard. Gracie had an unexpectedly difficult time with first-round opponent Kimo Leopold.
	In November, George Foreman becomes the oldest man in history (45) to win the world heavyweight title with a shocking knockout of champion Michael Moorer.
1995	In April 1995, at UFC 5 Royce Gracie and Ken Shamrock fight to a 36-minute draw in the organization's first-ever "superfight."
1996	The United States Congress passes the Professional Boxing Safety Act of 1996, which imposed comprehensive safety regulations on the sport.
1997	The Japan-based mixed martial arts organization PRIDE holds its first-ever event in Tokyo at the Tokyo Dome.
	Maurice Smith, a world-class kickboxer, surprises the combat sports world by defeating Mark Coleman at UFC 14 to win the UFC heavyweight championship.
2000	Cuba's Felix Savon wins a gold medal at the 2000 Olympic Games in Sydney, Australia—the third consecutive Games at which he has taken top honors.
	Congress passes the Muhammad Ali Boxing Reform Act in an effort to reform certain exploitative financial practices by boxing promoters, as well as addressing other problems in the sport.
2001	Zuffa purchases the UFC for $2 million dollars and later turns the company into the most successful mixed martial arts organization in history.
2003	Fedor Emelianenko wins the PRIDE heavyweight championship by defeating Antonio Rodrigo Nogueira.
2005	Spike TV airs the first season of *The Ultimate Fighter,* a television series of mixed martial artists competing for a UFC contract. The show contributed to a marked increase in the popularity of mixed martial arts.
	In April, Chuck "the Iceman" Liddell kayoes Randy Couture to win the UFC light heavyweight championship.
2007	In March, Randy Couture pulls the upset by defeating Tim Sylvia over five rounds to regain the UFC heavyweight championship at the age of 43.
2008	Fedor Emelianenko unleashes his power in devastating fashion at Affliction's first card by submitting former UFC heavyweight champion Tim Sylvia in 36 seconds.
2009	Fedor Emelianenko cements his status in the eyes of many in the combat sports world as the greatest fighter in mixed martial arts by knocking out former UFC heavyweight champion Andrei Arlovski in the first round.

BIBLIOGRAPHY

Books

Ali, Muhammad with Richard Duncan. *The Greatest: My Own Story*. New York: Random House, 1975.

Allen, David Rayvern. *Punches on the Page: A Boxing Anthology*. Edinburgh, Scotland: Mainstream Publishing, 1998.

Anderson, Dave. *In the Corner: Boxing's Greatest Trainers Talk about Their Art*. New York: William Morrow & Company, 1991.

Armstrong, Henry. *Gloves, Glory and God*. Westwood, NJ: Fleming H. Revell Company, 1956.

Ashe, Arthur, Jr. *A Hard Road to Glory: A History of the African-American Athlete: Boxing*. New York: Amistad Press, 1993.

Atlas, Teddy, and Peter Alson. *Atlas: From the Streets to the Ring: A Son's Struggle to Become a Man*. New York: Ecco, 2006.

Bak, Richard. *Joe Louis: The Great Black Hope*. New York: De Capo Press, 1997.

Berger, Phil. *Punchlines: Berger on Boxing*. New York: Four Walls Eight Windows, 1993.

Bingham, Howard L., and Max Wallace. *Muhammad Ali's Greatest Fight*. London: Robson, 2004.

Blewitt, Bert. *The A–Z of World Boxing: Authoritative and Entertaining Compendium of the Fight Game from its Origins to the Present Day*. London: Robson Books, 1996.

Bodner, Allen. *When Boxing Was a Jewish Sport*. Westport, CT: Praeger, 1997.

Boyd, Herb, with Ray Robinson II. *Pound for Pound: A Biography of Sugar Ray Robinson*. New York: Amistad Press, 2006.

Brenner, Teddy, and Barney Nagler. *Only the Ring was Square*. Englewood Cliffs, NJ: Prentice-Hall, 1981.

Bromberg, Lester. *Boxing's Unforgettable Fights*. New York: Ronald Press, 1962.

Bromberg, Lester. *World Champs*. New York: Retail Distributors, 1958.

Brunt, Stephen. *Facing Ali: Fifteen Fighters, Fifteen Stories*. Guilford, CT: Lyons Press, 2004.

Buchanan, Ken. *Buchanan: High Life and Hard Times*. London: Mainstream Publishing, 1986.

Buchanan, Ken. *The Tartan Legend*. London: Headline Book Publishing, 2000.

Cantwell, Robert. *The Real McCoy: The Life and Times of Norman Selby*. New York: Auerbach Publishers, 1971.

Carpentier, Georges. *The Art of Boxing*. New York: George H. Doran Company, 1926.

Carter, Rubin. *The Sixteenth Round: From Number 1 Contender to #45472*. New York: Penguin Global, 1991.

Cavanaugh, Jack. *Tunney: Boxing's Brainiest Champ and His Upset of the Great Jack Dempsey*. New York: Ballentine Books, 2006.

Century, Douglas. *Barney Ross*. New York: Schocken, 2006.

Chaiton, Sam, and Terry Swinton. *Lazarus and the Hurricane: The Freeing of Rubin "Hurricane" Carter*. New York: St Martin's, 2000.

Collins, Mark. *The 100 Greatest Boxers: The Ultimate Boxing Who's Who to Settle Every Argument and Start 100 More!* London: Generation Publications, 1999.

Collins, Nigel. *Boxing Babylon: Behind the Shadowy World of the Prize Ring*. New York: Citadel Press, 1990.

Cottrell, John. *Man of Destiny: The Story of Muhammad Ali/Cassius Clay*. London: Muller, 1967.

Couture, Randy, with Loretta Hunt. *Becoming the Natural: My Life In and Out of the Cage*. New York: Simon Spotlight Entertainment, 2008.

Crigger, Kelly. *Title Shot: Into the Shark Tank of Mixed Martial Arts*. Auberry, CA: Victory Belt Publishing, 2008.

DeLisa, Michael C. *Cinderella Man*. London: Milo Books, 2005.

Dibble, Roy F. *John L. Sullivan: An Intimate Narrative*. Boston: Little, Brown, and Company, 1925.

Dundee, Angelo. *My View From the Corner*. New York: McGraw Hill, Inc., 2007.

Early, Gerald, ed. *The Muhammad Ali Reader*. New York: Harper Perennial, 1999.

Edwards, Robert. *Henry Cooper: The Authorized Biography of Britain's Greatest Boxing Hero*. London: Chivers, Windsor, Paragon and Camden, 2003.

Ercole, Andy, and Ed Oconowicz. *Tiberi: The Uncrowned Champion*. Wilmington, DE: Jared Co., 1992.

Erenberg, Lewis. *The Greatest Fight of Our Generation: Louis v. Schmeling*. New York: Oxford University Press, 2005.

Evans, Gavin. *Prince of the Ring: The Naseem Hamed Story*. London: Robson, 1998.

Fair, James. *Give Him to the Angels: Story of Harry Greb*. New York: Smith and Durrell, 1946.

Farr, Finis. *Black Champion: The Life and Times of Jack Johnson*. New York: Charles Scribner's Sons, 1964.

Fields, Armond. *James J. Corbett: A Biography of the Heavyweight Boxing Champion and Popular Theater Headliner*. Jefferson, NC: McFarland and Company, 2001.

Fitzgerald, Mike. *The Ageless Warrior: The Life of Boxing Legend Archie Moore*. Champaign, IL: Sports Publishing LLC, 2004.

Fitzgerald, Mike. *Tale of the Gator: The Craig Bodzianowski Story*. Milwaukee, WI: Lemieux International, 2000.

Fleischer, Nat. *50 Years at Ringside*. New York: Fleet Publishing Corporation, 1958.

Fleischer, Nat. *The Heavyweight Championship: An Informal History of Heavyweight Boxing from 1719 to the Present Day* (rev. ed.). New York: G.P Putnam's Sons, 1961.

Fleischer, Nat. *Max Baer: The Glamour Boy of the Ring*. New York: C J O'Brien, 1942.

Foreman, George, and Joel Engel. *By George: The Autobiography of George Foreman*. New York: Simon & Schuster, 2000.

Franklin, Rich, and Jon F. Merz. *The Complete Idiot's Guide To Ultimate Fighting*. New York: Alpha Books, 2007.

Fraser, George McDonald. *Black Ajax*. New York: Carroll & Graf, 1999.

Frazier, Joe, and Phil Berger. *Smokin Joe: The Autobiography of a Heavyweight Champion of the World, Smokin' Joe Frazier*. New York: MacMillan General Reference, 1996.

Fried, Ronald K. *Corner Men: Great Boxing Trainers*. New York: Four Walls Eight Windows, 1991.

Fullerton, Hugh. *Two Fisted Jeff: Life Story of James J. Jeffries World's Greatest Heavyweight Champion*. Chicago: Consolidated Book Publishers, 1929.

Gentry, Clyde. *No Holds Barred: Ultimate Fighting and the Martial Arts Revolution*. London: Milo Books, 2002.

Giudice, Christian. *Hands of Stone: The Life and Legend of Roberto Duran*. London: Milo Books, 2006.

Goldstein, Alan. *A Fistful of Sugar: The Sugar Ray Leonard Story*. New York: Coward, McCann & Geoghegan, 1981.

Graziano, Rocky, with Ralph Corsel. *Somebody Down Here Likes Me Too*. New York: Stein & Day, 1981.

Hague, Jim. *Braddock: The Rise of the Cinderella Man*. New York: Chamberlain Brothers, 2005.

Hales, A. G. *Black Prince Peter: The Romantic Career of Peter Jackson*. New York: Wright & Brown, 1931.

Harrison, Audley. *Audley Harrison: Realising the Dream*. London: Andre Deutsch, 2001.

Haskins, James. *Sugar Ray Leonard*. London: Robson Books, 1989.

Hatton, Ricky. *The Hitman: My Story*. London: Ebury Press, 2007.

Hauser, Thomas. *The Black Lights: Inside the World of Professional Boxing*. Fayetteville: University of Arkansas Press, 2000.

Hauser, Thomas. *The Lost Legacy of Muhammad Ali*. Toronto: Sport Media Publishing, 2005.

Hauser, Thomas. *Muhammad Ali: His Life and Times*. New York: Simon & Schuster, 1992.

Heinz, W. C., ed. *The Fireside Book of Boxing*. New York: Simon & Schuster, 1961.

Heinz, W. C. *What A Time It Was*. Cambridge, MA: Da Capo Press, 2001.

Heller, Peter. *Bad Intentions: The Mike Tyson Story*. Cambridge, MA: Da Capo Press, 1995.

Hietala, Thomas. *Jack Johnson, Joe Louis and the Struggle for Racial Equality*. New York: ME Sharpe, 2002.

Hirsh, James S. *Hurricane: The Miraculous Journey of Rubin Carter*. Boston: Houghton Mifflin, 2000.

Holmes, Larry, with Phil Berger. *Larry Holmes: Against the Odds*. New York: St. Martin's Press, 1998.

Holyfield, Evander, and Bernard Holyfield. *Holyfield: The Humble Warrior*. Nashville, TN: Thomas Nelson, 1996.

Holyfield, Evander, with Lee Guenfeld. *Becoming Holyfield: A Fighter's Journey*. New York: Simon & Schuster, 2008.

Hudson, David L., Jr., and Mike Fitzgerald, Jr. *Boxing's Most Wanted: The Top Ten Book of Champs, Chumps and Punch-Drunk Palookas*. Washington, D.C.: Brassey's, 2004.

Hughes, Brian. *Willie Pep: The Will o' the Wisp*. Manchester, England: Collyhurst and Hughes, 1997.

Hughes, Matt, with Michael Malice. *Made in America: The Most Dominant Champion in UFC History*. New York: Simon Spotlight Entertainment, 2008.

Isenberg, Michael. *John L. Sullivan and His America*. Urbana: University of Illinois Press, 1988.

Jarrett, John. *The Champ in the Corner: The Ray Arcel Story*. London: Tempus Publishing, Ltd., 2007.

Jarrett, John. *Dynamite Gloves: The Fighting Lives of Boxing's Big Punchers*. London: Robson Books, 2002.

Jarrett, John. *Gene Tunney: The Golden Guy Who Licked Jack Dempsey Twice*. London: Robson Books, 2003.

Johansson, Ingemar. *Seconds Out of the Ring*. London: Sportsmens Book Club, 1961.

Johnson, Jack. *My Life and Battles*, ed. Chris Rivers. Westport, CT: Praeger, 2007.

Johnston, Alexander. *Ten and Out! The Complete Story of the Prize Ring in America*. New York: Ives Washburn, 1943.

Kaye, Andrew M. *The Pussycat of Prizefighting: Tiger Flowers and the Politics of Black Celebrity*. Athens: The University of Georgia Press, 2004.

Kearns, Jack 'Doc,' and Oscar Fraley. *The Million Dollar Gate*. New York: The MacMillan Co., 1966.

Kennedy, Paul. *Billy Conn: Pittsburgh Kid*. Bloomington, IN: AuthorHouse, 2007.

Kent, Graeme. *The Great White Hopes: The Quest to Defeat Jack Johnson*. Gloucester, England: Sutton Publishing, 2005.

Kimball, George. *Four Kings: Leonard, Hagler, Hearns, Duran and the Last Great Era of Boxing*. Ithaca, NY: McBooks Press, 2008.

Kram, Mark. *Ghosts of Manila: The Fateful Blood Feud Between Muhammad Ali and Joe Frazier*. New York: HarperCollins, 2001.

Krauss, Erich, and Brett Aita. *Brawl: A Behind-the-Scenes Look at Mixed Martial Arts Competition*. Ontario: ECW Press, 2002.

LaMotta, Jake, with Joseph Carter and Peter Savage. *Raging Bull: My Story*. New York: Da Capo Press, 1997.

Lane, Mills, with Jedwin Smith. *Let's Get It On*. New York: Crown Publications, 1998.

Larnder, Rex. *The Legendary Champions*. New York: American Heritage Press, 1972.

Layden, Tim. *The Last Great Fight: The Extraordinary Tale of Two Men and How One Fight Changed Their Lives*. New York: St Martin's Press, 2007.

Lewis, Lennox. *Lennox Lewis: The Autobiography of the WBC Heavyweight Champion of the World*. London: Faber & Faber, 1994.

Liddell, Chuck, with Chad Millman. *Iceman: My Fighting Life*. New York: Dutton, 2008.

Liebling, A. J. *The Sweet Science*. New York: Grove Press, 1956.

Lipsyte, Robert, and Peter Levine. *Idols of the Game: A Sporting History of the American Game*. Atlanta: Turner Publishing, Inc., 1998.

Loiseau, Jean Claude. *Marcel Cerdan*. Paris: Flammarion, 1989.

Long, Bill, and John Johnson. *Tyson-Douglas: The Inside Story of the Upset of the Century*. Alexandria, VA: Potomac Books, 2006.

MacKinnon, Timothy J. *Jens Pulver and the Wednesday Group That Will Change the World*. Bloomington, IN: iUniverse, 2007.

Magriel, Paul, ed. *The Memoirs of the Life of Daniel Mendoza*. London: B T Batsford Ltd., 1951.

Makinde, Adeyinka. *Dick Tiger: The Life and Times of a Boxing Immortal*. Tarentum, PA: Word Association Publishers, 2005.

Marantz, Steve. *Sorcery at Caesar's: Sugar Ray's Marvelous Night*. Portland, OR: Inkwater Pres, 2008.

Margolick, David. *Beyond Glory: Joe Louis v. Max Schmeling, and a World on the Brink*. New York: Vintage, 2005.

Marqusee, Mike. *Redemption Song: Muhammad Ali and the Spirit of the 60s* (2nd ed. London: Verso, 1999.

Mayeda, David T., and David E. Ching. *Fighting for Acceptance: Mixed Martial Artists and Violence in American Society*. Bloomington, IN: iUniverse, Inc., 2008.

Mayes, Harold. *Rocky Marciano*. London: Panther Books, 1956.

McCaffery, Dan. *Tommy Burns: Canada's Unknown World Heavyweight Champion*. Toronto, Ontario: Lorimer, 2001.

McCallum, John. *World Heavyweight Boxing Championship: A History*. Radnor, PA: Chilton Book Co., 1974.

McCullough, Wayne. *Pocket Rocket: Don't Quit, The Autobiography of Wayne McCullough*. London: Mainstream Publishing, 2005.

McGuigan, Barry, Gerry Callan, and Harry Mullan. *Barry McGuigan: The Untold Story*. London: Arrow Books, 1992.

McIlvaney, Hugh. *The Hardest Game: McIlvaney on Boxing*. New York: MacGraw Hill, 2001.

McRae, Donald. *Dark Trade: Lost in Boxing*. Edinburgh, Scotland: Mainstream Publishing, 1996.

Mee, Bob. *Boxing: Heroes and Champions*. London: Book Sales, 1997.

Mee, Bob. *Bare Fists*. Warwickshire, England: Lodge Farm Books, 1998.

Moore, Archie. *Any Boy Can: The Archie Moore Story*. Englewood Cliffs, NJ: Prentice-Hall, 1971.

Moyle, Clay. *Sam Langford: Boxing's Greatest Uncrowned Champion*. Seattle, WA: Bennett & Hastings, 2008.

Mullaly, Frederic. *Primo: The Story of 'Man Mountain' Carnera*. London: Robson, 1999.

Mullan, Harry. *Boxing: Inside the Game*. Cambridge, MA: Icon Books, 1998.

Mullan, Harry, with Bob Mee. *The Ultimate Encyclopedia of Boxing*. London: Carlton Books, 2007.

Murray, Michael. *The Journeyman*. Edinburgh, Scotland: Mainstream Publishing Company, 2002.

Myler, Patrick. *Gentleman Jim Corbett: The Truth Behind a Boxing Legend*. London: Robson Books, 1998.

Myler, Patrick. *Ring of Hate: Joe Louis v. Max Schmeling: The Fight of the Century*. New York: Arcade Publishing, 2006.

Newfield, Jack. *Only in America: The Life and Crimes of Don King*. New York: William Morrow and Company, 1995.

O'Connor, Daniel, ed. *Iron Mike: A Mike Tyson Reader*. New York: Da Capo Press, 2002.

Odd, Gilbert. *Boxing: The Great Champions*. London: Hamlyn Publishing Group, 1974.

Odd, Gilbert. *Debatable Decisions*. London: Nicholson & Watson, 1953.

Odd, Gilbert. *Encyclopedia of Boxing*. New York: Crescent Books, 1983.

Ortiz, Tito, with Marc Shapiro. *This Is Gonna Hurt: The Life of a Mixed Martial Arts Champion*. New York: Simon Spotlight Entertainment, 2008.

O'Toole, Andrew. *Sweet William: The Life of Billy Conn*. Champaigne: University of Illinois Press, 2007.

Otty, Harry. *Charley Burley and the Black Murderers Row*. Liskeard, Cornwall, England: Exposure Publishing, 2006.

Patterson, Floyd, and Milton Gross. *Victory Over Myself*. New York, NY: Scholastic Book Services, 1966.

Peligo, Kid. *The Gracie Way: An Illustrated History of the World's Greatest Martial Arts Family*. Montpelier, VT.: Invisible Cities Press, 2003.

Penn, B. J., with Glen Cordozo and Erich Krauss. *Mixed Martial Arts: The Book of Knowledge*. Auberry, CA: Victory Belt Publishing, 2007.

Pep, Willie, with Robert Sacchi. *Willie Pep Remembers*. New York: F. Fell Publishers, 1973.

Pepe, Phil. *Come Out Smokin': Joe Frazier, The Champ Nobody Knew*. New York: Coward McCann & Geoghegan, 1972.

Pitluck, Adam. *Standing Eight: The Inspiring Story of Jesus 'El Matador' Chavez Who Became Lightweight Champion of the World*. Cambridge, MA: Da Capo Books, 2006.

Pitt, Nick. *The Prince and the Prophet: The Rise of Naseem Hamed*. London: Four Walls Eight Windows, 1999.

Pollack, Adam J. *John L. Sullivan: The Career of the First Gloved Heavyweight Champion*. Jefferson, NC: McFarland Press, 2006.

Pulver, Jens, with Erick Krauss. *Little Evil. One Ultimate Fighter's Rise to the Top*. Ontario, Canada: ECW Press, 2003.

Remnick, David. *King of the World: Muhammad Ali and the Rise of an American Hero*. New York: Vintage Books, 1999.

Rendell, Jonathan. *This Bloody Mary Is The Last Thing I Own*. London: Faber & Faber, 1998.

Ribalow, Harold Uriel. *Fighter from Whitechapel: The Story of Daniel Mendoza*. London: Farrar, Straus and Cudahy, 1962.

Roberts, James B., and Alexander G. Skutt. *Boxing Register: International Boxing Hall of Fame Official Record Book* (4th ed). Ithaca, NY: McBooks Press, Inc., 2006.

Roberts, Randy. *Papa Jack: Jack Johnson and the Era of White Hopes*. New York: Free Press, 1985.

Robinson, Sugar Ray, and Dave Anderson. *Sugar Ray*. New York: Viking Press, 1970.

Rosenfeld, Allen S. *Charley Burley: The Life and Hard Times of an Uncrowned Champion*. Bloomington, IN: AuthorHouse Publishing, 2007.

Ross, Barney, and Martin Abramson. *No Man Stands Alone: The True Story of Barney Ross*. New York: Lippincoff, 1957.

Ross, Ron. *Bummy Davis vs. Murder Inc.: The Rise and Fall of the Jewish Mafia and an Ill-Fated Prizefighter*. New York: St. Martin's Press, 2003.

Rotella, Carlos. *Cut Time: An Education at the Fights*. New York: Houghton Mifflin, 2003.

Sammons, Jeffrey. *Beyond the Ring: The Role of Boxing in American Society*. Champaign: University of Illinois Press, 1988.

Samuels, Charles. *The Magnificent Rube: The Life and Gaudy Times of Tex Rickard*. New York: McGraw Hill, 1957.

Schaap, Jeremy. *Cinderella Man: James J. Braddock, Max Baer and the Greatest Upset in Boxing History*. New York: Houghton Mifflin, 2005.

Schmeling, Max, and George Von Der Lippe. *Max Schmeling: An Autobiography*. Santa Monica, CA: Bonus Books, 1998.

Shamrock, Ken, with Richard Hanner and Calixtro Romias. *Inside the Lion's Den: The Life and Submission Fighting System of Ken Shamrock*. North Clarendon, VT: Tuttle Publishing, 1998.

Shamrock, Ken, and Erich Krauss. *Beyond the Lion's Den*. North Clarendon, VT: Tuttle Publishing, 2005.

Shavers, Earnie, with Mike Fitzgerald and Marshall Terrill. *Welcome to the Big Time*. Champaign, IL: Sports Publishing LLC, 2002.

Sheridan, Jim. *Leave the Fighting to McGuigan: The Official Biography of Barry McGuigan*. New York: Penguin Books, 1986.

Sheridan, Sam. *A Fighter's Heart: One Man's Journey Through the World of Fighting*. New York: Atlantic Monthly Press, 2007.

Shropshire, Kenneth. *Being Sugar Ray: The Life of Sugar Ray Robinson, America's Greatest Boxer and First Celebrity Athlete*. New York: Basic Civitas Book, 2007.

Snowden, Jonathan. *Total MMA: Inside Ultimate Fighting*. Toronto, Ontario: ECW Press, 2008.

Steen, Rob. *Sonny Boy: The Life and Strife of Sonny Liston*. London: Methuen, 1993.

Strauss, Darin. *The Real McCoy*. New York: Plume Books, 2002.

Sugar, Bert Randolph. *Boxing's Greatest Fighters*. Guilford, CT: Lyons Press, 2006.

Sugar, Bert Randolph, and the Editors of *Ring* Magazine. *The Great Fights: A Pictorial History of Boxing's Greatest Bouts*. New York: Rutledge Press, 1981.

Suster, Gerald. *Lighting Strikes: Lives and Times of Boxing's Lightweight Champions*. London: Robson Books, 1994.

Thomas, James J. *The Holyfield Way: What I Learned Courage, Perseverance and the Bizarre World of Boxing*. Champaign, IL: Sports Publishing LLC, 2005.

Torres, Jose. *Fire and Fear: The Inside Story of Mike Tyson*. New York: Warner Books, 1989.

Torres, Jose. *Sting Like a Bee: The Muhammad Ali Story*. New York: McGraw Hill, 2001.

Tsyzu, Kostya. *Kostya: My Story*. Sydney, Australia: ABC Books, 2003.

Wall, Jeremy. *UFC's Ultimate Warriors Top 10*. Ontario, Canada: ECW Press, 2005.

Walsh, Peter. *Men of Steel: The Lives and Times of Boxing's Middleweight Champions*. London: Robson Books, 1993.

Ward, Geoffrey. *Unforgiveable Blackness: The Rise and Fall of Jack Johnson*. New York: Alfred A. Knopf, 2004.

Webb, Dale. *Prize Fighter: The Life and Times of Bob Fitzsimmons*. Edinburgh, Scotland: Mainstream Publishing, 2000.

Wells, Jeff. *Boxing Day: The Fight That Changed the World*. New York: Harpers Collins, 2000.

Wertheim, L. Jon. *Blood in the Cage: Mixed Martial Arts, Pat Miletich, and the Furious Rise of the UFC*. Boston: Houghton Mifflin, 2009.

Youmans, Gary B. *The Onion Picker: Carmen Basilio and Boxing in the 1950s*. Syracuse, NY: Campbell Road Press North, 2007.

Zirin, Dave. *Muhammad Ali Handbook*. London: MQ Publications, 2007.

Magazines

Black Belt http://www.blackbeltmag.com
Boxing Monthly http://www.boxing-monthly.co.uk
Elite Fighter http://www.elitefightermag.com/
FIGHT! http://www.fightmagazine.com/
FightSport http://www.fightsportusa.com/
Fight Zone http://www.fightzonemagazine.com/
KO (out of print)
MMA Worldwide http://www.mmaworldwide.com/
Real Fighter http://www.realfightermag.com/
The Ring (*Ring* magazine) http://www.thering-online.com/
Tapout http://www.tapoutmagazine.com/
Ultimate Grappling http://www.ultimategrapplingmag.com/
World Boxing
Wrestling Observer Newsletter

Web Sites/Blogs

Bad Left Hook http://www.badlefthook.com/
Bloody Elbow http://www.bloodyelbow.com/
Boxing Scene http://www.boxingscene.com/
Boxing Talk http://www.boxingtalk.com/
BoxRec http://www.boxrec.com
Bragging Rights Corner http://www.braggingrightscorner.com/
Cyber Boxing Zone http://www.cyberboxingzone.com/
Doghouse Boxing http://www.doghouseboxing.com/
East Side Boxing http://www.eastsideboxing.com/
Fight Hype http://www.fighthype.com/
Fightnews http://www.fightnews.com
Five Ounces of Pain http://fiveouncesofpain.com/
Heavyweight News http://www.heavyweights.co.uk/
KO Corner http://www.kocorner.com/
MaxBoxing http://www.maxboxing.com/

MMA Junkie http://mmajunkie.com/
MMA Weekly http://www.mmaweekly.com
SecondsOut http://www.secondsout.com/
Sherdog http://www.sherdog.com/
The Sweet Science http://www.thesweetscience.com/
Wrestling Observer http://www.f4wonline.com/

INDEX

Boldface page numbers refer to main entries in the encyclopedia.

About the Author

DAVID L. HUDSON, JR. is the author or co-author of 20 books, many on law and sports. His works include *The Rehnquist Court: Understanding Its Impact and Legacy* (Praeger, 2006), *The Handy Supreme Court Answer Book* (2007), *Women in Golf: The Players, the History, and the Future of the Sport* (Praeger, 2007), and *Boxings Most Wanted: The Top Ten Book of Champs, Chumps and Punch Drunk Palookas* (2003). He serves as First Amendment Scholar for the First Amendment Center located on the Vanderbilt University campus, and teaches adjunct classes at Middle Tennessee State University, Nashville School of Law, and Vanderbilt Law School.